THE OXFORD ENGLISH GRAMMAR

The Oxford

English Grammar

SIDNEY GREENBAUM

In memoriam

OXFORD UNIVERSITY PRESS

OXFORD

UNIVERSITY PRESS

Great Clarendon Street, Oxford OX2 6DP

Oxford University Press is a department of the University of Oxford.
It furthers the University's objective of excellence in research, scholarship,
and education by publishing worldwide in

Oxford New York

Athens Auckland Bangkok Bogotá Buenos Aires Calcutta
Cape Town Chennai Dar es Salaam Delhi Florence Hong Kong Istanbul
Karachi Kuala Lumpur Madrid Melbourne Mexico City Mumbai
Nairobi Paris São Paulo Singapore Taipei Tokyo Toronto Warsaw

with associated companies in Berlin Ibadan

Oxford is a registered trade mark of Oxford University Press
in the UK and in certain other countries

Published in the United States
by Oxford University Press Inc., New York

British Library Cataloguing in Publication Data
Data available

Library of Congress Cataloging in Publication Data
Data available
ISBN 0-19-861250-8

10 9 8 7 6 5

Printed in Great Britain by
Butler & Tanner Ltd.,
Frome, Somerset.

FOR AVRAHAM AND MASHA

Preface

This book is addressed primarily to native speakers of English and others who use English as their first language. It is a comprehensive account of present-day English that is chiefly focused on the standard varieties of American and British English, but it also refers frequently to non-standard varieties and it draws on the history of the language to illuminate and explain features of English of today. It offers a description of the language and is not intended to prescribe or proscribe.

This work is unique in its coverage for native speakers of the language. It is written to be accessible to non-specialists, but students of the English language and related subjects will also find it of interest and value. It serves as a reference work and can also be used as a textbook. Each chapter is prefaced by a list of contents and a summary of the chapter. You may wish to read through a whole chapter or to consult particular sections. The Glossary at the end of the book will provide you with succinct explanations of terms that are frequently used in the book.

In writing this book, I have drawn on my many years of experience in teaching, research, and writing. I have taught English language in a range of institutions and to different age-groups: at primary schools, at a secondary (grammar) school, at a college of further education, and at universities. My university teaching has encompassed a British university, universities in the United States, and a university in a country where English is a foreign language. I have been in English language research for over thirty years, and have directed a research unit (the Survey of English Usage) for the last twelve years. My books have ranged over various types of writing: monographs, reference works (including co-authorship of the standard reference grammar of English), textbooks, and books addressed to the general public.

Numerous citations appear in this book. Many of them come from American and British newspapers, magazines, and books. Most are taken from two sources: ICE-GB (the British million-word component of the International Corpus of English, drawing on language used in the period 1990–3) and the *Wall Street Journal* (about three million words from this American newspaper for 1989, provided in a CD-ROM by the Association for Computational Linguistics Data Collection Initiative).

ICE-GB was tagged and parsed with the assistance of programs devised by the TOSCA Research Group (University of Nijmegen) under the direction of Professor Jan Aarts. ICE-GB was compiled and computerized, with extensive mark-up, by researchers at the Survey of English Usage, who also undertook substantial manual work on the outputs of the TOSCA programs as well as manual pre-editing for parsing. The following Survey researchers were involved in the creation of ICE-GB or in the subsequent grammatical processing: Judith Broadbent, Justin Buckley, Yanka Gavin, Marie Gibney, Ine Mortelmans, Gerald Nelson, Ni Yibin, Andrew Rosta, Oonagh Sayce, Laura Tollfree, Ian Warner,

Vlad Zegarac. I am especially grateful to Gerald Nelson for overseeing the compilation of ICE-GB and the grammatical processing. He is also responsible for drawing up the annotated list of sources for ICE-GB texts in the Appendix. The work on ICE-GB was supported in the main by grants from the Economic and Social Research Council (grant R000 23 2077), the Leverhulme Trust, and the Michael Marks Charitable Trust. Financial support was also received from the Sir Sigmund Sternberg Foundation and Pearson Plc.

I am indebted to Akiva Quinn and Nick Porter, colleagues at the Survey, for ICECUP, a software concordance and search package, which I used extensively for searching ICE-GB for words and grammatical tags. I am also much indebted to Alex Chengyu Fang, another colleague at the Survey, for the application of two programs that he created: AUTASYS was used for tagging the Wall Street Journal Corpus, and so gave me access to grammatical information from an American corpus, and TQuery was invaluable for searching for structures in the parsed corpus.

Thanks are due to a number of colleagues for their comments on one or more draft chapters: Judith Broadbent, Justin Buckley, Alex Chengyu Fang, Gerald Nelson, Ni Yibin, Andrew Rosta, Jan Svartvik, Vlad Zegarac. I am also grateful to Marie Gibney for typing the drafts.

Contents

List of Tables

List of Figures

Pronunciation Table

Consonants

voiceless

p	pen	s	sit
t	top	ʃ	she
k	cat	tʃ	chip
f	few	h	he
θ	thin		

voiced

b	but	m	man
d	dog	n	n
g	get	ŋ	ring
v	van	l	leg
ð	this	r	red
z	zoo	w	we
ʒ	vision	j	yes
dʒ	jar		

Vowels

a	cat	ə	ago
ɑː	arm (RP) arm (GA)	ʌɪ	my
ɛ	bed	aʊ	how
əː (RP)	her	eɪ (RP) eː (GA)	day
ɜ (GA)	her	əʊ (RP) o: (GA)	no
ɪ	sit	ɛː	hair (RP) hair (GA)
iː	see	ɪə (RP) ɪ (GA)	near (RP) near (GA)
ɒ (RP) ɑː (GA)	hot	ɔɪ	boy
ɔː	saw	ʊə (RP) ʊ (GA)	poor (RP) poor (GA)
ʌ	run	ʌɪə (RP) ʌɪ (GA)	tire (RP) tire (GA)
ʊ	put	aʊə (RP) aʊ (GA)	sour (RP) sour (GA)
uː	too		

The pronunciation symbols follow those used in *The New Shorter Oxford English Dictionary* and in the latest edition of *The Concise Oxford Dictionary*.

RP (Received Pronunciation) is an accent that is typical of educated speakers of British English, though by no means all educated speakers use it. GA (General American) is an abstraction from what is typical of English pronunciation in the United States in contrast to RP. Most of the differences for vowels between RP and GA are due to the [r] being separately pronounced in GA after a vowel. For more detailed discussion of the pronunciation of consonants and vowels, see 10.3–8.

Syllabic consonants (consonants that constitute a syllable by themselves) are marked by a subscript vertical line: l̩, n̩.

Primary stress is marked by (') before the syllable, and secondary stress by (,) before the syllable: 'capita,lize. See 10.10–12.

The ends of tone units are marked by vertical lines, and the nuclear syllable is in capitals:

UnFORtunately| I've caught a COLD|

The direction of the tone is shown by an arrow before the nuclear syllable. See 10.15 f.

Abbreviations and Symbols

A	adverbial
GA	General American
ICE-GB	British corpus of ICE (International Corpus of English)
M	main clause
NP	noun phrase
O	object
P	predicative
PP	prepositional phrase
RP	Received Pronunciation
S	subject
sub	subordinate clause
V	verb

( )	comment or explanation after citation; optional letter(s) or word(s)
[ ]	comment or explanation within citation; phonetic transcription
/ /	phonemic transcription (cf. 9.36)
{ }	morphemic transcription (cf. 9.38); alternatives, e.g.:

$$\left.\begin{matrix} \text{a piece of} \\ \text{a bit of} \end{matrix}\right\} \left\{\begin{matrix} \text{bread} \\ \text{information} \end{matrix}\right.$$

Explanations of Corpora Citations

All citations preserve the original wording. If anything is omitted (to avoid irrelevant distractions), the omission is indicated by [...].

A few citations come from the American component of ICE (International Corpus of English). They are cited by references beginning ICE-USA-SIA and are direct (face-to-face) conversations.

Citations from the *Wall Street Journal* are for issues published in 1989. References consist of three sets of digits, for example 890929-0070-49. The first set indicates the date by year, month, and day; the second set is the identity number for the item; the third set identifies the sentence.

Citations for ICE-GB, the British component of ICE, are for language used during the years 1990–3. Pauses are indicated by <,>, a short pause (the equivalent of a single syllable uttered at the speaker's tempo), and by <,,>, a long pause (the equivalent of two or more syllables uttered at the speaker's tempo).

Citation references for ICE-GB begin either 'S' (spoken texts) or 'W' (written texts). The major divisions within these two categories are:

S1	dialogue
S1A	private conversations
S1B	public dialogues
S2	monologue
S2A	unscripted monologues
S2B	scripted monologues
W1	non-printed writing
W1A	student essays
W1B	letters
W2	printed writing
W2A	informational (learned)
W2B	informational (popular)
W2C	informational (reportage)
W2D	instructional
W2E	persuasive (press editorials)
W2F	creative (novels/stories)

There are 500 texts (samples) in ICE-GB, each text containing about 2,000 words, for a total of about one million words. The spoken texts number 300. Fifty of the spoken texts are scripted (written down and read aloud); the scripted texts are transcribed from the spoken recordings. Many of the texts are composite; that is, they are composed of several subtexts (shorter samples), such as a text comprising a number of personal letters.

Citation references for ICE-GB consist of three sets, for example S1B-046-63. The first set is the major category, in this instance a public dialogue (S1B); the second set is for the identity number of the text, which in this instance is a broadcast interview (in the subcategory S1B-041 to S1B-050), the third set is for the number of the text unit. The basic unit for reference in each text is the text unit. In written texts, the text unit corresponds to the orthographic sentence. In spoken texts, it is the approximate equivalent of the orthographic sentence, though there may be more than one equivalent in writing and sometimes a spoken text unit is grammatically incomplete.

A list of the sources of all texts, including any subtexts, in ICE-GB appears in the Appendix at the end of the book.

Chapter 1
The English Language

Summary

Chapter 1 Summary

- English is used in most countries of the world as a first language, a second language (for communication between inhabitants), or a foreign language. It is essentially a Germanic language introduced by invading tribes from the European continent into what later became known as England. It spread from there throughout the British Isles and subsequently to the United States and other territories colonized by the British, almost all of which are now independent countries. Since the end of the Second World War English has been the foremost language for international communication.

- The standard varieties of American and British English have influenced those of other countries where English is a first language and they have generally been the models taught to foreign learners. In the past they have also been the models for English as a second language, but in recent decades some second-language countries have begun to develop their own standard varieties.

- Standard English is remarkably homogeneous across national boundaries, particularly in the written language. It admits less variation than non-standard varieties. Its repertoire offers choices according to type of activity engaged in through language, medium of communication, and degree of formality. Correct English is conformity to the norms of standard English. Good English is good use of the resources of the language: language used effectively and ethically. Sensitivity to the feelings of others requires avoidance of offensive and discriminatory language.

English throughout the World

1.1
English internationally

The geographical spread of English is unique among the languages of the world, not only in our time but throughout history. English is the majority first language in twenty-three countries. It is an official language or a joint official language in about fifty other countries, where it is used in addition to the indigenous first languages for a variety of public and personal functions. It is also used as a second language, though without official status, in countries such as Bangladesh and Malaysia. Countries where English is a first or second language are located in all five continents. The total population of these countries amounts to around 2.5 billion, about 49 per cent of the world's population. Where English is a first or second language, it is used internally for communication between nationals of the same country. In addition, English is used extensively as a foreign language for international communication by people who do not ordinarily employ it when speaking or writing to their compatriots.[1]

The number of first-language speakers of English has been estimated at well over 300 million, of whom over 216 million live in the United States. The United Kingdom has about 53 million, Canada over 17 million, and Australia about 14 million. Countries where English is a majority first language may have large percentages of bilingual speakers and speakers for whom English is a second language. For example, Canada has a large minority of unilingual French speakers (nearly 17 per cent) as well as an almost equal percentage of speakers who are bilingual in French and English.

Most countries with second-language speakers of English are former British colonies, such as India and Nigeria. English has been retained as an official language in the majority of these countries after independence because none of the indigenous languages was accepted by all citizens as the sole national language. As an official second language, English is used in a variety of public functions: in government, in the law courts, in broadcasting, in the press, and in education. In many African and Asian countries it serves as the means of interpersonal communication between speakers of different indigenous languages. Because of both its national and its international reach, English is often used for literature, sometimes in forms that draw heavily on local colloquial forms of English. Writers and politicians in some African and Asian countries are ambivalent about the role of English: English may be viewed as an imperialist language, imposed by colonial oppressors and impeding the role of indigenous languages, or as the language of liberation and nationalism in countries divided by tribal loyalties.

The problem in calculating the numbers of second-language speakers is how to decide who counts as a speaker of the language. Should we include in our totals those who have a rudimentary knowledge of vocabulary and grammar but can make themselves understood only in certain types of exchanges—for example, giving street directions or offering goods for sale? If so, we might recognize as second-language speakers perhaps most of the 2.5 billion that live in countries where English is used as a second language. On the other hand, conservative estimates, requiring much greater competence in the language, tend to put the number at about 300 million.

A similar problem arises in calculating the numbers of users of English as a foreign language. Estimates have ranged wildly—from 100 million to 600 million. English is extensively studied as a foreign language. It is a compulsory subject or the preferred optional language in most countries where it is not a first or second language. It has been estimated that over 150 million children are studying English as a foreign language in primary or secondary schools. Many millions of foreigners listen to BBC broadcasts in English, and many millions follow the BBC English lessons on radio and television. 'Follow Me', the BBC English by Television 60-programme course for beginners, produced in 1979 with a consortium of European television stations, has been shown in over 80 countries. It attracted vast audiences in countries throughout the world in the 1980s, and in China alone it had an estimated audience of over 50 million. Over half a million visitors, mostly from the European continent, currently visit the United Kingdom each year to study English as a foreign language. A poll conducted in December 1992 showed that English is the most popular language in the European Union (then called the European Community) among young people (aged 15 to 24), and while 34 per cent of that age group spoke English in 1987 the figure in 1990 had risen to 42 per cent. A European Commission report for 1991–2 showed that 83 per cent of secondary school students in the European Union were learning English as a second language, compared with just 32 per cent learning French, the nearest competitor.

1.2
The spread of English in the British Isles

From the middle of the fifth century and for the next hundred years, waves of invading tribes from the European continent—Angles, Saxons, Jutes, and Frisians—brought their Germanic dialects to Britain, settling in the country and driving the Celtic-speaking Britons westward to Wales and Cornwall. Isolated from other Germanic speakers, the settlers came to acknowledge their dialects as belonging to a separate common language that they called English.[2]

Germanic is a branch of the Indo-European family of languages, from which have descended—among others—Latin and its Romance derivatives, Greek, Celtic, and Sanskrit. The Germanic dialects of the settlers belonged to West Germanic, the parent language also of modern German, Dutch, Flemish, and Frisian. From the middle of the ninth century England suffered large incursions by Danish Vikings, intent on settling as well as plundering. Their Scandinavian language belonged to North Germanic. The Danes came close to capturing the whole country, but were defeated overwhelmingly by the English under the leadership of King Alfred the Great. The Treaty of Wedmore signed in the same year (878) confined the Danes to the east of a line roughly from London to Chester, an area known as the Danelaw. There were further Danish invasions in the late ninth century, and finally from 1014 to 1042 the whole of England was ruled by Danish kings. The Scandinavian language introduced a considerable number of common loanwords into English and contributed to present dialectal differences in the north and east of the country. Much of the population in those areas must have been bilingual and it has been suggested that bilingualism may have hastened the reduction of inflections in English since the stems of words were often similar in the two Germanic languages.

In 1066 William the Conqueror, Duke of Normandy, invaded England and became its king. The Norman conquest established a French-speaking ruling class. French was the language of the royal court, the nobility, the church leaders, parliament, the law courts, and the schools. Most of the population continued to speak English, but bilingualism became common. Bilingualism resulted in an enormous influx of French words into English. From the late fourteenth century English displaced French for most purposes, and during the next century a standard English language emerged to meet the needs of the central bureaucracy, the printers, and the educators. Latin, however, was the language of learning throughout the Middle Ages—as in the rest of Europe— and remained so in England as late as the seventeenth century.

English arrived early in Scotland. By the seventh century the northern English kingdom of Bernicia had extended its territory—and its dialect—into what is now Southern Scotland. This dialect is the source of Scots, an ancient dialect of English that may be viewed as parallel with Modern English in their common derivation from Old English. By the middle of the sixteenth century Scots was becoming influenced by English in word forms and spellings, a process encouraged by the use of English Bibles in Scotland in the absence of a Scots Bible. When James VI of Scotland succeeded Queen Elizabeth I in 1603 to become James I of England, combining the thrones of the two kingdoms, there was a quickening of the pace of adoption of English in Scotland for writing and by the gentry for speech. The final blow to Scots as the standard dialect of Scotland was the Act of Union in 1707, when the two kingdoms were formally united. Despite attempts at reviving Scots, it remains restricted mainly to literary uses and to some rural speech. It has, however, influenced Scottish English, the standard variety of English in Scotland. About 80,000 people speak Scottish Gaelic, a Celtic language that is confined to the West Highlands and the Western Isles of Scotland, but nearly all of them are bilingual in Gaelic and English.

Wales was England's first colony. It was ruled from England as a principality from the beginning of the fourteenth century, and was incorporated into England by the Acts of Union of 1535 and 1543, which promoted the use of English for official purposes. The standard variety of English in Wales is thought to be identical with that in England. There are, however, distinctive Welsh English accents. According to a 1991 census, over half a million inhabitants of Wales above the age of 3 (19 per cent) speak Welsh, a Celtic language, most of whom are bilingual in Welsh and English. As a result of current education policies, the number of Welsh speakers among the young is now increasing.

English was permanently introduced into Ireland when the Normans invaded the country during the twelfth century and settled French and English speakers in the eastern coastal region, though many of their descendants adopted Irish (or Irish Gaelic), the Celtic language of the native inhabitants. In the sixteenth century the Tudor monarchs began a policy of bringing to Ireland large numbers of English settlers, and later also Scottish settlers, to displace the Irish from their land. By 1800 English was the language of half the population. The famines of 1846–8 led to mass emigration from Ireland, most of those who emigrated being Irish speakers, the poorer part of the population. During the nineteenth century English was promoted in the Catholic education system in opposition to the use of Irish by Protestant proselytizing societies. Despite attempts since independence to revive the use of Irish in the Republic of Ireland, there are few Irish monolinguals and perhaps only 2 per cent of the population use Irish regularly.

The United Kingdom, but particularly England, has a high proportion of speakers of immigrant languages. A 1981 survey, covering all pupils in primary and secondary schools under the control of the Inner London Education Authority, found that nearly 45,000 pupils (about 14 per cent) spoke a language at home other than English or in addition to English. The five most frequently reported languages, in order of frequency, were Bengali, Turkish, Greek, Spanish, and Gujerati.[3] British-born descendants of Caribbean immigrants, mostly from Jamaica, may speak a variety of English (related to Jamaican Creole) that has been termed British Black English.[4]

1.3
The spread of English in other first-language countries

Beginning in the early seventeenth century, the English language was transported beyond the British Isles by traders, soldiers, and settlers. During the next two centuries Britain acquired territories throughout the world. In some of these territories, British settlers were sufficiently numerous to dominate the country linguistically as well as in other respects, so that the indigenous population came to adopt English as their first or second language. More importantly for the future of English, the numbers of the early settlers were swelled enormously by waves of immigration and even when the newcomers brought another language their descendants generally spoke

English as their first language. All the major countries outside the British Isles where English is the dominant language have succeeded in assimilating linguistically their immigrants from non-English-speaking countries: the United States, Canada, Australia, and New Zealand.

The first permanent English settlements were established in the New World, beginning with the founding of Jamestown in 1607. The colonial period came to an end when the American colonies rejected British rule in the War of Independence (1776–83). Both before and after their independence, the Americans acquired territories that were occupied by speakers of other languages—Amerindian languages, Dutch, French, and Spanish. These have influenced American English, together with the languages of immigrants in later periods—notably German and Yiddish. It is estimated that over 27 million United States residents speak a language other than English at home, about half of whom use Spanish. Every year over half a million new immigrants enter the United States, most of them from non-English-speaking countries and most of them Spanish speakers.

Political independence of the United States led to cultural—including linguistic—independence, and hence to the growth of a separate standard American English that no longer looked to Britain for its norms. Though regional differences in pronunciation are conspicuous, American English is more homogeneous than British English in vocabulary and grammar, because of its shorter history and because of past migrations across the American continent and present easy mobility. As a result, dialect differences have not had as great an opportunity to become established and there has been much mixing of regional dialects. Black English, originally restricted regionally as well as ethnically, is used by most black speakers in a range of standard and non-standard varieties.[5]

Canada became a British possession in 1763, wrested from the French. After the American War of Independence, large numbers of loyalists settled in Canada, followed during the next century by waves of immigrants from the United States and the British Isles. Canada has a large minority of unilingual French speakers (nearly 17 per cent), concentrated in the province of Québec, as well as an almost equal percentage of bilingual speakers in French and English, which are the joint official languages of Canada. Virtually all Canadians speak English or French, apart from some rural indigenous or immigrant communities.

In 1770 Captain James Cook claimed the eastern coast of Australia for Britain. Soon afterwards, penal colonies were established to which convicts were transported from Britain. Until after the Second World War, immigration from Asian countries was restricted and most immigrants were English-speaking. Many of the Aborigines (the indigenous population before British colonization), who number fewer than 200,000, speak only English.

The first British settlement in New Zealand was in 1792. New Zealand became part of New South Wales and then after 1840 a British colony in its own right. Most settlers have been English-speaking. The indigenous Maori language, spoken by about 300,000, has official status in the courts.

Most of the other countries where English is the majority language are islands with relatively small populations located in the Atlantic or Caribbean (for example, Bermuda and Grenada) and were once—or still are—British colonies. The inhabitants are mainly of African origin, whose ancestors were brought in as slaves and adopted the language of their masters (cf. 1.5).

1.4
The spread of English in second-language countries

Of the countries where English is primarily a second language, South Africa has the largest number of people who speak English as their first language—over 1,800,000. At the time of writing there are eleven official languages: English and Afrikaans, a language related to Dutch, and nine African languages. Dutch settlements began in the Cape in 1652 and were well-established when the British arrived in 1795 and then annexed the Cape in 1814. Many of the Dutch-speaking Boers soon moved away to establish their own republics, but after two wars won by the British the Boer republics were absorbed in the Union of South Africa in 1910 as a dominion of the British Empire. In 1931 South Africa became an independent country within the British Commonwealth and in 1961 a republic outside the Commonwealth. It has recently rejoined the Commonwealth. Blacks, who constitute the majority of the population (about 70 per cent), speak a variety of indigenous languages. White first-language speakers of English, mainly of British descent, number about 1,120,000. The Indian community (about 400,000) are first-language speakers, as are increasing numbers of the ethnically mixed coloureds, who have been shifting their language loyalty from Afrikaans to English. In addition, about 1,750,000 Afrikaners and 5,500,000 blacks are bilingual in English. Afrikaans is associated with the ideology of apartheid, and therefore English is more popular in the non-Afrikaner population. In the absence of a common indigenous language, English is likely to survive the recent political and social changes in South Africa, at least as a second language.

English first came to South Asia (the Indian subcontinent) through trade. In 1600 Elizabeth I granted a charter to some London merchants giving them a monopoly on trade with India and the East. The East India Company gradually gained control over most of India, but in 1859 it was replaced by direct British rule. English was first introduced through Christian missionary schools, and its study was then encouraged by those Indian scholars that saw it as a means of gaining access to Western culture and science. In 1835 Lord Macaulay produced an official Minute that favoured English as the medium of education for the élite, a policy that was adopted and put into practice by the British administration. After the partition of British India into India and Pakistan in 1947, Hindi became the official language of India and English remained as an associate official language for the country as a whole as well as an official language in some states; in Pakistan, English is an official language alongside the national language Urdu. It is not an official language in Bangladesh, which seceded from Pakistan in 1971, but it has continued to play an important role there. Sri Lanka, as it is now called, became the British colony of Ceylon in 1802. As in India, English was first taught through Christian missionary schools. It became the language of administration, a medium for higher education, and a neutral language linking the Sinhalese majority and the Tamil minority, descendants of Indian labourers brought from South India by the British to work on plantations. In 1948 Ceylon became a British dominion and in 1972 the independent republic of Sri Lanka. English was replaced in its former official functions by Sinhala in 1956, sparking language riots. However, there have been some recent moves to enhance the status and use of English in Sri Lanka. In 1988 the Sri Lankan government proclaimed English to be a link language between the two major communities and is attempting to promote its use, particularly in education. In the other three South Asian countries, English is a primary foreign language. Nepal was never part of the British Empire, but the Maldives was a British protectorate (1887–1965) and part of Bhutan was annexed by the British (1865–1907).

Only tiny fractions of the populations of South Asian countries have ever had English as their first language, but there are sizeable numbers of second-language speakers who can claim to be bilingual. According to one estimate, only 4 per cent of the population of India use English regularly. However, that percentage translates into 30 million people, making India the third largest English-speaking country after the United States and the United Kingdom. India also ranks third for the publication of books in English and offers over 3,000 daily newspapers in English.

English and French are official languages in Mauritius, a small island in the Indian Ocean. At one time a French colony, it was a British colony from 1810 until it gained its independence in 1968.

Three former British colonies or protectorates are located in South East Asia: Brunei, Malaysia, and Singapore. Brunei was a British protectorate from 1888 until its independence in 1984, and it has retained English as a joint official language with Malay. Britain competed for control over Malaysia from the sixteenth century onwards, formally incorporated parts into the British Colony of the Straits Settlements in 1826, and established protectorates over other parts in the late nineteenth century. Malaya gained its independence in 1957 and, after other countries joined it, the federation of states became the Federation of Malaysia in 1963. Singapore left the Federation in 1965 to become an independent city state. English is no longer an official language in Malaysia, though it is a compulsory subject in primary and secondary schools and is used in the media and in higher education. English remains an official language in Singapore (jointly with Mandarin Chinese, Malay, and Tamil), used extensively both internally and externally for business. The Philippines, also located in South East Asia, became an American colony in 1898 and a self-governing commonwealth in 1935. The country gained independence from the United States in 1946. English remains an official language, jointly with Filipino, but its functions are becoming restricted.

The joint official languages in the British colony of Hong Kong, located in East Asia, are English and Cantonese, though only a minority of the population use English. Hong Kong Island was ceded by China to Britain in 1842, and the mainland New Territories were leased to Britain in 1898. Hong Kong is due to be returned to China in 1997, but its importance as a centre for international trade is likely to ensure the survival of English in its business community for the foreseeable future.

In the late nineteenth century and early twentieth century, the European powers competed for territories in Africa. English is an official language in seventeen former British colonies:

West Africa:	Cameroon (with French), Gambia, Ghana, Nigeria, Sierra Leone
East Africa:	Kenya (with Swahili), Sudan (with Arabic), Tanzania (with Swahili), Uganda
South Africa:	Botswana, Lesotho (with Sesotho), Malawi (with Chichewa), Namibia, South Africa (with ten other languages, as noted at the beginning of this section), Swaziland, Zambia, Zimbabwe

In addition, English is an official language in Liberia, created in 1822 as a homeland for freed American slaves.

Some island territories where English is a second language are located in the Pacific. In all the following, English is a joint official language: Cook Islands (with Polynesian languages), Fiji (with Fijian), Guam (with Chamorro), Papua New Guinea (with Hin Motu, an indigenous pidgin, and Tok Pisin, an English-based pidgin), Solomon Islands (with Solomon Islands Pidgin). Except for Guam, which is still a territory of the United States, these were all colonies or protectorates of Britain, Australia, or New Zealand.

In much of Spanish-speaking Central America, English or English Creole (cf. 1.5) is commonly spoken. English is an official language in the Central American state of Belize (formerly British Honduras), which was a British colony from 1862 until its independence in 1981. The Spanish-speaking Caribbean island of Puerto Rico was ceded by Spain to the United States in 1898 and since 1952 has been a semi-autonomous commonwealth linked to the United States. Because of its links with the United States, many Puerto Ricans are bilingual in Spanish and English.

English is an official language in two locations in Europe outside the British Isles: Malta (jointly with Maltese) and Gibraltar. The Republic of Malta, which comprises several islands in the Mediterranean Sea, was a British colony from 1802 and became an independent republic in 1974. The British colony of Gibraltar, a peninsula on the south-west coast of Spain, was ceded by Spain to Britain in 1713. Spain claims sovereignty, but Gibraltarians generally prefer to remain British or to become an independent territory within the European Community.

1.5
English pidgins and creoles

Pidgins are languages that are not acquired as mother tongues and that are used for a restricted set of communicative functions. They are formed from a mixture of languages and have a limited vocabulary and a simplified grammar. Pidgins serve as a means of communication between speakers of mutually unintelligible languages and may become essential in multilingual areas. A creole develops from a pidgin when the pidgin becomes the mother tongue of the community. To cope with the consequent expansion of communicative functions, the vocabulary is increased and the grammar is elaborated.

There are about thirty-five English-based pidgins and creoles, English-based because they draw heavily on English vocabulary.[6] They can be divided into Atlantic and Pacific varieties. The Atlantic varieties are linked to West African languages. They were established in West Africa and also developed in the Caribbean as a result of the slave trade when slaves speaking different West African languages were deliberately mixed on the transport ships and in the Caribbean plantations to reduce the risk of rebellions. The Pacific varieties developed later, mainly in the nineteenth century, and continue to flourish in Hawaii, Papua New Guinea (where the pidgin is called Tok Pisin), and other Pacific islands.

A pidgin may be creolized, becoming a mother tongue for some of its speakers, as happened in many areas of the Caribbean and has been happening to a limited extent with Tok Pisin in Papua New Guinea. A creole may be decreolized, when speakers adopt features of standard English, as is common in Jamaica and in Hawaii; it may be repidginized through use as a link language in contact areas, as has been occurring to Krio of Sierra Leone, or it may develop as a language in its own right, as has happened to Sranan, an English-based creole in Surinam, which has survived in the absence of a standard English. Recreolization may also take effect, a process that seems to be happening in London Jamaican, whose speakers were born in Britain and can speak their regional British English but have adopted features different from, though influenced by, Jamaican Creole.

Where a creole and the standard variety of English coexist, as in the Caribbean, there is a continuum from the most extreme form of creole to the form that is closest to the standard language. Linguists mark off the relative positions on the creole continuum as the basilect (the furthest from the standard language), the mesolect, and the acrolect. In such situations, most creole speakers can vary their speech along the continuum and many are also competent in the standard English of their country.[7]

1.6
English as an international language

The pre-eminence of English for international communication is in part indebted to the spread of English (outlined in 1.3–5) as a first or second language for internal communication in numerous countries that were once part of the British Empire. The role of English as an international language has gathered momentum since the end of the Second World War through the economic and military global dominance of the United States and the resources it deploys for scientific and technological progress. The United States remains by far the richest country in the world as measured by gross domestic product, which amounted in 1992 to 5,905 billion dollars, compared with 3,508 billion for Japan, its nearest rival.[8]

In developing countries, English is regarded as the language of modernization and technological advancement. Most of the world's scientific and technical journals are in English. It is commonly required for international trade and at international conferences, and is the official medium for communication at sea and in the air. Television programmes in English are viewed in many countries where English is a foreign language, and when demonstrators wish to achieve the maximum international impact they chant and display their slogans in English.[9]

The English taught to foreign learners is generally British or American English in their standard varieties. Except for pronunciation the differences between the two are relatively minor, as indeed they are between the standard varieties in any of the countries where English is the majority first language. The mass media are ensuring, if anything, the smoothing of differences and are encouraging reciprocal influences, though the influence of American English is predominant. Despite some trivial variation in spelling and punctuation, and some more important variation in vocabulary, the standard first-language varieties of written English are remarkably homogeneous. Predictions that they will diverge to become mutually unintelligible are implausible. It is reasonable to speak of an international standard written English. It is also reasonable to speak of an international standard spoken English if we limit ourselves to the more formal levels and if we ignore pronunciation differences. Even pronunciation differences—which of course exist within each national variety—do not constitute a major obstacle, once speakers have tuned into each other's system of pronunciation.

The situation in countries where English is primarily a second language is fluid and varies. In the past these countries have looked to British or American English for language norms. But there are indications that in some countries—such as India, Nigeria, and Singapore—local models of English are being sought that are based on their own educated varieties. This nativization of English augurs well for the continued use of English for internal functions in those countries.

At present, there are no established and generally acknowledged standard varieties in second-language countries. As a result, teachers and examiners are uncertain as to the norms towards which teaching should be geared: those of the evolving local standard or those of some external standard. In some areas the insecurity of teachers is exacerbated by inadequacies in their acquisition of English. Institutionalization of national standards will require research by grammarians and lexicographers into the language of educated speakers and the agreement of educational and governmental authorities.[10] The standard will then be codified in dictionaries, grammars, and usage guides, and incorporated in textbooks and in school and college examinations. The likelihood is that, as in Britain and the United States, only a minority will be fully competent in the national standard and that there will be a continuum of non-standard variation linked to it. We may hope that the new national standards will take their place as constituents of an International Standard English, preserving the essential unity of English as an international language and therefore its continuing value for that role.

The continuance of English as a second language or its demotion to a foreign language depends on government policies. In some countries the decision has been taken to promote a local language as the national language to the detriment of the role of English in administration and education. Thus, Swahili is being promoted in Tanzania, Bahasa Malaysia in Malaysia, Burmese in Burma, and Filipino in the Philippines. But governmental policies can change, as they have in some countries—at least for higher education—where the decline of English has been viewed with concern and the need has been accepted for an élite that is proficient in English. It is likely, however, that in some countries English will no longer be used for internal purposes. The lack of a legal official status need not in itself affect all the uses to which English is put within second-language countries. After all, English is not an official language in the United States, though there are current moves to designate it as such.

The present role of English as an international language derives from its geographical spread and the prestige and practical value it has acquired through the United States in the last few decades. It cannot be attributed to the intrinsic superiority of English over potential other candidates. It is possible to point to some features that appear to make English easier to learn than some other languages. English has few inflections, so foreign learners do not have to memorize declensions and conjugations. It has natural rather than grammatical gender, so learners do not need to memorize the gender of each noun and do not have to cope with ensuring gender agreement between the noun and an accompanying article or adjective. For most Europeans at least, the Germanic and Romance elements that constitute the bulk of English vocabulary provide welcome help. On the other hand, the absence of inflections has increased the importance of prepositions and the burden of memorizing the preposition that goes with a particular verb, noun, or adjective in a particular meaning: *look at* and *look to*, *pride in* and *proud of*, *afraid of* and *alarmed at*. English also confronts the learner with a multitude of idiomatic combinations, particularly verbs with adverbs; *get by*, *do in*, *turn up*, *make out*. The frequent absence of correlation between pronunciation and spelling is a serious obstacle for learning to read and write (cf. Chapter 12).

There is no method of weighing the advantages and disadvantages of English in comparison with other languages for foreign learners. Ultimately their motivation for learning English is pragmatic, depending on the value they expect to gain from doing so.

The Standard Language

1.7
Standard English

Standard English is the national variety of the language inasmuch as it is not restricted to any region within the country. It is taught throughout the education system, and is identified with educated English. It is the public language of official communication—in central and local government, in parliament and the law courts, and generally in the mass media. It is pre-eminently the language of printed matter; indeed, only the standard language has an established orthography. It is the variety that is taught to foreign learners.

No English-speaking country has a language academy to monitor changes in the standard language and to pronounce on their acceptability. To some extent the functions of an academy have been adopted by writers on usage in newspaper columns or in guides to usage.[11] Grammars of English focus on the standard language, paying minimal attention to differences in non-standard varieties—partly because there has been less research in those varieties and partly because grammars of the standard language have applications in the teaching of English to foreigners. Except for specialized dictionaries of dialect and slang, dictionaries too encode the standard language. Although they generally proclaim themselves to be descriptive, in practice they evaluate through their usage labels and they often include notes on usage problems.[12]

National standard varieties in countries where English is a first language are remarkably homogeneous, particularly in written English. The homogeneity is explained by their common descent from the British English of the seventeenth century. It is only in the late eighteenth century that the United States—the first of the states originally settled by British colonists—began to develop its own language norms. The influence of print, and more recently of radio, television, and film, have contributed to prevent the national standards of English-speaking countries from drifting far apart. If anything, under these influences and the ease of international travel the national standards have tended to converge.

1.8
Variation in standard English

A major characteristic of standard varieties is that they admit relatively less variation than non-standard varieties. Nevertheless, their uniformity should not be overstated. There are of course the well-known usage disputes: *Whom do you want?* and *Who do you want?*; *It is I* and *It is me*; *hopefully* in the sense 'I hope that'; *different from, different to,* and *different than.* Such variants represent changes in progress within the standard variety that have not been accepted by all speakers or that have not spread across the informal–formal continuum. But most variants are noticed only by English language specialists. In the following pairs, the **[a]** sentence is probably satisfactory for all English speakers, whereas the **[b]** sentence may be considered odd by some:

[1a] Who (*or* whom) did they give the prize to?

[1b] Who (*or* whom) did they give the prize?

[2a] I want you to say nothing about it.

[2b] I want that you should say nothing about it.

[3a] They're keeping an open mind on the appointment.

[3b] They're keeping open minds on the appointment.

[4a] That looks like being the best solution.

[4b] That looks to be the best solution.

[5a] My family donated to the college a well-equipped gymnasium.

[5b] My family donated the college a well-equipped gymnasium.

A different kind of variation within standard English relates to the choices available for different uses.[13] One dimension of use is the type of activity engaged in through language. Varieties defined by this dimension are sometimes termed registers, though the term is also extended to use varieties of all dimensions. Instructions typically resort to imperatives, as in cooking recipes: *Bring to the boil, then pour over the meat* rather than *You should bring . . .* Also typical is the omission of the direct object: *Bring to the boil* rather than *Bring the gravy to the boil.* Such omissions are also usual for instructions on labels: *Do not freeze; Stand upright; Keep out of reach of children.* We can immediately recognize as legal language the following sentence extracted from the instructions accompanying the issue of a credit card:

> No delay by the Bank in debiting the Account for any Card Use or part thereof shall affect or prejudice the Bank's right to do so subsequently.

The sentence illustrates prescriptive *shall,* archaic *thereof,* and the legal sense of *prejudice.* The unusual capitalization of *Account* and *Card Use* is conspicuous. The vocabulary items convey unmistakably the provenance of the sentence.

Many registers have been recognized apart from the language of recipes and the language of legal documents. For example: literary language, religious language, academic prose (including scientific writing), technical writing, business writing, the language of advertising, the language of newspaper headlines, journalistic writing. When such specialized registers irritate non-specialists by their obscurity, they are sometimes referred to by pejoratives such as journalese, officialese, gobbledygook, legalese, computerese. More generally, they are disparagingly called jargons.[14]

Another dimension is the medium: whether the communication is in speech or in writing. Most speech is in the form of dialogue, an instantaneous interaction not occurring in writing. Most dialogue is spontaneous conversation, contrasting with the planning and revision that is usually possible in writing. Speech communicates also through intonation and paralinguistic features and when the participants are visible to each other also through body language. On the other hand, there are some punctuation and graphic features that are unique to the written language. (See also 11.1.)

A third dimension is the formality of the language. The appropriate choices depend on the attitude of the speaker (or writer) to the listener (or reader), to the topic, and to the purpose of the communication. Much vocabulary is neutral in this dimension. Here is an opening sentence of a formal, coldly distant letter:

> Further to my letter of 10 December 1993, the Interest Review Unit have considered your representations.

A more friendly and more informal letter would have begun:

> Thank you very much for your reply to my letter of 10 December 1993. The Interest Review Unit have taken account of what you have written.

Contrast the casualness of *Sorry about what I said* with the more formal and polite *I apologize for my remarks*.

The three dimensions—type of activity, medium, and level of formality—overlap. Most speech tends to the less formal end of the formality continuum. Legal documents are necessarily in writing and are generally formal. Scientific articles in learned journals are formal, though popular scientific articles are much less so. The young discipline of computer science is happier with greater informality.

1.9
Correct English

Correct English is the notion of correctness applied to standard English. It is legitimate to speak of mistakes in the use of standard English affecting spelling, punctuation, vocabulary choice, and grammar. At the same time, there are a relatively few disputed usages, and about those there may be legitimate disagreements on which variant is correct.

More controversial are views that would extend the notion of correctness to pronunciation. Standard English in the sense of the term used in this book may be pronounced by a variety of accents. The nearest to a non-localizable

British accent is Received Pronunciation or RP (also known more popularly as BBC English, Oxford English, or the Queen's English), an accent with some variability used by those in the upper socio-economic ranges in England (cf. 10.6). All English-speaking countries have accents that are indicative of the socio-economic class of the speakers. In some countries, these vary regionally. For example, in the United States there is no non-localizable upper-class accent, but presenters in the major networks use a homogenized accent (Network English) that avoids regional associations.

Also controversial is the view that children should be taught to speak standard English as well as write it. Most educationists—though not all those in authority over education—advocate tolerance of non-standard dialects and all accents in speech while encouraging the acquisition of written standard English. They similarly support the maintenance of bilingualism, viewing the retention of an immigrant language as a valuable asset.

Just as English cannot claim intrinsic superiority as the reason for its international role, so the choice of the dialect that developed into our present standard English was not motivated by its superiority over other dialects of the period. It originated in the dialect that was common in London in the fifteenth century. London educated speech was a mixture of dialects among which predominated the East Midlands dialect, which was spoken by more people than any other dialect. The London dialect was a supra-regional dialect that reflected the status of London as the seat of the royal court and the political, judicial, and commercial capital of the country. Had it not been for the Norman Conquest, the standard language might have arisen from the Wessex dialect, which because of the dominance of the West Saxon kingdom under King Alfred and his successors had become the literary language.

The London dialect was not intrinsically superior to other dialects of the fifteenth century, and any other dialect or mixture of dialects might have suited just as well as the basis from which the standard language emerged. However, because of the functions it has been required to fulfil, standard English has become elaborated in grammar and vocabulary to an extent far beyond any of the non-standard dialects. In particular it alone can be used for the range of writing that is essential in a modern society.

1.10
Good English

Good English is sometimes equated with correct English, but the two concepts should be differentiated. Correct English is conformity to the norms of the standard language. Good English is good use of the resources available in the language. In that sense we can use a non-standard dialect well and we can use the standard language badly.

By good English we may mean language used effectively or aesthetically: language that conveys clearly and appropriately what is intended and language that is pleasing to the listener or reader. In the last few decades, lack of clarity in government writing and legal documents has been the target of movements for plain English in several English-speaking countries and they have achieved some successes in promoting legislation and in changing the attitudes of governments and businesses.

By good English we may also mean language used ethically. Commentators have highlighted and criticized doublespeak, the dishonest language employed by some political and military leaders to conceal their actions by obfuscations or to manipulate their followers in explaining away their policies. Protection is in some instances offered through legislation or overseeing agencies to prevent advertisers from lying about products or services.

Bad language is usually equated with swearing, which violates taboos against certain expressions referring (in the main) to sex and excretion. The use of swear-words and tolerance of their use have varied across time, region, and social class. In most countries where English is a majority first language greater tolerance has been extended in recent decades to swearing and obscenities when they occur in realistic portrayals of characters in literature, film, and television drama. But the taboos generally remain in force for at least their use by children as well as by adults where both sexes are present, particularly in middle-class society or on public formal occasions. Swearing by politicians and sports celebrities still evokes scandalized comments, even when not intended for public hearing.

Recent decades have seen a heightened awareness of another aspect of bad language. Attention has been drawn to language that is likely to give offence to particular groups and that might result in discrimination against them. As a result, positive or neutral expressions have been offered to replace language considered sexist or racist and nomenclature considered hurtful to those with physical or psychological disabilities. Excesses in the advocacy of such replacements have given rise to the disparaging terms *political correctness* and *politically correct*. The politically correct movement—particularly strong in American universities—has been viewed by many outside it as repressive and punitive and has evoked protest and ridicule.

There is now a vocabulary of terms in *-ism* and *-ist* to denote behaviour and attitudes that are considered to be offensively discriminatory and that refer to people who are thought to be prejudiced or to discriminate. In addition to the well-established terms *racism* and *sexism*, we can find designations such as *ableism* (discrimination in favour of able-bodied people), *ageism* (discrimination on grounds of age), *animalism* (discrimination against animals), *classism* (discrimination on grounds of social class), *handism* (discrimination against the left-handed), *heterosexism* (discrimination against homosexuals), *lookism* (discrimination because of a person's looks), *sizism* (discrimination because of a person's size).

Among expressions that have been coined, or given greater currency, to avoid language that was thought to be prejudicial are *humankind* ('mankind'), *humans* or *human beings* (generic 'man'), *chair* or *chairperson* ('chairman'), *flight attendant* ('steward' or 'stewardess'), *supervisor* ('foreman'), *gender reassignment* ('sex change'), *differently abled* ('handicapped'). Compounds with *challenged*—such as *physically challenged* ('crippled') and *intellectually challenged* ('unintelligent')—have been created to denote people who suffer from disabilities or to refer to the disabilities themselves, since *disabled* and *handicapped* were felt to be objectionable. This compounding has given rise to jocular inventions, such as *sartorially challenged* applied to a British politician who is notorious for slovenly clothing.

The perception, promoted by the feminist movement, that English has an in-built bias against women has had the most repercussions, and some of the proposals for change have won wide acceptance in several of the countries where English is a majority first language. In particular, the generic use of *man* and *men* to include women is now avoided. Whereas the American Declaration of Independence asserted in 1776 that 'all men are created equal', as far back as 1948 the Universal Declaration of Human Rights declared unambiguously that 'All human beings are born free and equal in dignity and rights'.

One major target for attack has been a feature in grammar. English has a gender distinction for the third person singular pronoun: masculine *he* and feminine *she*. It does not have a gender-neutral singular pronoun when generic reference is intended to include both men and women. Numerous proposals, reaching back more than a hundred years, have been offered for an epicene pronoun; for example: *thon, tey, en*. None has gained acceptance. The present fluidity of usage may be seen in extracts from the 1990 regulations of a School in the University of London. The first citation follows the traditional prescription to use the masculine:

[1] No student will be admitted to any course until *he* has paid the requisite fees. [W2D-007-7]

This use has been denounced as reinforcing the stereotype of men as dominant and in some contexts (for example, job advertisements) it may be interpreted as excluding women. The alternatives *he or she* (sometimes written *s/he, him/her, his/her*) may serve as a satisfactory substitute:

[2] No student is allowed to register or study concurrently for more than one examination of the University of London or of the School unless *he or she* has previously obtained in writing the permission of the Director of the School. [W2D-007-11]

If alternative forms are needed more than once, the result can be clumsy:

[3] A candidate who wishes to enter the School before *his or her* eighteenth birthday may be asked to write to state *his or her* reasons. [W2D-007-45]

Resort can be had instead to *they, them,* or *their* as generic singulars, a common usage in speech:

[4] This certificate lists the four courses for which the student was registered, showing letter grade assessments of *their* work over the year and grades for *their* examination performance. [W2D-007-76]

Some people object to this use of the *they*-pronouns as singulars, despite the convenience. Another method is to use the plural throughout, thereby sanctioning the use of *they*:

> **[5]** *Students* failing to disclose this fact are liable to have *their* registration cancelled. [W2D-007-13]

Or to avoid using pronoun forms:

> **[6]** Every student is allocated a tutor, who will advise in the selection of courses and act throughout the session as supervisor. [W2D-007-70]

In **[6]** the direct object pronoun has been omitted after *advise*, and possessive pronouns have been omitted before *courses* and *supervisor*.

Some writers—usually women writers—have employed a mixture of stratagems, including the use of *she* as a generic. Professor Jean Aitchison, a linguist, explicitly mentions this in the preface to a recent book:

> **[7]** One further point: in this edition, I have tried to avoid the sexist linguistic usages found in the earlier versions, which misleadingly implied in places that only males of our species could talk. I have done this partly by using the plural (*people* instead of *he*), partly by using indefinites (*a person, anyone*) followed by a plural pronoun (*if anyone is surprised, they should see how increasingly common this usage is*), and partly by interchanging *he* and *she* in places where a neutral between sexes pronoun is required. [Jean Aitchison, *Teach Yourself Linguistics* (London: Hodder & Stoughton, 1992), p. viii.]

The previous edition was published in 1987, only five years earlier. It is likely that people will continue to choose from the existing variants rather than adopt a new pronoun and that *they* will increasingly become acceptable as the generic singular even in formal style.[15]

Chapter 2
The Scope and Nature of Grammar

Summary

Chapter 2 Summary

- The word *grammar* is used variously, both in everyday language and as a technical term. It may refer to a book or to the contents of a book. Its scope may be restricted to syntax (the ways in which words combine into structures of phrases, clauses, and sentences) or it may include many other aspects of language. Grammars may be primarily intended as reference works or as textbooks; they may be aimed at native speakers or foreign learners. Descriptive grammar describes the rules of the language objectively whereas prescriptive grammar evaluates and advises.

- In one technical sense, a grammar is a theory of language description that can be applied to individual languages. Universal grammar concerns the properties that are common to all human languages. Traditional grammar adopts terms and approaches to language description, derived from Latin grammars, that were common in previous centuries.

- The most influential—and controversial—figure in theoretical linguistics in recent times has been Noam Chomsky, who conceives the goal of linguistics to be a description of the mental grammar of native speakers: the system of rules and principles that characterize the mental structures that underlie their ability to speak and understand their language. Chomsky hypothesizes that human beings have an innate language faculty that enables children to acquire a mental grammar quickly when they are exposed to a particular language. The object of research is the linguistic competence of the ideal native speaker, who knows the language perfectly, which is to be distinguished from linguistic performance. Grammaticality is related to competence, whereas acceptability is related to performance.

- Sentences may be unacceptable for various reasons; for example, because they are factually or logically nonsensical or because they are stylistically clumsy. Technically, a sentence is ungrammatical only in relation to a particular model of grammar; it is ungrammatical if that grammar does not account for it as a grammatical sentence of the language.

- For their data, linguists may draw on samples of actual use of the language, their own knowledge of the language, and judgements about the language elicited from native speakers. Theoretical linguists have tended to rely solely on introspection and their own evaluations.

- The study of language has a strong claim to be included in the curriculum as part of general knowledge. There are also applications for the study of language generally and for the study of syntax in particular.

- The tradition of English grammatical writing is based on the Latin grammars that were produced in the medieval and renaissance periods. Their influence persists in current terminology and approaches to grammar.

What is Grammar?

2.1
Types of grammar books

The word *grammar* is used in a number of ways. It may refer to a book, in which case a grammar is analogous to a dictionary. And just as we have many English dictionaries, which vary in the number of their entries and the quality of their definitions, so we have many English grammars (or grammar books), which vary in their coverage and their accuracy. The largest English dictionary is the scholarly twenty-volume *Oxford English Dictionary*, which traces the history of words and their meanings. Similarly, there are large scholarly grammars, notably the seven-volume *Modern English Grammar on Historical Principles*, published at intervals between 1909 and 1949 and still consulted by scholars, and the more recent *Comprehensive Grammar of the English Language*, published in 1985, that extends to nearly 1,800 pages.[1]

In the concrete sense of the word *grammar*, a grammar is a book of one or more volumes. We of course also use *grammar* for the contents of the book. When we compare grammars for their coverage and accuracy, we are referring to the contents of the book: a grammar is a book on grammar, just as a history is a book on history.

Grammars vary in their coverage. They are sometimes restricted to syntax, the ways in which words combine into structures of phrases, clauses, and sentences. But grammars may also include descriptions of one or more other aspects of language: morphology (the internal structure of words), word-formation (how new words are formed from more basic elements), phonetics (the possible sounds and sound patterns), phonology (the distinctive sounds and sound patterns), orthography (the conventional spellings), vocabulary, semantics (the meanings of words and sentences), and pragmatics (the interpretation of utterances in their contexts). This grammar treats all these aspects of language, but the term *grammar* is used in Chapters 3–5 in a common popular and technical usage as a synonym of *syntax*.

A distinction is often made between a reference grammar and a pedagogical grammar. Like a dictionary, a reference grammar is intended for individual consultation; it is not expected to be read or studied from beginning to end. Some reference grammars resemble dictionaries closely in being organized alphabetically rather than (as is usual) thematically.

Pedagogical grammars, on the other hand, are textbooks, chiefly intended for class use under the guidance of a teacher. The material in pedagogical grammars is graded according to the level and ability of the expected users and is generally presented in sections that can reasonably be absorbed within a class period. A topic is usually revisited in later sections in greater detail. It is assumed that sections will be studied in consecutive order.

In practice, the distinction between these two types of grammars is not always clear-cut. Reference grammars—or chapters from them—are sometimes used in class, and the more advanced pedagogical grammars may explicitly aim to serve also as reference works. Some pedagogical grammars are intended additionally—or chiefly—for self-study.

Further distinctions can be drawn that apply to both pedagogical and reference grammars. Some English grammars are primarily intended for native speakers and others primarily for non-native learners. And just as there are bilingual dictionaries, so there are grammars of English that point out problems for (say) German or Swedish speakers or interesting contrasts with what occurs in their own language.

Finally, grammars have different general objectives and their readers differ in their interests. Some readers study grammar because they wish to improve their use of the language. Others feel themselves competent in the language and are interested, or also interested, in learning about the language—in studying grammar for its own sake and not necessarily for practical applications.

2.2
Descriptive and prescriptive grammar

A distinction is often made between descriptive grammar and prescriptive grammar. Descriptive grammar attempts to describe the rules of the language objectively, accounting for what actually occurs. Prescriptive grammar is evaluative, guiding readers as to what is correct or incorrect. For example, a prescriptive grammar may prescribe that *none* takes a singular verb or it may allow either singular or plural; it may proscribe the adverb *badly* after a copula verb as in *We feel badly about it* (insisting on the adjective *bad*), *can* in the permission sense as *Can I leave now?* (requiring *may* instead), and *like* as a conjunction in *They behaved like they know me* (prescribing *as if*). Prescriptive grammar focuses on phenomena that are in divided usage in standard English, such as whether *data* is to be treated as singular or plural, or features that occur chiefly in non-standard usage, such as the multiple negation in *I didn't say nothing about nobody* (corresponding to *I didn't say anything about anybody* in standard English).

Evaluations as to what is correct or incorrect are intended for those who want to use standard English and are unsure about particular points. Evaluations may vary, since prescriptive writers rely largely on their own feelings. They do not necessarily accept evidence of what most educated people use or even of the usage of those considered to be the best writers or speakers.

Guides to usage are predominantly prescriptive. Many grammars contain both descriptive and prescriptive rules. The most sensitive guides and grammars point to stylistic variation, noting (for example) that the conjunction *like* is common in speech in standard English but not in writing. Pedagogical grammars are inherently prescriptive when their purpose is to tell their users—for example, foreign learners of English—what to say or write, but the best are based on accurate descriptions of current uses.

Descriptive grammars that are concerned with stylistic variation sometimes refer to prescriptive rulings, since the rulings reflect attitudes to usages that may result in stylistic restrictions; for example, confinement of the usages to speech or to formal writing. Descriptive grammars generally describe the standard variety, though some may occasionally refer to different practices in non-standard varieties. In recent decades, major reference grammars of English have dealt with both the American and the British national standards, sometimes noting differences in other national standards. Descriptive grammars that are restricted to descriptions of standard varieties may be viewed as covertly prescriptive in that by ignoring non-standard varieties they implicitly downgrade their value. It is possible to formulate grammars of non-standard varieties, though there is greater variation in these varieties.[2]

2.3
Theories of grammar

Every grammatical description presupposes an underlying theory, though many descriptions do not make their theoretical basis explicit and some are eclectic in drawing on more than one theory. In one technical sense, a grammar is a theory of language description. Grammatical theories make assumptions about the nature of natural languages (the languages that human beings acquire naturally, as opposed to artificial languages, such as computer languages), present goals for describing them, and develop methods of argumentation, formulation, and explanation. Among the many current general theories of language are Transformational-Generative Grammar, Tagmemic Grammar, Systemic Grammar, and Word Grammar. Some designations refer to a set of theories that share objectives but differ in many important respects. For example, generative grammars include Government and Binding Theory, Generalized Phrase Structure Grammar, and Lexical-Functional Grammar.

Grammatical theories are applied to the descriptions of individual languages. Sometimes the purpose of the application is to develop the theory, to demonstrate how the theoretical framework can cope with the language data and to investigate what changes in the theory are required for it to be successful.

Universal grammar concerns the properties that are common to all human languages (including potential languages) and that may therefore be taken to be defining and necessary properties of human language. In another approach, requiring studies of large numbers of languages, language universals may be absolute without exceptions (for example, that all languages have nouns), or there may be universal tendencies that admit a relatively few exceptions (for example, that the basic word order is for the subject to appear before the object in a sentence, in the sequences subject–verb–object or subject–object–verb or verb–subject–object). Typological linguistics is the study of the characteristics shared by groups of languages (for example, that in one language type the subject normally precedes the verb whereas in another type it normally follows the verb) even though the languages are not necessarily related historically. On the other hand, historical linguistics (also called comparative grammar) deals with the characteristics of languages that are related historically, and traces the development of families of languages from a common source or traces the development of individual languages.

Traditional grammar adopts the approaches and descriptive categories used, particularly in school grammars, in the eighteenth and nineteenth centuries. Traditional grammars describe solely, or chiefly, the written language and are indebted to Latin grammars for some of their analyses of English. Scholarly reference grammars of the first half of the twentieth century, such as the major work by Otto Jespersen (cf. n. 1), have also been considered traditional grammars. Traditional grammars typically make use of notional criteria; for example, defining a noun as the name of a person, place, or thing rather than by formal criteria such as that nouns typically take plural inflections or that they typically may be introduced by *the*. Grammars that make frequent use of notional definitions are notional grammars.

A distinction is sometimes drawn between formal grammars and functional grammars. Formal grammars describe the formal rules and structures of the language. Functional grammars also describe how the language is used, taking account of communicative purposes and of stylistic and social factors.

Chomsky and Theoretical Linguistics

2.4
Grammar in the mind

During the last forty years, the most influential figure in theoretical linguistics has been Noam Chomsky. Even linguists who oppose his views have been influenced by them and have been compelled to react to them.

Chomsky conceives the goal of linguistics to be a description of the internalized grammar of native speakers—their mental grammar. This is the knowledge of rules and principles that underlies their ability to speak and understand their language. It is an unconscious knowledge and is to be distinguished from the conscious knowledge that we obtain if we study grammar. As native speakers, we acquire our unconscious knowledge through exposure to the language during childhood. We do not need to study grammar to be able to communicate in our own language. After all, people were speaking and writing English long before the first English grammars appeared at the end of the sixteenth century. In any case, though English is the language that has been most intensively researched, linguists are nowhere near to having uncovered a complete grammar of English, so it would not be possible to learn all the highly complex rules even if we could imagine making use of conscious knowledge of them as we speak.

Chomsky draws a distinction between competence in language and performance in language. Competence is the underlying knowledge, whereas performance is the actual use made of that knowledge. Performance is affected by factors that are assumed to have nothing to do with language; for example, limitations on memory and a person's mental state at the time. Chomsky restricts the goal of linguistics to a description of linguistic competence. Since mental grammars are not directly observable, evidence for a description of competence must be derived from some aspects of performance, such as the judgements of native speakers on whether the constructions are ambiguous and on whether a set of sentences are similar in meaning. Chomsky's belief that progress in linguistics requires researchers to concentrate on competence is controversial and so are his views on what data constitute evidence for his theory. Chomsky's conception of competence in most of his work is restricted to the knowledge that enables a native speaker to produce an indefinitely large number of sentences, some of which are novel in the sense that they do not replicate sentences that the speaker (and perhaps anybody else) has produced before. For example, it is unlikely that the previous sentence has ever been written in exactly that wording. Many linguists have argued that competence should include (for example) knowing how to use sentences in context, since that knowledge may affect the form of sentences (particularly their intonation) and the interpretation of sentences. In his more recent work, Chomsky has implicitly taken account of some of this criticism.

We can assume that individual speakers of the language have different mental grammars. It is obvious, for example, that people vary in the number of words they know and the meanings they ascribe to them. We might expect them to vary also in the range of constructions that they can use and understand. Chomsky is not concerned with language variation. For him the goal of linguistic description is a description of the ideal speaker-hearer's intrinsic competence. Just as a perfect dictionary would ignore the limitations on the knowledge of actual speakers (and of course all our present incomplete dictionaries discount those limitations), so a perfect grammar must ignore the limitations and idiosyncrasies in their actual grammars. Linguists have traditionally generalized, abstracting from variation in use, but this abstraction has been carried to great lengths by Chomsky and his followers.

Chomsky claims psychological reality for the formulations of his theory. His grammar is intended to represent the mental grammar of the native speaker. The model of this mental grammar that the theory constructs undergoes changes as additional data are discovered and accounted for, and the theory may need to be amended drastically. At one time, it was thought that the rules postulated for the grammar would correspond to the mental operations in the production and recognition of speech, but attempts to find evidence for the psychological reality of the rules in the encoding–decoding processes have been frustrated. Psychological reality is claimed only for the representation of the knowledge of the rules. But that claim is highly significant, for it asserts that a successful representation reflects the structure of that part of the human mind that deals with language.

Chomsky also claims that his theory explains how children acquire the ability to speak at an early age despite the complexity of the rules and despite their exposure to fragmentary and imperfect data. Children hear incomplete sentences, hesitations, and false starts, and yet are able to construct an internalized grammar that abstracts from the data that they are exposed to. Chomsky hypothesizes that human beings have a language faculty separate from other mental faculties. This faculty—referred to as universal grammar—is species-specific (limited to human beings) and innate. Because children are equipped with this innate faculty, they are able to construct an internalized grammar quickly when they are exposed to a particular language. Many psychologists and linguists are sceptical of the belief that there is a language faculty distinct from other structures of the mind. They view linguistic knowledge as part of general knowledge, and consider that language acquisition as well as language processing should be investigated within the same framework as other types of cognitive acquisition and processing.

According to Chomsky, the principles required to abstract from the raw data to construct an internalized grammar are universal, pertaining to universal grammar. Chomsky and his followers have been exploring the extent to which rules can be assigned to universal grammar, reducing what needs to be described for individual languages. It is hypothesized that in addition to innate absolute universals that are common to all languages, there is also an innate set of parameters that vary among languages. When exposed to a particular language, children have to recognize which settings of parameters are applicable to that language. One parametric setting (or value) allows an unstressed subject pronoun to be dropped in a language such as Hebrew—but not in English—and the same setting regularly marks the verb with the person and the number (and in some instances the gender) of the subject. Another parametric variation applies to the ordering of verbs and objects. In languages such as English, the verb ordinarily comes before the object, but the reverse order is normal in a language such as Japanese. Research into parametric variation has been making important contributions to linguistic typology, though the psychological underpinning is not generally accepted.

Not all linguistic theories present claims for the psychological reality of their grammar. Some theories have a sociological bias, striving to explain the functions of language in human interaction. Other theories have practical aims, attempting descriptions that can be best applied to teaching of languages to foreign learners, to translations, or to natural language processing on computers. Some theories, such as Chomsky's, make claims for the truth of their grammars. Others are happy to be judged by criteria such as economy, simplicity, and elegance or by the successes they achieve when they are applied in other fields.[3]

2.5
Transformational-generative grammar

Chomsky's theory is a type of transformational-generative grammar, first advocated in his classic work *Syntactic Structures* (published in 1957) and modified in various stages. *Generate* is a term introduced into linguistics from mathematics, where it means 'provide a precise specification for membership in a set'. A generative grammar is intended to specify precisely the membership of the set of all the grammatical sentences in the language, excluding from the set all the possible ungrammatical sentences. It is a formal grammar that ideally consists of all the rules required to specify the structures, interpretations, and pronunciation of all the grammatical sentences. Informal grammars rely heavily on the knowledge of the language possessed by their users to fill gaps in the specifications. In a generative grammar the specifications are of the kind that would be required by computer programs.

The formulations of rules in Chomsky's theory have changed radically, but an early formulation may illustrate what is meant by precise specification. The very simple set of rules in [1] generates a large number of sentence structures:

[1]   (i)   S → NP + VP

       (ii)   NP → (Det) + (Adj) + N

       (iii) VP → V + (NP)

These are rewrite (or expansion) rules for phrase structure. The rules are instructions for rewriting the symbol on the left of the arrow as a string of one or more symbols on the right of the arrow. The symbols stand for Sentence, Noun Phrase, Verb Phrase, Determiner, Adjective, Verb, and Noun. Rule (i) is read as 'Rewrite S as NP plus VP'. Put informally, rule (i) specifies that a Sentence consists of a Noun Phrase and a Verb Phrase. Rule (ii) specifies that the Noun Phrase is a Noun preceded optionally by a Determiner and/or an Adjective. Rule (iii) specifies that the Verb Phrase consists of a Verb plus an optional following Noun Phrase. NP in rule (iii) allows the second application of rule (ii). Many complexities are here omitted; for example, that nouns may be singular or plural, verbs may be present or past, and adjectives may be comparative or superlative.

The lexicon (ideal mental dictionary) has a list of all the possible words in the language, their word category, and the structures they can fit in. Some examples, again in a highly simplified version, are given in [2]:

[2] Det: *a, the*

      Adj: *clever, large, old, tall*

      N: *book, child, man, Norman, Sheila*

      V: *bought, called, loved, saw, took*

The combination of the rules in **[1]** and the vocabulary in **[2]** allows the following sentences, among many others:

[3] Norman loved Sheila.

     Sheila saw Norman.

     Sheila called the child.

     The tall man bought a book.

     The clever child took a large book.

The structures of the sentences in **[3]** are given by the rules in **[1]** and **[2]**. The organization is hierarchical in that the words are grouped into constituents of the sentences: *Norman* is an NP consisting of just an N; *loved Sheila* is a VP consisting of a V (*loved*) and an NP that in turn consists of just an N (*Sheila*). The constituent structure or phrase structure can be represented by a tree diagram, as in **[4]** (**Fig. 2.5.1**):

Fig. 2.5.1 Tree diagram

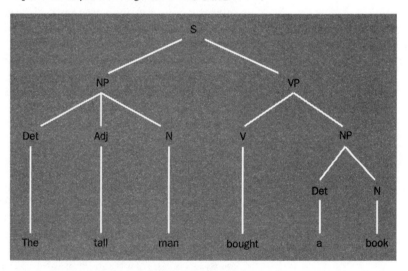

A transformational grammar makes use of transformations to relate structures. Chomsky claimed that phrase structural rules alone were inadequate for language description and that transformational rules were also needed to capture generalizations and to provide simpler and more elegant descriptions. Four types of transformational rules were proposed: these change one structure into another by moving, inserting, deleting, and replacing items. The nature of these rules has changed in the various stages of Chomsky's work and they remain a matter of considerable controversy.

A typical early transformation was the rule for changing an active sentence into a passive sentence. Though no longer a current rule, passivization is a useful illustration of a transformation. Passivization converts the active sentence **[5]** into the passive sentence **[6]**:

[5]   Martha may take the newspaper.

[6]   The newspaper may be taken by Martha.

The transformation operates on the structural description **[7]** that specifies the structure to which the rule applies:

[7] NP_1—AUX—V—NP_2

The structural change is shown in **[8]**:

[8] NP_2—AUX + *be* + *en*—V—*by* + NP_1

The rule involves several components of change, which can be illustrated for sentences **[5]** and **[6]**:

1. The second NP (*the newspaper*), which was the object of the verb in **[5]**, is the subject of the verb in **[6]** and has accordingly been moved to the front of the sentence.
2. The first NP (*Martha*), which was the subject of the verb in **[5]**, becomes part of a prepositional phrase introduced by the preposition *by*, and that phrase follows the verb.
3. *May take*, which consists of the auxiliary (AUX) *may* and the infinitive *take*, is expanded by the addition of a form of the auxiliary *be* (here simply *be*), and the main verb is changed into the passive participle form ending in *-en* (*taken*).

Further rules apply, which will not be discussed here. For example, the choice of the verb *be* depends on the preceding auxiliary. In **[9]** it is *been*, in **[10]** *being*, and in **[11]** *was*:

[9]   The newspaper has been taken by Martha.

[10]   The newspaper is being taken by Martha.

[11]   The newspaper was taken by Martha.

The ending *-en* is an irregular inflection for the passive participle, which regularly ends in *-ed*:

[12]   The newspaper may be borrowed by Martha.

Other examples of irregular forms of the participle are illustrated in **[13]** and **[14]**:

[13]   The newspaper will be read by Martha.

[14]   The newspaper may have been torn by Martha.

The rules will also have to allow for the optional deletion of the *by*-phrase:

[15]   The newspaper may have been borrowed.

The passive transformation was intended to capture the relationship between the active and the passive: the agent of the action (*Martha*), the thing affected by the action (*the newspaper*), and the action itself are the same in both **[5]** and **[6]**. The rules for the structures of constituents in the two sentences are identical. The passivization rule obviates the need for repeating independently the structural rules and the selectional restrictions. Selectional restrictions disallow the co-occurrence of certain semantic classes of words in specified syntactic relations. They exclude (for example) *The newspaper may drink Martha* and its passive *Martha may be drunk by the newspaper*.

Early in his work, Chomsky postulated two levels of syntactic structure: deep structure and surface structure. The operation of phrase structure rules resulted in deep (or underlying) structure, and the operation of transformational rules on deep structure resulted in surface structure. Identical deep structures were posited for sets of sentences such as those in **[16]**–**[19]**:

[16] I consider her my best friend.
I consider her to be my best friend.

[17] That you haven't ever met him is surprising.
It is surprising that you haven't ever met him.

[18] We have turned off all the lights.
We have turned all the lights off.

[19] She writes better than you write.
She writes better than you do.
She writes better than you.

On the other hand, sentences **[20]** and **[21]** are ambiguous. The ambiguities were said to reflect different deep structures.

[20] Visiting relatives can be a nuisance.

[21] It's too hot to eat.

The ambiguity of **[20]** is dissolved when we replace *can be* by *is* and *are*:

[22] Visiting relatives is a nuisance.

[23] Visiting relatives are a nuisance.

In **[22]** *visiting relatives* can be paraphrased by 'to visit relatives', whereas in **[23]** it is synonymous with 'relatives who visit'. In **[21]** *it* can be the general pronoun found in *It's sunny* and *It's raining*, or it can refer to a baby or living animal, or it can refer to food. The ambiguities are revealed by expansions:

[24] It ['the weather'] is too hot for us to eat anything.

[25] It ['the dog'] is too hot for it to eat anything.

[26] It ['the food'] is too hot for anyone to eat it.

In the sense of **[25]** the subject *it* in **[21]** is identical with the underlying subject of *eat*, whereas in the sense of **[26]** *it* is identical with the underlying object of *eat*.

Traditional grammars devoted attention to many of the transformations posited in the earlier stages of transformational-generative grammar, though they did not set up a formal descriptive apparatus for the correspondences. They considered active sentences as basic, and passive sentences were described in relation to them. Similarly, negative sentences were related to positive sentences, and questions to statements. Research on transformations has been valuable in discovering relationships between structures. However, most current linguistic theories have dispensed with transformational rules and do not recognize a distinction between surface and deep structure.[4]

2.6
Grammatical and acceptable

In everyday use, a sentence is said to be grammatical when it conforms to what are thought to be the norms of the language. Critics may condemn *Tell it like it is* as ungrammatical or not correct because *like* is being used as a conjunction, contrary to what they think is correct or proper in standard English. They may similarly condemn constructions such as *people what live in this neighbourhood* and *It ain't right.*

As a technical term in linguistics, *grammatical* is used to designate conformity to the rules of a grammar based on a particular grammatical theory. Such a grammar applied to a non-standard dialect of English may include *people what live in this neighbourhood* as a grammatical construction.

A generative grammar attempts in its formulations an explicit account of the rules that differentiate grammatical or well-formed sentences from ungrammatical, ill-formed, or deviant sentences. The boundaries between the well-formed and the ill-formed are fuzzy. It is obvious that *Little a boy the ran street up* is not an English sentence, but judgements among both linguists and non-linguists have differed on the status of sentences such as *The talking about the problem saved her* and *I didn't believe it, although Sid asserted that Max left.* In their eagerness to reach the boundaries of the language, some generative linguists have discussed extremely clumsy sentences they thought should be included, such as *Max wanted Ted to persuade Alex to get lost, and Walt, Ira.*

Judgements on whether sentences are well-formed or not are judgements on their acceptability. In a generative grammar, sentences are either grammatical or ungrammatical—either included by the rules or excluded. Acceptability, however, is scalar: not only are there disagreements among native speakers, but also they may evaluate certain sentences as neither completely acceptable nor completely unacceptable.

Chomsky has maintained that grammaticality and acceptability are distinct concepts: grammaticality relates to competence, whereas acceptability relates to performance. A sentence may be unacceptable because of its length or complexity, reasons having to do with style or limitations on human memory. But such sentences are to be treated as grammatical because they cannot be excluded from the set of grammatical sentences without excluding acceptable sentences. For example, certain rules apply recursively and there is no obvious limit to the recursion. Examples of recursion are co-ordination in **[1]** and relative clauses in **[2]**:

> **[1]** Peter is happy and Joan is tired and Carol is angry and Norman is cold and . . .

> **[2]** This is the man that hit the dog that bit the cat that ate the mouse that frightened the child that . . .

Since there is no definable limit to the number of co-ordinate or relative clauses, the grammar will allow an infinite number, but in practice nobody would continue to produce them indefinitely or be happy with sentences that went on too long. In certain types of embedding of relative clauses within other relative clauses, the degree of unacceptability increases with each recursion, but generative grammars may find it inappropriate or uneconomical to handle the increase in terms of grammaticality. Compare the differences in acceptability in **[3]**, **[4]**, and **[5]**:

> **[3]** The woman who(m) the detective questioned lives in my apartment building and is an old friend of mine.
>
> **[4]** The woman who(m) the detective who(m) the students recognized questioned lives in my apartment building and is an old friend of mine.
>
> **[5]** The woman who(m) the detective who(m) the students who(m) I teach recognized questioned lives in my apartment building and is an old friend of mine.

Grammars vary in what types of unacceptability they can account for or want to account for. They tend to exclude types for which it is difficult or impossible to generalize. Sentences may be factually nonsensical, as in **[6]**, or logically nonsensical, as in **[7]**:

> **[6]** The earth is flat.
>
> **[7]** Two and two are five.

Unacceptability may depend on one's beliefs:

> **[8]** His parents are atheists, and mine are eccentric too.

We may reject a sentence because it seems implausible or absurd:

> **[9]** Your daughter has just swallowed a whale.

But it is often possible to imagine contexts or interpretations where a sentence such as **[9]** makes sense; for example, the whale was a toy or cake in the form of a whale. Metaphorical uses override absurd literal interpretations. Sentences that are nonsensical under a normal interpretation are commonly found in children's literature, fables, and poetry. We might dismiss **[10]** as ridiculous, but a recent work of fiction fits the sentence into a plausible context:

> **[10]** Give the lad a happy story to drink.[5]

The Study of Grammar

2.7
The data for grammar

Scholars researching into grammar can draw on a number of sources for their data. One obvious source is examples of actual use of the language. The examples may be collected to investigate a particular point; for instance, negative constructions in English (*I don't have any money, I have no money, I think it's not right, I don't think it's right*). These may be collected systematically (for example by reading through a set of newspapers) or casually (by noting examples that one reads or hears) or by a combination of these two approaches. For the voluminous *Oxford English Dictionary* some 800 voluntary readers supplied citations on slips from their casual reading, which were added to the citations that were more systematically collected from specified early works. Scholarly grammarians in the first half of this century (such as Otto Jespersen, cf. n. 1) amassed enormous numbers of citation slips for their research.

The recent availability of increasingly powerful small computers has promoted the creation of large corpora (collections of electronic texts) that are distributed internationally, providing data for researchers that were not involved in their compilation. A corpus may be limited in its scope (say, to dramatic texts or runs of particular newspapers) or it may attempt a wide coverage. Some English corpora now run into many millions of words. A few contain transcriptions of the spoken language, material that is not easily obtainable by individual researchers. Some corpora are annotated for grammatical or other features of the language, enabling researchers to retrieve such information as well as specified words or combinations of words. Corpus linguistics has become a major area of linguistic research. Studies in computer corpora have resulted in numerous publications.

Corpus studies have obvious attractions for linguists who are not native speakers of the language, since they can be confident that their material is reliable. Those who are native speakers still find it useful to check corpora for their generalizations. Corpora are essential for studies of varieties of language, since differences between varieties are generally exhibited in the relative frequencies with which particular linguistic features occur.

It may be a matter of chance whether relatively uncommon constructions or language features appear in even a very large corpus in sufficient quantities—or at all—to provide adequate evidence. Linguists can supplement corpus data by drawing on their own knowledge of the language. Indeed, it has been common practice among theoretical linguists in the last thirty years to rely solely on data drawn from introspection. They use their knowledge of the language to create a set of samples for their own investigation, and evaluate the samples for acceptability, similarities of meaning, and ambiguities, and draw on their intuitions for decisions on grammatical structure.

Linguists may be biased or unsure in their judgements. It has been a common practice to consult the judgements of others, often native informants who would not know the purpose of the investigations. Some linguists have devised elaborate elicitation procedures under controlled conditions, asking large groups of informants for their judgements or requiring them to perform specified tasks. For example, when 175 British informants were asked to complete a sentence beginning *I badly*, most of them used either *need* (65 per cent) or *want* (28 per cent), indicating that these were the favourite verbs when the intensifier *badly* was in pre-verb position. In another experiment, eighty-five American informants were asked to use *probably* with the sentence *He can not drive a car*; 70 per cent of them positioned it before the auxiliary *can*, evidence that this is its normal position in a negative sentence.

2.8
Reasons for studying grammar

From time to time there are public debates about the teaching of grammar in schools. Educational fashions change, and after a period of over twenty-five years since the formal teaching of grammar was abandoned in most state schools there have been recent calls in both Britain and the United States for the reintroduction of grammar teaching as part of 'a return to basics'.

There are sound arguments for teaching about language in general and the English language in particular. An understanding of the nature and functioning of language is a part of the general knowledge that we should have about ourselves and the world we live in. In this respect, linguistics deserves a place at all levels of the curriculum at least as much as (say) history, geography, or biology. For language is the major means by which we communicate with others and interact with them, and our attitudes to our own variety and the varieties of others affect our image of ourselves and of others. Linguistics is a central discipline that has bearings on many other disciplines: psychology, sociology, anthropology, philosophy, literature, and computer science. Vocational applications are found in areas as diverse as the teaching of foreign languages, speech therapy, and information technology.

Study of the English language can help students develop their ability to adjust their language appropriately to different contexts. They should be aware of the expectations that standard English is the norm for public writing, and they will need to learn to adopt the conventions for public writing in grammar, vocabulary, spelling, and punctuation.

Grammar (in the sense of 'syntax') is generally regarded as central to linguistics, and it should therefore be included in a linguistic curriculum on its own terms. Many educationists have denied that a study of grammar can improve the ability to write English correctly and effectively, but (as with all subjects) it depends on what is taught and how it is taught. It would seem reasonable to suppose that written style can be improved through learning about the resources for grammatical structures, word order, and the devices for connecting sentences and paragraphs. Certainly, that kind of knowledge would be helpful at the editing stages to improve the style of earlier drafts and to correct grammatical errors.

There are other applications of a knowledge of grammar both in and out of the classroom: the interpretation of texts—literary or non-literary—sometimes depends on grammatical analysis; recognition of grammatical structures is often required for punctuation; and a study of one's own grammar is helpful in studying the grammar of a foreign language.

2.9
The tradition of English grammatical writing

The Western tradition for the study of grammar derives from the Greek philosophers, who treated it in their discussions of logic and rhetoric, and the study was taken up by Roman scholars. This tradition continued in the works on Latin grammar that were produced in the medieval and renaissance periods, when Latin was the language of learning. The grammar that was taught in the early grammar schools in England was Latin grammar, not English grammar.

The earliest known grammar of English was by William Bullokar, published in 1580, who wanted to show that English was as capable of grammatical analysis as was Latin. By 1800, a total of 112 grammars were published, excluding later editions. Most of these were slight, containing lists of letters and syllables and their pronunciation, definitions of parts of speech with their inflections, and treatments of punctuation and versification, and a very little on syntax. The traditional analyses for Latin grammar were generally applied to English grammar, including the Latin case names for nouns and the tenses for verbs, even though English does not have analogous inflections. There were exceptional authors such as John Wallis (one of the founders of the Royal Society), who treated English in its own terms in his 1653 grammar.

Most of the eighteenth- and nineteenth-century grammarians were prescriptive, setting out rules for correct speech and writing. By the twentieth century, both scholarly grammarians and textbook writers focused on the analysis of clauses. The emphasis on historical linguistics by the late nineteenth century added a new dimension, mainly in scholarly grammars: the writing of grammars of English that traced the history of forms and constructions. The most influential contemporary approach is exemplified in *A Comprehensive Grammar of the English Language* published in 1985 (cf. n. 1), an eclectic work drawing on the scholarly traditional grammars and on various recent linguistic theories. It is restricted to the two major national standards of American and British English in their present state, and has taken account of the spoken as well as the written language and of other types of stylistic variation. A notable feature is that it goes beyond the sentence to incorporate the influence of the context, both the linguistic context and the situational context.[6]

Chapter 3
An Outline of Grammar

Summary

Chapter 3 Summary

- Words, phrases, clauses, and sentences are grammatical units that constitute a hierarchy in which the sentence is at the highest level, though exceptions are common in the hierarchical relationship. Some grammatical phenomena apply across sentences, and some morphemes (constituents of words), such as inflections, need to be treated in the grammar.

- Sentences can be classified in various ways: (1) simple, compound, complex; (2) declarative, interrogative, imperative, exclamative; (3) statement, question, directive, exclamative; (4) assertion, request, offer, apology, and other kinds of speech act; (5) positive, negative; (6) active, passive.

- The basic structures of sentences always have a subject and a verb as constituents. The main verb may also require or permit one or two complements. The possible complements are direct object, indirect object, subject predicative, and object predicative. In addition, sentences usually have one or more adverbials, which are optional constituents. The constituents have semantic roles, indicating the part they play in the description of the situation. For example, the subject may be the agent of an action. The basic structures can be arranged in various ways.

- Part of the structure of a sentence may be omitted without affecting the acceptability of the sentence or its interpretation. The interpretation of the ellipsis may depend on information in the situation as well as the words of the sentence. For textual ellipsis the interpretation depends solely on the words that come before the ellipsis (anaphoric ellipsis) or those that come after it (cataphoric ellipsis).

- There are five types of phrases: noun phrases, verb phrases, adjective phrases, adverb phrases, prepositional phrases. The major division in word classes (or parts of speech) is into open classes (nouns, verbs, adjectives, adverbs) and closed classes (such as pronouns and auxiliaries). The open classes readily admit new words and therefore most words belong to the open classes.

- Seven grammatical categories apply to verbs (main verbs and auxiliaries), affecting the forms that verbs can have: mood (indicative, imperative, subjunctive), modality (modal auxiliaries), tense (present, past), aspect (perfect, progressive), voice (active, passive), number (singular, plural), person (first, second, third).

- Two categories apply to nouns: number (singular, plural) and case (common, genitive). Four categories apply to pronouns: number (singular, plural), person (first, second, third), case (subjective, objective, genitive), gender (masculine, feminine, non-personal).

- The semantic category of comparison applies to adjectives and adverbs that are gradable. These may have inflections for comparatives (e.g. *taller*) and superlatives (e.g. *tallest*) or periphrastic forms (e.g. *more wealthy, most wealthy*).

■ Phrases may be linked by co-ordination or apposition.

The Scope of Grammar

3.1
The grammatical hierarchy

Here and in the next three chapters, *grammar* is employed, in one of its common uses, as a synonym of syntax: the study of the ways in which words combine into structures of phrases, clauses, and sentences.[1]

Those four grammatical units—words, phrases, clauses, and sentences—constitute a hierarchy. The sentence is at the highest level in the hierarchy, the word is at the lowest level. Within the hierarchy:

> a sentence consists of one or more clauses
> a clause consists of one or more phrases
> a phrase consists of one or more words

Let us start with the sentence. In **[1]** the sentence consists of just one clause:

[1] His account contains many historical solecisms. [W2A-001-26]

We can divide that sentence into three phrases:

[2] His account
contains
many historical solecisms

The phrases in **[2]** consist of one or more words. Each phrase has a head (or principal word). The three heads are the noun *account*, the verb *contains* (the only word), and the noun *solecisms*. The three phrases are named after their heads:

[2a] His account   **noun phrase**
contains   **verb phrase**
many solecisms   **noun phrase**

Each phrase can be assigned a grammatical function in the clause:

[2b] His account   **subject: noun phrase**
contains   **verb: verb phrase**
many solecisms   **direct object: noun phrase**

As we can see from **[2b]**, a noun phrase can function as either the subject or the direct object. However, a verb phrase can function only as the verb of the clause or sentence.[2]

Just as a sentence may consist of only one clause so a phrase may consist of only one word. This may seem peculiar, since in everyday usage we think of phrases as having more than one word. The reason for the grammatical usage is economy. Rules that apply to a phrase apply equally whether the phrase consists of one word or more than one word. By allowing one-word phrases, grammarians can avoid having to repeat the same rules for one-word phrases and multi-word phrases. We can see that this is so, since we can reduce each phrase in **[2b]** to one word and preserve its grammatical functions.

[2c] It   **subject: noun phrase**
     contains   **verb: verb phrase**
     solecisms   **direct object: noun phrase**

You will notice that in **[2c]** the pronoun *it* is taken as the head of a noun phrase. That is because pronouns are essentially a subcategory of nouns.

The grammatical hierarchy is subverted in two ways: at the same level and across levels. A grammatical unit can contain other units at the same level in the hierarchy. Compounds are words composed of more than one word (usually only two words), e.g. the noun *headache* and the verb *babysit*. Phrases commonly contain other phrases. To take a simple example, the subject of **[3]** is the noun phrase *the title of the course*:

[3]   *The title of the course* was Woodland Ecology [S1A-036-162]

The noun phrase (NP) contains within it the prepositional phrase (PP) *of the course* (headed by the preposition *of*), which in turn contains the noun phrase *the course*. These relationships are expressed schematically in **[3a]**:

[3a] the title of the course   NP
            of the course   PP
              the course   NP

A clause can also contain another clause:

[4]   *If* you've been given a voucher *because* you have a low income, the value of your voucher may be reduced. [W2D-001-106]

The *if*-clause ends at *income*, and the *because*-clause is within the *if*-clause ('if you've been given a voucher for that reason'). Finally, a sentence can be embedded within a sentence in direct speech, as in the sentence marked off by quotation marks in **[5]**:

[5]   Prince Charles duly walked down the line, shook hands with who was there, and then, showing a rather splendid sense of humour said 'You know, I could have commanded him to be here tonight.' [W2B-004-32]

Units at a higher level in the grammatical hierarchy can function within units at a lower level. For example, the clause *pay as you earn* can be embedded in the noun phrase *the pay-as-you-earn policy*. More commonly, the embedded clause follows the head noun; for example, the *that*-clause in **[6]**, which modifies the noun *things*:

[6]   I had *a whole list of things that I wanted to buy eventually* [S1A-013-102]

3.2
Above the sentence and below the word

The sentence is the highest unit that is normally treated in grammar. However, some grammatical phenomena apply equally across sentences. For example, pronouns may refer to words in a preceding sentence, as in [1]:

> [1] *Organic farming* takes its cue from traditional agriculture. *It* makes use of the best ideas from the past and grafts onto them a scientific approach coupled with modern techniques that were unheard of in our grandfather's day. [W2B-027-17 f.]

The initial pronoun *it* in the second sentence refers back to the initial phrase *organic farming* in the first sentence, and the choice of *it* rather than (say) *she* or *they* is determined by the reference to that phrase. If we were to combine the two sentences by introducing the subordinating conjunction *since* between them, the same reference of *it* to *organic farming* would be across clauses but within one sentence. This type of reference also occurs within a clause: in the first sentence of [1] *its* also refers back to *organic farming*. Here is an example with *it*:

> [2] *Moussaka*'s got aubergines in *it* [S1A-063-23]

The unit below the word is the morpheme. Words consist of one or more morphemes; for example, we can divide the word *grandfather* into the morphemes *grand* and *father*. For most purposes, the word is the lowest unit that is treated in grammar. However, there is one important respect in which the grammar needs to refer to morphemes. Inflections are morphemes that signal the grammatical variants of a word; the inflectional *-s* at the end of *ideas* indicates that the noun is plural; the inflectional *-s* at the end of *makes* indicates that the verb is the third person singular, so that we say *she makes* but *I make* and *they make*. In addition, some affixes signal the part of speech to which a word belongs: the prefix *en-* in *enslave* converts the noun *slave* into a verb, and the suffix *-ize* converts the adjective *modern* into the verb *modernize*.

Sentences

3.3
Simple, compound, and complex sentences

Traditionally, sentences are classified as simple, compound, or complex according to their internal clause composition. A sentence consisting of one clause is a simple sentence. Hence, [1] is a simple sentence, and so is the much longer [2], which has phrases that are more complex than those in [1]:

> [1] I went there last week [S2A-024-9]
>
> [2] My Right Honourable Friend the Secretary of State met health authority

chairmen on the tenth of July and more recently at a briefing seminar in Cardiff on the nineteenth of October [S1B-056-3]

Clauses are units that, like sentences, can be analysed in terms of constituents functioning as subject, verb, direct object, etc.

A compound sentence consists of two or more clauses at the same grammatical level. Each of the clauses is a main clause, and typically each could be an independent sentence:

[3]   It has only been a week *and* I feel lonesome without you. [W1B-001-36]

In [3] the two main clauses are linked by the co-ordinator *and*.

A complex sentence contains a subordinate clause as one of its constituents. In the complex sentence [4] the subordinate clause functions as a direct object of the verb *understood*. The clause is introduced by the subordinator *that*:

[4]   Men of rank and education in the provinces understood *that* the preponderance of Roman strength doomed resistance or revolt to failure. [W2A-001-58]

It is perhaps easier to see that the *that*-clause is a direct object if we replace it with the pronoun *that*, as in [4a]:

[4a] Men of rank and education in the provinces understood *that*.

Unlike [4], [4a] is a simple sentence, since it consists of only one clause.

The traditional classification of sentences into simple, compound, and complex is a simplification of the clausal patterns in sentences, since it does not take into account frequent clause relations such as the co-ordination of subordinate clauses and subordination within one or more of the main clauses in a compound sentence. In addition, the spoken language in particular commonly contains utterances that cannot be analysed in terms of clauses. These issues are discussed in 6.1–7.

3.4
Declarative, interrogative, imperative, and exclamative sentences

We can distinguish four types of sentences with respect to their major uses in communication:

1. declaratives, or declarative sentences, for statements
2. interrogatives, or interrogative sentences, for questions
3. imperatives, or imperative sentences, for directives
4. exclamatives, or exclamative sentences, for exclamations

Declaratives are the most common type. They are also the basic type, in that the others can be most easily described by their differences from declaratives.

The four sentence types are illustrated by the following four related simple sentences:

[1]	They work hard.	(declarative)
[1a]	Do they work hard?	(interrogative)
[1b]	Work hard.	(imperative)
[1c]	How hard they work!	(exclamative)

3.5
Interrogative sentences

The two major types of interrogatives are *yes–no* questions and *wh*-questions.[3] *Yes–no* questions are generally intended to elicit the reply *yes* or *no*:

[1] Do you always work very quickly [S1B-023-65]

[2] Have you got an Uncle Victor [S1B-026-29]

[3] Would you quarrel with that [S1B-028-80]

[4] Can you remember how you felt when you heard that she died [S1B-046-71]

[5] Are there any other matters arising [. . .] [S1B-077-90]

[6] Is this call for maturity amongst our politicians and communicators naïve? [W2A-017-38]

The response may be more informative than a simple *yes* or *no*:

[7] A: Do you drink quite a lot of it ⟨ , ⟩

   B: Use it as a mixer for my uhm ⟨ , ⟩ lemonade ⟨ , , ⟩ and lime lemon lime and someone introduced it to me the other day [S1A-009-47 ff.]

The word order in *yes–no* questions differs from that in declaratives. In declaratives the subject comes before the verb, as in the declarative corresponding to **[2]**:

[2a] You have got an Uncle Victor.

In the *yes–no* question **[2]** the auxiliary verb is placed before the subject *you*. This change is subject–operator inversion, the operator generally being the first or only auxiliary. If the question does not have an auxiliary, *do* is inserted as a dummy auxiliary, as in **[1]**. For example, the *yes–no* question in **[8a]** corresponds to the declarative in **[8]**:

[8] It interferes with your life.

[8a] Does it interfere with your life [S1B-026-209]

Does in **[8a]** has the appropriate inflection (3rd person singular present tense) corresponding to the inflection of the verb *interferes* in **[8]**. The insertion of *do* in **[1]** and *does* in **[8a]** ensures that the question begins with the sequence verb followed by subject.[4]

Negative questions generally convey the speaker's expectation that the response should be positive:

[9] Isn't that a little irregular? [W2F-004-133] ('Surely it is')

[10] Haven't they got that the wrong way round [S1B-048-31]

[11] Can't you wait until everybody's finished having their lunch [S1B-049-38]

[12] Am I not allowed friends any more? [W2F-008-128]

Wh-questions expect a reply that supplies the information that the *wh*-word indicates as required. They are called *wh*-questions because the *wh*-words generally begin with *wh*-, the exception being *how*. The *wh*-word may be a pronoun **[13]**–**[15]**, an adverb **[16]**–**[21]**, or a determiner (introducing a noun phrase) **[22]**:

[13] *What* made you write them [S1B-048-8]

[14] *What* did he mean [S1B-047-23]

[15] *Who*'s next [S2A-054-92]

[16] Uhm but *why* isn't it in French [S1B-026-89]

[17] *Where* did it all begin? [W2B-010-158]

[18] *How* will this embarrassing confrontation end? [W2E-009-24]

[19] [. . .] *when* should the allies according to you cease hostilities [S1B-027-76]

[20] *How* deep is the snow [S2B-024-79]

[21] And uh ⟨ , , ⟩ *how* long did that go on for [S1B-066-70]

[22] *Which* bit do you want to start with first [S1B-071-1]

The *wh*-word is generally at the beginning of the question. If the *wh*-word or the phrase it is part of is the complement of a preposition, in formal style the preposition moves to the front together with its complement:[5]

[23] First of all *to what companies* does that scheme apply [S1B-062-81]

In less formal style, the preposition remains at the end:

[23a] First of all *what companies* does that scheme apply *to*?

The rule of subject–operator inversion applies generally to *wh*-questions. For example in **[24]** the direct object *what* begins the question and is followed by the dummy operator *do* and the subject *you*:

[24] What do you think? [W2F-013-9]

However, if the *wh*-expression is the subject of the sentence, there is no inversion. The normal declarative subject–verb order is retained:

[25] The crucial and fundamental question then arises: Who communicates about the threat and for what purposes? [W2A-017-27]

If the question seeks more than one piece of information, it may contain more than one *wh*-expression:

[26] Who is sampling who [S2B-023-6]

In the spoken language, the normal subject–verb order is sometimes retained even when the *wh*-expression is not the subject:

[27] You took which car?

[28] You did what next?

These may occur in an interview in a sequence of abrupt questions, they may be simple requests to repeat information, or they may express disbelief.

In addition to *yes–no* questions and *wh*-questions there are alternative questions. Alternative questions offer two or more options for the responses. One type of alternative question resembles a *yes–no* question **[29]**–**[31]** and the other type a *wh*-question **[32]**–**[33]**:

> **[29]** But is that a reflection on them ⟨ , ⟩ or on us [S2B-032-118]
>
> **[30]** Do we ask too much or too little of our police [S2B-032-119]
>
> **[31]** And uh that extrusion would it take place on a flexion injury or an extension injury or could it take place uh on either [S1B-068-80]
>
> **[32]** What are you doing for the summer, staying in Paris or going home? [W1B-001-109]
>
> **[33]** Uh which you ask is the more authentic the more mandated by tradition religious moderation ⟨ , ⟩ or religious extremism [S1B-047-69]

3.6
Tag questions

Tag questions are attached to clauses that are not interrogatives. The most common type of tag question is the abbreviated *yes–no* question:

> **[1]** Your heroines are very much of a type *aren't they* [S1B-048-147]
>
> **[2]** I can't be sure, *can I*? [W1B-001-9]

The tag may occur in the middle of a sentence:

> **[3]** So on going back to your to your childhood it was your mother *wasn't it* who was the driving force behind all of this behind this sort of intellectual rigour [S1B-046-48]

Tag questions generally consist of an operator followed by a pronoun. The operator echoes the previous auxiliary and the pronoun is co-referential with the previous subject. If there is no previous auxiliary, the dummy operator *do* is introduced, as with all *yes–no* questions (cf. 3.5).

> **[4]** And I think your mum likes company *doesn't she* [S1A-048-84]

A positive declarative generally takes a negative tag question **[1]** and **[3]**–**[4]**, whereas a negative declarative generally takes a positive tag question **[2]**.

The nuclear tone (distinct pitch movement) on the tag operator may be a rise or a fall. A rise is neutral in attitude, inviting the hearer to decide whether the preceding proposition is true. A fall invites the hearer to agree with the proposition.

Here are some further examples of tag questions:

> **[5]** But it's understated violence *isn't it* [S1B-048-144]
>
> **[6]** Yes they're always thrown in at the deep end *aren't they* [S1B-048-153]
>
> **[7]** He's not gone *has he*? [W2F-001-30]

[8] There's another story there, *isn't there?* [W2F-001-81]

[9] You don't mind, *do you?* [W2F-003-81]

[10] I can write *can't I?!!* [W1B-003-40]

Innit is an occasional informal variant of *isn't it*:

[11] [. . .] it's good news for you though *innit* [. . .] [S1A-019-320]

[12] Bit cheeky *innit* [S1A-078-165]

Both the declarative and its tag question are sometimes positive:

[13] So that's really unrealistic *is it* wanting to do to teach English [S1A-033-148]

[14] What's this funny thing What's this thing It's a foil *is it* [S1A-074-311]

[15] You're going to be transcribing all this *are you* [S1A-053-134]

[16] You've marked it *have you* [S1A-026-7]

This type of tag question points to a conclusion that the speaker has drawn on the basis of what was previously said or seen.

Tag questions may also be used with imperatives **[17]**–**[18]** and exclamatives **[19]**–**[20]**:

[17] Take a seat, *won't you?*

[18] Let me have a look, *will you?*

[19] What a mess he was in, *wasn't he?*

[20] How well she played, *didn't she?*

There are several tag questions that have the same form whatever appears in the previous declarative or exclamative. *Is it* appears to be a recently coined fixed tag:

[21] You mean about Felicity and her achievements *is it* [S1A-010-210]

[22] She looks she looks Puerto Rican or something *is it* [S1A-058-8]

[23] So you put you put in the sedative *is it* [. . .] [S1A-089-66]

Some well-established fixed tags are exemplified below:

[24] So you're not coming in *right* [S1A-008-152]

[25] Well what the hell *eh* [S1A-039-196]

[26] It must be peculiarly disconcerting, *don't you think*, to be left for someone entirely different from oneself? [W2F-011-92]

3.7
Imperative sentences

Second person imperatives—the typical and by far the most frequent imperatives—generally do not have a subject, but *you* is implied as subject:

[1] Just look at the beautiful scenery here [S2A-016-30]

[2] Never lecture with ⟨ , ⟩ animals or children and never ever try to do chemistry experiments live [S2A-053-63]

[3] As for whatever I said on the phone about our relationship, well if you can remember any of it still *please forget it* [S1B-003-169]

[4] Stir the spices into the meat, and season with salt and pepper. [S2D-020-86]

You can be added either for contrast or for some kind of emphasis (entreaty or warning):

[5] You pay now and I'll pay next time.

[6] You tell me. [W2F-001-53]

Occasionally, third person subjects occur:

[7] Nobody say anything.

[8] Those without letters from their parents raise their hands.

First and third person imperatives are formed with *let*. *Let* may be a main verb ('allow'), but *let's* must be the imperative auxiliary:[6]

[9] Uhm let me find you something ethnic [S1A-018-184]

[10] Let me put it this way [S1B-063-226]

[11] Let's have a closer look at some of those manœuvres [S2A-054-739]

[12] Let's get really drunk [S1A-048-119]

[13] Let us be clear, though, that a mature attitude to communications about national identity and international threat is possible. [W2A-017-71]

[14] Now ⟨ , ⟩ let me say again that is not a bad record by the police [S2B-037-84]

[15] The motto of the market is 'Let the buyer beware'. [W2A-019-70]

[16] In the long term, it is the replacement of Arab dictatorships by democracies that will be the best guarantee of freedom, stability and peace in the Middle East. Let Iraq be the first. [W2E-001-60 f.]

Do is placed before the imperative verb or auxiliary to make it less abrupt and more persuasive:

[17] Do bear in mind that unit values, and their income can fall as well as rise. [W1B-022-90]

[18] Do come in. [W2F-004-61]

[19] Do let's have another game.

Don't or *do not* is placed initially to negate second person and third person imperative sentences:

[20] But don't underestimate the problems [S2A-023-60]

[21] Don't be intimidated by vehicles following too close behind [S2A-054-165]

[22] Do not hesitate to contact me if you need any more information. [W1B-018-129]

[23] Don't let anybody in except me [S1B-048-120]

First person imperatives may be negated simply by inserting *not* after the pronoun:

[24] Oh let's not get touchy touchy [S1A-038-224]

[25] Let me not fall into temptation.

Alternatively, *don't* is inserted before *let's* or *let me* (especially in British English) or after *let's* (especially in American English):

[26] Don't let's tell the police [S1B-048-117]

[27] Don't let me think about it.

[28] Let's don't tell anyone.

3.8
Exclamative sentences

Exclamative sentences begin with *what* or *how*. *What* introduces noun phrases. Otherwise, *how* is used.

[1] What strong words you use. [W1B-003-160]

[2] What an idea you've got [S1A-032-230]

[3] And what an opportunity 〈 , 〉 this is for the youngster [S2A-003-81]

[4] What a star you are—as you would say! [W1B-002-25]

[5] How she how she talks [S1A-010-204]

[6] How clever he is [S1A-055-46]

[7] How sweet they were [. . .] [890929-0089-3]

[8] How well she plays.

Like the interrogative *wh*-phrase, the exclamative phrase is fronted. Otherwise, the word order is that of declaratives. Unlike questions, there is no subject–operator inversion (cf. 3.5). For example, the declaratives corresponding to **[1]** and **[6]** are:

[1a] You use such strong words.

[6a] He is so clever.

Such in **[1a]** is a determiner introducing a noun phrase, and *so* in **[6a]** is a premodifier of an adjective and can also premodify an adverb. Like *such* in **[1a]** and *so* in **[6a]**, *what* and *how* are intensifiers. In the absence of evaluative expressions in the context they may be interpreted as conveying either a high degree or a low degree. Thus, *what an idea* in **[2]** may be interpreted as 'an excellent idea' or as 'a terrible idea'. Similarly, *how she plays* may be interpreted as 'she plays excellently' or 'she plays badly'.

Exclamatives are often abbreviated to just the exclamative phrase:

[9] What a shame [S1A-006-278]

[10] What an admission from an actor. [W1B-003-11]

[11] How stupid [S1A-014-187]

[12] How nice for you [S1A-041-355]

In the following example, the *that*-clause is subordinate to the abbreviated exclamatory phrase *How wonderful*:

[13] How wonderful that this man has gotten a position in a university to help undo all the silly things that secretaries do when arranging luncheons, meetings, etc. [890725-0141-2]

3.9
Statements, questions, directives, exclamations

We have seen (cf. 3.4) that sentences fall into four main types that differ in form and that these four types are associated with four major uses in communication:

1. declaratives   statements
2. interrogatives   questions
3. imperatives   directives
4. exclamatives   exclamations

However, there is not a complete correlation between the sentence types and the communicative uses.

For example, rhetorical questions have the form of a question but the communicative function of a statement. If the rhetorical question is positive the implied statement is negative, and vice versa. The implied statement is the mental answer that the speaker intends the hearer to infer from the rhetorical question. Rhetorical questions are a persuasive device, and they are particularly common in persuasive discourse such as political speeches and newspaper editorials. They make take the form of *yes–no* questions **[1]–[2]** or *wh*-questions **[3]–[5]**:

[1] Don't I waffle on? [W1B-004-37] ('I certainly waffle on')

[2] My question is: is there any point in having a democracy when it can elect and keep on electing such a ludicrous government as we have had for the last ten years [W2B-014-41] ('There certainly isn't any point')

[3] What else is there to do? [W2C-014-97] ('There's nothing else to do')

[4] It has been a while since we spoke, but not too long for me to forget you—*how could I forget you*. [W1B-008-126] ('I couldn't possibly forget you')

[5] A: But sorry is this the right example Is this correct now

B: *Who knows* I really don't know [S1B-002-160 ff.]

Here is a series of rhetorical questions from an editorial:

[6] Even though the changes were more than he planned, we see no evidence that Mr Major's limited game of musical chairs is the shot in the arm his government badly needs. Does sending Gillian Shephard to agriculture make any more sense than sending John Gummer to environment? Where, apart from Mr Clarke's move, is the flair, the dash, the new blood and the supreme self-confidence the Tories need to sustain them through a troubled fourth term? Is John Redwood, the Thatcherite MP for Wokingham, really the man for Wales when his only link with the principality until now has been the M4? [*The Sunday Times*, 30 May 1993, p. 2.3]

In contrast to rhetorical questions, declarative questions have the form of a declarative but the force of a question. In writing they end in a question mark and in speech—as in A's question in **[8]**—they end with a rising intonation.

[7]   With all the bits of work you've done over the years, your CV must be full? [W1B-001-149]

[8]   A: A gentleman from the bank came down to see you

       B: That's right [S1B-061-14 f.]

Finally, exclamations may take the form of declaratives **[9]**–**[11]**, imperatives **[12]**–**[15]**, and interrogatives **[16]**–**[18]**:

[9]   I've not had a permanent job for almost two years now! [W1B-001-23]

[10] You can only have showers on week-days after supper, and you have to pay 5 Francs each time—I couldn't believe it! [W1B-002-126]

[11] He is also the most unsexy Spaniard I have ever seen! [W1B-005-99]

[12] I don't mean to sound religious, *God forbid no!* [W1B-001-13]

[13] Don't think that for one minute [S1B-049-43]

[14] [. . .] Do something exotic, wet and wild! [W1B-011-47]

[15] Shoot him! [W2F-012-130]

[16] Have you managed to have time away from wife-to-be!?! [W1B-002-134]

[17] What the hell is this? [W1B-005-41]

[18] So isn't the weather gorgeous? [W1B-005-47]

The nearest in force to exclamatives are sentences with the intensifiers *such* and *so* (cf. 3.8).

[19] The country created *such* a strong impression on us! [W1B-013-82] ('What a strong impression the country created on us')

[20] Oh that was *so* funny [S1A-018-258] ('How funny that was')

3.10
Speech acts

The four major communicative uses discussed in 3.9 distinguish uses at a very general level. We can make numerous more refined distinctions when we examine the utterance of sentences in actual contexts. When we utter a declarative, we generally do more than state something. We may simply inform somebody of something, as perhaps in this response of a patient to the doctor's query:

[1]   A: Now uh the rest of your health is okay I mean are you generally well
       B: *I feel fine* [S1A-051-134]

But we use declaratives for numerous purposes. For example, we can use declaratives to praise [2], to request [3], to apologize [4], to advise [5], to give permission [6], and to make an offer [7]:

[2]   I'm very happy with your work.

[3]   I should like some sugar, please.

[4]   I'm sorry for the interruption.

[5]   You should use another route.

[6]   You may have another piece.

[7]   I can lend you a hand with the washing-up.

We can express similar kinds of communication by using other sentence forms:

[2a]   How splendid your work is!

[3a]   Pass the sugar, please.

[4a]   Will you forgive my interruption?

[5a]   Shouldn't you use another route?

[6a]   Help yourself to another piece.

[7a]   Can I lend you a hand with the washing-up?

At the same time, these utterances retain their general communicative force. For example, [5a] is more polite than [5] because it is framed as a question that more easily allows the hearer to reject the advice.

When we speak or write, we are performing communicative actions. These actions, expressed in words, are speech acts, which are intended to convey communicative purposes to the intended hearers or readers.[7] The communicative purpose depends on the particular context. For example *It's going to rain* may be simply a prediction, or it may be intended as a warning to take an umbrella, or it may be intended to indicate that a projected excursion should be cancelled.

Speakers occasionally convey their purpose by using performative verbs, which explicitly denote their communicative purpose:

[8]   I *apologize* for the interruption.

[9]   I *predict* that it will rain this afternoon.

[10]   Talking to the driver is *forbidden*.

[11]   I must *inform* you that your time is up.[8]

[12]   I *sentence* you to three months' imprisonment.

[13]   We *advise* you to avoid becoming involved.

A sentence may convey more than one communicative purpose:

[14] I'm sorry for the interruption, but I should like to use the phone.

The first clause conveys an apology, and the second a request.

3.11
Positive and negative sentences

Sentences are either positive or (less commonly) negative. The most frequent method of negating sentences is to insert *not* or the contracted form *n't* in the verb phrase:

[1]   He would not stay long. [W2F-018-81]

[2]   Such communication was not part of the proceedings. [W2C-001-7]

[3]   The countries around the world do not fit into neat and precise categories of climate and weather. [W2B-026-2]

[4]   Well, that bit wasn't true, but he certainly didn't go to the première. [W2B-004-31]

Like questions (cf. 3.5 and n. 4), negative sentences require an operator. *Not* is positioned after the operator **[1]**–**[3]**, and *n't* is attached to the operator. In **[1]** the operator is the first—and, in this instance, only—auxiliary (*would*); it is the main verb *was* in **[2]**; and it is the dummy operator *do* in **[3]**. In the two clauses of **[4]** *n't* is attached to the operators *was* and *did*. As **[4]** demonstrates, negation may apply to more than one clause in a sentence.

In negative questions, contracted *n't* is attached to the operator and therefore comes before the subject **[5]**, whereas *not* generally follows the subject **[6]**–**[8]**:

[5]   Listen can't we do this at some other time [S1A-038-102]

[6]   [. . .] can we not have his forecast of the underlying rate of inflation excluding mortgage interest at the end of next year the fourth quarter [S1B-052-35]

[7]   Does novel-writing not come easily to you [S1B-048-42]

[8]   Why did they not speak out? [W2C-001-15]

But *not* may also occasionally come between the operator and the subject:

[9]   Do not the police really remain ⟨ , ⟩ as to many they appeared in nineteen eighty-one to have become ⟨ , ⟩ a white male force encased in technology [. . .] [S2B-037-36]

Sentences may be negative because of negative words other than *not*:

[10] Things *never* work out the way we would like them to. [W1B-001-37]

[11] At the time of the original meeting *nobody* had any idea of what would happen [S1B-061-126]

[12] There's *no* surer way to lose a good friend than to marry her. [W2F-018-10]

[13] However, I have heard *nothing* formally. [W1B-024-34]

In standard English, two negative words occasionally occur in the same sentence (or clause), but in that case they make a positive:

[14] None of the countries have no political prisoners. ('All the countries have some political prisoners.')

Non-standard dialects use more than one negative to emphasize the negation:

[15] Nobody told me nothing.

[16] We don't want none, neither.

The equivalents of **[15]** and **[16]** in standard English are:

[15a] Nobody told me anything.

[16b] We don't want any, either.

Double or multiple negation was common in earlier English, but by the eighteenth century it was no longer acceptable in standard English.

Negation may affect a phrase, without making the sentence negative:

[17] They spent a not unpleasant time at my place, didn't they?

[18] They were no doubt shocked to read some of the reports.

[19] I was greeted by none other than the mayor, and so was my assistant.

A tag question accompanying a negative sentence or clause is typically positive, as in **[17a]**; *some* (or its compounds such as *somebody*) is typically replaced by *any* (or its compounds) in negative sentences, as in **[18a]**; *so* in [19] requires to be replaced by *nor* or *neither* in **[19a]**.

[17a] They didn't spend a pleasant time at my place, *did they?*

[18a] They were not shocked to read *any* of the reports.

[19a] I was not greeted by the mayor, *nor* was my assistant.

As speech acts, negative sentences are used to deny something that has been mentioned:

[20] A: I mean four of the five sabbaticals were missing
　　　 B: That's irrelevant
　　　 A: It *isn't* irrelevant [S1A-068-157 ff.]

[21] But he was saying it as if it was my job to do it whereas of course it *isn't* [S1A-069-49]

More commonly, what is denied is an assumption that is not made explicit:

[22] A: Rugby ⟨ , , ⟩ the girls are just treated like a few honorary girls but they're *not* integrated
　　　 B: At King's Canterbury they are integrated but it *isn't* too free it's still quite academic [S1A-054-72 f.]

Negative sentences are also used to reject an offer or invitation:

[23] A: Have some banana bread ⟨ , ⟩
　　　 B: Look I'm not much of a banana bread eater [S1A-010-170 ff.]

Negative *yes–no* questions generally convey an expectation of a positive response, though the expectation may be frustrated:

[24] 'Don't you know snails are a delicacy?'
'I don't want to know anything,' I said, turning on my side and closing my eyes. [W2F-013-56 f.]

Why don't you and the abbreviated *why not* convey advice or offers:

[25] So why don't you knock on his door [S1B-007-55]

[26] Other times you say hey look I mean there's no point in competing why don't you come in with us [S1B-005-105]

[27] Why don't you have some Guinness [S1B-079-192]

[28] We are happy to give a randomly selected jury power over the life or death of individuals, so why not give a similarly randomly selected panel power over the nation? [W2B-014-71]

3.12
Active and passive sentences

An active sentence contains an object as one of its constituents (cf. 3.16). Active sentences can generally be made passive. The changes required by the transformation of active to passive are illustrated in the contrast of active **[1]** with passive **[1a]**:

[1] One of the lecturers recommended us to do this at the university.

[1a] We were recommended to do this at the university by one of the lecturers [S1A-013-135]

Some of the changes affect the verb phrase. An additional auxiliary (generally the auxiliary *be*) is added, which in **[1a]** is *were*; and the main verb is made into a passive participle, which for *recommended* is the same form as the past. The active object *us* becomes the passive subject *we*; the active subject is moved to the end, where it is introduced by the preposition *by*.

Get is used less commonly as a passive auxiliary:

[2] And just under half get invited to staff meetings [S1B-077-29]

[3] [. . .] and that's why I got sent home the night when other people didn't turn up and ended up going ⟨ , ⟩ to Cambridge [S1A-011-124]

A valid reason for resorting to the passive is that it is then possible to omit any mention of the agent (or cause) of the action, which is expressed in the active by the subject. Indeed, the *by*-phrase referring to the agent is commonly omitted, as in **[2]** and **[3]** above and **[4]** below:

[4] [. . .] I'm not trained as a ⟨ , ⟩ as a therapist [S1A-004-86]

The usual motivation for omitting mention of the agent is that identification of the agent is irrelevant or intended to appear so. The identity of the agent may also be unknown, as in **[5]**:

[5]   Oh she's called Jennifer [S1A-006-119]

Or the agent may not be a specific person:

[6]   I think it's how you're introduced to them [S1A-016-180]

Similarly in **[7]**, where *it* refers to a film:

[7]   It's set in the future [S1A-049-236]

In scientific and technical writing it is quite common for writers to resort to the agentless passive to avoid frequent use of the personal pronouns *I* and *we* and thereby maintain a more impersonal style:

[8]   For observation by bright field and interference microscopy urediniospores scraped from erumpent pustules and macerated or hand-sectioned telia *were mounted* in lactic acid and *heated* to boiling point. [W2A-028-41]

[9]   This approach *was* therefore *considered* and *found* to be far more attractive. [W2A-038-45]

The agentive passive can be used to good purpose, despite the availability of the more common active:

[10]   The story was inspired by a tip-off from an officer of the SB (the Polish secret police, which had been harassing Gowing for a few months), that Soviet hardliners, backed by the KGB, were trying to depose General Jaruzelski. [W2B-005-32]

The passive is preferable in **[10]** for two reasons. First, the active would produce a clumsy unbalanced sentence in which the part before the verb was much longer than the object (*the story*):

[10a]   A tip-off from an officer of the SB (the Polish secret police, which had been harassing Gowing for a few months), that Soviet hardliners, backed by the KGB, were trying to depose General Jaruzelski inspired *the story*.

Secondly, *the story* refers to what has been mentioned before and comes naturally at the beginning of the sentence as a link to the new information about the tip-off. In **[11]** *Kim Philby* is placed at the end of the passive *which*-clause as the climax:

[11]   It is noteworthy that the section in which Greene worked was that of the Iberian sub-section of Section V of the SIS, which was controlled by none other than Kim Philby. [W2B-005-141]

The Constituents of Sentences

3.13
The basic sentence structures

A sentence consisting of just one clause is a simple sentence. The basic structures of a clause are therefore identical to those of a simple sentence.

For a first approach to the grammar of the sentence and clause, it is sensible to examine the basic structures of simple sentences that are declarative (typically making a statement), positive (rather than negative), active (rather than passive), and complete (rather than elliptical). The constituents of the basic structures appear in their normal order, and they consist of phrases that do not themselves contain clauses. Each basic structure constitutes the nucleus of a simple sentence:

[1]   I'm sending you this card.

[2]   He shrugged his shoulders.

We can add one or more adverbials, which are optional constituents:

[1a] I'm sending you this card *to stand in your bedroom.* [W1B-006-51]

[2a] He *merely* shrugged his shoulders. [W2B-012-20]

In analysing the basic structures, we disregard adverbials.

The basic structures have two obligatory constituents: a subject and a verb, denoted by the symbols SV. Below are examples of sentences consisting of just a subject and a verb in that order. The two constituents are indicated by the parenthesized symbols that follow them.

[3]   All the flowers (S) have disappeared (V).

[4]   The enemy tanks (S) are retreating (V).

[5]   You (S) should be working (V).

[6]   All my friends (S) laughed (V).

The verb (V) of the sentence takes the form of a verb phrase. The verb phrase consists of one or more auxiliaries (or auxiliary verbs) plus the main verb, which is the head of the verb phrase.[9] The main verbs in [3]–[6] are *disappeared, retreating, working,* and *laughed.* It is the main verb that determines which constituents may follow it, and these constituents are the complements of the verb. In [3]–[6] there are no complements.

The types of complements are:

direct object   O
indirect object   O
subject predicative   P
object predicative   P

The complements are discussed in later sections (3.14–20). They are exemplified in the sentences below:

> **[7]**   I (S) hate (V) this noise (O).
>
> **[8]**   The idea (S) could make (V) her (O) a fortune (O).
>
> **[9]**   The party treasurer (S) is (V) very hospitable (P).
>
> **[10]** They (S) drove (V) us (O) crazy (P).

Complements may be obligatory, as in **[9]**, or at least obligatory in the intended sense of the verb, as in **[10]**. More important is the link between the complement and the verb. Only one instance of a particular complement type (direct object, indirect object, etc.) can occur in the same clause. This restriction does not exclude co-ordination of two phrases, since the co-ordinated unit as a whole functions as a complement:

> **[10a]** They (S) drove (V) us and everybody else (O) crazy (P).

Some verbs allow more than one type of complementation. For example: the verb *drive* can have no complements, or just a direct object, or a combination of direct object with an object predicative:

> **[11]**   He (S) is driving (V).
>
> **[11a]** He (S) is driving (V) his father's car (O).
>
> **[11b]** He (S) is driving (V) me (O) mad (P).

Traditionally, sentences have also been divided into two parts: the subject and the predicate. The predicate consists of the verb and its complements and also most adverbials. Excluded from the predicate are sentence adverbials, which point to logical links with what precedes **[11a1]** or express a comment by the speaker or writer **[11b1]**:

> **[11a1]** Nevertheless (A), he is driving his father's car.
>
> **[11b1]** Frankly (A), he is driving me mad.

3.14
Subject and verb

The verb is the easiest constituent to recognize, because of its formal characteristics. The verb of the sentence takes the form of a verb phrase, and the first or only word in the verb phrase indicates present or past tense. Thus, *like* is present in **[1]** and *liked* is past in **[1a]**:

> **[1]**   I *like* the music.
>
> **[1a]** I *liked* the music.

In **[2]** *have* is present tense even though *have thanked* refers to past time:

> **[2]**   I *have* thanked them for the gift.

In contrast, *had* is past tense:

[2a] I *had* thanked them for the gift.

In **[2a]** *had thanked* is the verb phrase, and *thanked* is the main verb. The phrase can be replaced by the one word *thanked*, in which case *thanked* is past tense and its corresponding present is *thank*:

[2b] I *thanked* them for the gift.

[2c] I *thank* them for the gift.

We can identify the subject easily if we change a declarative into a *yes–no* question, since the change involves the movement of the subject (cf. 3.5). For example, the declarative **[3]** can be turned into the interrogative **[3a]**:

[3] *His manner* was often intense.

[3a] Was *his manner* often intense?

The subject is *his manner* in both **[3]** and **[3a]**. Similarly, the subject is *the education minister* in both **[4]** and **[4a]**:

[4] *The education minister* managed the rare feat of antagonizing all the teaching unions.

[4a] Did *the education minister* manage the rare feat of antagonizing all the teaching unions?

If an adverbial (A) is present at the beginning of the declarative it is often moved to a later position in the interrogative:

[5] Last week (A) she (S) began (V) a campaign against journalistic clichés (O).

[5a] Did she begin a campaign against journalistic clichés last week?

But some types of adverbial generally occur initially:

[6] Anyway (A), would you necessarily get the job [S1A-093-115]

3.15
Subject

The subject has a number of characteristics, two of which we have seen in 3.14. Here is a list of the major characteristics:

1. In declaratives, the subject normally comes before the verb:

[1] I (S) might go (V) back to Cambridge early.

It need not come immediately before the verb, since an adverbial may intervene:

[2] I (S) just (A) remembered (V) the letter.

2. In interrogatives, the subject generally comes after the operator, the verb used for forming interrogatives (cf. 3.5); the rest of the verb phrase (if it

consists of more than the operator) follows the subject. In the examples, the operator is indicated by 'v' and the rest of the verb phrase (if any) by 'V':

[3]   *Are* (v) *they* (S) aware of your views?

[4]   What *did* (v) *you* (S) *get* (V) out of it?

[5]   *Is* (v) *everything* (S) *being changed* (V)?

There is no change in the declarative order in *wh*-interrogatives if the interrogative *wh*-expression is itself the subject:

[6]   *Who* (S) *did* (V) most of the driving?

[7]   *What* (S) *made* (V) them angry?

[8]   *What sort of physical activities* (S) *were* (V) available?

3. In second person imperatives (the most common type), the subject *you* is normally omitted:

[9]   *Turn* (V) it off.

4. The verb agrees in number and person with the subject where the verb has distinctive forms in the present or past tense:

[10]   *I* (S) *am* (V) in sympathy with her position.

[11]   *We* (S) *are* (V) very concerned about you.

[12]   *All their children* (S) *were* (V) in good shape.

[13]   *He* (S) *seems* (V) nervous.

The agreement applies only to the first verb in the verb phrase if there is more than one:

[14]   *Your friends* (S) *are* being (V) bitchy.

5. The subject decides the form of a reflexive pronoun (e.g. *myself, herself, themselves*) functioning as the object, when the subject and object refer to the same person or thing:

[15]   *You* (S) can cut *yourself*.

[16]   *They* (S) washed *themselves*.

6. Some pronouns have a distinctive form when they function as subject (cf. 3.18, 4.35):

[17]   *She* (S) is at college, so you can't see *her* now.

[18]   *We* (S) very rarely worked with them, though they contact *us* sometimes.

She and *we* are subjective forms, contrasting with *her* and *us*.

7. When we change an active sentence into a passive sentence (cf. 3.12), we change the subjects:

[19]   *The young producer* (S) proved all the critics wrong.

[19a]   *All the critics* (S) were proved wrong by the young producer.

8. In an active sentence that expresses the notion of an agent ('doer of the action'), the agentive role is taken by the subject:

[20] *My aunt* (S) gave me a mower for my wedding.

3.16
Direct object

When the main verb does not have a complement, it is intransitive. When it has a direct object (O), it is transitive. Many verbs can be either intransitive or transitive:

[1] *I* (S) *am eating* (V).

[1a] *I* (S) *am eating* (V) *my lunch* (O).

If a sentence has only one complement of the verb and that complement is a direct object, its basic structure is SVO.

We can identify the direct object in a declarative sentence if we can elicit it as a response to a question beginning with *who* or *what* followed by the operator (cf. 3.5) and the subject:

[2] *She* (S) *would have asked* (V) *her parents* (O).

[2a] *Who* (O) *would* (v) *she* (S) *have asked* (V)? [W2F-019-112]

[3] *They* (S) *speak* (V) *Welsh* (O) at home.

[3a] No but at home *what* (O) *do* (v) *they* (S) *speak* (V) [S1A-069-113]

In formal style, *whom* is used as the direct object in place of *who*.

[2b] *Whom* would she have asked?

Here are some major characteristics of the direct object.

1. The direct object normally comes after the verb, as in **[1a]**, repeated below:

[1a] *I* (S) *am eating* (V) *my lunch* (O).

The main exceptions to this rule occur in *wh*-questions (cf. 3.5) and in relative clauses (cf. 5.9). If the *wh*-expression in a question is a direct object, it is fronted:

[4] *What sort of dance training* (O) *did* (v) *you* (S) *have* (V) [S1A-004-67]

[5] *Which car* (O) *did* (v) *you* (S) *take* (V) [S1A-009-210]

Similarly, if the relative expression in a relative clause is a direct object it is fronted:

[6] [. . .] I had to meet this girl *who* (O) *I* (S) *haven't seen* (V) for ten years from my school [S1A-062-167]

[7] If you want a large black pencil ⟨ , ⟩ that's a marker pencil *which* (O) *you* (S) *have* (V) there [S1B-002-96]

2. Some pronouns have a distinctive form when they function as direct objects:

> **[8]**   My shoes are killing *me. I* don't like them at all.
>
> **[9]**   Nobody can catch *them. They* are hardened smugglers.

Contrast objective *me* and *them* with subjective *I* and *they.*

3. If the object and the subject refer to the same person or thing, the direct object is a reflexive pronoun (which ends in *-self* or *-selves*):

> **[10]**   *I* (S) could kick *myself* (O).
>
> **[11]**   *She* (S) has completely cut *herself* (O) off from me.

4. When we change an active sentence into a passive sentence, the active object becomes the passive subject:

> **[12]**   *The massive costs* (S) harm *the film industry* (O).
>
> **[12a]**   *The film industry* (S) is harmed by the massive costs.

3.17
Indirect object

We have so far encountered two basic structures: SV and SVO, exemplified in **[1]** and **[2]**:

> **[1]**   *My glasses* (S) *have disappeared* (V).
>
> **[2]**   *Our country* (S) *is absorbing* (V) many *refugees* (O).

The verb *disappear* here is an intransitive verb, since it does not have a complement. The verb *absorb* is here a transitive verb, since it has a direct object as its complement.

Some transitive verbs can have two objects, an indirect object as well as a direct object. In **[3]** *sending* has just one complement, a direct object; in **[3a]** it has two complements, an indirect object followed by a direct object (O). Both objects are indicated by 'O':

> **[3]**   I am sending *an official letter of complaint* (O).
>
> **[3a]**   I am sending *you* (O) *an official letter of complaint* (O).

Here are some other examples of verbs with these two complements:

> **[4]**   Well if you give *me* (O) *it* (O) tomorrow I might be able to do some tomorrow morning [. . .] [S1A-038-155]
>
> **[5]**   [. . .] we tell *each other* (O) *everything* (O) [S1A-054-1]
>
> **[6]**   Tea he makes tea he makes phone calls he makes gets *me* (O) *lollipops* (O) [S1A-074-368]
>
> **[7]**   [. . .] and what I would suggest is that we make *you* (O) *an appointment to go and see one and talk it through* (O) [S1A-078-89]

[8] [. . .] that teaches *one* (O) a *lesson about predicting things* (O) [. . .] [S1B-036-78]

[9] [. . .] the public sector health service buys *you* (O) *free private care* (O) [S1B-039-83]

[10] Can you pick a photograph that uh shows *us* (O) *the position* (O) [S1B-069-53]

[11] [. . .] and that earns *United* (O) *a free kick* (O) [S2A-003-95]

[12] Uh and it certainly isn't sitting there thinking that it owes *us* (O) *a living* (O) [S2A-023-32]

[13] Acting is a source of additional behavioural phenotypic flexibility, 'intelligence' permits *individual organisms* (O) *an increased capacity either to avoid change, or to track change, or both* (O). [W1A-009-64]

[14] [. . .] and I wish *you* (O) *success in finding a suitable career opening* (O). [W1B-019-48]

The indirect object can generally be paraphrased by a phrase introduced by *to* or *for*, but that phrase follows the direct object. For example:

[5a] We tell *everything* (O) *to each other*.

[9a] The public sector health service buys *free private care* (O) *for you*.

Sometimes the direct object is absent and the indirect object alone is the complement of the verb:

[15] [. . .] and we shall I promise *you* (O) ⟨ , ⟩ bring our own forces back home just as soon as it is safe to do so [S2B-030-58]

[16] Only God knows if there is absolute truth, and God doesn't tell *us* (O). [890825-0089-47]

When there is one object, the basic structure is SVO; when there are two objects it is SVOO, the first object being indirect and the second direct. A verb taking one object is monotransitive, a verb taking two objects is ditransitive.

Like the direct object, the indirect object can be questioned by *who(m)* or *what*:

[17] Easterly winds bring *us* (O) *this extreme cold* (O).

[17a] *What* (O) do easterly winds bring *us* (O)?

[17b] *Who* (O) do easterly winds bring *this extreme cold* (O)?

However, many people prefer to use the construction with a preposition in questions such as **[17b]**:

[17c] *Who* do easterly winds bring this extreme cold *to*?

[17d] *To whom* do easterly winds bring this extreme cold? [formal]

The indirect object shares characteristics with the direct object, a reason for calling both of them objects:

1. The indirect object comes after the verb:

[18] The waiver clause *denied* (V) *them* (O) *their rights* (O).

When both objects are present, the indirect object comes before the direct object.[10]

2. As with the direct object, some pronouns have a distinctive form when they function as indirect object. The objective forms *me* in **[4]**, and *us* in **[10]** contrast with the subjective forms *I* and *we*.

3. If the indirect object and the subject refer to the same person or thing, the indirect object is a reflexive pronoun:

> **[19]** *They* (S) asked *themselves* (O) the same question.

4. When we change an active sentence into a passive sentence, the active indirect object can become the passive subject. Compare repeated **[3a]** with **[3b]**:

> **[3a]** I am sending *you* (O) *an official letter of complaint* (O).

> **[3b]** *You* (S) are being sent *an official letter of complaint* (O).

The active direct object (*an official letter of complaint*) is retained in the passive of **[3b]**. The direct object can also become the passive subject:

> **[3c]** *An official letter of complaint* (S) is being sent *you* [O].

In **[3c]** the active indirect object (*you*) is retained in the passive. More commonly, the corresponding prepositional phrase replaces the passive indirect object:

> **[3d]** An official letter of complaint is being sent *to you*.

The indirect object typically refers to a person or some other animate being that is the recipient or beneficiary of the action.

3.18
Subject predicative

So far we have seen three basic structures: SV, SVO, SVOO. They are exemplified in **[1]**–**[3]**:

> **[1]** *My glasses* (S) *have disappeared* (V).

> **[2]** *Our country* (S) *is absorbing* (V) *many refugees* (O).

> **[3]** *I* (S) *am sending* (V) *you* (O) *an official letter of complaint* (O).

In **[1]** the main verb *disappeared* is intransitive, whereas in **[2]** and **[3]** the main verbs *absorbing* and *sending* are transitive. *Absorbing* in **[2]** has one complement: the direct object; *sending* in **[3]** has two complements: the indirect object and the direct object.

Some verbs are neither intransitive (without any complement), nor transitive (accompanied by one or two objects as complements). Such verbs are copular (or linking) verbs. The most common copular verb is *be*. The complement of a copular verb is the subject predicative (P).[11]

[4]   *The water-bed* (S) *was* (V) *very comfortable* (P).

[5]   *The baby tortoise* (S) *was* (V) *the size of a large soup plate* (P).

Copular verbs can refer to a current situation, e.g. *be*, or to a changed situation, e.g. *become*. Contrast:

[6]   The disastrous consequences *are* obvious.

[6a] The disastrous consequences *became* obvious.

Here are examples of subject predicatives with copular verbs :

[7]   My name is *Amanda* (P) [S1A-014-82]

[8]   It just sounds *a little affected* (P) [S1A-044-170]

[9]   Yes you were *in Brunei* (P) that year [S1A-056-245]

[10] [. . .] I feel *so self-conscious* (P) in high heels [S1A-042-291]

[11] The Third World (3W) constitutes *most of Asia (excepting Japan) Africa and Latin America* (P) [. . .] [W1A-015-62]

[12] I mean the audience used to go *mad* (P) as soon as he came on [. . .] [S1A-044-335]

[13] And of course I always wax *poetic* (P) about it to you [. . .] [S1A-094-38]

[14] They the owners were demanding payment of instalments as they fell *due* (P) or became *due* (P) up to the date of the award [S2A-065-59]

[15] [. . .] I remember I wasn't *there* (P) [S1A-002-138]

[16] Neither we nor, almost certainly, President Bush and Mr Major know how much of Iraq's armoury remains *intact* (P) [. . .] [W2E-005-78]

[17] It seems *a pity* (P) to waste it on an unappreciative audience. [W2F-011-15]

[18] "We have no useful information on whether users are *at risk* (P)," said James A. Talcott of Boston's Dana-Farber Cancer Institute. [891102-0191-9]

[19] Big mainframe computers for business had been *around* (P) for years. [891102-0171-9]

[20] The recent explosion of country funds mirrors the "closed-end fund mania" of the 1920s, Mr. Foot says, when narrowly focused funds grew *wildly popular* (P). [891102-0159-8]

[21] Some of his observations about Japanese management style are *on the mark* (P). [891102-0156-33]

Copular verbs other than *be* or *become* can be replaced by *be* or *become*, though the other verbs may contribute an additional element of meaning.

Copular verbs typically take an adjective phrase as their complement; for example: **[8]**, **[10]**, and **[12]**–**[14]** above.

The subject predicative is characterized in these ways:

1. The subject predicative comes after the verb, as in all the above examples.

2. The subject predicative cannot become the passive subject of the sentence, unlike the direct and indirect objects, since the distinction between active and passive applies only to sentences with transitive verbs. If the copular verb is *be* and if the subject predicative identifies the subject, the subject and subject predicative can change places:

> **[22]** *The president* (S) *was* (V) *Bill Clinton* (P).
>
> **[22a]** *Bill Clinton* (S) *was* (V) *the president* (P).

3. If the subject predicative is a pronoun with distinctive subjective and objective forms, we have a choice. The subjective form tends to occur in formal style:

> **[23]**   It is *I* (P). [formal]
>
> **[23a]** It's *me* (P).

The subject predicative typically characterizes the person or thing referred to by the subject. It also commonly identifies the subject or the location of the subject.

3.19
Object predicative

We have seen four basic structures: SV, SVO, SVOO, and SVP:

> **[1]** *My glasses* (S) *have disappeared* (V).
>
> **[2]** *Our country* (S) *is absorbing* (V) *many refugees* (O).
>
> **[3]** *I* (S) *am sending* (V) *you* (O) *an official letter of complaint* (O).
>
> **[4]** *The water-bed* (S) *was* (V) *very comfortable* (P)

In **[1]** the main verb is intransitive, in **[2]** and **[3]** transitive (in **[2]** monotransitive and in **[3]** ditransitive), and in **[4]** it is copular.

The fifth basic structure contains a transitive verb with two complements: a direct object (O) and an object predicative (P), normally in that order (cf. 3.22):

> **[5]**   *I* (S) *have made* (V) *my position* (O) *clear* (P).

A verb that has a direct object and an object predicative is a complex-transitive verb. Both complex-transitive verbs and ditransitive verbs have two complements. One fundamental difference between the two sets of complements is that there is a predicative relationship between the direct object and the object predicative. The relationship is analogous to that between the subject and the subject predicative. Thus, for **[5]** the relationship is shown when we introduce a copular verb between the direct object and the object predicative **[5a]**, and similarly for **[6]** and **[6a]**:

> **[5a]** *My position* (S) *became* (V) *clear* (P).
>
> **[6]**   *They* (S) *called* (V) *it* (O) *freelance teaching* (P).
>
> **[6a]** *It* (S) *was* (V) *freelance teaching* (P).

The other difference is that only the direct object in an SVOP structure can be made the subject of a passive sentence:

> **[5]**   *I* (S) *have made* (V) *my position* (O) *clear* (P).
>
> **[5b]** *My position* (S) *has been made* (V) *clear* (P).

Since the object predicative is not an object, it cannot be made a passive subject. In contrast, both complements in an SVOO structure—the indirect object and the direct object—can be made passive subjects:

[3]   *I* (S) *am sending* (V) *you* (O) *an official letter of complaint* (O).

[3a]   *You* (S) *are being sent* (V) *an official letter of complaint* (O).

[3b]   *An official letter of complaint* (S) *is being sent* (V) *you* [O].

Here are some further examples of the SVOP structure:

[7]   But state courts upheld a challenge by consumer groups to the commission's rate increase and found *the rates* (O) *illegal* (P). [891102-0179-15]

[8]   But Asian nations' harsh memories of their military domination by Japan in the early part of this century make *them* (O) *fearful of falling under Japanese economic hegemony now* (P). [891102-0149-12]

[9]   The department placed *a moratorium* (O) *on the research* (P), pending a review of scientific, legal and ethical issues. [891102-0145-9]

[10]   They call *it* (O) *"photographic"* (P). [891102-0092-26]

[11]   In July, closely held Hearst, based in New York, put *the paper* (O) *on the block* (P). [891102-0078-6]

[12]   Many felt Hearst kept *the paper* (O) *alive* (P) as long as it did, if marginally, because of its place in family history. [891102-0078-16]

[13]   You're getting *cheese* (O) *on your* ⟨ , ⟩ *jumper* (P) [S1A-061-86]

[14]   [. . .] she found *him* (O) *really frustrating* (P) because he didn't seem bothered [S1A-014-120]

[15]   [. . .] you're driving *independents* (O) *out of business* (P) [S1B-005-112]

[16]   [. . .] police and customs kept *the Defiant* (O) *under observations* (P) [S1B-063-233]

[17]   Uhm as soon as I took *my leg* (O) *out of the water* (P) it fell straight open [S1B-066-26]

[18]   The German press dubbed *him* (O) *honest John* (P) today [. . .] [S2B-002-89]

[19]   The allies' ability to attack powerfully and accurately at night caught *the Iraqis* (O) *at a disadvantage* (P) [S2B-008-29]

[20]   [. . .] he still thought *a leadership challenge* (O) *unlikely* (P) [S2B-017-36]

If the object predicative is a prepositional phrase, it may not be possible to make a simple paraphrase of the relationship between the direct object and the predicative. The paraphrase, however, can be established by omitting the preposition **[21]**–**[22]** or replacing it by another preposition **[23]**:

[21]   [. . .] I first got *a millionaire* (O) *for my neighbour* (P) at twenty-four twenty-five years old [S1A-028-220] ('A millionaire is my neighbour')

[22]   Maybe I'll just treat *it* (O) *as a work of art* (P) [. . .] [S1A-64-68] ('It is a work of art')

[23]   The French initiative threw *the United Nations Security Council* (O) *into confusion* (P) [. . .] [S2B-010-22] ('The United Nations Security Council is in confusion')

3.20
Complements and adverbials

We have so far encountered five basic structures: SV, SVO, SVOO, SVP, SVOP. The constant constituents are the subject and the verb. The other constituents are the complements of the verb: direct object, indirect object, subject predicative, and object predicative. Complements of the verb can be clauses as well as phrases (cf. 6.16).

The basic structures can be expanded by adverbials, which are optional constituents of the sentence. They are not complements, because their occurrence is not dependent on the main verb in the sentence. They are optional in the sense that the sentence remains well-formed when they are omitted. However, they are usually important informationally in the context, and in that sense they cannot be omitted without damaging the communication. Here are some examples of adverbials (A) that show their informational value. The examples also illustrate the possibility for more than one adverbial to occur in a sentence.

[1]   It was quite a nice do *otherwise* (A) [S1A-019-72]

[2]   I met a girl *on the train* (A) *today* (A) [S1A-020-1]

[3]   *In the summer* (A) you can take a car and four people *for a hundred and twenty pounds* (A) [S1A-021-97]

[4]   You need a lot of strength *in the right hand* (A) [S1A-022-295]

[5]   *Well* (A) *presumably* (A) she called him [S1A-023-127]

Adverbials are usually adverbs (e.g. *presumably* in **[5]**), prepositional phrases (e.g. *on the train* in **[2]**), or clauses (cf. 6.13 f.). They may also be noun phrases:

[6]   I had a really good supper *last night* (A) [S1A-011-241]

[7]   Give me a warning *next time* (A) [S1A-091-303]

[8]   In the 'good old days' our great-great-grandmothers walked *several miles* (A) to the village, [. . .] [W2B-022-4]

[9]   Oh Cath was in *this afternoon* [. . .] (A) [S1A-009-105]

Some constituents that resemble adverbials semantically are complements, since they are obligatory and are dependent on the main verb. These are predicatives (P). For example, *last night* in **[10]** is required to complete the sentence, unlike *last night* in **[6]**:

[10] *Our committee meeting* (S) *was* (V) *last night* (P).

In **[10]**, the subject predicative completes a sentence beginning with a subject and a verb. The basic structure of the sentence is SVP. Similarly, in **[11]** the object predicative is an adverb:

[11] [. . .] yeah you put *it* (O) *here* (P) [S1A-010-13]

Elsewhere *here* may be an adverbial, but in **[11]** it is an object predicative that is required to complete the sentence. The basic structure of **[11]** is SVOP.

The five basic structures are listed below in full:

SV   Subject + Verb
SVO   Subject + Verb + Direct or Indirect Object
SVOO   Subject + Verb + Indirect Object + Direct Object
SVP   Subject + Verb + Subject Predicative
SVOP   Subject + Verb + Direct Object + Object Predicative

Here are examples of the five structures:

[12] *My glasses* (S) *have disappeared* (V).

[13] *Our country* (S) *is absorbing* (V) *many refugees* (O).

[14] *I* (S) *am sending* (V) *you* (O) *an official letter of complaint* (O).

[15] *The water-bed* (S) *was* (V) *very comfortable* (P).

[16] *I* (S) *have made* (V) *my position* (O) *clear* (P).

There is one further element that is optionally added to the basic structure—the vocative (cf. 5.15):

[17] *Robin* what do you think [S1A-020-230]

Agreement between the subject and verb in number and person is discussed in 5.14.

3.21
Semantic roles

Sentences—and the clauses within them—are used to describe situations. Each constituent of a sentence or clause plays a role in the description. It is not clear how many roles should be distinguished, nor is there space to discuss the roles in detail, but some indication is here given of the major roles that have been identified and of the verb types that are typically involved.

A. Subject

If the verb is transitive or intransitive the subject typically has the agentive role, referring to the doer of an action:

[1] Will *anyone* (S) congratulate me on my cooking [S1A-020-266]

[2] *You* (S) picked her up [S1A-020-20]

[3] Does *she* (S) play tennis [S1A-020-207]

If the verb is copular, the subject typically has the identified role (referring to someone or something identified through the subject predicative) **[4]–[5]** or it has the characterized role (referring to someone or something characterized by the subject predicative) **[6]–[7]**:

[4] [. . .] *this* (S) is my daughter Felicity [S1A-010-214]

[5] *The difficulty* (S) is the travel [S1A-019-350]

[6] So *this one* (S) was ⟨ , ⟩ lower middle-class in that case [S1A-020-47]

[7] *You* (S) 're not a neurotic wreck on the other hand uhm [S1A-020-257]

72 AN OUTLINE OF GRAMMAR

If the verb is transitive, the subject may have the experiencer role, referring to someone who has experienced a sensation, an emotion, or cognition:

[8] As he climbed *he* (S) smelled roasting lamb on the damp wind and heard harsh shouts above the cries of children. [W2F-018-57]

[9] *I* (S) find him quite appealing [S1A-053-26]

[10] Uhm ⟨ , ⟩ have *you* (S) considered until now the effects that having an absent father may have had on your childhood [S1A-075-25]

If the verb is intransitive, the subject may have the affected role, referring to the person or thing directly affected by the action:

[11] In the past few years *many dolphins* (S) have drowned in fishing nets [. . .] [W2B-029-100]

[12] He clutched at it and *his trousers* (S) slipped onto his hips. [W2F-001-71]

The passive subject typically has the affected role:

[13] *My D H Lawrence* (S) was swept away [S1A-018-67]

[14] *Some* (S) were drafted into the army if they were suitable for that [. . .] [S2A-059-38]

The subject sometimes has the eventive role, referring to an event:

[15] *The last meeting* (S) was in the European championship in nineteen eighty-eight [. . .] [S2A-001-135]

[16] *The crash of Polly Peck* (S) is the biggest in British corporate history, but only in nominal terms. [W2E-002-71]

English grammar requires that a sentence or clause have a subject, though it may be absent in imperatives (cf. 3.7) or it may be ellipted (cf. 3.23). If there is no role to be assigned to the subject, *it* is added to serve as subject. This prop *it*, supporting the subject function, is used in particular with time and weather expressions (cf. 4.38):

[17] *It* (S)'s a bit late now [S1A-022-168]

[18] But unfortunately both Saturday and Sunday *it* (S) was really foggy [S1A-036-149]

B. **Direct object**

The direct object typically has the affected role, noted above for the subject:

[19] And someone came and locked *the gate* (O) after us [S1A-009-246]

[20] Now put *him* (O) outside nicely ⟨ , ⟩ and then brush *him* (O) out [S1A-032-50]

Like the subject, it may have the eventive role. Typically, the noun in the object is derived from a verb and carries the main meaning, while the verb has a general meaning (e.g. *do, have, make, take*).

[21] He had *a stroke* (O), didn't he [S1A-028-240]

[22] We did *some good praying* (O) [S1A-068-258]

[23] I made *a note* (O) at the time and afterwards [S1B-068-11]

[24] From the start our College took *a conscious decision that it would not resort to compulsory redundancies.* [W1B-024-78]

The direct object sometimes has the resultant role, referring to something that comes into existence as a result of the action of the verb:

[25] Well ⟨ , , ⟩ uhm ⟨ , ⟩ I wrote *my thesis* (O) in such a way that it's ⟨ , , ⟩ considerably more accessible than most people's [S1A-066-109]

[26] So they built themselves *a magnificent amphitheatre for popular sporting activities* [S2B-027-21]

C. **Indirect object**

The indirect object typically has the roles of recipient **[27]** or beneficiary **[28]**:

[27] That reminds us Tom hasn't paid *us* (O) yet [S1A-039-222] ('Tom hasn't paid money *to us*')

[28] The people we were staying with they ⟨ , , ⟩ uh cooked *us* (O) a traditional Normandy dinner (O) [S1A-009-118] ('They cooked a traditional Normandy dinner *for us*')

In **[28]** *us* is the indirect object and *a traditional Normandy dinner* is the direct object. Where the indirect object comes before an eventive direct object, it is likely to have the affected role (cf. **[21]**–**[24]** above):

[29] Stephen straightened unsteadily and gave *him* (O) *a push.* [W2F-015-90] ('Stephen pushed *him*')

[30] Give *me* (O) *a fright* (O) [S1A-042-21] ('Frighten *me*')

D. **Predicative**

Predicatives typically characterize the subject **[31]**–**[32]** or object **[33]**–**[34]**:

[31] I was *lucky* (P) [S1A-001-78]

[32] That was *a bit sad* (P) [S1A-006-277]

[33] I find *it* (O) *fascinating* (P) [S1A-001-26]

[34] The iron castings and the cast steel hour and declination axles were in sound condition and I considered *its restoration* (O) *a worthwhile challenge* (P) [W2A-040-42]

They may also identify the subject **[35]**–**[36]** or object **[37]**:

[35] He was *the first person in a wheelchair that I'd ever met* (P) [. . .] [S1A-004-101]

[36] It was the gauge that was *the killer* (P) in the first place [S1A-010-120]

[37] [. . .] the college paper published something on my work and called *it* (O) *Psychotherapy* (P) [S2A-027-19]

Another common role is locative, designating the place of the subject **[38]** or object **[39]**:

[38] This was *in America* [S1A-004-100]

[39] She put *her hand* (O) *on Dee's arm* (P) [. . .] [W2F-006-74]

E. Verb

The major distinction in verbs is between those that are stative and those that are dynamic.

Stative verbs are used in referring to a state of affairs:

[40] It *is* quite popular of course [S1A-035-22]

[41] It still *sounds* ridiculous [S1A-030-10]

[42] And parents *have* different expectations about boys from girls [S1A-012-123]

[43] Every war *possesses* a grim rhythm. [W2E-005-69]

[44] He may not even have *liked* his brother [. . .] [W1B-003-146]

Dynamic verbs are used in referring to a happening:

[45] He *walked* through the town *giving* out blessings and absolution to all sinners [S2B-027-65]

[46] We *discussed* extensively our needs for computing [. . .] [S1B-075-136]

[47] The last few days haven't been quite so hot and on Friday night it actually *rained*. [W1B-005-146]

[48] I *paid* it off in one large lump [S1A-039-201]

[49] One eye-witness I *spoke* to said six people had *died* [S2B-005-146]

Some verbs can be used both statively and dynamically. For example, the verb *be* is usually stative, but in **[50]** it is dynamic:

[50] I hope life is *being* kind to you and you kind to yourself. [W1B-008-132]

Similarly, whereas *taste* in **[51]** and **[52]** is stative, in **[53]** and **[54]** it is dynamic:

[51] [. . .] he could *taste* warm blood in his mouth from the lip he had just bitten. [W2F-012-152]

[52] The hamburgers *taste* good.

[53] *Taste* the fish.

[54] Do you want to *taste* the soup?

3.22
Rearranging the basic structures

We have noted several instances where the basic declarative structures are rearranged: the focused element is fronted in *wh*-questions (cf. 3.5), exclamatives (cf. 3.8), passives (cf. 3.12), and relatives (cf. 3.16, 5.9). There are three types of drastic rearrangement:

A. cleft sentences
B. sentences with extraposed subjects
C. existential sentences

A. **Cleft sentences**

Cleft sentences, as the term suggests, involve a split. It is the basic structure that is split. The previous sentence is itself a cleft sentence. Its basic structure is **[1]**:

[1]   *The basic structure* (S) is split.

The cleft sentence begins with *it* and a copular verb, generally *be*. The focused part comes next and then the rest of the sentence, which is introduced by a relative such as *that*, *which*, or *who*. In **[1a]** the focus is the subject of **[1]**:

[1a] It is *the basic structure* that is split.

Here is a further example:

[2]   He felt a sharp pain *then*.

[2a] [. . .] it was *then* that he felt a sharp pain [S2A-067-54]

For more on the cleft sentence, see 4.38 on cleft *it*.

B. **Sentences with extraposed subjects**

Clauses that are functioning as subject are commonly moved to the end and replaced by *it*. In **[3]** the *that*-clause is subject. In **[3a]** the clause is extraposed and replaced by *it*:

[3]   *That anything can be proved* is hardly probable.

[3a] *It* is hardly probable *that anything can be proved* [. . .] [W2F-001-2]

For more on extraposed subjects and objects, see 4.38 on anticipatory *it*.

C. **Existential sentences**

Existential sentences are introduced by *there*. **[4a]** shows the effect of this rearrangement on the basic structure **[4]**:

[4]   *Other telecommunications companies* are in this country.

[4a] *There* are *other telecommunications companies* in this country [S1A-069-147]

For more on existential sentences, see 4.39.

Another kind of rearrangement involves the use of pronouns. There are two types (cf. 5.11):

D. left dislocation
E. right dislocation

D. **Left dislocation**

In left dislocation, an introductory noun phrase is not integrated into the sentence structure and a pronoun appears in the position that the noun phrase might have occupied:

[5]   *Nuclear reactors they*'re not environmentally friendly [. . .] [S1A-088-121]

[6]   *My ex-boyfriend Phil he* got me interested [S1A-081-101]

E. Right dislocation

In right dislocation, the noun phrase appears at the end:

[7] *They*'ve got a pet rabbit ⟨ , ⟩ *Laura and her boyfriend Simon* [S1A-017-119]

[8] *That*'s a nice area isn't it *Leatherhead* [S1A-081-87]

There are two types of inversion, which result from the fronting of a sentence constituent:

F. subject–verb inversion
G. subject–operator inversion

F. Subject–verb inversion

Subject–verb inversion occurs when a complement is fronted:

[9] *At the back of the house* (P), overlooking the garden, *was* the large room Eleanor used as her study. [W2F-009-26]

[10] *Far worse* (P) *was* the spectre of youth unemployment looming on the horizon. [W2B-012-155]

Complements can sometimes be fronted without inversion:

[11] *A royal wedding British-style* (P), it is not [*The Sunday Times*, 6 June 1993, p. 1.24]

[12] *Tea* (O) he makes *tea* (O) he makes *phone calls* (O) he makes gets me lollipops [S1A-074-368]

Subject–verb inversion is an option, generally in fiction writing, for reporting clauses used with direct speech (cf. 6.17):

[13] 'We are not celebrating anything,' *said* the woman in the chair. [W2F-018-72]

G. Subject–operator inversion

Subject–operator inversion is common in questions (cf. 3.5). Otherwise, it mainly occurs (a) when negative expressions are fronted **[14]–[15]**, (b) when the conjunctive adverbs *nor* and *neither*, and the additive adverb *so* introduce a clause **[16]–[17]**:

[14] *No more did* they speak of the importance of reducing public expenditure [. . .] [W2B-012-93]

[15] *Never were* slaves so numerous as in Italy during the first century B.C. [W2A-001-31]

[16] *Nor would* she mention her discovery to a soul, not even Mrs Staples. [W2F-005-127]

[17] Social attitudes, such as the desire for insurance in one's old age, encourage this. *So* too *does* the teaching of the dominant Catholic Church. [W2A-019-10 f.]

H. **Exchanged positions of direct object and object predicative**

The direct object may follow the object predicative if the object is long, so that the SVOP structure changes to a SVPO order:

[18] Let me first make *clear* (P) 〈 , 〉 *certain important points on which I have* 〈 , 〉 *no disagreement* 〈 , 〉 *with my right honourable friend* (O)
[S2B-050-27]

On the postponement of the postmodification in a noun phrase, see 5.7.

3.23
Ellipsis

Ellipsis is the omission of part of the structure of a sentence. We can interpret the sentence despite the omission because we know what has been ellipted either from the situational context or from the textual context, though in some cases the distinction between these two sources may be blurred.

Situational ellipsis is typical of conversation, but it also occurs in informal writing or in written dialogue. Here are some examples, with the position of the ellipsis indicated by a caret:

[1] A: They can't uh 〈 , 〉 keep tracks on everybody

B: ^ Shouldn't think so [S1A-007-284 f.]

[2] Oh we'll find something I mean a quid ^ Doesn't matter if it's really crap 〈 , 〉 ^ Haven't wasted much cash [S1A-006-190 ff.]

[3] What do you think anamnesis means ^ Got any idea [S1A-053-109 f.]

[4] ^ Just spoken to you on the phone and heard your news [W1B-010-3]

[5] ^ Really looking forward to seeing you my dear [W1B-011-83]

[6] How are you? ^ Looking forward to your move to Cambridge? [W1B-013-92 f.]

The first three examples come from conversations and the last three from social letters. The situational context as a whole (including the structure and content of the sentences) provides the clues to the interpretation of the ellipsis. All six sentences have deficiencies in their structure because of the ellipsis. In **[1]** and **[2]**, subjects are missing; in **[3]**–**[6]** both subjects and auxiliaries are missing. Yet the sentences are quite normal and are easily understood.

In textual ellipsis, the interpretation is crucially dependent on the words that precede or follow the ellipsis. In **[7]** the interpretation depends on what comes beforehand:

[7] A: I'd just wondered if you'd seen it
B: Yes I have ^ [S1A-006-64 ff.]

We understand B's response as 'Yes I have seen it'. The antecedent of the ellipsis—the part of the linguistic context that determines the interpretation—is 'you'd seen it' in A's query. When the antecedent comes before the ellipsis, the ellipsis is anaphoric. Here are other examples of anaphoric ellipsis:

> **[8]** A: Didn't there used to be deer in Richmond Park
> B: Yeah there still are ^
> A: Are there ^ [S1A-006-225 ff.]

> **[9]** A: But I'll have to drive
> B: How far ^
> A: ^ About three miles probably [S1A-006-291 ff.]

> **[10]** A: [. . .] we found the tiles ⟨ , ⟩
> B: What tiles ^ [S1A-007-124 f.]

> **[11]** A: When's your Mum coming back
> B: Uh ⟨ , ⟩ ^ Friday I think
> A: Uh huh ⟨ , ⟩
> B: ^ Friday very early morning [S1A-006-301 ff.]

> **[12]** Luke offers the excuse that they're worn out by grief Matthew and Mark don't ^ [S2B-028-105 f.]

> **[13]** A: I've never had one
> B: Who you ^ Nor've I ^ [S1A-007-262 ff.]

> **[14]** Uh it may well be there's been a change in policy I think if there has ^ he owes to the House to make that clear [S1B-056-44 f.]

> **[15]** A strange silence fell on the house and suddenly there was a big space and you weren't here and weren't going to be ^. [W1B-006-6]

One conspicuous though relatively infrequent kind of anaphoric ellipsis is gapping, where the verb is elided in co-ordinated clauses:

> **[16]** All schools in the state system are being given budgetary freedom and their boards of governors ^ strengthened powers so that they can encourage the best and respond to local circumstances [S2B-035-39]

In cataphoric ellipsis, the antecedent comes after the ellipsis, so that the interpretation is held in suspense until the antecedent is reached:

> **[17]** If you don't want to ^, I'll prepare lunch.

> **[18]** When they can ^, they will show us around.

Phrases and Words

3.24
Phrase types and word classes

There are five types of phrases, named after the head of the phrase:

1. noun phrase   *a weak government*   (head: noun *government*)
2. verb phrase   *may have succeeded*   (head: verb *succeeded*)
3. adjective phrase   *far more enjoyable*   (head: adjective *enjoyable*)
4. adverb phrase   *too noisily*   (head: adverb *noisily*)
5. prepositional phrase   *in a wine bar*   (head: preposition *in*)

Chapter 5 is devoted to phrases.

Word classes, such as noun and verb, are traditionally called parts of speech. We can divide word classes into open classes and closed classes. Open classes readily admit new words, and therefore they contain most words in the language. Closed classes, on the other hand, rarely admit new words, so that it is possible to list all the words belonging to them. For example, we can list all the pronouns. However, it is impossible to list all the nouns, not only because they are so numerous but primarily because new nouns are being created all the time. The resistance to adding words to closed classes is highlighted in the failure of attempts to introduce a new personal pronoun that is neutral between *he* and *she* (cf. 1.10).

There are four open classes:

noun	*Texas, freezer, hygiene*
verb (or main verb)	*remember, depend, become*
adjective	*personal, afraid, mere*
adverb	*lavishly, luckily, consequently*

Chapter 4, which deals in greater depth with word classes, recognizes seven closed classes and distinguishes their subclasses:

auxiliary (or auxiliary verb)	*will, have, be*
conjunction	*and, if, although*
preposition	*of, by, into*
determiner	*the, no, some*
pronoun	*she, none, some*
numeral	*five, twentieth, one-sixth*
interjection	*oh, ouch, wow*

In this chapter we will be looking just at auxiliaries and pronouns.

3.25 Verbs

Seven categories apply to verbs (main verbs and auxiliaries), affecting the forms that verbs take:

A. mood
B. modality
C. tense
D. aspect
E. voice
F. number
G. person

Verbs that function as operators (cf. 5.18) may be contracted and attached as enclitics to preceding words (e.g. *'s* from *is*, *'ll* from *will*) and they may have negative forms in which *n't* is attached or fused with them (e.g. *isn't*, *won't*).

A. **Mood**

Three moods are distinguished for English: indicative, imperative, and subjunctive. The indicative mood applies to most verbs used in declaratives, and to verbs used in interrogatives and exclamatives. Imperatives (cf. 3.7) and present subjunctives (cf. 5.25 f.) have the same uninflected form of the verb, and the past subjunctive is confined to *were*. Here are examples of the three moods:

Indicative
[1] Envy *is* deep and agonizing.
[2] *Could* that be a joke?
[3] How preposterous the poem *seemed*!

Imperative
[4] *Pay* me next time.

Subjunctive
[5] God *help* America
[6] So *be* it!
[7] If I *were* you, I would complain.
[8] We insisted that she *be* in charge.
[9] It is important that he *sign* the petition.

B. **Modality**

Modality, which is sometimes used to include mood, is a semantic category that deals with two types of judgements: (1) those referring to the factuality of what is said (its certainly, probability, or possibility); (2) those referring to human control over the situation (ability, permission, intention, obligation). The judgements are grammaticalized through the modal auxiliaries: *can, could, may, might, shall, should, will, would, must, ought to* (cf. 5.24). The same auxiliaries are used for the two types of judgements. Here are some examples:

[10] This *may* come as a surprise to those who associate organic food with vegetarianism. [W2B-027-5] [possibility]
[11] In the meanwhile, *may* I just confirm a few administrative details. [W1B-030-85] [permission]
[12] You *must* have been a very fast driver [S1A-028-138] [certainty]
[13] I *must* remember to put that away [S1A-039-130] [obligation]
[14] There is still a long way to go before it *can* be said that the ethnic minorities are adequately represented in the membership of the police [S2B-037-60] [possibility]
[15] Not everybody has the time to foster but everyone *can* help [S2B-038-109] [ability]

[16] I was woken first by another relation who sounded like Pam's Mum and just kept saying "*Can* I speak to Pamela?" [W1B-007-36] [permission]

Modality can also be expressed by means other than by auxiliaries: nouns **[17]**, main verbs **[18]**, adjectives **[19]**, and adverbs **[20]**:

[17] There may be cars passing you from behind 〈 , 〉 and the *possibility* of pedestrians too [S2A-054-177]

[18] Were this a Yoshizawa book, the designs would be yet more beautiful, but western writers are not usually *permitted* to publish the very best of his work. [W2D-019-34]

[19] If it continues I'll be *able* to have my first shorts and burgers Bar-B-Q on my balcony in no time at all. [W1B-002-104]

[20] Because they were giving away free wine it *probably* went on for a reasonable length of time [S1B-066-71]

C. **Tense**

Tense is a grammatical category referring to the time of a situation. English has two tense categories indicated by the form of the verb: present and past. The tense distinction is made on the first or only verb in the verb phrase:

Present   *speaks, is* speaking, *has* been speaking

Past   *spoke, was* speaking, *had* been speaking

We also use auxiliaries for distinctions in time; for example, *will* and *be going to* (*I am going to write to you soon*) refer to future time. On tense, see 5.20–3.

D. **Aspect**

Aspect is a grammatical category referring to the way that the time is viewed by the speaker or writer. English has two aspects: perfect and progressive (cf. 5.27–32). Aspect is indicated by a combination of an auxiliary and a following verb form. The perfect aspect requires the perfect auxiliary *have* and a following *-ed* participle (also called the past participle or the perfect participle):

has call*ed*   may *have* call*ed*   could *have* be*en* called
had writt*en*   will *have* writt*en*   should *have* be*en* written

The progressive (or continuous) aspect requires the progressive auxiliary *be* and a following *-ing* participle (also called the present participle):

is call*ing*   may *be* call*ing*   *is* be*ing* called
was writ*ing*   will *be* writ*ing*   *was* be*ing* written

A common use of the present perfect is to refer to a situation beginning in past time and extending to the present:

[21] They are gathered in a building which 〈 , 〉 stands on a site where there *has been* worship for perhaps fifteen hundred years [S2A-020-95]

The past perfect refers to a situation that precedes another past situation:

[22] He didn't know if Sally *had heard* him or not, but she went over to Anne and Tommy and encircled them with her arms. [W2F-002-76]

A common use of the progressive is to view the situation as in progress:

[23] A couple of months ago we reported how medical ethics *is being taught* at St Mary's Hospital Medical School in London [S2B-038-59]

[24] The whole system makes it difficult to offer any assessment of what *is going* on in the Soviet economy [S2B-039-8]

E. **Voice**

The grammatical category of voice distinguishes active, the basic type, from passive. The distinction, discussed earlier (cf. 3.12), affects other parts of the sentence as well as the verb. The passive requires the passive auxiliary *be* (or, less frequently, *get*) and a following -*ed* participle (also called the passive participle):

is call*ed*	may *be* call*ed*	has *been* call*ed*
was writt*en*	will *be* writt*en*	had *been* writt*en*

F. and G. **Number and person**

For all verbs except *be* (whether *be* is a main verb or an auxiliary), number and person are categories that affect only the present tense. The -*s* form is used for the third person singular and the base or uninflected form is used for the rest:

[25] My children *write* letters home every day.

[26] My daughter *writes* to me regularly.

The base form *write* is used whether the subject is a plural noun phrase such as *my children* or one of the personal pronouns *I, we, you,* or *they*. The -*s* form *writes* is used when the subject is a singular noun phrase such as *my daughter* or one of the personal pronouns *he, she,* or *it*. The verb *be* makes a further distinction in the present tense—*am* for the first person singular:

am	1st person singular
is	3rd person singular
are	others

Be also has two forms in the past:

was	1st and 3rd person singular
were	others

3.26
Nouns and pronouns

Nouns and pronouns share certain distinctions.

Two categories apply to nouns:

A. number
B. case

A. Number in nouns

The category of number distinguishes between singular and plural nouns (cf. 4.4 f.). Number contrast does not ordinarily apply to proper nouns, such as *Caroline* or *the Netherlands*. Common nouns can be either count (or countable) or non-count (or uncountable or mass). Count nouns have number contrast: *house/houses, nurse/nurses*. Non-count nouns generally do not have a plural form: *wine, information*; but many of them are occasionally converted into count nouns to refer to kinds or quantities: *French wines, two teas* ('two cups of tea').

B. Case in nouns

Case is a grammatical category that distinguishes differences in grammatical function. Present-day English has only two cases for nouns: the common case and the genitive (or possessive) case (cf. 4.10). In irregular nouns such as *woman*, the combination of case with number yields four forms of the noun:

common singular	woman	the *woman* next door
genitive singular	woman's	the *woman's* husband
common plural	women	all the *women* in the family
genitive plural	women's	the *women's* grievances

Regular nouns make the four-way distinction only in writing:

common singular	nurse	the *nurse* in charge of the ward
genitive singular	nurse's	the *nurse's* patients
common plural	nurses	the *nurses* in the hospital
genitive plural	nurses'	the *nurses'* pay

In speech, the distinction is apparent only between *nurse* and the other three, since *nurse's, nurses,* and *nurses'* are pronounced identically.

Pronouns

Four categories apply to pronouns:

number
person
case
gender

A. Demonstratives

The demonstratives (cf. 4.45) have only a distinction in number:

singular *this, that* **plural** *these, those*

B. **Personal pronouns**   All personal pronouns (cf. 4.34 f.) have distinctions in person: first, second, and third. Most also have distinctions in number (singular and plural) and in case (subjective, objective, and genitive). The third person singular also has distinctions in gender: masculine, feminine, non-personal. Broadly speaking, the subjective case is used when the pronoun functions as the subject, and the objective case is used otherwise (but cf. 3.18). In general, *he* refers to males, *she* to females, and *it* to all else.[12] *She* and (less commonly) *he* are occasionally used to refer to inanimate objects such as cars, boats, and computers. *It* is used for babies and animals where the sex is unknown or disregarded.

> **1st person**   **singular** I, me, my   **plural** we, us, our
> **2nd person**   you, your
> **3rd person**   **masculine singular** he, him, his
>   **feminine singular** she, her
>   **non-personal** it, its
>   **plural** they, them, their

You may be singular or plural, and subjective or objective. *Her* may be either objective or genitive, and *it* may be either subjective or objective.

C. **Possessive pronouns**   The genitives of the personal pronouns are also called possessive pronouns (cf. 4.34 f.). There is generally a distinction in form between those that are dependent on a noun and those that can function independently. The contrast between the dependent and the independent possessives is illustrated by the difference between dependent *my* in *my book* and independent *mine* in *That book is mine.* Here is the full set of contrasts:

> **1st person**   my, mine; our, ours
> **2nd person**   your, yours
> **3rd person**   his, her, hers; its; their, theirs

There is no contrast between dependent and independent in the third person singular masculine *his* and the non-personal *its.* The independent function is rare for *its.*

D. **Reflexive pronouns**   Reflexive pronouns (cf. 4.34 f.) generally parallel the personal pronouns in person and number:

> **1st person**   myself, ourselves
> **2nd person**   yourself, yourselves
> **3rd person**   himself, herself, itself, themselves

However, unlike the personal and possessive pronouns, the reflexives make a distinction in number in the second person: singular *yourself*, plural *yourselves.*

E. **Relative pronouns**

The *wh*-relative pronouns (cf. 4.43) display distinctions in gender and case. The gender contrast is between personal *who* or *whom* and non-personal *which*:

the friends *who* give me advice
the book *which* I have just read

The case contrast applies only to subjective *who* and objective *whom*, though *whom* tends to be restricted to formal style:

the teacher *who* taught me English
the teacher *whom* (or *who*) you met

Relative *that* does not have distinctions in gender or case:

the friends *that* give me advice
the book *that* I have just read

Genitive *whose* is mainly used for personal reference, but it is also sometimes used for non-personal reference:

the friend *whose* daughter you know
the house *whose* owners you know

F. **Interrogative pronouns**

The personal interrogatives *who*, *whom*, and *whose* (cf. 4.43) also display distinctions in case:

Who taught you English?
Who (or *whom*) did you interview?
Whose is that book?

3.27
Adjectives and adverbs

The semantic category of comparison applies to adjectives and adverbs that are gradable (cf. 4.24). They are gradable when we can view them as on a scale; for example, for the adjective *cold*: *a bit cold, somewhat cold, rather cold, very cold, extremely cold*. We can also express comparisons for gradable adjectives or adverbs: *as cold (as), less cold (than), more cold (than), (the) most cold*.

Comparison is a grammatical category that can be expressed by inflections in many gradable adjectives and in a few gradable adverbs. The inflectional forms end (usually) in *-er* and *-est*:

absolute	comparative	superlative
tall	taller	tallest
wealthy	wealthier	wealthiest

Comparatives are required in standard English for a comparison involving two only (*Sam is taller than Richard*) and superlatives for a comparison involving more than two (*the tallest of the three girls*).

The inflectional comparatives and superlatives are used with monosyllabic words, such as *tall* and *young*, and some disyllabic words, such as *wealthy* and *clever*. Monosyllabic words generally take the inflectional forms, disyllabic words take either the inflectional forms or the periphrastic forms with *more* and *most* (*more wealthy, most wealthy*), and longer words take only the periphrastic forms (*more beautiful, most beautiful*). Adverbs that have the same forms as adjectives can also take inflectional forms: (work) *harder*, (work) *hardest*. A few common adjectives and adverbs have irregular forms:

good, better, best
badly, worse, worst

3.28
Co-ordination and apposition

Co-ordination links items of equivalent grammatical status. Previously in this chapter (cf. 3.3) we have seen an example of co-ordination of clauses in a compound sentence:

[1] It has only been a week *and* I feel lonesome without you. [W1B-001-36]

The two clauses of **[1]** have equivalent grammatical status since each can stand alone as an independent sentence (cf. 6.2–8):

[1a] It has only been a week. I feel lonesome without you.

Phrases, including just the head words, can also be co-ordinated. (For co-ordination of noun phrases, see 5.12 f.) As with co-ordination of clauses, the central co-ordinators are *and, or*, and *but* (cf. 4.30), though only *and* and *or* can link more than two units:

[2] [. . .] they've sort of got rice *and* carrots *and* things in there [S1A-055-146]

[3] [. . .] they work out a sum that they think is reasonable for you to pay back every week *or* every month [S1A-078-104]

[4] When did you last have your teeth seen *and* cleaned [S1A-087-204]

[5] It's turned upside down *and* back to front [S1B-015-184]

[6] I knew that the fault lay not with our young people *but* the quality and type of education they had received. [W2B-012-121]

Units may be co-ordinated without a co-ordinator being present. In **[7]** *dingy* and *stagnant* are considered to be co-ordinated because the co-ordinator *and* is implied:

[7] They only thrive in *dingy* ⟨ , ⟩ *stagnant* areas where the oxygen levels are fairly low [S1A-087-158]

Co-ordination with a co-ordinator is syndetic co-ordination, co-ordination without a co-ordinator is asyndetic co-ordination.

The co-ordinated phrases must be identical in function, but they need not be identical in type of phrase. In **[8]** *themselves to themselves* (noun phrase plus prepositional phrase) is co-ordinated with *well away from the roads* (adverb phrase plus prepositional phrase); both are subject predicatives (cf. 3.18):

[8]   They tend to keep themselves to themselves *and* well away from the
          roads [S1A-006-266]

Apposition (cf. 5.11) is similar to co-ordination in that it links items of equivalent grammatical status. The difference between them is that the linked appositives are identical in their reference (refer to the same person or same thing) or they overlap in their reference (one appositive included in the reference of the other). Typically, the units in apposition are noun phrases. Here are some examples:

[9]   But in fact uhm most of us know it's really a version of *that huge robust
          plant the acanthus* ⟨ , ⟩ which many of you may have in your gardens [S2A-
          024-69]

[10] For the average property, the cistern should have a capacity of *230 litres
          (50 gallons).* [W2D-012-33]

[11] Inside was *the engine—his engine.* [W2F-007-4]

[12] *My sister Mary Jane* squeezed in beside me at the rail. [W2F-013-7]

Appositives may be linked by the co-ordinators *and* or (more usually) *or*:

[13] The single layer net can be seen as a crude emulation of a *neural cell, or
          neuron,* in the brain. [W2A-032-67]

This is co-ordinative apposition, since *neural cell* and *neuron* refer to the same thing.

Chapter 4
Word Classes

Summary

Prepositions (4.31)

Determiners and pronouns (4.32–45)

Numerals (4.46)

Interjections (4.47)

Chapter 4 Summary

■ Word classes (or parts of speech) are either open or closed. Open classes are by far the largest because they readily admit new words. The open classes are noun, verb, adjective, and adverb. The closed classes are auxiliary, conjunction, preposition, determiner, pronoun, numeral, and interjection. Many words belong to more than one class.

■ Word classes are established on the basis of three types of criteria: notional (meanings), morphological (forms), and grammatical (relations with other words and larger units).

■ Nouns by themselves or with determiners and modifiers typically function as subject and direct object. Nouns are either common or proper, count (having both singular and plural forms) or non-count. They may be in the common case or the genitive case, for which there is a corresponding *of*-phrase. Gender differences (masculine, feminine, non-personal) are signalled only through some associated pronouns.

■ Verbs (or main verbs) by themselves or preceded by auxiliaries (or auxiliary verbs) function as the verb of a sentence or clause. Verbs have five form-types: base (without inflections), -*s* form (for the present tense), -*ing* participle, past, and -*ed* participle. In regular verbs the past and the -*ed* participle are identical, but they are distinguished in some irregular verbs.

■ Adjectives by themselves or with modifiers typically function both attributively as premodifiers of nouns and predicatively as subject predicative. Nominal adjectives (e.g. *the poor*) serve as head of a noun phrase. Most adjectives are gradable: they can take intensifiers (e.g. *very*) and comparison (e.g. *taller, tallest; more difficult, most difficult*).

■ Adverbs by themselves or with modifiers typically function as premodifiers of adjectives and other adverbs, as adverbials, or as complements of verbs. Sentence adverbials are either conjuncts (logical connectors, e.g. *therefore* and *nevertheless*) or disjuncts (commenting on the stance of the speaker or the content of the sentence, e.g. *frankly, fortunately*). Adjuncts are adverbials (e.g. referring to space, time, or manner) that are more closely linked to the processes or circumstances described in the sentence.

■ Auxiliaries fall into two major sets: primary auxiliaries (*be, have, do*) and modals (e.g. *can, will, must*). They precede verbs to express notions such as time, permission, possibility. As operators they play a role in sentence processes such as negation and interrogation.

■ Conjunctions are either co-ordinators or subordinators. Co-ordinators (*and, or, but*) link units of equal status. Subordinators (e.g. *if, although*) link subordinate clauses to their host clauses.

- Prepositions (e.g. *of, in*) function as the first constituent of prepositional phrases and are typically followed by noun phrases as their complements. They may be simple (consisting of one word, e.g. *of, to*) or complex (e.g. *according to, as well as*).

- Determiners (e.g. *the, your*) introduce noun phrases, whereas pronouns (e.g. *she, anybody*) function as noun phrases by themselves or with modifiers. Many words may be either determiners or pronouns. The definite article *the* and the indefinite article *a(n)* are only determiners. The major sets of pronouns/determiners are the primary pronouns (personal, possessive, reflexive), the *wh*-pronouns (interrogative, exclamative, relative, nominal relative, *wh*-conditional), and the indefinite pronouns (assertive, non-assertive, negative, universal, quantifying). Other sets of pronouns or determiners are demonstratives, reciprocals, pronoun *one*, existential *there*.

- Numerals may function as pronouns or determiners. There are three types: cardinals (e.g. *two, ten thousand*), ordinals (e.g. *first, twentieth*), fractions (*a half, two-thirds*).

- Interjections are exclamatory emotive words that are loosely attached to the rest of the sentence, e.g. *ah, ouch, sh, wow*.

Determination of Word Classes

4.1
Open and closed classes

Grammatical descriptions require reference to word classes (or parts of speech), such as noun and verb. Further distinctions may be made within word classes; for example, within nouns the distinction between common nouns and proper nouns. Grammarians have varied on the number of classes and subclasses. The more comprehensive and detailed their descriptions, the more classes and subclasses they require.

Word classes fall into two categories: open classes and closed classes. Open classes readily admit new members and therefore are by far the largest classes. There are four open classes:

noun
verb
adjective
adverb

The seven closed classes recognized in this grammar are:

auxiliary
conjunction
preposition
determiner
pronoun
numeral
interjection

As with the open classes, the closed classes may be divided into subclasses. For example, conjunctions are subdivided into co-ordinators (or co-ordinating conjunctions) and subordinators (or subordinating conjunctions).

Items may belong to more than one class. In most instances we can only assign a word to a word class when we encounter it in context. *Looks* is a verb in 'It *looks* good', but a noun in 'She has good *looks*'; *that* is a conjunction in 'I know *that* they are abroad', but a pronoun in 'I know *that*' and a determiner in 'I know *that* man'; *one* is a generic pronoun in '*One* must be careful not to offend them', but a numeral in 'Give me *one* good reason'.

Some members of a class are central (or prototypical), whereas others are more peripheral. *Tall* is central to the class of adjectives, because it conforms to all the characteristics of adjectives; in particular it can be attributive (premodifying a noun) as in *that tall building* and predicative (functioning as subject predicative) as in *That building is tall*. *Afraid*, on the other hand, is peripheral, because it can only be predicative as in *He was afraid*.

Some members of a class consist of more than one word. *Book review* and *cable car* are compound nouns, *no one* and *one another* are compound pronouns, *because of* and *in spite of* are complex prepositions, *as well as* and *in order that* are complex conjunctions. Compounds may be written as orthographic words, either solid or hyphenated. The pronouns *nobody* and *yourself* are written solid (though *yourself* is separated in *your good self*), and *no one* is sometimes hyphenated as *no-one.*

Roughly corresponding to the distinction between open-class and closed-class words is that between lexical or content words, on the one hand, and grammatical or function words, on the other. These terms acknowledge the importance of most of the closed-class words in the grammatical relations between words or higher units. It would be wrong, however, to think of closed-class words as lacking content. The preposition *into* contrasts with *out of* in the sentence 'He went *into* the kitchen and she went *out of* the kitchen', and the pronouns *nobody* and *everybody* are obviously different in their meaning.

Some words do not fit well into any of the classes. Among them are:

1. the negative particle *not* and its contraction *n't*, which are used to form negative sentences (cf. 3.11);
2. the infinitive particles *to*, *so as to*, and *in order to*, which are followed by an infinitive verb;
3. the infinitive particles *for* and *in order for*, which introduce the subject of an infinitive clause (cf. 4.30):

    [1] And I mean it's you know a bit difficult *for* people to get there [S1A-019-345]

    [2] *In order for* a closure to be carried 〈 , 〉 there have to be a hundred honourable members for the closure [S1B-051-17]

4. *with* and *without*, when they introduce the subject of a non-finite or verbless clause (cf. 4.30):

    [3] I put it on *with* the zip done up [S1A-042-174]

    [4] You'll never get a word in *with* me talking [S1A-081-41]

    [5] We're riding here *with* our visors up as it was a very cold and humid day [S2A-054-123]

5. existential *there* (cf. 4.39):

    [6] *There*'s a certain amount of academic snobbery attached to UNIX I always feel [S1A-029-166]

4.2
Criteria for word classes

Word classes have been established on the basis of three types of criteria: notional, morphological, and grammatical.

Notional (or semantic) criteria involve generalizations about the meaning of words in a class. Notional definitions have often been applied to English nouns and verbs. A common notional definition of the noun class is that nouns are names of persons, things, and places. To some extent it is a satisfactory notional definition in that many central nouns refer to persons, things, and places. But it is inadequate in that it excludes many words that we wish to place in the same class as *child, book,* and *city* because they behave in the same way grammatically. The notional definition of nouns excludes abstract nouns such as *action, destruction, morality, time, authorship, happiness, existence, contradiction*—to mention just a few. Verbs have been notionally defined as expressing an action or a state. The definition is undermined by the very words *action* and *state*: *action* is a noun, and so is *state* as used in the definition.

Morphological criteria refer to the forms of words that belong to one class. These may be inflectional forms of the same lexical item: plurals of nouns (*book/books, child/children*), variant forms of verbs (*steal/steals/stole/stealing/ stolen*), comparatives and superlatives of adjectives (*happy/happier/happiest*). Or they may be affixes, usually suffixes, that identify particular classes. For example: *-ness* or *-ity* for nouns (*goodness, normality*), *-ize* or *-ify* for verbs (*specialize, dignify*), *-able* or *-less* for adjectives (*suitable, careless*), *-ly* for adverbs (*mostly*).

Morphological criteria are inadequate for differentiating word classes in English for several reasons. First, many words are invariable in English, and do not admit inflections. This is so particularly for the closed classes. Secondly, even with the classes that admit inflections, many words are invariable. Nouns such as *chess* and *information* do not have plural forms. Adjectives with more than two syllables (*beautiful, interesting*) do not have inflected forms, nor do many with two syllables (*famous, hopeful*). Most adverbs are not inflected for comparison. Only verbs are virtually always inflected.[1] Thirdly, most words are not marked by affixes as belonging to particular classes. The forms of the words do not identify *speech* as a noun, *come* as a verb, *nice* as an adjective, or *here* as an adverb, though potentialities for inflections differentiate the first three words. Finally, since it is often possible to convert words from one class to another, some affixes that are characteristic of a particular class remain when the words are converted to another class: the noun suffix *-tion* (*prevention, education*) remains when certain nouns are converted to verbs (*condition, proposition*); the adjectives *disposable* and *hopeful* are converted into the nouns *disposable/disposables* and *hopeful/hopefuls*. When they are in isolation, we cannot tell whether *look* and *looks* are nouns or verbs, though we know that *looked* and *looking* are verb forms.

Morphological criteria alone are generally insufficient to establish word classes or to identify the word-class membership of a word in isolation.

However, in context the inflectional potential of a word is a guide to its word class, where inflectional variants are available. We know that *make* in **[1]** is a noun because we can add a plural inflection:

[1] How would you know what *make* it was [S1A-008-134]

[1a] How would you know what *makes* they were?

And we know that *make* is a verb in **[2]** because we can inflect it as a verb:

[2] If you're a stone and a half it must *make* some difference [S1A-038-72]

[2a] If you're a stone and a half it must have *made* some difference.

[2b] If you're a stone and a half it must be *making* some difference.

[2c] If you're a stone and a half it *makes* some difference.

Since verbs are almost always inflected, inflectional potentiality is a useful criterion for verbs.

Grammatical (or syntactic) criteria involve the grammatical functions of the word in its relation to other words. The criteria are invoked to establish the actual functions in context or the potential functions in isolation. As head of a noun phrase, a noun may function as subject, direct object, indirect object, etc. It may be introduced by determiners, premodified by adjectives, and postmodified by prepositional phrases and relative clauses. As head of an adjective phrase, an adjective may function as premodifier of a noun and as subject predicative and it may be premodified by adverbs. Similar criteria may be applied to all the word classes. Grammatical criteria are the most reliable criteria for establishing word classes, though peripheral members may not conform to all the criteria.

In practice, morphological criteria are employed together with grammatical criteria where inflectional variants or affixal characteristics are available. Central members of the noun class can function as subject, be preceded by the determiner *the*, and take plural forms.

Notional criteria are often a useful entry to a recognition of a class, as indeed is simply a list of examples. Notional criteria are valid for establishing equivalences in word classes across unrelated languages, since morphological resemblances are likely to be absent and grammatical resemblances may sometimes be insecure.

Nouns

4.3
Characteristics
of nouns

As the head of a noun phrase, a noun has a range of functions (cf. 5.3). For example, the noun *teachers* is the head of the subject noun phrase of [1] and the noun *dinner* is the head of the object noun phrase in [2]:

> [1]   *The teachers* aren't perhaps aware of how they can work with the disabled student [S1A-001-96]

> [2]   The people we were staying with they ⟨ , , ⟩ cooked us *a traditional Normandy dinner* [S1A-009-118]

Typically, nouns are introduced by a determiner (cf. 4.32 ff.): the definite article *the* in [1] and the indefinite article *a* in [2]. They may be premodified: in [2] by the adjective *traditional* and the noun *Normandy*. They may also be postmodified: the relative clause *we were staying with* postmodifies *people* in [2] and the prepositional phrase *in the building* postmodifies *room* in [3]:

> [3]   And they were saying wait until summer and you'll get the benefit then ⟨ , ⟩ because it's the coolest *room in the building* [S1A-017-93]

The typical noun has both singular and plural forms: *teacher/teachers, dinner/dinners, building/buildings.*

Here are some typical noun endings:

-age:	*postage, pilgrimage, patronage, savage, courage, beverage*
-ation, -tion, -sion, -ion:	*explanation, education, nation, division, invasion, objection*
-er, -or:	*writer, painter, player, actor, doctor*
-ing:	*building(s), saving(s), shaving(s), writing(s), gathering(s), wandering(s)*
-ity:	*reality, immunity, disparity, eternity*
-ment:	*appointment, deferment, experiment, establishment, embarrassment, ointment*
-nes:	*awkwardness, eagerness, giddiness, happiness, lawlessness, readiness*
-ist:	*atheist, soloist, apologist, biologist, capitalist, specialist, realist, dramatist*

Some of these endings were endings of the words when they were borrowed from other languages. For noun suffixes in word formation, see 9.21 f.

4.4
Proper nouns

Nouns are either common or proper.

Proper nouns name specific people, animals, institutions, places, times, etc. They have unique reference, and in writing they begin with a capital letter; *Bill Clinton, Jerusalem, Christmas, December*. Names may consist of a combination of a proper noun with other words (adjectives, common nouns, prepositional phrases), and it is usual for the initial letters of each open-class word in the name to be written in capitals, and also the definite article *the* if it is part of the name:

The Hague	*Queen Elizabeth*
The New York Times	*Scotland Yard*
Lake Michigan	*Great Britain*

Closed-class words, such as the definite article (when not part of the name) and prepositions, are generally in lower case:

the Pacific	*the United States of America*
the University of Michigan	*the King of Belgium*

Proper names are non-count: they have no contrast in number. Generally, they have only a singular form, but some place-names have only a plural form:

the Netherlands	*the Bahamas*
the Alps	*the Andes*
the United Nations	*the British Isles*

Proper names are treated as common nouns when they do not have unique references, though they retain capitals in writing. They can then be in the plural and take determiners that are confined to count nouns:

[1]   I bet it's busy on *Sundays* [S1A-006-250]

[2]   I've got a lot of *Julians* in my class [S1A-032-277]

[3]   It's about a group of latterday *Rip Van Winkles* who in a Bronx hospital in 1969 were briefly awakened from a catatonic state in which they'd existed for 30 or even 40 years [S2B-033-6]

[4]   But you're *a bit of a Bertie Wooster* yourself [S1B-042-43]

[5]   So this is a very common sight ⟨ , ⟩ on *a Saturday* at Paestum [S2A-024-21]

4.5
Count and non-count nouns

Common nouns are either count (or countable) or non-count (or uncountable or mass). Count nouns have both a singular and a plural and they can be introduced by determiners that accompany distinctions in number. For example:

a			*two*	
one			*several*	
every	} *picture*		*few*	} *pictures*
either			*many*	
this			*these*	

Non-count nouns indicate entities that are viewed as uncountable. They are singular in form and are treated as singular for subject–verb agreement (cf. 5.14). They are introduced by a restricted set of determiners (cf. 4.32 ff.). For example:

the			*my*	
this			*whose*	
some	} *information*		*which*	} *sugar*
any			*what*	
no			*whatever*	

Like plural count nouns, non-count nouns may head a noun phrase without an overt determiner, the zero article (cf. 4.33):

[1] I think they're not too good on *music* [S1A-033-115]

[2] She was an enthusiastic gardener, a collector of *old furniture* ('Not antiques,' Eleanor once said to her), a hoarder of books and records, photographs and silly mementoes. [W2F-009-25]

[3] *Honesty* is appreciated a lot [S1A-037-206]

[4] You even have to pay extra if you want *bread* with your meal. [W1B-002-127]

The count/non-count distinction correlates to some extent with the distinction between concrete and abstract nouns. Concrete nouns are used to refer to entities that are typically perceptible and tangible, whereas abstract nouns refer to those that are not perceptible and tangible, such as qualities, states of mind, and events: *morality, happiness, belief, disgust, pursuit.* When concrete nouns are non-count, the entities they refer to are viewed as an undifferentiated mass: *furniture, bread, cheese, coffee, whisky.*

We can often achieve countability with non-count nouns (particularly concrete nouns) through partitive expressions. There are general partitive expressions, such as *a piece of/pieces of* and *a bit of/bits of*:

a piece of	*bread*
a bit of	*sugar*
some pieces of }	*cheese*
two pieces of	*information*
	advice
	evidence
	news

There are also partitive expressions that tend to go only with certain non-count nouns:

two *slices* of bread/cheese/cake/meat

a *lump* of sugar/coal
a *bar* of chocolate/soap/gold
a *glass* of water/soda/whisky
three *cups* of coffee/tea

We can also use measurements:

two *pounds* of sugar/coffee/tea
a *ton* of coal
a *litre* of brandy

Some nouns can be either count or non-count, sometimes with a difference of meaning:

[5]   How would we do it if it was *paper* [S1A-077-21] (non-count)

[6]   It's gonna be difficult cos all my *papers* are in a mess in my desk [S1A-074-342] (count)

[7]   That's exactly what happens in our eyes and that's why the nasal retina actually sees *light* ⟨ , ⟩ from the lateral field [S1B-015-185] (non-count)

[8]   At the beginning death was seen as a *light*, now he seems to be praising it as a darkness. [W1A-018-27] (count)

[9]   Do you want *cake* [S1A-019-90] (non-count)

[10] Mm that's a wonderful walnut *cake* [S1A-056-195] (count)

[11] Is that because you were having *difficulty* remembering things [S1A-059-17] (non-count)

[12] They might be in financial *difficulties* [S1B-065-3]

[13] One loses *interest* in everything when one has children [S1A-032-11] (non-count)

[14] I mean Thames and Hudson have expressed an *interest* and it's possible I would be able to publish something out of that but you know all that takes a very long time [S1A-066-106]

More generally, many concrete nouns that are normally non-count can be treated as count nouns in two uses:

1. When the noun refers to different kinds or qualities:

[15] I don't like *sparkling wines* all that much [S1A-019-14]

[16] We bought *Italian cheeses*, fresh pasta and olives [. . .] [W1B-013-29]

2. When the noun refers to quantities in a situation where the units are obvious:

[17] *One sugar* only, please.

[18] I'll have *two coffees*.

4.6
Regular plurals

Count nouns make a distinction between singular and plural. Singular denotes one, and plural more than one:

[1]   It weighs one *pound* exactly.

[1a] It weighs at least one and a half *pounds*.

In writing, the regular plural ends in -*s*:

cat/cats   book/books   house/houses

Some spelling rules affect the addition of the regular -*s* inflection:

1. If the singular ends in a sibilant (see below) that is not followed by -*e*, add -*es*:

pass/passes   buzz/buzzes   bush/bushes   church/churches   box/boxes

A few nouns ending in -*s* have a variant in which the consonant is doubled before the inflection:

bus/buses or *busses   bias/biases* or *biasses   focus/focuses* or *focusses*
gas/gases or *gasses*

If a sibilant is followed by -*e*, only -*s* is added:

cage/cages   disease/diseases   grudge/grudges

2. If the singular ends in a consonant plus *y*, change the *y* to *i* and then add -*es*:

spy/spies   curry/curries   worry/worries

Proper nouns are exceptions:

the Kennedys   Bloody Marys

If a vowel precedes the final *y*, the plural is regular:

toy/toys   play/plays

3. For some nouns ending in -*o*, add -*es*. Here are common examples:

echo/echoes   hero/heroes   potato/potatoes   tomato/tomatoes
veto/vetoes

In some instances there is variation between -*os* and -*oes*; for example:

cargo/cargos or *cargoes   motto/mottos* or *mottoes   volcano/volcanos* or
volcanoes

The regular -*s* plural inflection is pronounced as /ɪz/, /z/, or /s/ depending on the final sound of the singular.

1. /ɪz/ if the singular ends in a sibilant:

   /s/   *bus/buses   box/boxes*

> /z/   buzz/buzzes
> /ʃ/   bush/bushes
> /tʃ/   church/churches
> /ʒ/   barrage/barrages
> /dʒ/   grudge/grudges

2. /z/ if the singular ends in a vowel or a voiced consonant (cf. 10.3) other than a sibilant:

> ray/rays   study/studies   key/keys   attitude/attitudes   dog/dogs
> barn/barns

3. /s/ if the singular ends in a voiceless consonant (cf. 10.3) other than a ◂ sibilant:

> cat/cats   cake/cakes   tramp/tramps   tourist/tourists

4.7 Irregular plurals

1. Voicing of final consonant

Some nouns ending in -f or -fe form their plurals by changing the ending to -ves. They include:

> calf/calves   life/lives
> half/halves   loaf/loaves
> knife/knives   self/selves
> leaf/leaves   thief/thieves

Others have regular plurals as well:

> dwarf/dwarves or dwarfs
> handkerchief/handkerchiefs or handkerchieves
> hoof/hooves or hoofs
> scarf/scarves or scarfs
> wharf/wharves or wharfs

Some nouns ending in -th have the regular plural in spelling, but the pronunciation of th is voiced /ð/ and therefore followed by /z/. However, in most cases, the regular pronunciation /θs/ is a variant:

> baths   oaths   paths   sheaths   truths   wreaths   youths

A change of voicing also occurs from the voiceless /s/ ending in singular house to the voiced ending in /zɪz/ in plural houses.

2. Mutations

In a few nouns, the plural is formed by mutation (a change in the vowel):

> man/men   woman/women   tooth/teeth
> foot/feet   goose/geese
> mouse/mice louse/lice

Children, the plural of *child,* combines a vowel change and the irregular ending *-en* (a survival of an Old English plural inflection). A similar combination appears in *brethren,* a specialized plural of *brother.* The older plural ending is found without vowel change in *ox/oxen.* In American English there are also variant plurals of *ox:* regular *oxes* and the unchanged form *ox.*

3. Zero plurals

Count nouns that have the same form for singular and plural are said to have zero plural. These include the names of some animals, particularly *cod, deer, sheep*; nouns denoting quantity when they are premodified by a numeral or other quantifier and particularly when they are attached to a noun head: *two hundred (people), three dozen (plants), several thousand (dollars).* The measure nouns *foot* (length unit), *pound* (unit of weight or of British currency), and *stone* (British weight unit) optionally take zero plurals: *six foot two, twenty pound, fifteen stone.*

4. Foreign plurals

Some nouns borrowed from other languages (in particular from Latin and Greek) may retain their foreign plurals, but generally only in technical usage. In non-technical usage, the regular plural is normal in some of the instances listed below:

(a) nouns in *-us,* with plural in *-i*:
    alumnus/alumni   bacillus   locus   nucleus
(b) nouns in *-us,* with plural in *-a*:
    corpus/corpora   genus/genera
(c) nouns in *-a,* with plural in *-ae*:
    alga/algae   antenna   formula   vertebra
(d) nouns in *-um,* with plural in *-a*:
    addendum/addenda   bacterium   curriculum   erratum   ovum
(e) nouns in *-ex* or *-ix,* with plural in *-ices*:
    appendix/appendices   codex   index   matrix
(f) nouns in *-is,* with plural in *-es*:
    analysis/analyses   axis   basis   crisis   diagnosis   ellipsis   hypothesis   oasis   parenthesis   synopsis   thesis
(g) nouns in *-on,* with plural in *-a*:
    automaton/automata   criterion   phenomenon
(h) nouns in *-eau,* with plural in *-eaux*:
    bureau/bureaux

The regular plural is normal with *bureau* and other such words borrowed from French (e.g. *plateau, tableau*). Some French words ending in *-s* have the same spelling for their plural, but are pronounced regularly with /z/ (e.g. *corps, rendezvous*).

(i) nouns in *-o,* with plural in *-i*:
    tempo/tempi   virtuoso

Certain nouns in -*a* are regularly treated as singular, though the ending represents an original plural: *agenda, insignia*. The use of other nouns in -*a* as singulars is controversial. They include *criteria, media, phenomena, strata*. *Media* in the sense 'mass media' is often treated as singular:

[1] This is a call for a more mature leadership, a more mature *media* and a more mature constituency. [W2A-017-83]

[2] And maybe the *media* plays a part in all this [S1B-030-52]

[3] The way-up *criteria* is a phenomenon used to establish which way the rocks were originally deposited. [W1A-020-3]

[4] Many LA countries, including Brazil, Argentina and Chile, opted for import-substitution industrialization, a *phenomena* where manufactured goods are made in the country for a domestic market instead of importing them from abroad. [W1A-015-68]

[5] Schmidt (1982) explained this *phenomena* by describing the motor program for walking—in animals—as being innate [. . .] [W1A-016-56]

Data is commonly used as a non-count noun in scientific discourse:

[6] In this context inertia is ⟨ , , ⟩ is a combination of how much *data* we've got and then how and how far away it is from the average [S1B-017-215]

[7] Uhm in order to contextualise what I want to say I just want to play you a little bit of *data* [S2A-030-17]

[8] Regression is commonly used by statisticians to calculate the best-fit through a set of data points in order to establish how close the *data* is to the ideal. [W2A-036-86]

[9] Now the SPDIF link is a single channel, where all this *data* plus other information on subcodes, emphasis, etc, is encoded. [W2B-040-21]

5. Uninflected plurals, without singulars

cattle   livestock   people (as plural of *person*)
police   poultry   vermin

6. Binary plurals

Some nouns with plural inflection refer to instruments or articles of clothing that consist of two parts that are joined together. For example:

binoculars   clippers   glasses   scissors   spectacles
briefs   jeans   pants   shorts   trousers

They take a plural verb:

[10] If you need glasses because your sight has changed or because your *glasses* are worn out [. . .] [W2D-001-102]

7. Inflected plurals, without singulars

Some nouns have the regular plural inflection but do not have a corresponding singular, at least in the relevant sense. For example:

arms ('weapons')
clothes ('garments')
customs ('tax')

manners ('behaviour')
premises ('building')

8. Collective nouns

Singular collective nouns refer to a group of people or animals or to institutions. They may be treated as either singular or plural. They are treated as plural (more commonly in British English than in American English) when the focus is on the group as individuals rather than as a single entity. They may then take a plural verb, and plural pronouns may be co-referential with them (cf. 5.14):

[11] The Argentine *team are* in possession now inside *their* own half [S2A-010-213]

Citation **[12]** illustrates a change in the treatment of the collective noun *class* from singular to plural. In the first two uses, *a class* is conceived of as an entity ('cohesive', 'which is made up of people'), whereas in the third use, *a class* refers to individuals ('who own most of the land'). There is a conspicuous switch from non-personal *which* for the singular to personal *who* for the plural:

[12] I was brought up in New Zealand and I've never forgotten how odd it seemed to me when I arrived in this country to find a society which is dominated by a ruling class *a class which is* cohesive and self-defining *a class which is* made up of people who look different often because they're actually taller and bigger and sound different because they speak in a different tone or accent who enjoy better health and longer life expectancy who live in different sorts of houses who send their children to different sorts of schools who are educated in different sorts of universities *a class who dominate* all the best jobs *who own* most of the land *control* most of the wealth *exercise* most of the power and *whose* dominant position is underpinned by a dense and complex class structure which effectively insulates *them* against challenge [S2B-036-6 ff.]

Here are some common examples of collective nouns:

administration	enemy	majority
army	family	minority
audience	firm	mob
class	gang	nation
committee	government	public
company	group	swarm
crew	herd	team
crowd	jury	

9. Plurals of compounds

Compounds generally follow the regular rule by adding the regular *-s* inflection to their last element:

gunfight/gunfights
pop group/pop groups

two-year-old/ two-year-olds
gin-and-tonic/ gin-and-tonics

Compounds ending in an adverb also generally follow the regular rule:

close-up/ close-ups
take-over/ take-overs
stand-in/ stand-ins

Though having the plural inflection at the end, these two break the spelling rule by retaining *y* before the inflection:

lay-by/ lay-bys
stand-by/ stand-bys

The following two compounds are exceptional in taking the inflection on the first element:

passer-by/ passers-by
listener-in/ listeners-in

A few compounds ending in *-ful* usually take the plural inflection on the last element, but have a less common plural with the inflection on the first element:

mouthful/ mouthfuls or *mouthsful*
spoonful/ spoonfuls or *spoonsful*

Compounds ending in *-in-law* allow the plural either on the first element or (informally) on the last element:

sister-in-law/ sisters-in-law or *sister-in-laws*

Some compounds consisting of a noun plus a postmodifying adjective also allow both alternatives:

court martial/ courts martial or *court martials*
attorney general/ attorneys general or *attorney generals*
poet laureate/ poets laureate or *poet laureates*

Other compounds with a postmodifying adjective or prepositional phrase have the plural inflection only on the first part:

heir apparent/ heirs apparent
notary public/ notaries public
commander-in-chief/ commanders-in-chief
right-of-way/ rights-of-way

4.8
Non-standard plurals

Non-standard dialects may differ from standard dialects in the plurals of nouns. Among the differences found in various non-standard dialects are:

1. **Zero plurals**

   After numerals or quantifiers, count nouns may have a zero plural (the same form as in the singular):

   thirty year, many mile

2. **Regular plurals**

   Nouns that have irregular plurals in standard dialects may take regular plurals:

   mouses, louses, sheeps, swines, deers

3. **Double plurals**

   Nouns that have irregular plurals in standard dialects may have an added regular plural:

   mens, childrens, mices

   Some regular plurals in standard dialects may take a second regular plural:

   bellowses, beasteses (with an intrusive /ɪ/)

4. **Mutation plurals**

   Like standard *mice* is non-standard mutation plural *kye* ('cows'), a survival of an older plural. Double plurals of the same word are also found: *kyes* and (with older -*en* plural ending) *kine*.

5. **Plurals in -*(e)n***

   The older plural ending in -*(e)n* found in standard *oxen* is also found in non-standard *een, eyen* ('eyes'); *shoon, shoen* ('shoes'); *flen* ('fleas'); *housen* ('houses').

6. **Plurals in -*(e)r***

   The older plural ending in -*(e)r* found in the standard double plural *children* is found in non-standard regularly formed *childer*.

4.9
Gender

Gender is a grammatical category by which nouns are divided into two or more classes that require different agreement in inflection with determiners and adjectives, and perhaps also with words of other classes, such as verbs. There is often an association between gender classes and meaning contrasts such as in sex, animacy, and size.

Old English had three genders: masculine, feminine, and neuter.

Determiners, adjectives, and co-referring pronouns agreed with nouns in gender. For example, the determiner equivalent to present-day *the* and *that* assumes three different forms in agreement with singular nouns from different genders functioning as subject:

sē cyning ('king'—masculine)
sēo lufu ('love'—feminine)
þæt land ('land'—neuter)

The assignment of nouns to gender classes in Old English cannot be predicted from their meaning. For example, *mere* ('lake') and *hām* ('home') are masculine, *miht* ('might') and *stōw* ('place') are feminine, *folc* ('people') and *land* ('land') are neuter. Nor do they necessarily reflect contrasts in sex: *wīf* ('woman', 'wife') is neuter, whereas *wīfmann* ('woman') is masculine.

Nowadays, English has no classes of nouns that signal gender differences through their inflections, nor do determiners or adjectives vary according to the gender of nouns. English no longer has grammatical gender. (See Ch. 3, n. 12.) It can be said to have natural gender, in that certain pronouns expressing natural contrasts in gender are selected to refer to nouns in accordance with the meaning or reference of the nouns:

he, him, his, himself	masculine
she, her, hers, herself	feminine
who, whom, whoever, whomever	personal—either masculine or feminine
it, its, itself, which	non-personal

In **[1]** *hers* is chosen because it refers back to *Natalie* ('the same as Natalie's letter'), whereas in **[2]** *his* is chosen because it refers back to *Shakespeare* ('Shakespeare's plays'):

[1] Well, if you've seen *Natalie*, this letter will probably be very boring, as it will contain much the same as *hers*! [W1B-002-113]

[2] Who can remember who was Secretary of the Council when *Shakespeare* wrote *his* plays [S1B-022-48]

The choice of pronouns does not depend on differences in the word classes of *Natalie* and *Shakespeare*. It relates to differences in the sex of Natalie and Shakespeare. We know that Natalie is a name applied to females and that the playwright Shakespeare was a male.

There are male and female pairs of nouns. Some of these are not marked morphologically:

father—mother	*boy—girl*
brother—sister	*man—woman*
son—daughter	*king—queen*
uncle—aunt	*monk—nun*
nephew—niece	*bachelor—spinster*

Spinster is not generally used nowadays for young unmarried women, because of its connotation of a woman unlikely to be married. *Single* is preferred, and used for both women and men.

Some pairs are morphologically marked, usually with the suffix for the female noun:

host—hostess	*prince—princess*
waiter—waitress	*emperor—empress*
actor—actress	*hero—heroine*
god—goddess	*usher—usherette*

The male noun has the morphological marking in these two pairs:

bride—bridegroom   widow—widower

Since these endings are found in only a few nouns, they cannot be regarded as signalling gender classes. Furthermore, increasingly the male noun is used to refer to both sexes in some instances, e.g. *waiter, actor,* or a neutral noun replaces the pair, e.g. *attendant* for *usher—usherette.*

Similar male and female pairs are found for some animals. For example:

bull—cow	*ram—ewe*
dog—bitch	*lion—lioness*
stallion—mare	*tiger—tigress*

Pet-owners and those who have close dealings with the animals may use *he* and *she* as appropriate and perhaps *who*, whereas others will use *it* and *which* for all animals. Similarly, *it* and *which* might be used to refer impersonally to a child or baby, particularly if the sex is not known or is irrelevant:

> **[3]** He had fathered a child upon an unknown woman, for some reason it had been impossible for them to marry—or of course either he or she had not wanted to marry—and they got rid of *the baby* almost as soon as *it* was born. [W2F-014-12]

The personal pronoun *she* may be used to refer to countries and also (though occasionally *he* occurs) to inanimate entities such as ships, cars, and planes:

> **[4]** So *France* one of the world's biggest arms suppliers and by reputation the West's most promiscuous salesman will still allow *her* customers to buy secrecy along with their kit [S2B-034-39]

> **[5]** Within the last twenty years *the People's Republic of China* ⟨ , ⟩ became so fearful of the population outstripping the means of subsistence within *her* frontiers ⟨ , ⟩ that Peking if I can still call it like that ⟨ , ⟩ decreed restraint of parenthood ⟨ , ⟩ under penalty ⟨ , ⟩ to one child for each couple [S2B-048-67]

> **[6]** In the predawn on Sept. 25, 1967, the Cunard Line's Queen Mary, outbound from New York, passed *her* sister ship the Queen Elizabeth heading west. [890928-0168-1]

4.10
Case

Case is an inflected form of the noun that coincides with certain syntactic functions (such as subject) or semantic relations (such as possessor).

In Old English, nouns distinguished five cases—nominative, accusative, genitive, dative, and instrumental—though the distinction between dative and instrumental was neutralized inflectionally and other distinctions were often neutralized in particular declensions (sets of nouns with the same inflections). For example, singular *cyning* ('king') has the same form for the nominative and accusative, as well as for the dative and instrumental:

nominative/accusative	*cyning*
genitive	*cyninges*
dative/instrumental	*cyninge*

In Old English, determiners and premodifying adjectives agreed with the noun in case as well as gender. All five cases of the noun are differentiated in the following examples of the singular masculine noun *cyning*. The differentiation is signalled by the different inflectional forms of the adjective *gōd* ('good'), though there are only three inflectional forms of the noun:

nominative	*gōd cyning*
accusative	*gōdne cyning*
genitive	*gōdes cyninges*
dative	*gōdum cyninge*
instrumental	*gōde cyninge*

In the course of time, most case inflections were lost. The two remaining cases for nouns are the common case and the genitive case. The common case is the one that is used ordinarily, whenever the genitive case is not required.

Apart from the *-es* inflection, Old English had other genitive singulars: *-e*, *-an*, *-a*, and an uninflected genitive. During the Middle English period, the *-es* or *-s* inflection became dominant, spreading to nouns which originally did not have this inflection. Similarly, the plural *-es* or *-s* inflection became the only inflection for the plural, including the genitive plural. In some non-standard dialects (e.g. Black English and in the north Midlands of England) the genitive is often not inflected: *your wife sister, that man coat*.

In speech, the genitive is signalled in singular nouns by an inflection that has the same pronunciation variants as for plural nouns in the common case (cf. 4.6):

1. /ɪz/ if the singular ends in a sibilant

    the *church's* membership

2. /z/ if the singular ends in a vowel or a voiced consonant other than a sibilant

    the *boy's* father   my *dog's* lead

3. /s/ if the singular ends in a voiceless consonant other than a sibilant

    the *student's* parents

There is no difference in speech between the genitive singular, the common case plural, and the genitive plural for regular nouns, though they are differentiated by means of the apostrophe in writing:

	singular	plural
common case	*girl*	*girls*
genitive case	*girl's*	*girls'*

Nouns with irregular plurals are differentiated for all four possibilities:

	singular	plural
common case	*child*	*children*
genitive case	*child's*	*children's*

For the punctuation of the apostrophe, see 11.32.

Genitives may be dependent or independent. The dependent genitive is dependent on the head of the noun phrase. It functions like a possessive pronoun (cf. 4.34 f.):

Estelle's eldest daughter   (dependent genitive)
her eldest daughter   (possessive pronoun)

The independent genitive is not dependent on a following noun, but a noun is implied. The implied noun may be recovered from the context:

[1]   [. . .] there's a possibility of giving up my car ⟨ , ⟩ and taking on *my dad's* [S1B-080-252] ('my dad's car')

[2]   Well ⟨ , , ⟩ uhm ⟨ , ⟩ I wrote my thesis in such a way that it's ⟨ , , ⟩ considerably more accessible than *most people's* [S1A-066-109] ('most people's theses')

Again, possessive pronouns may be used if their reference is clear: 'taking on *his*' in **[1]** and 'more accessible than *theirs*' in **[2]**.

The independent genitive is also used with reference to places. Possible place references are given in parentheses:

[3]   So you're not going to go back and work in *the publisher's* and serve tea ⟨ , ⟩ and stuff [S1A-018-118] ('the publisher's office')

[4]   They are always singing in *the men's* [S1A-043-274] ('the men's room')

[5]   And you can get them from Marks & Spencer's [S1A-017-327] ('Marks & Spencer's store')

[6]   If they uh produce as good a cricketer as you and you took advantage of those nets at *Lord's* you'd put put the fear of God into a few of the players there [S1B-021-53] ('Lord's cricket ground')

[7]   I stood on a pair of scales at *my cousin's* [S1A-038-66] ('my cousin's home')

The dependent genitive usually corresponds to an *of*-phrase with the definite article *the* in the first noun phrase:

Estelle's eldest daughter
the eldest daughter of Estelle

The two constructions are occasionally combined:

a daughter of Estelle's

This double genitive construction—genitive plus *of*-phrase—generally has an indefinite first noun phrase, introduced (for example) by the indefinite article *a* or *an*. Sometimes, however, the demonstratives *this* or *that* are used:

[8] *That hall of Martin's* is quite big actually [S1A-073-99]

[9] *That new film of Joey Jodie Foster's* looks quite good [S1A-049-321]

The present-day English genitive is treated here traditionally as a case that is signalled by inflectional suffixes. In an alternative analysis, the genitive is regarded as an enclitic, a word joined onto a preceding word (as with contracted *n't* in *isn't*). The analysis is motivated by the fact that the genitive is not necessarily attached to one particular word. It may serve a co-ordinated phrase, as in [10]–[14]:

[10] There were some amusing moments but I felt that we were starting to laugh at opera singers popping their heads through curtains and uh little songs where you could almost hear *Gilbert and Sullivan's* patter songs coming through [S1B-044-16]

[11] Seven rounds of talks have already failed to produce an agreement mainly because of *France and Germany's* refusal to accept a proposal from the European Commission for cuts of thirty percent [S2B-007-34]

[12] Three o'clock and Doctor Finley is up again after just *an hour and a half's* sleep [S2B-011-69]

[13] For the last two years Joe's father has visited him regularly at *Peter and Sheila's* home and on Friday nights Joe goes to his father's for the weekend [S2B-038-85]

[14] It's this kind of immediate help that enables *children and young people's* views to be heard and hard-pressed foster families to go on fostering [S2B-038-108]

Paraphrases with an *of*-phrase show that the genitive applies to the co-ordinated noun phrases and not simply to the noun it is attached to. For [14], for example, the paraphrase is 'views of children and young people'.

Similarly, the genitive at the end of a postmodifying prepositional phrase may apply to the whole of the noun phrase and not just to the noun that comes before the genitive:

[15] Trevor Emms *the Duke of Norfolk's* agent and Sir Leslie Scott a land commissioner were level-headed men with a lifetime of land management behind them [S2B-025-80] ('the Duke's agent', not 'Norfolk's agent')

[16] The cost of compensating dockers made compulsorily redundant by the Government's abolition of the Dock Labour Scheme is likely to be more than five times *the Department of Transport's* original estimate. [W2C-001-21] ('the Department's original estimate', not 'Transport's original estimate')

The genitives in [10]–[16] are group genitives.

The genitive is the head of a genitive noun phrase and may therefore take its own determiners and modifiers:

a layperson's point of view ('the point of view of a layperson')
your mother's mother ('the mother of your mother')
the doctor's daughter ('the daughter of the doctor')
different people's experience ('the experience of different people')
my youngest child's computer ('the computer of my youngest child')

4.11
Genitive and
of-phrase

The genitive is preferred to the corresponding *of*-phrase when the noun phrase denotes persons, animals, or human institutions:

[1] Each has its place in *the designer's* studio [W2D-016-71]

[2] The unions say they accept that a twenty percent drop in passenger traffic justifies *the management's* action [S2B-002-64]

[3] Then he said they wanted to try and get to *the air defence system's* command [S1B-038-9]

[4] Well now the Japanese are trying harder in the executive car market as well ⟨ , ⟩ and *Mitsubishi's* new Sigma is priced directly to compete with *BMW's* five series [S2A-055-20]

[5] In the dawn greyness she had listened to *the birds'* first brave cheepings and had given way to her overpowering urge to confront Lesley once more. [W2F-003-8]

The genitive is commonly used with noun phrases referring to time or place:

[6] And the first performance will be ⟨ , ⟩ in about *a month's* time [S1A-004-124]

[7] So I think from *today's* session you've realised I hope that you shouldn't start somebody on life-long anti-hypertensive therapy based upon one single blood pressure measurement [S1B-004-267]

[8] This investment was intended to provide the infrastructure necessary to *Hong Kong's* continued economic development [W2E-008-45]

The genitive is also commonly used with noun phrases that denote entities, states, and activities associated with human beings:

[9] The Frenchman said *my heart's* desire is to be married to a woman so beautiful that everybody in the room is jealous of me [S2B-047-58]

[10] The aim of the Corpus Definition sub-system is to enable the definition of a corpus structure to be entered by *the program's* user. [W1A-005-10]

[11] She's called the Alpha Challenge and the arbitrators were asked to decide questions of principle arising out of *the vessel's* arrest and detention [. . .] [S2A-066-65]

[12] Genesis also favoured *the meletron's* unique sound ⟨ , ⟩ and they featured it heavily on many of their classic early seventies albums [S2B-023-11]

[13] Different theorists dispute the role and relative importance of these factors in our feeling *an emotion's* intensity and differentiation of emotions. [W1A-017-7]

[14] To establish the soundness of a theory in principle, *the methods'* feasibility need be demonstrated just in principle. [W2A-035-59]

The genitive sometimes occurs with noun phrases where none of the above conditions applies:

[15] Chromosomes are made up of protein and DNA, and the latter comprises *the cell's* genetic material [W2B-030-108]

[16] They're not smooth like *an apple's* flesh [S1A-009-159]

[17] That means you're not keeping it there but you'd rather do it for *simplicity's* sake [S1B-080-65]

If the noun that might take the genitive has restrictive postmodification (cf. 5.8), the *of*-phrase is preferred to the group genitive (cf. 4.10):

[18] And they were all uh reproductions *of a* ⟨ , , ⟩ *particular period in art history* [S1A-013-159]

[19] [. . .] Gaveston's ⟨ , ⟩ description of the King of England as being interested in plays and masques and poetry uh uh immediately makes him as far as I can uh see in the eyes *of most people who read that play* effeminate [S1B-045-32]

The alternative group genitive construction would be clumsy: for **[18]** *a particular period in art history's reproductions* and for **[19]** *most people who read that play's eyes.*

The *of*-phrase may be preferred for reasons of communicative importance. The more important information tends to be placed last. In **[20]** the *of*-phrase is used in '*the head of a cat*', when the noun *cat* is introduced, but the genitive is used in '*the cat's* head', since the new point being introduced is about the head:

[20] And he showed that he could in fact measure absorption changes across the head *of a cat* and *the cat's* head's about four or five centimetres diameter [S2A-053-38]

4.12
Meanings of genitive and *of*-phrase

The genitive has also been called the possessive, since one of its meanings has been to denote the possessor of what is referred to by the second noun phrase, as in '*the couple's* home'. But possession has to be interpreted liberally if it is to cover many instances of the genitive and the *of*-phrase. In a liberal interpretation, we could count as possession any connections between the two nouns where the verbs *possess* or *have* can be used in a paraphrase; for example, family relationships: *Tom's son* ('the son that Tom has').

Here are other examples of the possessive genitive:

Mexico City's population
Tom's shock of blond hair
Napoleon's army
the local team's morale
hunger's most acute form
the world's food reserves
Peter's illness
the manufacturer's name and address
my son's bedroom
Japan's importance
the owner's privacy

If the second noun is derived from a verb, the relationship between the genitive phrase and the second noun phrase may correspond to that between subject and verb or that between object and verb. The subjective relationship is more common for the genitive. For example, *the people's choice* corresponds to *The people chose*, where *The people* is subject, and hence *the people's* in *the people's choice* is a subjective genitive. On the other hand, *Kennedy's* in *Kennedy's assassination* is an objective genitive ('Somebody assassinated Kennedy').

The *of*-phrase may also be subjective or objective. But when the genitive and the *of*-phrase co-occur, the genitive phrase is subjective and the *of*-phrase is objective:

God's choice *of Israel* ('God chose Israel')
the reviewer's analysis *of the play* ('The reviewer analysed the play')
my neighbour's criticism *of my children* ('My neighbour criticized my children')
the judge's presentation *of the facts* ('The judge presented the facts')
the country's abolition *of slavery* ('The country abolished slavery')
the Department's acceptance *of the need for reform* ('The Department accepted the need for reform')

Although there may be ambiguity when constructions with the genitive or *of*-phrase are viewed in isolation, the context or general knowledge will resolve the ambiguity. Both factors contribute to interpreting *women's* in *women's subjection* as objective in **[1]**:

[1]   In this novel, both sides to the question of women's rights and *women's subjection* are presented through various characters by the concealed narrator, and the reader can draw her own conclusions. [W2B-009-76]

A *by*-phrase will show that the genitive is objective, as in this sentence that appears earlier in the same text:

[2]   Thus the narrator, through Baruch's simplistic exaggerations, is putting
          across one of the more neglected aspects of political feminism: how to
          make an analysis of *women's subjection by men* in relation to subjection
          according to class. [W2B-009-68]

The *by*-phrase corresponds to the *by*-phrase in passive sentences:

women's subjection by men ('Women are subjected by men', 'Men subject
women')

The subjective *by*-phrase therefore contrasts with the objective *of*-phrase:

women's subjection of men ('Women subject men')

Compare:

the subjection of men by women

The genitive noun phrase may also be the subject of an *-ing* participle
clause (cf. 6.10, 6.16), especially when the noun phrase is a pronoun or a
proper noun. Here are some examples with proper nouns:

[3]   There is something inherently suspect about *Congress's* prohibiting the
          executive from even studying whether public funds are being wasted in
          some favored program or other. [891102-0080-33]

[4]   If successful, the offer would result in *McCaw's* owning a total of slightly
          more than 50% of LIN's common shares on a fully diluted basis. [891011-
          0158-21]

[5]   The future depends on *Algeria's* finding more efficient ways to run its
          factories and farms, perhaps with the help of foreign companies it has
          largely rejected since independence. [881103-0111-107]

[6]   He said various "normal investment banking fees" were discussed as
          part of *Shearson's* joining the KKR team. [881027-0004-25]

The *-ing* participle in such constructions is called a gerund.

The genitive and *of*-phrase can have several other meanings. The temporal
genitive denotes a period of time or a duration of time:

a session's legislation	('legislation passed during a session')
today's lower standards	('the lower standards that apply today')
this season's games	('the games during this season')

The source genitive denotes such relationships as authorship and origin:

Coleridge's poetry	('the poetry written by Coleridge')
the consultants' views	('the views expressed by the consultants')
Bill Clinton's speech	('the speech made by Bill Clinton')
Australia's exports	('the exports that come from Australia')
the sun's rays	('the rays emanating from the sun')

In most of its uses, the dependent genitive phrase functions in the same way
as determiners such as *the* and *her.*

$$\left.\begin{array}{l} \text{her} \\ \text{Carol's} \\ \text{my daughter's} \end{array}\right\} \text{children}$$

Central determiners cannot co-occur, so that we cannot say *the her children*. Similarly, genitive phrases cannot co-occur with central determiners, so that we cannot say *the my daughter's children*. However, the head of the noun phrase is implicitly definite: *my daughter's children* corresponds to *the children of my daughter* and *a friend's children* to *the children of a friend*. The central determiners *my* and *a* in those examples belong to the genitive phrase and not to the head of the noun phrase, as the paraphrases show. And of course *a* in *a friend's children* could not apply to *children* because *a* can only be a determiner with singular count nouns.

The descriptive genitive differs grammatically from the other uses of the genitive. It is a modifier. The determiner that precedes a descriptive genitive applies to the whole noun phrase and not to the genitive. For example, *girls'* is a descriptive genitive in *a girls' school* ('a school for girls') and its function is equivalent to that of *local* in *a local school*. A modifier that precedes the descriptive genitive may belong either to the genitive or to the head of the noun phrase. *A good girls' school* is ambiguous between 'a school for good girls' and its more plausible interpretation 'a good school for girls'.

Here are some examples of descriptive genitives:

cow's milk	('milk produced by cows')
a warm *summer's* day	('a warm day in summer')
a *ten minutes'* walk	('a walk lasting ten minutes')
the *lion's* share of the booty	('the largest share')

Descriptive genitives may form part of an idiomatic phrase, as in *lion's share* above and in *dowager's hump* and *dog's dinner* below:

[7]   [. . .] the typical bent spine of osteoporosis has been given the name of '*dowager's hump*'. [W2B-022-12]

[8]   Well the thing I'm worried about more than anything is having to go into his office dressed up like *a dog's dinner* [S1A-042-165]

Some descriptive genitives can be replaced by nouns that are not in the genitive: *a warm summer day, a ten minute walk*. Nouns are regularly used to premodify other nouns, as in this noun phrase: *a plastic cat litter scoop*. Generally, the singular form of the noun is used in premodification.

Verbs

4.13
Characteristics of verbs

Verbs (or main verbs or lexical verbs or full verbs) function as the head of a verb phrase, either alone or preceded by one or more auxiliaries (cf. 4.29, 5.17 ff.). For example, the main verb *prepare* in its various forms:

[1] They *prepared* the meal.

[2] They *may prepare* the meal.

[3] They *should have prepared* the meal.

[4] They *may have been preparing* the meal.

In [1]–[4] the verb phrases function as the verb of the sentence.[2]
Here are some typical verb endings:

-ate:	*translate, incorporate, abbreviate, contaminate, assassinate, demonstrate*
-en:	*sicken, happen, madden, toughen, strengthen, listen*
-ify:	*magnify, clarify, beautify, objectify, typify, amplify*
-ise, -ize:	*baptise, agonise, popularise, legalize, summarize, computerize*

Some of these endings were present when the words were borrowed from other languages. For verb suffixes in word formation, see 9.19.

4.14
Form-types of verbs

Verbs have five form-types. In all regular verbs (such as *prepare*) and in many irregular verbs (such as *make*), two of the form-types have the same form. In some regular verbs (e.g. *put*) three form-types have the same form. The full set of five forms appears in the irregular verb *write*.

Form-types				
1. base	*prepare*	*make*	*put*	*write*
2. *-s*	*prepares*	*makes*	*puts*	*writes*
3. *-ing* participle	*preparing*	*making*	*putting*	*writing*
4. past	*prepared*	*made*	*put*	*wrote*
5. *-ed* participle	*prepared*	*made*	*put*	*written*

The highly irregular verb *be* has eight forms, three of which have informal contracted forms. There are also informal contracted negative forms ending in *n't*. Some of the forms have stressed and unstressed pronunciations. Both are given below; the stressed pronunciation first and then the unstressed (with reduced vowels).

1. base	*be* /biː/, /bɪ/
2. present—1st person singular	*am* /am/, /əm/
	'm /m/
—in questions	*aren't* /aːnt/ or /aːrnt/
— 3rd person singular	*is* /ɪz/
	's /z/ or /s/
	isn't /ɪzn̩t/
—others	*are* /aː/ or /aːr/
	're /ə/ or /ər/
	aren't /aːnt/ or /aːrnt/
3. *-ing* participle	*being* /biːɪŋ/
4. past—1st and 3rd person singular	*was* /wɒz/ or /wəz/
	wasn't /wɒzn̩t/
—others	*were* /wəː/ or /wəːr/
	weren't /wəːnt/ or /wəːrnt/
5. *-ed* participle	*been* /biːn/, /bɪn/

Is corresponds to the *-s* form-type in all other words, but *am* and *are* correspond to the present tense uses of the base form-type. For *'s*, contracted from *is*, and also the contracted forms of *has* and *does* (see below), /z/ follows a voiced sound and /s/ a voiceless sound (cf. 4.15). The alternatives with or without /r/ depend on whether the accent is rhotic or non-rhotic (cf. 10.5).

The irregular verb *have* also has informal non-negative and negative contracted forms:

1. base	*have* /hav/, /həv/, or /əv/
—for present tense	*'ve* /v/
	haven't /havn̩t/
2. *-s* form	*has* /haz/, /həz/, or /əz/
	's /z/ or /s/
	hasn't /hazn̩t/
3. *-ing* participle	*having* /havɪŋ/
4. past	*had* /had/, /həd/, or /əd/
	'd /d/
	hadn't /hadn̩t/
5. *-ed* participle	*had* /had/, /həd/, or /əd/

The alternative unstressed pronunciation without initial /h/ is quite common. It accounts for misspellings of *have* in combinations such as *could of* (instead of *could have*) or *should of* (instead of *should have*).

The paradigm for the irregular verb *do* is shown below with informal contracted forms and with stressed and unstressed pronunciations:

1. base	*do* /duː/, /dʊ/
—for present tense	*don't* /dəʊnt/
2. *-s* form	*does* /dʌz/, /dəz/
	's /s/ or /z/
	doesn't /dʌzn̩t/

3. -*ing* participle	*doing* /duːɪŋ/
4. past	*did* /dɪd/
	didn't /dɪdn̩t/
5. -*ed* participle	*done* /dʌn/

The contracted form *'s* is only occasionally found in writing: *Who's she take after?*, *What's he say?* It is more common in informal speech.

The contracted forms of *be*, *have*, and *do* are used also when they function as auxiliaries. For the contracted forms of the modal auxiliaries, see 4.29. Two of the contractions have more than one expansion: *'s* can represent *is*, *has* or *does* (as well as the genitive marker), and *'d* can represent *had* ('I'd paid last month') or *would* ('I'd like another portion').

Five form-types are distinguished even when there are only three or four distinctions in form, because the fivefold distinction is made in some verbs and it coincides with differences in grammatical relations. The additional distinctions made in the verb *be* are not incorporated, because they are unique to that verb and do not affect grammatical relationships for other verbs.

A. **Base form-type**

The base form-type has the following uses:

1. **Present tense,** except for the third person singular (cf. 5.21 f.):

    [1] Of course you ⟨ , ⟩ you get better repeatability the more readings you *take*
    [S1B-004-266]

2. **Imperative** (cf. 3.7.):

    [2] *Tell* me about your life [S1A-075-27]

3. **Present subjunctive** (cf. 5.25):

    [3] I urged in my previous letter that these research staff *be* treated as their present colleagues and *be* permitted to apply for a redundancy payment when their contracts expire. [W1B-024-31]

For verbs other than *be*, the present subjunctive can only be distinguished from the present tense indicative in the third person singular, which has the -*s* form. Hence, there is not a distinctive subjunctive form in:

    We recommend that they *repay* the full amount.

The subjunctive form can appear in the third person singular:

    We recommend that he *repay* the full amount.

The present tense form here would be *repays*. British English rarely uses the present subjunctive except for the verb *be*, as in **[3]**. It uses instead *should* (*he should repay*) or the present tense -*s* form (*he repays*). Here is an example from an American source of the present subjunctive with a verb other than *be*:

    [4] Israel insists that it *remain* in charge on the borders [. . .] [*International Herald Tribune*, 24 January 1994, p. 8]

4. **Infinitive** (cf. 5.19), which has two major uses:

    (a) bare infinitive (without *to*), follows a modal auxiliary (cf. 4.29):

        [5] I must *write* that message [S1A-039-113]

    (b) *to*-infinitive is the main verb in infinitive clauses (cf. 6.10):[3]

        [6] I'd like to *write* something on process theology [S1A-053-24]

B. *-s* form-type

The *-s* form-type is restricted to the third person singular present tense:

    [7] It *comes* with a small remote control and all the usual features, including wired and optical outputs [W2B-040-33]

    [8] It still *is* very very difficult for me to be monogamous ⟨ , , ⟩ and to have a satisfying ongoing sexual relationship with anybody [S1A-072-210]

C. *-ing* participle

The *-ing* participle is used in:

1. **Progressive aspect,** following the auxiliary *be* (cf. 5.31):

    [9] I think somebody's been *leading* you up the garden path [S1A-008-223]

2. ***-ing* participle clauses,** as the main verb (cf. 6.10):

    [10] Those involved in the deal are keeping details secret to avoid *putting* the sale in jeopardy. [W2C-020-39]

D. **Past**

The past is used for the past tense (cf. 5.21 f.):

    [11] You *mentioned* that any lump should be excised. [S1B-010-61]

    [12] The photograph I thought *was* absolutely terrible [S2A-027-50]

E. *-ed* participle

The *-ed* participle is used in:

1. **Perfect aspect,** following the auxiliary *have* (cf. 5.27 ff.):

    [13] We have *been* waiting for Her Majesty the Queen to arrive and we've *discovered* that there has *been* a fault in her transport arrangements [S2A-020-84]

2. **Passive voice,** following the auxiliary *be* (cf. 3.12):

    [14] I feel sure that some day it will be *published* [S1B-026-243]

3. ***-ed* participle clauses,** as the main verb (cf. 6.10):

    [15] The applications will then be published to enable public consultation, with winners *announced* in October and any newcomers taking over from January 1993. [W2C-017-46]

The past subjunctive (cf. 5.26) is *were*, and it can only be distinguished from the past indicative when the subject is *I* or third person singular:

[16] If I *were* you, I'd apply for the York position just for the experience. [W1B-074-43]

[17] Of course, BS would squeal, but it could hardly complain if closure *were* its only aim. [W2C-007-22]

In these instances the past indicative is *was*, which often replaces subjunctive *were*, particularly in less formal use:

[18] [. . .] I'd go to the Palmer one if I *was* you. [S1A-005-54]

4.15
The -s form

For both regular and irregular verbs the spelling and pronunciation of the *-s* form is virtually always predictable from the base form. The rules for deriving the *-s* form from the base form are similar to those for adding the plural inflection to singular nouns in regular plurals (cf. 4.6).

The regular spelling of the *-s* inflection is *s*:

run/runs   put/puts   revere/reveres

Here are additional spelling rules for particular cases:

1. If the base ends in a sibilant sound (see below) that is not followed by *-e*, add *-es*:

buzz/buzzes   pass/passes   catch/catches   fax/faxes   rush/rushes

For a few words ending in *-s*, there is a variant in which the *-s* is doubled before the inflection:

bus/buses or *busses   bias/biases* or *biasses   focus/focuses* or *focusses   gas/gases* or *gasses*

Where sibilants are followed by *-e*, only *-s* is added:

force/forces   grudge/grudges   rise/rises

2. If the base ends in a consonant plus *y*, change the *y* to *i* and then add *-es*:

worry/worries   fly/flies   bury/buries   deny/denies

If a vowel precedes the final *y*, the spelling is regular:

play/plays   annoy/annoys

3. For some verbs ending in *-o*, add *-es*:

go/goes   do/does   echo/echoes   veto/vetoes

Derivatives with *go* and *do* also have -*es*:

undergo/undergoes   overdo/overdoes

4. There are two irregular forms:

have/has   be/is

The -*s* inflection is pronounced /ɪz/, /z/, or /s/ depending on the final sound of the base:

1. /ɪz/ if the singular ends in a sibilant:

   /s/   *pass/passes   fax/faxes*
   /z/   *buzz/buzzes*
   /ʃ/   *rush/rushes*
   /tʃ/   *catch/catches*
   /ʒ/   *camouflage/camouflages*
   /dʒ/   *judge/judges*

2. /z/ if the singular ends in a vowel or a voiced consonant (cf. 10.3) other than a sibilant:

pay/pays   pursue/pursues   hum/hums   drive/drives   rebuild/rebuilds

3. /s/ if the singular ends in a voiceless consonant (cf. 10.3) other than a sibilant:

cook/cooks   convert/converts   worship/worships

4. There are irregular pronunciations:

   (a) *do* /duː/ → *does* /dʌz/; so also for the derivatives of *do*, such as *overdoes*
   (b) *say* /seɪ/ → *says* /sɛz/

4.16
The -*ing* participle

As with the -*s* form, the spelling and pronunciation of the -*ing* participle is virtually always predictable from the base form of both regular and irregular verbs.

The inflection is spelled -*ing*, which is added to the base:

pass/passing   carry/carrying   go/going   be/being

Here are additional spelling rules for particular cases:

1. If the base ends in -*e*, drop the -*e* before the -*ing*:

drive/driving   make/making   deceive/deceiving   co-operate/co-operating

But if the base ends in *-ee*, *-oe*, or *-ye*, keep the final *-e*:

> *see/seeing   disagree/disagreeing   hoe/hoeing   dye/dyeing*

Also, *singe* keeps the *-e* in *singeing*, distinguishing it from *singing*, the *-ing* participle of *sing*. *Binge* and *tinge* have the variants *binging* or *bingeing; tinging* or *tingeing.*

2. If the base ends in *-ie*, change the *i* to *y* and drop the *-e*:

> *die/dying   tie/tying   untie/untying   lie/lying*

Contrast *die/dying* with *dye/dyeing.*

3. In general, double the consonant letter before *-ing* if all these three conditions apply:

(a) the base ends in a single consonant letter
(b) a single vowel comes before that consonant letter
(c) the final syllable of the base is stressed, as it must be if the base is monosyllabic.

All three conditions apply in these examples:

> *tip/tipping*   *permit/permitting*
> *rob/robbing*   *defer/deferring*
> *sag/sagging*   *forget/forgetting*
> *hum/humming*   *upset/upsetting*
> *bet/betting*   *forbid/forbidding*

There is no doubling if:

(a) the base ends in two or more consonant letters:

> *sing/singing   fight/fighting   kick/kicking   remind/reminding*

(b) there are two vowel letters before the final consonant of the base:

> *read/reading   reveal/revealing   despair/despairing*

(c) the final syllable of the base is not stressed:

> *limit/limiting   differ/differing   deliver/delivering*

The letters *y* and *w* count as vowel letters when they come at the end of the base (and are pronounced as vowels), and they are therefore not doubled:

> *apply/applying   fly/flying   show/showing*

There are some exceptions to the rules for doubling:

(a) A few words ending in *-s* have variants with or without the doubling:

> *bus/busing* or *bussing   gas/gasing* or *gassing   bias/biasing* or *biassing   focus/focusing* or *focussing*

Busing and *gasing* are irregular, and so are *biassing* and *focussing.*

(b) British English generally doubles the consonant letter if the base ends in -*l* even though the final syllable of the base is not stressed:

marvel/marvelling   model/modelling   quarrel/quarrelling
travel/travelling

American English generally follows the regular rule and does not double the consonant:

marveling   modeling   quarreling   traveling

British and American English differ in the same direction for a few bases ending in -*m(e)* or -*p*:

British	*programme/programming diagram/diagramming*
	kidnap/kidnapping worship/worshipping
American	*program/programing diagram/diagraming*
	kidnap/kidnaping worship/worshiping

However, in both British and American English, *handicapping* and *humbugging* are usual, even though the final syllable of the base is not stressed.

(c) If the base ends in -*c*, the *c* is in effect generally doubled as *ck* even though the final syllable of the base is not stressed:

mimic/mimicking   panic/panicking   picnic/picnicking   traffic/trafficking

The pronunciation of the -*ing* inflection by speakers of standard English is generally /ɪŋ/, at least in their careful speech. A common non-standard pronunciation is /ɪn/, which is sometimes represented in writing as -*in'*, e.g. *singin'*. Some non-standard dialects prefix the -*ing* participle with *a*- before consonants: *a-huntin', a-comin', a-runnin'*. The *a*-prefix is usually explained as a reduced form of the preposition *on*, originally attached to verbal nouns ending in -*ing* and then generalized to -*ing* participles.

4.17
The -*ed* form in regular verbs

The -*ed* form in regular verbs and in many irregular verbs represents two form-types: the past and the -*ed* participle (cf. 4.14):

past:	We *saved* some money.
-*ed* participle:	We have *saved* some money.

The -*ed* form in regular verbs is virtually always predictable from the base form.

The regular spelling of the -*ed* form in regular verbs is -*ed*:

play/played   talk/talked   disturb/disturbed   distinguish/distinguished

Here are additional spelling rules for particular cases, which largely coincide with those for the -*s* form (cf. 4.15) or the -*ing* participle (cf. 4.16):

1. If the base ends in -*e*, drop the -*e* before adding -*ed*:

   deceive/deceived   save/saved   co-operate/co-operated

But if the base ends in -*ee*, -*oe*, -*ie*, or -*ye*, keep the final -*e*:

   disagree/disagreed   hoe/hoed   die/died   dye/dyed

2. If the base ends in a consonant plus *y*, change the *y* to *i* and then add -*ed*:

   worry/worried   cry/cried   apply/applied   deny/denied

If a vowel precedes the final *y*, the spelling is regular:

   play/played   annoy/annoyed

There are exceptions where the *y* changes to *i* even though a vowel precedes the *y*:

   lay/laid   pay/paid

Derivatives of *lay* and *pay* are also exceptions:

   mislay/mislaid   underpay/underpaid

The verb *say* is similar to these two verbs in spelling:

   say/said

But *said* is irregular in pronunciation /sɛd/.

3. The rules for doubling the final consonant letter of the base are identical with those required before the -*ing* inflection (cf. 4.16), and they may therefore be restated here briefly. In general, double the consonant letter before -*ed* if all these three conditions apply:

   (a) the base ends in a single consonant letter
   (b) a single vowel comes before that consonant letter
   (c) the final syllable of the base is stressed

All three conditions apply in these examples:

   rob/robbed   permit/permitted   defer/deferred

Exceptions:

   (a) A few words ending in -*s* have variants with or without the doubling:
        bus/bused or *bussed   bias/biased* or *biassed*
        focus/focused or *focussed   gas/gased* or *gassed*

   (b) If the base ends in -*l* or for a few words in -*m(e)* or -*p*, British English generally doubles the consonant letter whereas American English generally follows the regular rule:

British	*marvelled modelled quarrelled travelled programmed*
	diagrammed kidnapped worshipped
American	*marveled modeled quarreled traveled programed*
	diagramed kidnaped worshiped

However, in both American and British English, *handicapped* and *humbugged* are usual.

(c) If the base ends in *c*, the *c* is generally doubled as *ck* even though the final syllable of the base is not stressed:

mimic/mimicked   panic/panicked   picnic/picknicked   traffic/trafficked

The rules for the pronunciation of the -*ed* inflection are analogous to those for the -*s* inflection (cf. 4.15). The inflection is pronounced /ɪd/, /d/, or /t/ depending on the final sound of the base:

1. /ɪd/ if the base ends in /d/ or /t/:

/d/   *mend/mended   fade/faded   defend/defended*
/t/   *net/netted   visit/visited   hesitate/hesitated*

2. /d/ if the base ends in a vowel or a voiced consonant (cf. 10.3) other than /d/:

flow/flowed   try/tried   revise/revised   save/saved

3. /t/ if the base ends in a voiceless consonant (cf. 10.3) other than /t/:

walk/walked   notice/noticed   fix/fixed   help/helped

4.18
Irregular verbs

There are five form-types (cf. 4.14). Apart from the highly irregular verb *be* (which has eight forms), irregular verbs may have three, four, or five forms, depending on whether one form is used for two or three form-types. The -*s* form and the -*ing* participle are always available and can be predicted from the base for all verbs except the verb *be* (which has the unpredictable -*s* form *is* as well as the unpredictable present tense forms *am* and *are*). Except for the verb *be*, we therefore need list only three forms to show irregularities in the verb: the base, the past, and the -*ed* participle. These three forms are known as the principal parts of the verb.

For example, the principal parts of the verb *see* are *see* (base), *saw* (past), and *seen* (-*ed* participle). We can additionally derive from the base the remaining forms *sees* (-*s* form) and *seeing* (-*ing* participle). The principal parts of the verb *make* are *make*, *made*, *made*; the five form-types are therefore *make* (base), *makes* (-*s* form), *making* (-*ing* participle), *made* (past), *made* (-*ed* participle). The principal parts of the verb *put*, which has only three forms, are *put, put, put*; the base, the past, and the *-ed* participle are identical, and the additional forms are *puts* and *putting*. Dictionaries list the principal parts of irregular verbs and of regular verbs that have spelling changes across the principal parts, such as doubling of the consonant before the inflection or the change of *y* to *i*.

We can establish seven classes of irregular verbs according to whether or not four features apply to their principal parts:

1. The past and *-ed* participles are identical, as in regular verbs.
2. The past has a *-d* or *-t* inflection, as in regular verbs, and the same inflection may also be found in the *-ed* participle.
3. The vowel in the base form is identical with the vowel in the other two principal parts, as in regular verbs.
4. The *-ed* participle has an *-(e)n* inflection, which is not found in regular verbs.

Table 4.18.1 sets out in columns the four features and indicates whether they apply (+) or not (−) to each of the seven classes of irregular verbs. The '±' for class II indicates that some verbs in the class do not have the specified feature.

Two irregular verbs do not fit into the seven classes. The present-day forms of the verb *be* derive historically from different verbs: the past tense *was* and *were*; the present tense *am*, *is*, *are*; and *be*, *being*, *been* (cf. 4.14). The verb *go* takes its past form *went* from a different verb; the principal parts are *go*, *went*, *gone*.

Table 4.18.1 Classes of irregular verbs

	past = participle	*-t/-d* inflection	all vowels identical	*-n* inflection
I. *bend bent bent*	+	+	+	−
II. *show showed shown*	−	+	±	+
III. *buy bought bought*	+	+	−	−
IV. *break broke broken*	−	−	−	+
V. *hit hit hit*	+	−	+	−
VI. *find found found*	+	−	−	−
VII. *begin began begun*	−	−	−	−

Examples of verbs in the seven classes follow, together with some brief comments.

I. *bend bent bent*   *burn burnt burnt*
   build built built   *learn learnt learnt*
   have had had   *smell smelt smelt*
   make made made   *spell spelt spelt*
      spoil spoilt spoilt

The inflections are irregularly attached. The *-t* inflections follow a voiced sound, contrary to the general rule (cf. 4.17). Those in the second column also have regular variants: *burn, burned, burned* and *spoil, spoiled, spoiled.* The regular variants are usual in American English.

II.　　*show showed shown*　　*shear sheared shorn*
　　　　mow mowed mown　　*swell swelled swollen*
　　　　sew sewed sewn
　　　　saw sawed sawn

The past is formed regularly, but the participle has the *-(e)n* inflection. Those in the second column have a different vowel in the participle, hence the '±' in the table. All the verbs also have regular variants for the participle: *show, showed, showed.*

III.　　*buy bought bought*　　*dream dreamt dreamt*
　　　　hear heard heard　　*kneel knelt knelt*
　　　　lose lost lost　　　*lean leant leant*
　　　　say said said　　　*leap leapt leapt*
　　　　feel felt felt
　　　　keep kept kept

Despite the identity of spellings in some instances, the vowel sounds of the past and participle always differ from that of the base. Those in the second column also have regular variants: *dream, dreamed, dreamed.*

IV.　　*break broke broken*　　*see saw seen*
　　　　speak spoke spoken　　*take took taken*
　　　　blow blew blown　　*tear tore torn*
　　　　hide hid hidden　　*write wrote written*
　　　　lie lay lain　　　*bite bit bitten*

All three forms differ. The past lacks an inflection, but the participle has the *-(e)n* inflection. The verbs vary in their sameness of vowels. For example, *blow* has the same vowel in the base and the participle (*blown*), *tear* has the same vowel in the past and the participle (*tore, torn*), and the vowels are different in all three principal parts of *write.*

V.　　*hit hit hit*　　　*fit fit fit*
　　　　burst burst burst　　*rid rid rid*
　　　　hurt hurt hurt　　*quit quit quit*
　　　　let let let　　　*sweat sweat sweat*
　　　　set set set　　　*wet wet wet*
　　　　put put put　　　*wed wed wed*
　　　　cut cut cut
　　　　cast cast cast

All three parts are identical. Those in the second column also have regular variants: *fit, fitted, fitted. Cost* belongs to this class, but it is regular in the sense 'estimate the value or cost of'.

VI.   *find found found*   *get got got*
      feed fed fed   *hold held held*
      read read read   *strike struck struck*
      bleed bled bled   *stand stood stood*
      fight fought fought   *wind wound wound*
      dig dug dug   *light lit lit*
      win won won   *speed sped sped*
      sting stung stung   *hang hung hung*

The past and participle are identical, as in the regular verb, but there is a change in the vowel and there are no inflections. A few verbs in this class also have regular variants: *light, lighted, lighted; speed, speeded, speeded.* In American English, *get* has two participles: *got* and *gotten;* the tendency is for *have got* to denote possessing something and *have gotten* to denote obtaining something. *Hang* also has a regular variant—*hang, hanged, hanged*—which tends to be used to denote suspension by the neck, especially in an official execution.

VII. *begin began begun*   *come came come*
      drink drank drunk   *run ran run*
      sing sang sung
      ring rang rung
      shrink shrank shrunk
      swim swam swum

Those in the first column have three different forms for the principal parts and no inflections. Those in the second column have the same form for the base and the participle.

4.19
Non-standard verb forms: present tense

A historical perspective is helpful for understanding the variations in verb forms in non-standard dialects and their differences from standard English.

The present tense in Old English distinguished the three persons in the singular. The inflections for the present can be generalized as follows (where *þ* is equivalent to present-day *th*, and the parentheses indicate variant omissions):

1st person singular   *-e*
2nd person singular   *-(e)st*
3rd person singular   *-(e)þ*
plural   *-aþ*

The present subjunctive was *-e* for the singular and *-en* for the plural.

The Northumbrian dialect of Old English eventually developed a somewhat different system for the present tense:

1st person singular	*-o, -e*
2nd person singular	*-as*
3rd person singular	*-es, -as*
plural	*-es, -as*

Phonological changes led to the neutralization of the unstressed vowels in the inflections to *e* /ə/ and then to the loss of final *-e*. By about 1300, the verb paradigms for the present tense had developed separately in the Middle English dialects:

	North	*Midland*	*South*
1st person singular	*-(e)*	*-e*	*-e*
2nd person singular	*-es*	*-es(t)*	*-est*
3rd person singular	*-es*	*-eþ/-es*	*-eþ*
plural	*-es*	*-en/-es*	*-eþ*

The Midland dialects had adopted the subjunctive plural inflection *-en* as an alternative for the indicative plural. The *-es* inflection for the third person singular infiltrated into the Midland dialects from the North.

By the late fourteenth century, the London standard (which drew on various dialects) had the following paradigm for the present tense:

1st person singular	*-(e)*
2nd person singular	*-(e)st*
3rd person singular	*-eth*
plural	*-e(n)*

At the same time, a variant *-(e)s* inflection (spread from the North) was used in London for the third person singular as well as the *-eth* inflection (*she giveth, she gives*).

During the next two centuries there were losses of final *-e* in the first person singular and of final *-n* and then final *-e* in the plural, so that these assumed the base form that they now have in standard English. By the end of the seventeenth century, the *-s* form was the dominant form for the third person singular in the increasingly standardized English, though *doth* and *hath* continued to be used until well into the eighteenth century as a spelling convention rendered by /s/ in speech, as was perhaps often the case with other verbs in the seventeenth century. Plurals in *-s* are also occasionally found in the seventeenth and eighteenth centuries. By the nineteenth century, the distinctive second person singular was abandoned for general use as a result of the supplanting of *thou* by *you*; *thou* and the *-st* form (*thou walkst, thou knowest*) have continued to appear in the restricted domains of poetry and prayer. They are occasionally used facetiously; and so is the *-eth* inflection, as in this epigram advertising a lager:

> The Lord giveth. The Landlord taketh away. [*The Independent Magazine*, 6 August 1994, pp. 14 f.]

Present-day standard English retains only two forms in the present tense: the *-s* form for the third person singular and the base form for the rest. Hence, the anomaly in standard English that -*s* signals the singular in the present tense of verbs but the plural in nouns:

The studentslisten.

The student listens.

Non-standard dialects vary in how they treat the present tense. Commonly, the paradigm has been regularized to extend the -*s* form to all persons in the singular and to the plural (*I knows, we knows*, etc.). Alternatively, the uninflected base form has been extended to the third person singular (*she know*). Old inflected forms have been retained to a limited extent in some non-standard dialects: the -*eth* inflection for the third person singular (*she knoweth*) and the -*en* inflection for the plural (*they knowen*). Some non-standard dialects that have kept a distinctive *thou/thee* pronoun for the second person singular have also retained the -*st* inflection that accompanies it.

Dialect variation is particularly acute with the verb *be*, whether as a main verb or an auxiliary verb. In some non-standard dialects, the paradigm has been regularized by using *be* throughout (*I be, you be*, etc.). In some, regularization is achieved through *is* (*I is, you is*, etc.). There are also non-standard dialects that have *bin* or *are* (*I bin, I are*, etc.). In others, the verb *be* may be omitted in the present tense whenever it can occur in a contracted form (*They my friends*, corresponding to *They're my friends*), though omission does not usually apply to *am*.

Ain't is a much stigmatized negative present tense form for *be* (both main verb and auxiliary verb) and for auxiliary *have* (*She ain't angry, I ain't telling, They ain't done it*). In standard English there is no corresponding negative verb for *(I) am not* in the declarative, though *aren't (I)?* serves the purpose in the interrogative, especially in British English. Earlier spellings of *ain't* included *an't, a'n't, i'n't, e'n't* for *be*, and *ha'n't* for *have*; they represent earlier pronunciations that more closely represent the positive forms. *Ain't* is stigmatized in both British and American standard English, though it is used informally in speech in certain contexts, particularly by speakers of standard American English. American politicians may use *ain't* in public speeches to convey a folksy tone. In [1] the casualness is enhanced by the use of the double negative:

[1] The state leaders of United We Stand America, meeting in Dallas to debate their future, faced serious questions about whether Mr. Perot's claim last week that the country "*ain't* seen nothing yet" was more than an idle boast. [*International Herald Tribune*, 8 February 1994, p. 3]

In non-standard dialects *ain't* is common, but *in't* is preferred in some dialects for tag questions. Some non-standard dialects have *amn't* for *am not*, and others use *aren't* for *am not* in the declarative (*I aren't*). Some Black English dialects use *ain't* also to correspond to *didn't*.

4.20
Non-standard verb forms: past tense and -*ed* participles

The past tense inflections in Old English can be generalized as follows, where the parentheses indicate variant omissions:

1st person singular	-*(e)*
2nd person singular	-*e*, -*(e)st*
3rd person singular	-*(e)*
plural	-*on*

The past subjunctive had -*e* or -*en* for the singular and -*en* for the plural.

As a result of phonological changes (reduction of unstressed vowels to *e* /ə/ and subsequent loss of final -*e* and also loss of final -*n*), the emerging London standard looked like this by the late fourteenth century:

1st person singular	-*(e)*
2nd person singular	-*(est)*, -*(e)st*
3rd person singular	-*(e)*
plural	-*e(n)*

By the nineteenth century, continuation of the phonological processes and abandonment of a distinctive second person singular had resulted in the levelling of the whole past paradigm to one form. Non-standard dialects generally display the same results. Some that retain the *thou*/*thee* pronoun also retain the -*st* inflection for the second person singular. Some non-standard dialects may use the base form in combination with past time adverbials ('I *like* the movie I saw yesterday').

The distinctions in the past tense of the verb *be* in present-day standard English can be traced back to Old English, if we take account of phonological changes:

1st person singular	*wæs*	*was*
2nd person singular	*wǣre*	*were*
3rd person singular	*wæs*	*was*
plural	*wǣron*	*were*

Old English subjunctives were singular *wǣre* and plural *wǣren*. They were distinctive only in the first and third person singular, as in present-day standard English.

Most non-standard dialects have generalized the forms of the past tense of *be*, either using *was* (*we was*, *you was*) or *were* (*I were*, *it were*). Some have used *was* for the positive (*we was*, *she was*) and *were* for the negative (*we weren't*, *she weren't*).

Old English had two major classes of verbs. Weak verbs formed their past and -*ed* participles by the addition of inflections, generally containing *t* or *d*. Strong verbs did so by changing the vowels and adding an -*en* inflection to the participle, as in present-day *ride*, *rode*, *ridden*. The weak verbs were by far the more numerous, but many of the strong verbs occurred very frequently. However, since it was easy to add inflections to weak verbs, it was usual to create new verbs on the model of the weak verbs and to adapt borrowed verbs to that model. Nowadays all newly formed or borrowed verbs follow regular processes of adding inflections for the past tense and the -*ed* participle. In the course of time the tendency to regularize the verb forms led to many strong verbs becoming weak. Among common verbs that have changed from strong to weak since the Old English period are *climb, help, melt, step, walk, wash*. There are relatively few changes in the opposite direction. Among common verbs that have changed from weak to strong by analogy with other verbs are *dig, fling, hide, spit,* and *wear*. In some instances, strong verbs adopted forms from another class of strong verbs; for example, *spoke* has replaced the earlier *spake*, which is found in the King James Bible. Some strong verbs also had alternative weak forms, such as *knowed*, that have not survived in standard English.

Non-standard dialects have irregular verb patterns that vary among themselves and differ from standard English. On the whole, the tendency is to generalize or regularize further than in standard English. Occasionally older forms have been retained; for example: *crope* as past of *creep* and *croppen* as participle. Here are examples of different treatments of the principal parts of verbs in non-standard dialects (cf. 4.18):

1. past generalized to participle:
    go, went, went
    hide, hid, hid
    take, took, took
    write, wrote, wrote

2. participle generalized to past:
    see, seen, seen
    do, done, done
    swim, swum, swum

3. base generalized to past and participle:
    come, come, come
    give, give, give
    run, run, run

4. regularization:
    know, knowed, knowed
    creep, creeped, creeped
    see, seed, seed
    catch, catched, catched

5. new irregular form introduced:
    write, writ, writ
    bring, brang, brung
    ride, rid, rid

The generalization and regularization tendencies are also found in present-day standard English (cf. 4.18). Some irregular verbs have regular variants, and speakers of standard English are sometimes unsure whether verbs such as *sing* and *drink* have distinctive forms for the past and *-ed* participle.

Adjectives

4.21
Characteristics of adjectives

Adjectives serve as the head of an adjective phrase (cf. 5.39 ff.). Used alone or with one or more modifiers, they have two characteristic functions (cf. 4.22): premodifier of a noun **[1]** and subject predicative **[2]**:

> **[1]** In short, she was one of those *happy* natures who find life 'fun' and never take offence if they are asked out to dinner at six o'clock. [W2F-017-12]

> **[2]** Weather's been great these last few days so I'm *happy*! [W1B-002-9]

Here are some typical adjective endings:

-able, -ible	*acceptable, suitable, capable, credible*
-al	*accidental, seasonal, dictatorial, political*
-ed	*frenzied, crooked, wicked, kindhearted*
-ful	*careful, faithful, doubtful, lawful*
-ic	*romantic, dramatic, historic, dynamic*
-ish	*childish, foolish, smallish, feverish*
-ive	*active, comprehensive, defective, affirmative*
-less	*careless, reckless, hopeless, harmless*
-ous	*famous, glorious, ambitious, erroneous*
-y	*tasty, moody, heavy, hungry.*

Some of these endings were endings of the words when they were borrowed from other languages. For adjective suffixes in word-formation, see 9.20.

4.22
Attributive and predicative adjectives

Most adjectives can be used both attributively (as premodifiers of nouns) and predicatively (as subject predicative). Attributive adjectives attribute a quality or characteristic to what is denoted by the noun they modify: *pleasant company, pleasant dreams*. Predicative adjectives are part of the predicate, linked to the subject by a copular verb such as *be* or *seem*: *The company was pleasant, Your dreams seem pleasant.*

Some adjectives are attributive only:

[1] I usually think that advertising and publicity is a complete and *utter* waste of money [. . .] [S1B-078-21]

[2] At encounters like this the *sheer* power which the United States can exert is glaring [S2B-040-105]

[3] Harry hurled himself at the soldier, knocking him off his feet and right out of the vehicle, leaving Harry as the *sole* occupant and in the driving seat. [W2F-012-122]

[4] He will continue to report to Donald Pardus, president and *chief* executive officer. [891102-0174-2]

[5] She's sitting there at this *very* moment saying why doesn't he ring me at this moment [S1A-020-126]

[6] A defense lawyer thought this testimony an "*atomic* bomb" in the face of the prosecution. [891004-0118-29]

Many adjectives that are only attributive are so when they are used in a particular sense. For example, *real* is attributive only in the sense 'rightly so called' **[7]**–**[8]** but is a central adjective in the sense 'actually existing' **[9]**–**[10]**:

[7] And it's a chance to bring back Alan Ball who's uhm a *real* exponent and expert on Greek football [S2A-018-67]

[8] Is Yiddish a *real* language [S2B-042-60]

[9] He said there was a *real* danger of massacres in the absence of civil authority [S2B-004-124]

[10] The possibility that the conducting filament is a mixture of microcrystallites and dielectric is *real*. [W2A-034-65]

Similarly, *criminal, late,* and *old* are only attributive in **[11]**–**[13]** but central adjectives in **[14]**–**[16]**:

[11] [. . .] one of the ⟨ , ⟩ main principles of *criminal* law is judge the act not the actor [S2A-044-105]

[12] Under the *late* dictator Gen. Franco, many Basques supported the radical nationalist organization ETA; now, ETA finds itself isolated. [891011-0113-25]

[13] I have defeated them, these two *old* enemies of lovers [S1B-007-129]

[14] It is unfortunate that some people are not exposed to better opportunities than welfare or *criminal* activities. [891005-0114-24]

[15] *Late* payment of bills is the latest problem to surface as a result of the desktop-computer maker's much publicized switch to a new system for providing its management with information. [891011-0060-2]

[16] He's got a wrinkled *old* face [S1A-015-58]

Adjectives that are only attributive tend to be intensifiers (e.g. *utter*), restrictives (e.g. *only*), related to adverbials (e.g. *old* **[13]** 'of old'), or related to nouns (e.g. *criminal* **[11]** 'dealing with crime').

Some adjectives are only predicative:

[17] Caroline is *afraid* of Nellie's attempts to get her to join in the nude dancing and runs off. [W2B-009-101]

[18] [. . .] I was getting quite *fond* of him [S1A-049-19]

[19] Her office personality is a positive one; but she is not *aware* of this, any more than she is *conscious* of her breakfast-time vagueness. [W2F-019-32]

Many of these predicative adjectives resemble verbs in their meanings: *afraid of* 'fear', *fond of* 'like', *aware that* 'know that'.

Central adjectives can be attributive **[20]** or predicative **[21]**. They can also function as an object predicative **[22]** (cf. 3.19) and postmodify nouns **[23]** or indefinite pronouns **[24]**.

[20] I spent some time looking for a *suitable* menu package to use to do this, but could not find a wholly *suitable* system [W1A-005-33]

[21] Some were drafted into the army if they were *suitable* for that and some went into palace service [S2A-059-38]

[22] Thus it can be seen that choropleth has its advantages—good visual impression, easy to construct (in some ways) easy interpretation (also restricted) which may make it *suitable* for certain purposes in statistical analysis. [W1A-006-76]

[23] Reliance acquired a 7% UAL stake earlier this year at an average cost of $110 a share, and reduced its stake to 4.7% after UAL accepted the bid at prices *higher* than $282 a share. [891102-0042-11]

[24] The moral is, try and learn what everybody else is using and then try something *better* or at least different. [W2D-017-22]

4.23
Nominal adjectives

Adjectives can serve as the head of a noun phrase (cf. 5.3).

Adjectives as heads of noun phrases are nominal adjectives. They are generally introduced by a definite determiner, commonly the definite article *the*. Nominal adjectives do not take plural inflections, but they can be plural in meaning. We can distinguish nominal adjectives that have plural reference from those that have singular reference.

Plural nominal adjectives refer to animate beings, generally human, and they have generic reference (cf. 5.16):

[1] The vital decisions we reach on human fertilisation and embryology and subsequently pregnancy termination must affect how we regard the status of each individual ⟨ , ⟩ his or her human rights the treatment of *the handicapped* the fate of *the senile* and *the terminally ill* [S1B-060-34]

[2] A recent estimate puts the proportion of *the literate in Egypt* at around ⟨ , ⟩ half of a percent certainly no more than one percent [S2A-048-28]

[3] For the first time the 1991 census will include a question about long-term illness to help plan services and facilities for *long-term sick* and *elderly* [S2B-044-60]

[4] In South East Asia and in South America there's less of a tradition of democracy less articulation of the consequences of the birth rate among *the very poor* but there's also less evident inadequacy of natural resources [S2B-048-72]

[5] It is *the 'old old'* or those over 75 who are most likely to experience major health and mobility problems. [W2A-013-7]

[6] There was a professional pessimism about the ability to help *the so called 'chronic sick'* and so the neglect of their services seemed justified [S2A-013-41]

[7] So I thought this is an interesting ⟨ , ⟩ uhm idea of bringing *disabled* and *abled* together [. . .] [S1A-002-7]

[8] All three are located in the mythified undifferentiated home counties and feature a common cast of supporting characters choleric retired generals do-gooding vicars absent-minded professors domineering cooks and assorted spinsters with bees in their bonnets and bats in their belfries the *dog-loving the boy-hating* the busybody the scatterbrain *the short-sighted the long-winded* [S2B-026-11]

[9] And what the Government should have done straightaway to ease our collection problems is introduced one hundred per cent rebates as of April the first this year for *the poorest of society* [S1B-034-106]

In most of the above citations the determiner is *the*, but determiners are absent in the co-ordinated phrases of **[3]** and **[7]**. Nominal adjectives may be premodified by adverbs, as is usual for adjectives: *terminally ill* **[1]**, *very poor* **[4]**. But like nouns, they may be premodified by adjectives—*old old* **[5]**, *so-called 'chronic sick'* **[6]**—and by nouns or noun phrases—*the long-term sick* **[3]**. They may be postmodified by prepositional phrases: *the literate in Egypt* **[2]**, *the poorest of society* **[9]**. The superlative *poorest* **[9]** shows that, like other adjectives, nominal adjectives can be inflected for comparison. In their potential for inflection and modification, nominal adjectives share features that are characteristic of both nouns and adjectives.

Some plural nominal adjectives are nationality or ethnic adjectives. They all end in a sibilant sound: *-(i)sh*, (*British, Welsh*), *-ese* (*Portuguese*), *-ch* (*French*), *-s* (*Swiss*).

[10] The imperial family's remoteness from *ordinary Japanese* will be underlined by the absence of a coronation procession. [W2C-008-42]

[11] Seventy years on, *the Chinese* are suddenly objecting to the plans for the new airport. [W2E–008–50]

[12] There were Celts of course in the British Isles the ancient Britons and *the ancient Irish* [S2A-022-11]

Singular nominal adjectives generally refer to abstractions:

[13] It looks as though she's verging on *the dreamy* [S1A-067-142]

[14] [. . .] somebody may be doing *the dirty* on me ⟨ , ⟩ behind my back [S1A-067-194]

[15] There is a hidden plane of meaning (*the unconscious* for Freud; the imagination, perhaps *the divine*, in Symbolism). [W2A-002-22]

[16] So now ⟨ , , ⟩ can he keep *his cool* and really ⟨ , ⟩ make his mark here [S2A-008-31]

[17] Tonight I hope you'll not mind if I eschew *the academic* and pursue a more earthy albeit reflective tack analyzing the soil within which citizenship can root and thrive [S2A-039-11]

[18] In fact if anything *the opposite* is true [S2B-032-47]

[19] Please let me have everything for the brochure by August 21 at *the very latest*, and information for the factsheets by September 30. [W1B-019-123]

[20] The concrete and steel chicane was meant to slow vehicles down for the customs check, not to stop them completely like the tank traps of *old*. [W2F-012-139]

[21] Besides which, there's distinct evidence to *the contrary*. [W2F-016-64]

[22] By contrast, the new technocratic internationalism is shrewd in fusing principles of US and Western self-interest with *the good* of the coming world order [891011-0115-12]

[23] Among other things, it included checking, safe deposit box and credit card—all for *free*—plus a good deal on instalment loans. [891102-0107-5]

[24] These questions in turn raise others about those buildings which, at *best*, fail to engage our admiration, or, at *worst*, repel us. [W2A-005-33]

[25] But GMAC approved the Buick program, he says, because the American Express green card requires payment in *full* upon billing, and so doesn't carry any finance rates. [891102-0076-21]

The features applying to plural nominal adjectives apply to the singular too. Determiners are absent in some instances where the singular nominal adjective is the complement of a preposition **[20]** and **[23]**–**[25]**.

Some nominal adjectives that have the form of *-ed* participles do not convey generic reference. They may be either singular or plural with specific reference:

[26] We shouldn't be concerned with the character and disposition of *the accused* [S2A-004-106]

[27] We trust *the enclosed* is satisfactory, but if you have any queries, please do not hesitate to contact *the undersigned*. [W1B-022-105]

[28] At the graveside the curate adhered to the bald form of the funeral service, without any diversionary extolling of *the deceased's* particular merits as a human being. [W2F-010-72]

[29] Mrs Mandela, whose husband Mr Nelson Mandela is deputy president of the African National Conference, and *her co-accused* deny the charges. [W2E-019-62]

This type of nominal adjective can take the genitive *the deceased's* **[28]**. *Her co-accused* **[29]** could be singular, but the wider context shows that there were three co-accused. *The enclosed* **[27]** has concrete non-human reference.

4.24
Gradability and comparison

Most adjectives are gradable. We can use intensifiers to indicate their point on a scale: *somewhat long, quite long, very long, incredibly long.* We can also compare things and say that something is longer than, or as long as, something else.

There are three directions of comparison:

1. higher
   (a) Frank is *taller* than Paul. (comparative)
   (b) Frank is the *tallest* of the boys. (superlative)
2. same
   Frank is *as tall* as Paul.
3. lower
   (a) Frank is *less tall* than Paul.
   (b) Frank is the *least tall* of the boys.

There is a three-term contrast in degrees of comparison:

1. absolute   *tall*
2. comparative *taller*
3. superlative *tallest*

The comparative (*taller*) is used for a comparison between two units or sets of units and the superlative (*tallest*) where more than two units or sets of units are involved. *Less* is a comparative adverb in *less tall* and *least* is a superlative adverb in *least tall*.

Degrees of comparison are expressed either through the inflections -*er* and -*est* or periphrastically through the premodifiers *more* and *most*:

	absolute	comparative	superlative
inflection	*calm*	*calmer*	*calmest*
premodifier	*difficult*	*more difficult*	*most difficult*

Monosyllabic words (e.g. *calm, tall, great*) generally form their degrees of comparison through inflections. Many disyllabic words (e.g. *polite, noisy, friendly*) can have either inflections or premodifiers. Words of three or more syllables (e.g. *difficult, beautiful, impolite*) require premodifiers, except that some words of three syllables with the negative prefix *un-* (e.g. *uncommon, unhappy, unhealthy*) can go either way. The inflectional option was available for adjectives of three or more syllables as late as the seventeenth century and is still found in some non-standard dialects.

Some spelling rules apply to adjectives taking the inflections (cf. 4.17):

1. If the base ends in -*e*, drop the -*e* before the inflection:

   polite/politer-politest   close/closer-closest

2. If the base ends in a consonant plus *y*, change the *y* to *i* and then add the inflection:

   sexy/sexier-sexiest   healthy/healthier-healthiest

3. Double the consonant letter before the inflection if all three conditions apply:

   (a) the base ends in a single consonant letter
   (b) a single vowel letter comes before that consonant letter
   (c) the final syllable of the base is stressed

   fat/fatter-fattest   wet/wetter-wettest

A final syllabic / ḷ / in the base, as in *subtle* and *gentle*, is not pronounced as syllabic when inflections are added. The final /r/ of the base is pronounced when inflections are added even by speakers who do not pronounce final /r/, as in *cleverer, cleverest*.

A few very frequent adjectives have irregular forms for their comparatives and superlatives:

good	*better*	*best*
well ('healthy')	*better*	*best*
bad	*worse*	*worst*
far	*farther*	*farthest*
	further	*furthest*

As late as the seventeenth century periphrastic *more* and *most* were commonly combined with the inflectional forms for emphasis: *more lovelier, most unkindest*. These combinations—double comparatives and double superlatives—persist in non-standard dialects.

The irregular comparison forms of *bad* are treated variously in non-standard dialects. In place of comparative *worse* we find *badder* (a regularized form), *worser* (double comparative form), and *worserer* (treble comparative form). In place of superlative *worst* we find the double superlative forms *worsest* and *worstest*.

4.25
Adjectives as unmarked term

Gradable adjectives can be used as the unmarked (or neutral) term in *how*-questions. The unmarked term is used for a question relating to the whole scale and not just to the particular adjective. For example, *old* in **[1]** does not mean that the speaker assumes that Nell is old:

[1] *How old* is Nell now [S1A-031-46]

On the other hand, *How young is she?* would mean that the speaker assumes that she is young. The unmarked term is the adjective that refers to the top of the scale: the end that denotes the greater extent of the quantity or quality.

Here are other examples of adjectives as the unmarked term in independent and subordinate *how*-questions (cf. 6.12):

[2] And *how competent* do you think that system is [S1B-030-96]

[3] And I don't know *how accurate* it is [S1B-041-158]

[4] *How legitimate* is it [S1B-045-36]

[5] Did you personally uhm take any steps to see *how reliable* a sort of man he was [S1B-067-61]

[6] They claimed authority over all Britanny but how *effective* was this claim? [W1A-003-69]

In contrast *disinflationary* is a marked term in **[7]**:

[7] If his forecasts this year go even slightly astray just *how disinflationary* will two hundred billion pounds of spending be [S1B-052-39]

Some gradable adjectives are also used in measure expressions as the unmarked term: *deep, high, long, old, tall, thick, wide*. Here are some examples:

[8] They're standing *nine ten deep* [S2A-019-34]

[9] It's *sixteen feet long six feet high six feet wide* [S2A-019-34]

[10] Anna *seven years old* clings to any adult she meets [S2B-038-8]

[11] When finished, shape into rolls, *about 4–5 inches long* and *1 inch thick* and put these, if there is time, in the fridge to chill for 1/4 hour. [W2D-020-72]

Adverbs

4.26
Characteristics
of adverbs

Adverbs are a heterogeneous class, varying greatly in their functional and positional ranges. They constitute a series of overlapping subclasses, and some of them belong to more than one subclass. For example, the adverb *very* is an intensifier that functions only as a premodifier (*very large, very carefully*), whereas *too* is an intensifier when it functions as a premodifier (*too small, too quickly*), but it has a different meaning ('in addition') when it functions as an adverbial ('The food was good, *too*'). We may regard as complex adverbs certain fixed expressions that have the form of prepositional phrases, such as *of course* and *as a result*.

The terms *adverb* and *adverbial* are distinct. *Adverb* is the name of a word class (or part of speech), so adverbs can be contrasted with adjectives. An adverb phrase is a phrase headed by an adverb; for example, *very carefully*, headed by the adverb *carefully*. *Adverbial* is the name of a constituent of a sentence or clause, so adverbials can be contrasted with complements of the verb such as subject predicatives and direct objects. An adverb phrase may function as an adverbial:

> **[1]**   I met my husband *here*.

But so can other linguistic units, such as a prepositional phrase or a clause:

> **[1a]** I met my husband *in San Francisco*.
>
> **[1b]** I met my husband *where he was working*.

Used alone or with one or more modifiers, adverbs have two characteristic functions. One is as premodifier of an adjective **[2]**–**[3]** or of another adverb **[4]**–**[5]**:

> **[2]**   One foot's *slightly* bigger than the other though [S1A-017-285]
>
> **[3]**   The truly disturbing aspect is that the CIA itself was also *laughably* amateurish in not challenging his obvious breaches of accepted procedure. [*The Sunday Times*, 27 February 1994, p. 1.18] ('to a degree that was laughable')
>
> **[4]**   This really takes things *too* far doesn't it [S1A-019-1]
>
> **[5]**   Well I used to get it *very* badly at night but if I take one of those tablets it's they help [S1A-051-64]

As premodifiers or postmodifiers, adverbs are generally intensifiers, indicating degree or extent above or below an assumed norm: *slightly* (*bigger*) **[2]**, *laughably* (*amateurish*) **[3]**, *too* (*far*) **[4]**, *very* (*badly*) **[5]**.

The other characteristic function is as adverbial in sentence or clause structure (cf. 3.20). There is often more than one adverb functioning as adverbial in the same sentence:

> **[6]**   *Actually* you *probably* wouldn't have enjoyed it *here* [S1A-010-199]
>
> **[7]**   *Funnily enough*, many patients who show such learning *consequently* deny *ever* having done the task *before*! [W1A-004-71]

Though important informationally, adverbials are optional constituents of the sentence or clause, in the sense that if they are omitted the sentence remains well-formed:

> **[6a]** You wouldn't have enjoyed it.
>
> **[7a]** Many patients who show such learning deny having done the task.

Adverbs are obligatory constituents when they function as complements **[8]**–**[9]**:

> **[8]**   I thought he was *here* [S1A-005-187]
>
> **[9]**   If the place grabbed me then I recreated it and put a story *there* [S1B-048-109]

Adverbs functioning as adverbials and as complements are discussed in 4.27 f. The full range of functions of adverb phrases is listed in 5.44. Modification of adverbs is illustrated in 5.45 f.

As with the other word classes, many adverbs do not have suffixes: *now, here, often, therefore, however*. The most common adverb ending is *-ly*, which is added to adjectives to form adverbs:

openly, madly, carefully, notably, frequently

If the adjective ends in *-ic*, the suffix is generally *-ically*:

romantically, heroically, electrically, sceptically, axiomatically

The exception is *publicly*.

Less common are adverb endings in *-ward* or *-wards* and *-wise*. The ending *-wards* usually has a directional meaning. The ending *-wise* generally has either a manner meaning or a viewpoint meaning:

-wards	*forward(s), upward(s), skywards, northward(s), inward(s), straightforward(s), afterward(s)*
-wise	*likewise, otherwise, lengthwise, snakewise, marketing-wise, stomachwise, pricewise*

Likewise and *otherwise* also have other meanings. *Clockwise* and *anticlockwise* combine manner with direction.

An Old English genitive inflection in *-es* is preserved in some adverbs ending in *-s*, e.g. *homewards, besides, needs* (as in *needs be*), *sideways, days* ('by day') and *nights* ('by night') in *They work nights*. The genitive inflection is obscured in *since, else, once, twice*.

A grammatically important class of adverbs are the *wh*-adverbs, so called because most of them are written with an initial *wh-*, the exceptions being *how* and its compounds (such as *however*). Several of them introduce relative clauses (cf. 5.9): *when, where, why* and (less commonly) *whereby, whereupon*, and the archaic *whence, wherein*. Here are examples of their use with relative clauses:

[10] Her father was in the oil business in Pennsylvania at a time *when* it was expanding very rapidly [S1B-005-14]

[11] Uhm ⟨ , ⟩ the best cheese was probably the brie at the farmhouse *where* we were staying because uhm it was the local one [S1A-009-318]

[12] The reason *why* a revived Halloween is approved is because it is a massive new advertising opportunity, in particular in the children's market. [W2E-003-71]

[13] If organisations operated according to classical free-market theory, *whereby* firms are guided by 'market forces' to make appropriate decisions, there would be no organisation problem. [W2A-011-027]

The *wh*-adverbs *how, when, where*, and *why* introduce interrogative sentences and clauses (cf. 3.5, 6.12):

[14] *How* does that suit you [S1A-012-46]

[15] *Why* are you looking at me Bobby ⟨ , ⟩ I've never borrowed a hardback [S1A-013-96]

[16] *How* long did you stay there [S1A-014-77]

[17] I don't even know *where* Jesus College is [S1A-039-132]

[18] [. . .] do you know *when* his office hours are [S1B-007-66]

[19] Work is going well; I really enjoy it, though there is still so much that I don't know *how* to do yet! [W1B-002-114]

The adverbs may be postmodified by *else* and *otherwise* and by intensifiers; for example: *how else, when otherwise, why on earth, where in the hell, why ever.* The adverb *how* also introduces exclamative sentences and clauses (cf. 3.9):

[20] *How* true that is [S1A-079-106]

[21] I was just saying outside ⟨ , ⟩ *how* these six months go round so rapidly [S1A-087-16]

[22] I can remember going there and being amazed *how* pimply ⟨ , ⟩ the conscripts were [S1A-014-21]

The *wh*-adverbs *how, when, why,* and *where* are used with nominal relative clauses (cf. 6.12):

[23] So that depends on *how* you want to do it [S1A-012-178]

[24] I mean that's *why* I like faxes [S1A-015-17]

[25] The most important thing you will ever learn is *how* to use your brakes effectively [S2A-054-100]

Finally, *however* is used with *wh*-conditional clauses (cf. 6.14):

[26] You really are relatively speaking in comparison with the other two very inexperienced *however* talented you may be [S1B-043-21]

In all these constructions *how* and *however* may modify adjectives or adverbs: *how long* **[16]**, *how true* **[20]**, *how pimply* **[22]**, *however talented* **[26]**.

In Old English, adverbs were derived from adjectives chiefly by adding *-e* or *-līce*. As a result of phonological processes, the suffix *-e* was dropped so that the adverb and adjective came to have the same form, and *-līce* developed into present-day *-ly*. Some adverbs still have the same form as corresponding adjectives; for example: *hard, long, fast, early, daily, kindly*. In other instances, adverbs have forms both with and without the *-ly* suffix, though sometimes differing in meaning:

[27] It's a bit *late* now [S1A-022-168]

[28] Have you seen any of the others *lately*? [W1B-002-97]

[29] Incorporated in the great wooden beams which descended *deep* into the mine-shaft was a revolutionary 'man-engine', the first of its kind in the country. [W2F-007-8]

[30] Thought of Jeff and how *deeply* he cares about the political situation in this country. [W1B-003-48]

[31] I think you're doing *fine* [S1A-075-1]

[32] Put the onions into the bowl and chop *finely* [. . .] [W2D-020-85]

[33] Don't be intimidated by vehicles following too *close* behind [S2A-054-165]

[34] One item *closely* matches your theme [S1B-007-16]

[35] God that came out *quick* didn't it eh [S1A-056-211]

[36] I'll just *quickly* show you one or two more [S2A-046-47]

Only the *-ly* form can precede the verb.

Adjective forms of adverbs are more common in informal English:

[37] Dobrovolski getting away on the left hand side gets in the cross and Kalivanov gets in the first *real* good effort of the evening [S2A-010-43]

In informal American English, *real* and *sure* are commonly used as intensifiers and *good* and *bad* as manner adverbs:

[38] I *sure* like them.

[39] He plays *real good*.

Non-standard dialects extend the use of adverbs (particularly manner adverbs) without the *-ly* suffix:

[40] They sing *terrible*.

[41] You don't talk *proper*.

Many adverbs are gradable, but most require the comparative to be expressed periphrastically through the premodifiers *more* and *most* (cf. 4.24). Those adverbs that take comparative inflections are generally identical with adjectives. Here are adverbs with irregular forms for their comparatives and superlatives:

badly	*worse*	*worst*
well	*better*	*best*
little	*less*	*least*
much	*more*	*most*
far	*farther*	*farthest*
	further	*furthest*

Here are some examples with regular inflections:

fast	*faster*	*fastest*
hard	*harder*	*hardest*
often	*oftener*	*oftenest*
soon	*sooner*	*soonest*

Like gradable adjectives (cf. 4.25), gradable adverbs can be used as the unmarked (or neutral) term in *how*-questions:

[42] I'm just wondering *how quickly* I can read this book [S1A-053-1]

[43] And we can do that with female speakers and male speakers and children ⟨ , ⟩ to see *how well* they can perceive pitch differences [S2A-056-89]

[44] The first decision to be made is *how frequently* recordings should be made. [W2A-016-21]

Badly is the marked term in [45]:

[45] *How badly* do the children have to behave before they are hit? [W2B-017-66]

4.27
Adverbs as adverbials

Grammatically, we can distinguish three major functions of adverbs (alone or with modification) as adverbials:

conjuncts
disjuncts
adjuncts

Because conjuncts and disjuncts may relate to the sentence as a whole, they have been called sentence adverbials.

Adverbs that are conjuncts (conjunctive adverbs) are logical connectors that generally provide a link to a preceding sentence [1] or clause [2]. They involve a great deal of compression of meaning, as paraphrases can show. For example, *therefore* in [1] is to be interpreted as 'because the more demanding the work the sooner fatigue sets in'.

[1] The more demanding the work the sooner the fatigue sets in. It is *therefore* necessary to encourage the operators to take short breaks to keep them properly alert. [W2B-033-81 f.]

[2] If he was not taken in procession to the prison gates, as happens both to Samuel Pickwick and to William Dorrit, the relief and celebration must *nevertheless* have been much the same. [W2B-006-32]

The unit in which the conjunct is positioned may be part of a clause:

[3] It'll mean traders will be able to offer a discount for cash ⟨ , ⟩ or *alternatively* charge extra to customers using credit cards [S2B-019-28]

[4] Could a tumour not cause obstruction and *hence* swelling [S1B-010-77]

Here are examples of conjuncts, listed semantically:

first, second, . . .; firstly, secondly, . . .; next, then, finally, last(ly); in the first place . . .; first of all, last of all; to begin with, to start with, to end with
equally, likewise, similarly, in the same way
again, also, further, furthermore, moreover; what is more; in addition; above all
in conclusion, to conclude, to summarize
namely, for example, for instance, that is (to say)
so, therefore, thus; hence, consequently; as a result, as a consequence, in consequence
otherwise, else
rather, alternatively, in other words
on the contrary, in contrast, in comparison, on the other hand
anyhow, anyway, besides, however, nevertheless, nonetheless, still, though, yet; in any case, at any rate, after all, at the same time, all the same
incidentally, by the way

Disjuncts provide comments on the unit in which they stand. Two major types of disjuncts are distinguished: style disjuncts and content disjuncts.

Style disjuncts can be paraphrased by a clause with a verb of speaking; for example, the style disjunct *frankly* by the paraphrase 'I say to you frankly', in which *frankly* functions as a manner adverb 'in a frank manner':

[5] Americans may say they'd like the idea of a simple President leading a simple life without all the trappings and paraphernalia of a world leader but *frankly* that's nonsense [S2B-021-11]

[6] And the second uh purpose is in fact involved in sex or *more strictly* I suppose the exchange of DNA [S2A-051-25]

[7] *Briefly* then the Sigma makes sensible use of its technology ⟨ , ⟩ it cruises very well and it comes with a three-year warranty [S2A-055-63]

[8] But *simply* if I took a starting point as 1880 and the end-point as 1980 what would be the difference between the temperatures in those two dates [S1B-007-173]

[9] *Personally* I agree with H G Wells that it is a great mistake to regard the head of state as a sales promoter [S2B-032-45]

Here are examples of style disjuncts, listed semantically:

approximately, briefly, broadly, crudely, generally, roughly, simply
bluntly, candidly, confidentially, flatly, frankly, honestly, privately, strictly,
    truly, truthfully
literally, metaphorically, personally

There are a number of fixed prepositional phrases that function as style disjuncts. For example:

in brief, in all fairness, in general, in all honesty, in short

Style disjuncts are also expressed by fixed clauses of various types. For example:

to be candid, to be fair
to put it bluntly, to speak frankly
strictly speaking, crudely speaking
put simply, put briefly
if I may be candid, if I can speak confidentially, if I can put it bluntly

Most of the adverbs and prepositional phrases that function as style disjuncts can also function as manner adverbs within their sentence:

[10] [. . .] I am going to speak *very honestly* [S1B-051-53]

Honestly and *frankly* can also shade into a predominantly emphatic function:

[11] I don't *honestly* know [S1A-068-32]

Content disjuncts may be modal (commenting on the truth-value) **[12]**–**[13]** or evaluative (making a value judgement) **[14]**–**[19]**:

[12] This is *probably* a woman's size [S1A-022-628]

[13] He *obviously* felt he was being tested in some way [S1A-037-16]

[14] Opposition candidates boycotted the vote. *Unmysteriously*, President Gnassingbe Eyadema won, with 96.5% of the vote. [*The Economist*, 4 September 1993, p. 69]

[15] *Not surprisingly*, the socially depriving conditions had an adverse effect on children. [W2B-019-27]

[16] Progress has *naturally* been patchy ⟨ , ⟩ for confidence in the police is a fragile growth [S2B-037-54]

[17] Major accidents and pollution incidents, which *thankfully* are rare, often create very special trans-frontier pollution problems. [W2A-030-2]

[18] *Touchingly*, the prime minister seems to believe that the Italian public understands him, and that direct appeals will head off plummeting polls. [*The Sunday Times*, 14 August 1994, p. 1.14]

[19] Moreover, Irish voters have *wisely* never given him an overall parliamentary majority. [W2E-004-95]

Wisely **[19]** makes a value judgement on the subject of the sentence as well as on the content of the sentence as a whole: 'Irish voters were wise never to have given ...' and 'That Irish voters have never given ... was wise'.

Here are examples of content disjuncts that are (a) modal, (b) evaluative, (c) evaluative and subject-related:

(a) *admittedly, certainly, clearly, evidently, indeed, obviously, plainly, surely, undoubtedly; apparently, arguably, (very, etc.) likely, maybe, perhaps, possibly, presumably, probably, supposedly; actually, basically, essentially, ideally, nominally, officially, ostensibly, really, superficially, technically, theoretically*

(b) *fortunately, happily, luckily, regrettably, sadly, tragically, unhappily, unfortunately; amazingly, curiously, funnily, incredibly, ironically, oddly, remarkably, strangely, unusually; appropriately, inevitably, naturally, predictably, understandably; amusingly, hopefully, interestingly, significantly, thankfully*

(c) *cleverly, foolishly, prudently, reasonably, sensibly, shrewdly, unwisely, wisely; rightly, justly, unjustly, wrongly*

Adjuncts are more integrated into sentence or clause structure. Four major subclasses of adverbs as adjuncts are distinguished:

space
time
process
focus

The first two subclasses relate to the circumstances of the situation described in the sentence or clause; the third involves the process denoted by the verb and its complements; the fourth consists of adverbs that focus on a particular unit.

Space adjuncts include position **[20]**–**[21]** and direction **[22]**–**[24]**:

[20] Why have I got such a terrible collection of letters *here* [S1A-010-55]

[21] There are cockroaches crawling around *inside* even if you have grates [S1A-063-150]

[22] Well we could go *there* for about five minutes but then I have to leave again [S1A-098-239]

[23] So I said don't worry about this and we ran *back* to my car [S1A-028-81]

[24] Shall I move these *away* [S1A-012-33]

Time adjuncts include position in time **[25]**–**[27]**, duration **[28]**–**[29]**, and frequency **[30]**–**[33]**:

[25] And have you *recently* had antibiotics for anything [S1A-089-122]

[26] Ring her *tomorrow* and invite her out [S1A-020-95]

[27] You mean you haven't shaved it off *since* [S1A-017-175]

[28] *How long* has he lived in this country [S1B-080-135]

[29] Some fields remain grass *permanently*, others stay in grass for only a few years at a time before being ploughed up. [W2B-027-54]

[30] None the less, it constitutes a sanctuary that *occasionally* helps more than 1,000 refugees. [W2C-002-89]

[31] The craving for more freedom of expression was *all too often* reduced to a need to call oneself by the name of one's nationality. [W2B-007-88]

[32] After all the party that controls the White House *invariably* loses ground in the mid-term elections for Congress and *usually* much more ground than has been lost this year [S2B-006-14]

[33] We were in telephone contact *daily* [S1B-061-186]

Process adjuncts relate to the process conveyed by the verb and its complements. Adverbs functioning as process adjuncts are mainly manner adverbs, which convey the manner in which the action is performed:

[34] And I thought the overall impression in the hall was a bad speech *badly* delivered [S1B-039-29]

[35] Apply the brake *very smoothly* and put it back on its side stand [S2A-054-37]

[36] Cassie crouched forward, holding her arms *tightly* around her as if suffering from stomach pain. [W2F-001-164]

[37] The pup looked up and wriggled *happily* at the sound of his name. [W2F-006-233]

[38] Firstly, he suggests that the diagnostic process is non-comparable, in that, physical illnesses are assessed *objectively* and mental illnesses are assessed *subjectively*. [W1A-007-60]

Wh-adverbs often function as adjuncts. They have the special function of introducing certain types of clauses: interrogative, exclamative, relative, nominal relative, and *wh*-conditional (cf. 4.26). *How* and *however* can also function as premodifiers:

[39] *How* many classes are there that disabled people can go to [. . .] [S1A-002-60]

[40] And so *however* conservative their intention the ultimate effect of these philosophies was to weaken the idea of any moral authority beyond the self [S2B-029-87]

Focusing adjuncts focus on a particular unit in a sentence or clause. The major semantic types are:

additive
particularizer
exclusive
intensifier

Additive adverbs emphasize that what is said applies also to the focused part. They include:

also	*neither*	*as well*
both	*too*	*in addition*
either	*yet*	
even		

[41] Besides being an academic sociologist ⟨ , ⟩ Mike Grierson is *also* the warden of a small block of flats for people diagnosed as suffering from schizophrenia [S2B-038-45]

[42] It's part of the complication of the countryside that it's *both* an ideal and a hard economic fact [S1B-037-7]

[43] Did you intend then *even* then to become a writer [S1B-046-107]

[44] I think he worked in a bank *too* at one stage [S1A-033-45]

[45] [. . .] The photon travels through without being *either* absorbed or reflected [S1B-015-96]

Particularizer adverbs emphasize that what is said is restricted chiefly to the focused part. They include:

chiefly	*particularly*	*at least*
especially	*predominantly*	*in particular*
largely	*primarily*	
mainly	*principally*	
mostly	*specifically*	
notably		

[46] And those forty or so jobs you've applied for have they *mainly* been in response to vacancies that you've seen advertised [S1A-034-197]

[47] They speak of continuing racial harassment *especially* of young black men [S2B-037-24]

Exclusive adverbs emphasize that what is said is restricted entirely to the focused part. They include:

alone	*precisely*
exactly	*purely*
just	*simply*

merely   solely
only

[48] You know there are *only* three vegetarian dinners here [S1A-011-231]

[49] Well you should *just* stay till Sunday night [S1A-011-143]

[50] Is that *simply* a question of money and cost [S1B-050-56]

Intensifiers denote a place on a scale of intensity, either upward or downward. Intensifier adverbs are particularly numerous. They include:

almost	*fully*	*quite*	*a bit*
badly	*greatly*	*rather*	*a little*
barely	*hardly*	*slightly*	*a little bit*
completely	*highly*	*somewhat*	*a lot*
considerably	*immensely*	*strongly*	*at all*
deeply	*incredibly*	*thoroughly*	
enough	*less/least*	*totally*	
entirely	*much/more/most*	*utterly*	
extremely	*nearly*	*well*	

[51] [. . .] she says there's now a change to re-allocate money to areas that *badly* need it [S2B-015-75]

[52] The police have *greatly* improved their training and equipment ⟨ , ⟩ for handling public disorder [S2B-037-80]

[53] I've got another number and I don't like it *very much* [S1A-041-245]

[54] But this *hardly* worries the recording industry, who want to deter multi-generation copying. [W2B-038-112]

4.28
Adverbs as complements

Adverbs often function as complements of the verb *be*, in which case they are subject predicatives (cf. 3.18). Generally, the adverbs have a spatial meaning, though the meaning may be extended metaphorically:

[1] [. . .] my friend who gets these seats is *away* she's ill [S1A-045-145]

[2] But the potential is *there* certainly [S1B-014-48]

[3] The flag is *up* for an offside decision [S2A-003-50]

[4] If you are *abroad* for more than six months in any tax year you will not be given automatic credits for any week in that tax year. [W2D-004-79]

[5] I was *up* before her though ⟨ , ⟩ yesterday [S1A-019-199]

[6] A: Is it flashing
B: No But it is *on* [S1A-049-147]

[7] I wish it was *over* now [S1A-038-232]

The complements of *be* may also have a temporal meaning:

> **[8]**   Well, that was *then*, this is *now*. [W1B-001-64]

The adverbs of phrasal verbs and phrasal-prepositional verbs (cf. 5.34 f., 5.37) are complements of the verbs and have spatial meaning, literal or metaphorical:

> **[9]**   How did that come *about* [S1A-004-57]
>
> **[10]**   But it went *off* okay last night did it [S1A-005-199]
>
> **[11]**   I would hold my breath if your arrival could be speeded *up* by doing so. [W1B-007-111]
>
> **[12]**   Drop *in* on the way in [S1A-043-231]
>
> **[13]**   In which case we'd better get you to fill *in* one of these forms [S1A-089-248]
>
> **[14]**   I think you'd know if you'd put *on* a lot of weight [S1A-011-194]
>
> **[15]**   And I thought well now where shall I poke him to wake him *up* [S1A-018-261]
>
> **[16]**   But when the two leaders emerged from their meeting they played *down* their differences [S2B-002-97]
>
> **[17]**   Turn the heat *down* to low [. . .] [W2D-020-89]
>
> **[18]**   Never do anything you can get *away* with not doing [S1A-030-171]
>
> **[19]**   Is this the guy that was breaking *out* into a sweat [S1A-037-170]
>
> **[20]**   And he thinks his wife is having it *off* with someone else [S1A-063-177]

For some phrasal verbs the effect of the adverb is completive, indicating that the action has concluded and the result has been achieved: 'put *on* a lot of weight' **[14]**, 'wake him *up*' **[15]**. In **[11]** *up* is intensifying: 'could be speeded *up*'.

A few verbs other than phrasal verbs require a complement, usually one with spatial meaning. Here are some examples with adverbs:

> **[21]**   Seven successive popes lived *here* before the papacy returned to Rome [S2B-027-79]
>
> **[22]**   [. . .] by the time I got *home* they'd already phoned my agent [S1A-092-47]

Here is an instance where the adverb has a manner meaning:

> **[23]**   So I don't think they have behaved *well* at any stage frankly [S2B-013-61]

Complex-transitive verbs take adverbs as object predicative (cf. 3.19), again usually with spatial meaning:

> **[24]**   Yes but obviously by the fact that she wanted him *back* as I said to you she obviously wasn't leaving him [S1A-080-144]
>
> **[25]**   Just as they were about to become corrupted or softened by a posting, orders moved them *somewhere else*. [W2F-009-116]
>
> **[26]**   Larry O'Connell calls them *together* [S2A-009-5]
>
> **[27]**   It's to Dubrolsky in the end who plays it *through* [S2A-019-209]

Here is an example where the adverb has a manner meaning:

> **[28]**   So how come you've been treated *differently* [S1A-060-8]

Auxiliaries

Auxiliaries (or auxiliary verbs) fall into two major sets:

1. the primary auxiliaries:
   be, have, do
2. the modals (or modal auxiliaries or secondary auxiliaries):
   can, could
   may, might
   shall, should
   will, would
   must

Be, have, and *do* are also main (or lexical or full) verbs. Their informal contracted forms are given in 4.14. The modals also have informal non-negative and negative contracted forms. Some of the modals have stressed and unstressed pronunciations. Both are given below, the stressed pronunciation first and then the unstressed (with reduced vowels).

can	/kan/, /kən/	*can't*	/kɑːnt/ or /kant/
could	/kʊd/, /kəd/	*couldn't*	/kʊdn̩t/
may	/meɪ/	*mayn't*	/meɪnt/ (British)
might	/mʌɪt/	*mightn't*	/mʌɪtn̩t/
shall	/ʃal/, /ʃəl/	*shan't*	/ʃɑːnt/ (British)
should	/ʃʊd/, /ʃəd/	*shouldn't*	/ʃʊdn̩t/, /ʃədn̩t/
will	/wɪl/	*won't*	/wəʊnt/
'll	/əl/ or /l/		
would	/wʊd/, /wəd/	*wouldn't*	/wʊdn̩t/
'd	/əd/ or /d/		
must	/mʌst/	*mustn't*	/mʌsn̩t/

The alternative pronunciations of *can't* are British /kɑːnt/ and American /kant/. In British English, *shan't* is sometimes used as a negative contracted form of *shall*, and *mayn't* is very occasionally found as a negative contracted form of *may*.

Auxiliary *be* combines with a following *-ing* participle to form the progressive aspect (cf. 5.31 f.); e.g. *was playing*. It also combines with a following *-ed* participle to form the passive voice (cf. 3.12); e.g. *was played*. Auxiliary *have* combines with a following *-ed* participle to form the perfect aspect (cf. 5.27 ff.); e.g. *has played*. Auxiliary *do* is the dummy operator: in the absence of any other auxiliary, it functions as the operator to form (for example) interrogative and negative sentences; e.g. *Did they play? They didn't play.*

The modals are followed by an infinitive, e.g. *can play.* They convey notions of factuality, such as certainty (e.g. *She could be at the office*), or of control, such as permission (e.g. *You may play outside*).

The modals differ from the primary auxiliaries in several ways:

1.   They do not have an *-s* form for the third person singular present:

> He *may* be there.
>
> She *can* drive.

2.   They do not have non-finite forms and therefore must be the first verb in the verb phrase.

3.   Their past forms are often used to refer to present or future time:

> He *might* be there now.
>
> She *could* drive my car tomorrow.

Must has only one form.

All the auxiliaries are used as operators for negation, interrogation, emphasis, and abbreviation (cf. 5.18). For negation, *not* is placed after the auxiliary or the negative contracted form is used:

[1]   Uhm ⟨ , ⟩ I think I remember being with a girl ⟨ , ⟩ that I'd met ⟨ , ⟩ uhm ⟨ , ⟩ who I was just impressing and she wanted me to ⟨ , , ⟩ go all the way when I was about sixteen and I just ⟨ , ⟩ *could not* just *couldn't* [S1A-072-179]

[2]   He *doesn't* think he'll even be at the talk [S1A-005-126]

For interrogation, the operator is placed before the subject in *yes–no* questions and in most *wh*-questions (cf. 3.5):

[3]   *Does* an artist have to live with an artist [S1A-020-233]

[4]   So why *didn't* you do the exam [S1A-008-37]

The operator may be used for emphasis. In speech the emphatic function is signalled by placing the nuclear tone (a distinctive movement of pitch) on the operator. *Do* is introduced as the dummy operator for emphasis:

[5]   It *does* sound good [S1A-079-47]

The operator may be used as an abbreviatory device to avoid repetition:

[6]   I'll try and show you if I *can* [S1A-088-148]

[7]   A: It looks a good vehicle yeah
          B: It *does* [S1A-041-82]

Do and *do not* (or *don't*) are used in front of imperatives (cf. 3.7):

[8]   *Do* hand your coat up if you'd like to [S1A-066-7]

[9]   *Do* not hesitate to call us. [W2D-009-164]

Let is used for first and second person imperatives (cf. 3.7):

[10]   *Let's* stop for the moment [S1A-001-45]

In standard English, two modals cannot co-occur. However, in non-standard dialects some double modals can co-occur; for example: *might could, might should, won't can't, would could, should can, may can, will can.* They are used also after the infinitival *to*; for example: *have to can, used to could, going to can, would like to could, have to can.* The second modal is usually *can* or *could.*

There are several marginal auxiliaries, marginal in that they are also used as main verbs. When used as main verbs they require the dummy operator *do*. The marginal auxiliaries are *used to, ought to, dare,* and *need*; the informal negative contracted forms are *usedn't to, oughtn't to, daren't,* and *needn't. Used to* is used as an auxiliary mainly in British English:

[11] Yeah we *used to* buy Mum a vase every year for her birthday [S1A-019-98]

In **[12]** *used to* (also spelled *use to*) is used as a main verb with *do* as dummy operator:

[12] *Didn't* there *used to* be deer in Richmond Park [S1A-006-225]

[13] I mean I *did use to* go down to Bournemouth [S1A-097-200]

Like *used to* and unlike the other auxiliaries, *ought* is generally followed by infinitival *to*. It is used as an auxiliary in **[14]–[16]**:

[14] I don't know if I *ought to* say this [S1A-068-49]

[15] There were of course other casualties of war as well it *ought not to* be forgotten [S2A-019-84]

[16] *Ought not* the government *to* be planning to spend more? [W2C-008-89]

In non-standard dialects and sometimes in informal standard English, it is used as a main verb with *do* as dummy auxiliary: *didn't ought to.*

Dare and *need* are used as auxiliaries mainly in interrogative and negative sentences:

[17] And *dare* I ask as to the presence of a man in your life [S1A-098-21]

[18] We *dare not* let that happen again [S2B-050-90]

[19] Or *daren't* you ask [S1A-098-268]

[20] You *needn't* read every chapter [S1A-053-9]

[21] Nor *need* I look further than my own city of Sheffield ⟨ , , ⟩ where the percentage of termination of pregnancy continues to be considerably higher than the average for England and Wales [. . .] [S1B-060-18]

As main verbs, *dare* and *need* may take the *-s* and past forms and infinitival *to* as well as dummy auxiliary *do*:

[22] I can't distinguish between my different daydreams because I don't have any. I *don't dare* to have! [W1B-003-9 f.]

[23] *D'you need to* know anything else [S1A-017-261]

[24] I think this is the first action that *needs to* be taken and we *need to* take it very soon [S2A-031-20]

[25] Something obviously *needed to* be done [S2B-025-14]

The main verb *dare* may also be without infinitival *to*:

[26] I wouldn't *dare* look [S1A-061-160]

There are also a number of other auxiliary-like verbs that convey notions of time, aspect, or modality; for example: *be going to, have to, start, had better* (cf. 5.33).

Other auxiliaries are found in some non-standard dialects:

1. habitual *be* and (with verbs other than *be*) habitual *do*:

> They *be* out every night, but we don't *be* out.
>
> He *do* work for me.

2. completive *done* (to indicate completion):

> They *done* painted it.

Conjunctions

4.30
Conjunctions

There are two classes of conjunctions: co-ordinators (or co-ordinating conjunctions) and subordinators (or subordinating conjunctions).

Co-ordinators link units of equal status. The central co-ordinators are *and, or,* and *but*:

[1]   Well he'd better not get drunk *and* tell Jo what happened in the week-end ⟨ , ⟩ in the hope that she'll finish with me [S1A-030-267]

[2]   He married a girl from the Soviet Union *and* she followed him [S1A-014-150]

[3]   This was calibrated before flight using Freon 12, Freon 22 *and* filtered air [. . .] [W2A-029-51]

[4]   All right then I'll see you later *or* I'll speak to you on the phone [S1A-090-129]

[5]   Intuitively the first mechanisms to account for mass movement in the situation of the device structure would be electromigration, *or* diffusion *or* a combination of both [S2A-034-45]

[6]   She would be drenched with a bucket of water, fall through a trap door, get blown up, *or* find herself shot from a cannon. [W2B-010-55]

[7]   I like mineral water *but* I don't like fizzy water [S1A-019-13]

[8]   I wear this occasionally *but* very rarely now [S1A-022-217]

The conjoins (co-ordinated units) may be clauses **[2]**, **[4]**, **[7]**; the main verb (finite or non-finite) with its complements **[1]**, **[6]**; or various kinds of phrases (including those consisting of just one word) **[3]**, **[5]**, **[8]**. Only *and* and *or* can link more than two conjoins **[3]**, **[5]**, **[6]**; the co-ordinator can be repeated between each conjoin **[5]**, or it can be inserted only between the last pair of conjoins **[3]**, **[6]**. See also 5.12 f.

The conjunctions *and* and *but* have both stressed and unstressed pronunciations. They are shown below, the stressed pronunciation coming first:

and /and/, /ən/ or /n̩/
but /bʌt/, /bət/

And is occasionally abbreviated in writing to '*n* or '*n*', generally in fixed expressions:

bed 'n breakfast
rock 'n' roll

It is also abbreviated as the ampersand &, a representation of Latin *et*, 'and'.

The co-ordination can be emphasized by initial correlative expressions: *both . . . and; either . . . or; not (only) . . . but (also)*:

[9] But unfortunately *both* Saturday *and* Sunday it was really foggy [S1A-036-149]

[10] Well nobody in their right mind wants war *either* in the Middle East *or* anywhere else [S1B-035-59]

[11] It means that somehow or other religion in the modern world has been marginalised and that other agencies have taken over *not only* the bodies *but* souls of human beings [S1B-028-9]

The marginal co-ordinator *nor* may be emphasized by the preceding correlative *neither*:

[12] We have also seen in the last few days that there was *neither* time *nor* reason to delay the land battle any longer [S2B-014-20]

Conjunctions that in certain respects are closer to co-ordinators than subordinators include *for* and *nor*. Unlike the other co-ordinators, however, *for* can only link clauses. For many speakers of English *nor* can be preceded by a co-ordinator, which in effect performs the linking of the conjoins in such instances:

[13] So you didn't have a lot of religious pressure *but nor* did you have a lot of religious thought [S1A-076-150]

[14] I would simply say to them ⟨ , ⟩ we won't forget those young men ⟨ , ⟩ *and nor* in my judgement will we forget what they were out there to achieve ⟨ , ⟩ what they accomplished [S2B-004-63]

There are a large number of subordinators. Some of them consist of more than one orthographic word: *in order that, in that, rather than*. Some are historically composed of more than one word, but are now written as one word: *although, because, until, whereas*. Some are also used as prepositions (cf. 4.31): *after, as, before, like, since, than, till, until*. Some combine with other words to form complex prepositions: *because of, in case of. After, before, once, since*, and *though* are also used as adverbs.

Subordinators generally appear at the beginning of a subordinate clause:

[15] We can get that out *if* you want [S1A-006-159]

[16] Well Toni's put an order in ⟨ , ⟩ today *as* I said [S1A-017-89]

[17] But I have such a thin skin I'm always terribly easily hurt and I find it very hard to forgive *although* I do ⟨ , , ⟩ eventually [S1A-031-103]

[18] He does seem to be a good laugh *once* he's here in the house [S1A-041-279]

[19] Laura likes tea bags you see *after* they've had taken some of the strength out [S1A-042-44]

[20] *As* you say it's right at the heart of the process isn't it [S1B-020-43]

[21] *Before* he was Prime Minister he was a great one for offering other people jobs that weren't at his disposal [S1B-040-26]

[22] *Although* fungi are routinely observed in ponds in small numbers, little is known of their role and ecology. [W2A-021-65]

[23] It looks *as though* it might have been open for quite a long time [S1A-065-310]

[24] Would I be right in thinking *that* you're quite possibly marginally bored by what you're doing for work this week [S1A-098-299]

[25] But I'll see *if* I can sort out some guest list [S1A-099-358]

The subordinate clauses in **[15]**–**[22]** are adverbial clauses. They typically follow their host clauses **[15]**–**[19]**, but they may also precede them **[20]**–**[22]**. The subordinate clauses in **[23]**–**[25]** are complements of the preceding verb. Complements virtually always follow the verb.

Some of the subordinators are used to introduce non-finite or verbless clauses:

[26] Add the meatballs to the tomato sauce, partially cover the pan, and simmer for another 15 minutes *while cooking the spaghetti.* [W2D-020-106]

[27] Cassie crouched forward, holding her arms tightly around her *as if suffering from stomach pain.* [W2F-001-164]

[28] Can you describe to me *if possible* a typical day in your home when you were a boy of less than fourteen [S1A-076-75]

[29] We never spoke much, though that doesn't really matter as words are often inappropriate *when in the presence of feeling.* [W1B-008-57]

Some subordinators are restricted to certain types of non-finite or verbless clauses: *for, in order to, in order for, so as, with, without. For, in order for, with,* and *without* introduce the subject of the clause.

[30] I shall try to prepare myself *for you turning up on our shores six foot tall.* [W1B-015-12]

[31] It will be impracticable *for them to be available as often as the media will now demand.* [W2E-005-18]

[32] I sometimes wonder whether Stephen actually went to prison ⟨ , ⟩ deliberately *in order to have something to talk about when he came on this show* [S1B-042-97]

[33] *In order for the disc to be extruded* what type of force has to be applied to it [S1B-068-77]

[34] So far as Muslims are concerned, the normal method of slaughtering is known as dhabh and it involves cutting the throat of the animal or fowl while it is still conscious *so as to allow the blood to start flowing out while it is still alive.* [W2B-020-86]

[35] I put it on *with the zip done up* [S1A-042-174]

[36] You'll never get a word in *with me talking* [S1A-081-41]

[37] But they said because you've got to tell someone in advance you can't just put it on *without them knowing* [S1A-047-77]

[38] I didn't mention this, however, for Mary Jane would have insisted on turning back and *with the sun out in full force* I was already too hot to be bothered. [W2F-013-105]

[39] Less than fifty feet away a US military jeep was flying through the air, headed straight for him, *with a demented Harry Benjamin as its pilot.* [W2F-012-145]

What with also introduces the subject of non-finite or verbless clauses:

[40] *What with his gambling debts and a son away at some expensive school near London*, he's hard-pressed for money to live on. [W2F-007-71]

Prepositions

4.31
Prepositions

Typically, prepositions function as the first constituent of a prepositional phrase. The second constituent is the complement (or object) of the prepositional phrase. Thus, *in a hurry* is a prepositional phrase, in which *in* is the preposition and *a hurry* is its complement. Prepositions chiefly take as their complements noun phrases [1], nominal -*ing* participle clauses [2] (cf. 6.12), and nominal *wh*-clauses [3] (cf. 6.12).

[1] And every single person *without a computer background* failed [S1A-005-161]

[2] That's a good way *of trying to get to know each other* [S1A-017-250]

[3] It's just a question *of which is the more efficient approach* [S1A-029-196]

On the possible complements of prepositions and on constructions where the complement is either fronted or absent, see 5.47. On premodifiers of prepositions and prepositional phrases, see 5.49. On prepositional verbs and phrasal-prepositional verbs, see 5.34, 5.36 f.

Simple prepositions consist of just one word. Here is a list of simple prepositions:

aboard	concerning	out	versus (*also* 'v.'
about	considering	outside	*and* 'vs.')

above	between	like	since
across	beyond	minus (*also* '–')	than
after	but	near	through
against	by	nearby	throughout
along	circa (*also* 'c.')	next	till
amid	cum	notwithstanding	times (*also* '×')
amidst	despite	of	to
among	down	off	toward
amongst	during	on	towards
anti	except	onto	under
apropos	excepting	over	unlike
around	excluding	past	until
as	failing	pending	unto
at	following	per	upon
atop	for	plus (*also* '+')	via
bar	from	post	vis-à-vis
before	given	pro	with
behind	in	qua	within
below	including	re	without
beneath	inside	regarding	worth
beside	into	round	
besides	less	save	

The most frequent simple prepositions are *about, after, as, at, before, between, by, during, for, from, in, into, like, of, on, over, than, through, to, under, with, within, without.* Some have both stressed and unstressed forms. They include the following, where the stressed form is given first:

as	/az/, /əz/
at	/at/, /ət/
for	/fɔː/ or /fɔːr/, /fə/ or /fər/
into	/ɪntʊ/, /ɪntə/
of	/ɒv/, /əv/ or /ə/
than	/ðan/, /ðən/
to	/tuː/, /tʊ/ or /tə/

The alternatives for *for* with /r/ are for those with a rhotic accent (cf. 10.5).
    Here are examples of the use of some infrequent simple prepositions:

[4]   Well I'm a bit *anti* it [. . .] [S1A-054-53]

[5]   [. . .] I conclude with the inescapable fact that, *bar* the Tantric tradition, it is the sexuality of the Goddess, and consequently the real women, that has suffered most in the transition that the Aryan heroes brought into the world's symbolic art forms so variously enshrined in each religious tradition. [W1A-008-11]

[6]   In particular, the varied pattern of incident, interval and allusion is of interest and compares well with the unimaginative and depressing grid plans offered by Foster Associates and by Richard Rogers Partnership, and with the animal-maze *cum* rural open-prison *cum* Japanese factory exercise-yard sketched out by MacCormack, Jamieson, Prichard & Wright. [W2A-005-84]

[7] Access by sea is straightforward *given* the recognised hazards of the time such as storm wreck and piracy [S2B-043-12]

[8] These make up the normal weekly income, which (*less* any disregards) will be taken into account in calculating your Family Credit. [W2D-005-127]

[9] We ourselves are having problems again at the moment because something else has threatened to be built *next* us [S2A-027-118]

[10] We'll get that *out* the way tomorrow [S1A-030-173]

[11] Uhm the esterase *plus* the water gives you the acid and the alcohol [S2A-034-34]

[12] *Post* 1945, there was a general agreement by the western world to an obligation to help the development of the Third World and also to arrest the spread of communism. [W1A-015-6]

[13] I just feel sorry for them now: they're *pro* Boris Yeltsin. [W1B-013-88]

[14] [. . .] nothing remains of the chapels *save* the curved outer wall and window, producing the maximum enlargement of the window surface. [W2B-003-26]

[15] It's mass *times* the distance from the centre if one's being pedantic about it [S1B-017-235]

Many simple prepositions are also used in other word classes. They are functioning as conjunctions when they introduce clauses other than nominal *wh*-clauses and nominal *-ing* participle clauses; conjunctions include *after, as, before, but, except, since, than, till, until.* Some simple prepositions are used as *-ing* or *-ed* participles; e.g. *concerning, failing, following, given, granted. Given* and *granted* are used also as conjunctions. Many of the simple prepositions are used also as adverbs; e.g. *around, before, down, inside, off, out, over, under.*

Complex prepositions consist of more than one word. Here is a selected list:

according to	in comparison with	on account of
along with	in conjunction with	on behalf of
apart from	in connection with	on grounds of
as a result of	in contact with	on pain of
as for	in contrast to	on the part of
as opposed to	in favour of	on top of
as to	in front of	out of
as well as	in keeping with	outside of
away from	in lieu of	owing to
because of	in line with	prior to
by means of	in regard to	rather than
by way of	in respect of	regardless of
care of (*also* c/o)	in response to	relative to
close to	in return for	save for
contrary to	in spite of	short of

down to	in terms of	so far as
due to	in the case of	subject to
except for	in the course of	subsequent to
for the sake of	in the face of	such as
further to	in the light of	thanks to
in accordance with	in the wake of	together with
in addition to	in view of	up to
in case of	instead of	with reference to
in charge of	irrespective of	with regard to
in common with	next to	with respect to

The prepositions *close to, like, near, unlike,* and *worth* share a feature typical of adjectives: they can be premodified by *very. Close to* and *near* can also be inflected for comparison: *closer to/closest to, nearer/nearest,* while *like, unlike,* and *worth* can take the periphrastic comparison forms: *more/most (un)like, more/most worth.*

The variants *amongst, towards, round* (in place of *around*) are more common in British English than in American English. *Atop* ('on top of') is mainly American English. *Outwith* ('outside', 'beyond') is a common Scottish preposition that is beginning to be found in other varieties of British English.

In many non-standard dialects, *off of* is frequently used in place of simple *off* ('He took it *off of* me'), and a prepositional *while* is found in some non-standard dialects with the meaning 'till'.

There is not a sharp boundary between complex prepositions, which act as a unit, and sequences of (for example) preposition plus noun plus preposition. Some complex prepositions are fixed expressions that allow no variation, such as *because of* and *so far as.* Others allow some variation, such as *as a result of* (cf. *as a direct result of*), *in front of* (cf. *in the front of*), *in comparison with* (cf. *in comparison to*).

One indication of the degree of cohesiveness of complex prepositions is whether other words can be inserted within them. Those that permit insertions are less cohesive:

> **[16]** I think probably what he meant is that the Jewish community in this country *in common* I should say *with* the United States community and maybe that in Israel ⟨ , ⟩ is becoming religiously quite polarised [. . .] [S1B-047-25]

The same applies to those that allow ellipsis of part of the complex preposition. *Even to* in **[17]** is to be interpreted as *even up to*:

> **[17]** But I don't think it should be *up to* us even *to* the alliance that fought Saddam Hussein in this case to make the decision about war crimes or whether there should be a prosecution [S1B-036-22]

The prepositional complement generally takes the objective form, where this is available in pronouns: *about me, for her, to him, from us, with them.* However, subjective *who* and *whoever* are commonly used except in formal style. Objective *whom* is more usual when the preposition precedes its complement:

[18] Do you have long-term plans, such as where (—and *with whom?*—if anyone) you eventually want to settle? [W1B-015-62]

Determiners and Pronouns

4.32
Characteristics of determiners and pronouns

Determiners introduce noun phrases (cf. 5.2). They express such notions as number or quantity and the kind of reference of the noun phrase. *This* and *any* may be determiners:

[1] So when was the sell-by date of *this* soup [S1A-061-159]

[2] Programming the areas is relatively easy and, as the speech is digitised, *any* vocabulary in *any* language may be used. [W2B-039-93]

Pronouns are in effect closed sets of nouns. They are typically deictic, pointing to entities in the situation or pointing to linguistic units in the previous or following context (cf. 7.9). Typically they are not introduced by determiners and are not modified. *This* and *any* may be pronouns:

[3] Yes if the anterior ligament is intact and there's injury disruption to the posterior ligament ⟨ , ⟩ then *this* is incurred in a flexion injury ⟨ , ⟩ when the head is moving forward [S1B-068-64]

[4] *Any* of these matters may serve as 'mitigating circumstances' reducing the defendant's moral responsibility and thus calling for a degree of leniency in fixing the appropriate sentence. [W2B-020-53]

As examples [1]–[4] indicate, words that function as determiners may also function as pronouns. This combination of potential functions is sufficiently common that it is economical to set up one pronoun-determiner word class for most pronouns and determiners. Some pronouns in the pronoun-determiner class have only pronominal functions, e.g. *I, someone, themselves*; some have only determiner functions, e.g. *no, your, every*; most have both pronominal and determiner functions, e.g. *some, that, which.*

The major sets of pronouns/determiners may be grouped as follows:

primary pronouns/ determiners (cf. 4.34 f.)	{	personal	e.g. *I, you, she*
		possessive	e.g. *my/mine, you/yours*
		reflexive	e.g. *myself, herself, ourselves*

wh-pronouns/ determiners (cf. 4.43)	{	interrogative	e.g. *what, whose*
		exclamative	*what*
		relative	e.g. *who/which*
		nominal relative	e.g. *who, whatever*
		wh-conditional	e.g. *whatever, whichever*

| indefinite pronouns/ determiners (cf. 4.44) | ⎧ assertive
 ⎪ non-assertive
 ⎨ negative
 ⎪ quantifying
 ⎩ universal | e.g. *some, somebody*
 e.g. *any, anyone*
 e.g. *none, nothing*
 e.g. *few, many*
 e.g. *all, everyone* |

In addition, there are smaller sets or individual items:

reciprocal pronouns/determiners: *each other, one another* (cf. 4.42)
demonstrative pronouns/determiners: *this, that, these, those* (cf. 4.45)
generic pronoun *one* (cf. 4.36)
substitute pronoun *one* (cf. 4.37)
existential *there* (cf. 4.39)

The numerals (cf. 4.46) also function as pronouns or determiners.

Finally, the important class of the definite and indefinite articles (cf. 4.33) function only as determiners.

4.33
Definite and indefinite articles

The definite and indefinite articles are determiners. The definite article is *the*, usually pronounced /ðə/ but pronounced /ðiː/ when stressed. The indefinite article is represented by two variants: *a* (/ə/ or stressed /eɪ/) or *an* (/ən/ or stressed /an/).

The choice between the variants of the indefinite article depends on the initial sound, not the spelling, of the following word. *A* is used before a consonant sound: *a way, a video, a huge house, a one-off event, a unit, a U-turn, a eunuch. An* is used before a vowel sound: *an idea, an architect, an hour, an honorary member, an MBA, an H-bomb, an x-ray.* There are a few words beginning with *h* that some people pronounce with an initial vowel sound (an older pronunciation): *an hotel, an historian.*

The definite article serves as a determiner with singular or plural count nouns and with non-count nouns:

the issue/issues   the information

The indefinite article can only be used with singular count nouns, reflecting its historical derivation from the numeral *one*:

an issue

The analogous indefinite reference for plurals and non-count nouns is conveyed through the absence of a determiner (sometimes termed the zero article) or through the presence of *some* (pronounced /səm/):

(some) issues   (some) information

The definite article is used when the speaker (or writer) assumes that the hearer (or reader) can identify the reference of a noun phrase:

[1] Uhm ⟨ , ⟩ a couple of people can't make *the performances* but *the majority of them* yes [S1A-004-132]

The indefinite article is used when that assumption cannot be made:

[2] It was *a fourteenth or thirteenth century chateau* and we just sort of wandered in [S1A-009-248]

The distinction between the two articles is neutralized for generic noun phrases. For example, **[3]** could be replaced by **[3a]** without affecting the meaning:

[3] *The sandflats* are regarded as the province of *marine biologists*, while *the dunes* are investigated by *terrestrial biologists*. [W2A-022-9]

[3a] *A sandflat* is regarded as the province of *the marine biologist*, while *a dune* is investigated by *the terrestrial biologist*.

As can be seen, the distinction between singular and plural is also neutralized in generic phrases. Fur further discussion of the definite and indefinite articles, see 5.16.

4.34
Forms of personal, possessive, and reflexive pronouns

The three primary sets of pronouns—personal, possessive, and reflexive—are interrelated. They exhibit contrasts in person (first, second, third), number (singular, plural), gender (masculine, feminine, non-personal), and case (subjective, objective). These contrasts are not available in all instances.

The usual forms of these sets of pronouns in standard English are displayed in Table 4.34.1. The possessive pronouns fall into two types: dependent (with determiner function) and independent (with pronominal function).

Some of the pronouns have stressed and unstressed pronunciations. Common unstressed pronunciations are given below, preceded by stressed pronunciations:

me	/miː/, /mɪ/
my	/mʌɪ/, /mɪ/
we	/wiː/, /wɪ/
he	/hiː/, /hɪ/ or /ɪ/
her	/hə:/ or /hə:r/, /hə/ or /hər/ or /ə/ or /ər/
him	/hɪm/, /hɪm/ or /ɪm/
his	/hɪz/, /hɪz/ or /ɪz/
she	/ʃiː/, /ʃɪ/
them	/ðɛm/, /ðəm/

Table 4.34.1 Primary pronouns

person	number and gender	personal		possessive		reflexive
		subjective	objective	dependent	independent	
1st	singular	*I*	*me*	*my*	*mine*	*myself*
	plural	*we*	*us*	*our*	*ours*	*ourselves*
2nd	singular	*you*	*you*	*your*	*yours*	*yourself*
	plural	*you*	*you*	*your*	*yours*	*yourselves*
3rd	masc. singular	*he*	*him*	*his*	*his*	*himself*
	fem. singular	*she*	*her*	*her*	*hers*	*herself*
	non-pers. singular	*it*	*it*	*its*	*its*	*itself*
	plural	*they*	*them*	*their*	*theirs*	*themselves*

Note: For the informal contractions *'s* ('us') and *'em* ('them'), see **[6]**–**[9]**.

The unstressed pronunciation of *my* is sometimes represented in fictional dialogue by the spelling *me*:

[1]   "*Me* brother Sam gives it another twelvemonth, m'm." [W2F-005-42]

The possessive pronouns were originally the genitives of the personal pronouns. During the Middle English period the two functions—dependent and independent—came to be distinguished in form. A genitive inflection -*(e)s* was attached to the possessive to yield *your(es)*, *our(es)*, etc. In other areas, -*(e)n* was attached by analogy with *mīn* ('mine') and *þīn* ('thine') to form *his(e)n*, *our(e)n*, *your(en)*, etc. as independent possessives. On the other hand, the dropping of the final -*n* gave rise to the new forms *my* and *thy*, which were used as dependent possessives.

The possessive pronouns can be emphasized by a following *own*. It functions as a determiner when it follows the dependent possessive pronoun within a noun phrase:

[2]   He showed my children love something that *their own* father hadn't shown them [S1B-049-164]

Own can help to avoid ambiguity. In **[3]** *his own* emphasizes that Galiamin is in Galiamin's half, not in Chernishkov's half:

[3]   Chernishkov in the end plays the ball forward to Galiamin who's eight yards inside *his own* half [S2A-010-187]

Own can be intensified by *very*: *my very own*, etc.

Own cannot combine with the independent possessive (*mine*, *theirs*, etc.), but it functions as a pronoun in combination with the dependent possessive:

[4]   But ⟨ , ⟩ people who can converse in languages other than *their own* ⟨ , ⟩ as I can not ⟨ , ⟩ advance the cause of civilization [S2B-048-39]

As in the double genitive construction (cf. 4.10), the combination of possessive and *own* can combine with the *of*-phrase:

[5]   Later I was surprised to be consulted by him on *a scheme of his own* an entirely original scheme for electronic scanning [S2A-041-87]

Compare *a scheme of his own* with *his own scheme*, and the analogous comparison of *a scheme of his* with *his scheme*.

There are alternative forms to those displayed in Table 4.34.1.

1. *'s* is a contracted form of *us* in *let's*, the combination with the imperative auxiliary *let*:

[6] Well it's not that wonderful a film really ⟨ , ⟩ *let's* be honest [S1A-006-164]

[7] But before we look at the paintings *let's* look at the technique that the Egyptians used for decorating these tombs [S2A-052-65]

2. *'em* is an informal alternative to *them*:

[8] The previous year there had been a disc called 'Sock it to *'em*, J.B.' by Rex Garvin with Mighty Craven [. . .] [W2B-010-62]

[9] 'He gets angry with Lottie and Jacob sometimes, but he wouldn't see *'em* without a roof over their heads, even though they've nothing to do with him.' [W2F-007-105]

This is usually explained as a survival of a Middle English form *hem*, which was gradually replaced by *them*. The *th*-forms (*they, them, their*) derive from Scandinavian and fully ousted the older *h*-forms for the third personal plural. The objective *hem* was the last to give way, but has been preserved in contracted *'em*, which is now generally felt to be a contraction of *them*.

3. In some regions, there are informal combinations for the second personal plural: *you all* or *y'all* (genitive *y'all's*), *you guys* (American), *you lot* (British). These compensate for the absence of number contrast in present-day second personal forms.

4. *themself* has been introduced in recent decades as a singular gender-neutral pronoun, analogously to this use of *they, them*, and *their*, but it seems to be of rare occurrence so far.

[10] Or the person who's trying not to drink so much and beats *themself* up when they slip back and get drunk! [Linda Stoker, *Having It All*, p. 145. London: Bloomsbury]

5. Archaic second personal forms sometimes appear in poetry and religious language, and are otherwise occasionally used facetiously. They are displayed in Table 4.34.2.

[11] A: Can I create staff shortages please as well as snow ⟨ , ⟩
    B: Do as *thou* wills *thou* wilt please [S1A-070-274 f.]

Non-standard dialects exhibit many variants. In some dialects the objective forms of the personal pronouns (*me, us*, etc.) are commonly used as subject, and occasionally the reverse occurs (e.g. *I* and *he* as objects). The objective forms are common in all dialects when the subject consists of co-ordinated phrases, and they sometimes appear in the informal speech of speakers of standard English:

[12] Because *me and John* said [. . .] [S1A-005-4]

[13] *Xepe and me* have had about ten minutes yeah ten minutes over the last week or something [S1A-008-8]

Table 4.34.2 Archaic second person forms

	personal		possessive	
	subjective	objective	dependent	independent
singular	*thou*	*thee*	*thy*	*thine*
plural	*ye*	*you*	*your*	*yours*

Masculine and feminine pronouns are used in some dialects to denote inanimate objects and to refer to inanimate noun phrases. *Youse* or *you'uns* are found in some dialects as the second personal plural.

The possessive *thy* and *thine* survive in some dialects for the second personal singular. Some dialects have preserved the older forms *hisn, hern, ourn, theirn* as independent possessives. Others have regularized *mine* to *mines* by analogy with *yours, ours*, etc. The dependent possessive pronoun *me* is commonly used in non-standard dialects.

Regularization has similarly affected the paradigm of reflexive pronouns in non-standard English. By analogy with *myself, yourself*, etc. (which combine the possessive with *self*) there are the widespread non-standard forms *hisself* and *theirselves. Thyself* has been preserved in some non-standard dialects together with the other second personal singular *th*-pronouns.

4.35
Person, number, gender, case

Contrasts in person apply to all three primary sets of pronouns. The first person (e.g. *I, we, my, ourselves*) includes the speaker or speakers (in written language, the writer or writers). The second person (e.g. *you, your, yourselves*) includes the person or persons addressed but excludes the speaker. The third person (e.g. *he, her, themselves*) excludes the speaker and the person or persons addressed.

Noun phrases other than pronouns are in the third person and are so treated for subject–verb agreement (cf. 5.14). In standard English, conventional politeness requires that in co-ordinated phrases the second person comes first and the first person last:

> my husband and I
> you and your husband
> you, Mary, and me
> you and me

In informal speech the first person is sometimes put first:

> **[1]** This man suddenly fled past *me and Martin Meredith* and all these Falange started firing at him [S2A-050-117]

In **[2]**, cited from fictional dialogue, the prior mention of *me* is motivated by the superior (parental) role of the speaker:

> **[2]** I suppose he's right, but it don't make things any easier for *me and the kids* when there's no money coming in. [W2F-007-103]

Notice, however, the use of non-standard *don't* instead of standard *doesn't*.

Inclusive *we* is the use of *we* to include also the person or persons addressed. It combines first and second persons.

> **[3]** I'm saying I mean I could meet you here tomorrow night and then *we* could go off [S1A-043-205]

The contracted pronoun *'s* is generally inclusive in *let's*:

> **[4]** Right let*'s* see how many words *we* can think of beginning with D [S1A-085-244]

Inclusive *we* is commonly used in writing to draw the reader into closer involvement with the written work:

> **[5]** As *we* have seen, reassertion of identification with the Plantagenet past also took place at this time. [W2A-010-58]

Exclusive *we* excludes the person or persons addressed. It generally combines first and third persons:

> **[6]** I was out with some friends and *we* got talking about books [. . .] [S1A-013-214]

> **[7]** A: First of all ⟨ , ⟩ uh how do you see the future of the group ⟨ , , ⟩
> B: Uhm ⟨ , ⟩ well *we*'re sort of working towards our first performance [. . .] [S1A-003-120]

Exclusive *we* may also represent the speech or writing of more than one person, as in prayer or in joint authorship.

The plural personal pronoun *we* is sometimes used with singular reference. The authorial *we* may be preferred in formal lectures or learned writing by single authors to avoid using *I*, which is felt by some to be too intrusive. Citations **[8]** and **[9]** are excerpted from works by single authors:

> **[8]** In this chapter *we* shall develop some of the issues dealt with in Chapter 2.1. [W2A-001-8]

> **[9]** *We* are currently engaged in measuring these rates in Professor Shetty's subjects. [W2A-024-25]

We and the pronoun *us* or *'s* in combination with *let* can refer to a single speaker in situations of unequal relationship; for example, a doctor or dentist speaking to a patient or a teacher speaking to a student. The intention is to convey a friendly tone, although it is increasingly regarded by some as patronizing.

> **[10]** Well *we*'ll just check your blood pressure [S1A-051-42]

> **[11]** There may be a little tartar build up as well which has cracked off so ⟨ , ⟩ low levels of tartar which I'll just clean Yes *we* saw you in July about six months ago [S1A-087-13 f.]

> **[12]** Let*'s* have a look at your throat just now [S1A-051-49]

In informal conversation, *us* is sometimes used in place of *me* between equals in certain expressions, especially with the verb *give*:

[13] Nigel you couldn't give *us* a hand could you [S1B-074-206]

In a jocular use, the first personal plural can refer to a single hearer:

[14] A: God you really know how to put someone down don't you
B: Oh let's not get touchy touchy [S1A-038-224]

In British English, *one* is sometimes used as the equivalent of the first person singular pronoun, usually by speakers of the upper social classes or in argumentative spoken or written contexts:

[15] It's been a mixture of ⟨ , ⟩ extreme pleasure I've had hundreds of letters from all sorts of people who have enjoyed the book ⟨ , ⟩ and considerable irritation because of being constantly interviewed And the phone never stops going And ⟨ , ⟩ people offer *one* goodies Not that *one* doesn't get offered nice things [S1B-046-2 ff.]

[16] No I think I would certainly want to live with someone that could understand *one's* own angst and anxieties [S1A-020-251]

[17] And *one* has to say straightaway I won't say it again during this programme but all three ⟨ , ⟩ who've just spoken are active supporters of the Labour Party [S1B-022-70]

The gender contrasts apply to the use of the third personal singular pronouns to refer to entities in the situation **[18]** or to an antecedent in the linguistic context **[19]**:

[18] Look at *him*!

[19] He married *a girl* from the Soviet Union and *she* followed him [S1A-014-150]

In general, *he* refers to males, *she* to females, and *it* to all else. *She* and (less commonly) *he* are occasionally used to refer to inanimate objects such as cars, boats, and computers. *It* is used for babies and animals where their sex is unknown or disregarded:

[20] A: So I was left with the baby
B: How old is *it* [S1A-039-69 f.]

[21] But you couldn't have *a dog* leaving *it* all day could you [S1A-019-170]

The absence of a gender-neutral singular personal pronoun has posed problems. On the various methods of dealing with the problem, see 1.10.

The contrasts in case apply to the personal pronouns. In general, the subjective case is used for the subject of a sentence or finite clause and the objective case in all other instances, as in these contrasts between subjective *I* and objective *me*:

[22] Can *I* find out the computer data you hold about *me*? [W2D-010-35]

[23] I'm sure that you are expecting *me* to say something stimulating thought-provoking and original [S2A-045-9]

[24] But *I* think really what made my mind up was when my husband Terry gave *me* an ultimatum [. . .] [S1B-049-32]

There is, however, variation in case when the pronoun is the complement of the verb *be*. The formal variant is the subjective form and the less formal variant is the objective form:

[25] His name was Trophemus and it was *he* who introduced Christianity to this land [S2B-027-39]

[26] The reason that this is such a sacred place is because the two Marys remained in the Camargue with Sarah the servant and it is *she* who has become the most important person for the gypsies [S2B-027-110]

[27] Hello it's *me* again [S1A-098-220]

The objective form is also normal in abbreviated responses in the spoken language:

[28] A: Well I don't suppose she knows how many people are living in the whole property
B: *Me* [S1A-007-239]

We and *you* function as determiners when in combination with a following noun or nominal adjective:

[29] [. . .] we are an endangered species *we* men and *we* sportsmen [S1B-021-45]

[30] [. . .] Jules was going around saying *you* bloody men *you* hypochondriacs [. . .] [S1A-080-257]

For the third person, demonstrative *those* is used in standard English, but non-standard dialects use the third person pronouns *them* or *they* (cf. 4.45).

Personal pronouns are sometimes modified by relative clauses:

[31] And *we* who happen to be in a better position than the others to be able to send any troops have sent some troops [S2B-013-65]

Other possibilities (mainly for first person plural and second person) are modification by adjectives in exclamatory phrases (*poor you*), and by adverbs (*we here*), and prepositional phrases (*you at the back*, mainly in vocative phrases). *It* and *they* are not modified by adjectives or relative clauses. Demonstrative *those* is used instead of *they* with relative clauses.

4.36
Generic pronouns

Generic reference may be conveyed by the generic pronoun *one* (genitive *one's*, reflexive *oneself* or *one's self*) and the personal pronouns *we*, *you*, and *they*.

The generic pronoun *one* is formal and tends to be replaced by the personal pronouns *we*, *you*, and *they* in less formal contexts. They all refer generally to people, though the reference may be restricted by the context. Here are some examples of generic *one*:

[1] *One* loses interest in everything when *one* has children [S1A-032-11]

[2] Or the stresses may be psychological ones uhm bereavement divorce or marriage come to that ⟨ , ⟩ loss of *one's* job [S2A-033-37]

[3] In other words, within the pluralist society, *one* is free to choose to be unconfronted by choice; *one* may find *oneself* choosing from the variety to have no variety. [W2A-012-52]

Generic *we* has the widest extent in that it must include the speaker as well as those addressed. *You*, the most common generic pronoun in speech, generally includes the person or persons addressed. *They* excludes the speaker and those addressed.

[4] *We* don't have a constitution which says Congress shall pass no law restricting the freedom of press or Congress shall pass no law uhm discriminating against religions [S1B-011-149]

[5] *We* should not underestimate the defence of honour or the realization of claims to certain titles, rights and privileges as motivating factors leading to the outbreak of open and public war during this period. [W2A-010-16]

[6] God *you* do have to be careful don't *you* [S1A-023-26]

[7] When *you* select these modes, the Page up/down buttons allow *you* to step through their software pages, while the data entry controllers allow *you* to edit the parameters. [W2B-031-67]

[8] A: And is Japan the one that doesn't like beards or long hair
B: So *they* say [S1A-097-234 f.]

Here are examples of the alternative reflexive forms of *one*—*oneself* and the less frequent *one's self*:

[9] And will he take it from me and my own experience that it's a very satisfactory way of employing *oneself* and serving the customer [S1B-059-73]

[10] It must be peculiarly disconcerting, don't you think, to be left for someone entirely different from *oneself*? [W2F-011-92]

[11] The solutions must involve a re-emphasis of the values that have helped many blacks succeed: respect for the family, for the community, for *one's self*. [891011-0117-70]

To avoid repeating *one*, some speakers and writers switch to another generic pronoun, such as *you*:

[12] [. . .] *one* feels that if *you* create too many if *you* secrete too many of *your* own endorphins ⟨ , ⟩ *you* get addicted to *your* own ⟨ , ⟩ home-made opiates and then have to keep producing them [S2A-027-68]

In American English, *one* was traditionally followed by *he*:

[13] If *one* is wise, *he* should not put all *his* savings in one place.

However, many would now not use generic *he*, to avoid charges of sexism.

4.37
Substitute pronoun *one*

Apart from generic *one* (cf. 4.36) and the numeral *one*, there are two uses of *one* as a substitute pronoun.

One may be a substitute for an indefinite noun phrase:

[1] Uhm ⟨ , ⟩ the movement language that's being developed is *one* which involves different people with different skills to talk to each other [S1A-001-34]

[2] A: Why are you looking at me Bobby ⟨ , ⟩ I've never borrowed a hardback
B: You mean you've never borrowed *one* off me love never [S1A-013-97]

[3] A: Well I could have parties and things
B: She's planning *one* [S1A-019-329 f.]

In [1] *one* substitutes for *a movement language*, in [2] for *a hardback*, and in [3] for *a party*. The plural of this use of *one* is the indefinite pronoun *some*.

In the second use, *one* substitutes for the head of a noun phrase and perhaps also one or more of its modifiers:

[4] A: Oh what sort of a park is it ⟨ , ⟩
B: It's quite a huge *one* [S1A-006-229 f.]

[5] And then the suitors will try for her hand and those who don't make it will be killed and the *one* who gets through will marry her [S2A-059-83]

[6] A long-lived scar on the American psyche second only I suspect to the *one* marked Vietnam bore the name of Iran [S2B-034-99]

In [4] *one* substitutes for *park*, in [5] for *suitor*, and in [6] for *scar on the American psyche* (the head with its postmodifier). The plural of this use of *one* is *ones*:

[7] The most commonly used model of psychopathology is the medical model as opposed to the dynamic, behavioural, phenomenological and ethical *ones*, for example. [W1A-007-14]

[8] A: Who are your favourite poets ⟨ , , ⟩
B: Well ⟨ , ⟩ different *ones* for different times I think [S1B-048-22]

[9] Consequently, all the early types of video recording, and most of the later *ones*, have attempted to achieve a high writing speed without an excessive actual tape speed. [W2D-014-71]

In [7] *ones* substitutes for *models* (the head only), in [8] for *favourite poets* (the head and its premodifier), and in [9] for *types of video recording* (the head and its postmodifier).

One and *ones* may serve as pronouns without reference to any preceding noun phrase:

[10] In England it doesn't matter because ⟨ , ⟩ he can get help as he's uh the only *one* allowed to drive that car [S1A-009-224]

[11] Here too are the families of those who lost loved *ones* during the conflict [. . .] [S2A-020-70]

4.38
It

The pronoun *it* has four uses:

1. referring *it*
2. anticipatory *it*
3. cleft *it*
4. prop *it*

1. Referring *It*

Referring *it* is exemplified in **[1]**–**[3]**:

> **[1]** A: How long did you do *English* for
> B: Uh I did *it* for about half a term [S1A-006-1 f.]

> **[2]** And so Bob drafted *this questionnaire* and gave *it* to Dick [S1A-008-97]

> **[3]** I had *a really really good supper* last night *It* was lovely [S1A-011-24l f.]

It can also refer to the whole or part of a sentence or clause:

> **[4]** *I was very alert* yesterday *It*'s a bit unlike me [S1A-019-214 f.]

> **[5]** I hope you don't mind my *rubbing my hands* I think perhaps *it*'s a nasty gesture but I find they get cold [S1A-022-136 f.]

> **[6]** [. . .] I don't think *we can run A-REV on Apples* ⟨ , , ⟩ I think *it*'s unlikely [S1A-029-144 f.]

> **[7]** A: So *you're going tonight* then yeah
> B: I'm thinking about *it* uh [S1A-038-180 f.]

2. Anticipatory *It*

Anticipatory *it* is used when a clause (generally one that might have functioned as subject) is postponed to provide a more balanced sentence, a sentence where what precedes the verb is shorter than what follows it. Anticipatory *it* then serves in the position that might have been occupied by the clause. For example, anticipatory *it* is the subject in **[8]** and the extraposed clause (the clause taken out of its position and moved to the end) is *he's not going to be back here*:

> **[8]** *It*'s a shame *he's not going to be back here* [S1A-042-32]

As a less common alternative, the clause could have been the subject, though in this instance the omitted conjunction *that* would have to be restored.

> **[8a]** *That he's not going to be back here* is a shame.

Extraposition is normal with clausal subjects. But subject -*ing* clauses usually occur in the initial position. Here is an example of an -*ing* clause that has been extraposed:

> **[9]** So a lot of my friends were in one-parent families as well so *it* didn't seem particularly odd *not having a father* ⟨ , , ⟩ I think [S1A-076-67]

> **[9a]** *Not having a father* didn't seem particularly odd.

Here are some further examples of extraposed clauses:

> **[10]** *It*'s a funny thought isn't it *that I was embarrassed* [S1A-032-37]

[11] *It* is hardly probable *that anything can be proved*; *it* is even possible *that there is nothing to prove*; and unwarranted investigation might cause undeserved distress. [W2F-001-2]

[12] *It* was extraordinary *what you went through to to get the picture in those circumstances* [S1A-052-144]

[13] *It* is physically impossible *to force myself to work* sometimes [S1A-040-122]

[14] *It* would be a waste of time *for people watching this programme to think that this is a party political split across the board* [S1B-022-115]

[15] How difficult is *it* going to be *for her to find employment* [S1B-062-138]

If after a complex-transitive verb (one having both object and object predicative; cf. 3.19) the object clause is a *that*-clause, it is generally extraposed:

[16] And did he make *it* clear *that he wasn't putting in any money* [S1B-061-21]

Compare:

[16a] Did he make *his decision* clear?

To-infinitive object clauses are also generally extraposed. Here are other examples of extraposed object clauses:

[17] And will he take *it* from me and my own experience *that it's a very satisfactory way of employing oneself and serving the customer* [S1B-059-79]

[18] But I have such a thin skin I'm always terribly easily hurt and I find *it* very hard *to forgive* although I do ⟨ , , ⟩ eventually [S1A-031-103]

3. Cleft *It*

Cleft *it* serves as subject of a cleft sentence or cleft clause. The sentence is split to put the focus on some part of it. The cleft sentence is introduced by cleft *it* followed by a verb phrase whose main verb is a copular verb, generally *be*. The focused part comes next, followed by the rest of the sentence introduced by a relative item. Here are examples of cleft *it*:

[19] *It* is *the ability to do the job* that matters not where you come from or what you are [S1B-043-103]

[20] Now I ask you if you could explain why *it's not until twelfth of January* that you signed that application form [S1B-061-94]

[21] *It* uh looks like *Justin Channing* who's receiving treatment [S2A-003-52]

[22] And *it* was *then* that he felt a sharp pain [S2A-067-54]

[23] *It's this kind of routine work* where she says her concentration is most affected [S2B-011-71]

[24] *It* was *not nominal electoral mass but political contacts* which gave clout [S2B-025-27]

[25] *It's in the scenes when De Niro fighting against an on-rush of uncoordinated tics and twitches is beginning to relapse into the coma from which he'd been recently aroused* that he and Williams are particularly impressive [S2B-033-20]

The focused part is occasionally fronted for additional emphasis:

> **[26]** *Semione it* is who chips the ball in [S2A-010-162]

The relative item may be a zero relative (omitted relative *that*):

> **[27]** And *it*'s *these motions* we're designing for [S2A-025-21]

> **[28]** *It*'s *the young miner* I feel sorry for, especially one with a young family. [W2F-007-82]

Generally zero relative is not used when the focused part is the subject of the rest of the cleft sentence, but it is occasionally found in informal conversation:

> **[29]** *It*'s *his Mum* falls in love with him [S1A-006-125]

The focused part may be a clause:

> **[30]** *It* is *what you put in and what you achieve* which counts [S2B-035-4]

> **[31]** But *it* was *as we moved on to consider the crucial monetary issues* ⟨ , ⟩ *in the European context* ⟨ , ⟩ that I've come to feel increasing concern [S2B-050-13]

> **[32]** But *it*'s *when the happy little game strays into the field of advertising* that hackles are bound to rise. [W2E-006-52]

> **[33]** *It* wasn't *till I was perhaps twenty-five or thirty* that I read them and enjoyed them [S1A-013-216]

Standard English does not allow the focused part of a cleft sentence to be the subject predicative after copula *be* or to be a part of a verb phrase. Both these are allowed in non-standard dialects of Irish English:

> **[34]** *It*'s *lucky* she is.

> **[35]** It *must have been smoking* they were.

4. Prop *it*

Prop *it* (or empty *it*) is used to fill the place of a required function—generally the subject—but has little or no meaning. It is particularly frequent in expressions referring to weather and time:

> **[36]** Anyway if *it*'s really bad weather we'll just ⟨ , , ⟩ you know stay in [S1A-006-205]

> **[37]** *It*'s really hot in here [S1A-017-202]

> **[38]** One day we went up on the chair-lift and *it* was bright sunshine [S1A-021-227]

> **[39]** But unfortunately both Saturday and Sunday *it* was really foggy [S1A-036-149]

> **[40]** I think *it*'s going to rain [S1A-073-302]

> **[41]** *It*'s a bit late now [S1A-022-168]

> **[42]** *It*'s so near Christmas [. . .] [S1A-039-13]

> **[43]** *It*'s past midnight and what have I said? [W1B-001-74]

> **[44]** No idea what time *it* is! [W1B-008-2]

> **[45]** A: Sorry about this
> B: *It*'s alright [S1A-026-93]

[46] *It*'s just been all work and no play [S1A-040-228]

[47] I may well be tempted into the party that Helen was talking about depending how much work I have to do, you know how *it* goes [S1B-004-68]

Prop *it* also occurs in functions other than as subject, including some idiomatic expressions:

[48] Actually you probably wouldn't have enjoyed *it* here [S1A-010-199]

[49] I'm not really in favour of boys' schools taking on girls in the sixth form and that's *it* [S1A-012-198]

[50] Uh Rebecca can't make *it* tomorrow [S1A-099-78]

[51] And when I started again in the September I said now if nothing comes you've had *it* chum [S1B-026-60]

[52] The constraints on member governments would be purely political so in practice probably wouldn't prevent individual governments going *it* alone as they did in the Gulf [S2B-013-30]

[53] Yes we are creating a classless Britain and a first-class Britain one which can compete and where everyone can make *it* wherever they come from whatever their backgrounds [S2B-035-54]

[54] [. . .] his ambition is not to make money but to play the Casanova but hasn't the confidence to hit *it* off with the streetwise town women. [W1B-012-42]

[55] I'm taking *it* easy myself, at least while the summer weather lasts. [W1B-014-54]

4.39
Existential *there*

Existential *there* is to be distinguished from the spatial adverb *there*. The two can co-occur. In **[1]** the first *there* is existential and the second *there* is spatial:

[1] When I went through Romania ⟨ , , ⟩ *there* were guards *there* as well [S1A-014-26]

Existential *there* has some of the characteristics of a pronoun, as we will see later in this section.

Ordinarily, some of the information in a sentence (or clause) is known to the hearer or speaker, perhaps from the situation or linguistic context. The subject of the sentence or clause is usually known information. Existential *there* is used as a device for rearranging the sentence so as to present the subject (at least) as new information. The rearrangement involves postponing the subject and replacing it by existential *there*, which is followed by a verb phrase (generally with *be* as the main verb):

[2] *There* were *a lot of idiots* on the road [. . .] [S1A-019-138]

In **[2]** *there* is the grammatical subject and *a lot of idiots* is the notional subject. Without existential *there* the sentence would be:

[2a] *A lot of idiots* were on the road.

Since the notional subject is new information, it is commonly an indefinite noun phrase; that is to say, a noun phrase with an indefinite determiner (such as *a*, *some*, *any*) or no determiner, or an indefinite pronoun such as *someone*, *nobody*, *any*. But a definite noun phrase may occur if it is new information:

[3]   Uhm ⟨ , ⟩ there may be some funds that the department knows how to tap ⟨ , ⟩ *There* may be *the odd scholarship* [S1A-035-93 f.]

The existential sentence sometimes has only the notional subject following the verb, as in **[3]** above. In that case, only the existential form of the sentence is possible if the verb is *be*. Here are some further examples:

[4]   *There* were *hundreds of cabins* [S1A-021-62]

[5]   I don't think *there*'s *anything quite like Toblerone* [S1A-023-190]

[6]   Oh I think *there*'s *a lot of that* [S1A-031-115]

[7]   [. . .] *there* are *various places where you can do that* [S1A-035-34]

[8]   *There*'s *too much of me talking* [S1A-037-247]

[9]   *There*'s *no problem* [S1A-038-159]

[10]   *There*'s still *time* [S1A-079-64]

More usually, there are elements other than the notional subject in the existential sentence. They may precede or (more commonly) follow the notional subject:

[11]   [. . .] but within the beech and oak woods *there* are *different kinds* [S1A-036-200] ('Within the beech and oak woods are different kinds')

[12]   I thought *there* was *safety* in numbers [S1A-072-208] ('Safety was in numbers')

[13]   I'll leave the bastard and then he'll realise that *there*'s *something* wrong [S1A-080-148] ('Something is wrong')

The notional subject may be followed by an -*ing* participle and perhaps its complements. The participle would be the main verb in the corresponding non-existential sentence.

[14]   *There*'s *a road* going up the side [S1A-071-47] ('A road is going up the side')

[15]   Otherwise *there* would've been *two groups* sitting there waiting for me to lecture on Tuesday [S1A-082-44] ('Two groups would've been sitting there . . .')

[16]   *There* should be *quite a few people* coming tomorrow [S1A-099-296] ('Quite a few people should be coming tomorrow')

Another type of existential sentence has a noun phrase followed by a relative clause. As in the cleft sentence, the effect is to give greater prominence to the element preceding the relative clause:

[17]   Well *there* are *five* who've got forms with me so far [S1A-069-244]

[18]   *There* is *one thing* that truly disturbs me, and I speak as a Methodist clergyman. [891012-0145-7]

[19]   And *there* were *these weird organisms* that are well preserved [S1B-006-255]

In this construction, the noun phrase may have functions other than as notional subject:

[20] It's very flat and *there*'s *a lot of things* I'm ignoring [S1B-08-118] ('I'm ignoring a lot of things')

[21] And *there* are *weeks* when you can get struck down [. . .] [S1B-012-10]

[22] You notice that halfway down this trail *there*'s *a line* I've drawn [S1B-017-122]

In **[23]** there is a zero relative (omitted relative *that*). As with cleft sentences, the zero relative occurs in informal speech even though it is the subject of the relative clause (cf. 5.9):

[23] Uh ⟨ , ⟩ so *there* was *something* happened at that boundary which is of significance although we don't know what it is [S1B-006-264] ('Something that happened at that boundary . . .')

Existential *there* has some of the characteristics of pronouns. It can occur as the subject of its sentence or clause. This is evident in questions, where it is positioned after the operator (cf. 5.18):

[24] Is *there* anything else [S1B-017-158]

[25] Are *there* any particular events that you can remember about your father [S1A-075-131]

Similarly, like personal pronouns it acts as the subject of a tag question:

[26] There wouldn't be any point would *there* [S1A-029-182]

[27] There's no problem is *there* [S1B-013-21]

Like other grammatical subjects it often determines number concord, taking a singular verb even though the notional subject is plural. This usage is common in informal speech:

[28] [. . .] *there* was elements of it that were fun [S1A-076-125]

[29] No I mean *there*'s no seats left on that day [S1A-074-188]

[30] But honest to goodness *there*'s all these numbers that you can dial for all ⟨ , ⟩ all the different sexual pleasures that you want [S1A-027-162]

The alternative plural concord with a plural notional subject also occurs frequently:

[31] But it shouldn't be too difficult because *there* are always loads of jobs going [S1A-097-231]

4.40
Primary reflexive pronouns

Reflexives (*myself, yourself,* etc.) have two uses:

1. The primary reflexive is used in place of a personal pronoun to signal that it co-refers with another nominal in the same sentence or clause;

that is to say, they both refer to the same entity. Primary reflexives may be either obligatory or optional.

2. The emphatic reflexive is used in addition to another nominal to emphasize that nominal. The addition is always optional.

The primary reflexive usually co-refers with the subject. The reflexive may be the direct object **[1]**, the indirect object **[2]**, the subject predicative **[3]**, the object of a prepositional verb **[4]**, or the agent in a *by*-phrase **[5]**:

[1] U.S. trade negotiators argue that *countries with inadequate protections for intellectual-property rights* could be hurting *themselves* by discouraging their own scientists and authors and by deterring U.S. high-technology firms from investing or marketing their best products there. [891102-0173-7]

[2] The first chapter asks about your daydreams and then as an exercise *you* have to write *yourself* an obituary one which in your wildest dreams you would love to have. [W1B-003-6]

[3] One of the great motifs of moral thought in the last century ⟨ , ⟩ has been the crucial importance of private space the territory in which *we*'re simply free to be *ourselves* [S2B-029-126]

[4] *The word dissemination*, I decided, referred only to *itself*. [891102-0084-41]

[5] Takeover experts said they doubted *the financier* would make a bid by *himself*. [891102-0012-21]

The subject with which the reflexive co-refers may be implied from a host clause. This commonly occurs in subordinate non-finite clauses without a subject:

[6] After your first three weeks of sleep deprivation, you are scarcely in touch with reality; without psychiatric treatment, *you* may well be unable to fend for *yourself* ever again. [891102-0087-35]

[7] Following the acquisition of R.P. Scherer by a buy-out group led by Shearson Lehman Hutton earlier this year, *the maker of gelatin capsules* decided to divest *itself* of certain of its non-encapsulating businesses [891102-0168-2]

[8] *He* also charged that the utility lobby was attempting to all but buy votes with heavy campaign contributions to *himself* and his colleagues. [891102-0070-10]

[9] Starting in late November, *the Conservative government* intends to raise about $20 billion from divesting *itself* of most of Britain's massive water and electricity utilities. [891012-0055-3]

In **[10]** the subordinate clause is initial, so that the reflexive is cataphoric (cf. 7.9) since it precedes the pronoun (*she*) with which it co-refers:

[10] Believing *herself* to be by nature unbusiness-like—for her husband deals with all the household bills, investments and tax demands—*she* does her best to suggest efficiency by her appearance. [W2F-019-21]

The subject may be implied in a subordinate clause even when there is no co-referring noun phrase in a host clause:

[11] It is physically impossible to force *myself* to work sometimes [S1A-040-122]

[12] And will he take it from me and my own experience that it's a very satisfactory way of employing *oneself* and serving the customer [S1B-059-73]

[13] He and I share a belief that walking is not simply therapeutic for *oneself* but is a poetic activity that can cure the world of its ills. [890906-0016-23]

Similarly, the subject may be implied in subject-less independent sentences:

[14] Why not do it for *ourselves*?

It is implied regularly in second personal imperatives:

[15] Don't compare *yourself* with anyone else [S1A-042-139]

[16] So stir *yourselves* tonight. [W2E-003-074]

Less commonly, the reflexive may co-refer with a nominal other than the subject; for example, the direct object **[17]**–**[19]** and the subject predicative **[20]**–**[21]**:

[17] [. . .] you've neither judged or encouraged me but you have allowed *me* to be *myself* and make my choices. [W1B-005-18]

[18] "Learn what the white man has to teach *us*—then do it for *ourselves*," says Derrick Malloy, eight minutes older than his brother. [89725-0133-9]

[19] Will not someone out there save *him* from *himself*? [890814-0026-51]

[20] [. . .] they were very much in the shadows ⟨ , ⟩ and it was *him* ⟨ , ⟩ all by *himself* on this stage you know [S1A-045-4]

[21] It is *every man* for *himself*. [890929-0014-53]

When there is co-reference with a subject, the reflexive is required if it functions as an object (including prepositional object, cf. 5.36) or complement of the verb. Hence, the subject and the direct object refer to two different people in **[22]** but to the same person in **[23]**:

[22] *He* taught *him* to play the piano.

[23] *He* taught *himself* to play the piano.

Exceptionally the personal pronoun is used instead, to convey the impression of two aspects of a person—in **[24]** the giver and what is given:

[24] *You* have given me *you* and you have restored to me myself. [W1B-006-12]

The reflexive is also required in many instances in the complement of a preposition. These include instances where the prepositional phrase modifies a noun that denotes a picture, work of literature, etc.:

[25] The princess is drawing a *picture of herself* and it's going to be pinned on the palace door [S2A-059-82]

[26] Two Dallas schoolteachers sent him a *videotape of themselves* and told him, "If you do not like what you see, pass it along to your buddies." [890817-0011-55]

[27] You could commission *prints of yourself* [S1A-015-34]

[28] All the same, he gives an extremely good *account of himself* [. . .] [890927-0182-41]

The reflexive is also required in a prepositional phrase that is a part of an idiomatic expression [29]–[33]:

[29] Could the United States slide into a technical race against *itself* now there are no new generations of Soviet MIGs to mesmerise the Pentagon's planners [S2B-034-103]

[30] Do you really feel bad about *yourself*? [W1B-003-161]

[31] Schumacher likened the ideal business structure to a series of balloons freely floating *by themselves* with a hand at the centre lightly holding the strings to keep them all together. [W2B-013-65]

[32] Her father had commissioned it: that *in itself* was unusual. [W2F-003-27]

[33] The very witnesses to the death of God at Auschwitz sometimes, *despite themselves*, write at moments of Providence and faith. [890112-0098-35]

There are a number of reflexive verbs. These require a reflexive as direct object. Common reflexive verbs are *absent, avail, busy, content, pride*:

[34] Regarding Paternoster, the consortium [. . .] then sought to *avail itself* of the opportunity for intensive development by planning to build a million square feet of office space within the 4.3 acre site. [W2A-005-65]

[35] We like to *pride ourselves* on the care which we lavish on our children, so, why is child abuse not an issue of popular debate, other than around the times of extensive media coverage? [W2B-017-30]

Some verbs that may take reflexives as direct objects may omit them with little or no effect on the meaning. They include *adjust, behave, dress, hide, prepare, shave, undress, wash*:

[36] I shall try to *prepare myself* for you turning up on our shores six foot tall. [W1B-015-12]

[37] The seat belts automatically *adjust themselves* to your shoulder height [S2A-055-10]

Reflexives optionally replace personal pronouns after some prepositions:

[38] After the Last Supper Jesus wrapped a towel *around himself* poured water into a basin and washed the feet of his disciples [S2A-020-15]

[39] She has always dismissed chess as being too intellectual a game for someone *like herself*, but it is a chessplayer's mind which she is bringing to bear on these situations. [W2F-019-29]

[40] The German Generalissimo in London might be no more civilized than Attila himself, but he would soon feel the difference *between himself* and Attila. [891011-0109-16]

They also optionally replace first and second person pronouns in co-ordinated constructions. *Myself* is particularly common, since it is felt to be less assertive than *I* or *me*:

[41] And the dispute lay between both Indiana on one side of the Atlantic *and myself* on the other [S2A-042-95]

[42] When you have identified these people please ask either Mrs Robinson *or myself* to come over and have a short session with them (approximately 1 hour) to discuss their role and responsibilities. [W1B-017-103]

[43] Hong Kong had obviously been very carefully planned with Peter *and myself* in mind [W2B-004-96]

In this use the co-ordinate construction may be the subject of its clause:

[44] You have there the front and the back ⟨ , , ⟩ of a letter from North Sakara on which Professor Smith and *myself* are working [S2A-048-62]

The two parts of the reflexives can be separated by an intervening word, but then the possessive pronoun is used in the first part:

[45] He doesn't sound *his* normal *self*. [W2B-001-108]

The separation may also occur without any intervening word:

[46] He is most satisfying on the famous dead, whom he meets halfway—something he does not always do with his living subjects—revealing more of *his self*. [890906-0016-46]

In headlines and other abbreviated styles of language, *self* alone may be used as the reflexive:

[47] Enfield Corp. President Improperly Put *Self* on Board, Judge Rules [890927-0145-5]

4.41 Emphatic reflexive pronouns

Emphatic reflexives function as a kind of appositive (cf. 5.11) to a noun phrase, which they emphasize. If that noun phrase is the subject, the reflexive may either immediately follow the subject **[1]** or occur at various later positions in the clause **[2]–[5]**:

[1] *Mr. McGovern himself* had said repeatedly that he intended to stay on until he reached the conventional retirement age of 65, "unless I get fired." [891102-0083-33]

[2] The House and Senate are divided over whether the United Nations Population Fund will receive any portion of these appropriations, but *the size of the increase* is *itself* significant. [891102-0091-10]

[3] They also provided videotapes, which *they* selected *themselves*, of the high points of her interrogation. [891012-0105-24]

[4] Astrophysicist John N. Bahcall, who thinks a lot about how the sun shines (the "solar neutrino problem"), says his kids are "deeply opposed" to the deer hunt, but *he* has no opinion *himself*. [891012-0044-33]

[5] *The new structures* wouldn't *themselves* conceal policy differences [S2B-013-22]

As with the primary reflexives (cf. 4.40), the subject of a non-finite clause may be implied in a host clause **[6]–[7]** or from the context as a whole **[8]**:

[6] To survive a squeeze *himself*, *Mr Spitalnick* has switched most of his operation into the private-label business, making garments that carry a store's brand. [891012-0104-12]

[7] And the Greeks looked down on *the Romans* as being upstart barbarians *themselves* [S2A-022-51]

[8] He said to us it's strange to get used to having to make the decisions *yourselves* [S2B-047-41]

If the reflexive is appositive to a noun phrase other than the subject, it must follow that phrase immediately:

[9] In 1989, as often as not, the principal fights in the major campaigns are prompted by *the ads themselves.* [891102-0151-8]

[10] [. . .] whether the relevant indemnity should be signed or countersigned by the bank rather than by the charterers *themselves* without any countersignature. [S2A-065-23]

[11] It is taken for granted that any letter addressed only to either Will or to *Cathy herself* will be passed across the breakfast table as soon as it is read [. . .] [S2A-065-23]

4.42
Reciprocal pronouns

The reciprocal pronouns are *each other* and the less frequent *one another* and their respective genitives, *each other's* and *one another's*. Like the primary reflexives (cf. 4.40), the reciprocals co-refer with a noun phrase; but unlike the primary reflexives, they co-refer only with noun phrases that are plural in form or meaning:

[1] Oh I suppose it's a question *lots of people* ask *each other* [S1A-050-26]

[2] [. . .] *Chris and I* ⟨ , ⟩ suited *each other* [S1A-054-3]

[3] It's caused by *two germs* that live together ⟨ , ⟩ and scratch *each other's* back [S1A-087-155]

[4] [. . .] we *none of us* poach *each other's* business [S1A-027-62]

[5] Anyhow *you and Harriet* know *one another* [. . .] [S1A-094-75]

[6] Nell's a very prim little thing, *they*'ll be good for *one another.* [W2F-007-138]

As with the primary reflexives, the reciprocals usually co-refer with the subject, but they may co-refer with noun phrases in other functions, such as direct object:

[7] Now you should be able to stack *all of these columns* on top of *each other* [S2A-046-10]

[8] In programming, getting the sound you want typically involves constantly moving to and fro between different parameters, fine-tuning *them* against *one another.* [W2B-031-9]

In **[9]** the noun phrase *the banks* is the complement of a preposition and the reciprocal pronoun is within the postmodifier (*to each other*) of that phrase:

[9] Second, there is a reduced risk because the gross exposure of *the banks* to *each other* has been cut. [W2C-016-28]

As with the primary reflexives, the co-referring subject *you* is implied in subject-less imperatives **[10]** and may be implied from a host clause **[11]**–**[12]**:

[10] Love *one another* [S2A-020-63]

[11] And then the prophet comes in and says well even if *we* all have one father that's no excuse for betraying *each other* and in particular for men to betray their wives and to take foreign wives [S2A-036-58]

[12] On Wall Street *men and women* walk with great purpose, noticing *one another* only when they jostle for cabs. [891102-0153-12]

Constructions with *each other* correspond to constructions in which the two parts of the pronoun are separated into *each . . . other*. The separation places greater emphasis on the reciprocity:

[13] They will *each* know when to involve *the other* in responding to the task in hand. [W1B-029-60]

[14] Fortunately, this doesn't lead to *each* program looking like every *other* [. . .] [W2B-036-37]

The corresponding constructions with the reciprocals are:

[13a] They will know when to involve *each other* in responding to the task in hand.

[14a] Fortunately, this doesn't lead to the programs looking like *each other*.

4.43
Wh-pronouns and determiners

The *wh*-pronouns and determiners are so called because they are spelled with an initial *wh*, the exceptions being *how* and its compounds. They fall into five sets according to the type of sentence or clause in which they occur:

A. interrogative
B. exclamative
C. relative
D. nominal relative
E. *wh*-conditional

Some of them are used both as pronouns and as determiners. The *wh*-words or phrases with the *wh*-word are initial in their sentence or clause. Hence, if they are not the subject, they are generally fronted:

They gave me *an expensive gift* for my birthday.

What an expensive gift they gave me for my birthday.

For *wh*-adverbs, see 4.26.

A. **Interrogative**

Interrogative *wh*-pronouns and *wh*-determiners introduce *wh*-questions. They represent a piece of missing information that the speaker wants the hearer to supply. The pronoun is illustrated in **[1]** and the determiner in **[2]**:

> **[1]**   A: *Who*'s that then ⟨ , , ⟩
> B. Well she's called Lynn [S1A-037-69]

> **[2]**   A: *whose* project is it
> B: Uhm ⟨ , , ⟩ I'm not sure [S1A-066-90]

Citations **[3]** and **[4]** illustrate their uses in subordinate clauses:

> **[3]**   A: I want to ask you *what* you think about the role of the father today
> ⟨ , , ⟩
> B: Thank you very much [S1A-072-28 f.]

> **[4]**   A: Do you know *what* word is used to mean that something is life-giving
> or supportive in its function
> B: Growth factor [S1B-009-133 f.]

There are five interrogative pronouns:

who   whom   whose   which   what

Three of these are also determiners:

which   what   whose

Who and *whom* differ in case: *who* is subjective and *whom* is objective (cf. 4.35). But in practice *who* is commonly also used for object functions **[5]**–**[6]** except in formal style, where it is replaced by *whom* **[7]**:

> **[5]**   *Who* didn't you like [S1A-037-53]

> **[6]**   Anyway so ⟨ , , ⟩ *who* else can we nominate [S1B-079-61]

> **[7]**   When was it last serviced, by *whom*, and what service agreements or
> guarantees exist? [W2D-012-56]

There are some gender contrasts between personal (masculine or feminine) and non-personal (cf. 4.35). *Who* and *whom* are only personal. Both as pronoun **[8]** and as determiner **[9]**, *whose* also has only personal reference:

> **[8]**   *Whose* is that book?

> **[9]**   *Whose* standards are you ⟨ , , ⟩ invoking [S1A-062-58]

Which, on the other hand, can be personal or non-personal both as pronoun **[10]**–**[11]** and as determiner **[12]**–**[13]**:

> **[10]**   I mean *which* is better to do this and clean clean the wax out of your ears
> or to go round with wax in your ears [S1A-080-61]

> **[11]**   *Which* of your friends are you closest to?

> **[12]**   "In a credit crunch," Citicorp Chairman John S. Reed warns, "financial
> institutions would be faced with a choice: *Which* customers do you take
> care of? [. . .]" [891012-0081-37]

> **[13]**   *Which* car did you take [S1A-009-210]

The gender of *what* varies according to its function. As a pronoun, *what* is only non-personal:

> **[14]** *What* were the first symptoms [S1A-040-278]
>
> **[15]** *What* are other people doing [S1A-014-242]

As a determiner, *what* can introduce personal **[16]** as well as non-personal noun phrases **[17]**–**[18]**:

> **[16]** *What* politicians have you met?
>
> **[17]** By *what* right do we impose our values on the residents of Colombia? [890929-0138-24]
>
> **[18]** Why *what* size feet have you got [S1A-017-288]

The speaker uses *which* to indicate an assumption that the hearer has a restricted set from which to make a response. In using *what*, the speaker assumes an open-ended set.

The interrogative pronouns may be postmodified by *else* or *otherwise* (*who else*, *what otherwise*) and by *ever* (*who ever*, *what ever*) and various intensifying phrases (*who the hell*, *what the devil*).

B. **Exclamative**

What is used as an exclamative determiner. It may precede the indefinite article:

> **[19]** And he's just been acquired by the slavers and they are washing him in ⟨ , ⟩ in a stream and they're finding out *what* a very beautiful young man he is [S2A-059-58]
>
> **[20]** [. . .] if it were me I would rather spend the money on something else given *what* a cramped flat we have. [W1B-009-97]
>
> **[21]** *What* a mess she was in, *what* a labyrinth of lies and half-truths was closing around her, her own and those of a generation gone. [W2F-003-96]

If the noun is non-count or plural, *what* is the only determiner:

> **[22]** *What* nonsense I'm writing.
>
> **[23]** *What* strong words you use. [W1B-003-160]

The exclamative noun phrase is often used alone:

> **[24]** *What* a ridiculous letter. [W1B-010-106]
>
> **[25]** *What* an appropriate introduction to San Francisco! [W1B-012-15]
>
> **[26]** Oh *what* a nightmare [S1A-038-247]
>
> **[27]** *What* fun [S1A-069-327]

Exclamative *what* has intensifying force similar to that of intensifying *such* (cf. 4.45). But, unlike *such*-phrases, *what*-phrases are always initial in their clause, and they can introduce subordinate clauses, as in citations **[19]** and **[20]** above.

C. **Relative**

Relative pronouns and determiners are used in the construction of relative clauses, which postmodify nouns (cf. 5.9). They normally come at the beginning of relative clauses:

[28] Oh my God I went to have dinner with this girl called Kate *who*'s on my
course [S1A-038-20]

But if the relative item is a *wh*-pronoun and it is the complement of a
preposition, the preposition may precede the pronoun:

[29] Again I'm not so much concerned with meaning but the ways *in which* the
satire is ⟨ , ⟩ achieved [S1B-014-5]

Similarly, a preposition may precede a noun phrase that has the relative
determiner:

[30] Outside the Church's boundaries lay the truly independent congregations,
of whose political importance, small numbers and doctrinal divisions
something has already been said. [W2A-006-74]

There are three *wh*-relative pronouns:

who, whom, which

There are two *wh*-relative determiners:

whose, which

In addition, relative clauses may be introduced by the relative pronoun *that*,
which is sometimes omitted. When *that* is omitted, the relative is said to be the
zero relative pronoun.

Like the interrogative pronouns, *who* and *whom* differ in case: *who* is
subjective and *whom* is objective. As with the interrogative pronouns, *who* is
commonly also used for object functions **[31]–[32]** except in formal style,
where it is replaced by *whom* **[33]–[34]**:

[31] [. . .] there's a group called Coimbre Flamenco *who* I saw at Sadler's
Wells [S1A-044-353]

[32] [. . .] I wouldn't want to live with someone *who* I didn't have any sex life
with [S1A-050-84]

[33] Aeneas suffers perpetual isolation as he wanders from place to place,
having lost those *whom* he loved. [W1A-010-16]

[34] Now ⟨ , ⟩ as for actually ⟨ , ⟩ how ⟨ , , ⟩ or to *whom* you send the messages
⟨ , ⟩ there's a standard convention ⟨ , ⟩ used ⟨ , ⟩ for addresses for e-mail
[S2A-028-76]

As with the interrogative pronouns, there are some gender contrasts. *Who*
and *whom* are personal, as illustrated in **[31]–[34]**. *Which* is non-personal
[35]–[36]:

[35] They can't fit me in for a week so I'm going to do it for a day *which* is
useless really but ⟨ , ⟩ I just heard today [S1A-099-57]

[36] All these are the dates of the context in *which* the artefact was found not
the date that they think the artefact belongs to [S1B-017-46]

The older use of the pronoun *which* for personal reference ('Our Father *which*
art in Heaven') is preserved in archaic forms of religious language.

That and the zero relative pronoun (symbolized by '[Ø]') are used for both
personal and non-personal reference:

[37] Maybe they are people *that* have just never thought about it [S1A-037-6]

[38] Your father actually is up to just about every trick *that*'s in the book [. . .] [S1A-065-135]

[39] The people [Ø] we were staying with they ⟨ , , ⟩ uh cooked us a traditional Normandy dinner [S1A-009-118]

[40] What's happened to the door [Ø] we had out there [S1A-007-38]

Neither *that* nor the zero relative may be the complement of a preceding preposition. Citation **[36]** illustrates this difference between them and the *wh*-relatives. In **[36]** *which* is the complement of the preceding preposition in *the context in which . . .*; but the preposition *to* is stranded at the end of the relative clause introduced by *that*: *the date that they think the artefact belongs to*. The zero relative pronoun does not function as the subject of the relative clause.

The determiner *whose* is used for personal and non-personal reference:

[41] It is for example clear ⟨ , ⟩ that pharaonic Egyptian society did not contain people *whose* status was so elevated that they felt writing to be beneath them [S2A-048-31]

[42] So in the case of the sensory system which deals with the sensation from the whole body the primary neuron the central neuron is the neuron that aligns itself in the dorsary ganglia and *whose* axons make up peripheral nerves and dorsal roots [S1B-015-28]

The determiner *which* is normally used for non-personal reference:

[43] It may be that the potential obstacles are not insurmountable, in *which* case I look forward to hearing from you to discuss things further. [W1B-018-117]

Only the *wh*-relatives are normally used in non-restrictive relative clauses, including sentential relative clauses (cf. 5.9 f.):

[44] They also provided videotapes, *which* they selected themselves, of the high points of her interrogation. [891012-0105-24]

[45] There are charges that these culminated in the kidnapping and execution of former Premier Aldo Moro, *whose* insistence on defying an American veto on admitting Communists into the Cabinet infuriated Washington. [W2C-010-23]

Non-standard dialects often use *what* or *as* as relative pronouns for personal or non-personal reference:

That's the woman *what* told me.

Here's the car *as* I bought yesterday.

In some dialects, genitive *what's* is sometimes used as the determiner:

They're the people *what's* children are causing all the noise.

The relative pronoun is commonly omitted in non-standard dialects when it is subject of the relative clause:

I'm taking the bus [Ø] goes to Manchester.

Resumptive pronouns are sometimes introduced, echoing the relative pronoun:

They're making a birthday party for their youngest, *which* I'm invited to *it*.

D. **Nominal relative**

Nominal relatives introduce nominal relative clauses (cf. 6.12), which function like noun phrases as subject, direct object, etc.

> **[46]** Excuse me I've got to do *what I did last time* [S1A-001-17] ('. . . the thing that I did last time')

There are twelve nominal relative pronouns:

who	*which*
whom	*whichever*
whoever	*whichsoever*
whomever	*what*
whosoever	*whatever*
whomsoever	*whatsoever*

Which and *what* and their compounds can also be determiners. The difference between the two sets parallels that for the interrogative determiners *which* and *what*. Those ending in *-soever* are archaic, except for *whatsoever*.

Here are some further examples of the nominal relative pronouns:

> **[47]** You saw *what* happened [S1A-008-48]

> **[48]** No ⟨ , , ⟩ but it pays *what* I would call a part-time wage [S1A-011-17]

> **[49]** And ⟨ , ⟩ I mean ⟨ , , ⟩ he'll have to think about *who* will look after Nell when she gets home from school [S1A-031-44]

> **[50]** I can't remember *who* he was talking to [. . .] [S1B-016-140]

> **[51]** I was just wondering if it was worth complaining to *whoever* was in charge or not bothering [S1A-69-178]

> **[52]** Because she's still wondering ⟨ , ⟩ why you haven't acknowledged *whatever* it was she last sent you [S1A-095-289]

> **[53]** I want to see *what* happens next [S1B-026-207]

Here, as elsewhere, the *who* pronouns (*who, whoever, whosoever*) are subjective and the *whom* pronouns are objective, but the *who* pronouns are generally used for object functions except in formal contexts.

Here are examples of nominal relative determiners:

> **[54]** He has chosen from the scribe's pattern books *what* scenes he wishes in his tomb [S2A-052-78]

> **[55]** But it's really quite arbitrary *which* by-elections they are [S1B-029-117]

> **[56]** So you will only see a very little of *whatever* fabric you choose at the sides [S1A-086-21]

> **[57]** The reason by-elections are given this great significance is that *whichever* by-elections occur before a general election are always seen as having been the pointers [S1B-029-115]

Who, *whom*, and *what* may also be used in nominal relative *to*-infinitive clauses:

> **[58]** It outlines some of the opportunities that are available at our main branches and *who* to contact for more information [S2B-044-81]

[59] They were called media response teams which I thought was an interesting new development in which journalists were really carried around and shown *what* to report and told *what* to report effectively [S1B-031-110]

E. *Wh*-conditional

Wh-conditional pronouns and determiners are compounds ending in -*ever*. They introduce *wh*-conditional clauses (cf. 6.14), which denote a range of possible choices. The clauses function not as nominal clauses but as adverbial clauses:

[60] *Whatever* you've been doing you've been doing the right thing [S1A-087-42]

There are six *wh*-conditional pronouns. *Whosoever* and *whomsoever* are archaic. *Whatever* and *whichever* are also used as determiners; the difference between them parallels that for the interrogative and nominal relative determiners *what* and *which*. As elsewhere, the *who* pronouns (*whoever* and *whosoever*) are subjective and the *whom* pronouns are objective, but the *who* pronouns are used for objective functions except in formal contexts.

Here are some further examples of the pronouns:

[61] *Whoever* you are I'm not going to bother wasting my time [S1B-026-61]

[62] I used to set so much a day either so many hours or so many words *whichever* came first [S1B-048-55]

[63] *Whatever* people say I've noticed they are distinctly different [S1A-094-179]

[64] Piracy and robbery and fraud could occur between individuals at any time *whatever* treaties said [S2B-043-57]

Here are examples of the determiners:

[65] *Whatever* problem comes up you always have this issue in experimental psychology of how we test it [S1B-016-29]

[66] You will be surprised how much knowing you are using the best quality bait will do for your confidence and success, *whichever* species you are after. [W2D-017-35]

The pronouns can be used in verbless clauses:

[67] *Whatever* the reason, the result has been only too predictable. [W2E-009-36]

They can also be used alone to indicate indeterminate additions or alternatives:

[68] I couldn't say well I'm personnel manager here or I'm this or that or *whatever* [S1A-060-161]

[69] And she knew an ex-professor because she did some M.Sc. in shipping trade and finance *whatever* and she's saying she's going to get no problem ah [S1A-038-25]

[70] They will then be passed on to another company that will make them into some sort of product and finally go to an end customer ⟨ , ⟩ something like NASA or *whoever* [S2A-029-57]

Whatsoever can function as an intensifier:

[71] The referee had no doubts *whatsoever* [S2A-014-259]

4.44
Indefinite pronouns and determiners

The indefinite pronouns and determiners are so called because they have a general reference. Many items function both as pronouns and determiners. Compounds in *-one*, *-body* or *-thing* function only as pronouns, and so does *none*. *No* is only a determiner.

The indefinites fall into two sets. The primary set consists of four interrelated subsets:

> assertive
> non-assertive
> negative
> universal

The second set consists of the quantifiers (or quantifying indefinites).

Table 4.44.1 Primary indefinite pronouns and determiners

Assertive		Non-assertive		Negative		Universal	
pronoun	determiner	pronoun	determiner	pronoun	determiner	pronoun	determiner
some	some	any	any	none	no	all	all
someone		anyone		no one		everyone	
somebody		anybody		nobody		everybody	
something		anything		nothing		everything	
		either	either	neither	neither	both	both
						each	each
							every

Table 4.44.1 displays the four subsets of the primary indefinites. All the compounds in *-one* and *-body* have genitives; for example: *someone's, anybody's, no one's*.

The compounds in *-one* and *-body* have personal reference, the compounds in *-thing* have non-personal reference. All the others (including *none*) can have either personal or non-personal reference. The primary indefinites vary in countability and number. For example, *some, any, none, no,* and *all* can be used as non-count as well as count; *some wine, any money, none (of the information), no butter, all (of the evidence)*. Some primary indefinites are count only: they may be singular (e.g. *everyone*), plural (e.g. *both*), or dual (*either, neither, both*).

The non-assertives have a negative force, and they tend to occur in non-assertive contexts, particularly in negative, interrogative, and conditional clauses. The question in **[1]** indicates that the speaker expects a negative answer:

> **[1]**   No uhm were you using *any* form of contraception [S1A-089-156]

Here are further examples of non-assertives:

> **[2]**   I said I don't want to do *any* more essays [S1A-090-150]

[3] Uh ⟨ , ⟩ I might come in on Tuesday depending if I've got *anything* to do [S1A-008-160]

[4] *Anybody* else like a piece of *anything* that they can see on here that I haven't given them [S1A-012-48]

[5] But uh hardbacks I wouldn't lend to *anyone* [S1A-013-85]

[6] Did you see *either* of those two gentlemen on *any* occasion in 1987 [S1B-065-34]

The non-assertives can also be used emphatically (e.g. 'any at all', 'anybody no matter who') outside non-assertive contexts:

[7] This is always a question in psychology for *any* area [S1B-016-28]

[8] And so it's ⟨ , ⟩ totally accessible ⟨ , ⟩ for *anybody* [S1A-003-47]

[9] The cat will attack *anyone* [. . .] [S1A-019-152]

The negative force is in the implied contrast. For **[9]** the meaning conveyed is that the cat will attack not just certain people. Similarly, in **[10]** the implication is that nobody has more fault than the speaker:

[10] It's my fault as much as *anybody* else's more than *anybody* else's [S1A-026-244]

The assertives have a positive force. This is most obvious in questions. In **[11]** *some* indicates an expected positive response:

[11] Dad will you have *some* more juice [S1A-022-233]

Here are some further examples of assertives:

[12] Listen can't we do this at *some* other time [S1A-038-102]

[13] Oh well I've never been *something* like that [S1A-014-148]

[14] Oh please eat *something* [S1A-023-120]

[15] Oh that was *someone* else [S1A-032-185]

[16] So I think from today's session you've realised I hope that you shouldn't start *somebody* on life-long anti-hypertensive therapy based upon one single blood pressure measurement [S1B-004-267]

Here are examples of negative indefinites:

[17] There have been six federal presidents since the birth of the federal state and *none* has been as popular as the present president [S2B-021-93]

[18] We all know in our own lives what changes the last ten years have brought but *none* of us knows the picture overall and that's what the census supplies [S2B-044-18]

[19] There are many origami yachts, boats and ships, but *none* are as simple or as full of movement as this wonderful design by Japan's First Lady of origami, Mrs Toshie Takahoma. [W2D-019-64]

[20] What worries me about regional theatres at the moment is that almost *none* of them have permanent companies [S1B-050-55]

[21] *Nobody* ever makes it like she used to make it [S1A-057-131]

[22] At the same time *neither* party can afford to ignore the two main messages from the electorate [S2B-006-21]

> **[23]** *Neither* of these two types of new religious movements is likely to permit much in the way of 'internal pluralism'. [W2A-012-29]

It has been argued that *none* is singular because of its etymology. In practice, it is treated as both singular **[17]**–**[18]** and plural **[19]**–**[20]**.

Here are examples of universal indefinites:

> **[24]** He denied *all* knowledge of it [S1A-014-4]

> **[25]** And she said *all* I want is a vase [S1A-019-81]

> **[26]** The ocean currents carrying warm water could reach *both* polar regions entirely unobstructed. [W2B-025-37]

> **[27]** So *each* party has its own different rules for election of its leader [S1B-011-95]

> **[28]** Environment is *everything* that happens to you which you sense happening to you as you grow up through life [S1B-016-95]

> **[29]** And the imposition of calendar age on *everybody* ⟨ , ⟩ by social life and by bureaucracy is something which I think we're right strongly to resist [S2A-038-39]

Finally, we come to the quantifiers, some of which are compounds. The primary quantifiers can function either as pronouns or as determiners:

1. *many, more, most, a few, fewer, fewest, several, enough*
2. *much, more, most, a little, less, least, enough*
3. *few, little*

Subset (1) quantifiers are count, and subset (2) quantifiers are non-count. However, *less* is often treated also as count ('*less* people'). Subset (3) quantifiers are negative; *few* is count and *little* is non-count.

Here are examples of the quantifiers in their three sets—**[30]**–**[33]**, **[34]**–**[35]**, and **[36]**–**[37]**:

> **[30]** And *many* of these earthquakes are caused by a rupture along a single fault [. . .] [S2A-025-51]

> **[31]** So we switched on and off uh *several* times which is uh the best way of coping with temperamental printers [S1A-024-22]

> **[32]** And I've got so *many* events to go to I mean I know that sounds a bit odd but I mean I've got *a few* [S1A-039-285]

> **[33]** This is a false belief you've been having for *a good few* years now and I think it's time ⟨ , ⟩ that you got rid of this [S1A-069-52]

> **[34]** You may have *a little* trouble getting in [S1A-027-90]

> **[35]** And such wilderness as we do have is actually wearing out because we have so *much* access [S1B-037-66]

> **[36]** There was *little* time for research and there were *few* research students [S2A-041-14]

> **[37]** There are very *few* clubs now which're exclusively male [S1B-021-46]

In addition, there are a number of compound quantifiers used only as pronouns; for example: *a bit, a lot, a couple*. Like the primary quantifiers, they can combine with a following *of*-phrase to denote quantity.

Indefinite pronouns may be postmodified mainly by relative clauses **[38]**, and prepositional phrases **[39]**:

[38] And *anybody* who thinks that there is great glory in war as such uh is off his head [S1B-031-31]

[39] Michele on Sunday was sort of pronouncing *some* of the Latin names [S1A-036-222]

The compounds in *-body*, *-one*, and *-thing* can also be postmodified by reduced relative clauses:

[40] Well Karen reckons that she's kind of jealous of Karen and Ian because she's got *nothing* out there apart from Salvatore [S1A-036-37]

[41] [. . .] the parent turns out to be *somebody* quite murderous [S1B-030-101]

[42] I can never think of *anything* to say when I'm being being under stress [S1A-038-46]

Some of the primary quantifiers can be premodified by intensifiers, such as *very* and *so*.

4.45
Demonstratives

There are four primary demonstratives:

this   that   these   those

They can function either as pronouns **[1]** or as determiners **[2]**:

[1] Oh you have to pay for *these* [S1A-030-49]

[2] Do you have one of *those* houses with a view [S1A-031-18]

The primary demonstratives present two types of contrast. The first is a contrast in number: *this* and *that* are singular, *these* and *those* are plural. The second is a contrast in proximity: *this* and *these* indicate relative nearness, *that* and *those* indicate relative remoteness. The proximity may be in space **[3]–[4]** or in time **[5]–[6]**:

[3] But in the presence of a scattering material the light has travelled a very convoluted path perhaps three or four times the distance between *this* side of the bottle and *that* side [S2A-053-91]

[4] *This* paper builds on *that* study to propose a mapping to allow Mascot 3 to be used with Occam. [W2A-038-6]

[5] Lewis with a kind of half smile playing around his lips ⟨ , , ⟩ and just dropping off his work rate a bit in *this* second round after *that* fast start to it [S2A-009-82]

[6] They would set out what *these* policy areas would be and then the foreign ministers of the twelve would implement *those* policies on the basis of majority voting [S2B-013-26]

This is also used in informal speech as an indefinite determiner, roughly corresponding to *a* or *some*:

> **[7]** And there'd be *this* guy that always used to snore with his mouth wide open in the tree and they the others used to pop acorns in through his mouth [S1A-046-325]

Similarly, *these* may be indefinite, introducing new information rather than referring to something in the situational or linguistic context:

> **[8]** There's all *these* horror stories about it happening but I've never actually heard of it 〈 , 〉 actually happened to anybody [S1A-100-208]

Such may have a demonstrative sense ('like that') as a pronoun **[9]** or (more frequently) as a determiner **[10]–[11]**:

> **[9]** [. . .] I'd like to do it every day 〈 , , 〉 but you know *such* is life [S1A-003-101]
>
> **[10]** Do I understand you to be saying that in *such* an accident uh a passenger would be thrown uh first of all forwards and then backwards [S1B-068-50]
>
> **[11]** He is entitled to *such* payments subject only to the limited category of cross-claims which the law permits to be raised as defences by way of set-off in *such* circumstances [S2A-065-33]

In **[10]** the determiner *such* precedes the indefinite article.

Some non-standard dialects have a three-term system for the demonstratives. Distance further off than *that/those* is indicated by *yon* and *thon*, among several variants.

Common non-standard alternatives to *those* as determiner are *they* and particularly *them*:

> **[12]** What was Moses doing going off in *them* wild jeans [S1A-040-9]

There are also non-standard compounds in which *here* is added to *this/these* ('*this here* house') and *there* to *that/those* ('*that there* tree') and their variants (e.g. '*them there* politicians').

The demonstratives may be preceded by determiners:

> **[13]** I don't know what *all this* is about [S1A-024-18]
>
> **[14]** Oh well let me take *both those* points uh at once [S1B-043-11]
>
> **[15]** They must not lay the paper upon which they are writing on *any such* book, etc, open or closed. [W2D-006-38]

The demonstrative pronouns may also be postmodified, particularly *that* and *those*:

> **[16]** Conditions within the sands of the embryo dunes are similar to *those at the top of the intertidal zone.* [W2A-022-68]
>
> **[17]** But to *those who knew the river in its heyday* it's dead [S2B-022-6]
>
> **[18]** Is this an indication that the social structure within the church mirrored *that in society*? [W1A-002-25]
>
> **[19]** Perhaps the most promising view is *that which suggests that amnesia is the result of damage to a specific systemic component of episodic memory.* [W1A-004-91]

The singular demonstrative pronouns generally have only non-personal reference. The exceptions are when they are subject and the speaker is providing or seeking identification:

[20] [. . .] *this* is my daughter Felicity [S1A-010-214]

[21] Is *that* Jane Warren [S1B-078-90]

Numerals

4.46
Numerals

There are three types of numerals:

A. cardinal
B. ordinal
C. fraction

Numerals constitute a closed system in that they comprise a restricted set of items, but there is no limit on the combination of these items. They may function as pronouns or determiners. They may be written out as words or as digits.

A. Cardinals

Cardinals (or cardinal numerals) refer to quantity. They include *zero* and its synonyms: *nought* or *naught*, *cipher* or *cypher*, and the terms used in various games—*nil*, *nothing*, *love*, and (in American English) *zip*. They also include *dozen* and *score*.

Here are examples of cardinals as pronouns **[1]**–**[3]** and as determiners **[4]**–**[6]**:

[1] She wakes me up at *six* every morning [S1A-019-190]

[2] That was a mistake by a factor of *ten* [S1A-024-28]

[3] Uhm ⟨ , ⟩ the reason for doing that is the *five* of us spread out over a little distance in the wood and we each took a patch [S1A-036-184]

[4] Stay in and watch *two* videos [S1A-006-208]

[5] Oh we had a long discussion about it on *one* occasion [S1A-023-73]

[6] Well the book's about *two hundred and fifty* pages long [. . .] [S1A-008-7]

Cardinal pronouns can be plural:

[7] It does affect *millions* of people [S1B-022-15]

[8] He took me to what he called a place round the corner, a kind of club where youngish men, all civilians, sat in *twos* and *threes* at little tables with drinks in front of them, talking in low voices. [W2F-014-49]

> **[9]** Further north I came across *dozens* of Iraqi soldiers wandering slowly towards their border [S2B-004-85]

The plural may indicate a range:

> **[10]** He was in his late *forties* I would say [S1B-067-59]
>
> **[11]** They are wishing him back to the form that he showed throughout the *nineteen-eighties* [S2A-007-70]
>
> **[12]** In the *1990s*, who knows what may happen? [W2B-037-129]

A range is also indicated by numerals that are hyphenated or linked by slashes:

> **[13]** Similar situations apply in India, a country in the World Bank's lower middle-income group of *35–40* countries. [W1A-014-21]
>
> **[14]** This is a mixed age group party rather than the planned *17–35* but will hopefully still be a much needed enjoyable relaxing break. [W1B-006-128]
>
> **[15]** Sunday work is *2pm–6pm* but is paid as a full day. [W1B-016-80]
>
> **[16]** At some time in the near future we will have to decide as to whether to allocate the pension payments to *1991/92* or relate them back to *1990/91*. [W1B-023-62]

Cardinals can be premodified by intensifiers:

> **[17]** I had it in that garage for *nearly thirty* years [S1A-007-78]
>
> **[18]** But I mean my only recollection of it is sleeping in a wood for *about four or five* hours [S1A-014-53]
>
> **[19]** Most people's vocabulary is *over fifteen thousand* words [. . .] [S1B-003-33]
>
> **[20]** They arrived *some two* minutes ago [. . .] [S2A-020-6]
>
> **[21]** If a satellite is placed in orbit *around 41,000* km away and its motion is parallel to that of the Earth's rotation, its velocity matches that of the Earth and it remains above a fixed point on the surface. [W2A-037-35]
>
> **[22]** For example, on average Cambridge has something like a dozen days a year when the temperature will reach 25 °C (77 °F), whereas Lerwick in the Shetland Isles can sometimes go *a full twelve* months without registering as high as 18 °C (64 °F). [W2B-026-26]
>
> **[23]** It's *a good two* weeks' time [S1A-040-222]

Approximation is also indicated by the postmodifying *odd* and by *or so*:

> **[24]** He's *forty odd* I would have thought [S1A-061-52]
>
> **[25]** And of those *forty or so* jobs you've applied for have they mainly been in response to vacancies that you've seen advertised [S1A-034-197]
>
> **[26]** You've been in high office now only *three years or so* [S1B-043-19]

Cardinals functioning as pronouns can also be postmodified:

> **[27]** In Mexico City motor vehicles *three million of them* produce eighty percent of the contamination in the air [S2B-022-132]
>
> **[28]** Gildas dates the Saxon revolt to *446 A.D.* (which was later amended to *449 A.D.* by Bede). [W1A-001-34]

[29] Of the countries creating a diverse manufacturing economic base there are *four which have surpassed many of the others in economic development.* [W1A-015-15]

[30] When you write at *12.35 at night* that's what happens. [W1B-006-76]

[31] *One of the four nuclear reactors at the plant* was badly damaged by a chemical explosion after it seriously over-heated and went out of control. [W2A-030-7]

It is conventional to write out a numeral in words at the beginning of a sentence. Numerals of ten or under are normally written out except in formulae or in tables, but some publishers extend the rule to all numerals under 100.

B. Ordinals

Ordinals (or ordinal numerals) refer to positions in a sequence. The primary ordinals are items such as *first, second, fifteenth, twenty-third.*

Here are examples of the primary ordinals as pronouns **[32]–[33]** and as determiners **[34]–[35]**:

[32] I've only mentioned the *first* of the analyses [S1B-017-175]

[33] Two scans are made; the *second* being closer to the position of the teats as indicated by the *first.* [W2A-033-80]

[34] It was the *first* time I'd met anyone in a wheelchair [. . .] [S1A-004-112]

[35] Well now let's move beyond Elgar into the early years of the *twentieth* century [S1B-032-65]

A number of other items have a grammatical function and a meaning similar to those of the primary ordinals, including:

additional	*further*	*other*	*same*
another	*last*	*others*	*subsequent*
following	*latter*	*preceding*	
former	*next*	*previous*	

All of these can function as determiners. Most can also function as pronouns; the exceptions are *additional, further,* and *subsequent.* Here are some examples:

[36] One and a half billion babies will be born over the *next* ten years [S2B-022-73]

[37] Unemployment had increased by over 400,000 in the *last* four months alone. [W2B-012-108]

[38] And Andy Smith who won his *previous* race is currently struggling at the back [S2A-012-63]

[39] But before we get on to those let's just consider one *other* aspect of the climate system [S2A-043-74]

The ordinals may have either singular or plural reference, except that *another* is only singular and *others* is only plural.

First, next, last, and *same* may be premodified by *very:*

[40] [. . .] today's ⟨ , ⟩ lecture ⟨ , ⟩ the *very last* lecture before Christmas ⟨ , ⟩ uh is The Ancient Celts Through Caesar's Eyes [S2A-022-2]

[41] Strong rumours were around about a reshuffle the *very next* day [. . .]
[W2B-012-37]

[42] And what arouses one's suspicions is that that *very same* Hebrew form Malachi ⟨ , ⟩ means my messenger [. . .] [S2A-036-72]

The ordinals functioning as pronouns may be postmodified:

[43] Incorporated in the great wooden beams which descended deep into the mine-shaft was a revolutionary 'man-engine', the *first of its kind in the country.* [W2F-007-8]

[44] The findings of Rothwell (1985, p.375) are not encouraging in this regard, showing decisions on technology to be usually 'top-down' in character, to the extent that supervisors and end-users are often the *last to know about the nature of the changes proposed.* [W2A-011-87]

C. **Fractions**

The fractions refer to quantities less than one. They include *(a) half, two halves, a quarter, three-quarters,* and compounds of a cardinal number with an ordinal, such as *two-thirds, three-fifths, one-eighth.*

The fractions can be pronouns **[45]**–**[47]** or determiners **[48]**–**[51]**:

[45] In some areas, it states, as many as *one third* of homes have already been sold. [W2C-015-32]

[46] Each one of these is about ten milliseconds *ten thousandths* of a second [S2A-056-106]

[47] And just under *half* get invited to staff meetings [S1B-077-29]

[48] Uh I did it for about *half* a term [S1A-006-2]

[49] It's probably *half* the population at best that are covered [S1B-058-52]

[50] At an altitude of 60 miles (96 kilometres)—the maximum height the V-2 reached—the air has about *one-millionth* the density at sea level, so the V-2 can be considered to have been in space for a brief period. [W2B-035-29]

[51] Even now jets can only operate up to about *one-sixth* satellite speed. [W2B-035-47]

Cardinals may be co-ordinated with fractions:

[52] *One and a half billion* babies will be born over the next ten years [S2B-022-73]

[53] And that was how I flew, with the rest of the unit, to Hong Kong for *three and a half* wonderful weeks. [W2B-004-87]

Fractions may be premodified by intensifiers:

[54] The society in which we live is one in which two percent of the society own *about half* the wealth and it's getting worse the gap between the rich and the poor [S2B-036-51]

[55] *Nearly three-quarters* of the water used is for agricultural purposes, and the area of irrigated land is increasing steadily each year. [W2B-024-62]

[56] John Turner who ⟨ , ⟩ is playing the organ today has been Cathedral Organist here for *over quarter* of a century [S2A-020-77]

Further examples appear in the citations given above: *as many as one third* [45], *under half* [47], *up to about one-sixth* [51].

Interjections

4.47 Interjections

Interjections are exclamatory emotive words that are loosely attached to the rest of the sentence. They are common in the spoken language and in representations of conversation. Here is a list of common interjections:

ah	ho-ho	sh
aha	hooray	shooh
ahem	humph	tsk
boo	oh	tut-tut
eh	oho	ugh
gee	ooh	uh-huh
ha	oops	uh-uh
ha-ha	ouch	whew
hello	ow	whoops
hey	phoo	wow
hi	pooh	yippee
ho	psst	yuk

A few have been converted into nouns or verbs; for example: *boo* (noun or verb), *pooh-pooh* (verb), *shooh* (verb), *tut-tut* (noun and verb), *wow* (verb). *Cor* /kɔ:(r)/ is British.

There are also a number of hesitation noises, which may be represented by these spellings:

hm	uh
mhm	uhm
mm	um

In addition, there are many exclamatory words and phrases that have been considered interjections, though they are related to other words in the language. Here are some examples:

blimey (British)	gosh
bottoms up (British)	hear, hear
cheerio (British)	heck (American)
cheers (British)	right on (American)
crikey	so long
damn	sure

| doggone it (American) | well done |
| drat | well, well |

Some exclamatory words or phrases are borrowed from foreign languages; for example: *ciao, skol.*

Chapter 5
The Grammar of Phrases

Summary

Chapter 5 Summary

- Five types of phrases are distinguished, each named after the word class of the head of the phrase: noun phrase, verb phrase, adjective phrase, adverb phrase, and prepositional phrase.

- The head of a noun phrase is a noun, a pronoun, a nominal adjective, or a numeral. It may be introduced by one or more determiners, and it may be modified by one or more premodifiers and by one or more postmodifiers.

- Noun phrases commonly have one of the following functions: subject, direct object, indirect object, subject predicative, object predicative, complement of a preposition, premodifier of a noun, vocative. The most common premodifiers of nouns are adjectives, nouns, genitive noun phrases, participles, and numerals. The most common postmodifiers of nouns are prepositional phrases and relative clauses (finite or non-finite).

- Modification of nouns may be restrictive or non-restrictive, a distinction depending on the meaning intended by the speaker/writer. Restrictive modification restricts the scope of the reference of the noun phrase, whereas non-restrictive modification does not do so but instead contributes further information. Sentential relative clauses, which are non-restrictive, have as their antecedent not a noun head but the whole or part of what precedes them in the sentence.

- Appositives are typically non-restrictive noun phrases that have the same reference as the preceding noun phrases.

- Noun phrases may be co-ordinated syndetically (with co-ordinators) or asyndetically (without co-ordinators). In polysyndetic co-ordination, co-ordinators are inserted between each pair of noun phrases. Co-ordination is segregatory if a paraphrase shows that each noun phrase could function independently. Co-ordination is combinatory when the noun phrases function as a unit that cannot be separated in that way.

- The verb agrees with the subject in number and person wherever such distinctions are featured in the verb. Agreement is expected to be with the head of the noun phrase, but the number of the verb is sometimes attracted to that of another noun in the phrase, usually one that is nearer. Singular collective nouns may be treated as plural (especially in British English) when the focus is on the group as individuals.

- Vocatives are predominantly noun phrases. They are optional additions to the basic sentence structures, and are used to address (usually) people, either to single them out from others or to maintain some personal connection with them.

- Three types of contrast can be established for the reference of noun phrases: definite/non-definite, specific/non-specific, generic/non-generic.

- The head of a verb phrase is a main verb, which may be preceded by up to four auxiliaries in a specific sequence.

- Operators are used for negation, interrogation, emphasis, and abbreviation. The functions of the operator can be performed by the first auxiliary in the verb phrase or by the main verb *be* (in British English especially, also *have*) when it is the only verb in the verb phrase. In the absence of another potential operator, *do* is introduced as a dummy operator.

- Verbs may be finite or non-finite. A verb is finite if it is marked for the distinction in tense between present and past. In a finite verb phrase the first or only verb is finite.

- The two tenses (as shown by verb inflections) are present and past. The two aspects are perfect and progressive.

- The simple past is primarily used when the situation was completed before the time of speaking or writing. The simple present is primarily used for situations that include the time of speaking or writing.

- The most common ways of expressing future time in the verb phrase are with *will* (or its contraction *'ll*) and *be going to.*

- The present subjunctive has the base form of the verb; it is mainly used in *that*-clauses. The past subjunctive is *were*, used in hypothetical constructions.

- Each of the modals has two kinds of meanings: deontic (referring to some kind of human control) and epistemic (a judgement of truth-value).

- The perfect (auxiliary *have* plus the *-ed* participle) is used to indicate that a situation occurs within a period preceding another period or point of time. For the present perfect, the period extends from the past to the present time. For the past perfect, the period precedes another situation in the past.

- The progressive (auxiliary *be* plus the *-ing* participle) primarily focuses on the situation as being in progress.

- There are a large number of idiomatic verb combinations. A phrasal verb combines a verb and an adverb. Phrasal verbs may be intransitive, transitive, or copular. A prepositional verb combines a verb and a preposition. Prepositional verbs may be monotransitive (with a prepositional object), doubly transitive (with a direct object and a prepositional object), or copular. A phrasal-prepositional verb combines a verb, an adverb, and a preposition. Phrasal-prepositional verbs may be monotransitive (with a prepositional object) or doubly transitive (with a direct object and a prepositional object).

- The head of an adjective phrase is an adjective, which may be preceded by premodifiers and followed by postmodifiers. A sequence of adjectives may constitute a hierarchy of modification or the adjectives may be co-ordinated (asyndetically or syndetically). The two major functions of adjective phrases are as premodifier of a noun and as subject predicative. The most common premodifiers of adjectives are intensifying adverbs. The most common postmodifiers of adjectives are prepositional phrases and clauses.

■ The head of an adverb phrase is an adverb, which may be preceded by premodifiers and (less commonly) followed by postmodifiers. The major functions of adverb phrases are as premodifiers of adjectives and adverbs and as adverbials. Adverbs can be premodified by intensifying adverbs and they can be postmodified by adverbs, comparative clauses, and prepositional phrases.

■ A prepositional phrase consists of a preposition and its complement. Prepositional complements are chiefly noun phrases, -*ing* participle clauses, and *wh*-clauses. Prepositional phrases may have the following functions: postmodifier of noun or adjective, subject predicative, object predicative, adverbial, and complement of verb. Prepositions and prepositional phrases may be premodified by intensifying adverbs.

Types of Phrases

The five types

The five types of phrases are named after the class of the word that is the head of the phrase. The phrase types are exemplified below in the order that they are discussed in this chapter.

1. noun phrase   *recent deluges of reports* (head: *deluges*)
2. verb phrase   *might have been accepted* (head: *accepted*)
3. adjective phrase   *surprisingly normal* (head: *normal*)
4. adverb phrase   *more closely* (head: *closely*)
5. prepositional phrase   *for a moment* (head: *for*)

Prepositional phrases always consist of two constituents: a preposition and the complement of the preposition. In the prepositional phrase *for a moment*, the constituents are the preposition *for* and its complement *a moment*, a noun phrase with two constituents—the indefinite article *a* and the noun *moment*. Other phrase types may consist of just one word as head (cf. 3.1); for example, in **[1]**–**[4]**, the noun phrase *lectures*, the verb phrase *brought*, the adjective phrase *cold*, and the adverb phrase *badly*.

[1]   *Lectures* begin at nine.

[2]   They *brought* me a box of chocolates.

[3]   I'm feeling *cold*.

[4]   They are behaving *badly*.

Noun Phrases

The structure of the noun phrase

A noun phrase has as its head a noun, a pronoun, a nominal adjective, or a numeral. See 4.3 ff. for nouns, 4.32 ff. for pronouns, 4.23 for nominal adjectives, and 4.46 for numerals.

The noun phrases in **[1]** are indicated by italics:

[1]   *Female spotted hyenas* are so much like *males* that *it*'s hard to tell *them* apart. Now, *scientists* believe *they* know why.
     Solving *a centuries-old puzzle*, *California researchers* have reported in *the journal Science* that *high levels of male hormone absorbed before birth* turn *female spotted hyenas* into *large aggressive animals* and make *the male hyena a second-class citizen of his own clan*. [*International Herald Tribune*, 1 July 1993, p. 9]

The noun phrases at the end of [1]—the *male hyena* and *a second-class citizen of his own clan*—are two separate noun phrases ('make *the male hyena* into *a second-class citizen of his own clan*').

Some of the noun phrases in [1] consist of a single word; for example, in the first paragraph the nouns *males* and *scientists*, and the pronouns *it*, *them*, and *they*. Most of the noun phrases in [1], however, have more than one word.

Noun phrases that have a noun as their head are often introduced by the definite article *the* or the indefinite article *a* or *an*. *The* and *a* are the most frequently used members of the class of determiners, which includes also *some*, *both*, and *this* (cf. 4.32–4, 4.43, 5.4). The second paragraph in [1] has several noun phrases introduced by the indefinite or definite article; for example *a centuries-old puzzle* and *the male hyena*.

Noun phrases may have modifiers. These may add information that characterizes more specifically what the head refers to. In [1] *California* modifies *researchers*: the researchers in question are restricted to those from California. Because it precedes the head noun *researchers*, *California* is a premodifier. In the noun phrase *high levels of male hormone absorbed before birth*, there is both premodification and postmodification: the noun head is *levels*, which is premodified by *high* and postmodified by *of male hormone absorbed before birth*. Modifiers are dependent on the head and can be omitted without disturbing the structure of the sentence, but like adverbials (cf. 3.20) they are usually important informationally and in that sense they cannot be omitted without damaging the communication.

We can now represent the structure of the typical noun phrase (NP) that has a noun as its head **(Fig. 5.2.1)**. The parentheses indicate the elements of the structure that may be absent.

Fig. 5.2.1 Structure of a noun phrase

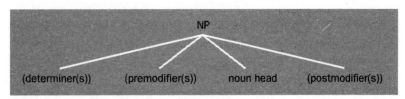

These four constituents are exemplified in the noun phrase *a second-class citizen of his own clan*:

determiner:	*a*
premodifier:	*second-class*
noun head:	*citizen*
postmodifier:	*of his own clan*

More than one determiner can introduce a noun phrase (cf. 5.4); for example, *all* and *our* in [2]:

[2]   In the initial sorties *all our aircraft* have returned safely [S2B-008-15]

A noun head may have more than one premodifier. There are two sets of premodifiers in [1], which differ in their relationship to the noun head: *female spotted hyenas* and *large aggressive animals*. *Spotted* modifies *hyenas*, and *female* modifies the unit *spotted hyenas*. On the other hand, *large* and *aggressive* separately modify the head *females*, since we can reverse their order (*aggressive large females*) and we can co-ordinate them (*large and aggressive females*). The structural difference is displayed in **Fig. 5.2.2**.

Fig. 5.2.2 Premodifiers and NP heads

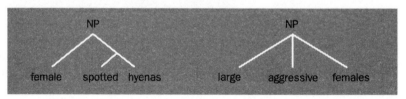

A noun head may also have more than one postmodifier. Two postmodifiers are exhibited in **[3]**:

> **[3]** [. . .] I think it is a pity that LB is *the only major corporation I have worked for where this has been a problem.* [W1B-020-24]

The noun head is *corporation* and the two postmodifiers are *I have worked for* and *where this has been a problem*. The second postmodifier modifies the whole of the preceding noun phrase, including the first postmodifier, since clearly the writer does not want to generalize by extending the reference to major corporations where he has not worked. On the other hand, the two postmodifiers in **[4]** modify the head separately:

> **[4]** [. . .] we could not trace *the invoice dated 22nd March 1990 for £43.13.*
> [W1B-021-37]

We could reverse the order of the postmodifiers without changing the meaning:

> **[4a]** We could not trace *the invoice for £43.13 dated 22nd March 1990.*

If we ignore the internal structure of the postmodifiers by using the convention of triangles, we can show the difference in the relation of the postmodifiers to the head in **Figs. 5.2.3** and **5.2.4**.

Fig. 5.2.3 Postmodifiers and NP head: Sentence [3]

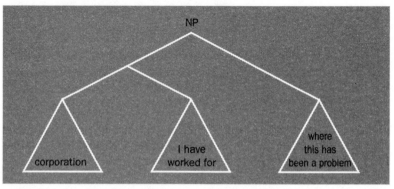

Modification of nouns can be very complex. Here is an example of the heaping up of premodifiers in the headline in a local London weekly paper:

Fig. 5.2.4 Postmodifiers and NP head: Sentence [4]

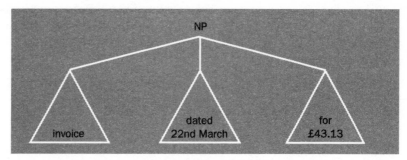

[5]   *Dog row sword death jury* told trial man 'didn't intend any harm' [*Hackney Gazette*, 21 April 1989, p. 5]

As commonly in headlines, grammatical words such as *the* and *was* (cf. 8.19) are omitted, so that a full version of the headline sentence might read as in **[5a]**:

[5a] The dog row sword death jury was told that the trial man 'didn't intend any harm'.

The noun phrase subject is virtually unintelligible without the information supplied in the first paragraph of the news item:

[5b] An alleged murderer has denied deliberately plunging a sword into an unarmed man after a row over a dog fight.

Complex noun phrases usually have heavy postmodification. Here is an example, where everything after *What is* constitutes one noun phrase:

[6]   What is *the single mechanism or dual mechanisms that allows a conducting filament to grow in the vertical direction immediately after breakdown and then at a later time and with the reapplication of a higher current to undergo radial growth to a lower resistance state*? [W2A-034-37]

The structure of a noun phrase may be extended through co-ordination or apposition. In co-ordination (cf. 5.12), two or more noun phrases are joined by a co-ordinator to form one compound noun phrase, as in **[7]**:

[7]   If you have left *school, college or an approved training course* you may be credited with contributions in one of the relevant tax years to help you to get benefit. [W2D-002-11]

In apposition (cf. 5.11), two noun phrases are typically juxtaposed. The second noun phrase typically refers to the same entity as the first noun phrase:

[8]   Another tropism that may be of widespread occurrence, and which is also particularly evident in roots is *a directional response to injury, traumatropism*. [W2A-025-25]

In **[8]**, *traumatropism* is in apposition to (or an appositive of) *a directional response to injury*. The appositive here (*traumatropism*) is the technical term for what is described in the first noun phrase.

5.3
Functions of noun phrases

The possible functions of noun phrases are listed below:

1. Subject

[1] And *my earliest memory of the theatre* is going to the Hippodrome in Ipswich [. . .] [S1B-023-33]

2. Direct object

[2] [. . .] sign *your name* there [S1B-026-152]

3. Indirect object

[3] I always tell *people* I am not a musical person [S1B-046-22]

4. Subject predicative

[4] Uh faith has been *a gift* for me [S1B-041-113]

5. Object predicative

[5] I called this little talk *a survey of global bifurcations* [S2A-033-70]

6. Complement of a preposition

[6] Uhm but why isn't it in *French* [S1B-026-89]

7. Premodifier of a noun or noun phrase[1]

[7] Simon's on this *revision* course [. . .] [S1A-093-229]

[8] So a lot of my friends were in *one parent* families as well [. . .] [S1A-007-175]

8. Vocative

[9] You're a snob *Dad* [S1A-007-175]

There are a number of other functions performed by restricted ranges of noun phrases.

9. Adverbial

Noun phrases function as adverbials in expressions of time, location, direction, manner, and intensification:

[10] But you have to wait *a long time* [S1A-062-111]

[11] The flag goes up *far side* [S2A-018-66]

[12] Some of it's coming out *this way* [S2A-053-78]

[13] [. . .] and would certainly not have been designed *that way* today [S2A-025-90]

[14] The loss in nineteen seventy hit him *a great deal* [. . .] [S1B-040-81]

10. Premodifier of adjective

[15] The plane was *4 hours* late. [W1B-009-75]

[16] It's *sixteen feet* long *six feet* high *six feet* wide [S2A-055-77]

11. Premodifer of preposition

[17] He revealed that Washington had informed the Kremlin *an hour* before the start of the assault [S2B-008-57]

[18] Two sleek, grey bodies were effortlessly riding our bow wave *just a foot or so* beneath the surface. [W2B-029-94]

12. Premodifier of adverb

[19] Now Mercedes have always been good at insulating their car but they've gone *a stage* further with this [S2A-055-13]

13. Postmodifier of noun

[20] Women may suffer from lack of "acceptable partners" because too many of the men *their age* are dead [. . .] [Betty Friedan, 'Intimacy's Greatest Challenge', *The Times*, 19 October 1993, p. 2]

14. Postmodifier of adjective

[21] We're short *fifteen dollars*.

Pronouns and nominal adjectives can perform the first six of the functions listed above for noun phrases. Clauses that serve the functions performed by noun phrases are termed nominal clauses (or noun clauses) (cf. 6.12).

5.4 Determiners

Determiners come at the beginning of a noun phrase. They convey various pragmatic and semantic contrasts relating to the type of reference of the noun phrase and to notions such as number and quantity (cf. 4.33, 4.43–6, 5.16). Determiners are distinguished according to the positions they can occupy relative to other determiners. They are also distinguished according to their co-occurrence with types of nouns.

A. Predeterminers, central determiners, postdeterminers

A noun phrase can be introduced by more than one determiner. It is usual to distinguish three sets of determiners that may co-occur in this sequence: (1) predeterminers, (2) central determiners, (3) postdeterminers. Here are examples with all three kinds of determiners:

all(1) *my*(2) *many*(3) friends
twice(1) *every*(2) *other*(3) day

Just one or two of these kinds of determiners may be present:

all(1) casualties   *all*(1) *those*(2) friends
my(2) friends   *my*(2) *many*(3) friends
every(2) day   *every*(2) *other*(3) day

Many determiners can also be premodified by intensifiers:

hardly any (money)   *no fewer than* twenty (claims)
virtually no (trees)   *just about* every (viewpoint)
almost all (instances)   *far too* much (time)
more than half (my efforts) *so very* little (milk)
less than ten (per cent)

1.   Predeterminers

The predeterminers fall into four subsets:

(a) the subset *all, both, half* (cf. 4.44, 4.46)

all
both } the children
half

(b) multipliers (cf. 4.46) consisting of:

(i) the subset *once, twice,* and (archaic or literary) *thrice*

once
twice } { a day
thrice   every few weeks

(ii) the subset *double, treble, quadruple*

                    double
(They now earn) {   *treble*   } their previous salary
                    quadruple

(iii) multiplying expressions headed by *times*:

ten times the fatalities
three times a day
four times each month

(c) fractions other than *half*:

one-tenth the speed
one-millionth the density
two-thirds the time

(d) exclamative *what* (cf. 4.43), which can precede the indefinite article:

what { a day
         a happy occasion

Such and *many* can also precede the indefinite article:

such } { a friend
many   a good time

But *such* and *many* are not predeterminers, since they straddle the sets of determiners.[2] Both can be preceded by determiners from other sets. For example, *such* can follow the predeterminer *all*, central determiners such as *any*, and postdeterminers such as *several*:

$$
\left.\begin{array}{l}
\text{all} \\
\text{any} \\
\text{several}
\end{array}\right\} \textit{such parties}
$$

Many can follow central determiners:

$$
\left.\begin{array}{l}
\text{my} \\
\text{the} \\
\text{whose}
\end{array}\right\} \textit{many ideas}
$$

Many and *such* can also co-occur:

many such crises

The predeterminers do not co-occur. Those in subsets (a) and (c) also function as pronouns and can take partitive *of*-phrases:

all of my children
two-thirds of the time

Such and *many* can be similarly used:

such of your people
many of the cars

2.   Central determiners

Like the predeterminers, the central determiners do not co-occur. The central determiners are all closed sets:

(a) articles, comprising the definite article *the* and the indefinite article *a* or *an*, and the zero article (cf. 4.33, 5.16)
(b) demonstratives: *this, these; that, those* (cf. 4.45)
(c) possessive determiners: *my, our, your, his, her, its, their* (cf. 4.34 f.)
(d) interrogative determiners: *which, what, whose* (cf. 4.43)
(e) relative determiners: *whose, which* (cf. 4.43)
(f) nominal relative determiners: *which, whichever, whichsoever* (archaic); *what, whatever, whatsoever* (cf. 4.43)
(g) *wh*-conditional determiners: *whatever, whatsoever, whichever* (cf. 4.43)
(h) indefinite determiners: *some, any, either, no, neither* (cf. 4.44)

Enough can be a central determiner, but it can sometimes follow the head noun:

enough food
food *enough*

3.   Postdeterminers

The postdeterminers fall into four subsets:

(a) cardinals (cf. 4.46)

all my *six* children

(b) primary ordinals (cf. 4.46)

  her *twenty-first* birthday

(c) general ordinals: e.g. *another, last, next, other* (cf. 4.46)

  both her *other* daughters

(d) primary quantifiers: e.g. *many, several, few, little, much* (cf. 4.44)

  the *several* poems by Blake in our anthology
  your *few* suggestions
  the *little* information you gave me

B. Singular count, plural count, non-count

Nouns may be count or non-count (cf. 4.5), and count nouns may be singular or plural. Determiners can be distinguished according to which nouns they co-occur with.

1. With singular count only

central determiners: *a* or *an, each, every, either, neither*
postdeterminer: cardinal *one*

$$\left.\begin{array}{l} a \\ every \\ neither \\ one \end{array}\right\} \text{suggestion}$$

2. With plural count only

predeterminer: *both*
central determiners: *these, those*
postdeterminers: cardinals from *two* up; primary quantifiers *many, a few, few, several*

$$\left.\begin{array}{l} both \\ five \\ these \\ several \end{array}\right\} \text{books}$$

3. With non-count only

postdeterminers: *much, a little, little*

$$\left.\begin{array}{l} much \\ a \ little \end{array}\right\} \text{luck}$$

4. With singular count, plural count, and non-count

predeterminers: *all*, multipliers, fractions, exclamative *what*
central determiners: *the, no*, possessives, interrogatives, relatives, nominal relatives, *wh*-conditionals
postdeterminers: ordinals

$$\left.\begin{array}{l} \textit{all their} \\ \textit{half the} \\ \textit{which(ever)} \end{array}\right\} \left\{\begin{array}{l} \text{house} \\ \text{houses} \\ \text{furniture} \end{array}\right.$$

5. With singular count and non-count

central determiners; *this*, *that*

$$\left.\begin{array}{l} \textit{this} \\ \textit{that} \end{array}\right\} \left\{\begin{array}{l} \text{car} \\ \text{information} \end{array}\right.$$

6. With plural count and non-count

central determiners: zero article, *some* (stressed /sʌm/, unstressed /səm/), *any*, *enough*

$$\left.\begin{array}{l} \textit{some} \\ \textit{enough} \end{array}\right\} \left\{\begin{array}{l} \text{dollars} \\ \text{money} \end{array}\right.$$

Stressed *some* and *any* can also co-occur with singular nouns:

[1] He was obviously afraid of mentioning *some girlfriend* and offending the wife [S1A-037-24]

[2] And also in *any area* of teaching you look for uhm *any experience* you've had with the relevant age range [S1A-033-161]

5.5
Premodifiers of nouns

Adjectives are typical premodifiers of nouns, but other word classes are also used in this function. Nouns, participles, genitive noun phrases, and numerals are particularly common. Below are the types of premodifiers.

1. Adjective or adjective phrase

[1] So I think from today's session you've realised I hope that you shouldn't start somebody on *life-long anti-hypertensive* therapy based upon one *single* blood-pressure measurement [S1B-004-267]

2. Noun or noun phrase

[2] One of the *consortium* members uh ⟨ , ⟩ uh has all the files [S1A-024-62]

[3] And then I had the vegetarian option which was a wonderful *spinach cheese* thing with good uhm veggies [S1A-011-246]

[4] It's *a hundred and fifty pound* job to replace a door [S1A-007-107]

[5] My father had a *Church of Scotland* background [S1B-041-105]

3. *-ing* participle

[6] But I hope to throw the net further in the *coming* weeks and get to know other nationalities. [W1B-002-69]

4. *-ed* participle

[7] The results of that in pollution and *wasted* natural resources every year is shameful. [W2B-013-69]

5. Genitive noun phrase (cf. n. 1)

[8] That's *the old soldier's* way isn't it [S1A-009-180]

6. Numeral

[9] Only do *six* essays not twelve [S1A-053-59]

[10] Unfortunately, at the time the *first* launchers were required, jets could operate only up to about *one-tenth* satellite speed, so they could not be used to solve the problem. [W2B-035-46]

7. Adverb

[11] In the first week of May 1988 William Millinship, the *then* managing editor of the Observer, took me aside—it was on the pinky-grey editorial floor of the paper's new building over Chelsea Bridge—and spoke to me with unaccustomed force, even severity. [W2B-015-4]

8. Prepositional phrase

[12] Both accords follow months of *behind-the-scenes* negotiations between PLO and Israeli officials, with Norway acting as a go-between. [*International Herald Tribune*, 10 September 1993, p. 1]

9. Clause

[13] It is required to allow updating and track entries by data from several sensors using a *read and lock* procedure call (prior to writing) and a *write and unlock* procedure call (to complete writing). [W2A-038-127; bold in original]

[14] Had the *what-can-you-do*—? *Carry-a-card*—? problem again! [W1B-010-93]

Apart from *then* **[11]**, a few place adverbs and (before some pronouns and determiners) intensifying adverbs are used as premodifiers (cf. the adverbs as postmodifiers in 5.6). For example:

an *overhead* projector	*quite* a crowd
the *downstream* current	*quite* some time
offshore deposits	*rather* a good mathematician
the *inside* doors	*just about* everybody
overseas broadcasts	*nearly* everything
the *above* diagram	*almost* nothing
our *downstairs* tenants	*virtually* all the immigrants

Premodifying prepositional phrases and clauses tend to be *ad hoc*, and are generally hyphenated. A few premodifying clauses, such as *keep-fit* in *keep-fit class*, are established expressions. Here are two other examples:

pay-as-you-earn tax   *do-it-yourself* store

5.6
Postmodifiers of nouns

The typical postmodifiers of nouns are prepositional phrases and relative clauses. Below are the types of postmodifiers.

1. **Prepositional phrase** (cf. 5.47 ff.)

    [1] It's just a question *of* ⟨ , , ⟩ *which is the more efficient approach*
    [S1A-029-196]

2. **Finite relative clause** (cf. 5.9)

    [2] We don't have a constitution *which stops* ⟨ , , ⟩ *government from legislating certain things* [S1B-011-148]

3. **Relative *-ing* participle clause** (cf. 5.9)

    [3] The air mass *bringing the coldest temperatures* is the polar continental mass which comes in from the Soviet Union. [W2B-026-74]

4. **Relative *-ed* participle clause** (cf. 5.9)

    [4] An intake shaft would provide higher ventilation efficiency for the more extensive layout *planned for the mine.* [W2A-031-38]

5. **Relative infinitive clause** (cf. 5.9)

    [5] And again Fred when is the best time *to do it* [S1B-025-58]

6. **Appositive finite clause** (cf. 5.11)

    [6] It's really shorthand for the view *that well-being depends on more than the absence of disease* [S2B-038-2]

7. **Appositive infinitive clause** (cf. 5.11)

    [7] And finally today marks the beginning of a week of Christian unity ⟨ , ⟩ so it's an opportunity *for Christians everywhere to at least unite in prayer for a speedy end to the war in the Gulf* [S2B-023-57]

8. **Adverb**

    [8] [. . .] So you arrived the day *before* did you [S1B-066-120]

9. **Adjective**

    [9] Uhm let me find you something *ethnic* [S1A-018-184]

    [10] As well as the bonfire *proper* there was a second, more seriously built fire, where men were turning a sheep on a spit. [W2F-018-84]

10. **Noun phrase**

    [11] And yet in his address *this morning* President Bush referred to destroying his nuclear capability and destroying his chemical warfare capability [S1B-027-7]

Adverbs, adjectives, and noun phrases are more restricted in their use as postmodifiers of nouns. Most adverbs and noun phrases in this function refer to time or place.[3] Time reference:

a month *ahead*	a day *later*
a year *ago*	the meal *last night*
some time *afterwards*	my appointment *the following day*

Place reference:

the weather *outside*	your way *home*
our journey *overseas*	the park *nearby*
the rooms *upstairs*	the road *that way*
the point *here*	the houses *this side*

Postmodifying adjective phrases can usually be treated as reduced relative clauses: *something ethnic*—'something that is ethnic'; *the best way possible*—'the best way that is possible'. Compound indefinite pronouns and compound indefinite adverbs (which behave in some respects like pronouns) can only be postmodified:

somebody *taller*	somewhere *quiet*
nothing *interesting*	nowhere *better*
anyone *knowledgeable*	anywhere *cheap*

If the adjective itself has a postmodifier (cf. 5.42), then the adjective phrase generally postmodifies the noun or pronoun:

students *good at athletics*	the books *easiest to read*
those *sure of themselves*	a computer *powerful enough to cater*
candidates *confident that they will*	*for your needs*
be interviewed	an income *greater than mine*

But if the postmodifier of the adjective is a *to*-infinitive clause or a comparative construction, we can put the adjective before the noun and its postmodifier after the noun:

the *easiest* books *to read*
a *greater* income *than mine*

In a small set of noun phrases, the adjective always follows the noun. These derive from French or are based on the French word order; for example:

heir *apparent*
attorney *general*
president *elect*
court *martial*

(For the plurals of these compounds, see 4.7.) *Proper* in the sense 'in a strict designation' also always follows the noun, as in *the bonfire proper* in [10]. Similarly, *present* and *absent* follow the noun when they are equivalent to relative clauses: *the members present*—'the members who were present'; *the people absent*—'the people who were absent'.

11. Comparative constructions

> **[12]** After five years of decline, weddings in France showed a 2.2% upturn last year, with *6,000 more* couples exchanging rings in 1988 *than in the previous year*, the national statistics office said. [891102-0155-47]

A noun may be modified by a combination of a determiner *more, less,* or *as* before the noun and a comparative construction after the noun. In **[12]** the determiner is itself modified (*6,000 more*) and the comparative construction is *than in the previous year*, the two parts forming a discontinuous unit: *6,000 more than in the previous year.* Here are other examples:

> **[13]** Moreover, the Japanese government, now the world's largest aid donor, is pumping *far more* assistance into the region *than the U.S. is.* [891102-0149-38]

> **[14]** He also claims the carrier costs less and takes up *less* space *than most paper carriers.* [891102-0090-25]

> **[15]** The cells are broken off ⟨ , , ⟩ so I wasn't able to do *as* good an operation *as I would have wished* ⟨ , ⟩ on that lady [. . .] [S1B-010-23]

The combination may also involve a premodifying adjective:

> **[16]** In part, this may reflect the fact that 'she speaks a *more progressive* language' *than her husband*, as Columbia's Prof. Klein puts it. [891102-0097-3] ('a language more progressive than her husband speaks')

An inflected form of an adjective may be used:

> **[17]** In particular, Mr. Coxon says, businesses are paying out a *smaller* percentage of their profits and cash flow in the form of dividends *than they have historically.* [891102-0102-38]

Four of the primary quantifier pronouns may also be postmodified by comparative constructions: *much/more, few/fewer, little/less.* The absolute forms of the pronouns are used in constructions introduced by *as*:

> **[18]** I was surprised to see more of them here than in NY, maybe *as* many *as in London* [W1B-011-44]

The comparatives are used in constructions introduced by *than*:

> **[19]** Now you've been in *more* of this building *than I have* [S1A-013-219]

5.7
Extraposed postmodifiers

Postmodifiers of noun phrases need not be attached directly to the noun that is head of the phrase. This is trivially so when two postmodifiers relate to the same noun, since the second postmodifier is distanced by the first:

> **[1]** The Foreign Office has rejected a call *by families of British hostages in Lebanon* ⟨ , ⟩ *for the restoration of diplomatic ties with Syria* [S2B-019-32]

Both the *by*-phrase and the *for*-phrase postmodify *call*. In **[2]** there is only one postmodifier of *concerns*: the *on*-phrase, which stretches to the end of the sentence. However, the postmodifier is separated from *concerns* by the parenthetic remark that is enclosed in dashes:

> **[2]** We do have *concerns*—and believe staff should too—*on the more extreme agreements which sometimes get drafted by companies who are relatively unfamiliar with CASE contract norms.* [W1B-029-34]

Postmodifiers may be extraposed (moved outside their normal position) to the end of a sentence or clause, leapfrogging over other constituents:

> **[3]** However, *new sets* soon appeared *that were able to receive all the TV channels.* [W2B-034-81]

Citation **[3]** contains a typical example of extraposition. The noun phrase (all of which is italicized here and in subsequent examples) is the subject of the sentence and the predicate (*soon appeared*) is considerably shorter than the subject. If the postmodifier were not extraposed, the sentence would be clumsy:

> **[3a]** However, *new sets that were able to receive all the TV channels* soon appeared.

The stylistic principle of sentence (or clause) balance requires that the part before the verb should not be much longer than the part after the verb (cf. 3.22). Another principle is also involved. The principle of end focus encourages the placement of the most important information at the climax of the sentence. *Appeared* is a verb that expresses the notion of coming into existence, which is relatively light informationally.

Extraposition of the postmodifier in the subject tends to occur in contexts where the extraposed postmodifier cannot be misanalysed as modifying another noun.[4] Favourable contexts are where there is no competing noun. Such contexts occur where the verb is intransitive **[3]** or passive **[4]**, or where the verb is copular and followed by an adjective phrase **[5]**:

> **[4]** *A tape recording* was then published *in which Mr Lenihan freely admitted he had rung the president.* [W2E-004-82]

> **[5]** The format has a slight drawback in that *few VCRs* are available *that accept its tapes*; there are also few prerecorded Video 8 tapes available. [W2D-014-103]

As in **[3]**, the verb *was published* in **[4]** expresses the notion of coming into existence, while the predicate *are available* in **[5]** expresses the notion of being in existence. Here are some other examples of extraposition from a noun phrase that is the subject of a sentence or of a clause within a sentence:

> **[6]** *A hunt's* begun *for two gunmen who burst into a pub in South London and opened fire on drinkers killing two* [S2B-016-3]

> **[7]** *Repeated attempts* were therefore rightly made *to fulfil the purposes of the United Nations without conflict* [S2B-030-71]

[8]   *The real nation* he contended already existed in Eastern Europe *possessed of an authentic Jewish culture passed down through the medium of the Yiddish language* [S2B-042-67]

[9]   The cause of ice ages is still a controversial subject, and *debates* continue *about the precise climatic effects of individual cycles.* [W1A-006-26]

Less frequently, extraposition takes place from noun phrases that are the direct object **[10]**–**[11]**, the subject predicative **[12]**, or the complement of a preposition **[13]**:

[10]   They call *anything* a burger *that you slap into a roll* [S1A-055-187]

[11]   The invoice shows no deposit as having been paid; but in fact I paid *a deposit of £903.87* to Mr Swan on 11 December *in the form of a cheque which has since been cleared through my bank.* [W1B-027-111]

[12]   I once had a fan letter from Neil Kinnock saying *what a good way* it was *to start Monday morning* and asking me how I got away with it. [W2B-001-11]

[13]   If she ever found herself in *a position*, by raising her little finger, *to save him from a painful and lingering death*, she hoped (she said) that she would still have the common humanity to raise it; but to be candid, she felt some doubt on the matter. [W2F-011-89]

5.8
Restrictive and non-restrictive modification

Modification of nouns may be restrictive or non-restrictive. The distinction is essentially a distinction of the meaning intended by the speaker or writer, though it may correlate with differences in intonation or punctuation.

Modification is restrictive when the modifier is intended to restrict the reference of the noun phrase. Modification is non-restrictive when the modifier does not restrict the reference, but instead contributes information about what is referred to in the rest of the noun phrase. The distinction between the two types of modification is illustrated in **[1]** and **[2]**:

[1]   The *poor* areas of Mexico City are awash with polluted water [S2B-022-107]

[2]   He was obviously afraid of mentioning some girlfriend and offending the wife So eventually I had to help the *poor* guy out [S1A-037-24 f.]

Poor in **[1]** is restrictive, since it is used to distinguish one set of areas of Mexico City from other areas. On the other hand, *poor* in **[2]** is non-restrictive, since it is used to make an evaluative comment on the person in question and is not intended to distinguish him from other persons. In speech, restrictive premodifiers tend to be stressed; in writing, there is no difference in punctuation between the two types of premodification.

Whether a premodifier is restrictive or non-restrictive usually depends on the context beyond the noun phrase itself, sometimes the situational context as well as the linguistic context. In **[2]**, *light blue* is a non-restrictive premodifier of *carpet* if we assume—as seems likely—that there is only one carpet in the room:

> **[3]** The room is hot and my feet are hot even though they are barely touching the *light blue* carpet. [W1B-006-41]

On that assumption we can paraphrase *the light blue carpet* by a non-restrictive relative *which*-clause separated by punctuation marks (cf. 5.9): 'the carpet, which is light blue'. In **[3a]**, on the other hand, *light blue* is a restrictive premodifier of *carpet*, since its function is to distinguish the carpet from other carpets:

> **[3a]** I've decided to buy the *light blue* carpet, though my husband prefers the dark blue one.

Proper nouns are generally not modified restrictively, since they are generally identified uniquely. However, they may be modified restrictively when some kind of specification is needed. For example, in **[4]** one person named John is specified by the modification, in **[5]** one part of July is singled out, in **[6]** two types of Greek are contrasted, in **[7]** post-war Japan is implicitly contrasted with pre-war Japan, and in **[8]** the implicit contrast is with the present condition of the United Nations.

> **[4]** That's the *only* John *I know* [S1A-032-285]
>
> **[5]** They come out *late* July August [S1A-033-108]
>
> **[6]** One of the ⟨ , ⟩ synoptic gospels is written in *more or less colloquial* Greek ⟨ , ⟩ sort of as it would be spoken rather than *literary* Greek [S1A-053-99]
>
> **[7]** *Postwar* Japan, pacific, industrious and in its own way democratic, belongs in the best, not the worst, traditions of the 20th century. [W2C-008-58]
>
> **[8]** They will continue to work for a *stronger more effective* United Nations. [S2B-041-13]

Non-restrictive postmodifiers are often marked by punctuation or intonation separation from the rest of the sentence as a kind of parenthesis, as in **[9]** and **[10]**:

> **[9]** I will begin with a look at the weather of our own country, *which is part of a temperate climate*, before moving on to the different very varied climates of the world. [W2B-026-6]
>
> **[10]** The eagerly awaited gala première of the Pink Panther Strikes Again, *at the end of 1976*, made the front pages twice. [W2B-004-21]

In **[10]** the writer chose to insert the commas, thereby treating *at the end of 1976* as a separate piece of information, but he could equally have omitted them without affecting the non-restrictive sense of the phrase. For example, *of Russia* and *of Japan* in **[11]** are non-restrictive despite not being separated by punctuation, since the two named leaders are uniquely identified without the prepositional phrases:

> **[11]** Moving to thaw long-frosty relations, President Boris N. Yeltsin *of Russia* and Prime Minister Kiichi Miyazawa *of Japan* agreed Thursday to discuss

the two nations' territorial dispute in a summit meeting here in October, raising the prospect of stepped-up Japanese aid. [*International Herald Tribune*, 9 July 1993, p. 1]

If [**11**] had read *the President of Russia* and *the Prime Minister of Japan*, the two *of*-phrases would have been restrictive, since they would have been required to identify which President and which Prime Minister were being referred to. Although *of Russia* and *of Japan* are non-restrictive in [**11**], they are not separated from the rest of the sentence by punctuation. The absence of punctuation is usual if the non-restrictive postmodifiers are brief prepositional phrases.

5.9
Restrictive and non-restrictive relative clauses

Wh-relatives, such as *which* and *who*, are normally the only relatives used with non-restrictive clauses. Intonation or punctuation separation is a signal that the clause is non-restrictive:

[1]   There will be a break from 12.30 pm till 1.30 pm for lunch, *which will not be provided.* [W1B-017-52]

[2]   The other six include Diana Turbay, daughter of a former Columbian president, *who edits a leading news magazine.* [W2C-001-90]

Punctuation separation is sometimes absent from what are obviously non-restrictive clauses, as in [**3**] (where Dr Funk of Tahiti is the name of a baby tortoise) and the two clauses in [**4**]:

[3]   Finally, into the garage to inspect Dr Funk of Tahiti *who was hibernating in a box of straw.* [W2B-004-37]

[4]   If you get a certificate AG3 *which shows you can contribute less than £11.20*, you should ask the optician for form ST(V) *on which you can apply for help with the cost of a private sight test.* [W2D-001-64]

Sometimes, however, punctuation makes a difference. The insertion of a comma after *prisoners* in [**5**] would indicate that the *who*-clause is non-restrictive and therefore that all prisoners breach rules:

[5]   The department is also likely to look at ending the dual role of the Prison Board of Visitors, who act as prison watchdogs as well as fulfilling a disciplinary role against prisoners *who breach rules.* [W2C-001-74]

Restrictive relative clauses may also be introduced by *wh*-relatives. There are two restrictive relative clauses in [**6**], one beginning with *who* and the other (embedded within it) beginning with *under which*:

[6]   In the meantime, I can give you the following list of commentators *who are on contracts under which they retain copyright*: [. . .] [W1B-016-99]

That is commonly used in restrictive relative clauses instead of the *wh*-pronouns:

[7]   I enjoyed the time *that I was given to study and to explore* [S1A-001-29]

The two types of relatives may co-occur in the same sentence:

[8]   [. . .] tumours *which grow slowly* are less radio-sensitive than tumours *that grow rapidly* [. . .] [S1B-010-92]

Indeed, *that* and the *wh*-pronoun may modify the same noun:

[9]   There are two directories *that I can direct you to* uhm *which will give you the first lead on that* [S1A-035-127]

But there are stylistic objections to the use of both *that* and a *wh*-pronoun when the relative clauses are co-ordinated:

[10]   [. . .] it was part of the anomalous froth now being blown off a boom *that* had run for 10 years *and which* had thrown up the usual number of excesses. [W2E-002-73]

Relative *wh*-words may be preceded by a preposition. The preposition may be fronted with the *wh*-word, which is the complement of the preposition:

[11]   Now ⟨ , ⟩ as for actually ⟨ , ⟩ how ⟨ , ⟩ or *to whom you send the messages* ⟨ , ⟩ there's a standard convention ⟨ , ⟩ used ⟨ , ⟩ for addresses for e-mail [S2A-028-76]

Compare with **[11]**: 'You send the messages *to them.*' *That*, however, cannot be preceded by a preposition. Instead, the preposition is stranded, i.e. left at the end in its usual place (cf. 5.47):

[12]   I knew my Wagner and my Beethoven and my Brahms very well but uh I saw that there were a great number of British composers *that I hadn't heard of* [S1B-032-14] (Cf. '*I hadn't heard of* a great number of British composers.')

[13]   Your instructor will also point out many things *that you haven't even thought about* [S2A-054-125] (Cf. '*You haven't even thought about* those things.')

If the relative is a *wh*-word, the preposition can either be fronted or left stranded. Compare **[13a]** and **[13b]**:

[13a]   Your instructor will also point out many things *about which you haven't even thought.*

[13b]   Your instructor will also point out many things *which you haven't even thought about.*

Fronting of the preposition, as in **[11]**, tends to occur more frequently in formal style.

The prepositional phrase may itself be the postmodifier of a noun in the relative clause:

[14]   Other people will have to pay for their sight test, *the cost of which may vary from one optician to another*, so it may pay you to shop around. [W2D-001-12]

The antecedent of *which* in **[14]** is *sight test*, so *the cost of which* corresponds to 'the cost of the sight test'. In a somewhat clumsy variant of **[14]**, the prepositional phrase is fronted:

[14a] Other people will have to pay for their sight test, *of which the cost may vary from one optician to another*, so it may pay you to shop around.

A construction similar to that in **[14]** appears in **[15]**:

[15] This assumption is supported by the nature of the Latin used in the Llandaff Charters, *some of which have been shown to date from the second quarter of the sixth century* [. . .] [W1A-001-74]

Relative *that* may be readily omitted from restrictive clauses if it is not the subject of the clause. In such cases it is usual to speak of a zero relative. In **[16]** the noun *tie* is modified by two restrictive relative clauses. The first clause has a zero relative pronoun and the second has the relative pronoun *that*:

[16] And she'd actually described the tie *he was wearing that I'd given him for his Christmas before* [S1B-026-15]

In **[16]** *that* is required to mark the beginning of the second clause. It could be omitted (since it is not the subject) if the second clause was the only one:

[16a] And she actually described the tie *I'd given him for his Christmas before*.

Relative *that* is not omitted from the second clause in **[17]** because it is the subject:

[17] The worst *I've done* is like ⟨ , , ⟩ why I can't think of anything *that's like approaching that really* [S1A-097-160]

Relative words other than pronouns are also used to introduce relative clauses. The relative determiner *whose* is exemplified in **[18]** and **[19]**. In **[18]** *whose* is personal ('his face') and in **[19]** it is non-personal ('its achievement'). Although there are brief pauses before both relative clauses, the clause in **[18]** is non-restrictive and the clause in **[19]** is restrictive:

[18] Above him is the Byzantine emperor ⟨ , ⟩ *whose face has been somewhat rubbed* but one sees a little bit of the under drawing with a big black moustache and a baggy turban [S2A-059-8]

[19] Our successor as Chancellor of the Exchequer ⟨ , ⟩ has during the last year ⟨ , ⟩ had to devote a good deal of his considerable talent ⟨ , ⟩ to demonstrating exactly how those Madrid conditions have been attained ⟨ , ⟩ so as to make it possible to fulfil a commitment ⟨ , ⟩ *whose achievement has long been in the national interest* [S2B-050-24]

The relative adverbs *where*, *when*, and *why* are exemplified in **[20]**–**[22]**. Of these citations, **[20]** is non-restrictive and **[21]**–**[22]** are restrictive:

[20] A similar scenario occurs around the margins of the Amazon basin, *where farmers are forced to encroach onto the forest margins in order to subsist.* [W1A-013-62]

[21] We hear little of the day-to-day successes but only of the odd occasion *when conflict arises* [S2B-031-53]

[22] But that was one reason *why I never wanted to do that again* actually [S1A-008-63]

The relative adverbs can be replaced by relative pronouns or by prepositional phrases with relative pronouns as complements. For example, *where* in **[20]** can be replaced by *in which*; *when* in **[21]** by *on which*; and *why* in **[22]** by *that* or zero.

The non-restrictive/restrictive distinction applies equally to non-finite relative clauses: *-ing* participle clauses **[23]** and **[26]**, *-ed* participle clauses **[24]** and **[27]**, and infinitive clauses **[25]** and **[28]**. The first in each of these pairs is non-restrictive and the second restrictive:

[23] Sometimes it carries red Saharan dust which falls with rain, *leaving a reddish film over buildings and parked vehicles in Southern England.* [W2B-026-80] ('which leaves . . .')

[24] The Prison Department's stance is likely to encourage Lord Justice Woolf to include proposals for minimum standards when he finally produces his report, *expected early next year.* [W2C-001-84] ('which is expected . . .')

[25] Please see attached notes, *to give you an idea of what we require.* [W1B-019-122] ('which will give you . . .')

[26] We are, of course, fully aware of the very difficult financial situation *facing your College. . . .* [W1B-024-76] ('that faces . . .')

[27] An intake shaft would provide higher ventilation efficiency for the more extensive layout *planned for the mine.* [W2A-031-38] ('that is planned . . .')

[28] Indeed if some of my former colleagues are to be believed I must be the first minister in history *to have resigned because he was in full agreement with government policy* [S2B-050-2] ('that has resigned . . .')

For postmodifying adjective phrases as reduced relative clauses, see 5.6. For non-standard relative pronouns, see 4.43.

5.10
Sentential relative clauses

Sentential relative clauses do not postmodify nouns, but it is convenient to deal with them at this point because in their form they resemble other non-restrictive relative clauses. In a sentential relative clause, the antecedent of the relative is the whole or part of what comes before it in the sentence. In **[1]**, for example, the antecedent of *which* is everything that precedes *which*:

[1] None of the three cities mentioned by the Anglo-Saxon Chronicle demonstrates any signs of habitation after the late fifth century (*which throws serious doubt on the usefulness of the Chronicle at this stage*). [W1A-001-63]

In **[2]**, the antecedent includes everything except the first word *certainly*:

[2]   Certainly he was soon reapplying for retirement, *which suggests that he was no longer happy with the work upon which he had been engaged for some nineteen years.* [W2B-006-46]

The sentential relative clause is non-restrictive, and therefore it is generally separated from what precedes it by an intonation break or pause in speech and by a punctuation mark in writing.

Here are some further examples with sentential relative *which*:

[3]   But the big tune at the centre of the Rhapsody and the blues melody in An American in Paris (given an upbeat reading) are lacking in sensuous warmth, *which means that a dimension is missing in both works.* [W2B-008-48]

[4]   He feels at ease with such people, *which is not true of all Indian politicians,* and that may explain why he decides to retain the external affairs portfolio for himself in his first government after the elections. [W2B-011-13]

[5]   He left BSC shortly after I did to tackle the problems of the redirection of the Ocean Shipping Group, *which he did with no little success.* [W2B-016-71]

[6]   Chimps can grow as big as you or me, *which is something that most people do not realise.* [W2B-021-14]

In all these instances **[1]–[6]** it would be possible to transform the sentential relative clause into an independent sentence in which the demonstrative pronoun *that* has the same reference back to the preceding part of the sentence.[5] For example:

[6a] Chimps can grow as big as you or me. *That is something that most people do not realise.*

The relative may be the complement of a preposition **[7]** or the determiner of a noun phrase **[8]–[9]**:

[7]   You may find the above questions obvious, *for which I apologise,* but I feel they are sufficiently critical to be worth emphasising. [W1B-030-58]

[8]   It may be that the potential obstacles are not insurmountable problems, *in which case* I look forward to hearing from you to discuss things further. [W1B-018-117]

[9]   What you should do is order one first and then eat it and then carry on from there ⟨ , ⟩ *by which time* you wouldn't want a second anyway [. . .] [S1A-018-27]

Relatives other than *which* can introduce relative clauses. They include *whereupon, whence* (formal style), and *when* in combination with a preceding preposition.

[10] The Social Democrats did not have the sense to call off the visit, but they swore to confront the East Germans with 'reform' demands—*whereupon* they suffered the supreme humiliation: The communists withdrew their invitation. [890918-0062-6] ('as a result of which')

[11] I finally got the parcel at the end of August, *since when* several factors [. . .] have all delayed my writing to Edinburgh University Press . . . [W1B-015-47 ff.]

5.11
Appositives

Appositives may be either restrictive or non-restrictive. Typically, appositives are non-restrictive noun phrases, separated by an intonation break in speech and by punctuation in writing:

[1] Hong Kong has not forcibly deported any Vietnamese since the international outcry over an operation of December, 1989 when 51 protesting boatpeople were put on a plane to the Vietnamese capital, *Hanoi*, under armed police guard. [W2C-019-75]

[2] David, *an apprentice mechanic*, was a natural athlete, played for Cheltenham Rugby Club's under-16 team and was also a keen cricketer. [W2C-020-80]

[3] Your sight can be tested only by a registered ophthalmic optician (*optometrist*) or an ophthalmic medical practitioner. [W2D-001-2]

[4] This pipe is usually a 25mm (*1 in*) diameter steel pipe, wrapped with special tape to protect it from rusting, and buried to protect from frost. [W2D-012-38]

[5] Jordan, too, which maintains close military and political links with Iraq, might have used her strong army to take Hijaz, *the Saudi region in which the holy cities of Medina and Mecca stand*. [W2E-001-46]

[6] Inside was the engine—*his engine*. [W2F-007-4]

The appositive may consist of a set of co-ordinated noun phrases:

[7] He wanted to break up their home, the fragile and wholly superfluous objects of their shared life—*mirrors, tables, the chiming clock, her idiotic, hated thimbles*—suddenly taking on a sinister appeal. [W2F-08-113]

Left and right dislocation (cf. 3.22), found mainly in informal speech, can be viewed as special kinds of apposition. In left dislocation, an anticipatory noun phrase is followed by a pronoun in the normal position for the noun phrase:

[8] '*Your mother, she* was just misunderstood. *Time and patience, it* wouldn't have taken any more than that—' [W2F-010-24 f.]

[9] *The Household Division they* wear these ⟨ , ⟩ Tudor coats in the presence of Her Majesty the Queen [S2A-011-85]

[10] The hideous exterior looks might lead you to think that it's a tractor but *the innards* ⟨ , ⟩ well *they* suggest otherwise [S2A-055-92]

In right dislocation, an anticipatory pronoun is in the normal position and an explanatory noun phrase appears later in the sentence:

[11] And there were still hundreds of people on it but *it* was so big *this boat* that you didn't meet them [S1A-021-63]

[12] *They*'re not great social animals *computer scientists* [S1A-014-251]

[13] It looks like *him* you know *the father* [S1A-041-30]

The postponed noun phrase may itself be a pronoun—for example, the demonstrative pronoun *that* in **[14]**:

[14] *It*'s a tremendous amount of money *that* [S1B-074-233]

The appositive may be separated from its antecedent apart from the special instances of left and right dislocation illustrated in **[8]**–**[14]**.

[15] A tremble spread outward from her spine until *the earth itself* seemed to shake, *an earth where the same sun rose as yesterday, the same scents drifted on the wind*; only she was so different that she didn't belong there any more. [W2F-015-44]

The separation may be due to the presence of apposition markers—such as *for example, that is to say, namely,* and *such as*—which introduce appositives:

[16] I mean for instance when Trevor and I did the whole of the Roman plays *that's to say Titus Andronicus Coriolanus Anthony and Cleopatra Julius Caesar* I used curved Roman trumpets which I've specially made [S1B-023-131]

[17] I then find that there is an impossible situation in the family ⟨ , ⟩ *say an unfaithful husband or something like that* [S1B-070-26]

[18] Some satellites *for example the satellite known by its acronym as SPOT* ⟨ , ⟩ can view the same place from two directions [S2A-029-103]

For co-ordinative apposition, see 5.12.

In restrictive apposition, the appositive is not separated by punctuation or intonation. Three types of restrictive apposition occur with noun phrases. In the first type, the first noun phrase starts with a determiner and the second noun phrase, which is more specific, is usually a name:

[19] The unsuccessful intervention of Magnus Maximus into continental politics between 383–88 A.D., along with a considerable portion of the British army, set a dangerous precedent, which the usurper *Constantine III* followed in 407 A.D. with disastrous consequences. [W1A-001-15]

[20] In some cases, as with my agent *Dennis Selinger*, they are also obliged to play the part of best man, godfather to the children and lifelong friend. [W2B-004-9]

[21] Steffi Graf's three-year winning reign at the Australian Open ended when the Czech *Jana Novotna* beat her 5–7, 6–4, 8–6 in a gripping quarter final at Flinders Park. [W2C-014-89]

The first type is also used with words that are cited and with the titles of works:

[22] Mary Jane tells me I shouldn't use the word *half-caste* [S1A-080-182]

[23] Now in the present case the phrase *interim award* has been used or may have been understood to be used uh in another sense [S2A-063-43]

[24] Kevin Kostner's epic film *Dance with Wolves* has been nominated for twelve Oscars [S2B-016-106]

[25] It's actually the second play I've written for them uhm ⟨ , ⟩ which is kind of based on the uhm the Browning poem *The Pied Piper* [S1A-096-27]

The first noun phrase is often ellipted in this type of apposition. For cited words (e.g. *half-caste* **[22]** and *interim award* **[23]** above), the ellipted noun phrase would be expressions such as *the word, the phrase, the sentence, the expression, the slogan,* whereas for works it would be *the play, the film, the novel,* etc.

[26] Well I don't think you can negotiate if by *negotiations* you mean can we allow Saddam Hussein to hold on to part of Kuwait [S1B-035-68]

[27] *Disraeli*'s a proper noun [S1A-085-292]

[28] '*That was laid on with a trowel*' appears in Shakespeare's As You Like It (I, ii, 98) which the Arden edition glosses as '*slapped on thick and without nicety, like mortar*'. [W2B-010-108]

[29] It's a short step from these to Ronald Reagan's '*Let's make America great again*' in 1980. [W2B-010-187]

[30] *Twins* is definitely a film to watch [S1A-049-304]

[31] In *Babes in Arms* (1939)—the only one in the genre I have looked at— Rooney and Garland play the teenage children of retired vaudeville players who decide to put on a big show of their own. [W2B-010-179]

[32] But to say this is from the *New York Times* therefore it's American English is not very helpful lexicographically cos sort of ninety percent of the matter is common English of the world [S1B-076-52]

The assumed ellipsis of *the film* explains why in **[30]** the verb is singular though *Twins* is plural.

The second type of restrictive apposition is the same as the first, except that the determiner is missing in the first noun phrase. This type commonly occurs in news reports:

[33] "Italy has never questioned the need for unity of command in the United Nations Operation in Somalia," Foreign Minister *Andreatta* said Thursday. [*International Herald Tribune*, 16 July 1993, p. 2]

[34] Financial adviser *David Innes*, who is now the centre's general manager, explained that staff were "very mindful" that the lifeline was being viewed as their last chance. [W2C-009-40]

[35] Art Student *Mulvey* and his tutor at Kingsway College in central London decided he would make the graffiti study as a project for his diploma, a court heard. [W2C-020-56]

[36] Forest's equaliser in the 75th minute had an element of good fortune, Terry Wilson's drive spinning off defender *Richard Shaw* and looping over goalkeeper *Nigel Martyn* into the net. [W2C-014-37]

Family designations are often found in this second type:

[37] This is Cousin *Renee* who is not to be confused with Auntie *Renee* [S2B-024-115]

The second type resembles titles, except that titles are well-established whereas many of these appositives are *ad hoc* and outside news reports they follow the first or third types. Titles generally precede the name:[6]

Senator Richard G. Lugar	*Prince* Charles
Chairman Mao	*Dr* Kissinger
Mr Clinton	*Emperor* Akihito
President Boris Yeltsin	*Chief* Buthelesi
Admiral Crowe	*The Reverend* Martin Luther King, Jr

When the titles are modified, they may follow the name, but in that case they are appositives rather than titles:[7]

[38] Mikhail Gorbachev's meeting yesterday with Boris Yeltsin, *president of the Russian Federation*, came none too soon. [W2C-008-3]

Two titles may be combined:

His Royal Highness Prince Charles
Her Majesty Queen Elizabeth
Mr Chief Justice

The third type of restrictive apposition is the reverse of the first: the name comes first and is followed by a noun phrase that is less specific and is introduced by a determiner:

[39] Dad slowly rolled the belt round his wrist and pulled at the other end as if it were the old razor strop used in Perkins *the barber's* down the road. [W2F-001-98]

[40] Simon doesn't pay but Laura *the student* does [S1A-007-225]

The non-restrictive/restrictive distinction applies to appositive clauses as well as relative clauses.[8] The finite clause in **[41]** is non-restrictive, the finite clause in **[42]** and the infinitive clause in **[43]** are restrictive:

[41] It will not be long before he asks his regular question: *'What would you like for your birthday?'* [W2F-019-105]

[42] Well is there very much that you can't do under DOS I mean given the fact *that machines get much faster* [S1A-029-162]

[43] Most of the time though the tendency of the blood *to clot* must be resisted ⟨ , ⟩ but not so firmly that it won't clot at all ⟨ , ⟩ [S2B-038-32]

Appositive clauses are treated as complements of the noun head in 6.16.

5.12
The co-ordination of noun phrases

Co-ordinated noun phrases are at the same level of structure and constitute a unit, a compound noun phrase. Typically, noun phrases are co-ordinated explicitly by means of a co-ordinator. The usual co-ordinators for noun phrases are *and* and *or*, less frequently *nor* and *but*.

If co-ordinators are present, the co-ordination is syndetic:

[1] What is it like to be back home studying again in the company of *close friends and family*? [W1B-001-129]

The two noun phrases may be separated by an intonation break in speech or by a comma in writing to emphasize a separate unit of information:

[2] His only answer to *his errors, and those of others*, is to isolate them. [W1A-010-78]

[3] It was *attacks by their neighbours, or the fear of such attacks,* that gave early Rome the pretexts or motives for reducing them to submission; in addition, by confiscating some of their lands, the Romans were able to satisfy the land-hunger of their own peasantry. [W2A-001-3]

More than two noun phrases may be co-ordinated in syndetic co-ordination. In that case, it is normal for the co-ordinator to appear only between the last two phrases:

[4] Mr. Mandela has in turn been *activist, prisoner, martyr, statesman and conciliator.* [*International Herald Tribune*, 20 July 1993, p. 2]

Punctuation usage varies as to whether a comma is inserted between the penultimate noun phrase and the co-ordinator. The comma is often omitted on the assumption that it is not necessary, since the co-ordinator is sufficient to signal the co-ordination. American usage omits the comma in journalistic writing, as in **[4]**, but otherwise retains it:

[5] For someone bound by classical concepts of *motion, inertia, and gravity,* it is hard to appreciate the self-consistent world view that went with Aristotle's understanding of a pendulum. [*Chaos: Making a New Science,* by James Gleick (New York: Penguin, 1988), p. 40]

British usage tends to omit the comma **[6]**, but sometimes retains it **[7]**:

[6] Ideas that come to mind are *workload, allocation of the 1% flexibility element from the last salary settlement and the new College admissions procedure.* [W1B-024-8]

[7] When I think of children I think of *imagination, generosity, and tantrums that are basically harmless.* [W2B-004-3]

Co-ordination is polysyndetic when co-ordinators are repeated redundantly between each pair of noun phrases when there are more than two:

[8] The mixture of warm air and moisture creates thunderstorms at altitude—maybe 3,000 metres (10,000 feet)—bringing *thunder and sheet lightning and heavy downpours* from France, often at night. [W2B-026-44]

[9] It was agreeable, he thought, to have no ties, not to have to rush back to wife and family as did, for instance, Herbert, always in a hurry to fit in *the children's holidays or Venice or Paris* because Victoria must go between the children's half-terms, and still constantly travel for his own work. [W2F-018-16]

The redundancy emphasizes that each item is a separate entity.

Co-ordination is asyndetic when the phrases are not linked by co-ordinators but co-ordinators could have been inserted, as in this example of left dislocation (cf. 5.11):

[10] *Defence, international relations, economic management, honours, appointments, law enforcement*—all are excluded. [*The Economist,* 17–23 July 1993, p. 25]

Co-ordination may be hierarchical, with one level of co-ordination embedded in another level:

[11] So this is showing you this interesting balance in this classical Ottoman painting ⟨ , ⟩ between *naturalism or pretend naturalism* ⟨ , ⟩ *and stylisation* [S2A-059-20]

In **[11]** the compound noun phrase *naturalism or pretend naturalism* is co-ordinated with the simple noun phrase *stylisation*.

The co-ordinated noun phrases may include or consist of pronouns **[12]**, nominal adjectives **[13]**, and numerals **[14]**:

[12] The optician cannot say that *he or she* will only test your sight if you buy glasses from *him or her*. [W2D-001-41]

[13] We're at the moment when there's about to be a struggle between *the earthly and the divine* and that's why this episode illuminates a world that we know [S2B-028-96]

[14] It was easterly winds which brought the severe cold of the winters of *1947 and 1962/3*—two of the coldest winters this century in the British Isles. [W2B-026-48]

Co-ordinators other than *and* and *or* are exemplified below:

[15] The risk is not imposition ⟨ , ⟩ *but* isolation [S2B-050-59]

[16] When I was a young and inexperienced gardener a thing that really whetted my appetite is a is a very dumpy thick tome or a series of tomes that you can't get your hands on for love *nor* money now which was sold in four and sixpenny weekly instalments called the Marshall Cavendish Encyclopedia of Gardening [S1B-025-115]

[17] But, as has already been suggested, the pluralism of modern society also embraces options that are internally monolithic in belief *and/or* practice. [W2A-012-51]

And/or is an abbreviatory device ('*and* or *or*').

In co-ordinative apposition, the two noun phrases linked by *and* or *or* are co-referential. The co-ordinators can be regarded as markers of apposition:

[18] Deng Rong, 43, *the book's author and Mr. Deng's youngest daughter*, makes clear that her aim is not to write a tell-all unauthorised biography but rather something closer to a Communist hagiography. [*International Herald Tribune*, 20 August 1993, p. 1]

[19] The impulses that occur in the brain produce certain recognized patterns on an electroencephalogram (*eeg, or brain wave trace*). [W2B-023-5]

[20] With V-2 engines such a vehicle would have a maximum speed of only *about 6,000 miles per hour (9,600 kilometres per hour) or about one-third of satellite speed.* [W2B-035-42]

5.13
Segregatory and combinatory co-ordination

Co-ordination of noun phrases may be segregatory or combinatory. The co-ordination is segregatory when each noun phrase could function independently in the clause, perhaps with some changes, such as in the number of the verbs. For example, **[1]** is roughly equivalent to **[1a]**:

[1] *Bomb warnings and drugs courier baggage* were mentioned. [W2C-001-48]

[1a] *Bomb warnings* were mentioned and *drugs courier baggage* was mentioned.

The co-ordination is combinatory when the noun phrases function semantically as a unit and cannot be paraphrased in a co-ordination of clauses:

[2] This unscheduled stop provoked some consternation in the United States, coming so soon after *Rajiv and President Reagan* had met at the United Nations in New York, and just a month before the first Reagan–Gorbachev summit in Geneva. [W2B-011-25]

[3] The remark certainly didn't seem to bother Pete, as a week later, in Paris, *he and Lynne* were married. [W2B-004-50]

[4] Anyhow *you and Harriet* know one another [. . .] [S1A-094-75]

[5] They have their own companions, Frankenstein has a very caring family and the opportunity to make friends at University, *Adam and Eve* have each other, whilst the inhabitants of the Wasteland miss the chance to form meaningful relationships amongst themselves. [W1A-010-42]

One another **[4]** and *each other* **[5]** are explicit indicators of combinatory co-ordination. They can be inserted in **[2]** ('had met each other') and **[3]** ('were married to one another'). On the other hand, *both* and *neither* are common indicators of segregatory co-ordination of noun phrases:

[6] *Both Wales and the North* had never progressed beyond being military zones, so that there was no structure of government to be destroyed and consequently they were much harder to subdue. [W1A-001-83]

[7] We have also seen in the last few days that there was *neither time nor reason* to delay the land battle any longer [S2B-014-20] ('there was not time and there was not reason')

Co-ordinated modifiers of noun phrases are also open to the distinction between segregatory and combinatory co-ordination. In **[8]**, *the beech and oak woods* is shown to be segregatory because of the previous mention of *your beech woods and your oak woods*:

[8] So uhm so then that means like you get your get *your beech woods and your oak woods* but within *the beech and oak woods* there are different kinds [S1A-036-200]

Out of context, *the beech and oak woods* could have a combinatory interpretation: 'the woods containing both beeches and oaks'. In **[8]**, however, the context makes it clear that the phrase is elliptical for 'the beech woods and the oak woods'.

Segregatory co-ordination may involve ellipsis of some part or parts of the noun phrase.

[9] Poplar, as one of the most poverty-stricken boroughs in London, attracted the attention of *Beatrice and Sydney Webb* in 1914. [W2B-019-10] ('Beatrice Webb and Sydney Webb')

[10] Tape is the recording medium used by *both audio and video recorders*. [W2D-014-61] ('both audio recorders and video recorders')

[11] Nor, to turn to *Marxist or quasi-Marxist interpretations*, is there any evidence that slavery was a decisive factor. [W2A-001-29] ('Marxist interpretations or quasi-Marxist interpretations')

In combinatory co-ordination, there is no ellipsis:

[12] Add *the tomato and onion mixture* then bring to the boil before adding the contents of the tin of beans. [W2D-020-88] ('the mixture containing tomatoes and onions')

[13] For example, *the diagnostic and statistics manual* (DSM) has been updated twice, once in 1968, and again in 1980, with a revised version in 1986. [W1A-007-79]

[14] She had *egg and bacon breakfast* and it seemed enough, but she wants some milk. [W2F-003-79]

[15] Ultimate power would lie with the jury of 12 randomly selected *good men and true*. [W2B-014-73]

5.14 Subject–verb agreement

The verb agrees with the subject in number and person wherever such distinctions are featured in the verb. Subject–verb agreement applies to the first verb in the verb phrase, whether it is a main verb or an auxiliary. Except for the verb *be*, the distinctions appear only in the present tense, which has two forms: the -*s* form (ending in -*s*) and the base (or uninflected) form. The -*s* form is used for the third person singular, and the base form is used otherwise. Subject–verb agreement varies in non-standard dialects, where some verb forms are merged (cf. 4.19 f.).

If the noun phrase has a noun as its head, the relevant distinction is only in number, since all such noun phrases are in the third person. The general rule then is that singular noun phrases require the -*s* form and plural noun phrases require the base form:

[1] His account *contains* many historical solecisms. [W2A-001-26]

[2] Many terrestrial soils, in contrast, *contain* large proportions of very small particles made up of clay minerals. [W2A-022-83]

Agreement is expected to be with the head of the noun phrase, the plural *schools* in **[3]**:

[3]   In recent years several schools of thought *have* emerged, each
       championed by leading exponents of the period. [W1A-001-8]

Modal auxiliaries (cf. 4.29, 5.24) do not have an -*s* form, so the agreement
rule does not apply to them. For example, modal *will* is used with a singular
subject in [4] and with a plural subject in [5]:

[4]   My door *will* always be open to you. [W1B-001-133]

[5]   Our relationship is just beginning—growing pains *will* be part of its growth.
       [W1B-001-41]

Personal pronouns have distinctions in person as well as number. The third
person singular pronouns *he*, *she*, and *it* take the -*s* form and the other
personal pronouns—*I*, *we*, *you*, and *they*—take the base form:

[6]   Well he *has* this stupid girl he *falls* in love with doesn't he or something
       [S1A-006-109]

[7]   And she *wants* to know when to move it uh before or after the budding
       [S1B-025-44]

[8]   So ⟨ , ⟩ I don't really want to go anyway so ⟨ , , ⟩ I don't see it *makes* a
       difference ⟨ , ⟩ really [S1A-006-325]

[9]   I *hate* this [S1A-001-18]

[10]   Life goes on Matthew doesn't it regardless of the turmoil we *find*
       ourselves embroiled in. [W1B-001-23]

[11]   Uhm ⟨ , ⟩ and really you *need* it all through your life [S1A-003-17]

[12]   And as you can see they *look* ⟨ , ⟩ quite different [S2A-028-42]

Whether used as a main verb or as an auxiliary, the verb *be* has further
distinctions, which extend to the past tense. In the present tense, it has three
forms, adding a distinctive form *am* for the first person singular in agreement
with the pronoun *I*.

[13]   At the moment I *am* at home doing some work on a word processor. [W1B-
       001-121] (1st person singular)

[14]   Well you *are* going to be a doctor [S1A-039-104] (2nd person singular)

[15]   The other thing *is* uhm ⟨ , , ⟩ do you confide in her [S1A-031-166] (3rd person
       singular)

[16]   Like fallen leaves that the wind sweeps to and fro, we *are* indiscriminately
       swayed by our unsubstantial and frivolous emotions. [W1B-001-38] (1st
       person plural)

[17]   Regards to your family—I hope you *are* all well. [W1B-004-139] (2nd person
       plural)

[18]   More and more people *are* being arrested [S2A-005-23] (3rd person plural)

The verb *be* is the only verb to display distinctions in number and person
for the past tense. *Was* is used for the first and third persons singular, and *were*
is used otherwise:

[19]   Also, on reflection, I *was* baffled by the logic. [W2B-004-47] (1st person
       singular)

[20] However, one had to make allowances for youth, as Lynne *was* actually younger than one of the children she *was* talking about. [W2B-004-49] (3rd person singular)

[21] Well we *were* wondering about that [S1A-073-67] (1st person plural)

[22] Robert Runcie it's it's wonderful meeting you just at this point after ten years is it when you *were* just leaving Saint Albans [S1B-041-46] (2nd person singular)

[23] And within the dance field that you *were* both ⟨ , ⟩ in before this ⟨ , ⟩ uhm ⟨ , ⟩ would you say the attitude is is fairly ⟨ , ⟩ uhm ⟨ , , ⟩ rigid towards no not even thinking about including disabled people [S1A-002-48] (2nd person plural)

[24] And they have a conventional cooker as well which they *were* using [S1A-009-183] (3rd person plural)

Nominal clauses (cf. 6.12) functioning as subject generally take a singular verb:

[25] That his people believe that after last night *is* doubtful [S2B-008-85]

[26] Once you've sent a message onto the e-mail system ⟨ , ⟩ receiving them ⟨ , ⟩ *is* as simple as sending them [S2A-028-65]

[27] To say actors are childlike *is* to pay them a compliment. [W2B-004-02]

Nominal relative clauses (cf. 6.12), however, vary in number according to whether the nominal relative pronoun is interpreted as singular **[28]** or (far less usually) as plural **[29]**:

[28] What was interesting *was* the uh breakfast petit déjeuner uhm [S1A-009-129]

[29] What we're going to have now *are* speeches [S1B-079-82]

The subject is plural if it consists of two or more noun phrases co-ordinated by *and*:

[30] The truth the truth is Mister Speaker ⟨ , ⟩ that in many aspects of politics ⟨ , ⟩ *style and substance* ⟨ , ⟩ complement each other [S2B-050-3]

If, however, the two noun phrases are viewed as referring to a single entity, they take a singular verb:

[31] *The Stars and Stripes* was draped over Mr. Kempner's coffin last Tuesday at his funeral in Johannes Kirche in Berlin, the same Lutheran chapel where he was baptized and confirmed. [*International Herald Tribune*, 31 August 1993, p. 5]

Similarly, if the co-ordinated noun phrases are in co-ordinative apposition (cf. end of 5.12), and therefore refer to the same single entity, they take a singular verb.

If two singular noun phrases are co-ordinated by *or* or by *nor*, they generally take a singular verb:

[32] [. . .] as far as Jordan is concerned will my honourable friend make Her Majesty's Government's position clear as follows that if either Iraq or Israel *invades* or *uses* Jordanian territory our attitude towards any such incursions would be the same as our attitude towards Iraq's incursion into Kuwait [S1B-060-88]

[33] Neither blanket television nor 24-hours-a-day radio news *is* well suited to reporting events that drag on, let alone a war with no clear time limit. [W2E-007-10]

If the noun phrases differ in what verb form they would take separately, the plural is more usual:

[34] Neither you nor your partner *have* to be a parent of the child or children provided they live with you as members of your family. [W2D-005-25]

Singular collective nouns, which denote a group of people or things, are sometimes treated as plural in British English (less commonly in American English) when the focus is on the group as individuals rather than as a single entity:

[35] The Argentine team *are* in possession now inside *their* own half [S2A-010-213]

[36] And his reaction to this uh mention of Mr Lampitt's company was that he was surprised that Mr Lampitt's company *were* on the acquisition trail *themselves* [S2A-070-12]

[37] Uhm so people are still confused because they keep telling me the Government *are* confused about what *they* want to do [S1B-034-29]

[38] Commenting on the timing of the two reports, Mr Kreindler said that they had surfaced just as his group *were* gathering critical evidence. [W2C-001-52]

[39] The public *have* been fair [S2B-031-19]

[40] The enemy *have* brought forward *their* elephant ⟨ , ⟩ to trample down the bridge but one of the Moguls has managed to shoot the elephant [S2A-059-113]

Titles of works and citations (cf. 5.11), even if plural in form, take a singular verb:

[41] Larry Niven's "The Integral Trees" *is* not set in the same universe as his delightful Big-Dumb-Object Novel "Ringworld". [*The Economist*, 24–30 July 1993, p. 87]

[42] Thus *sandshoes is* the word found in our Northeast area, while *gollies is* found in our Merseyside area. [*The Dialects of England*, by Peter Trudgill (Oxford: Basil Blackwell, 1990), p. 101]

The pronoun *none* is treated as either singular or plural:

[43] We all know in our own lives what changes the last ten years have brought but none of us *knows* the picture overall and that's what the census supplies [S2B-044-18]

[44] Anomalous innervation may suggest motor recovery where none *has* actually occurred. [W2A-026-29]

[45] I wonder who supplies them at the moment because uh uh certainly none of the locals *do* [S1A-027-33]

[46] There are many origami yachts, boats and ships, but none *are* as simple or as full of movement as this wonderful design by Japan's First Lady of origami, Mrs Toshie Takahama. [W2D-019-64]

The variation exists irrespective of whether there is a postmodifier of *none* with a plural—*none of us* **[43]** and *none of the locals* **[45]**. The singular verb *has* is required in **[44]** because the antecedent of *none* (*motor recovery*) is a singular non-count noun.

Existential *there* (cf. 4.39) is often followed by a singular verb, especially in informal speech, even when the noun phrase that follows the verb is plural:

[47] There'*s* books as presents books for the children and so on [S1A-013-52]

[48] There *is* £2 left which will be deducted from your spectacle voucher. [W2D-001-72]

Lack of number agreement between subject and verb sometimes occurs, especially in speech and in unedited writing, because of the influence of another noun or pronoun that intervenes between the head of the noun phrase and the verb.

[49] *Depopulation* due to plague and migration in the fifth and sixth centuries *appear* to be responsible for the demise of the lowland British kingdoms. [W1A-001-87]

[50] You are, no doubt, aware of the Smith & Jones cases, in which an age *limit* of 27 years and of 35 years (37 years for clinical staff) *were* found to be indirectly discriminatory against women, in the civil service and UGC New Blood Scheme, respectively. [W1B-024-24]

[51] The *results* of that in pollution and wasted natural resources every year *is* shameful. [W2B-013-69]

In **[49]** the head of the noun phrase is the non-count noun *depopulation*, but plural *centuries* immediately precedes the verb *appear*, which is therefore in the plural by attraction to the preceding plural noun. In **[50]** *were* is plural by attraction to the nearby plural *years* (and perhaps also the collective noun *staff*, which is often treated as plural in British English), though *limit*, the head of the relevant noun phrase, is singular. In **[51]**, on the other hand, singular *year* has probably led to the use of singular *is* by attraction, in disregard of plural *results*, the head of the noun phrase.

5.15
Vocatives

Vocatives are predominately noun phrases. They are optional additions to the basic sentence structures, and are used to address the person or persons spoken to, either to single them out from others **[1]** or to maintain some personal connection with them **[2]**:

[1]   *Robin* what do you think [S1A-020-230]

[2]   You're a snob *Dad* [S1A-007-175]

In its function of singling out a person, the vocative may constitute the whole utterance, as in broadcast panel discussions where the presenter singles out one of the speakers [3] or a member of the audience [4]:

[3]   Kenneth Clarke [S1B-027-2]

[4]   Gentleman with the beard ⟨ , ⟩ sir [S1B-027-134 f.]

The utterance in [4] combines two vocatives.

Vocatives may appear initially [1], finally [2], or medially [5]:

[5]   It may well be an outcome *Peter* devoutly to be desired [S1B-027-40]

In writing they are normally separated from the rest of the sentence by punctuation:

[6]   'You've done well too, *boy*. Your ma and me are proud of you.' [W2F-007-31 f.]

In speech, vocatives are generally marked by distinctive intonation, varying according to their position in the sentence.

Vocatives are commonly names (as in [1], [3], and [5] above), family terms [2] and [7], epithets [7]–[10], titles [11]–[13], and designations of respect [14]–[16]:

[7]   A: Will you have another cup of tea *grandpa*
       B: No thank you *sweetheart* [S1A-028-153 f.]

[8]   Well you can't ask for it back *dear* [S1A-007-87]

[9]   Right okay then *love* so I'll hear from you at the beginning of next week [S1A-095-327]

[10]   How are you *darling*? [W1B-002-111]

[11]   *My Lord* ⟨ , ⟩ the first passage is at page 229 [S1B-063-66]

[12]   *Officer* I think that uh you examined that uh Ford Cortina make of car which you found present at the scene of the accident [S1B-068-15]

[13]   *Mr Speaker* my right honourable friend is right [S1B-053-5]

[14]   A: Did you not know it
       B: I didn't know that at the time *sir* [S1B-061-176]

[15]   "That will do, Pritchard."
       "Thank you, *m'm*." [W2F-005-57 ff.]

[16]   'Can I help you, *miss*?' he said. [W2F-009-65]

Some noun phrases that do not belong to the above types are commonly used as vocatives:

[17]   Well good afternoon *ladies and gentlemen* [S2A-024-1]

[18]   I asked what he was doing.
       'Just attached here and there, *old boy*. It's hush-hush, I can't really explain.' [W2F-014-52 ff.]

[19]   'You'll bend over that table, *lad*,' he said. [W2F-001-95]

[20]   Stick to your guns stick to your gun *girl* [S1A-091-141]

[21]   Cor blimey I haven't spoken to you for a week *woman* [S1A-098-225]

[22] Uhm I'm sorry *everybody* then it looks like that was a that was a definite pick-up then [S1A-020-21]

Examples **[23]** and **[24]** are restricted to particular situations:

[23] Now *members of the jury* ⟨ , , ⟩ you and I tried this case ⟨ , ⟩ as a ⟨ , ⟩ team [S2A-061-1]

[24] *Students or staff who feel that a situation has not been satisfactorily resolved* please contact . . . [S2B-044-98]

Finally, it is conventional for the salutation that heads letters to be a vocative beginning with *Dear* followed by a name or names or by designations such as *Sir, Madam, Colleagues.*

Vocatives may also be addressed to non-humans (e.g. supernatural beings and pets) or to abstract entities (e.g. *Spring, Virtue, Beauty*).

Some of the noun phrases used as vocatives would otherwise require a determiner such as *the* when they are used in the singular. For example, contrast the use of *young man* as a complete noun phrase in **[25]** with *the young man* in **[25a]**:

[25] And Playatsky in fact took off his glasses looked at him and said *young man* ⟨ , ⟩ on what basis pray do you venture to contradict me [S2A-023-43]

[25a] *The young man* ventured to contradict me.

5.16
Reference of noun phrases

Noun phrases generally refer to entities in the world. We can establish three sets of contrasts for noun phrase reference:

1. definite versus non-definite
2. specific versus non-specific
3. generic versus non-generic

A speaker or writer uses a definite noun phrase on the assumption that the hearer or reader can identify its reference. For example, in **[1]** the first mention of *cigarette* is in an indefinite noun phrase, but since the second mention refers back to the previous mention, it is in a definite noun phrase:

[1] A: But you only had one hand because you'd got *a cigarette* in the other
B: No I was holding on with both hands but *the cigarette* was in my two fingers [S1B-066-16 f.]

The indefinite article *a* signals that *a cigarette* has indefinite reference (one of a type of object with that designation), and the definite article *the* that *the cigarette* has definite reference. Other signals of indefinite reference are indefinite determiners such as *some* (cf. 4.44) and the zero article (cf. 4.33).

Identification of the reference comes from three major sources:

1. The phrase refers to something previously mentioned, as in **[1]** above and in **[2]** below:

> **[2]** As the administration meanders, the House has sent to the Senate *a spending bill that chops away at what is already a tight aid request. The bill*'s huge engines—aid to Russia, Israel and Egypt—almost guarantee that most of the administration's money requests will safely pass through Congress in spite of overall budget constraints. [*The International Herald Tribune*, 30 July 1993, p. 6]

2. The identification comes from the modifiers in the noun phrase:

> **[3]** Now over the course of the season ⟨ , ⟩ *the steps to the swimming pool* might be used a very substantial amount mightn't they [S1B-067-95]

3. The phrase refers to something that the speaker or writer believes is uniquely identifiable to the hearer or reader, either from general knowledge or from knowledge of the particular situation:

> **[4]** Today is Sunday 14th April, it's mid-afternoon and *the sun* is shining. [W1B-001-123]
>
> **[5]** Far more than that number, I judge, now believe that they would have a better chance of holding their seats and keeping power under another leader. This includes the majority of *the Cabinet.* [W2C-003-65 f.]
>
> **[6]** I shall probably look in at *the College* once or twice during the autumn, and hope to see you then. [W1B-014-64]
>
> **[7]** 'I've got to take out *the dog,*' he said as finally as he could. [W2F-001-162]
>
> **[8]** Tanya appeared quite relieved as *the telephone* rang. [W2F-006-163]
>
> **[9]** Every Tuesday I stood there waiting by *the door* expecting you to come [S1A-040-372]

The definite article is not the only signal of definite reference. Proper names are intended to be uniquely identifiable, either because the reference is generally known (e.g. *Ronald Reagan, Paul McCartney*) or because the speaker/writer expects the particular hearer/reader to know who or what is referred to when there is more than one possibility (*Springfield, Mary*). The personal pronouns are also definite, and in most uses so are the demonstrative pronouns (cf. 4.45).

A noun phrase has *specific reference* when it refers to a specific person, thing, place, etc., even if the reference is not definite (i.e. the speaker/writer does not expect the hearer/reader to identify the reference). For example, the analysis in **[10]** is a specific analysis:

> **[10]** Although I publish quite a lot I discovered a couple of years ago that no mainstream publisher wanted to publish *a negative analysis of the British monarchy that I've written* [S2B-032-10]

On the other hand, *a historical novel* in **[11]** is non-specific, since it does not refer to a particular instance of a historical novel:

> **[11]** I'd always been interested in ancient history and I'd always wanted to write *a historical novel* [S1B-048-162]

A film in **[12]** is probably intended to be non-specific too, though it is possible that a particular film is intended:

[12] I had intended to take them dancing and to hear Colin sing but they wanted to see *a film* so I was outnumbered. [W1B-006-63]

Here is another clear example of non-specific reference:

[13] Your sight can be tested only by *a registered optician* (optometrist) or *an ophthalmic medical practitioner.* [W2D-001-2]

Noun phrases with non-specific reference normally have an indefinite determiner such as *a*, but *the* is also possible:

[14] I intended to write *the definitive study on the present British monarchy.*

Noun phrases with generic reference are used in generalizations:

[15] *Fractals* are wiggly lines which look equally wiggly whatever scale you examine them at. [*The Economist*, 24–30 July 1993, p. 84]

Fractals is generic in that it refers to all members of the class of fractals. Generic noun phrases are by definition non-specific. The distinctions of definite and indefinite and also of singular and plural are neutralized, so that approximating to **[15]** are **[15a]**, **[15b]**, and **[15c]**:

[15a] *The fractals* are wiggly lines which look equally wiggly whatever scale you examine them at.

[15b] *The fractal* is a wiggly line which looks equally wiggly whatever scale you examine it at.

[15c] *A fractal* is a wiggly line which looks equally wiggly whatever scale you examine it at.

The four versions are also available for the generic phrases in **[16]** and **[17]**:

[16] I don't see *a French writer* voluntarily writing in English [S1B-026-107]

[17] Okay ⟨ , ⟩ here's just a ⟨ , ⟩ few of the areas where ⟨ , ⟩ *collisions of electrons with molecules* play an important role [S2A-028-8]

In **[17]** the whole noun phrase is generic, and the noun phrases within it— *electrons* and *molecules*—are also generic.

The four versions of the generic noun phrase illustrated in **[15]**–**[15c]** are not always available. Non-count nouns (cf. 4.5) do not have a plural and they cannot be used in a generic interpretation with *the*. All the noun phrases in **[18]** are generic, and six of them—all except *soft drinks* and *sandwiches*—are non-count:

[18] *Coffee, tea, soft drinks, confectionery, sandwiches, fruit* and *other food and drink* do not mix well with *computing equipment.* [W2B-033-56]

However, plural generic noun phrases usually do not take *the* as a determiner. Although we could replace *sandwiches* in **[18]**, for example, with generic *a sandwich* or (more plausibly, in a sentence where it alone is subject) with generic *the sandwich*, we could not have *the sandwiches*. But plural generic noun phrases with nominal adjectives as their head do have *the*:

[19] *The French* report signs of chemical emissions after their bombing missions against chemical weapons plants [S2B-001-4]

[20] The vital decisions we reach on human fertilisation and embryology and subsequently pregnancy termination must affect how we regard the status of each individual ⟨ , ⟩ his or her human rights the treatment of *the handicapped* the fate of *the senile* and *the terminally ill* [S1B-060-34]

In **[21]** the generic *the Dutch* is co-ordinated with two plural generic nationality nouns:

[21] But now *the Danes*, *the Germans* and *the Dutch* are also having second thoughts about setting up such a bank before the 12 economies in the EC have achieved greater "convergence". [W2E-008-72]

The reference of generic noun phrases is interpreted as extending to those that are relevant in the context. In **[19]** *the French* does not refer to all the French people. In **[21]** the reference is presumably to the Danish, German, and Dutch governments.

Verb Phrases

5.17
The structure of the verb phrase

A verb phrase has as its head a main (or lexical) verb. The main verb may be preceded by up to four auxiliaries (or auxiliary verbs), but see 5.33 for semi-auxiliaries.

The auxiliaries fall into two major sets:

1. the primary auxiliaries:
2. the modals (or modal or secondary auxiliaries (cf. 4.29)):

In addition, there are several marginal auxiliaries (*dare, need, ought to, used to*; cf. 4.29) and a number of semi-auxiliaries such as *had better* and *had got to*.

The primary auxiliaries are *be, have,* and *do*. Auxiliary *be* has two functions: (1) it forms the progressive in combination with a following *-ing* participle, e.g. *is playing*; (2) it forms the passive in combination with a following *-ed* participle, e.g. *is played*. Auxiliary *have* forms the perfect aspect in combination with a following *-ed* participle, e.g. *has played*. Auxiliary *do* is the dummy operator: it functions as the operator to form (for example) interrogative and negative sentences in the absence of any other operator, e.g. *Did they play? They didn't play* (cf. 5.18).

The modal auxiliaries are *can, could, may, might, shall, should, will, would, must*. The modals convey notions of factuality, such as certainty (e.g. *They must be there*), or of control, such as permission (e.g. *You may play outside*). They are followed by an infinitive (cf. 5.24).

The auxiliaries appear in a set sequence:

modal—perfect *have*—progressive *be*—passive *be*—main verb

It is not usual for all to be present in one verb phrase, though it is certainly possible, as in **[1]**:

[1]   *should* (modal) *have* (perfect) *been* (progressive) *being* (passive) *played* (main verb)

In **[1]** each of the auxiliaries is followed by the required verb form:

should (modal) *have* (infinitive)
have (perfect) *been* (*-ed* participle)
been (progressive) *being* (*-ing* participle)
being (passive) *played* (*-ed* participle)

Here are examples of verb phrases with combinations of three auxiliaries:

[2]   Those who had parents who slapped their faces if they misbehaved *would have been making* judgements about my behaviour which were influenced by their own childhood memories. [W2B-017-85] (modal perfect progressive)

[3]   Well there's no doubt at all that we would have wanted to see sanctions run on for a longer period to see if Saddam *could have been removed* from Kuwait without war [S1B-027-143] (modal perfect passive)

[4]   If he were still alive, he *would*, at the very least, now *be being questioned* very searchingly by Scotland Yard. [*Evening Standard*, 26 June 1992, p. 8] (modal progressive passive)

As **[4]** illustrates, the sequence of verbs in the verb phrase may be interrupted by intervening adverbials. Here are further examples of such interventions:

[5]   Now *I've* just *been working* on this and and the problem has been to a certain extent the printer [S1A-024-3]

[6]   But uh if you had the choice would you prefer to have a meal which *has been* freshly *prepared* with uh fresh ingredients and so on [S1A-059-92]

[7]   The agreement *could* not even *have been considered* further unless it had been signed by all the members back in May [S1B-054-30]

In questions the operator precedes the subject and is therefore separated from the rest of the verb phrase:

[8]   '*Was* the Sharptor mine *being worked* the way it should have been, before it went out of business?' [W2F-007-45]

The first or only verb in the verb phrase is obligatorily marked for tense—a main verb in **[9]** and **[10]** and an auxiliary in **[11]** and **[12]**:

[9]   Doug *makes* quince jelly sometimes doesn't he [S1A-009-143]

[10]   There's one I was going to show you because it it *made* my hair stand on end [S1A-037-213]

[11]   But time *is* going slowly [S1A-017-12]

[12]   Officially I *was* doing a unit of English [S1A-006-10]

The first or only verb in the verb phrase is also marked for person and number where relevant:

[13] I *am* a secretary [S1A-014-86] (1st person singular)

[14] They *are* very very concerned [S1B-056-24] (3rd person plural)

The first or only verb in the verb phrase can function as the operator, for example in forming questions:

[15] *Can* you remember that [S1B-041-22]

The dummy operator *do* (cf. 5.18) is followed only (if at all) by the main verb in the infinitive:

do play   does go   did say

The only auxiliary that can be in the subjunctive (cf. 5.25 f.) is auxiliary *be*, which may function as the progressive auxiliary or the passive auxiliary:

if she *be acting* as lead   if I *were playing*
if it *be known*   if he *were told*

Semi-auxiliaries that begin with *be* (cf. 5.33) can also be in the subjunctive:

were I *to tell* you
if he *were going to write*

See 3.11 for negatives and 3.12 for passives.

5.18
Operators

The major characteristic of an auxiliary is that it can function as an operator when it is the first auxiliary in the verb phrase. When a form of the main verb *be* is the only verb in the verb phrase it can also function as an operator (e.g. '*Are* they upstairs?'); the same applies, especially in British English, to the main verb *have* (e.g. '*Have* you any children?'), although it is also treated as a main verb ('*Do* you have any children?'). In the absence of another potential operator, *do* is introduced as a dummy operator.

The operator is used for negation, interrogation, emphasis, and abbreviation.

A. Negation

To form a negative sentence or negative finite clause, *not* is placed after the operator:

[1] He says that there should be one national police force.

[1a] He says that there *should not* be one national police force [S1B-033-2]

[2] It was pasteurised milk.

[2a] It *was not* pasteurised milk [S1A-009-319]

[3] The countries around the world fit into neat and precise categories of climate and weather.

[3a] The countries around the world *do not* fit into neat and precise categories of climate and weather. [W2B-026-2]

Not can be contracted as *n't* and attached as an enclitic (cf. 4.29) to most operators:

[4] But *wouldn't* she remember him [S1A-006-134]

[5] You *can't* see from there [S2A-058-3]

[6] Perhaps this suggestion *isn't* absurd [S2B-029-114]

[7] He *didn't* play against England on Tuesday evening [S2A-014-29]

B. Interrogation

To form an interrogative sentence or interrogative finite main clause, the operator is placed before the subject:

[8] You can remember that.

[8a] *Can* you remember that [S1B-041-22]

[9] They will cope with the environmental problems that we have created.

[9a] How *will* they cope with the environmental problems that we have created [S2B-022-75]

[10] The poison is in that one.

[10a] *Is* the poison in that one [S1A-042-48]

[11] I told you.

[11a] *Did* I tell you [S1A-048-262]

[12] They went off to their parents.

[12a] Where *did* they go off to [S1A-039-65]

There is no subject–operator inversion in *wh*-questions if the *wh*-item is the subject (cf. 3.5).

Citation **[13a]** contains a negative question with subject–operator inversion. The operator *didn't* is negative:

[13] You didn't have enough sleep on the bus.

[13a] 'Honest to God, Dorothy—*didn't* you have enough sleep on the bus?' [W2F-013-33]

A more formal variant has the uncontracted negative particle *not* placed after the subject.

[13b] *Did* you *not* have enough sleep on the bus?

Another rarer formal variant has the uncontracted negative particle immediately after the operator, particularly if the subject is lengthy **[13c]**, but not only then **[14]**.

[13c] *Did not* all those travelling with you have enough sleep on the bus?

[14] For instance why did not the author(s) use this information to compare the relationship of social attributes and health? [W1B-025-6]

Subject–operator inversion also occurs with initial negative expressions:

[15] *No longer can* any member of the tribe of Levi ⟨ , ⟩ act as priest [S1B-001-9]

[16] *At no time were* they prepared to do so [S1B-014-19]

[17] *Never were* slaves so numerous as in Italy during the first century B.C. [W2A-001-31]

[18] *Rarely* in human history *has* the idea of an obligation imposed on us by others seemed so constricting and suffocating [S2B-029-127]

C. **Emphasis**

The operator may be used to convey emphasis. In speech, the emphatic function is signalled by placing the nuclear tone (a distinct pitch movement) on the operator; in writing, emphasis is occasionally signalled by italics or (mostly in manuscripts) by underlining. (The same methods are used to signal emphasis for words other than operators.) The emphasis on operator is usually intended to deny something that has been mentioned previously or that may have been assumed, or to reject what has been said by somebody else; e.g. an offer, invitation, advice, order. (See also 3.10.)

The emphatic function of the operator is unequivocally conveyed even in writing by the positive forms *do*, *does*, *did* when they are used in positive declarative sentences or clauses that are not abbreviated (see subsection D below):

[19] I *do* apologise for that [S1A-006-260]

[20] [. . .] it *does* actually face ⟨ , ⟩ south-west not west [S1A-023-250]

[21] Well I *did* think about it [S1A-039-215]

The non-emphatic equivalents are 'I *apologise*' for **[19]**, 'it actually *faces*' for **[20]**, and 'I *thought*' for **[21]**. Apart from such contexts, the operator *do* is not necessarily emphatic. For example, in **[22]** it is required as a dummy operator to form the *wh*-question:

[22] Why *did* you buy it [S1A-048-256]

Did in **[22]** may also be emphatic, but the emphasis would be conveyed by the intonation. Similarly, the negative forms of *do* (*doesn't, don't, didn't*) need not be emphatic, since they are used as dummy operators for negation.

Here are two examples of operators other than *do* that are used for emphasis. The context shows that they are intended to be interpreted as emphatic:

[23] I read that in the paper ⟨ , ⟩ so it *must* be true [S1A-063-185]

[24] "I think it will be all right," said Mr Hurd in a crowning sentence of elliptical emollience in which every word can have a different stress which renders a different overall meaning. But it *won't* be all right: the question is whether he, or any of the other questors after unity, can now help to make it so. [W2E-003-54 f.]

Here are some examples from writing where the operator is shown to be emphatic because it is in italics **[25]** or because it is underlined **[26]**–**[27]**:

[25] 'I want my d-daddy,' Tommy sobbed without looking up. 'He *is* alive. He *is*!' [W2F-002-49] [italics twice in original]

[26] Anyway, I really <u>must</u> go now. [W1B-013-105] [underline in original]

[27] You <u>can</u> be certain that I love you. [W1B-015-101] [underline in original]

D. Abbreviation

The operator may be used as an abbreviating device to avoid repetition of the verb phrase, perhaps together with other parts of the predicate:

[28] I've got to phone Liz because she said she was going to phone ⟨ , ⟩ on uh Monday night but she *hasn't* [S1A-093-203] ('she *hasn't phoned*')

[29] And W G Grace was coached by his mother and she didn't do a bad job and neither *did* he [S1B-021-78] ('neither *did* he *do a bad job*')

[30] A: Oh I wouldn't touch those ⟨ , , ⟩
B: No I *wouldn't* either [S1A-042-322 ff.] ('I *wouldn't touch those* either')

In British English an intransitive main verb *do* can be added to the abbreviating operator. It serves as a substitute for the rest of the predicate:

[31] Yes please don't bother for a moment because merely I wanted to know whether you disagree as I think you *might do* from what you've been saying with that passage that I've quoted from Dr Kendall's evidence [S1B-070-123]

[32] Thank goodness I didn't say anything awful ⟨ , ⟩ because I *could've done* [S1A-091-299]

Abbreviating operators are commonly used in tag questions (cf. 3.6):

[33] She's company though *isn't* she [S1A-019-162]

[34] Well you've got income coming in from the property I suppose *haven't* you [S1A-071-117]

[35] Apparently he dithers, hardly surprising being a politician *is* it? [W1B-001-22]

[36] But you can't just pick them up off the counter *can* you [S1A-079-217]

5.19
Finite and non-finite verb phrases

Verb phrases may be either finite or non-finite. In a finite verb phrase the first or only verb is finite. A verb is finite if it displays tense; that is, the distinction between present and past:

[1] What *stops* a Prime Minister ⟨ , ⟩ or government ⟨ , ⟩ from ⟨ , , ⟩ passing discriminatory legislation [S1B-011-143]

[2] He added that the car *stopped* almost immediately and the young man, who was in a "terrible state," told him he had hit two people. [W2C-017-33]

In [1] *stops* is a finite verb phrase consisting solely of a finite verb in the present tense, and in [2] *stopped* is likewise a finite verb phrase but this time the finite verb is in the past tense.

The finite verb phrases marked in **[3]**–**[8]** contain more than one verb, but only the first verb in the verb phrase is finite:

[3] British and Irish nurses at a Baghdad hospital *have stopped* work in protest at not being allowed to leave Iraq [S2B-019-7]

[4] Everything else *has been stopped* [S1A-012-237]

[5] The reason I have a new landlord is cos I'*m starting* work in Finchley today. [W1B-009-136]

[6] The new contractors *will be starting* the week of the 22nd. [W1B-028-48]

[7] Now before I *can start* the instrumentation we need to know a little bit from maths of how we go from absorption measurement into measurement of concentrations of haemoglobin and cytochrome [S2A-053-43]

[8] Silvie kept me there 1½ hours today and *did start* complaining about the electricity board. [W1B-006-88]

The three non-finite verb forms have been illustrated in **[3]**–**[8]** as functioning within a finite verb phrase:

1. *-ed* participle (*stopped*), functioning as perfect participle in *have stopped* **[3]** and as passive participle in *has been stopped* **[4]**
2. *-ing* participle (*starting*), functioning as progressive participle in *'m starting* **[5]** and *will be starting* **[6]**
3. infinitive (*start*), functioning after modal *can* in *can start* **[7]** and after dummy operator *did* in *did start* **[8]**

If a non-finite verb is the first or only verb in the verb phrase, the phrase is a non-finite verb phrase:

[9] Well will you tell her that you might save Rebecca from complete despair because *being exposed* twice within a month would be rather awful for her [S1A-021-151]

[10] It's right ⟨ , , ⟩ it's on a sort of hill ⟨ , ⟩ and you've got lovely views *looking* out the South Downs [S1A-036-148]

[11] I wouldn't really be looking forward to *be getting dressed* up on Friday [S1A-042-262]

[12] I broke my right wrist *riding* my bike in Germany [S1A-046-133]

[13] And I've got so many events *to go* to I mean I know that sounds a bit odd but I mean I've got a few [S1A-039-285]

[14] Yeah he said he seemed quite quite happy *to meet* you [S1A-008-155]

A finite verb phrase can function as the verb of a simple sentence **[15]**, the verb of a main clause within a compound sentence **[16]**, or the verb of a subordinate clause **[17]**–**[18]** (cf. 6.4):

[15] Tonight I'*m going* to my first cocktail party at the Commission, my dears! [W1B-002-85]

[16] Now I'*ve* just *been working* on this and and the problem *has been* to a certain extent the printer [S1A-024-3]

[17] Hackney has become fashionable among artists, actors and writers who *want* to live some way into London but who *don't have* much money. [W1B-011-16]

[18] We would get more information if they *were asked* for a doctor's letter to the College Occupational Physician. [W1B-018-87]

In **[16]** there are two co-ordinated main clauses, each with its own verb, the finite verb phrases *'ve been working* and *has been*. In **[17]** the finite verb phrases *want* and *don't have* function as the verbs in finite relative clauses (cf. 5.9), a type of subordinate clause, the main verb of the sentence being *has become*. In **[18]** the finite verb phrase *were asked* functions as the verb in a finite subordinate clause introduced by the subordinator *if*, the main verb of the sentence being *would get*.

A non-finite verb phrase normally cannot function as the verb of a simple sentence or as the verb of a main clause within a compound sentence.[9] It can, however, function as the verb of a non-finite subordinate clause:

[19] I don't recall *actually giving the name* [S1B-061-182]

In **[19]** *giving* is the verb of an -*ing* participle clause. It is a transitive verb, and its direct object is *the name*.

Imperative sentences and clauses are generally called finite, even though the verb does not display a distinction in tense:

[20] [. . .] just *feed* in some of your tapes and *say look* this is what you've got to do [S1A-056-19]

They are associated with other finite clauses because the imperative verb can be the verb of a main clause. The same applies to clauses whose verb is a subjunctive (cf. 5.25 f.).

5.20
Tense and aspect

Tense is a grammatical category referring to the location of a situation in time. Strictly speaking, English has only two tenses of the verb—present and past—if tense is defined as being shown by a verb inflection. However, English has many ways of referring to past, present, and future time. We use a number of auxiliary verbs in combination with main verbs to refer to time. Time is also conveyed with the help of adverbs (e.g. *nowadays, tomorrow*), prepositional phrases (e.g. *in 1990, before the next meeting*), noun phrases (e.g. *last week, this evening*), and clauses (e.g. *when we saw them, after the conflict is over*).

The aspect of the verb refers primarily to the way that the time of the situation is regarded rather than its location in time in absolute terms. English has two aspects: the perfect aspect and the progressive (or continuous) aspect. The aspects are expressed by a combination of an auxiliary and a following verb. The perfect aspect (as in 'I *have written* many times before now') is primarily used to place the time of one situation relative to the time of another situation.[10] The progressive aspect (as in 'I *am writing* a letter to my parents') primarily focuses on the duration of the situation.

Distinctions in tense are signalled by the inflections of the first or only verb in the verb phrase. For all verbs except the modals, the present tense distinguishes between the *-s* form (e.g. *saves*) for the third person singular and the base (or uninflected) form (e.g. *save*) for the rest. For regular verbs and many irregular verbs, the past tense has the *-ed* inflection (e.g. *saved*, cf. 4.17 f.).

Aspect is always combined with tense. So *has left* and *have left* are present perfect (because *has* and *have* are present tense), whereas *had left* is past perfect (because *had* is past). Similarly, *am leaving, is leaving,* and *are leaving* are present progressive, whereas *was leaving* and *were leaving* are past progressive. The two aspects are combined in *has been leaving*. Further complexity is introduced when the two aspects are combined with modals or passives (cf. 5.17).

5.21
Simple present and simple past

When there is only one verb in the verb phrase, the choice is between the simple present and the simple past:

simple present	(it) *computes*	(they) *compute*
simple past	(it/they) *computed*	

The simple present has the wider use. It has been called the non-past tense, signifying that it can be used whenever the past tense is inappropriate. The simple past is generally used to refer to past time, i.e. before the time of speaking or writing. Auxiliaries, such as *will*, and semi-auxiliaries, such as *be going to*, are used to refer to future time (cf. 5.23).

The simple past is primarily used when the situation was completed before the time of speaking or writing. This paragraph from the beginning of a novel follows one in which the narrator introduces himself:

> [1]   I *grew* up in Plano, a small silicon village in the north. No sisters, no brothers. My father *ran* a gas station and my mother *stayed* at home until I *got* older and times *got* tighter and she *went* to work, answering phones in the office of one of the big chip factories outside San Jose. [*The Secret History*, by Donna Tartt (London: Penguin, 1992), p. 5]

The narrator has introduced himself as 28 years old and it is therefore clear that he has finished growing up. The paragraph describes the situation during the time in which he was growing up ('I *grew* up in Plano'). Contemporaneous with that past situation is the situation of his father's work ('*ran* a gas station') and within that past situation are two sequences of other situations relating to his mother ('*stayed* at home' and '*went* to work') that are divided by a change

('I *got* older and times *got* tighter'). All the situations are set in a period before the narration and all are described with the simple past.

In this first paragraph of a news report **[2]**, the present situation described with present tense (*is transfixed*, a combination of present *is* and passive participle *transfixed*) is set in a background of past events, for which the past tenses *came* and *proclaimed* are used:

[2]   Four years after the Berlin Wall *came* down and leaders *proclaimed* a new
          era of freedom and prosperity, Western Europe *is* transfixed by gloom.
          [*International Herald Tribune*, 9 August 1993, p. 1]

The simple present is primarily used for situations that include the time of speaking or writing, as in these examples of the state present:

[3]   I *feel* like doing something exciting [S1A-048-209]

[4]   Well this *is* very tasty [S1A-057-120]

[5]   She *sounds* quite sensible actually [S1A-038-29]

[6]   There *is* no asbestos in our products now. [891102-0191-7]

[7]   It *employs* 2,700 people and *has* annual revenue of about $370 million.
          [891102-0187-4]

[8]   All four seats *have* memory devices [S2A-055-11]

[9]   Serbs and Croats *make* up the core of the Yugoslav population. [W2B-007-
          29]

[10] You *know* nothing [S1A-044-364]

[11] He said half plus half *equals* one [S1B-065-21]

The situations in **[3]**–**[11]** refer to a state that remains unaltered throughout. The duration encompassed in those situations varies immensely from the very brief periods in **[3]**–**[4]** to the timelessness in the simple arithmetic calculation in **[11]**.

In contrast to the state present in **[3]**–**[11]**, the recurrent present is used for events that happen repeatedly. The period includes the time of speaking or writing, but the events need not be happening at that time:

[12] Again there are eight over ninety this year four men and four women and
          the oldest is Robert Weston who's ninety-seven and still *walks* to church
          [S2A-020-36]

[13] I *work* in the Physiology Department [S2A-034-93]

[14] If you *appease* a bully you *pay* for it later ⟨ , ⟩ and you often *pay* more
          dearly [S2B-030-10]

[15] Just as the warm air rising up *pushes* other air out of the way and *sets*
          the atmospheric convection circulating, so the sinking cold water at high
          latitudes *pushes* other water out of the way, eventually ensuring that
          water *rises* to the surface in the tropics and *is warmed* by the Sun as it
          begins to move out towards the poles. [W2B-025-20]

[16] Seagrass *grows* in sand, silt or mud and resembles an underwater
          meadow. [W2B-029-67]

The instantaneous present is used with a single event that occurs simultaneously with the time of speaking or writing. Performative verbs (cf.

3.10), for example, describe the speech act that is being performed by the utterance itself:

[17] I *apologise* for the very short notice but I have only just received the final list of names myself. [W1B-022-18]

[18] After much consideration we *regret* that we are unable to offer you the post on this occasion. [W1B-019-71]

[19] Well I *thank* my honourable friend for that question [S1B-059-44]

[20] Smoking *is forbidden* in all parts of the building. [W2D-006-54]

Other common uses of the instantaneous present are in descriptions of events taking place simultaneously with the act of speaking:

[21] Now then Barnes *comes* inside on his right foot *waits twists turns feigns* to play to the left *clips* it nicely nicely to Platt on the far side [S2A-001-110 ff.]

[22] The field officer ⟨ , ⟩ Brigadier Braithwaite ⟨ , ⟩ *rides* ⟨ , ⟩ to face Her Majesty *salutes* with his sword ⟨ , ⟩ and *rides* away to take command of the parade again ⟨ , ⟩ as the quick march is The Thin Red Line [S2A-011-29]

[23] The processions *move* towards the first representatives of other Christian churches ⟨ , ⟩ as the sounds of this much loved hymn Praise to the Holiest in the Height *rise* to the height of the magnificent gothic vaulting of the nave almost a hundred and two feet [S2A-020-8]

[24] I *write* to confirm the reservation, which I made by telephone today, of a double room with bath for my wife and myself at the special rate of £126 per person for three nights (bed, breakfast and evening meals). [W1B-027-116]

[25] I *enclose* the correct record form, and would be grateful if you would complete it and send it back. [W1B-017-128]

5.22
Secondary uses of the simple tenses

Besides its primary use in reference to past time, the past tense has several secondary uses. They involve a distancing—a metaphorical use of pastness.

1. The backshift past is used in indirect speech or thought in a backshift from the present tense—the sequence of tenses (cf. 6.18):

[1] The US Defence Secretary Dick Cheney speaking to a conference in Washington said the war *was* going well for the allies [S2B-001-91]

The reporting verb *said* is in the past tense. The Defense Secretary may have actually said something like 'The war *is* going well for the allies.' Here are two other examples of backshift into the past tense:

[2] You see he told somebody I *was* weak [S1A-052-62]

[3] Television viewers in Manhattan earlier this month might have thought they *were* seeing double. [890928-0074-1]

2. The attitudinal past is used as a more polite or more tentative alternative to
   the present with verbs of thinking or wishing:

   [4] A: Hello Can I help you
           B: Yeah I just *wondered* if I can ⟨ , ⟩ if these are to take away . . . [S1A-
               077-266 ff.]

   [5] 'Can I help you, miss?' he said.
           'I *wanted* to know. Is it true about Mrs Hamilton?' [W2F-009-65 ff.]

   [6] A: And *did* you want third party fire and theft or ⟨ , , ⟩
           B: Do I want what [S1B-080-166 f.]

The distancing in time may be viewed as a metaphorical distancing in the
relation of the speaker to the hearer.

3. The hypothetical past is used mainly in hypothetical conditions that relate
   to present or future time, those that convey belief in the non-fulfilment of
   the condition (cf. 6.14):

   [7] I wish it *was* over now [S1A-038-232]

   [8] I feel that if only he *had* a home, secure and fulfilling job, close friends,
           he could bounce back easily. [W1B-015-95]

If the verb is *be*, the past subjunctive *were* (cf. 5.26) is used in formal contexts
in place of hypothetical past *was*:

   [7a] I wish it *were* over now.

The simple present is used for several purposes, apart from its reference to
include present time:

1. It can have future reference in subordinate clauses:

   [9] [. . .] when there *is* a withdrawal when there's the acceptance of the
           United Nations resolutions and all they stand for then the hostilities will
           end [S1B-027-20]

   [10] Well they won't learn anything if they *mess* about will they [S1A-083-60]

2. It can refer to the future for scheduled events.

   [11] You know you're welcome and the last No.38 *leaves* Haverhill at 3 pm!
           [W1B-009-112]

   [12] Mr Major who *flies* to Bonn on Monday said Britain was strongly
           committed to the European Community [S2B-005-124]

3. The historic present refers to past time. It is occasionally used in narration,
   to give a sense of immediacy: **[13]** comes from a novel, **[14]** from an
   unscripted talk, and **[15]** from a conversation.

   [13] 'No, it isn't necessary,' he *protests*, as, to the accompaniment of a
           tabret, she *begins* to imitate the pelican of the wilderness, reviving her
           young ones with her blood.
               He *holds* up a hand to stop her.
               She *reads* it.
               He *turns* his head.
               She *reads* that.

'No,' he *says*. [*The Very Model of a Man*, by Howard Jacobson (London: Penguin, 1993), p. 39]

[14] And then the prophet *comes* in and *says* well even if we all have one father that's no excuse for betraying each other and in particular for men to betray their wives and to take foreign wives [S2A-036-58]

[15] So he *moans* about money ⟨ , , ⟩ and the fact that the college haven't yet billed him for my services and if they don't do it before April they won't get the money anyway So this is nothing to do with me anyway so I just *sympathise* because I need the job and I sort of *try* to keep him happy [S1A-082-48]

4. The simple present refers to events in the very recent past time in newspaper headlines:

[16] Taiwan and China *Reach* Accord on Return of Hijackers [*International Herald Tribune*, 8 August 1994, p. 1]

[17] Bagwell *Hits* 39th, *Trumps* Williams' 42d [*International Herald Tribune*, 8 August 1994, p. 15]

The reports below these two headlines were in the simple past.

5. The simple present can also be used—as an alternative to the simple past—with verbs of communication or reception of communication when the message is still valid:

[18] Mary Jane *tells* me I shouldn't use the word half-caste [S1A-080-182]

[19] He *says* he'd feel less of a man if he didn't speak up for what he believes in. [W2F-007-102]

[20] I *hear* we're doing a gig together [S1A-096-7]

[21] I *understand* from our recent telephone conversation that your last certificate dates from September 1988 and that you would like to renew this by taking the refresher course this September. [W1B-018-61]

[22] It was, you may think, very natural and proper that she should take her mother's side, but I *gather* it went a good deal further than that. [W2F-011-97]

In an extension of this use, simple present can be used with past reference to writers, artists, musicians, etc., and their works:

[23] It's in the Bible that Abraham *stands* up and *argues* with God over the fate of the cities of the plain [S1B-047-92]

[24] Freud *wants* to avoid the suggestion, that Jensen, his contemporary, was consciously using his ideas. [W2A-002-65]

[25] [. . .] if you look at theorem minus three it *says* it is differentiable provided the derivative of that point is non-zero [S1B-013-203]

[26] If Beckett *makes* few value judgements in his text, it is because his whole position *is* one of assertive though ungrounded evaluation. In refusing to play the detached observer, Beckett *identifies* himself in a brashly partisan way with the text he *is* reading. [W2A-004-30 f.]

[27] In his book, A Plea for Reflectors, John Browning *describes* just such a telescope. [W2A-040-16]

5.23
Future time

The two most common ways of expressing future time in the verb phrase are with the modal *will* and its contraction *'ll* and with the semi-auxiliary *be going to*:

[1] A: *Is* the whole system *going to* grind to a halt over the next two years
     B: No I don't think it *will* because we know that there is a reasonable amount of collection of the present poll tax and I would be fairly confident that that *will continue* [S1B-034-110 f.]

[2] Please arrive at 8.45 am for registration as the first teaching session *will* start at 9.00 am promptly. [S2B-005-81]

[3] I won't be a second Richard I'*m* just *going to* go berserk for a while and I'*ll* then start again [S1A-001-20]

[4] I'm hoping I'*ll* be on the 'phone at home too in the very near future. [W1B-002-96]

Some speakers (in the south of England, in particular) use *shall* instead of *will* for the future when the subject is *I* or *we*:

[5] Well if I get bored with the company I *shall* come and find you [S1A-040-402]

[6] We *shall* be away on holiday from Wednesday 29 August to Tuesday 12 September (both dates inclusive). [W1B-027-76]

The simple present and the present progressive are both used to refer to future scheduled events:

[7] California politicians *face* a formidable opponent in the November elections: O.J. Simpson. [*International Herald Tribune*, 8 August 1994, p. 3] (The reference is to the trial of Simpson scheduled to start during the election campaign season.)

[8] So we have to decide who *is going* [S1B-077-109]

A number of auxiliaries and semi-auxiliaries may have future reference when used in the present tense, generally in combination with other meanings:

[9] I keep thinking I *must* do something about it [S1A-010-42]

[10] She said that she'd find out precisely whether I *should* get Book One or Book Two tomorrow so I'll ring her Wednesday morning. [S1A-043-177]

[11] We're at the moment when there'*s about to* be a struggle between the earthly and the divine and that's why this episode illuminates a world that we know [S2B-028-96]

[12] The spillage *is certain to* cause immense environmental damage. [W2E-001-12]

The auxiliaries and semi-auxiliaries may refer to a future within a past period when they are in the past tense:

[13] He was watching her being destroyed right in front of him. He *would* never thereafter know precisely why he did what he did next. [W2F-012-117]

[14] I was just thinking about art because I *was going to* get back to painting after not doing any for a year and a half [S1B-018-1]

[15] We *were due to* go back to collect our boat from Andraitx in Majorca where we had left it in May. [W2B-012-77]

[16] Uh as I understood the completion date *was to* be the third of February [S1B-061-146]

[17] I *was going* on holiday to Slovenia but HF (the walking hols. co.) cancelled this last weekend. [W1B-006-126]

The semi-auxiliaries in **[14]**–**[16]** allow the inference that the situation did not occur. In **[17]** the context indicates that that inference must be drawn. *Will* plus the perfect may also refer to a past period:

[18] Next to that there's a manuscript of about sixteen hundred uh which *will have been* made in Baghdad [S2A-059-40] ('I predict it was made in Baghdad')

[19] You *will have noticed* this isn't a synthesizer this is a human being [S2A-030-18]

For the use of *will* plus the perfect to refer to a past time within a future period, see 5.29.

5.24
Modal auxiliaries

When they appear, the modals (or modal auxiliaries) must be the first in the sequence of auxiliaries in a verb phrase (cf. 5.17) and they may function as operators (cf. 5.18). In standard English they function only as finite verbs and therefore only one modal may be present in a verb phrase, but in some non-standard varieties modals can co-occur (cf. 4.29). Unless they are functioning as operators, the modals are followed by an infinitive: *can be, may see*. Most of the modals have present and past forms: e.g. *can/could*.

Each of the modals has two kinds of meanings: deontic (or root or intrinsic) meanings and epistemic (or extrinsic) meanings. Deontic meanings refer to some kind of human control over the situation, such as permission or obligation. Epistemic meanings refer to some kind of judgement of the truth-value of the proposition, such as its possibility or necessity. Sometimes there is a merger of meanings:

[1] *Can* you tell us how you first got involved in this project [S1A-002-100]

Can you might be paraphrased by 'are you able to' (ability) or by 'is it possible for you to' (possibility).

The major meanings of the modals are listed below with examples.

A. *Can/could*

1. Ability

[2] I *can* just about carry it [S1A-019-244]

[3] I mean obviously I *can* write academic articles [S1A-066-123]

[4] *Could* you be a bit more specific than that [S1B-020-86]

2. Permission

> **[5]** *Can* I borrow yours [S1A-093-253]
>
> **[6]** You *can* take these [S1A-022-254]
>
> **[7]** *Could* I have the ⟨ , ⟩ slides on please and the lights out [S2A-040-1]

3. Possibility

> **[8]** *Can* this be sent [S1A-091-112]
>
> **[9]** These forces *can* be known and expressed only indirectly, through the condensations and displacements of dream imagery. [W2A-002-25]
>
> **[10]** I have not forgotten you—how *could* I. [W1B-008-93]

B. *May/might*

1. Permission

> **[11]** If I'm that interested I'll ask you if I *may* have a piece [. . .] [S1A-010-178]
>
> **[12]** In the meanwhile, *may* I just confirm a few administrative details. [W1B-030-05]
>
> **[13]** Having given you a brief outline of the scope of our interests and the way we are structured I wonder if I *might* now turn in more detail to the traditional examples of land management [. . .] [S2A-045-59]

In the permission sense, *may* and *might* are more formal than *can* and *could* and are used less frequently than they are, but *may* is sometimes prescribed.

2. Possibility

> **[14]** I *may* be staying around to the end of the week or I *may* go back tomorrow [S1A-098-48]
>
> **[15]** Uh ⟨ , , ⟩ it *may* be worth your while ⟨ , ⟩ [S1A-066-70]
>
> **[16]** You *might* be interested in it [S1A-032-144]

C. *Will/would*

1. Future prediction

> **[17]** He'*ll* be nineteen on Friday [. . .] [S2A-003-82]
>
> **[18]** And as she grows up she'*ll* see that her dislike of Gavin is irrational even if she can't admit it [S1A-054-39]

2. Present prediction

> **[19]** The procedure is very simple and *will* be familiar by now [S2A-054-197]
>
> **[20]** The tourist season *will* be over by now. [W2F-013-22]
>
> **[21]** You might still talk about a moral consensus but that hardly justified making illegal what a minority of the population sincerely believed was permissible That *would* be what John Stuart Mill called the tyranny of the majority [S2B-029-101]

3. Habitual prediction

> **[22]** Hence if you smile, you *will* feel happy. [W1A-017-32]
>
> **[23]** My door *will* always be open to you. [W1B-001-133]
>
> **[24]** [. . .] she'*ll* answer yes to every question you ask her [S1B-010-49]

[25] If an outcrop of a syncline/anticline occurs on a horizontal face then the outcrop pattern *will* be wider than the thickness of the fold strata [. . .] [W1A-020-93]

4. Volition

[26] *Will* you have another cup of tea grandpa [S1A-028-153] ('Do you want to have a cup of tea')

[27] I *will* answer you in a minute [S1A-038-263] ('I intend to answer you')

[28] Right I'*ll* ask her [S1A-017-40]

[29] [. . .] *would* you please sit back close your eyes and try and envisage the scene [S2A-044-45]

The combination *would like* is commonly used with volitional meaning.

[30] I *would like* it done on Wednesday if possible [S1A-038-152] ('I want it done . . .')

[31] Now ⟨ , ⟩ where *would* you *like* to have it [S1A-089-165]

D. *Shall/should*

The use of *shall* for the prediction and volition meanings is rare outside the English of Southern England. The regulative use, imposing an obligation, is largely confined to legal and administrative language.

1. Prediction (with 1st person subjects)

[32] I *shall* regret this for the rest of my life! [W1B-015-24]

[33] I *shall* have a fever by tonight, blood poisoning soon after. [W2F-015-121]

[34] As we *shall* discover, the concept of child abuse is an extremely elusive one and means different things to different people. [W2B-017-25]

The more common alternative is *will* or its contraction '*ll*.

2. Volition (with 1st person subjects)

[35] It is a far from boring topic, but there are so many favourite ways of doing it that I *shall* not add my own. [W2D-011-48]

[36] *Shall* I go first [S1A-002-2]

[37] [. . .] and we *shall* I promise you ⟨ , ⟩ bring our own forces back home just as soon as it is safe to do so [S2B-030-58]

The more common alternative is *will* or '*ll* in declarative sentences. Interrogative *shall I/we* can be replaced by *should I/we* or *do you want me/us to*.

Those who use *shall* with first person subjects in place of *will* may also use *should like* in place of *would like*:

[38] I *should like* to help you as much as I can [. . .] [W1B-0015-13]

3. Regulative

[39] The committee *shall* consider the case after hearing any representations which the teacher may make. [W2D-008-49]

[40] Congress learned during the Reagan administration that it could intimidate the executive branch by uttering again and again the same seven words: "Provided, that no funds *shall* be spent . . ." [891102-0080-1]

E. *Should, ought to*

1. Probability

[41] Lesions such as these *should* be capable of a good recovery in the long term. [W2A-026-71]

[42] [. . .] when you've won every major medal in the sport and held the world record nerves *shouldn't* be a problem [S2A-007-126]

[43] With a new labor force, service at Eastern Airlines is likely to improve sharply, and with its strong route structure, the Texas Air Unit *ought to* make a "spectacular turnaround," he says. [891005-0041-57]

2. Obligation

[44] I can remember when common sense said that for instance women were weaker than men women *shouldn't* wear trousers women *should* earn less than men [S1B-029-123]

[45] So does anybody else uhm have any topics that they feel we *should* pursue [S1B-077-44]

[46] Oh well I suppose I *ought* to go to bed, as it's work tomorrow. [W1B-013-100]

F. *Must, cannot/ can't, have to, have got to, need*

1. Certainty

[47] I read that in the paper ⟨ , ⟩ so it *must* be true [S1A-063-185] ('It is certain to be true')

[48] They *must* have been his daughters, *mustn't* they [. . .] [S1A-023-350]

[49] A Salomon managing director once said to me, "If you think a million dollars is good money, you *must not* have kids." [891012-0133-29] ('It is certain that you do not have kids')

[50] So ⟨ , ⟩ in all biochemical systems there *has to* be an off switch as well because otherwise ⟨ , ⟩ things would burn out [. . .] [S2A-034-112]

[51] Loose shirts over jeans *has got to* be a sort of ⟨ , ⟩ temporary prejudice hasn't it [S1A-054-120]

In this meaning, *must* is not usual in negative or interrogative clauses, especially in British English. Possible replacements are *can, have to,* and *have got to.*

[52] You see ⟨ , , ⟩ as I explained there on that diagram ⟨ , ⟩ if you get ⟨ , , ⟩ a swelling of the whole gland ⟨ , , ⟩ it *can't* be a tumour [. . .] [S1B-010-64]

[53] For a start the patients *cannot* have been brain dead ⟨ , ⟩ otherwise they *couldn't* have adapted so well when awakened [S2B-033-22]

The past of *must* in this meaning is *must have*:

[54] I *must have* lent it to somebody [S1A-045-47]

2. Obligation

[55] They *must* be fed and they *must* be fed with their stir fry or whatever it is [S1A-011-233]

[56] You *must* keep them moist [S1B-025-64]

[57] Oh we *mustn't* be too late then [S1A-099-118]

    [58]   Sorry we *have to* stop [S1A-004-43]

    [59]   Do we *have to* take a bottle of white wine [S1A-038-185]

    [60]   People *have got to* double their efforts. [W2C-014-78]

In this meaning, the equivalent past is *had to* or *had got to*:

    [61]   And she *had to* be back on duty that day [S1A-028-99]

3.   **Necessity**

As a modal, *need* is restricted to negative and interrogative clauses and to the present tense:

    [62]   You *needn't* read every chapter [S1A-053-9] ('It's not necessary for you to read every chapter')

    [63]   We do not want a conflict I *need* hardly tell you that [S2B-030-11]

    [62a] *Need* I *read* every chapter?

The necessity meaning is generally conveyed by the main verb *need to* and by the semi-auxiliaries *have to* and *have got to*:

    [64]   I just *need to* check your blood pressure [S1A-051-191]

    [65]   D'you *need to* know anything else [S1A-017-261]

    [66]   You *don't need to* bother [S1A-057-63]

    [67]   Do they *have to* sign on the back [S1A-070-52]

    [68]   Have the right change for your fare with you so that you *do not have to* fumble in your wallet or bag. [W2D-009-41]

The modal perfect *need have* is used for past time, but more commonly the main verb *need to* and the two semi-auxiliaries:

    [69]   You probably didn't expect me to say such things Francoise, but I *needed to* say them. [W1B-008-66]

    [70]   All I *had to* do was heat it up [S1A-020-271]

G. Past time reference of modals

The modal *must* and the marginal modals *need* and *ought to* do not have past tense forms, and the marginal modal *used to* does not have a present tense form. There are four pairs of modals with present and past forms: *can/could*, *may/might*, *shall/should*, and *will/would*. However, as we will soon see, the past forms often have special uses.

    Could and *would* may be used with past time reference:

    [71]   Free subjects of Rome *could* not legally be made slaves. [W2A-001-36]

    [72]   There were the usual witty remarks about 'one too many', but the sad fact was that even two was one too many, and perhaps even one. A glass of wine *would* make me incapable, but not drunk. [W2B-001-49 f.]

Used to occurs more frequently for this past habitual meaning of *would*:

    [73]   I *used to* say what I thought [S1B-046-94]

    [74]   At the start I *used to* get two or three abusive letters a week [S2B-025-17]

We have also noted earlier the past time reference of *had to*, *had got to*, and *needed to*.

Past time reference is normally conveyed by the modal perfect, a combination of a modal and the perfect auxiliary *have* (cf. 5.29). The modal itself may be in the present tense or in the past tense. The past tense in this combination is a special use of the past (cf. subsection H below). Notice that the pastness may relate to the auxiliary or to the main verb. Here are some examples:

[75] It *may have* saved his life [S2B-046-44] ('It's possible that it saved his life')

[76] So when he felt he *might have been* wrong, he didn't acknowledge it. [W2F-010-45]

[77] Uh I *could have* retired earlier [S1B-041-5] ('It was possible for me to retire earlier')

[78] From his window the young boy *would have* looked across the green fields to Camden Town [. . .] [W2B-006-42]

[79] The dreadful truth to come out of the Cullen enquiry is that the 167 *need not have* died. [W2C-007-113]

[80] They *must have* been his daughters, mustn't they [. . .] [S1A-023-350] ('It's certain that they were his daughters')

[81] There was a thick rubber lifebelt clamped around his chest, constricting his breathing when it *ought to have* helped [. . .] [W2F-001-2]

There is no modal perfect of *can*, and the modal perfect is generally not used for ability and permission meanings, for the obligation meaning of *must have*, or for the volition meanings of *shall* and *will*. On the modal perfect *will have*, see 5.23 and 5.29.

H. **Special uses of past modals**

The past tense of the modals is often used with present or future time reference, as a more tentative or more polite alternative to the present tense (cf. 5.22). These have been illustrated above in the list of meanings of modals: the present time reference of *could* for ability [4], permission [7], and possibility [10]; *might* for permission [13] and possibility [16]; *would* for volition [29]; *should* for probability [41].

The past tense modals *could*, *might*, *should*, and *would* are used for the backshifting of the present tense forms in indirect speech (cf. 6.19). For example:

[82] [. . .] it said that hysteria *could* not be ⟨ , ⟩ distinguished from malingering [S1B-070-43]

[83] She wondered how he *would* get back to Ramsford without a car [S1A-054-39]

All the past tense modals are used in the hypothetical past, particularly in conditions (cf. 5.22, 6.14). For example:

[84] It *would* help if we *could* just get some sleep [S1A-040-296]

[85] Oysters I *should* imagine [S1A-009-285] (In the first person, *should* is an alternative to *would*)

Would (for present and future time) and *would have* (for past time) are regularly used in the host clauses of conditions, as in **[84]** above and in **[86]** below:

[86] A judge told him and three others: 'If you had been older you *would have* gone straight to prison.' [W2C-020-65]

Putative *should* is used (especially in British English) in contexts that suggest that some situation may exist now or in the future:

[87] But they recommend that any work by the water, electricity and gas authorities *should* be done before the scheme is started. [W2C-017-82]

[88] It is disappointing, therefore, that the submitted design *should* fall far short of its clearly stated goal [. . .] [W2A-005-73]

Putative *should* is often used in British English instead of the mandative subjunctive (cf. 5.25).

5.25
Present subjunctive

There are two subjunctives: the present subjunctive and the past subjunctive. The present subjunctive is identical with the base form of the main verb:

[1] Israel insists that it *remain* in charge on the borders [. . .] [*International Herald Tribune*, 24 January 1994, p. 8]

Be is also used as the subjunctive of the progressive auxiliary **[2]** or passive auxiliary **[3]**:

[2] The technology of hard disk systems requires that the disk *be spinning* at about 3,000 revolutions per minute [. . .] [W2B-033-47]

[3] He proposed last June that American Medical *be acquired* by a new employee-stock ownership plan. [891012-0066-27]

Negation of the present subjunctive is achieved by placing *not* before it:[11]

[4] Consider the effect of requiring that ice *not be sold* for more than $1 a bag. [890927-0173-16]

The present subjunctive is used in three structures:

A. main clauses
B. adverbial clauses
C. *that*-clauses

The present subjunctive of verbs other than *be* is only distinct from the present indicative in the third person singular, where the indicative has the -*s* form. So *remain* in **[1]** is subjunctive because the indicative would be '(*it*) *remains*'. Its main use in present-day English is in *that*-clauses.

A. Main clauses

The optative subjunctive is used to express a wish. It is largely restricted to a few fixed expressions. There may be subject–verb inversion:

[5] Poll tax is dead, *long live* the council tax! [W2E-009-55]

[6] If they decide that it's necessary then *so be it* [S1B-036-24]

[7] [. . .] *far be it from me to* suggest that every politician or indeed every whip [. . .] has been uh pure and chaste over the last fifty years [S1B-024-134]

So also *So help me God*.

Normal word order is found with other expressions:

[8] [. . .] *woe betide* the incumbent who raises taxes [. . .] [S2B-006-22]

[9] At last, after all these years, I've learnt the truth about *Blue Peter*. *God rot* the grown-up who told me it was the name of the galleon in the programme's logo. ['Shep was not the only bitch', by Margot Norman, *The Times*, 1 October 1993, p. 18—*Blue Peter* in italics in original]

The following are probably subjunctives with an implied subject rather than imperatives:

[10] Andy, *bless* him, fixed my porch light up today [. . .] [W1B-003-54]

[11] *Damn* the Belgian refugees! [W2F-005-33]

An alternative—and less restricted—formulaic way of expressing a wish is with *may* and subject–operator inversion: *May you never have reason to regret your decision.*

B. Adverbial clauses

The suppositional subjunctive is occasionally used in adverbial clauses, particularly in conditional and concessive clauses (cf. 6.14):

[12] [. . .] the students would keep a record of what it is that's going on whether it *be* routine mundane day by day things or something out of the ordinary [S1B-044-109]

[13] But on the other hand if we're advancing 〈 , 〉 even though that *be* quite slow 〈 , 〉 quite different attitudes uh prevail [S2A-021-43]

If need be ('if need exists', 'if there is need') and *be it remembered* ('it should be remembered', with subject–verb inversion) are fixed expressions:

[14] [. . .] you can teach him *if need be* [S1A-043-99]

[15] The Labour Party's 1983 election manifesto, which committed it to a non-nuclear defence policy and, *be it remembered*, to withdrawal from the European Community, became known as the "longest suicide note in history". [W2E-004-51]

The present subjunctive is accompanied by subject–verb inversion in the absence of a subordinator:

[16] [. . .] there is very little tax manœuvre uh for the Chancellor *come* the budget [S2B-002-116] ('when the budget comes')

[17] If you opt for using the local supply, *be* it dirty, moderate or first-class, there is one exercise which will improve them all. [W2D-017-62] ('whether it be dirty, moderate or first-class')

The present indicative is far more usual than the subjunctive in these contexts.

C. *That*-clauses

The mandative subjunctive is used (especially in American English) in *that*-clauses that complement verbs, adjectives, or nouns (cf. 6.16) when the clauses convey an order, request, or intention. Citations **[2]** and **[3]** above are examples of the mandative subjunctive. Here are some further examples:

[18] Still, bankers expect packaging to flourish, primarily because more customers are *demanding* that financial services *be tailored* to their needs. [891102-0107-60]

[19] In November 1294, as war with Philip the Fair of France loomed, Edward was seeking the *prayers* of the Franciscan chapter-general assembled at Assisi that 'the present tempestuous time *be succeeded* by a more tranquil one'. [W2A-010-32]

[20] The lawyer, Thomas Ward, was arrested here last week by U.S. agents in response to a *request* from the British government that he *be extradited* for trial, according to U.S. officials. [891012-0006-2]

[21] The latest absurdity grows out of a *demand* by Mr. Fernandez's lawyers that for a fair trial they *be allowed* to use secret government data in his defense. [891004-0126-5]

In British English the usual—and more common—alternative to the mandative present subjunctive is *should* with the infinitive, but the indicative is sometimes used.

Here are examples of words followed by *that*-clauses with the mandative subjunctive:

verbs:	*ask* ('request'), *decide, demand, intend, insist, order, propose, recommend, request, require, suggest, urge*
nouns:	*decision, demand, insistence, proposal, recommendation, request, requirement, suggestion*
adjective:	*crucial, essential, imperative, important, necessary, vital*

5.26
Past subjunctive

The past subjunctive is the hypothetical subjunctive. It is restricted to *were*, and it is distinct from the past indicative of the main verb *be* only in the first and third personal singular, where the indicative is *was* (*I was, she was*):

[1] If it *were* correct it would make much twentieth-century social legislation for example rent acts confiscatory and it would deny our property [S2B-046-86]

Were is a subjunctive auxiliary—progressive **[2]** or passive **[3]**—when used as the first or third person singular:

[2] All this would be great news if oil *were selling* at $40 a barrel. [890928-0019-51]

[3] These options would look more attractive if the capital-gains tax *were* reduced. [890929-0070-65]

The same applies if *were* is part of a semi-auxiliary as in *were to*:

[4] He said Sony would not object even if Columbia *were to make* a movie critical of the late Emperor Hirohito, although he added that people in Japan might not want to see it. [891004-0011-6]

The past subjunctive *were* is used in hypothetical conditional clauses (cf. 6.14) and in some other hypothetical constructions:

[5] For example, suppose Congress *were to give* every woman whose family income is under $10,000 a year $100 a month for every child she is caring for under the age of 12. [891012-0103-9]

[6] Even if BDDP *were interested* in making a bid, it might be biting off more than it could chew. [891012-0025-8]

[7] If I *were* you, I'd apply for the York position just for the experience. [W1B-014-43]

[8] If my tabby, Genghis Khan, *were serenaded* by Mignon Dunn, he would speed down the fire escape never to return. [891005-0021-19]

[9] I felt as if I *were standing* in the grim grocery store Mr. Gumbel describes with such meaningful detail. [891004-0149-2]

[10] It's as though there *were* ⟨ , ⟩ a garden round him [. . .] [S2A-059-44]

[11] And this is a French Revolutionary satire which tells uh projects as it *were* the fate of the British government uh if the French were to invade ⟨ , ⟩ in seventeen ninety-three [S2A-057-90]

[12] In fact, I rather think you wish it *were* true. [W2F-008-75]

In **[13]**, the subjunctive is involved in subject–verb inversion:

[13] *Were* this a Yoshizawa book, the designs would be yet more beautiful, but western writers are not usually permitted to publish the best of his work. [W2D-019-34]

The past indicative *was* is more usual than subjunctive *were* in contexts that are not formal. The exception is the fixed expression *as it were*. In subordinate clauses referring to present time that are introduced by *as if* or *as though*, the present indicative is an alternative to subjunctive *were*.

5.27
Present perfect

The present perfect is a combination of the present tense of the verb *have* (*has*, *have*, and the contractions *'s*, *'ve*) with the perfect participle. Essentially, it refers to a situation in past time that is viewed from the perspective of present time.

The state present perfect refers to a state that began before the present time of speaking or writing and continues until that time, perhaps including it:

[1] And how long *have* you *had* a full licence [S1B-074-310]

[2] The last few days *haven't been* quite so hot and on Friday night it actually rained. [W1B-005-146]

[3] Eight of them *have remained* parked at the side of the runway all week [S2B-005-12]

[4] Estonia *has* until now *been* the calmest of the three Baltic republics [S2B-015-59]

[5] I miss you! It *has* only *been* a week and I feel lonesome without you. [W1B-001-36]

[6] Today *has been* slightly less of a nightmare though not much. [W1B-007-34]

[7] The food *has been* interesting so far. [W1B-010-161]

[8] These are major reasons why the cost of space transportation *has remained* extremely high. [W2B-035-62]

[9] I *have* never *felt* at home since Flora told me she had heard us discussing her. [W2F-018-25]

All of the citations [1]–[9] contain an expression denoting a period of time extending from some time in the past to the present. Generally the time expressions are adverbials, but *The last few days* [2] and *Today* [6] are subjects and in [8] it is the verb *remain* (*has remained*) that conveys the notion of duration to the present. Several of the citations—[1], [8], and [9]—suggest that the situation will continue into the future, but *until now* [4] and *so far* [7] imply an expectation of a change.

The recurrent present perfect resembles the state present perfect in referring to a period that extends from the past to the present time of speaking or writing, but the reference is to recurrent events and not to an unbroken state:

[10] The utility *has been collecting* for the plant's construction cost from its 3.1 million customers subject to a refund since 1986. [891102-0179-18]

[11] As individual investors *have turned* away from the stock market over the years, securities firms *have scrambled* to find new products that brokers find easy to sell. [891102-0159-16]

[12] The monthly sales *have been setting* records every month since March. [891102-0178-3]

[13] Attorneys *have argued* since 1985, when the law took effect, that they cannot provide information about clients who do not wish their identities to be known. [891102-0143-6]

[14]   The fact that the villagers *have* always (or at least for seventy years) *played* cricket on this site implies that they want (and are entitled) to continue to do so. [W2A-007-55]

The event present perfect refers to one or more events that have taken place in a period that precedes the present time of speaking or writing. The period within which the event or events took place is viewed as relevant to the present. It may be relevant because the event has just been revealed, as in news broadcasts **[15]** or reports in newspapers **[16]**:

[15]   The Democrats *have gained* a handful of additional seats in the House of Representatives where they already hold a big majority [S2B-006-11]

[16]   A man who killed his girlfriend more than 20 years ago *has* finally *confessed* after his wife complained of a foul smell coming from a cupboard in their home, Japanese police said yesterday. [W2C-019-82]

[17]   The company said it *has offered* to withdraw its bids in Hiroshima and Nagano. [891102-0141-29]

[18]   The Life Insurance Co. of Georgia *has* officially *opened* an office in Taipei. [891102-0131-1]

Or the event may have just happened:

[19]   Now very gradually release the clutch lever and as the engine starts to move forward ⟨ , ⟩ very very gently open up the throttle ⟨ , , ⟩ That's all right The bike *has stalled* ⟨ , ⟩ We will start again [S2A-054-69 ff.]

The past period may be relevant because it is viewed as still operative in the present:

[20]   It means that somehow or other religion in the modern world *has been marginalised* and that other agencies *have taken* over not only the bodies but the souls of human beings [S1B-028-9]

[21]   In this age of the microchip all sorts of gadgets *have been invented*, such as microwaves, video recorders and fax machines which were supposed to make life easier. [W2E-009-79]

[22]   She *has written* several books, some of which *have* recently *been translated* into English. [W2D-019-65]

[23]   A: *Have* you *seen* The Silence of the Lambs ⟨ , , ⟩
         B: Yes It's only just come out in the cinema [S1A-006-55]

In **[20]** the period in which the events have occurred ('in the modern world') includes the present. The present is invoked in **[21]** by 'in this age of the microchip'. The present perfect in **[22]** leaves open the possibility that the author may write additional books, which may also be translated. In **[23]** the present perfect indicates that it is still possible to see the film.

The present perfect competes with the past, which occurs more frequently. The present perfect is generally excluded if there are expressions that refer to a specific time in the past. Contrast:

[24]   I *worked* in New York *in 1990*.

[24a] I *worked* (or *have worked*) in New York for many years.

On the other hand, the past is generally excluded in the presence of expressions that refer to a period of time extending to the time of speaking or hearing:

[24b] I *have worked* in New York *since 1990*.

The present perfect is used less often in American English than in British English.

In citation **[25]**, the simple past in the first paragraph (repeated several times) contrasts with the present perfect in the second paragraph:

[25] In its two-month rampage, the great Midwest flood of 1993 *cut* an awesome destructive swath. It *took* 50 lives, *left* almost 70,000 people homeless, *inundated* an area twice the size of New Jersey, *caused* an estimated $12 billion in property and agricultural damage and *stirred* anew a debate over the nation's flood-control system and its policies.

The crest of the mighty flood, probably the worst ever to wash over the United States, *has roiled* down the Mississippi River past Cairo, Illinois, and from there south the swollen waters will steadily lose their deadly potency because the river bottom widens drastically.
[*International Herald Tribune*, 11 August 1993, p. 1]

The past in the first paragraph refers to a set of events occurring over a period of two months that were completed when the news item was written. These events had been reported previously, and therefore the present perfect was not appropriate. In the second paragraph the most recent event is reported—appropriately with the present perfect—and is followed by a prediction of a further event ('the swollen waters *will* steadily lose their deadly potency').

The present perfect can be used in subordinate clauses to refer to a time in the future:

[26] We shall make up our mind when the IMF *has reported* [S1B-053-94]

[27] But what if a massive build-up of armed strength occurs before a war *has started*? [W2C-003-77]

This use of the present perfect accords with the use of the simple present for future time reference in subordinate clauses (cf. 5.22):

[27a] But what if a massive build-up occurs before a war *starts*?

The corresponding forms in main clauses would be *will have started* in **[27]** and *will start* in **[27a]**, forms which occasionally occur also in subordinate clauses.

5.28
Past perfect

The past perfect (or pluperfect) is a combination of the past tense of the verb *have* (*had* or the contracted form '*d*) with the perfect participle. It is used to refer to a situation in the past that came before another situation in the past. The past perfect represents either the past of the simple past or the past of the present perfect. The distinction appears in **[1]**, where *had realised* is the past of the simple past and *hadn't been* is the past of the present perfect:

> **[1]** Uh, *had* you *realised* before this meeting that uh the Scott Coopers' surveyor *hadn't* yet *been* to the premises [S1B-069-146]

These two verbs can be seen as the past of the verbs in **[1a]**:

> **[1a]** *Did* you *realise* before this meeting that Scott Coopers' surveyor *hasn't* yet *been* to the premises?

Here are some clear examples of the past perfect as past of the past:

> **[2]** It now transpires that Mr Sigrani *had issued* a writ against Mr Daniel on the twenty-first of April 1989 [S2A-069-42]

> **[3]** Confronted, Mrs. Yeargin admitted she *had given* the questions and answers two days before the examination to two low-ability geography classes. [891102-0148-13]

> **[4]** In September, the department *had said* it will require trucks and minivans to be equipped with the same front-seat headrests that have long been required on passenger cars. [891102-0128-6]

When the past perfect is the past of the simple past, it can co-occur with specific expressions of time.

Here are some examples of the past perfect as past of the present perfect:

> **[5]** A USX spokesman said the company *had* not yet *received* any documents from OSHA regarding the penalty or fine. [891102-0089-10]

> **[6]** Equitable of Iowa Cos., Des Moines, *had been seeking* a buyer for the 36-store Younkers chain since June, when it announced its intention to free up capital to expand its insurance business. [891102-0035-2]

> **[7]** I knew my Wagner and my Beethoven and my Brahms very well but uh I saw that there were a great number of British composers that I *hadn't heard* of [S1B-032-14]

The backshift past perfect is used in indirect speech or thought in a backshift from the simple past, in **[2]** above and in **[8]**, or the present perfect, in **[5]** above and in **[9]** (cf. 6.18):

> **[8]** The company said local authorities held hearings on the allegations last spring and *had returned* the plant to "routine inspection" in August. [81102-0051-4]

> **[9]** In his return toast to Mr. Nixon, Mr. Yang said the relationship *had reached* a "stalemate." [891102-0099-16]

The hypothetical past perfect is used in hypothetical conditions that relate to past time, indicating the knowledge or belief that the condition was not fulfilled (cf. 6.14):

> **[10]** If a business *had made* the same mistake as the Government has made in introducing the poll tax against all informed advice I don't think we would allow them to run a business again . . . [S1B-034-96]

5.29
Modal perfect

The modal perfect is a combination of a modal (cf. 4.29, 5.24) with the perfect auxiliary *have* in the infinitive, e.g. *may have, could have*.

The modal perfect commonly serves to express the past time reference of the verb phrase:

[1] You *must have been* a very fast driver [S1A-028-138] ('It is certain that you were . . .')

[2] Uhm ⟨ , ⟩ have you considered until now the effects that having an absent father *may have had* on your childhood [S1A-075-26] ('possibly had')

[3] She *might have been* so damaged by her own experiences that she is unable to think about protecting other children—'No one protected me, so why should I care?' [W2B-017-84] ('possibly was')

[4] From his window the young man *would have looked* across the green fields to Camden Town, and to the Hampstead Road along which the old stage coaches still travelled. [W2B-006-42] ('probably looked')

Will have completed in **[5]** and *will have stopped* in **[6]** are future perfect, referring to a past within a future period:

[5] Applications for General Course registration will be considered from undergraduates who *will have completed* at least two years in a foreign university by the time of their enrolment at the School. [W2D-007-62]

[6] However, about 75 per cent of those affected *will have stopped* having attacks by the time they are twenty. [W2B-023-31]

The past modal perfect is often hypothetical:

[7] Protests about his policy or even complaints about its results *would have been punished* with death [S2B-030-77]

[8] Modern means of communication now make the manipulation of public opinion possible on a scale that even Goebbels *would have found* unimaginable. [W2B-014-43]

[9] Under Rome such men as Nehru or Nkrumah *would have been* eligible for the highest imperial offices. [W2A-001-85]

[10] You *should have insisted* it went ahead [S1A-095-22]

[11] There are many people, on both sides of the Atlantic, who wish it *could have been* different. [W2E-007-43]

Hypothetical *would have* is particularly common in the host clauses of unfulfilled conditions (cf. 6.14):

[12] Had they shown up, barristers *would have heard* a stirring account of how their leaders had routed the opposing army of the Law Society on the battlefield of the Courts and Legal Services Bill (now Act). [W2C-006-30]

[13] A judge told him and three other youths: 'If you had been older you *would have gone* straight to prison.' [W2C-020-65]

5.30
Perfect in non-finite phrases

The perfect in a non-finite verb phrase refers to a preceding time. For example, in **[1]** the causing of inconvenience preceded the expression of regret and in **[2]** the running preceded the breathlessness:

[1] I am sorry *to have caused* you some inconvenience by misreading the subscription information. [W1B-026-114]

[2] He was almost breathless from *having run* towards her uphill from, it could only be, the lake. [W2F-005-79]

Here are some further examples of the infinitive and *-ing* participle perfects in non-finite phrases:

[3] They were wearing ski-masks and dark clothing and are thought *to have escaped* in a red car [S2B-016-6]

[4] I'd have like not *to have worried* about the trembling fingers, but I was suddenly overwhelmed with a terrible feeling of sadness. [W2B-004-121]

[5] But *having taken* the first bend well Smith was never really in trouble after that [S2A-012-8]

[6] Her daughter Carol *having produced* coffee for the waiting reporters offered some thoughts on the matter [S2B-003-95]

[7] Funnily enough, many patients who show such learning consequently deny ever *having done* the task before! [W1A-004-71]

[8] The Occupational Health Service has suffered from *having acquired* a room at a time, with each room adapted to provide for what was most urgently needed at the time. [W1B-017-31]

[9] Faith in a supranational Communist ideology *having failed*, people fall back upon the collectivity to which they felt they belonged. [W2B-007-89]

5.31
Progressive

The progressive (or continuous) aspect consists of a form of the auxiliary *be* followed by an *-ing* participle. In this function, the participle may be termed the progressive participle. Here are examples of finite verb phrases with the progressive:

am making	may *be flying*
is writing	has *been running*
was playing	*are being* taught
were deciding	should have *been studying*

Here are examples of non-finite verb phrases with the progressive:

singing	to *be singing*
being explained	to *be being* explained
having *been listening*	to have *been listening*

The initial *being* that would be expected before *singing* and *being explained* is omitted as we can see from the corresponding infinitive phrases *to be singing* and *to be being explained* and the corresponding finite phrases *is singing* and *is being explained*. Presumably the omission is to avoid the juxtaposition of two -*ing* participles: *being singing*.

The progressive is primarily used to focus on the situation as being in progress at a particular time. Accordingly, it is not used to refer to a situation that is represented as a state. Hence, it is odd to say 'I am knowing English' or 'He is liking your sister'. Some verbs, such as *be*, are normally used in the depiction of states, but may occur in the progressive when they in fact depict an event in progress:

[1]   I'*m being* sarcastic [S1A-068-23]

[2]   By then she *was having* difficulty with her teeth [S2A-062-65]

[3]   Who *am* I *thinking* of [S1B-008-45]

The event progressive indicates that an event is or was in progress:

[4]   A: What *are* you *doing* Bert ⟨ , ⟩
       B: I'*m walking* into the dining-room so I can sit down [S1A-065-147 f.]

[5]   *Are* you *going* grey [S1A-068-103]

[6]   I *was working* in the lab on a simple piece of test equipment I'd designed and he came in and asked me some questions about it in a very friendly way [S2A-041-83]

[7]   I *was sitting* down and an Israeli soldier came up to me and he said why *are* you *sitting* here when history has been made [S2A-050-43]

[8]   She *was spooling* the programme on to the tape machine when the phone rang. [W2F-020-149]

[9]   When we *were walking* over the bridge Mary Jane stopped to take a shot of a woman on the other side of the road who *was dragging* a child along by the hand. [W2F-013-110]

[10]   He had his notebook out and *was flicking* the pages over, like a stage policeman. [W2F-009-105]

[11]   *Was* uhm John *appearing* distinctly sort of uneasy when uhm Kate was uhm all round him [S1A-069-29]

The progressive is often used to indicate that one event is in progress when another event occurred, as in [6]–[9]. For example, in [8] the ringing of the phone occurred at one point of time during the spooling. The progressive is also often used to indicate the simultaneity of an event with a state or another event depicted with the simple present or the simple past, as in [10] and [11].

The recurrent progressive refers to a set of recurrent events that are viewed as in progress over a limited period of time:

[12]   A: Where *are* you *working* now
        B: I'*m working* in a software house in Kilburn [S1A-079-69 f.]

[13]   She *is dressing* to suit her husband's taste and, as long as he continues to tell her how nice she looks, there is no reason to change style. [W2F-019-48]

One secondary use of the present progressive is to refer to a future scheduled event:

[14] *Are* you *coming* tonight to the meeting [S1A-068-224]

[15] Or perhaps you will speak to me shortly when you *are* either *opening* a bottle of champagne or a bottle of hemlock [S1A-095-150]

Another secondary use is as a more polite or more tentative alternative to the simple present or the simple past:

[16] I'*m hoping* to find out if there's a bus service (direct) from Haverhill to London and vice versa. [W1B-001-179]

[17] I'*m wondering* well what on earth is going to happen next [S1B-026-204]

[18] Mary Jane suggested that after we'd had some lunch we could take a stroll along by the river, but all I wanted was to lie down. 'Actually I *was thinking* of having a rest afterwards,' I said. [W2F-013-28]

This use tends to be employed with verbs of thinking. Because of its association with duration, the progressive suggests a less conclusive process of thinking than do the simple tenses. The progressive can be combined with the attitudinal past (cf. 5.22) to reinforce the tentativeness or politeness, as in **[18]** (if it has present reference) and in **[19]**:

[19] I *was wondering* ⟨ , , ⟩ would you like to do some sight singing [S1A-045-157]

5.32
Progressive in non-finite phrases

The progressive in a non-finite phrase usually expresses simultaneity when it is in a subordinate clause:

[1] Today is Sunday 14th April, and the mid-afternoon sun is illuminating my room—where I sit *facing* a WP screen *writing* you this letter. [W1B-001-95]

[2] Prince Charles duly walked down the line, shook hands with who was there, and then, *showing* a rather splendid sense of humour said, "You know, I could have commanded him to be here tonight." [W2B-004-32]

[3] Pete was always a Leica enthusiast and in the Leitz showroom he was having a marvellous time *trying* out all their latest equipment. [W2B-004-116]

[4] *Commenting* on the time of the two reports, Mr Kreindler said that they had surfaced just as his group were gathering critical evidence. [W2C-001-52]

[5] 'I wanted to go to the castle,' she said huffily, *shoving* the camera back into her bag as if she had no further use for it, 'but it seems I've no choice.' [W2F-013-119]

The time reference of the participle clause is inferred from the host clause—present in **[1]** and past in **[2]**–**[5]**.

A contrast is sometimes possible with the perfect. Contrast **[5]** with **[5a]** where the perfect *having shoved* points to an action that precedes her saying 'I wanted to go to the castle':

> **[5a]** 'I wanted to go to the castle,' she said huffily, *having shoved* the camera back into her bag.

The progressive is the only verb form possible in a non-finite clause functioning as the complement of a preposition (cf. 5.47):

> **[6]** He was obviously afraid of *mentioning* some girlfriend and *offending* the wife [S1A-037-24]

There are also some verbs that take the progressive, rather than the infinitive, as the verb in their complement (cf. 6.16):

> **[7]** I would consider *trying* that [S1A-059-95]

In instances where both the progressive and the infinitive are possible, the progressive may indicate that the event is viewed as having some duration or as recurring:

> **[8]** I heard you *speaking* Welsh yesterday [S1A-069-92]

Contrast **[8]** with **[8a]**:

> **[8a]** I heard you *speak* Welsh yesterday.

The progressive may be combined with the infinitive to indicate duration:

> **[9]** So you know just uhm that it would be healthier for me *to be doing* something [S1A-060-201]

Contrast **[9]** with **[9a]**:

> **[9a]** It would be healthier for me *to do* something.

There may also be a contrast with the perfect:

> **[9b]** It would be healthier for me *to have done* something.

The perfect refers to a hypothetical previous action. The addition of the progressive adds a reference to duration:

> **[9c]** It would be healthier for me *to have been doing* something.

5.33
Auxiliary-like verbs

A large number of verbs or verb combinations are similar in meaning to the auxiliaries in expressing notions of time, aspect, or modality, though they do not share all the characteristics of auxiliaries (cf. 4.29). Some have been illustrated (for example, *be going to, be to, be about to*) in 5.23.

Here are some other examples that are followed by an infinitive:

appear to	had rather
begin to	happen to
be supposed to	have to
get to	seem to
had better	tend to

And here are some that are followed by an -*ing* participle:

begin	keep
continue	start
go on	stop

The following citations illustrate their use in combination with other verbs:

[1] The next thing I *have to do* is have a drink of beer [S1A-026-285]

[2] Loose shirts over jeans *has got to be* a sort of ⟨ , ⟩ temporary prejudice hasn't it [S1A-054-120]

[3] He *happens to shave* three times a day [S1A-065-195]

[4] He then *continues to explain* what would happen. [W1A-018-43]

[5] Worst affected *is likely to be* the yellow-bellied sea-snake, which feeds on the surface. [W2B-029-91]

[6] Well when you said you've got one that *seemed to be* the implication [S1B-002-124]

[7] Actually today I'm nursing a very bad hangover so I decided I *had better stay* at home rather than throw up on the metro!! [W1B-009-31]

[8] I *kept saying* she will ring she will ring [S1A-040-377]

Unlike auxiliaries, most of these auxiliary-like verbs can be non-finite, so that they can form chains of verbs, sometimes in combination with auxiliaries:

[9] I'*m going to have to get* round to it [S1A-039-21]

[10] Well ⟨ , ⟩ you can't earn a living if they'*re going to keep cancelling* [S1A-083-55]

[11] I'*ll have to stop talking* about the place, it's bringing tears to my cheeks. [W1B-001-63]

[12] If so, Bush *had better stop talking* about Hitler and start explaining how containment would work. [W2E-010-27]

5.34
Phrasal and prepositional verbs

Multi-word verbs are combinations of verbs with other words that form an idiomatic unit, inasmuch as the meaning of the combination cannot be predicted from the meaning of the parts.[12]

There are degrees of idiomaticity. The contribution of both the verb and the particle may be opaque, as in *give in* ('surrender') and *carry on* ('continue'). Or the verb's contribution may be transparent but the particle is not predictable, as in *call on* and *accuse of.* Or only the particle's contribution is transparent, as in *turn off* (e.g. *the lights*). With some multi-word verbs there is a set of contrasting transparent particles: *turn* plus *on, off, up, down*. In some, the particle *up* has a completive meaning: *drink up, eat up, shut up, wake up*. In free combinations, the verbs and the particles are both transparent in meaning and they can be separately contrasted with other verbs and with other particles: *bring/send/take/push/lead*, etc., plus *in/out/up/down/along*, etc.

The most frequent types of multi-word verbs consist of a verb in combination with one or more particles, a term used for words that do not take inflections. The particles in such multi-word combinations are either adverbs or prepositions.

Seven types of multi-word verbs with particles are distinguished, which are discussed in the sections that follow (cf. 5.35–7):

1. intransitive phrasal verbs, e.g. *give in* ('surrender')
2. transitive phrasal verbs, e.g. *find* (something) *out* ('discover')
3. monotransitive prepositional verbs, e.g. *look after* ('take care of')
4. doubly transitive prepositional verbs, e.g. *blame* (something) *on*
5. copular prepositional verbs, e.g. *serve as*
6. monotransitive phrasal-prepositional verbs, e.g. *look up to* ('respect')
7. doubly transitive phrasal-prepositional verbs, e.g. *put* (something) *down to* ('attribute to').

In addition, there are various other idiomatic combinations with verbs (cf. 5.38).

The particles in phrasal verbs are adverbs and those in prepositional verbs are prepositions. In phrasal-prepositional verbs the first particle is an adverb and the second is a preposition. As the above examples show, for some multi-word verbs there are single-word verbs with approximately the same meaning, but these are generally more formal.

Phrasal verbs in particular have become a fertile field for new coinages in the twentieth century.

5.35
Phrasal verbs

Intransitive phrasal verbs consist of a verb and an adverb, and they do not have an object. Here are some examples:

[1] Uhm and he said can I *pop over* [S1A-008-249]

[2] I thought you were going to *shut up* [S1A-043-93]

[3] Was it alive do you think when she *set out* for the country [S1B-014-99]

[4] I hope everything has *turned out* well for you both, and I am sure you've had no trouble with passing your courses. [W1B-008-112]

[5] Much of that activity though *goes on* within the framework of competitive sport [S1A-004-65]

[6] See how you *get on* [S1A-022-255]

[7] You *end up* by feeling quite compromised [S1A-058-198]

[8] Well they won't learn anything if they *mess about* will they [S1A-083-60]

Transitive phrasal verbs also consist of a verb and an adverb, but they take a direct object. The adverb is generally separable in that it can appear either before or after the direct object. However, if the object is a personal pronoun it is normal for the adverb to follow the pronoun. Contrast:

[9] A: You *picked up* a girl on the train
 B: I did not pick *her* up [S1A-020-3 f.]

[10] It's difficult to imagine people picking ⟨ , , ⟩ *picking* women *up* . . . [S1A-020-185]

Here are some examples of transitive phrasal verbs:

[11] She said she'd *find out* precisely whether I should get Book One or Book Two tomorrow so I'll ring her Wednesday morning [S1A-043-177]

[12] Can we *put* this big light *off* [S1A-042-299]

[13] And Tarbull said he looked as if he was a man who was always on the lookout for enemies as if somebody was always trying to *do* him *down* [S1B-005-167]

[14] I mean the newspapers *make up* a story and then they obediently trot in and try and perform it [S1B-024-14]

[15] No dummies, the drivers *pointed out* they still had space on their machines for another sponsor's name or two. [891102-0184-16]

[16] Earlier this year, Japanese investors *snapped up* a similar, $570 million mortgage-backed securities mutual fund. [891102-0164-6]

[17] "What sector is stepping forward to *pick up* the slack?" he asked. [891102-0157-5]

[18] You can't *hold back* technology. [891102-0070-29]

The adverb particle comes before the object if the object is long, as in **[16]**, and particularly if it is a clause, as in **[11]** and **[15]**.

In some transitive phrasal verbs the position of the adverb particle is fixed. This occurs when the phrasal verb and its object constitute an idiomatic whole. Usually the adverb comes immediately after the verb. Here are some examples:

take up arms
let off steam
put on airs
shut up shop

Sometimes the adverb follows the object:

keep one's shirt on
put one's foot down
cry one's eyes out
keep one's hand in

There are also instances of fixed positions where various direct objects are possible:

> let out a cry
> carry off the trophy
> put up some resistance
> get somebody off ('get somebody released from punishment')

Like other transitive verbs, transitive phrasal verbs occur in the passive, in which case there is no direct object:

[19] As I understand it people in the City are still being *laid off* [S1B-021-114]

[20] The Dance Umbrella one of the the great dance festivals has been heavily *cut back* [S1B-022-26]

[21] It is being *put up* for sale without going on the market and without being advertised. [W2C-020-38]

The object may be fronted in a relative clause, and so be separated from the verb. In **[22]** the relative pronoun *which* is the object of *flesh out*:

[22] Diagrams can only show the bare bones of a design, which the folder through dedicated practice must *flesh out* and bring to life. [W2D-019-29]

If the relative is a zero pronoun (cf. 5.9), no object is present:

[23] First of all I think ⟨ , ⟩ relying on lecture notes alone is not enough for for any work you're going to *hand in* [S1B-007-1]

5.36
Prepositional verbs

Monotransitive prepositional verbs superficially resemble transitive phrasal verbs when the particle of the phrasal verb precedes the object, but only the particle of a phrasal verb can also follow the object:

[1] I *looked at* the words. [prepositional verb]

[1a] I *looked up* the words. [phrasal verb]

[1b] I *looked* the words *up*. [phrasal verb]

The reason for the difference is that the particle of a phrasal verb is an adverb, which can be moved more freely, whereas a preposition comes before its complement. On the other hand, the adverb particle normally cannot precede the object if it is a personal pronoun, so that *looked at* in **[1c]** is a prepositional verb:

[1c] I *looked at* them. [prepositional verb]

Monotransitive prepositional verbs have only one object. The prepositional complement serves as the object of the verb. It is a prepositional object, because it requires a preposition to introduce it.[13] Here are some examples:

[2]   Did you *apply for* anything in the final year [S1A-034-120]

[3]   Laura never *gets off* the phone [S1A-041-66]

[4]   I can't possibly *account for* it [S1A-045-196]

[5]   Tonight they're back in their constituencies doing it all again to try to *decide on* her successor [S2B-003-55]

[6]   The creation of a new elite and Soviet-style industrialization has *led to* large-scale social mobility. [W2B-007-76]

[7]   And after her father died, of course, Isabel's trust fund included quite a substantial holding in the company, and her husband could always *rely on* the trustees to support his decisions. [W2F-011-52]

[8]   Pamela Sebastian in New York *contributed to* this article. [891102-0157-74]

[9]   They *worry about* their careers, drink too much and suffer through broken marriages and desultory affairs. [891102-0157-74]

[10]   While giving the Comprehensive Test of Basic Skills to ninth graders at Greenville High School last March 16, she spotted a student *looking at* crib sheets. [891102-0148-2]

As with the objects of transitive phrasal verbs, the prepositional object may be absent or may be fronted, so that the preposition is left stranded (cf. 5.47):

[11]   The declaration by Economy Minister Nestor Rapanelli is believed to be the first time such an action has been *called for* by an Argentine official of such stature. [891102-0172-2]

[12]   Well I couldn't care less what the hell we *talk about* [S1A-038-10]

[13]   What was she *waiting for* [W2F-020-126]

[14]   I think that perhaps I could give them the backing to go out and win the election so that they can go on doing the jobs that they are so obviously ⟨ , ⟩ *succeeding at* [S2B-003-48]

In a more formal variant, the preposition is fronted with a relative *wh*-pronoun:

[14a]   . . . the jobs *at which* they are so obviously *succeeding*.

Doubly transitive prepositional verbs have two objects. The first object is a direct object and the second object is a prepositional object, introduced by a preposition:

[15]   No-one will *blame* you *for* a genuine mistake. [W2D-009-152]

[16]   According to Mr Pitkin, Isabel was a strikingly attractive woman who could have married anyone she wanted, but she *set* her heart *on* Albert Barnsley. [W2F-011-45]

[17]   She must not *put* him *through* that agony again. [W2F-019-108]

[18]   All manifestations of life, she felt, had validity; but interpreting that which was unconscious in terms which were conscious, she thought, was trying to *turn* an orange *into* a lemon. [W2F-020-139]

Some doubly transitive prepositional verbs combine with a direct object in an idiomatic combination:

[19] I think it's a great shame that the Tories have never actually said to the British people we're sorry ⟨ , ⟩ we *made a mess of* it ⟨ , ⟩ and now we're going to try and do better [S1B-034-35]

[20] It sounds that you're wanting to *take care of* yourself physically as well [S1A-059-58]

[21] One of the more consoling aspects of our present dark age is that we now *give much more attention to* the mentally and physically handicapped than we did even twenty-five or thirty years ago [S1B-060-55]

[22] But in the last forty years, agriculture has *lost touch with* its roots. [W2B-027-10]

[23] However, it did have some disadvantages, the main one being that slight changes in the phase of the signal *gave rise to* colour changes. [W2B-034-110]

Most of the doubly transitive prepositional verbs allow a passive with the direct object as subject (cf. **[11]** above):

[24] Uhm when they're *deprived of* exercise for two weeks the deprived group has many more symptoms of anxiety and insomnia [S2A-027-65]

[25] In other words, he accuses Mr Heseltine of ambition—as if that motive could ever be wholly *excluded from* politics—and lack of clarity. [W2E-004-21]

[26] They were *accused of* wasting public money and encouraging idlers. [W2B-019-105]

A few idiomatic doubly transitive prepositional verbs normally have passives with the direct object as subject, but may also allow the prepositional object as passive subject:

[27] [. . .] *insufficient attention* was *paid to* uh dictionary compilation [S2A-032-57]

[27a] Dictionary compilation was *paid insufficient attention to.*

In these prepositional verbs, the direct object is part of the idiom: *pay attention to, make a fuss of, make a mess of, keep an eye on, take offence at, make an attack on.* In a few others—such as *catch sight of, keep pace with, get hold of, give rise to*—the direct object is even more cohesive with the verb, and if these allow the passive it is normally only the prepositional object that can be passive subject:

[28] Currently, the small average net gain of 15 million tons worldwide in grain harvests is well below the 28 million tons required merely to *keep pace with* the population growth. [W2B-024-50]

[28a] The population growth is being *kept pace with.*

The doubly transitive prepositional verbs are not completely fixed, since most of them have some variability in the direct object: *give much more attention to* **[21]**, *pay insufficient attention to* **[27]**. Other examples of additions of determiners or adjectives to the nouns: *make a complete mess of, make a vicious attack on, take good care of, lose all touch with, give unexpected rise to.*

Stranding of the preposition belonging to doubly transitive prepositional verbs is illustrated in **[29]**, where the preposition is stranded at the end of a relative clause (cf. 5.47):

[29] So for example when you've been looking at the design of your process are there any uhm ⟨ , , ⟩ features of the equipment that you've had to *pay any particular attention to* [S1B-020-23]

In a more formal variant, the preposition is fronted with the relative if it is a *wh*-word (cf. **[14]** and **[14a]** above):

[29a] [. . .] features of the equipment *to which* you have had to *pay any particular attention*.

There are a few prepositional verbs that seem to express a copular relationship with their complement, which should be regarded as a subject predicative rather than a prepositional object and can therefore not be made a passive subject:

[30] But they failed to *act as* parents because they didn't actually see the child [S1B-030-112] (cf. 'They *are* parents')

[31] Any of these matters may *serve as* 'mitigating circumstances' reducing the defendant's moral responsibility and thus calling for a degree of leniency in fixing the appropriate sentence. [W2B-020-53] ('constitute')

[32] Economic dislocation has reached the point at which insubordination could *turn into* revolution as yesterday's extension of rationing in Moscow emphasised. [W2C-008-4] ('become')

[33] The uncompromising nature of Beckett's declared commitment to his subjects is such that he might with good reason *pass for* little more than an apologist. [W2A-004-42] ('seem')

[34] His Tokyo summit *looked like* a waste of time and money [S2B-040-41] ('seemed')

[35] I was woken first by another relation who *sounded like* Pam's Mum and just kept saying "Can I speak to Pamela?" [W1B-007-36]

[35] Dad was right and his stomach *felt like* water. [W2F-001-79]

5.37 Phrasal-prepositional verbs

Phrasal-prepositional verbs consist of a verb and two particles, the first an adverb and the second a preposition.

Monotransitive phrasal-prepositional verbs have just one object, a prepositional object:

[1] Have the police *come up with* anything yet? [W2F-020-168]

[2] Further to that we *got on with* the basic organisational work which was purely organisational work [S1B-054-26]

[3] And the Greeks *looked down on* the Romans as being upstart barbarians themselves [S2A-022-51]

[4] Why be good if you can *get away with* being bad [S2B-029-42]

[5] Germany *did away with* its monarchy in November 1918 [S2B-021-88]

[6] The Labour Party, among others, has not *faced up to* this reality. [W2E-007-51]

If the verb in a monotransitive phrasal-prepositional verb can by itself take a direct object, then the phrasal-prepositional verb can generally be in the passive. *Come up with* **[1]** cannot be made passive, but the verbs in the other citations can be. For example:

[3a] The Romans *were looked down on* as being upstart barbarians themselves.

[5a] Its monarchy *was done away with* in November 1918.

[6a] This reality *has not been faced up to* by the Labour Party, among others.

Like other prepositional verbs, the preposition in a monotransitive phrasal-prepositional verb can be stranded (cf. 5.47):

[7] I've got the French written paper on Thursday which I'm not *looking forward to* at all [S1A-09-176]

[8] It seems wrong to me (a retired civil servant) that people employed within any public service should, as its customers, be granted exemption from the limitations and delays that other customers have to *put up with*. [W1B-027-63]

A more formal variant is occasionally possible, in which the preposition is fronted with a *wh*-relative:

[7a] I have the French written paper on Thursday *to which* I am not *looking forward*.

But in most instances, the verb is too closely linked with both particles to allow separation.

Doubly transitive phrasal-prepositional verbs have two objects. In one type, the direct object either precedes or follows the first particle (an adverb), and the prepositional object follows the second particle (a preposition):

[9] They should be honest about it and *put* the plant *up for* sale. [W2C-015-8]

[9a] They should be honest about it and *put up* the plant *for* sale.

[10] The issue I would like to *take up with* you [. . .] [S1B-022-57] (cf. 'I would like to *take up* that issue *with you*')

Other verbs of this type are *put* (something) *down to* ('ascribe to') and *let* (somebody) *in on* ('allow to share'), *get* (something) *across to* ('communicate'), *fill* (somebody) *in on* ('acquaint with up-to-date information'). In another type, the direct object precedes the first particle and does not follow it:

[11] So it seems that if his captor dies exile is the only alternative to *keep* a politically undesirable person *out of* affairs. [W1A-002-90]

Other verbs of this type include *bring* (somebody) *up against* ('make (somebody) confront'), *put* (somebody) *up to* ('encourage to behave mischievously or illegally').

Doubly transitive phrasal verbs can be made passive. The direct object becomes the passive subject:

[12] The most influential writer on the English constitution Walter Bagehot warned that daylight should not be *let in on* the magic of the monarchy if its prestige is to be preserved [S2B-032-55]

5.38
Other multi-word verbs

In addition to phrasal and prepositional verbs, there are a number of other types of idiomatic verb combinations.

A multi-word verb may consist of two verbs and a preposition. The combination may function as a transitive verb and then takes a prepositional object:

[1] They offered it to someone else but he changed his mind so they had to *make do with* me [S2B-025-10]

[2] You can now *let go of* the front brake [S2A-054-49]

[3] *Get rid of* the infection and your symptoms will subside [S1A-087-172]

So also *have done with*, *put paid to*. The combination may consist of just the two verbs and function intransitively:

[4] But ⟨ , , ⟩ after all these years it's sort of slowly taking its course but ⟨ , ⟩ I still can't *let go* [S1A-050-23]

So also *make do, let be, get going, get started*.

A verb may enter into an idiomatic combination with an adjective functioning as subject predicative. Combinations include:

come true	ring true
fall ill/sick	run wild
go crazy/native	turn cold/sour

Examples:

[5] For some this so-called age of plunder is a dream *come true* ⟨ , ⟩ instant access to that guitar lick or drum pattern it would take years to play [S2B-023-2]

[6] But in the past manufacturers have also responded to requests for a return to dedicated knobs and sliders with claims that "it would cost too much" and "there are far too many parameters these days for it to be practical"—claims which never really *rang true*. [W2B-031-18]

There are many other types of idiomatic verb combinations that have relatively few members. One common idiomatic construction is *make sure* followed by a *that*-clause, though the subordinator *that* may be omitted:

[7]   *Make sure* that you don't miss out on Sunday April the twenty-first [S2B-044-69]

[8]   *Make sure* you've got your flak jacket with you [S1A-061-27]

Sure is an object predicative in this construction (cf. 3.19), but it precedes the direct object because the object is a clause.

Other types include *take* (something) *for granted, take place, steer clear of, fall in love with.*

Adjective Phrases

5.39
The structure of the adjective phrase

The adjective phrase has as its head an adjective, which may be preceded by premodifiers and followed by postmodifiers. The structure of the typical adjective phrase is shown at **Fig. 5.39.1**. The parentheses indicate the elements that may be absent.

Fig. 5.39.1 Structure of an adjective phrase

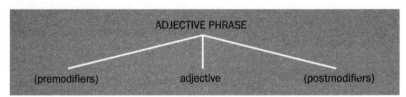

Adjectives may occur in sequence in a hierarchy of modification, where an adjective modifies the rest of the phrase that follows it:

[1]   *Big brown* bears thunder through the deep woods, closing in on a remote site where campers wait, ready to squirt them. [*International Herald Tribune*, 30 August 1993, p. 3]

[2]   We had some *nice crisp white* wine to go with it [S1A-009-309]

[3]   I mean I don't mind *sillyish American* films if they're *goodish sillyish Americanish* films [S1A-006-96]

In **[1]** *brown* modifies *bears* and *brown bears* is further modified by *big*. In **[2]** *wine* is first specified by *white* and then in turn by *crisp* and *nice*. Similarly, in **[3]** *American films* is first modified by *sillyish*, and then in the later phrase *sillyish Americanish films* is further modified by *goodish*.

A sequence of adjectives may be asyndetically co-ordinated. That is to say, a co-ordinator is not present but could be inserted:

[4] They only thrive in *dingy* ⟨ , ⟩ *stagnant* areas where the oxygen levels are fairly low [S1A-087-158]

[5] Don Boswell at the Record has an opening for a *bright vital young* reporter, Army reject ideally suitable, must be *honourable, fearless, eager*, all the things young reporters are. [W2F-014-73]

[6] Has it gone to a different degree of development in different aspects of human life *physical economic social* etcetera [W1B-028-13]

The adjectives may be syndetically co-ordinated, i.e. with a co-ordinator present:

[7] She was expecting to see a commanding sort of mogul type of figure and Rockfeller kind of wandered in looking *very thin ascetic and nervous* ⟨ , ⟩ and he sat with his back to the wall [S1B-005-166]

[8] We need to proceed with the greatest care therefore ⟨ , ⟩ for embryo research is a complex issue which involves the whole spectrum of *medical scientific ethical* ⟨ , ⟩ *and moral* issues [S1B-060-37]

In a sequence of adjectives, one adjective may modify the following adjective:

[9] It's got a *bloody great* Sony sticker there [S1A-008-135]

[10] It's usually *dark brown* ⟨ , ⟩ really [S1A-022-315]

Repetition of the same absolute adjective has an intensifying effect:

[11] He had been a monk at Kirkstall Abbey ⟨ , ⟩ *long long* time ago [S1B-026-73]

[12] Just a hint of a swelling starting and if the eye closes he's in *big big* trouble [S2A-009-134]

Repetition of the same comparative adjective, however, indicates incremental increase:

[13] It makes him ⟨ , ⟩ unhinges him and he just gets *weirder and weirder* and the film gets *weirder and weirder* [S1A-049-262]

[14] She hadn't returned since his birth, and she found it *harder and harder* to breathe as the afternoon wore on. [W2F-010-77]

The same applies if the comparison is expressed by *more and more*:

[15] I think it's become *more and more difficult* [S1B-050-61]

Co-ordination of *nice* (in particular), *good*, or *lovely* with another adjective may express intensification:

[16] She rearranges her nightdress and falls asleep almost immediately, thinking about how *nice and safe* she is lying next to her husband. [W2F-016-53]

[17] It's *nice and quiet* [S1A-019-322]

[18] London is *good and warm*, though I've never spoken to her, just the impression I get. [W1B-001-96]

5.40
Functions of adjective phrases

The two major functions of adjective phrases are as premodifier of a noun and as subject predicative. They are listed first below, followed by other functions.

1.   Premodifier of a noun

   [1]   Well it's a *much less popular* route [S1A-021-99]

2.   Subject predicative (cf. 3.18)

   [2]   No I mean Auden was *extraordinarily ugly* [S1A-015-53]

3.   Object predicative (cf. 3.19)

   [3]   He's opening his mouth *very wide* just now [S1A-023-115]

4.   Postmodifier of a pronoun (cf. 5.6)

   [4]   There would still be eyes watching and wondering from a distance but, briefly, there was no one *close.* [W2F-015-61]

5.   Postmodifier of a noun (cf. 5.6)

   [5]   To outsiders London seems one of the most vibrant cultural capitals of the world ⟨ , ⟩ a city *bright with theatres cinemas ballet opera art galleries and great museums* [S1B-022-2]

6.   Nominal adjective (cf. 4.23)

   [6]   Tonight I hope you'll not mind if I eschew *the academic* and pursue a more earthy albeit reflective tack analyzing the soil within which citizenship can root and thrive [S2A-039-11]

7.   Complement of a preposition (cf. 5.47)

   [7]   Kaye doesn't finish till *late* [. . .] [S1A-005-86]

5.41
Premodifiers of adjectives

Adjectives are premodified chiefly by adverbs. Generally, the premodifier is an intensifier (cf. 5.45):

   [1]   This is a *perfectly* good conversation as far as I'm concerned [S1A-008-111]

   [2]   I can remember going there and being amazed *how* pimply the ⟨ , ⟩ conscripts were [S1A-014-21]

   [3]   She's *sort of* broad in the chest and she's *sort of* stocky [S1A-019-160]

   [4]   That is *a bit* premature isn't it [S1A-019-195]

   [5]   I found it *rather* tight [S1A-022-257]

   [6]   Uhm ⟨ , ⟩ Dennis can we have your report which I trust won't be *too deeply* technical [S1B-078-5]

   [7]   Grand mal epilepsy is a *surprisingly* common condition, affecting between four and eight people in every thousand. [W2B-023-27] ('common to a surprising degree')

[8] I'd be *quite* keen to try anything like that really [S1A-035-55]

[9] What have you been doing then that's been *so* wild [S1A-040-227]

[10] They're all young and *very* wet behind the ears [S1A-010-26]

Very is the most common intensifier. Some of the intensifiers are combinations of words, such as *sort of* **[3]** and *a bit* **[4]**. The intensifier may itself be intensified; for example, *deeply* in **[6]** is intensified by *too*.

Intensifiers may also modify comparatives **[11]**–**[14]**:

[11] Actually Simon can't be *too much* older than us [S1A-017-53]

[12] I feel *so much* better now I know he's in London and he's not going to come round [S1A-042-20]

[13] So I think it's *slightly* lighter [S1A-099-167]

[14] I think it is *far* better to increase the amount of democracy rather than to go ahead and reduce it which I believe would be wrong at this time [S1B-053-41]

Very cannot intensify comparatives, though it can occur in intensifier combinations such as *very much*, where *very* is an intensifier of *much*. On the other hand, *very* is the most common intensifier of superlatives:

[15] My *very* best wishes to you both, take care. [W1B-008-119]

Other intensifiers of superlatives precede the determiner or follow the noun:

[16] And they are as I say *by far* the best side in Greece [S2A-018-85]

[17] Firstly I am the youngest *by miles*. [W1B-002-157]

[18] *Much* the best pastry we've ever had [S1A-057-155]

Focusing adverbs (cf. 4.27) are often used as premodifiers of adjectives. They include additive adverbs **[19]**–**[20]**, exclusive adverbs **[21]**–**[22]**, and particularizer adverbs **[23]**–**[24]**. The particularizer adverbs may also convey intensification.

[19] *Equally* important are the profoundly moral arguments over the origin of life ⟨ , ⟩ the status of the embryo and the freedom to experiment on and then destroy human life in its first fourteen days [S1B-060-2]

[20] The main problem confronting any study of the Picts is the complete lack of source material, or *even* archaeological evidence. [W1A-009-81]

[21] I'm *only* sorry that we aren't actually having a holiday in Provence [S1A-011-57]

[22] How do you get it *just* right [S1A-022-251]

[23] Is there anything *particularly* distinctive about that fermentor [S1B-020-31]

[24] Belgravia as an estate is *predominantly* residential with offices and commercial property around the perimeter [S2A-045-92]

Another type of premodifier of adjectives is the viewpoint adverb. For example, *morally* is a viewpoint adverb when it has the meaning 'from a moral point of view'. Here are some examples:

[25] In countries with *technically* advanced agriculture, milking is done by machine, rather than by hand. [W2A-033-10]

[26] The orthodoxies of our time are that morality is a private affair a matter of personal choice ⟨ , ⟩ and that the state must be *morally* neutral [S2B-029-105]

[27] You mean it's *theoretically* possible [S1A-062-56]

[28] It is *physically* impossible to force myself to work sometimes [S1A-040-122]

[29] They often have to cope with negative public attitudes towards the stereotyped image of the *mentally* ill, borne of ignorance and fear. [W1A-007-90]

5.42
Postmodifiers of adjectives

Adjectives are typically postmodified by prepositional phrases and various kinds of clauses. Below is a list of types of postmodifiers.

1. **Prepositional phrase**

   [1] I was afraid *of him* ⟨ , ⟩ didn't really know him and I was kind of glad when ⟨ , ⟩ he left [S1A-072-51]

2. ***That*-clause**

   [2] I feel sure *that some day it will be published* [S1B-026-243]

   [3] I expect you're glad *you're not a vegetarian* [S1A-055-128]

3. ***Wh*-clause**

   [4] Yes you have to be careful *what's available in what colour* [S1A-086-291]

   [5] I think that Jim felt ⟨ , ⟩ slightly embarrassed taking over from the man who had actually facilitated his becoming Prime Minister and he was uncertain *what to do* [S1B-040-8]

4. ***To*-infinitive clause**

   [6] If you have any questions then I would be happy *to hear from you*, but would you please allow me until Tuesday 7 May to give me a little time to sort things at this end. [W1B-016-34]

5. ***-ing* participle clause**

   [7] But police were busy *handing out letters about the operation to residents* and Supt Slater was happy with the result. [W2C-011-72]

6. **Comparative clause**

   [8] No I'm sure it's easier *than they say* [S1A-074-111]

7. **Adverb**

   [9] It certainly tasted strong *enough* [S1A-009-154]

The relation between an adjective and its postmodifier in types [1]–[5] often resembles that between a verb and its complement, and indeed such postmodifiers are often termed complements (cf. 6.16), as are those of type **[6]**. Compare the following pairs;

[10]   I am *afraid of him.*

[10a]   I *fear him.*

[11]   I'm *sure that it will be published.*

[11a]   I *know that it will be published.*

[12]   He was *uncertain what to do.*

[12a]   He did not *know what to do.*

[13]   I am *happy to hear from you.*

[13a]   I *rejoice to hear from you.*

Some adjectives require a postmodifying prepositional phrase with the specified preposition, at least in the relevant sense. For example: *accustomed to, bad at, bent on, fond of, free from, good at, short of, subject to, tantamount to. Conscious* takes either a prepositional phrase with *of* or a *that*-clause.

As with objects of verbs, *that* may be omitted from the postmodifying *that*-clause, as in **[3]**. *Wh*-clauses may be finite **[4]** or non-finite with an infinitive verb **[5]**.

Types **[2]–[5]** may have analogous constructions with anticipatory *it* as subject and an extraposed subject clause (cf. 3.22). The subject clauses are not postmodifiers of the adjectives:

[14]   But after two days *it* was obvious *that it wouldn't work* because he didn't want me to even pick the child up [S1B-049-75] (*that*-clause)

[14a]   *That it wouldn't work* was obvious.

[15]   Although a national park has been established at Morne Anglaise, *it* is doubtful *whether any of these large parrots live within its boundary.* [W2B-028-74] (*wh*-clause)

[15a]   *Whether any of these large parrots live within its boundary* is doubtful.

[16]   I detect in the United States' latest addition a realisation that *it* is important *to keep the United Nations Security Council consensus* and that I very much welcome [S1B-035-93] (*to*-infinitive clause)

[16a]   *To keep the United Nations Security Council consensus* is important.

[17]   Oh I see I thought you said *it* was very frightening *being able to understand what they were saying* [S1A-020-37] (*-ing* participle clause)

[17a]   *Being able to understand what they were saying* was very frightening.

In most instances of *to*-infinitive clauses, the implied subject of the clause is the same as the subject of the host clause, as in **[6]**, simplified as **[6a]**:

[6a]   *I* would be happy *to hear from you.* ('I will hear from you')

But with some adjectives, the subject of the host clause is identical with the implied object of the infinitive clause:

[18]   Generally motorbikes aren't as visible as cars and *their speed* is more difficult *to estimate* [S2A-054-192]

[18a] *To estimate their speed* is more difficult.

This construction in **[18a]** allows extraposition of the clause with an anticipatory *it* in subject position (cf. 4.38):

[18b] *It* is more difficult *to estimate their speed.*

A number of adjectives belong to the set that functions like *difficult* in constructions like **[18]**, **[18a]**, and **[18b]**. They include *easy, hard, impossible, nice, pleasant, tough, unpleasant.* The superficial resemblance of constructions with these two different kinds of sets of adjectives in *to*-infinitive clauses has led to the linguistic puzzle on the differences between **[19]** and **[19a]**:

[19]   John is *eager to please.*

[19a]   John is *easy to please.*

Another set of adjectives resembles *difficult* when they are in infinitive clauses in that the host subject is also the implied object of the infinitive clause but they do not admit extraposition of the clause:

[20]   Both Philips and Matsushita are now making DCC chip sets and the first batch of Philips chips were ready *to mount on a single board inside the stand-alone deck unit in time for CES at Las Vegas.* [W2B-038-76]

Other adjectives like *ready* in this respect include *available, free, hot, sufficient.* Since these can also function in constructions where the subjects are identical, there is potential ambiguity in isolation where both interpretations are possible:

[21]   *It* [i.e. the dog] is too hot *to eat.*

[22]   *It* [i.e. the food] is too hot *to eat.*

For **[21]** we can add an object to the infinitive clause:

[21a]   It is too hot *to eat any food.*

For **[22]** we can add a subject to the infinitive clause and optionally an object:

[22a]   It is too hot *for anyone to eat (it).*

The addition of the object is only possible when the subject is present. Analogous to **[21]** and **[22]** is a third interpretation, since *it* can be used to refer to the weather:

[23]   *It* [i.e. the weather] is too hot *to eat.*

We can in this interpretation add a subject or an object or both.

Only two adverbs are used as postmodifiers of adjectives, both of them intensifiers—*enough* and *indeed*:

[24]   Highway officials insist the ornamental railings on older bridges are not strong *enough* to prevent vehicles from crashing through. [891102-0090-5]

[25]   And so we were very lucky *indeed* to have a statutory body agree for us to have five hundred hours of ethics and politics for our nursing course [S1B-044-92]

[26]   Its a very good kick *indeed* [S2A-002-50]

The intensifier *indeed* commonly correlates with the premodifier *very*, as in **[25]**–**[26]**. However, it need not do so:

[27] While some but as yet pretty few women are at last achieving promotion to senior rank ⟨ , ⟩ senior black officers are rare *indeed* [S2B-037-62]

Comparative clauses and phrases correlate with a preceding *more* or the *-er* inflection, *less*, and *as*:

[28] Both agree that improvement is needed and should be *more* rapid *than is now the case* [S2A-021-36]

[29] The total of 18 deaths from malignant mesothelioma, lung cancer and asbestosis was far high*er than expected*, the researchers said. [891102-0191-16]

[30] Yet our efforts are somehow *less* noble *than those of an investment expert studiously devouring press clippings on each company he follows.* [891102-0073-60]

[31] You can be *as* personal *as you like* [S1A-017-357]

Combinations of premodifier and postmodifier are often possible, since an intensifier can usually be used with the adjective. Here is an example with *no* ('not at all'):

[32] The nature of the work that we do is *no* different ⟨ , ⟩ *from* ⟨ , ⟩ *any other creative arts group* [S1A-004-118]

Adverb Phrases

5.43
The structure of the adverb phrase

The adverb phrase has as its head an adverb, which may be preceded by premodifiers and (less commonly) followed by postmodifiers. The structure of the adverb phrase is shown at **Fig. 5.43.1**. The parentheses indicate the optional elements.

Fig. 5.43.1 Structure of an adverb phrase

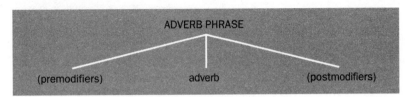

Adverbs may be co-ordinated to express repetition:

[1] Books that you come back to ⟨ , ⟩ *over and over and over and over* again [S1A-013-54]

[2] It goes *on and on* like this [S1B-022-126]

> **[3]** And there used to be islands and they used to go *round and round* and then one would stop at the top of the tree and they'd get on and experience whatever that land had to offer [S1A-046-321]

Repetition may also be conveyed by the co-ordination of contrasting directional adverbs:

> **[4]** Of course I assumed that as Mr Sainsbury was popping *in and out* from time to time that the scheme was proceeding anyway [S1B-061-129]

> **[5]** The side of the bed was weighed down with his father's bulk and his shoulder was being pumped *up and down*. [W2F-001-12]

> **[6]** Tommy had fallen asleep by the time Anne had calmed down and she rocked him gently *back and forth* in her arms. [W2F-002-80]

Adverb phrases may be co-ordinated with a co-ordinator:

> **[7]** We had to do something *structurally and radically* different. [891102-0100-8]

> **[8]** I have a right to print those scripts if I go there and *laboriously—but no longer surreptitiously—*copy them out in long hand. [891102-0084-54]

> **[9]** *Rightly or wrongly, but not necessarily rationally*, currency traders use the monthly figures as an excuse to buy or sell if the deficit is more or less than predictions, notes a Commerce Department official. [891013-0001-15]

Adverbs may also be co-ordinated asyndetically, without a co-ordinator (cf. 5.39):

> **[10]** "I think life is the exercise that can be a yogic practice, if you do it *lovingly, authentically, honestly*," he says. Or: "In ten years time, I hope I'm healthy—*physically, emotionally, psychologically, spiritually*." ['Jeff Goldblum, you've got to hand it to him', by Sabine Durant, *The Independent*, 22 July 1993, p. 13]

Co-ordination of comparative adverbs or of *more and more* with adverbs indicates incremental increase (cf. 5.39):

> **[11]** These become key issues in which the two groups become *further and further* divided [S1B-047-52]

> **[12]** That is happening and it's happening *more and more slowly* under John Major than it did under Mrs Thatcher [S1B-039-73]

Repetition of an adverb expresses intensification (cf. 5.39), and if the adverb itself is an intensifier the repetition reinforces the intensifying effect:

> **[13]** He's *desperately desperately* in love [S1A-069-31]

> **[14]** It escaped on the underground and it got out this poor wasp so *far ⟨ , ⟩ far* from home [S1A-067-43]

> **[15]** [. . .] I was talking to this this guy at college and uhm he's *really really really* boring and he *always always* says the same thing [S1A-091-51]

> **[16]** I'm going to rehearse it *very very* slowly [S1A-026-176]

> **[17]** And I've been applying *quite quite* regularly since [S1A-034-143]

5.44
Functions of adverb phrases

The major functions of adverb phrases are as premodifiers of adjectives and adverbs and as adverbials and complements of a verb. They are listed first below, followed by other functions.

1. **Premodifier of an adjective** (cf. 5.41)

   [1]   We're *far too* close to it [S1A-023-323]

2. **Premodifier of an adverb** (cf. 5.45)

   [2]   I'm going to give you a prescription to clear up the infection 〈 , 〉 then you need to have your teeth *extremely* thoroughly cleaned 〈 , 〉 as soon as possible [S1A-087-177]

3. **Adverbial** (cf. 3.20, 4.27)

   [3]   Refunds of fees are not *normally* available. [W2D-007-94]

4. **Subject predicative** (cf. 3.18)

   [4]   I thought he was *here* [S1A-005-187]

5. **Premodifier of a preposition** (cf. 5.49)

   [5]   But I have a feeling they might be *right* by the door but if they're not then it's not worth it [S1A-046-364]

6. **Premodifier of a pronoun** (cf. 5.5)

   [6]   When I look around at my friends, *virtually* all of them seem to have got careers. [W1B-001-167]

7. **Premodifier of a determiner** (cf. 5.4)

   [7]   Everybody knows that the results in fact have *absolutely* no meaning and can be interpreted any way you like [S1B-029-23]

8. **Premodifier of a numeral** (cf. 5.4)

   [8]   The chaps *around* forty to forty-five are all called John [S1A-032-281]

9. **Premodifier of a noun phrase** (cf. 5.5)

   [9]   This is really *quite* a problem I imagine [S1B-023-42]

10. **Postmodifier of a noun phrase** (cf. 5.6)

    [10]   Your friend *here* does she doodle a lot [S1A-017-97]

11. **Postmodifier of an adjective or adverb** (cf. 5.42, 5.46)

    [11] Well right that's fair *enough* then [S1A-005-209]

    [12] And oddly *enough* it's not only outsiders who ask it [S2B-042-6]

12. **Subject predicative** (cf. 3.18)

    [13] At least we're *outside*. [W2F-013-130]

13. **Object predicative** (cf. 3.19)

    [14] Shall I move these *away* [S1A-003-74]

14.   **Complement of a preposition** (cf. 5.47)

> **[15]** Oh I should have thought he'd've had one before *now* [S1A-007-256]

These functions are discussed elsewhere, as indicated.

5.45
Premodifiers of adverbs

Adverbs are premodified only by intensifying adverbs.[14] The most common premodifying intensifier is *very*.

> **[1]**   I wear this occasionally but *very* rarely now [S1A-022-217]

Here are examples of other intensifiers:

> **[2]**   And it's not *that* far away [S1A-006-290]
>
> **[3]**   I'm trying *so* hard to concentrate on this [S1A-038-244]
>
> **[4]**   But I did it *really* badly [S1A-050-166]
>
> **[5]**   I mean it worked *perfectly* well [S1A-056-164]
>
> **[6]**   We might die and then find ourselves going *straight* down [S1A-084-144]
>
> **[7]**   I think they did *pretty* well to get to ⟨ , ⟩ end up like that [S1A-095-86]
>
> **[8]**   Let's go through them *fairly* systematically [S1A-004-275]
>
> **[9]**   I could not myself have expressed it *as* well [S1B-052-67]
>
> **[10]**   You're sort of jumping *a bit* ahead [S1B-009-122]

There may be a sequence of intensifiers premodifying an adverb, each modifying the following intensifier:

> **[11]**   Don't know if it fits me *all that* well now [S1A-022-188]
>
> **[12]**   It takes *far too* long for us to get rid of the poll tax [S1B-034-92]
>
> **[13]**   The prophet responds to this by saying that God will show to them *all too* clearly how just he is by coming against them in judgement [S2A-036-62]

5.46
Postmodifiers of adverbs

Two adverb intensifiers—*enough* and *indeed*—commonly postmodify adverbs, as they do adjectives (cf. 5.42):

> **[1]**   It was quoted often *enough* in the recent debate in the other place [S1B-060-69]
>
> **[2]**   On that occasion he used the original scoring; on Telarc he is accompanied by a full symphony orchestra and is recorded very sumptuously *indeed*. [W2B-008-39]

Very normally premodifies the adverb when it is postmodified by *indeed. Ever* is an intensifying postmodifier of *never*:

[3] Never lecture with ⟨ , ⟩ animals or children and *never ever* try to do chemistry experiments live [S2A-053-63]

A few postmodifying adverbs are not intensifiers:

[4] Well do it somewhere *else* [S1A-010-145]

[5] Well it's not that far *away* [S1A-011-64]

As with adjectives (cf. 5.42), comparative clauses and phrases postmodify adverbs and they may correlate with a preceding *more* or comparative inflection, *less*, or *as*:

[6] I think he's feeling the time going *more* slowly *than I am* since he's the one left behind. [W1B-010-154]

[7] But you'd probably know that music scene *much* better *than I would* [S1A-033-102]

[8] Not everyone at the training sessions will be a complete novice so don't be discouraged if you don't pick things up *quite as* quickly *as everyone else* [S2A-054-97]

[9] Uhm ⟨ , ⟩ also another factor which I think is not often taken into account is they have very low population densities so epidemics go through the population *much less* regularly *than they do through an urban population or uhm a rural village-based population* [S2A-047-54]

[10] Indeed this dying month of March she has visited the Abbey on no less *than three occasions* [S2A-020-55]

Some attitudinal adverbs (cf. 4.27) can be postmodified by a prepositional phrase introduced by the preposition *for*:

[11] Unhappily *for Tanya*, the telephone was in a corner of the living-room. [W2F-006-169]

[12] And ⟨ , ⟩ very luckily *for us* this also this enzyme has an absorption spectrum that changes depending upon whether the enzyme is oxygenated or de-oxygenated [S2A-053-28]

[13] He didn't quite gather it cleanly the first time but uh thankfully *for Spurs* he got hold of it in the end and Adams was uh denied the chance [S2A-015-178]

Viewpoint prepositional phrases are also possible, such as *in my view, from their point of view, in my belief, in my opinion*:

[14] But literature actually interestingly *in my belief* ⟨ , ⟩ uh rather neglects it [S2A-031-61]

Independently is unique in that it can be postmodified by a prepositional phrase introduced by *of*:

[15] They then determined whether audience judgments varied independently *of the true status of the story*, by comparing audience guesses to each storyteller's claim about his or her story. [W2A-007-110]

Prepositional Phrases

5.47
The structure of the prepositional phrase

The prepositional phrase consists of two constituents: a preposition and the complement of the preposition. Optionally, the preposition may be premodified by an intensifying adverb (cf. 5.49). The structure of the prepositional phrase is shown in **Fig. 5.47.1**, with the optional intensifier in parentheses.

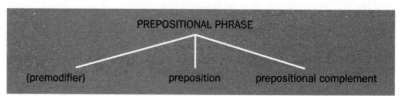

Fig. 5.47.1 Structure of a prepositional phrase

The prepositional complement is chiefly a noun phrase, an -*ing* participle clause, or a *wh*-clause. These are listed first below, followed by other linguistic units.

1. Noun phrase as complement

    [1] But I mean my only recollection of *it* is sleeping in *a wood* for *about four or five hours* [S1A-014-53]

2. -*ing* participle clause as complement

    [2] I mean instead of *getting people up so early* she could stick around and have breakfast for an hour or two [S1A-006-312]

For the use of the genitive case for the subject of the participle clause, see 6.16.

3. *Wh*-clause as complement

    [3] It's just a question of *how we organise it and what the numbers should be* [S1B-075-68]

4. Adverb as complement

    [4] I have to wait till *then*! [W1B-007-64]

5. Adjective as complement[15]

    [5] When the public feuding ended, the insults continued in *private*. [890921-0035-29]

6. Prepositional phrase as

    [6] That means he took one lamb burger out of there ⟨ , ⟩ from *under the grill* [S1A-095-225]

In certain constructions, the preposition is stranded—left by itself, without a following prepositional complement. Stranding may result from the absence of a complement or from the fronting of the complement.[16]

The complement is absent in three instances:

1. Where a prepositional verb or phrasal-prepositional verb is in the passive, the subject corresponds to what would be the prepositional complement in the active:

[7] All she meant, I feel, is that McQueen popularized the term, for it is generally held to be a negro phrase and *was talked about* before the film star came on the scene. [W2B-010-194] ('People talked *about that*')

[8] A bill will be introduced to enable applications for asylum in the United Kingdom *to be dealt with* quickly and effectively [S2B-041-41] ('They will deal *with applications for asylum*')

2. The subject of the host clause is the same as the implied prepositional complement in an infinitive clause (5.42):

[9] *Buses* are well lit, *easy to see into* from outside, and pick up and set down passengers at regular intervals, reducing the chances of violence or robbery. [W2D-009-81] ('It is easy to see *into buses*')

[10] [. . .] *they*'re rather *nice to look at* as you'll see later ⟨ , ⟩ I hope [S2A-046-34] ('It's rather nice to look *at them*')

3. The subject of the host clause is the same as the implied prepositional complement in an -*ing* participle clause (cf. 5.42):

[11] Well *the swimming pool*'s not *worth talking about* [. . .] [S1A-021-133] ('It's not worth talking *about the swimming pool*')

The complement of the preposition is fronted in three types of construction:

4. *wh*-questions (cf. 3.5)

[12] *What* did you have it *on* [S1A-009-162]

[13] *Which part*'s he *from* [S1A-014-12]

[14] *Who* is it *by* [S1A-043-64]

[15] *How long* did you do English *for* [S1A-006-1]

5. Relative clauses (cf. 5.9)

[16] Uhm ⟨ , , ⟩ had an exhibition *which* I forgot to invite you *to* [S1A-015-70]

[17] So anyway ⟨ , ⟩ then I found out he was going out with a woman *that* I was going out *with* you know [. . .] [S1A-052-71]

If the relative clause has a zero relative (cf. 5.9), the prepositional complement is of course absent:

[18] They may have to say that's the direction we were going *in* [S1B-039-46] ('. . . the direction *that* we were going *in*')

The preposition must be stranded in relative clauses if the relative is *that* **[17]** or zero **[18]** since the preposition can only precede a *wh*-relative. In *wh*-questions and in relative clauses with a *wh*-relative there is usually a choice. Generally, the prepositional complement alone is fronted and the preposition is stranded, as in **[12]**–**[16]**. In a usually more formal alternative, the preposition is fronted with its complement in a *wh*-question **[19]** or relative clause **[20]**:

[19] First of all *to what companies* does that scheme apply [S1B-062-81]

[20] There can't be many other countries for example where the retail price of a loaf of bread is lower than the wholesale cost of the ingredients *from which* it's made [S2B-039-14]

If the *wh*-question or relative clause is long, the preposition is more likely to be fronted. Contrast **[21]** with **[21a]**:

[21] You find me preparing for a concert organized by friends *at which* for half an hour I will be reading one of my poems to an audience 1000% of the size of the normal audience for poetry. [W1B-015-67]

[21a] You find me preparing for a concert organized by my friends *which* I will be reading one of my poems *at*.

6. The relative in a nominal relative clause (cf. 6.12) must always come first in that clause. The relative may be the same as the implied prepositional complement:

[22] I think that's *what* everybody ⟨ , ⟩ hopes for ⟨ , ⟩ within a working situation ⟨ , ⟩ uhm [S1A-002-97] ('Everybody hopes *for that*')

[23] *Whatever* you want to look *at*'s there really [S1B-074-203] ('You may want to look *at that*')

[24] I remember ⟨ , ⟩ long long ago telling my publishers that that's *who* I would like to be *like* [. . .] [S1B-048-130] ('I would like to be *like that person*')

A preposition can precede a nominal relative clause, but then the whole clause is the complement of the preposition:

[25] I was just wondering if it was worth complaining *to whoever was in charge* or not bothering [S1A-069-178] ('*She* was in charge')

[26] It's quite another for them to imagine that they can transfer or share the contract *with whoever they choose* [S2B-007-47] (cf: 'They will choose *him*')

In **[25]** *whoever* is the subject of the clause, whereas in **[26]** it is the object and could be replaced by the more formal *whomever*.

5.48
Functions of prepositional phrases

1. **Postmodifier of a noun**

   [1] Everybody questions the significance *of the results* [S1B-029-27]

2. **Postmodifier of an adjective** (cf. 5.42)

   [2] And also it is alleged that uh he was ignorant *of the crucial lack of an extradition treaty* [S2A-064-59]

3. **Subject predicative** (cf. 3.18)

   [3] Yesterday the sun was just as it is *in India* [S1A-017-203]

4.**Object predicative** (cf. 3.19)

>**[4]**From the time I brought her *out of hospital* she never slept [S1B-049-88]

5.**Adverbial** (cf. 3.20)

>**[5]**Every Tuesday I stood there waiting *by the door* expecting you to come
>[S1A-040-372]

Prepositional verbs (cf. 5.36) and phrasal-prepositional verbs (cf. 5.37) can be analysed alternatively as verbs with prepositional phrases. In that case the prepositional phrase is also a complement of the verb:

6.**Complement of a verb** (cf. 3.20)

>**[6]**There's a word beginning *with D* that would describe it [S1A-018-188]

Citations **[7]**–**[9]** contain other multi-word verbs that have a preposition as a component (cf. 5.34, 5.36 f.). These can similarly be analysed as single verbs with a prepositional phrase as their complement:

>**[7]**Did you apply *for anything* in the final year [S1A-034-120]

>**[8]**No-one will blame you *for a genuine mistake.* [W2D-009-152]

>**[9]**Have the police come up *with* anything yet? [W2F-020-168]

One argument in favour of this alternative analysis is that it is possible to separate the verb from the preposition by inserting an adverb or other linguistic unit between the two:

>**[10]**But I look forward *tonight* to a thorough debate on the orders ⟨ , ⟩ and on
>all aspects raised by the establishment of the new bank [S1B-054-11]

>**[11]**And the free world has reacted *quickly* to this momentous process and
>must continue to do so if it is to help and influence events [S1B-054-16]

>**[12]**We've been waiting *for so long* for it [S2A-009-96]

Another argument in favour of the alternative analysis is that it is possible to co-ordinate the prepositional phrases:

>**[13]**And and they were drawing inspiration *not from Palladio* ⟨ , ⟩ *not from
>Lutyens* ⟨ , ⟩ *not even always from Le Corbusier* ⟨ , , ⟩ *but from car
>production hovercraft balloons robots* [S2A-040-57]

>**[14]**The path followed by such an oceanic current depends *partly on the
>difference in temperature between the equator and the poles, partly on
>the effect of the Earth's rotation, and partly on the shape of the ocean
>basin itself.* [W2B-025-14]

The conjunction can also appear simply in front of a phrase that is not co-ordinated to another phrase:

>**[15]**Fish could be seen feeding *but not on hook baits.* [W2D-017-87]

5.49
Premodifiers of prepositions and prepositional phrases

Prepositions may be premodified by intensifiers. Here are some examples:

[1]   I don't think there's anything *quite* like Toblerone [S1A-023-190]

[2]   It's *so* near Christmas it's unbelievable [S1A-039-13]

[3]   The contribution of modern genetics has shown however that the genetic code is really a fundamental organising principle and there is a radical unity *long* before the fourteen-day stage [S1B-060-64]

[4]   The choir is placed *sharply* above the nave [. . .] [W2B-003-102]

[5]   This stance was somewhat hypocritical, as for many years, indeed *ever* since the war, all the major investment decisions in the industry had been agreed by, and, in the main, financed by, government. [W2B-016-15]

[6]   A button labelled Layer/Active, handily located *just* below the Tone Buttons, allows you to switch between the two functions. [W2B-031-31]

In some instances the intensifiers modify the whole prepositional phrase rather than the preposition. In such instances the prepositional phrases are close in meaning to adjective phrases:

[7]   I mean ⟨ , ⟩ you were *very* on time [S1A-022-28]

[8]   Your heroines are *very much* of a type aren't they [S1B-048-147]

[9]   Of course he was *all* for that and so was his family [S1B-049-23]

[10] What is happening is *perfectly* in order [S1B-051-15]

[11] Notice how this section is *somewhat* at odds with the earlier part of the chapter [. . .] [S2A-036-124]

[12] I supposed they must be friends, because they were *so* at their ease, and always seemed to be involving themselves with my mother. [W2F-010-94]

Chapter 6
Sentences and Clauses

Summary

The sentence (6.1)

Clause relationships (6.2–7)

Signals of clause relationships (6.8–9)

Subordinate clauses (6.10–16)

Reported speech (6.17–19)

Chapter 6 Summary

- The notional definition of a sentence as expressing a complete thought is too vague. Preference is given to a formal definition of a sentence as consisting of one or more grammatically complete clauses. Complete sentences are distinguished from elliptical sentences, unfinished sentences, and non-sentences.

- Clauses may be linked through co-ordination or subordination. Co-ordinated clauses are at the same grammatical level. Subordinate clauses are dependent on other clauses, either embedded in them or loosely attached to them.

- Traditionally, sentences are classified as simple (consisting of one main clause without subordination), compound (consisting of two or more main clauses that are co-ordinated), and complex (consisting of a main clause with one or more subordinate clauses). The classification is a simplification that does not take account of various patterns of co-ordination and subordination. The distinction between co-ordination and subordination can be subsumed under the broader distinction between parataxis and hypotaxis.

- Orthographic sentences are not necessarily the same as grammatical sentences, which are identified with a cluster of clauses (minimally one) that are interrelated by co-ordination or subordination.

- Co-ordination and subordination can sometimes express similar meaning relationships.

- Co-ordination is signalled by the actual or potential presence of co-ordinators between clauses.

- Subordination is generally signalled by subordinators and *wh*-words. Non-finite and verbless clauses are generally subordinate.

- Subordinate clauses are finite, non-finite, or verbless. The verb in a non-finite clause is an -*ing* participle, an -*ed* participle, an infinitive preceded by *to*, or a bare infinitive. Non-finite and verbless clauses may have their own subject or may be subjectless.

- Subordinate clauses function as nominal clauses, relative clauses, adverbial clauses, or comparative clauses.

- Nominal clauses are declarative, interrogative, exclamative, or nominal relative.

- Adverbial clauses express a range of meanings: place, time, condition, circumstance, concession, reason or cause, purpose, result, manner, proportion, similarity, and comment.

- Comparative clauses involve a standard of comparison and a basis of comparison. Comparatives are inflected forms or phrases constructed with *more.* They are used with a postmodifying *than*-clause to express higher degrees of comparison. Lower degrees are expressed by premodifying *less* with a postmodifying *than*-clause, and equivalent degrees by premodifying *as* with a postmodifying *as*-clause. Comparative clauses are often elliptical.

■ Nominal clauses can function as complements of verbs, adjectives, and nouns.

■ The major categories of reported speech (including reported thought) are direct speech and indirect speech. Indirect speech involves an orientation to the deixis of the reporting situation, generally resulting in shifts of (particularly) pronouns and a backshift in tense. Minor intermediate categories of reporting are free direct speech and free indirect speech.

The Sentence

6.1
Complete and incomplete sentences

The traditional definition of a sentence states that a sentence expresses a complete thought.[1] The trouble with this notional definition is that it requires us to know what a complete thought is. Does *God* or *our home* express complete thoughts? Is there just one complete thought in **[1]**?

> **[1]** Some 4,000 people (most of whom had heard about, but not actually read the book) wrote to Dr Robinson, telling him of their own faith, beliefs, convictions, feelings, or special knowledge concerning matters religious. [W2A-012-36]

We can easily rewrite **[1]** as at least three separate sentences, each complete in itself:

> **[1a]** Some 4,000 people wrote to Dr Robinson. They told him of their own faith, beliefs, convictions, feelings, or special knowledge concerning matters religious. Most of them had heard about, but not actually read the book.

Similarly, **[2]** can be rewritten as two complete sentences:

> **[2]** An example of conforming individualism was recently provided for me by my daughter when I noticed that she was wearing only one ear-ring. [W2A-012-121]

> **[2a]** An example of conforming individualism was recently provided for me by my daughter. It happened when I noticed that she was wearing one ear-ring.

We rightly feel that **[1]** and **[2]** have a unity and completeness, but we have the same feeling about the three sentences in **[1a]** and the two sentences in **[2a]**. What gives us that feeling is not that each sentence expresses one complete thought but that each sentence is grammatically complete.

The measure of grammatical completeness is the clause. The canonical sentence consists of one or more grammatically complete clauses. That is to say, each clause contains the constituents that must be present according to the general rules for constructing clauses—subject, verb, and complements of the verb (cf. 3.13)—except that the understood subject *you* is generally omitted in imperative sentences (cf. 3.7). Citation **[3]** is a simple sentence consisting of just one grammatically complete clause, and citation **[4]** is a sentence consisting of two grammatically complete clauses co-ordinated by *and*:

> **[3]** The conquest of Italy was certainly not a process of enslavement. [W2A-001-2]

> **[4]** Some peoples were actually given Roman citizenship, *and* their chief men secured high office at Rome. [W2A-001-7]

The writer of **[4]** could have punctuated the two clauses as separate orthographic sentences, the second sentence beginning with *and*, but they would remain grammatically linked by *and*. If the co-ordinator *and* is omitted, the two clauses constitute two independent sentences.

In **[5]**, by contrast, the subject *The Romans themselves* is shared by two predicates, one beginning *saw* and the other beginning *traced*:

> **[5]**   *The Romans themselves* saw in this practice a major factor in their rise to world power *and* traced it back to the legendary origins of their city. [W2A-001-8]

It is normal for the second subject to be omitted in such instances. We could say that **[5]** consists of two clauses: a complete clause (which could also be an independent sentence) and an incomplete clause—incomplete because the subject is omitted, though understood from the previous clause. Another way of analysing the sentence is to say that the sentence contains one subject and two co-ordinated predicates. This kind of analysis—stipulating co-ordination of parts of the sentence rather than ellipsis of parts—is adopted in this chapter wherever possible.

There are incomplete sentences where it would be reasonable to posit ellipsis. If the interpretation depends on the situational context, we have situational ellipsis. For example, **[6]** and **[7]** were uttered during a word game.

> **[6]**   Haven't got one [S1A-010-65]

> **[7]**   Got an e [S1A-010-76]

The interpretation of the ellipted subject as *I* in **[6]** and of the ellipted subject and auxiliary as *I've* in **[7]** depends on the situation, since the same incomplete sentences could have different ellipted words in a different situation: say, *we* in **[6]** or *she's* in **[7]**.

The other major type of ellipsis is textual ellipsis, which depends crucially on the linguistic context: we recover the ellipted words from what has been said or written before or after the ellipsis. In **[8]**, the elliptical sentence in B's utterance is interpreted by reference to the immediately preceding utterance by A:

> **[8]**   A: You told me at the time ⟨ , ⟩
>   B: Did I [S1A-007-276 f.]

Did I is incomplete since the main verb and its possible complements are missing. We readily understand *Did I* to mean roughly 'Did I tell you at that time?'

Elliptical sentences are incomplete sentences, but they are perfectly normal and acceptable. They are subject to rules. For example, while *Did I* is an acceptable response by speaker B in **[8]**, *Did* or *I* would be distinctly odd in that context. Elliptical sentences are particularly common in spoken dialogue and in written representations of dialogue.

A different type of incomplete sentence, very common in speech, is the unfinished sentence. Speakers may fail to complete a sentence for a variety of reasons. For example, they may restart a sentence to correct themselves **[9]**, or they may become nervous, excited, or hesitant [10], or they may lose the thread of what they are saying [11], or they may be interrupted by another speaker [12]:

> [9]   Right Friday morning *I will I am supposed to* go see Mrs Girlock [ICE-USA-S1A-004]
>
> [10] Well *you put it* uh yeah you put it here [S1A-010-121]
>
> [11] A: I mean he's a bit odd
>   B: Mm ⟨ , ⟩
>   A: *But* uh ⟨ , , ⟩ What was I saying God I've lost me thread ⟨ , ⟩ *I wanted*
>   B: About you wanted to keep the fea uh feature geometry stuff
>   A: Oh yeah [S1A-005-12 ff.]
>
> [12] A: Do you want to go and see the film that evening or ⟨ , ⟩ just have the ⟨ , ⟩
>   B: No [S1A-005-80 f.]

Unfinished sentences are not rule-governed, since speakers may fail to finish their sentences at any point. Grammars, therefore, cannot account for them. There are equivalents of unfinished sentences in writing, but writers have the opportunity to complete them or to delete them in the process of writing or at the later stage of editing.

Many utterances in speech are not analysable in terms of clause structures. They are complete in themselves, but they are non-clauses. Particularly common are backchannels, items intended to encourage the other speaker to continue, often also expressing agreement. Most frequent among these are *yes* and its variants (such as *yeah*) and *uh* and its variants (such as *uhm*). They may constitute complete utterances, in that they are all that a speaker says at that point in the conversation:

> [13] A: I mean she fell in love with him
>   B: *Yes*
>   A: the fifteen year old him
>   B: *Yes*
>   A: back in time
>   B: *Yes* [S1A-006-141 ff.]
>
> [14] A. [. . .] I'm afraid that I'm not going to hear him if he wakes up and I
>   B: *um*
>   A: don't want Jim to always be the one to get up and take care of him if he's up
>   B: *mm-hmm*
>   A: in the middle of the night [. . .] [ICE-USA-S1A-003]

After a negative sentence *no* can also be used as a backchannel and to express agreement:

> [15] A: I don't know what else I'll go to though ⟨ , ⟩
>   B: *No* ⟨ , ⟩
>   A: Because the thing is I'm going to be absolutely knackered [S1A-005-69]

Numerous other items are used as backchannels. They include *exactly, fine, good, okay, really, right, sure*, and interjections such as *ah, oh, uhuh* (sometimes combined with other words, as in *oh dear*). Some backchannels take the form of clauses, for example: *that's right, that's true, I see, I know.* Combinations also occur, such as *yes I know, well that's true.* Most of the non-clausal items, as well as others, may be used primarily as reactions to previous utterances to convey sentiments such as agreement, disagreement, acceptance, refusal, reservation, surprise. They may be linked to a following clause by conjunctions: *yes, if . . .; sure, and . . .; oh, but . . .* Clauses such as *you know* and *you see* are intended to elicit support from listeners.

Other non-clausal utterances that commonly occur in conversation include greetings (e.g. *hello, good afternoon, happy birthday*) and expletives (e.g. *gosh, damn, good*). Some phrases, particularly noun phrases, stand alone as speech acts and the force they convey is clear in the situational context, though they cannot be analysed as elliptical clauses because we cannot be sure what has been ellipted. For example: *Taxi!, Fire!* (noun), *Your place or mine?, Next, Not a sound.* In print too, non-clausal language may appear in informal letters, notices, headlines, headings, titles of publications, and labels.

The types of non-clausal examples that have been outlined are perfectly normal and acceptable, and they can be analysed for their phrase structure: *Happy Birthday*, for example, is a noun phrase in which the noun *Birthday* is the head and the adjective *Happy* is its premodifier.

In conclusion, we can distinguish:

1. complete sentences
2. elliptical sentences
3. unfinished sentences
4. non-clauses

Clause Relationships

6.2
Co-ordination of clauses

Clauses may be related through co-ordination or subordination.[2] Co-ordinated clauses are linked at the same grammatical level.

Two or more clauses may be co-ordinated to form a sentence. Such a sentence is traditionally termed a compound sentence, and the co-ordinated clauses are the main clauses of the sentence. In **[1]** there are two main clauses co-ordinated by *and*:

[1] The cause of ice ages is still a controversial subject, *and* debates continue about the precise climatic effects of individual cycles. [W1A-006-26]

The relationship of clauses is displayed in **Fig. 6.2.1**. The triangles represent the clauses, and M in the triangles stands for 'main clause'.

**Fig. 6.2.1 Co-ordination of two
main clauses: Sentence [1]**

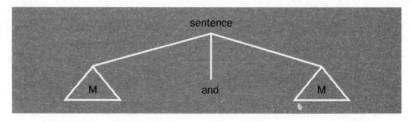

In **[2]** there are three co-ordinated main clauses:

[2] Crime was awful, test scores were low, *and* there was no enrollment in
honors programs. [891102-0148-58]

The clause composition of **[2]** is represented in **Fig. 6.2.2**.

**Fig. 6.2.2 Co-ordination
of three main clauses:
Sentence [2]**

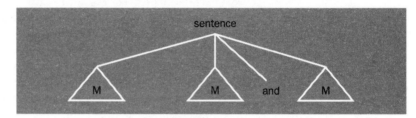

The three co-ordinated clauses are on the same level of co-ordination, but
often two of the co-ordinated clauses are more closely linked and as a pair they
are co-ordinated with the remaining clause. In **[3]**–**[4]**, the first two clauses
form a pair that is co-ordinated with the third—clearly indicated in **[4]** by the
reinforcing initial *Either*:

[3] Money is not everything, *but* it is necessary, *and* business is not
volunteer work. [891102-0098-8]

[4] *Either* defend the status quo *and* stop complaining about the resulting
costs, *or* rethink the status quo. [891004-0107-35]

In **[5]**–**[6]**, the first clause is co-ordinated with the pair that follows it—
indicated in **[6]** by the comma at the end of the first clause and the absence of
a comma between the last two clauses:

[5] We have tried to train the youngsters, *but* they have their discos and their
dances, *and* they just drift away. [891102-0103-13]

[6] Please read my enclosures carefully, *and* select the most appropriate
option *and* return the papers to me. [W1B-022-94]

Co-ordination may be either syndetic or asyndetic. It is syndetic when
co-ordinators are present, as in **[1]**–**[6]**. It is asyndetic when co-ordinators are
not present but can readily be inserted, for example, between the three units
of **[7]** that are separated by semicolons. The sentence in **[7]** lists the results of
damage to the ozone layer in the upper atmosphere.

[7] Agricultural crops would be scorched, and yields would fall; marine
plankton would be seriously affected; human health would suffer (there

would be more eye cataracts, more problems arising from damage to people's body immune systems.) [W2A-030-30]

The first part of **[7]** consists of two co-ordinated clauses. They constitute a unit within the structure of the clause, and their closer links are signalled by the syndetic co-ordination by *and*. The final parenthetic clause elaborates on the damage to human health mentioned in the previous clause.

Co-ordination of predicates is usual when the subject is shared:

[8] Criminals prefer anonymity *and* are less likely to get to work where there is a chance of being recognised. [W2D-009-82]

[9] Incorrect inflation pressures will cause abnormal tyre wear *and* may result in premature failure. [W2D-018-125]

In **[10]** the passive auxiliary *was* is shared and in **[11]** the modal auxiliary *will* is shared, in both cases together with the subject:

[10] The Lorillard spokeswoman said asbestos was used in "very modest amounts" in making paper for the filters in the early 1950s *and* replaced with a different type of filter in 1956. [891102-0191-11]

[11] [. . .] a strong solution around their newly developing roots will upset their osmotic balance *and* stop them developing properly. [W2D-011-35]

Gapping is a type of ellipsis that sometimes occurs in the middle of a co-ordinated clause. It affects the second clause and subsequent clauses. The main verb and/or an auxiliary is ellipted, possibly with any preceding auxiliaries and a following verb complement, such as a direct object, and an adverbial. The place of the gap is marked by a caret in the following examples. In **[12]** the main verb *is* is ellipted, in **[13]** the same main verb is ellipted in the second and third clauses, in **[14]** two auxiliaries—*will be*—are ellipted, and similarly in **[15]** two auxiliaries—*may be*—are ellipted.

[12] But because individual amounts are relatively small *and* the occurrence ^ commonplace, not much fuss is made. [W2B-029-18]

[13] The effect is of instability, in tone, literary register, genre, and idiom, the result ^ impermeability rather than clarity, *and* Beckett's language ^ a record of disruption rather than communication. [W2A-004-11]

[14] The major criticism will then be presented, *and* counter arguments ^ considered. [W1A-007-5]

[15] Frequently this covering may comprise large filamentous algae such as Phormidium or Stigeoclonium, and under these conditions the distribution of flow may be impaired *and* the ventilation ^ decreased. [W2A-021-13]

The first co-ordinated clause may have final ellipsis. In speech there is usually a distinct intonation break at the point of ellipsis and in the parallel point in the last of the co-ordinated clauses. In writing, these points are often marked by punctuation. In **[16]** the auxiliary *have* is at the point of ellipsis:

[16] We have ^, *and* I am sure others have, considered what our options are. [891102-0125-7]

Final ellipsis with three co-ordinated clauses is exemplified in **[16a]**:

> **[16a]** We have ^, you have ^, *and* I am sure others have, considered what our
> options are.

6.3
Subordination of clauses

Subordinate clauses can be constituents of other clauses. For example, they may function as subject **[1]**, or as complement of a verb **[2]–[5]**:

> **[1]** *Whether he speaks or not* remains to be seen [S2A-008-134]
>
> **[2]** [. . .] I've never wanted *to be a writer at all* [S1B-026-196]
>
> **[3]** No I've enjoyed *doing it* [S1B-026-214]
>
> **[4]** Do you think *that's possible* [S1B-026-228]
>
> **[5]** Guy the incredible thing is *that you've now written this year music for all Shakespeare's plays* [S1B-023-1]

Subordinate clauses can also be constituents of phrases.[3] For example, they may function as postmodifier within a noun phrase **[6]**, as complement of a preposition **[7]**, or as complement of an adjective **[8]**:

> **[6]** It's caused by two germs *that live together* ⟨ , ⟩ *and scratch each other's back* [S1A-087-155]
>
> **[7]** [. . .] you seem to have a capacity for *handling stress* [S1B-041-116]
>
> **[8]** By then I was sure *that he was not going to leave the Department* [W2B-012-52]

Subordinate clauses that function as subject, complement, or postmodifier are embedded within their host clause or host phrase. However, two types of subordinate clauses are attached to their clause in varying degrees of looseness: adverbial clauses and non-restrictive relative clauses (cf. 5.9 f.). Both play a role in the semantics of interclausal relationships that is akin to the role played by co-ordinated clauses or juxtaposed clauses. Adverbial clauses are illustrated in **[9]–[10]** and non-restrictive relative clauses in **[11]–[12]**. The paraphrases below the examples demonstrate their resemblance to co-ordinated clauses or juxtaposed sentences:

> **[9]** *Although the lectures are called The Persistence of Faith* ⟨ , ⟩ I did not speak about faith in the lectures [S1B-028-63]
>
> **[9a]** The lectures are called The Persistence of Faith, *but* I did not speak about faith in the lectures.
>
> **[9b]** The lectures are called the Persistence of Faith. However, I did not speak about faith in the lectures.
>
> **[10]** [. . .] tears always come to my eyes *when I hear these notes* [S1B-046-85]
>
> **[10a]** I hear these notes *and* then tears always come to my eyes.
>
> **[11]** As anticipated, she queried your desire to stay in Sun City, *which has little to offer except gambling and "dancing" girls.* [W1B-014-148]

[11a] As anticipated, she queried your desire to stay in Sun City. It has little to offer except gambling and "dancing" girls.

[12] The warnings, *issued to at least 100 criminal defense attorneys in several major cities in the last week*, have led to an outcry by members of the organized bar, *who claim the information is protected by attorney–client privilege.* [891102-0143-2]

[12a] The warnings have led to an outcry by members of the organized bar. They were issued to at least 100 criminal defense attorneys in several major cities in the last week. The members of the organized bar claim the information is protected by attorney–client privilege.

The first of the relative clauses in **[12]** is a non-finite reduced relative clause (cf. 5.9).

6.4
The interplay of co-ordination and subordination

Traditionally, sentences are classified as simple, compound, or complex, depending on their clause composition. A simple sentence consists of just one main clause:

[1] The tears ran down my face. [W2B-006-56]

A simple sentence need not be very short, since one or more of its phrases may be long; for example, the subject of the simple sentence in **[2]**:[4]

[2] *A scattering of glass fragments beneath the streetlamp opposite it* confirmed her worst suspicions. [W2F-006-20]

A compound sentence consists of two or more main clauses, generally linked by a co-ordinator such as *and*:

[3] Somewhat to her surprise, the doorbell was working *and* she could hear the sharp peal on the other side of the door. [W2F-006-32]

A complex sentence contains one or more subordinate clauses:

[4] She looked towards the door, *as though Connie might materialize there at any second.* [W2F-006-95]

This triple classification is a simplification of the clausal patterns in sentences. There may be subordination within co-ordination. In **[5]**, for example, the second main clause (M) contains a subordinate (sub) *if*-clause at the end:

[5] I will be out of College for the next two weeks, *but* please contact me after this *if you have any queries.* [W1B-024-112]

Similarly, there may be co-ordination within subordination, as in **[6]** (where the subordinate clauses are final) and **[7]** (where they are initial):

[6] The military claim *that* all nuclear reactors have been destroyed *and that* fourteen chemical and biological factories and storage areas have been destroyed or heavily damaged [S2B-001-78]

Fig. 6.4.1 Subordinate clause within a main clause: Sentence [5]

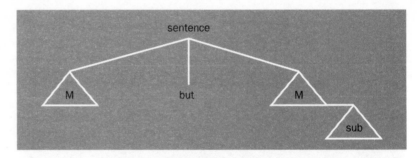

Fig. 6.4.2 Co-ordination of final subordinate clauses: Sentence [6]

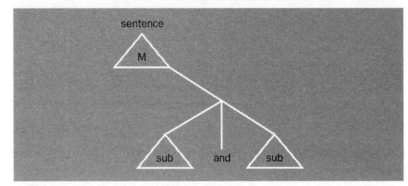

Fig. 6.4.3 Co-ordination of initial subordinate clauses: Sentence [7]

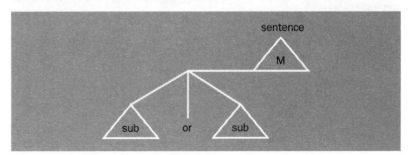

[7]   *Whether* this is necessary, *or whether* the prospect of being milked is sufficient inducement, is not yet known. [W2A-033-68]

There may be subordination within subordination. Sentence **[8]** contains a subordinate *if*-clause, which in turn contains a subordinate *because*-clause. The *if*-clause is host to the *because*-clause.

[8]   *If* you've been given a voucher *because* you have a low income, the value of your voucher may be reduced. [W2D-001-106]

Similarly, there may be co-ordination within co-ordination. Sentence **[9]** consists of three main clauses. The last two clauses (co-ordinated by *and*) are more closely linked, and are at a lower level of co-ordination (cf. 6.2):

[9]   This variation on the meatball theme was originally made with veal, *but* in America and in this country veal can be hard to come by *and* turkey breast makes a surprisingly satisfactory substitute. [W2D-020-1]

Fig. 6.4.4 Subordination within subordination: Sentence [8]

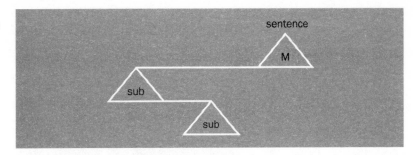

Fig. 6.4.5 Co-ordination within co-ordination: Sentence [9]

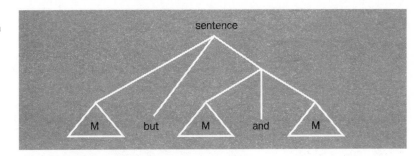

A subordinate clause may be linked jointly to two or more main clauses:[5]

[10] *Whatever you decide on*, it must be convenient, acceptable and affordable, *or* you will not stick at it. [W2B-022-54]

[11] *As Romanesque developed*, the roof of the structure was supported on piers *but* interior features were carried on the secondary support of columns. [W2B-003-35]

[12] *Now that we have had advance warning*, I have put your information around the relative departments *and* we could build it in to next year's budget. [W1B-019-39]

[13] [. . .] I'd go to that and I'd go to the Palmer one *if I was you* [S1A-005-54]

We can represent **[10]** by **Fig. 6.4.6**, and **[13]** by **Fig. 6.4.7**.

Fig. 6.4.6 Initial subordinate clause linked by two main clauses: Sentence [10]

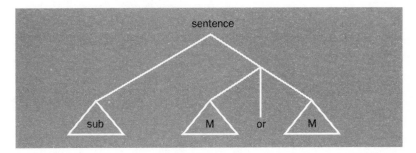

A further complication is exhibited in sentence **[14]**. The *and*-clause is parenthetic, expressing an elaboration of the point made in the initial subordinate *when*-clause. The *and*-clause itself contains two subordinate *whether*-clauses that are linked by *or*.

Fig. 6.4.7 Final subordinate clause linked to two main clauses: Sentence [13]

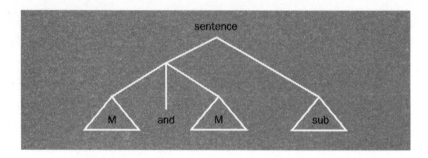

[14]   When you tie a standard rose *and this applies to any standard rose whether you do it yourself or whether you buy it* you really need two ties on it [S1B-025-77]

The structure of **[14]** can be represented by **Fig.6.4.8**, where the broken line indicates the parenthesis.

Fig. 6.4.8 Parenthetic *and*-clause containing co-ordination of subordinate clauses: Sentence [14]

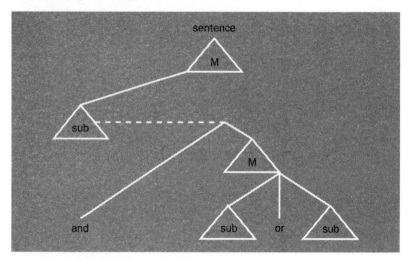

The second co-ordinated clause in **[15]** is similarly parenthetic. It expresses the stance that the writer is taking:

[15]   There is one thing that truly disturbs me, *and I speak as a Methodist clergyman.*

The clause can be paraphrased as a style disjunct, a type of sentence adverbial (cf. 4.27):

[15a]   There is one thing that truly disturbs me, *speaking as a Methodist clergyman.*

By conveying the stance with a co-ordinated clause rather than an adverbial, it gains greater emphasis because it is more independent grammatically.

The subordinate clauses that we have considered so far have been embedded in, or attached to, a host clause, but subordinate clauses may also be embedded in a phrase. In **[16]** the relative clause *she'd said this* is embedded as a postmodifier in the noun phrase *the first time she'd said this*:

[16] This was absolutely the first time *she'd said this.* [W1B-007-86]

If we ignore details of its embedding, we can simply show it as a triangle linked by an arrow to the inside of the clause, as **Fig. 6.4.9.**

Fig. 6.4.9 Embedded relative clause: Sentence [16]

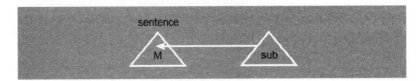

Here is a more complicated example of embedding in a phrase. In **[17]** there is one main clause. The verb of the sentence (*seek*) has an infinitive clause (beginning *to determine*) as its complement (more precisely, its direct object). That infinitive clause has as its direct object a noun phrase (beginning *the question*). The noun phrase has as its complement two co-ordinated clauses (both beginning *how far*) linked by *or*. The first of those clauses has an adverbial (beginning *as*).

[17] I shall not seek to determine the question *how far aggression or fears of aggression by Carthage or by Hellenistic kingdoms or later by northern or eastern peoples provided Rome with motives, as they often provided pretexts, for expansion or how far the real cause of expansion must be sought in the mere desire for power and glory, or in greed for the profits of empire* [. . .] [W2A-001-12]

Fig. 6.4.10 Embedded co-ordinated clauses functioning as noun phrase complements: Sentence [17]

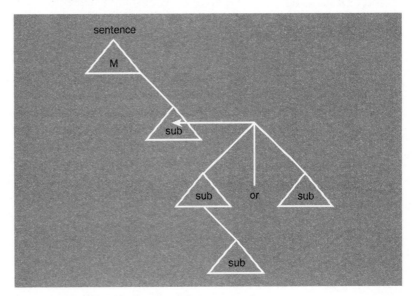

Finally, in **[18]** we see four *to*-infinitive clauses in asyndetic co-ordination (without a co-ordinator, cf. 6.2).

[18] Without compulsion, *though* sometimes encouraged by the Roman authorities, the natives began *to* adopt the Latin language, *to* build towns

Fig. 6.4.11 Four *to*-infinitive clauses in asyndetic co-ordination: Sentence [18]

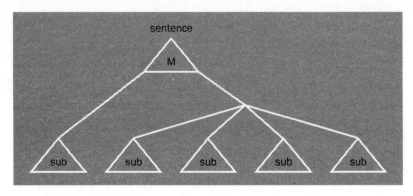

of the Italian type, *to* imitate Graeco-Roman architecture and sculpture, *to* copy the manners of the Romans. [W2A-001-63]

6.5
Parataxis and hypotaxis

The distinction between co-ordination and subordination can be encompassed under the broader distinction between parataxis and hypotaxis. Parataxis is the relation between two or more units of equal status, and hypotaxis is the relation between two units of unequal status, where one is dependent on the other.

Although here we are concerned with the relations between clauses, the distinction applies equally to structures below the level of clauses. Hence, *large houses* is a hypotactic structure, since *large* modifies *houses*. The relationship between *large* and *inexpensive* in *large inexpensive houses* or *large but inexpensive* is paratactic, since the two adjectives separately modify *houses* and they are not dependent on one another. On the other hand, *my first good meal* is a hypotactic construction, since *first* modifies *good meal* and not simply *meal*. Similarly, the relation between the premodifiers in the ambiguous *our French history teacher* is hypotactic; *French* is either dependent on *history* ('teacher of French history') or on *history teacher* ('history teacher who is French').

By definition a subordinate clause and its host clause or phrase are in a hypotactic relationship, since subordination implies that the two units are of unequal status.

Parataxis covers a variety of clause structures:

1. syndetically co-ordinated clauses
2. asyndetically co-ordinated clauses
3. juxtaposed clauses
4. a parenthetic clause and the clause to which it is attached
5. a tag question and the clause to which it is attached
6. a reported clause in direct speech and its reporting clause

The co-ordination of clauses has been illustrated in 6.2 and 6.4. The co-ordination is overt in syndetic co-ordination, where a co-ordinator is present. The co-ordination is implicit in asyndetic co-ordination, since a co-ordinator can be inserted between the clauses.

Juxtaposed clauses are paratactically related clauses that do not imply co-ordination. In the written language the clauses may be set out as separate orthographic sentences, as in **[1]**:

> **[1]** One wants as much information as it is possible to get. This is not the same as getting as much data as possible. The first decision to be made is how frequently recordings should be made. For example, one could record every minute of the operation and gain an enormous amount of data. [W2A-016-19 ff.]

However, the clauses may be linked by a comma or some other punctuation mark internal to an orthographic sentence so as to signal a close relationship between the clauses. In **[2]** a comma links the two juxtaposed clauses:

> **[2]** I'll have to stop talking about the place, it's bringing tears to my cheeks. [W1B-001-63]

The second clause in **[2]** provides the reason for what is said in the first clause. We could therefore insert a subordinator such as *because* or *since* between the two clauses to make their relationship explicit. In **[3]** three punctuation marks link the four clauses in the orthographic sentence—a colon, a semicolon, and a dash:

> **[3]** On organic farms, straw is used in a variety of ways: it can be fed to animals or used as bedding; it can also be used for roofing—thatchers claim that straw from organic farms is easier to work and lasts twice as long as the same stuff grown conventionally. [W2B-027-60]

The two clauses beginning *it* can be asyndetically co-ordinated. As a set, they are juxtaposed to the first clause, detailing the generalization made in that clause. The final clause is juxtaposed to the previous clause, explaining why organic straw is used for roofing. The two clauses in **[4]** provide a further example of juxtaposition:

> **[4]** Things have been mad I haven't had a moment to myself [S1A-040-223]

Independent parenthetic clauses (those not marked as co-ordinate or subordinate) enter into a paratactic relation with the host clause in which they are inserted:

> **[5]** The ten per cent we pay our agent rewards him for settling the terms regarding billing, salary *(note the order in which an actor puts priorities)* and accommodation. [W2B-004-6]

> **[6]** Barbara Hendricks is at her finest in the operatic numbers *(I loves you, Porgy is particularly eloquent),* and the warm beauty of the voice gives much pleasure throughout the programme. [W2B-008-138]

> **[7]** The first vehicle capable of reaching space—the V2 ballistic missile *(see right)*—demonstrates the essential simplicity of the principles behind the design of a rocket-propelled spacecraft. [W2B-035-13]

Some expressions function in dialogue to convey various kinds of interaction with other speakers, such as a positive response or softening the impact of what is said. Some of these expressions are clauses that allow little or no variation in their form; for example: *I mean, I think, you know, you see.* They are loosely attached to their host clauses or inserted inside them:

> **[8]**   But of course *you see I mean* if you say classical feature theory handles it then of course then you're back to all the old problems [. . .] [S1A-005-25]

Similar to the fixed parenthetical clause expressions in their interactive role are tag questions (cf. 3.6), which are generally intended to elicit confirmation or agreement from listeners:

> **[9]**   It's up to Laura really *isn't it* ⟨ , ⟩ in the end [S1A-099-131]

> **[10]**   I am a very strong swimmer but even the most confident swimmers can drown *can't they* my dear? [W1B-006-21]

Reported clauses function as syntactic units that are independent of the reporting clause (cf. 6.17). Reporting clauses may precede **[11]**, follow **[12]**, or interrupt **[13]** reported clauses:

> **[11]**   He looked slowly round at the crew and said, 'Anyone know if it's raining in Rio?' [W2B-004-108]

> **[12]**   'Blake Edwards is a sadist,' I said. [W2B-004-53]

> **[13]**   'Why,' asked Blake, 'are you here?' [W2B-004-69]

Reported speech can consist of more than one sentence:

> **[14]**   'Ah,' she said and looked at me with here huge dark eyes. 'Now if only Peter could give me a child like that I'd get pregnant tomorrow. The only trouble is . . .' her look now enveloped Peter as well, 'his children have turned out so badly.' [W2B-004-43 ff.]

6.6
Sentences and clause clusters

The orthographic sentence is not necessarily identical with the grammatical sentence. For rhetorical reasons it may incorporate two or more grammatical sentences, which are perhaps separated by semicolons, colons, or dashes:

> **[1]**   She was the widow of a curate from the south of France; with her daughter she kept a small day school and had a few paying guests. [W2B-002-14]

> **[2]**   The problem is easily solved if they rotate their crops: wild oats, for instance, cannot survive in a field of grass. [W2B-027-94]

> **[3]**   It all depends on the sun—a south-facing window will add more heat than it loses, winter or summer, though not always when you want it. [W2D-012-80]

Conversely, an orthographic sentence may be coterminous with a non-sentence or an incomplete sentence. Citation **[4]** is an extract from an informal personal letter, [5] from a newspaper editorial, [6] from a review in a newspaper:

[4]   Gill was also upset as they made no effort to speak to her new man. But enough of my news. What have you been doing this weekend? *Anything nice.* I'm trying to psyche myself up to do some computer theory revision. *BORING.* [W1B-005-76 ff.]

[5]   Resolve in the Gulf and determined leadership on the budget and the economy could still make Mr Bush the president nobody ever really thought he could be. The jury is still out, but not for long. *Your move, Mr President.* [W2E-010-53 ff.]

[6]   The cigarettes she puffs on during the play are tobaccoless. *Herbal. Nonaddictive.* [*International Herald Tribune*, 30 April 1994, p. 24]

The spoken language does not have oral sentences that correspond to the orthographic sentences of the written language. There are no equivalents in speech to the written signals of the beginnings and ends of orthographic sentences. Neither intonation nor pauses signal unequivocally the ends of speech units that might be thought to correspond to orthographic sentences. For that reason, some grammarians have preferred to abandon the term *sentence* for the grammatical structures of the spoken language.

Instead, we might refer to clause clusters or clause complexes to denote the equivalents of the canonical grammatical sentence. A clause cluster is a set of clauses that are interrelated by co-ordination or subordination, or simply just one clause if it is not linked to other clauses.[6]

The following is taken from a broadcast discussion. The speaker has been called upon to contribute to the discussion:

[7]   [a]   Yes I I think it's infinitely more entertaining
      [b]   And I think the only real value of politics is that you should make people laugh ⟨ , ⟩
      [c]   And uh so therefore I think that it adds greatly to the gaiety of the nation
      [d]   And what I think is is really funny about it is that these people are totally to follow the fiction that's written in the newspapers
      [e]   I mean the newspapers make up a story
      [f]   And then they obediently trot in and try and perform it [S1B-024-10 ff.]

The extract consists of two clusters. The first cluster consists of four co-ordinated main clauses [a]–[d], and the second of two co-ordinated main clauses [e]–[f].

The next extract is more complicated. It is a private conversation between two speakers:

[8]   [a]   A: We could come round with a bottle of something *and* I could bring the odd bottle of cider
      [b]   B: We could do that *but* then I can't actually take you to the station ⟨ , ⟩
      [c]   A: Uhm oh that's true
      [d]   *Or* Coke Coke will do ⟨ , ⟩
      [e]   B: Yes

> **[f]**   I could probably manage to take you back to the station on
>   some Coke [S1A-006-96 ff.]

Each of the first two clusters **[a]** and **[b]** consists of two co-ordinated main clauses. The third cluster **[c]** is a simple clause preceded by interjections. The fourth cluster **[d]** begins with the co-ordinator *or*, but *or* does not link to the immediately preceding clause; it in fact presents an alternative to what is said in the second main clause of **[a]**: *I could bring the odd bottle of cider. Or* in **[d]** is equivalent to *alternatively* and might be regarded as a connective adverb rather than as a true co-ordinator. *Yes* **[e]** is a response item—a non-sentence, since it does not have clause structure. The fifth cluster **[f]** is one main clause with a subordinate *to*-infinitive clause.

We could generally refer to clause clusters instead of sentences, even for the written language, so as to avoid confusing grammatical sentences with orthographic sentences. But *sentence* is preferred in this book to *clause cluster* because it is familiar to readers.

6.7
Meaning relationships in co-ordination and subordination

Similar meaning relationships are sometimes expressed through co-ordination and subordination. In **[1]** the subordinate *while*-clause is concessive and contrastive in meaning:

> **[1]**   *While* some politicians and communicators may identify themselves with
>   some transnational culture, many of them are great patriots. [W2A-017-60]

A similar meaning can be conveyed through co-ordination with *but*:

> **[1a]**   Some politicians and communicators may identify themselves with some
>   transnational culture, *but* many of them are great patriots.

The second clause may be juxtaposed and may more explicitly show the relationship through a conjunct such as *however*:

> **[1b]**   Some politicans and communicators may identify themselves with some
>   transnational culture. *However*, many of them are great patriots.

In **[2]** the clauses are in a cause–effect relation. They are asyndetically co-ordinated, linked by the conjunct *so* ('therefore'):

> **[2]**   The economies are too small to supply a large range of products now
>   universally sought and desired, *so* these have to be imported, at great
>   cost relative to the money earned by the primary sector. [W2A-019-33]

The two clauses could be syndetically co-ordinated by *and*: '*and so* these have to be imported'. Alternatively, the first clause could be subordinated, introduced by (for example) *since*, and the redundant conjunct *so* would then be omitted.

The cause–effect relationship in **[2]** can be emphasized by making the second clause explicitly identify the relationship:

[2a] The economies are too small to supply a large range of products now universally sought and desired. *That is why* these have to be imported, at great cost relative to the money earned by the primary sector.

Again, the two clauses can also be co-ordinated: *and that is why*.

Co-ordination, syndetic or asyndetic, is an option that is also available for the time relation exemplified in **[3]**:

[3] *When* Monsieur Savlon came back to clear the table he asked me in perfectly good English, 'You do not like snails?' [W2F-013-52]

The subordinator *when* makes the time relation explicit. If the clauses are co-ordinated by *and*, the assumption is that the two events (his return to the table and his question) are in chronological order:

[3a] Monsieur Savlon came back to clear the table *and* he asked me in perfectly good English, 'You do not like snails?'

Since the two clauses share an identical subject, it would be possible to omit the second subject *he*, so that we would now have co-ordination of the predicates. Alternatively, the two clauses could be set out as two orthographic sentences, and optionally *then* could be inserted after the subject *he* to make explicit the time relation between the clauses.

Similar meaning relationships can be conveyed at the level below the clause through nominalizations—noun phrases that correspond to clauses. For example, corresponding roughly to **[3]** is **[3b]**, where *return* is a noun converted from the verb *return*:

[3b] *On Monsieur Savlon's return to clear the table* he asked me in perfectly good English, 'You do not like snails?'

Co-ordination (syndetic or asyndetic) and juxtaposition put the clauses on the same grammatical level. Syndetic co-ordination emphasizes their connection. Subordination downgrades the subordinate clause grammatically in relation to the host clause or host phrase, and nominalization provides a further downgrading to the level of the phrase.

Signals of Clause Relationships

6.8
Signals of co-ordination

Co-ordination of clauses is signalled by the presence of a co-ordinator between the clauses (syndetic co-ordination) or by the potentiality for its presence (asyndetic co-ordination, cf. 6.2). The central co-ordinators are *and*

and *or*. They alone can link more than two clauses at the same level, and all but the final instance of the co-ordinator are then usually omitted. Thus in **[1]** *or* links four *to*-infinitive clauses:

[1] On the other hand I long to travel, to get out of London, to go to America *or* just to see wide open unspoilt spaces. [W1B-006-72]

In polysyndetic co-ordination, the co-ordinator *and* or *or* is repeated, contrary to normal practice. The effect is to emphasize the individuality of each of the clauses:

[2] Columba then prophesied that he would become a beggar *and* that his son would run from house to house with a half empty bag *and* that he would die in the trench of a threshing-floor. [W1A-020-53]

The other clear co-ordinator is *but*. Unlike the central co-ordinators, it can link only two clauses at the same level. Like them, it can also link subordinate clauses:

[3] When my plate was clean I asked her if she would mind telling him when she got the chance *that* I couldn't stand snails or garlic, *but that* this was no reflection on his excellent cooking. [W2F-013-90]

[4] Cut the meat into even-sized cubes, leaving on any fat *but* removing all gristle. [W2D-020-25]

There are several other items that are sometimes considered to be co-ordinators. *For* and *so that* ('with the result that') resemble the co-ordinators in not allowing a co-ordinator to precede them. We cannot, for example, add a second *for*-clause in **[5]** linking it to the first by *and, or, but*:

[5] 'It doesn't matter,' I said, *for* I didn't want to admit that I sometimes feel shy with foreigners. [W2F-013-92]

By contrast, we can co-ordinate two *because*-clauses:

[6] However, *because* in many cases the condition is well controlled by medication *and because* sufferers don't necessarily like to talk about their illness, most people are not aware of the extent of epilepsy in the population. [W2B-023-29]

For and *so that* can link only main clauses. Unlike the co-ordinators, they cannot link subordinate clauses or parts of clauses.

Other putative co-ordinators are *nor* and *yet*. Both of these can be preceded by a co-ordinator:

[7] So you didn't have a lot of religious pressure *but nor* did you have a lot of religious thought [S1A-076-150]

[8] But the fact is you're part of an alliance *and yet* you are acting unilaterally [S2B-010-110]

Because they can themselves be preceded by co-ordinators, both *nor* and *yet* are better regarded as adverbs, more specifically conjuncts (conjunctive adverbs, cf. 4.27).[7] In the absence of a co-ordinator, clauses linked by *nor, yet*, and other conjuncts are asyndetically co-ordinated:

[9] It's been available now for two decades *yet* in that time a hundred million children have died from diarrhoea [S2B-022-128]

Conjuncts such as *however*, *therefore*, and *nevertheless* are more removed from the co-ordinator class because they need not be positioned at the beginning of their clause:

[10] None of France's wine regions can steal a march on Burgundy, *however*. [891102-0121-25]

[11] But not all concerted action is *therefore* ineffectual. [891011-0146-53]

Like *nor* and *yet*, their clauses can be linked by co-ordinators:

[12] The early evidence suggests the strategy has worked *but nevertheless* Iraq's surviving aircraft and huge quantities of guns and missiles will be more effective in daylight [S2B-008-30]

6.9
Signals of subordination

There are two types of signals that a clause is subordinate: the identity of the initial item in the clause and the nature of the verb phrase or its absence.

A clause is subordinate if it is introduced by a subordinator (or subordinating conjunction) such as *if, because,* and *although* (cf. 4.30). Certain subordinate clauses are introduced by *wh*-words (cf. 6.12). Some of these *wh*-words are used only with subordinate clauses; for example: *whoever, whatever, however.* Others may also be used with interrogative main clauses; for example: *who, which, when, where, why, how.*

The subordinators *as, that,* and *though* are exceptional in that they occasionally do not come at the beginning of their clauses (cf. concessive clauses in 6.14).

That may be either a subordinator like *whether* **[1]** or a relative pronoun like *which* **[2]**:

[1] We decided *that* we would work together [. . .] [S1A-001-43]

[2] [. . .] I very much enjoyed the work *that* I was involved in [S1A-001-28]

As a subordinator, *that* can usually be omitted ('zero *that*') when its clause is not functioning as subject:

[1a] We decided we would work together.

In **[1a]** there is no overt signal of subordination for the complement *we would work together,* but we could point to the option of inserting the subordinator *that.* As a relative pronoun, *that* is functioning in place of *wh*-relative pronouns:

[2a] I very much enjoyed the work *which* I was involved in.

Like the subordinator, relative *that* can often be omitted ('zero relative'):

[2b] I very much enjoyed the work I was involved in.

Again, the covert signal of subordination in **[2b]** is the optionality of inserting *that*.

Subject–operator inversion may signal subordination without a subordinator, mainly in conditional clauses (cf. 6.15):

[3] It acts as a metaphor representing his early awakening for literature which could have been channelled into something better *had he been taught how*. [W1A-018-84] ('if he had been taught how')

If the verb in a clause is non-finite **[4]** or if there is no verb **[5]**, the clause is generally subordinate (cf. 6.10):

[4] She paused, sighed winsomely, *looking aged*. [W2F-008-7]

[5] He began running, feeling light and purposeful, scarcely seeming to touch the pavement with his feet, *his heart strong and amazingly compliant with his sudden awakening*. [W2F-008-95]

Subordinate Clauses

6.10
Forms of subordinate clauses

There are three major forms of subordinate clauses:

1. finite clause, whose verb is a finite verb (cf. 5.19):

[1] *When we were walking over the bridge* Mary Jane stopped to take a shot of a woman on the other side of the road *who was dragging a child along by the hand*. [W2F-013-110]

2. non-finite clause, whose verb is a non-finite verb (cf. 5.19):

[2] *To test the belt tension*, press the belt down at a point midway on the longest run between pulleys (Fig. A:25), *using firm thumb pressure*. [W2D-018-5]

3. verbless clause, which does not have a verb:

[3] In accordance with the principles of direct play the ball should be thrown forward *where possible*. [W2D-015-109]

Non-finite and verbless clauses are treated as clauses because we can analyse their structure in the same way as we analyse finite clauses. So in **[2]** the infinitive clause can be analysed as having a verb *to test* and a direct object *the belt tension*; similarly, the *-ing* participle clause has a verb *using* and a direct object *firm thumb pressure*. The analyses of the non-finite clauses can be compared with those for corresponding finite clauses (cf. 3.13 ff.):

[2a] You (S) test (V) the belt tension (O).

[2b] You (S) use (V) firm thumb pressure (O).

The structure of the verbless clause *where possible* **[3]** can be analysed as having a conjunction *where* and a predicative *possible*. Compare the corresponding subordinate finite clause:

[3a] . . . where [conj] that (S) is (V) possible (P)

A non-finite or verbless clause may be host to a finite clause:

[4] 'It doesn't matter,' I said, for I didn't want *to admit that I sometimes feel shy with foreigners.* [W2F-013-92]

The infinitive clause in **[4]** is host to the *that*-clause.

The verb in a non-finite clause may take any of four non-finite forms and the clause may be with or without a subject:

1. *-ing* participle clause with subject:

[5] I don't see *a French writer voluntarily writing in English* [S1B-026-107]

2. *-ing* participle clause without subject:

[6] Yes the thing is we we do notice very much that there's difficulty in *attracting younger members to the societies* [S1B-025-135]

3. *-ed* participle clause with subject:

[7] *This said,* the Isozaki scheme is not entirely without merit. [W2A-005-83]

4. *-ed* participle clause without subject:

[8] *Unless otherwise stated* the tuition fees will be charged on a simple hourly rate [. . .] [S2B-044-106]

5. *to*-infinitive clause with subject:

[9] Uh well do you want *me to tell you the truth* [S1B-029-41] ('that I should tell you the truth')

6. *to*-infinitive clause without subject:

[10] And I just thought well now where shall I poke him *to wake him up* [S1A-018-26]

7. bare infinitive clause with subject:

[11] But what made *him want to go to Disneyworld for the job* [S1A-065-255]

8. bare infinitive clause without subject:

[12] [. . .] I think it helps *support our style of policing structure* [S1B-033-13]

9. verbless clause with subject:

[13] *No soldiers here,* although those waiting squads in trucks were only minutes away. [W2F-015-34]

10. verbless clause without subject:

[14] Women, however, *although under subjection,* are not actually in a class of their own, but in an underrated grouping according to gender, which cuts across all classes. [W2B-009-69]

6.11
Functions of subordinate clauses

The functions of subordinate clauses can be consolidated into four major types:

  A. nominal clauses, which can have a range of functions similar to those of noun phrases (cf. 5.3)
  B. relative clauses, which postmodify noun phrases (cf. 5.9)
  C. adverbial clauses, which can have a range of functions similar to adverb phrases or prepositional phrases when these function as adverbials (cf. 5.44, 5.48)
  D. comparative clauses, which together with the comparative items *more*, *less*, or *as* or the comparative inflection *-er* function as intensifiers (cf. 5.41, 5.45).

A. Nominal clauses

All nominal clauses (cf. 6.12) may have the following first two functions in a host clause, and most nominal clauses may also have functions 3–5:

1. **Subject:**

   [1] *That his people believe that after last night* is doubtful [S2B-008-85]

   [2] *Whether a stock offering is in the best interest of Mr. Wisner or his shareholders* is unanswerable. [891004-0124-80]

   [3] [. . .] *to talk of it as a United States operation* simply misreads history or intentionally misinterprets history [S1B-027-109]

   [4] And *mastering this technique* can be a lot of fun [S2A-054-108]

2. **Complement of a verb,** chiefly as direct object (cf. 3.16):

   [5] Only nine per cent answered *that religious leaders played a significant part in their life* [S1B-028-24]

   [6] I don't know *what my mother would have done if we had not come out naturally bookish* [S1B-046-36]

   [7] [. . .] I've never wanted *to be a writer* at all [S1B-026-196]

   [8] Depending on who comes, you'll possibly need to bring sleeping bags and I hope you don't mind *sleeping on the floor.* [W1B-004-45]

   Most nominal clauses may also function as:

3. **Complement of an adjective** (cf. 5.42):

   [9] It's strange, I don't look like my mother and everyone here presumes I'm Spanish and is surprised *that I don't speak a word.* [W1B-003-114]

   [10] They are not sure *what did happen* [S2B-028-59]

   [11] I'm not quite sure *if that's right actually* [S1B-075-18]

   [12] And they say they're prepared *to take industrial action to back their demands for shorter hours* [S2B-011-20]

   Unlike these nominal clauses, noun phrases functioning as complements of adjectives require linking prepositions: *surprised at that, sure of that, prepared for that.*

4. **Complement of a preposition** (cf. 5.47):

> **[13]** At the time of the original meeting nobody had any idea of *what would happen* [S1B-061-120]
>
> **[14]** I'll come on to *when you went off to Germany* shortly [S1B-061-85]
>
> **[15]** [. . .] you seem to have a capacity for *handling stress* [S1B-041-116]
>
> **[16]** [. . .] you've talked in various articles over the years about *her making you feel utterly inadequate and and horrible* [S1B-046-63]

5. **Complement of a noun** (cf. 6.16):

> **[17]** [. . .] it had a lovely wood letter-rack and a sort of in-tray done in wood which I fancied despite the fact *that I haven't got anything to put in it* [S1A-014-216]
>
> **[18]** Police say they can't confirm a TV report *that the building had been hit by automatic fire* [S2B-016-95]
>
> **[19]** Many more people can look forward to a retirement in the knowledge *that in addition to the basic state retirement pension they will benefit from their employer or personal pension scheme* [S2B-035-23]
>
> **[20]** And uh she then said well look uhm you because you're a national figure you've been in eight million homes tonight uh you really must get used to the idea *that people will come up to you* [S2A-023-3]

B. **Relative clauses**

Relative clauses postmodify noun phrases. They can be restrictive **[21]** or non-restrictive **[22]**:

> **[21]** Individuals *who need professional help* are those *who cannot handle these problems themselves.* [W1A-007-44]
>
> **[22]** We can send two representatives and additional observers (*who can participate but not vote*). [W1B-024-60]

Reduced relative clauses have a non-finite verb:

> **[23]** It was a very contemporary version of the play [. . .] although most people *responding to it* didn't feel that it had been updated to a specific period [S1B-023-45] ('most people *who responded to it*')
>
> **[24]** Uh this is an action *authorised by the Security Council of the United Nations* [S1B-027-107] ('an action *that is authorised by the Security Council of the United Nations*')
>
> **[25]** But according to the United Bible Societies these figures don't tell the whole story ⟨ , ⟩ as some countries imported paper ⟨ , ⟩ *on which to print their own Bibles* [S2B-023-52] ('paper *on which they would print their own Bibles*')

Relative clauses are discussed in 5.10 and therefore need not be treated in this chapter.

C. **Adverbial clauses**

Adverbial clauses have two main functions in relation to their host clause (cf. 4.27):

1. **Disjunct:**

    [26] Do you know where it might be *because uhm Bob and I were talking about it the other day* [S1A-046-330] ('I'm asking the question for that reason')

    [27] *Broadly speaking*, there are three types of theories in scientific subjects. [W2A-035-15] ('I'm speaking broadly when I say this')

2. **Adjunct:**

    [28] But you said you're not familiar with it in practice 〈 , 〉 *because you're not working as a counsellor* [S1A-060-52]

    [29] Add the meatballs to the tomato sauce, partially cover the pan, and simmer for another 15 minutes *while cooking the spaghetti*. [W2D-020-160]

D. **Comparative clauses**

Comparative clauses (cf. 6.15) are introduced by the subordinators *than* or *as*. Together with a preceding correlative, the comparative clauses function as intensifiers. In **[30]** the preceding correlative of the *than*-clause is *more*:

[30] Both agree that improvement is needed and should be *more* rapid *than is now the case* [S2A-021-36]

The discontinuous intensifier *more . . . than is now the case* modifies the adjective *rapid* ('How rapid?'—'More than is now the case'). In **[31]** the inflection *-er* on *lower* combines with the *than*-clause to intensify the adjective *low*:

[31] In five out of the seven leading industrial nations industrial output is now low*er than it was a year ago* [S2B-041-65]

In **[32]** the preceding correlative is the intensifier *less*, a comparative of the adverb *little*. The intensified item is the noun *harm*:

[32] And the Ixtoc blow-out in the Gulf of Mexico—even though it gushed for months—did *less* harm *than it might have* because it was well out at sea and in deep, choppy, warm waters. [W2B-029-46]

The correlative of *as*-clauses is the adverb *as*:

[33] I'm perfectly happy for you to clap and sing and be *as* loud *as you want* [. . .] [S1A-068-235]

6.12
Nominal clauses

We can distinguish four types of nominal clauses:

A. subordinate declarative clauses
B. subordinate interrogative clauses
C. subordinate exclamative clauses
D. nominal relative clauses

The four types are exemplified below.

A. Subordinate declarative clauses

Subordinate declarative clauses that are finite are introduced by the subordinator *that*. They may function as complement of a verb **[1]**,[8] an adjective **[2]**, or a noun **[3]**:

[1] And she told me *that my father who'd died many years before was standing by my side* [S1B-026-14]

[2] I was quite surprised *that that argument is still playing* [S1B-039-115]

[3] Unexpected help for the prosecution comes from a young Japanese officer a Christian played by Noriyake Shioyi who had executed one of the airmen in the belief *that the order to do so had been lawfully issued* [S2B-033-52]

The conjunction *that* is generally omissible:

[4] Tell me this however ⟨ , ⟩ your lectures were widely noticed and I imagine *you've had a good deal of feedback since you delivered them* [S1B-028-2]

However, *that* must be retained when the clause serves as subject, since otherwise the subordinate clause may be misinterpreted as a main clause:

[5] *That his people believe that after last night* is doubtful [S2B-008-85]

Subject *that*-clauses are generally extraposed, and their subject position taken by anticipatory *it* (cf. 4.38). Since there is then little or no danger of misinterpretation, *that* can usually be safely omitted:

[6] We were advised to have our luggage ready as it was quite possible *we might be flying on to Rio de Janeiro.* [W2B-004-111]

Corresponding to the declarative *that*-clauses are non-finite clauses. Below are examples of -*ing* participle clauses **[7]–[8]**, *to*-infinitive clauses **[9]–[10]**, and bare infinitive clauses **[11]–[12]**:

[7] [. . .] the one piece of real good that could come out of all this is *the United Nations acting with authority* [. . .] [S1B-027-60] ('that the United Nations is acting with authority')

[8] And I find *myself sympathising very much with* ⟨ , ⟩ *this* [. . .] [S1B-028-87] ('that I sympathise very much with this')

[9] [. . .] secondly people expect *this countryside to be conserved* [S1B-037-78] ('that this countryside will be conserved')

[10] Uh well do you want *me to tell you the truth* [S1B-0-29-41] ('that I should tell you the truth')

[11] And that's the sort of thing that makes *one say well uhm I shall show em* [S1B-041-10] ('causes that one will say . . .')

[12] Uhm let *me bring you in Eric Groves a naval specialist on this* [S1B-038-92] ('allow that I bring you in . . .')

B. Subordinate interrogative clauses

Three types of subordinate interrogative clauses can be distinguished, corresponding to the three types of main interrogative clauses (cf. 3.5): *yes–no* clauses, alternative clauses, and *wh*-clauses.

Yes–no and alternative clauses are introduced by the subordinators *whether* and *if. Yes–no* clauses are exemplified in **[13]–[14]**:

[13] The whole purpose of meeting was to decide *whether it was worth going ahead at all* [S1B-061-124]

[14] I don't know *if you ever tried running a business* but it's very difficult [S1B-065-27]

The alternatives in alternative clauses are introduced by *or*:

[15] It doesn't matter *whether it's marsh or fen or heathland or bog or sand dunes or what* [. . .] [S1A-036-165]

[16] Well I didn't know for sure *if it was free or not* [S1A-039-262]

If is more restricted than *whether*. For example, only a *whether*-clause can be the complement of a preposition **[17]** and only *whether* can be followed immediately by *or not* **[18]**:

[17] There's no indication as to *whether the shots were aimed at the Soviet leader* [S2B-016-120]

[18] No ⟨ , ⟩ she said she was coming tomorrow to tell me *whether or not she could do the following week* [S1A-083-36]

Wh-interrogatives are introduced by *wh*-pronouns **[19]** (cf. 4.43), or *wh*-determiners (cf. 4.43), or *wh*-adverbs **[20]** (cf. 4.27):

[19] At another point during the hearing, Rep. Markey asked Mr Phelan *what would be discussed at a New York exchange board meeting today.* [891102-0104-30]

[20] A spokesman said he could not speculate as to *when a new proposal would be presented* or *how long it would take to complete*, and Ramada officials declined to elaborate. [891012-0117-13]

What would be a determiner in **[19]** if it were followed by (say) *issues*. As with main clauses (cf. 3.5), if the *wh*-element is the complement of a prepositional phrase, the preposition may be stranded at the end **[21]** or (in formal style) may be fronted with its complement **[22]**:

[21] I'm not sure *who I should speak to.*

[22] I am not sure *to whom I should speak.*

In standard English, subordinate interrogative clauses differ from main interrogative clauses in word order. Main clauses require subject–operator inversion except when a *wh*-element is the subject (cf. 3.5):

[13a] *Was it* worth going ahead at all?

[16a] *Was it* free or not?

[20a] How long *would it* take to complete?

Subordinate clauses, on the other hand, place the subject first, as in declarative clauses. However, non-standard dialects commonly have subject–operator inversion in subordinate clauses:

[13b] You can decide *was it* worth going ahead at all.

[16b] I didn't know *was it* free or not.

[20b] He didn't know how long *would it* take to complete.

In consequence, non-standard dialects omit in such cases the subordinators *whether* and *if*, which are redundant when the interrogative is signalled by inversion.

To-infinitive clauses may serve in all three types of interrogatives, as *yes–no* interrogatives **[23]**–**[24]**, alternative interrogatives **[25]**–**[26]**, and *wh*-interrogatives **[27]**–**[28]**. However, only *whether*—not *if*—can be used to introduce *yes–no* and alternative clauses.

[23] The municipalities said they have not decided *whether to try to force the company to go through with the contracts.* [891102-0141-30]

[24] As a result, Fed officials may be divided over *whether to ease credit.* [891102-0120-16]

[25] It is hard to know *whether to laugh at or cry about the impoverished woman who raises rabbits to sell as pets or as meat.* [890929-0055-21]

[26] During the coming weeks, President Bush must decide *whether to veto the bills containing them—or, alternatively, to sign these bills into law with a statement declaring their intrusions on executive power to be in violation of Article II, and thus void and severable.* [891102-0080-17]

[27] It is hard to know *what to do about drugs.* [890929-0138-57]

[28] These issues weigh on Mr. Clausen as he considers *whom to anoint as his successor.* [891002-0067-150]

Whether or *if* can be repeated in alternative clauses if the alternative clauses are in full:

[29] The issue is whether fleet requirements can be met by remanufacturing previously built aircraft *or whether additional new production is required.* [890911-0107-10]

If the alternative clause is infinitive, *whether* can be repeated when infinitival *to* is retained:

[25a] It is hard to know whether to laugh at *or whether to cry about* the impoverished woman who raises rabbits to sell as pets or as meat.

Or whether and *or if* introduce *yes–no* interrogative clauses when they are co-ordinated with a *wh*-interrogative:

[30] The indictment does not say how the alleged bid-rigging was to be done *or whether the two companies went through with the alleged scheme.* [890807-0101-19]

[31] How soon Wang will stage a comeback, *or if it will at all*, are still matters of debate. [891018-0120-2]

C. Subordinate exclamative clauses

As in main exclamative clauses (cf. 3.8), *what* introduces noun phrases **[32]** and *how* is used otherwise **[33]**. *What* and *how* are intensifiers in this use.

[32] And I know *what great joy he's brought not only to his family but to so many of his parents' friends* [S1B-060-50] ('very great joy')

[33] My agent called me in this morning to tell me *how good he was.* [W1B-003-131]

D. **Nominal relative clauses**

Nominal relative clauses (or independent relative clauses or free relative clauses) closely resemble noun phrases.[9] Like noun phrases and unlike other clauses, they can take a plural verb:

> **[34]** *'What the market wants to see* are deals in non-recessionary businesses,' said Brian Doyle, a senior analyst at Salomon Brothers. [890918-0054-41]

They can have concrete reference **[35]** and indeed personal reference **[36]**:

> **[35]** In two years, I probably have eaten *what looked like 20 different types of fish*, only to be informed each time that I was eating "snapper" or "garoupa." [890920-0116-21]

> **[36]** We bribe *whoever needs to be bribed to get on that plane* before anyone thinks we might try anything so crazy. [W2F-015-109]

> **[37]** So before the centralisation of the Temple ⟨ , ⟩ you had local officials where anybody could do *whatever they liked in them more or less* [. . .] [S1B-001-27] ('anything that they liked . . .')

> **[38]** And this is *where the eighty-nine earthquake occurred* [S2A-025-57] ('the place at which the eighty-nine earthquake occurred')

> **[39]** This enables you to get your weight evenly distributed, and to push off to *whichever side the ball comes.* [W2D-013-49] ('any side that the ball comes')

> **[40]** This is *how she put it* [S1A-040-321] ('the way that she put it')

To-infinitive clauses can also be nominal relative clauses:

> **[41]** "It is absurd that societies so stricken with crime should attempt to apply their standards to us and teach us *what to do*," he said. [*International Herald Tribune*, 25 April 1994, p. 4] ('that which we should do')

> **[42]** It outlines some of the opportunities that are available at our main branches and *who to contact for more information* [S2B-044-81] ('the person that you should contact . . .')

> **[43]** So ⟨ , ⟩ he directed me *where to go* [S1B-049-143] ('the place that I should go to')

> **[44]** You don't just learn words and grammar you learn *how to* uh *behave more generally* [S1B-003-088] ('the way that you should behave more generally')

Nominal clauses that are complements of verbs or adjectives may be fronted. The motivation for doing so is generally end-focus: to place at the climax the information that is new or at least relatively less familiar to the hearer. Here are two examples:

> **[45]** Uh the record of Saddam Hussein does not lead us to believe that *what he says he says he'll do* he necessarily will do [S1B-027-18]

> **[46]** I hope to go to the States sometime soon but *whether it will materialise* I don't know. [W1B-014-85]

6.13
Forms of adverbial clauses

Adverbial clauses may be finite, non-finite, or verbless, and the verb of a non-finite clause may be an *-ing* participle, an *-ed* participle, a *to*-infinitive, or a bare infinitive (cf. 6.10).

Adverbial clauses that are finite generally have a subordinator, such as *if* or *although*; exceptionally, subject–operator inversion may be used instead of the conditional subordinator *if* (cf. 6.14). Non-finite and verbless clauses may have a subordinator **[1]–[2]**, but they are commonly used without a subordinator **[3]–[4]**:

[1] Embarrassingly, my seat broke. *When reclined* it was not long enough for my legs [. . .] [*The Times*, 21 January 1993, p. 14]

[2] Defend yourself physically only *if really necessary.* [W2D-009-56]

[3] And you condemn the series *having seen a bit of one of them* [S1A-006-103]

[4] They met six years ago while both worked at a bank in Nazareth, *she a clerk and he a computer instructor.* [*International Herald Tribune*, 3 May 1994, p. 1]

In the absence of a subordinator, the meaning of the adverbial clause in relation to its host clause may be vague when the sentence is viewed in isolation. For example, the *-ing* participle clause in **[3]** might be temporal ('after you have seen a bit of one of them') or causal ('because you have seen a bit of one of them'). In the wider context it is clear that the clause is concessive ('though you have seen (only) a bit of one of them').

If the non-finite or verbless clause does not have a subject, its understood subject is normally interpreted as identical with the subject of the host clause. Thus, the subject of the *-ed* participle clause *When reclined* **[1]** is understood to be *it*: 'When it (i.e. my seat) was reclined'.

An adverbial participle or verbless clause is said to be dangling (or unattached) when its understood subject is not identical with the subject of the host clause. In **[5]** the subject of the verbless clause *If severe* is in the previous sentence—*these* (changes):

[5] Injury at any point along the length of the axon process produces biochemical and ultrastructural changes within the nerve cell body and *these* are more pronounced if proximal. *If severe*, nerve cell death may result. [W2A-026-6]

More commonly, the understood subject of a dangling clause can be deduced from some item in the host clause—*his* in **[6]**, yielding the interpretation 'When he was in the company of Bob Fagin and Paul Green':

[6] *When in the company of Bob Fagin and Paul Green*, no doubt *his* hurt was assuaged by routine duties and by companionship [. . .] [W2B-006-62]

Violation of the identical-subject rule is usually considered to be an error if it is noticed. But the rule is felt not to apply in certain cases. The main exceptions are:

1. If the dangling clause is a style disjunct that has the speaker's *I* as the understood subject (cf. 4.27):

> **[7]** *Broadly speaking,* the process followed reflected the revised priorities. [W2A-016-84] ('I am speaking broadly')

> **[8]** [. . .] and our links as we all know uh elsewhere uh are uh *to put it mildly* uh inadequate [S2A-023-28]

2. If the understood subject refers to the whole of the host clause:

> **[9]** I would like it done on Wednesday *if possible* [S1A-038-152] ('if it is possible')

> **[10]** Firstly, the head may twist sharply, *tearing and twisting the connections and membranes of the brain.* [W1A-004-15] ('the sharp twisting of the head will tear . . .')

3. In scientific usage, if the understood subject refers to the *I* or *we* of the speakers or writers:

> **[11]** Concentrations of substances below ten to the seventh cannot be measured *using these radioactive-based methodologies* [S2A-042-87]

> **[12]** Each question will be considered in turn *before looking at an alternative approach.* [W2A-016-17]

4. If the understood subject is a generic *you, we,* or *one* (cf. 4.36):[10]

> **[13]** It's the same deal *when setting off on a slippery surface* [S2A-055-53]

> **[14]** *Bearing in mind that many retired people can still contribute usefully to society,* it seems probable that the burden of a dependent child is, overall, at least as high as that of a retired person. [W2B-018-52]

Absolute clauses are adverbial participle clauses or adverbial verbless clauses that are not introduced by a subordinator and that have their own subject:

> **[15]** *Sanctions on Haiti having produced no useful results so far,* the United States is now considering whether to tighten them further. [*International Herald Tribune,* 21 January 1994, p. 6]

> **[16]** It may seem perverse to derogate AA, NA etc., *they being organisations which do fine and irreplaceable work in offering salvation to those afflicted by addiction.* [*The Independent Magazine,* 5 February 1994, p. 9]

> **[17]** There are populated areas all around the bay *the total population being in excess of ten million* [S2A-025-55]

> **[18]** While the government holds the towns, Unita controls much of the countryside, *its troops equipped with American-supplied ground-to-air missiles to deter air transport.* [W2C-002-82]

> **[19]** Lesley talked with animation, *the restraint of their first meeting all gone.* [W2F-003-67]

> **[20]** *College work aside,* I have just ended this strange relationship with the girl we spoke about in Paris. [W1B-008-86]

6.14
Meanings of adverbial clauses

Below are given, with examples, the major types of adverbial clauses according to their meaning relation with the host clauses. Some subordinators can be used with more than one type of clause; for example, *since* can serve with time or reason clauses, *so that* with purpose or result clauses.[11]

Place clauses

Place clauses may refer to position **[1]**–**[3]** or direction **[4]**–**[5]**:

[1]   They fired rockets and artillery last night but *where I was* they made no move to advance [S2B-014-81]

[2]   *Where the mighty Rhone river meets the Mediterranean Sea* its silt has created a spreading triangle of wild marshes 〈 , 〉 the Camargue [S2B-027-96]

[3]   DDT should still be used, with appropriate safeguards, *wherever pests can be well controlled*, and particularly when more expensive chemicals cannot be afforded. [890912-0079-85]

[4]   And Mr. McPhee is the envy of other writers for his ability to follow *wherever his fancy leads*. [890803-0142-12]

In **[5]**, the *where*-clause is the complement (object predicative) of the verb *put*:

[5]   [. . .] with the footballing folk of Newcastle urged to put their money *where their mouths are* [. . .] [W2C-004-69]

Temporal clauses

The situation in the host clause may occur before that of the temporal clause **[6]**–**[8]**, at the same time **[9]**–**[12]**, or at a later time **[13]**–**[15]**:

[6]   And she's advised them to get a good grounding *before they go* [S1A-005-136]

[7]   I didn't realise they were wisdom teeth *until someone pointed them out* [S1A-046-24]

[8]   What the chain does is sell even cheaper petrol to undercut this independent *till he's driven out of business or until he can be bought out by the main corporation* [S1B-005-101]

[9]   Mrs Mandela sat impassively *while Mr Kgase gave evidence in the court*, which was half-empty for the first time since the case opened last month. [W2C-019-64]

[10]   Uhm 〈 , 〉 and I think one of the things that I felt *when I was studying dance* 〈 , 〉 was I very much enjoyed the work that I was involved in [S1A-001-28]

[11]   [. . .] *whenever Adam and I hug and say hello* he sits on my knee and he you know he puts one leg on either side and we hug and we're close physically [S1A-003-112]

[12]   [. . .] it was supposed that a king had the right to rule only *as long as he was acting in the interests of his people*. [W2B-014-53]

[13]   Laura likes tea bags you see *after they've had taken some of the strength out* [S1A-042-44]

[14] So *when this nerve is cut* not only will you be numb in the area not only will the relevant muscles not be able to move but muscle will be all floppy through lack of tone [S1B-009-85]

[15] *Once we're convinced that we have the right to determine when life becomes human and when it ceases to be so* ⟨ , ⟩ then we stand in danger of creating a society that is potentially self-destructive [S1B-060-36]

When a *since*-clause and its host clause refer to a period leading up to the present (and perhaps including the present), the host clause generally takes the present perfect (cf. 5.27):

[16] Well I *'ve read* about three books *since I finished my degree* [. . .] [S1A-084-38]

[17] The Pentagon *has called* up more than thirty thousand reservists *since the crisis began* but most of them have been support units doctors cargo handlers mechanics [S2B-017-16]

Conditional clauses

Conditional clauses generally express a direct condition, indicating that the truth of the host clause (or apodosis) is dependent on the fulfilment of the condition in the conditional clause (or protasis).[12] However, some conditional clauses may express an indirect condition that is related to the speech act:

[18] And *if I remember rightly* you had jaundice didn't you [S1A-028-41] ('if I remember rightly it would be true to say')

[19] I mean *if I told you honestly* things can be really interesting [. . .] [S1A-048-8]

[20] [. . .] I did need to have a need to say ⟨ , ⟩ that I was doing something because uhm ⟨ , ⟩ otherwise I wouldn't be anybody *if you see what I mean* [S1A-060-159]

Direct conditions may be either open (or real) or hypothetical (or closed or unreal). Open conditions leave completely open whether the condition will be fulfilled:

[21] You're going to have huge trouble ⟨,⟩ *if you've infected me* [S1A-040-281]

In **[21]** the speaker does not give any indication whether he or she believes that the condition—the infection by the person addressed—has been fulfilled.

Hypothetical conditions, on the other hand, express the speaker's belief that the condition has not been fulfilled (for past conditions) or is not fulfilled (for present conditions) or is unlikely to be fulfilled (for future conditions). The hypothetical nature of the condition is conveyed through the verb forms, which are backshifted (cf. 6.18). Future and present hypothetical conditions take the past in the conditional clause and a past modal in the host clause. The future hypothetical condition is exemplified in **[22]**, where the modal *'d* (= *would*) appears in the host clause and the past *scratched* in the conditional clause:

[22] I *'d* be far more upset *if somebody* say *scratched one of my records* ⟨ , ⟩ *than tore one of my books* [S1A-013-175]

The present hypothetical condition is shown in **[23]**, where the modal *could* appears in the host clause and the past *had* in the conditional clause:

[23] Now *if I had an S* ⟨ , , ⟩ I *could* do a really clever word [S1A-010-60]

The past hypothetical condition takes the past perfect in the conditional clause and a modal past perfect in the host clause:

[24] I mean do you think she *would have been* different *if there'd been* ⟨ , ⟩ a supportive man in the home [S1A-072-215]

The modal in all three types of conditions is generally *would* or its contraction *'d*. It is used in the host clause unless some additional modal meaning is required, as with *could* in **[23]**, which can be paraphrased by 'would be able to'.

If the verb in the conditional clause of a present or future hypothetical condition is *be*, subjunctive *were* (cf. 5.26) is sometimes used instead of indicative *was* in the conditional clause, particularly in more formal contexts:

[25] [. . .] I would *if I were you* [S1A-095-300]

[26] It certainly provided a pretext, *if one were needed*, for the foreign tours he undertook to fifteen different countries during his first year after being elected to office. [W2B-011-14]

Conditional clauses may also have subject–operator inversion without a subordinator. In such cases the auxiliaries are usually *had*, *were*, or *should*:

[27] I think *had he won the 1970 election* he would have resigned in 1972 or 1973 [S1B-040-66]

[28] I am confident that I can deal with the problems uh of Prime Minister *were I to be elected* [. . .] [S1B-043-78]

[29] However, *should I briefly tire of cisatlantic life, and discover the means to journey to North America*—some conference might perhaps afford the opportunity—then perhaps, I trust, we might meet again. [W1B-015-55]

The most frequent conditional subordinator is *if*,[13] but there are others. Some are exemplified below.

[30] He says the country faces paralysis *unless a solution is found quickly* [S2B-011-119]

[31] The Democratic leadership agrees to relent, *provided the president asks for a modest tax increase—modest in the present year, but increasing rapidly thereafter.* [890929-0009-32]

[32] So *given that a micrometre is a thousandth of a metre* this'll normally be about point two five of a micrometre [S2A-051-16]

[33] The magazine will reward with "page bonuses" advertisers who in 1990 meet or exceed their 1989 spending, *as long as they spent $325,000 in 1989 and $340,000 in 1990.* [891102-0182-10]

[34] [. . .] *supposing she'd said that to a psychiatrist* what would they say [S1A-031-121]

Circumstantial clauses

Some place, time, and conditional subordinators may be used to introduce clauses that express a more general meaning of circumstances. In such cases, the subordinators *where, wherever, when, whenever*, and *if* are interchangeable.

> [35] So we believe in more investment better management some deregulation *where appropriate* to improve and expand those public services [S2B-035-46]

> [36] Finally, *when straw is combined with manure and composted*, it can be spread onto the land to return fertility to the farm. [W2B-027-61]

> [37] Avoid vigorous evening exercise *if possible*, as the increased adrenaline it produces may cause sleep problems, so try to take exercise in the morning or up to late afternoon. [W2B-022-69]

Alternative-conditional clauses

Alternative-conditional clauses express two or more stated possible conditions:

> [38] When you tie a standard rose and this applies to any standard rose *whether you do it yourself or whether you buy it* you really need two ties on it [S1B-025-77] ('if either condition applies')

> [39] I hope you'll think it's sensible law ⟨ , ⟩ but *whether you do or not* ⟨ , ⟩ uh you'll have to accept it from me because I am the judge ⟨ , ⟩ of the law [S2A-061-10]

> [40] *Whether or not we believe in God* we inhabit a culture in which religious teachings are marginal to many people's moral choices [S2B-029-8]

> [41] Furious, Peter assured all and sundry that, *Prince Charles or no Prince Charles*, he would boycott the premiere. [W2B-004-29]

> [42] The steering is just too vague and I'm still not convinced that two hundred horsepower and front-wheel drive ⟨ , ⟩ make desperately happy bedfellows ⟨ , ⟩ *trace control or no* [S2A-055-60]

> [43] When the Gothic designer was faced with an aedicular feature in a blank wall, *whether window, doorway, blank arch or niche*, he immediately began to anchor it into the wall by a system of mouldings, which swept up one side and down the other. [W2B-003-44]

Wh-conditional clauses

Wh-conditional clauses leave open the number of possible conditions:

> [44] *Whatever you've been doing* you've been doing the right thing [S1A-087-42] ('Whether you've been doing x, y, z, . . .')

> [45] *Wherever I now travelled around the country* I would hear complaints about the quality of young people leaving our schools: undisciplined, illiterate or innumerate were the mildest criticisms of them. [W2B-012-119]

> [46] You really are relatively speaking in comparison with the other two very inexperienced *however talented you may be* [S1B-043-21]

However, *whichever* offers a limited number of conditions, implied from the context:

> [47] The final film of the evening Fear is a cheerfully dopey thriller about this psychic Allie Sheedy ⟨ , ⟩ who can see into the minds of serial killers and thus help the otherwise baffled cops to bring them to justice or blow them away *whichever seems more convenient* [S2B-033-86]

Concessive clauses

Concessive clauses indicate that the situation in the host clause is unexpected in view of what is said in the concessive clause.

> **[48]** It is quite clear that *although individual sheets of papyrus* ⟨ , ⟩ *must have sat in piles in workshops* you could not go and buy them [S2A-048-57] ('It is surprising that you could not go and buy them')

> **[49]** The best parts of this building are seven hundred years old *though there has been worship here for a good deal longer* [S2A-020-92]

> **[50]** Good to see Willy Banks competing of course *even though he's no longer a challenger and won't of course be in the American Championships team for Tokyo* [S2A-007-73]

> **[51]** And *while some of the senior executives still remain from those early days* we now find it more effective to recruit locally [S2A-045-53]

Whereas clauses usually combine concession with contrast:

> **[52]** She now wears ⟨ , ⟩ size ten in clothes ⟨ , ⟩ *whereas formerly she wore size fourteen* [S2A-062-111]

Even if clauses combine conditional with concessive meaning.[14] We cannot therefore assume that what they describe is factual. In this respect they differ from *even though* clauses. The condition may be open **[53]** or hypothetical **[54]**:

> **[53]** Nevertheless, *even if the tax cut is made permanent*, its effects on the economy may be far less than its proponents anticipate. [890929-0070-49]

> **[54]** And, experts say, *even if oil were discovered there tomorrow*, none of it would enter the market until the next century. [891004-0113-52]

In concessive clauses introduced by the subordinators *as*, *though*, and *that*, the predicate is sometimes fronted except that auxiliaries and the verb *be* are stranded:

> **[55]** 'Prisoners for the All Highest's personal attention', their sergeant bawled at the gate guard, and, *tense as she was*, Jean felt a quite different shiver in her spine. [W2F-015-6]

> **[56]** *Unbelievable as it seems*, we are inundated with Russians. [*Evening Standard*, 6 May 1994, p. 24]

Reason clauses

Reason clauses express such notions as reason and cause for what is conveyed in the host clause. As with conditions, the reason may be indirect, related to the speech act or the belief of the speaker:

> **[57]** Well wouldn't it be a granular texture *because pears are granular aren't they* [S1A-009-158] ('I say that because of my belief that pears are granular')

Most reason clauses convey a direct reason or cause:

> **[58]** *Since you're not having anything else* you can have two of everything [S1A-067-66]

> **[59]** We need to proceed with the greatest care therefore ⟨ , ⟩ *for embryo research is a complex issue which involves the whole spectrum of medical scientific ethical* ⟨ , ⟩ *and moral issues* [S1B-060-37]

[60] I'm the patient and *as I don't know much about it* uhm he briefly explained what needed to be done [S1A-051-92]

[61] But the cancer tests are unique *in that they can be used to identify who in a family must be frequently monitored and who is free of the danger and need not be checked for symptoms.* [891012-0004-12]

Purpose clauses

Finite purpose clauses require a modal auxiliary (cf. 5.24), since they refer to an event that has yet to take place:

[62] Skilled ringers use their wrists to advance or retard the next swing, *so that one bell can swap places with another in the following change.* [891102-0103-32] ('in order that one bell can . . .')

[63] You'll just have to take an overnight bag with all the possibilities in *so you can zip up to the bathroom and change* [S1A-042-161]

[64] This problem is made all the more difficult with automated inspection because a large amount of data needs to be processed, preferably as quickly as possible, *in order that further, more detailed, inspection may be carried out on suspect regions if required.* [W2A-036-25]

Infinitival purpose clauses are more frequent than finite purpose clauses. The *to*-infinitive clauses are commonly used without a subordinator, but they may also be introduced by *in order to* and *so as to*:

[65] The other day she did it and disappeared *to use the phone* [S1A-040-4]

[66] I sometimes wonder whether Stephen actually went to prison ⟨ , ⟩ deliberately *in order to have something to talk about when he came on this show* [S1B-042-97]

[67] You'll learn assertiveness *so as not to be inhibited by other people's agendas* [S2B-029-118]

Result clauses

In contrast to purpose clauses, result clauses refer to a situation that is or was in effect, the result of the situation described in the host clause.

[68] [. . .] they actually said it was their fault you see *so that they paid all the costs and everything else* [S1B-074-16] ('with the result that they paid . . .')

[69] But the thing is you always have to write them in a slight code *so people don't know exactly what you are talking about* [. . .] [S1A-015-22]

So in **[69]** may be the conjunctive adverb, since the difference between the conjunction and the adverb is neutralized in asyndetic co-ordination (cf. 6.2). If the co-ordinator *and* is used, *so* is clearly an adverb:

[70] The final possibility is the electron can come in ⟨ , ⟩ and actually knock off an electron ⟨ , ⟩ which is bound to one of the atoms in the molecule ⟨ , ⟩ *and so* you get two electrons ⟨ , ⟩ coming away from the molecule [S2A-028-34]

Manner clauses

Manner clauses refer to the manner of the action expressed by the verb. Though treated here for convenience, they are complements of the verb (cf. 6.16):

[71] [. . .] and the lecturers do *as they're instructed* [S1A-082-27]

[72] [. . .] the dilemma was whether you carry on *as if he could take over* or you'd have to start all over again [S1A-062-4]

[73] It is misleading to talk *as though ninety percent are covered* [S1B-058-51]

Proportion and similarity clauses

Both proportion and similarity clauses involve kinds of comparison. A common type of proportion clause has comparatives in both clauses:[15]

[74] *The simpler* the business, *the better off* you are. [890817-0033-32]

[75] "He used to say that *the faster* he could sell MiniScribe, *the better*," recalls the former manager. [890911-0078-55]

[76] *The more sons* a man has *the more labour*, and so *the larger* he can make his herd. [W1A-011-314]

This type can be reduced to verbless clauses:

[75a] The faster, the better.

Somewhat similar is the verbless construction *so . . . so . . .*:

[77] I told her I was in a hurry, but I've transformed her house while she's taught Emily, *so far so good*. [W1B-006-89]

Another type of proportion clause is introduced by *as* or *just as*. The host clause begins with the correlative *so* and has subject–operator inversion:

[78] And *as lawsuits against directors and officers mushroomed in the mid-1980s*, so did the policy claims. [890814-0092-19]

[79] But *as fears of a recession in the near future fade*, so does the Fed's incentive to ease. [890815-0054-16]

Similarity clauses resemble the second type of proportion clause in form:

[80] *Just as the October 1987 "meltdown" in the stock market did not produce an economic recession (as we correctly predicted at the time)*, so the present strength in the stock market does not necessarily mean that the economy will avoid recession. [890905-0010-7]

[81] *Just as Newsday has had to acknowledge and cater to the differences between Long Island and New York*, so too must the Times appeal to the varying tastes of readers in far-flung communities. [890905-0102-19]

Comment clauses

Various types of parenthetical comment clauses are used, particularly in speech. The finite clauses are generally introduced by the subordinator *as*:

[82] Well now *as far as I know* I've never been raped or anything [. . .] [S1A-050-212]

[83] *As he said to me* well we didn't seem to be going anywhere fast [S1A-049-42]

[84] Uhm so I think he may not have the confidence to go ahead *as it were* [S1A-069-264]

[85] *As I remember* it used to be sort of like fairly common for a Tuesday ⟨ , ⟩ that I'd pretend to be sick ⟨ , ⟩ and so I didn't have to go to school [S1A-076-83]

[86] Assuming that post at the age of 35, he managed by consensus, *as is the rule in universities*, says Warren H. Strother, a university official who is researching a book on Mr. Hahn. [891102-0092-15]

Non-finite comment clauses are style disjuncts (cf. 4.27):

[87] *Broadly speaking*, there are three types of theories in scientific subjects. [W2A-035-15]

[88] *Put simply* ⟨ , ⟩ the principles of policing as asserted at the top ⟨ , ⟩ have not yet made in their view a sufficient penetration at all levels [S2B-037-25]

[89] *To be fair* you used to come when your Mum and Dad were still living in Portland Road but you haven't been since [S1A-027-117]

6.15
Comparative clauses

Comparative clauses involve a comparison with what is conveyed in the host clause. The comparative element signals the standard on which the comparison is made. In **[1]** the comparative element is *much more attention*:

[1] [. . .] we now give *much more attention* to the mentally and physically handicapped *than we did even twenty-five or thirty years ago* [S1B-060-55]

The standard of comparison is the amount of attention given to the mentally and physically handicapped. *Attention* is modified discontinuously: *much more . . . than we did even twenty-five or thirty years ago*. In **[1]** *more* is an irregular comparative form of *much* and is itself intensified by *much*. The basis of comparison is the situation twenty-five or thirty years ago, which is compared with the present situation.

Comparatives are either inflected forms (*older*) or phrases constructed with *more* (*more convenient*); cf. 4.24. They are used to express a higher degree of comparison, as in **[1]** above and in **[2]** below:

[2] [. . .] and here am I actually working *longer* hours *than I've ever worked in my life* [S1B-041-98]

A lower degree of comparison is expressed by premodifying *less* (itself a comparative of *little*) with a postmodifying *than*-clause:

[3] [. . .] guidelines have been issued by the various health authorities which dictate that if patients suffer heart attacks over the age of seventy they should receive *less* priority treatment *than those who suffer similar conditions under the age of seventy* [S1B-056-14]

An equivalent degree of comparison is expressed by premodifying *as* with a postmodifying *as*-clause:

[4] Many felt Hearst kept the paper alive *as* long *as it did*, if marginally, because of its place in family history. [891102-0078-16]

The comparative element may be a noun phrase **[5]**, an adjective phrase **[6]**, or an adverb phrase **[7]**:

[5] Yet however much one might prefer the trilogy over earlier texts, the criteria of purity, continuity and authenticity create *more problems* than they solve. [W2A-004-16]

[6] I'm so glad—she was *more despondent and depressed* than I've ever seen her when I left her to come home last September. [W1B-011-26]

[7] I think he's feeling the time going *more slowly* than I am since he's the one left behind. [W1B-010-154]

Comparative clauses are often elliptical, omitting elements that they share with their host clauses:

[8] The implication is that physical illnesses can be diagnosed more reliably *than can mental illnesses*. [W1A-007-61]

On the other hand, we can restore the elliptied elements of **[8]**:

[8a] The implication is that physical illnesses can be diagnosed more reliably *than mental illnesses can be diagnosed*.

We can also omit a further shared element in **[8]**, the auxiliary *can*:

[8b] The implication is that physical illnesses can be diagnosed more reliably *than mental illnesses*.

In **[8b]** we are left with only the subject of the comparative clause. In **[9]** only the direct object remains and in **[10]** only an adverbial:

[9] [. . .] if you hate these photographs more *than the one that's on the back of the album* I think you should leave the one that's on the back of the album [. . .] [S1A-100-15] ('than you hate *the one that's on the back of the album*')

[10] Pastoralism was much more widespread in the past than *at present* [W1A-011-3] ('than it is (widespread) *at present*')

When the only element left in the comparative clause is the subject and an auxiliary, the auxiliary functions as an operator (cf. 4.29). If the subject is not a pronoun, then subject–operator inversion is an option, as in **[8]** above and in **[11]**:

[11] When the scientists dosed forest land in Harvard, Mass., with a common nitrogen fertilizer, ammonium nitrate, they found the soil absorbed about 33% less methane from the air *than did unfertilized ground*. [890928-096-9]

The subject alone may be ellipted in the comparative clause:

[12] [. . .] the effects on San Francisco were much less *than would've occurred with the same earthquake at a closer distance* [S2A-025-39]

[13] Not all sects are new religious movements, but many of the new religions exhibit the sectarian characteristic of proclaiming an exclusive truth, and even those that claim that they do not do so may, in practice, turn out to be far less internally tolerant of diversity than *might at first appear*. [W2A-012-30]

[14]   But the increase cited in the API report was larger *than had been expected.* [891005-0046-20]

[15]   The government sells timber on a sustained basis, never selling more *than is grown.* [891005-0112-8]

However, in such instances the comparative clause seems to imply a relative clause:

[14a] . . . larger than (the increase that) had been expected.

[15a] . . . never selling more than (the timber that) is grown.

When the only element left is a pronoun that has both subjective and objective cases (cf. 4.34), the tendency is to use the objective case even when the pronoun would be the subject in a restored *than*-clause:

[16]   In fact she'd get somewhere quicker *than me* [S1B-049-94] ('than I would (get)')

But some writers are uneasy at using the objective case, as shown in **[17]** by the parenthetic question mark after *me*:

[17]   There are about 50 other girls, most appear younger *than me (?)* and are very unfriendly. [W1B-002-120]

The alternative is to use the subjective pronoun with the operator (cf. 5.18):

[18]   Now you've been in more of this building *than I have* [S1A-017-219]

More . . . than can also be used metalinguistically, to indicate a more accurate ascription:

[19]   [. . .] he was content to think that nature was *more acting than acted upon*, that the mind was more easily conceived as a thing made than a thing making. [W2A-003-19] ('more accurately described as acting than acted upon')

[20]   [. . .] I thought actually when he came on he was very blond but in fact he's *more ginger-haired than blond-haired* on this near side [S2A-017-4]

[21]   'I think you'll find the administrator *more than happy* to talk to you about his work,' he said, firmly overriding me. [W2F-004-125] ('happy to a degree that is not adequately described merely by the word *happy*')

[22]   The action however we should describe *more as painting than scribbling* [S2A-048-79]

[23]   Now this car coming up behind me is getting closer ⟨ , ⟩ so I'm making my intentions *more than clear* ⟨ , ⟩ and acting early [S2A-054-164]

Unlike the normal use of comparatives, this use can apply to verbs—for example, *acting* and *acted upon* in **[19]**. Metalinguistic *more* also occurs without the *than*-clause:

[24]   As he looked he knew this was not a woman about to achieve happy release, *more a woman about to be cast into damnation.* [W2F-012-108]

More cannot be replaced by an inflected form:

[25] His account of the motif further disguises the village of Voisins in the middle distance, makes the landscape appear *more wild than cultivated*, and all but effaces the acqueduct. [W2B-002-78] (not: '*wilder* than cultivated')

6.16
Complementation of verbs, adjectives, and nouns

Nominal clauses (cf. 6.12) can function as complements of verbs, adjectives, and nouns.[16]

The complement clauses can be *that*-clauses, and the subordinator *that* can be omitted. Here are examples with verbs **[1]**–**[2]**, adjectives **[3]**–**[4]**, and nouns **[5]**–**[6]**:

[1] Only nine per cent answered *that religious leaders played a significant part in their life* [S1B-028-24]

[2] I suppose *I was looking for something else* and just passed over it [S1B-062-134]

[3] Were you aware *that there came a time when a deposit had to be paid by Ward for the property* [S1B-061-102]

[4] You are sure *you informed us* [S1B-074-73]

[5] And I got the impression *that people only knew if they'd got one themselves* uhm [S1B-077-24]

[6] [. . .] I get the impression *people are borrowing lots of money as well to fund them because supposedly at the other end there's this big pay-off* [S1A-079-93]

In most complement *that*-clauses, the verb in the clause is indicative, but if the complement clause conveys the meaning of a directive, the present subjunctive is sometimes used instead, particularly in American English:

[7] I *urged* in my previous letter that these research staff *be* treated as their present colleagues and *be* permitted to apply for a redundancy payment when their contracts expire. [W1B-024-31]

[8] In the face of nuclear holocaust, not to mention the horrors of contemporary non-nuclear war, it is *imperative* that a new maturity *be* achieved in domestic and international communications. [W2A-017-43] (The *that*-clause is an extraposed subject. Compare 'That a new maturity be achieved is imperative'.)

[9] But *suggestions* that Saddam *be* given cash compensation, an oilfield or an island, would only encourage future extortion [. . .] [W2E-010-32]

Alternatives to the present subjunctive in such contexts are the modal *should* (particularly in British English) **[10]** and the indicative **[11]**:

[10] Although Somalis are *determined* that he *should* never be allowed to stage a come-back [. . .] [S2B-023-66]

[11] It was *essential* that the Pope *appeared* to be the most important ruler in the world [S2B-027-84] (Here too the *that*-clause is an extraposed subject.)

Another common alternative is to use a *to*-infinitive clause in place of a *that*-clause:

[12] Would you call into the station, or would you prefer *him to come to your house?* [W2F-009-107] (Compare the subjunctive in a finite clause: '. . . or would you prefer that he *come* to your house?')

Verbs, adjectives, and nouns may take as complements various types of *wh*-clauses: interrogative, exclamative, and nominal relatives (cf. 6.12). These may be either finite clauses or *to*-infinitive clauses:

[13] I wonder *why he's holding a globe* [S1A-067-109]

[14] Because she's still wondering ⟨ , ⟩ why you haven't acknowledged *whatever it was she last sent you* [S1A-095-289]

[15] I am not sure *if I want to become a Foster Corporate Parent*, but I am very interested. [891102-0105-44]

[16] [. . .] he was uncertain *what to do* [S1B-040-8]

[17] Mr Rogers you asked the question *when should the allies according to you cease hostilities* [S1B-027-76]

[18] On the basis of this already filtered and framed information the inspector takes a decision *whether to respond with an investigation.* [W2A-018-28]

The complement *wh*-clauses may also be linked to nouns by prepositions:

[19] It's just a question *of* ⟨ , , ⟩ *which is the more efficient approach* [S1A-029-196]

[20] In other words the notion of worsening educational standards reflects the decision *about how to interpret the evidence* ⟨ , ⟩ *rather than anything derived from the evidence itself* [S2A-021-69]

[21] There is also growing doubt *as to whether further embryo research is the best way forward* ⟨ , ⟩ and even increased recognition that assisting fertility does not depend on IVF alone [S1B-060-45]

Complements for verbs, adjectives, and nouns may be *to*-infinitive clauses and these may be without their own subject. The understood subject is generally identical with that of the host clause:

[22] I want *to see what happens next* [S1B-026-207]

[23] I certainly have no desire *to mislead anybody* [S1B-058-55]

But with nouns the understood subject may also be generic (cf. 4.36):

[24] The first is the notion that freedom *to experiment on human embryo* ⟨ , ⟩ is necessary *to help infertile couples* [S1B-060-39] ('freedom for one to experiment')

Or it may just be left vague:

[25] As far as Watson was concerned ⟨ , , ⟩ you had his ⟨ , ⟩ interviews when the decision *to seize the vessel* was taken on the twenty-second of August [S1B-063-63]

When a noun phrase intervenes between the host verb and the *to*-infinitive, it is often unclear whether the phrase belongs to the host clause or the complement clause. In either case, if it is a pronoun it is in the objective case.

Here are some examples:

[26] I don't want *her to catch your cold* [S1A-042-87]

[27] [. . .] I told *him to drive the forklift truck* [S2A-067-39]

[28] Could I ask *you to look at certain passages of his interviews* [S1B-063-65]

[29] [. . .] the data entry controllers allow *you to edit the parameters.* [W2B-031-67]

In **[26]** *her* belongs to the complement clause as its subject, so that we can refer to the clause including *her* by *that* **[26a]** and we can make the clause passive **[26b]**:

[26a] I don't want *that*.

[26b] I don't want *your cold caught by her*.

Other common verbs that resemble *want* in this respect are *hate, like, love,* and *prefer*. On the other hand, in **[27]** and **[28]** the pronouns do not belong to the infinitive clause. We can refer to the clause separately from the pronoun **[27a]**–**[28a]** and we can make the pronoun the passive subject of the host clause **[27b]**–**[28b]**:

[27a] I told him *that*.

[28a] Could I ask you *this*?

[27b] *He was told* to drive the forklift truck.

[28b] Could *you be asked* to look at certain passages of his interviews?

Like *tell* and *ask* are some other verbs that can take indirect objects; for example: *order, persuade, recommend, teach.* Finally, **[29]** is an example of a construction that does not fit either the *want* type or the *tell* type.

If we apply the previous tests, we find that **[29]** yields:

[29a] The data entry controllers allow *that* (i.e. *you to edit the parameters*).

[29b] The data entry controllers allow *the parameters to be edited by you*.

[29c] The data entry controllers allow *you that*.

[29d] *You will be allowed* to edit the parameters.

Many verbs fall into this intermediate range but they vary and do not necessarily share the features of the infinitival complementation of *allow*. They include *consider, encourage, expect, help, permit*.

Some verbs—but no adjectives or nouns—may take bare infinitive clauses (where the infinitive is without *to*) as complement. The verbs *help, let,* and *make* may take bare infinitive clauses that do not have their own subject:

[30] Japanese money will help *turn Southeast Asia into a more cohesive economic region.* [891102-0149-22]

[31] You can now let *go of the front brake* [S2A-054-49]

[32] They offered it to someone else but he changed his mind so they had to make *do with me* [S2B-025-10]

Let and *make* are restricted to certain verbs in their complements, mainly *let go, let fly, let be, make do*.

A somewhat larger number of verbs may take as complement a bare infinitive clause with its own subject. They include *get, have, let, make, feel, hear, see, watch, help*:

[33] Theoreticians would have *us believe that if digital audio data are transmitted correctly, the resulting audio must also be correct.* [W2B-040-17]

[34] [. . .] what would make *Guy de Maupassant decide to write through an Englishwoman* [S1B-026-90]

[35] I let *them have ten minutes to get there at Union Council yesterday* and you shouted at me [S1A-068-150]

[36] I had intended to take them dancing and to hear *Colin sing* but they wanted to see a film and so I was outnumbered. [W1B-006-63]

[37] Uhm ⟨ , ⟩ I saw *Heidi get out* ⟨ , ⟩ go and get a drink and I saw *her climb in miss the step* and then it was just ⟨ , ⟩ lot of commotion after that getting her out [S1B-066-151]

[38] Emma felt *her eyes prick suddenly.* [W2F-003-34]

Help may be followed by either a bare infinitive clause or a *to*-infinitive clause:

[39] Well a few drops helped *you remember* [S2A-027-13]

[40] He's a fifty-two-year-old business man and hotelier ⟨ , ⟩ who helped *to finance the United Somali Congress when it was first established in Rome* [S2B-023-79]

Some verbs—but again no adjectives or nouns—may take *-ed* participle clauses as complement. They include *get, have, make, feel, hear, see, watch, like, need, want.*

[41] [. . .] the person who booked me in had *his eyebrows shaved & replaced by straight black painted lines* [. . .] [W1B-011-72]

[42] They will find great difficulty in making *their wants known to those in authority* [. . .] [W2A-019-49]

[43] We've seen *our great piles of bricks built up* while the homeless grow [S2B-036-95]

[44] The council wants *the proposals "abandoned" until a means is found to replace temporary accommodation with permanent housing.* [W2C-009-8]

Most of these verbs also take bare infinitive clauses, which can serve as the corresponding actives of the *-ed* participle clauses:

[42a] They will find great difficulty in making *those in authority know their wants.*

If the verbs cannot be complemented by bare infinitive clauses, *to*-infinitive clauses may serve the same purpose:

[44a] The council wants *[people] to abandon the proposals.*

Some verbs may take *-ing* participle clauses as complements. With adjectives and nouns, the complement clause is typically introduced by a preposition. In this function the *-ing* participle is traditionally termed a gerund.

Common verbs with subjectless *-ing* participle clauses as complement include *avoid, (can't) bear, dislike, enjoy, hate, involve, like, love, mean, (not) mind, need, prefer, try:*

[45] Eleanor did not like *talking about herself,* and usually avoided personal questions. [W2F-009-44]

[46] The boys also enjoyed *seeing you* immensely. [W1B-014-13]

[47] Depending on who comes, you'll possibly need to bring sleeping bags and I hope you don't mind *sleeping on the floor* [W1B-004-45]

[48] This evidence involved *testing patients with spine severs.* [W1A-017-17]

[49] I'm sorry I missed *hearing your voice tonight.* [W1B-007-104]

[50] He increased the number of inspectors even though it meant *diverting manpower from inspections of domestically produced food.* [890927-0091-52]

[51] Twelve people also described *going through a mock execution* [S2A-034-91]

[52] I don't know if you ever tried *running a business* but it's very difficult [S1B-065-27]

Many of the same verbs may be complemented by an *-ing* participle clause with its own subject.

[53] Law enforcement duty ⟨ , ⟩ requires *a very real power over the citizen being entrusted to the policeman* [S2B-037-93]

[54] But it doesn't stop *people surging forward into the sea* [S2B-027-139]

[55] Yes it's easy to imagine *you doing all this.* [W1B-003-32]

[56] And I didn't in the least mind *you talking about Caroline.* [W2F-020-161]

[57] That need not mean *allied tanks and troops going all the way to Baghdad* [. . .] [W2E-002-41]

If the subject is a pronoun or proper name it is often in the genitive case **[58]**–**[59]** (more precisely, a possessive pronoun in **[58]** and **[59]**), though the objective case for pronouns **[55]**–**[56]** and the common case for names are also often used:

[58] I hope you don't mind *my rubbing my hands* [S1A-022-136]

[59] But most of the numbers are done in an upbeat style, which has the advantage of carrying the vocal introductions before the verse and preventing *their sounding superfluous out of stage context.* [W2B-008-129]

Nouns other than names generally take the common case, as in **[54]** and **[57]**.

Complementation of adjectives by *-ing* participle clauses is illustrated below. The clause may be without its own subject:

[60] I'm busy *eating* as a matter of fact [S1A-010-156]

[61] And he will be happy *sticking to blue wallpaper* won't he [S1A-086-144]

In **[60]**–**[61]** a preposition (here *with*) may be inserted between the adjective and the complement clause. For most adjectives the preposition is obligatory:

[62] He was afraid *of mentioning some girlfriend and offending the wife* [S1A-037-24]

If the clause has its own subject, the preposition is always obligatory:

[63] Once the instructor is happy *with you riding quiet roads with minimal traffic* ⟨ , ⟩ you'll both venture out onto busier roads [S2A-054-121]

[64] Well I was wrong *about it being a show-place* [. . .] [S2B-048-9]

[65] I could never get rid of the feeling that she was responsible *for his buying all the Prattertons*, and that through them she had somehow enticed him into marriage. [W2F-014-21]

The same options of case apply as with verb complementation. The possessive pronoun is used in **[65]** but the objective case of the personal pronoun in **[63]** and **[64]**.

Complementation of nouns by -*ing* participle clauses always requires a linking preposition, whether or not a subject is present. Examples are given below of complement clauses with their own subject:

[66] There is no question *of it being necessary or not* [. . .] [W2D-017-61]

[67] What are the chances *of it being* used? [W2C-003-78]

[68] Was there any realistic prospect ever *for it working* [S2B-014-96]

[69] Now that we have adopted a system *of my paying all expenses and then claiming*, the problem should be solved. [W1B-020-25]

[70] And it is sometimes coupled to a charge *of Coleridge collapsing through a drug-induced fatigue into a snug intellectual cocoon.* [W2A-003-13]

The possessive pronoun is used in **[69]** but the objective case in **[66]**–**[68]**. The common case *Coleridge* is employed in **[70]** rather than the genitive *Coleridge's*.

The citations that follow resemble those in **[53]**–**[57]**. They differ in that the noun phrase that immediately follows the verb is independent of the complement clause. As a consequence it can be made the passive subject of the host clause, as in a construction that corresponds to **[71]**:

[71] I saw *him smiling and pointing up* as the ⟨ , ⟩ fly-past came by [S2A-019-93]

[71a] *He* was seen *smiling and pointing up* as the fly-past came by.

Furthermore, since the noun phrase is independent of the complement clause, it can be a personal pronoun—as in **[71]**—but not a possessive pronoun. Verbs commonly used in this type of construction include verbs of perception (e.g. *feel, hear, see*), *catch, discover, find, get, have, leave*:

[72] I can feel *you beginning to buckle under the weight of all this sincerity.* [W1B-005-21]

[73] The most notable was EMI who soon had *an all electronic scanning system running.* [W2B-034-37]

[74] We've got *Dim Dimitri Conichev just moving forward in our picture there* [S2A-016-49]

[75] Not surprisingly we get uhm *the bulk of the heat coming in from the sun* [S2A-043-47]

[76] You saw *the pool being cleaned* when you arrived [S1B-066-81]

[77] I heard *the sound of a body hitting the car*—it's a very soft impact sound. [W2C-017-32]

[78] But for others it's a nightmare as they find *their work being used without permission* [S2B-023-3]

[79] [. . .] I will leave *that question* uhm ⟨ , ⟩ *hanging for now* [S2A-049-41]

[80] Keep *the indicator going* [S2A-054-170]

[81] She could feel *the lie making her blush.* [W2F-009-94]

For some verbs there is a choice of complement clause. The choice may be from two or three clause types: a finite clause, an -*ing* participle clause, or an infinitive clause. *Remember*, for example, may take all three:

[82] Most of the time I remember *I felt nothing at all* . . . [W1B-010-22]

[83] I remember *learning French* [S1A-053-324]

[84] We must remember *to get on that plane* you know [S1A-048-40]

The finite and -*ing* participle clauses **[82]**–**[83]** are factual, referring to some situation that has existed, whereas the infinitive clause **[84]** is non-factual, referring to a situation that may come into existence. It is possible to replace the finite clause in **[82]** by a participle clause and to replace the participle clause in **[83]** by a finite clause, in both instances preserving roughly the same meaning:

[82a] Most of the time I remember *having felt nothing at all.*

[83a] I remember *that I learned French.*

The finite *that*-clause is more flexible than the non-finite clauses. We can obtain a rough equivalent of the infinitive clause of **[84]** by inserting an appropriate modal auxiliary (in this instance the semi-modal *be to*) in the *that*-clause:

[84a] We must remember *that we are to get on that plane.*

Furthermore, *that*-clauses allow a range of tense and modal possibilities not open to the non-finite clauses:

[85] Remember *that alcohol affects your judgement of both people and situations.* [W2D-009-76]

[86] And one must also remember *that uh the same Arnold Bax has written poetry and I think plays under the pseudonym of Dermot O'Brien* [S1B-032-103]

[87] Remember *that other people may be just as apprehensive as you are* [. . .] [W2D-009-147]

Apart from the factual/non-factual distinction, -*ing* participle and infinitive clauses sometimes differ aspectually. The participle clause may indicate duration or iteration:

[88] I hate *being rushed.* [W2F-013-79]

[88a] I hate *to be rushed.*

In contrast with the infinitive clause in **[88a]**, the participle clause adds an indication of duration.

Reported Speech

6.17
Direct and
indirect speech

Reported speech conveys reports of acts of communication, including those of the reporters themselves. The reports may represent unspoken thoughts, either self-reports or deductions about the thoughts of others. In literature, the narrator is given the conventional licence (if the author so wishes) of knowing the thoughts and feelings of some or all the characters as well as what they say in private conversations from which the narrator is supposedly absent.

The two major categories of reported speech are direct speech and indirect speech.[17] Direct speech purports to convey the exact words that were spoken or written. Indirect speech conveys the content rather than the form. Of course, in both types only a part of the total communication may be reported. Citation [1] contains two examples of direct speech extracted from a fictional dialogue that presents a question and a response:

[1] One day the question that had dominated him all this time slipped from him, almost as if it had no meaning for him:
'Was the child mine?'
'Yes,' Susan said. *'Though I know I could never convince you of that.'*
[W2F-008-52 ff.]

A possible indirect report of the exchange in [1] would be:

[1a] He asked *whether the child was his*. She said *that it was, though she knew she could never convince him of that.*

The continuation of [1] provides an example of indirect speech, which represents the man's unspoken thought:

[2] Quietly doomed, he felt *he must continue.* [W2F-008-55]

A possible direct report of his feeling would be:

[2a] Quietly doomed, he felt, *'I must continue'.*

The reporter is held responsible for the accuracy of direct speech. By convention it is considered unnecessary to provide replications of pronunciation or the other speech features, though the manner of speaking is sometimes indicated (particularly in literature) by the choice of verb (e.g. *mumble, whisper, screech, sigh*) or by the addition of an adverbial (e.g. *hastily, placidly, sarcastically, indignantly, in trepidation*). In the written language, verbatim accuracy is generally expected (and may be legally required) in direct reporting. Omissions from quotations are supposed to be indicated by ellipsis periods and any changes by editorial comments.

In writing, direct speech is typically enclosed in quotation marks. The reporting clause, with any accompanying description or comment, may precede the direct speech [3], follow it [4], or come in the middle [5]:

[3] Cosmo said, *'Can I lend a hand?'*, and, pushing, asked, *'What is the picnic in aid of?'* [W2F-018-60]

[4] *'Where's the sea*?' I asked. [W2F-013-10]

[5] *'Something's wrong with Derek?'* Anne wailed, getting to her feet. *'I knew it. He's dead!'* She swayed back and forth on the spot, her shoulders shuddering. [W2F-002-166 ff.]

When the reporting clause is medial or final, its subject is not a pronoun, and its verb is in the simple present or simple past, then subject–verb inversion is sometimes used:

[6] 'It can't be far away,' *said Mary Jane*, swivelling her head. 'Isn't that a castle on the top of the cliff?' [W2F-013-12 f.]

For the punctuation of direct speech, see 11.30.

Reporting clauses are often omitted in fiction writing where there is a sequence of exchanges and it is clear who is speaking in each turn:

[7] She was spooling the programme on to the tape machine when the phone rang.
'Isobel? It's Bruno here.'
'What's that frightful noise in the background?' [W2F-020-149 ff.]

The reported speech, whether direct or indirect, may be introduced by a noun of speaking rather than a verb:

[8] A firm point of law can be seen in *the wife's statement* 'Take up the spike from the ground. If people, or if cattle should perish upon it, you yourself and I, with our children, will either be put to death, or be led into slavery'. [W1A-002-72]

[9] [. . .] the essence of religion ⟨ , ⟩ is *the answer to everybody's question* ⟨ , ⟩ what is the meaning of me and the other and the world [S1B-028-53]

[10] This reinforces *the earlier statement*, that man is blind to what he cannot see. [W1A-018-33]

[11] When did we last hear in a television discussion or a newspaper editorial *the simple assertion* that something was wrong because God or religious doctrine said so [S2B-029-9]

The reported speech may be connected to some nouns of speaking by a preposition:

[12] This is going to be *a question of* who you know not what you know [S1A-027-13]

[13] I can't give *a satisfactory explanation as to* why that should have occurred [S2A-068-26]

It may also be a predicative following the verb *be*:

[14] [. . .] you've anticipated my next question again because *my next question was* how do you think you viewed women at that time and how does that compare with your views today [S1A-072-197]

[15] *What I want to claim is* ⟨ , ⟩ that communication now extends far beyond language ⟨ , ⟩ because of technologies which have matured from infancy during the twentieth century [S2B-048-27]

A report may be partly in indirect speech and partly in direct speech. The mixture is clearer in writing, where the quotation marks can signal direct speech:

[16] The Motor-Cycle Crash Helmets (Religious Exemption) Act 1976 provides that any requirement imposed now or later by regulations under the 1972 Act shall not apply to any follower of the Sikh religion 'while he is wearing a turban'. [W2B-020-77]

Both direct and indirect speech may be hypothetical rather than a report of what was actually spoken, or they may present an abstraction of what might be said:

[17] If I say *I haven't done anything*, then you think I'm being deceitful. [W2F-008-77]

[18] I was going to tell you *Ginny's got engaged* but you knew that anyway [S1A-093-269]

[19] People would say *you've just got cold feet* [. . .] [S1A-050-181]

[20] They nearly said *they weren't going to op let me operate on her* [S1B-010-58]

[21] And everybody said *oh after dinner we're looking forward to hearing this* [S1B-032-115]

[22] I can remember when common sense said *that for instance women were weaker than men women shouldn't wear trousers women should earn less than men* [S1B-029-123]

6.18
Forms of indirect speech

Indirect speech is used to report declaratives, interrogatives, directives, and exclamatives (cf. 3.4). The nominal clauses reporting indirect speech are commonly complements of verbs of speaking or thinking, though they may also be complements of nouns (cf. 6.17).

Nominal *that*-clauses are used for indirect declaratives:

[1] General Schwarzkopf claims *that continuing the fighting a few days longer would have made no difference to the fate of the Kurds* [. . .] [W2E-009-72]

The subordinator *that* is often omitted after most of the verbs:

[2] You see he told somebody *I was weak* [S1A-052-62]

Some verbs also allow infinitive clauses [3]–[4] or *-ing* participle clauses [5]–[6] for indirect declaratives:

[3] But first he'd had to find out who claimed *to be speaking on behalf of the company its executives or the shareholders* [S2B-007-45]

[4] The communiqué warns that the reporters will be executed immediately if the police capture any of the traffickers' families to exchange for the

hostages; it also promises *to murder relatives of police officers and politicians.* [W2C-001-88]

[5] The patients were interviewed and tested in a laboratory and results consistently showed that the higher the spine sever the less patients reported *being able to 'feel' an emotion.* [W1A-017-20]

[6] He recalled *visiting both Yugoslavia and Indonesia as a boy with his grandfather and mother, the latter when he was only six years old.* [W2B-011-62]

Indirect questions are reported by various finite interrogative clauses; *yes–no* questions **[7]**, alternative questions **[8]**, and *wh*-questions **[9]** (cf. 3.5):

[7] In a reference to the Hindu claim over a mosque in the northern holy town of Iodia he asked *whether religious faith could be placed above the constitution and whether India was heading towards becoming a theocratic state* [S2B-006-49]

[8] Could you also inform me *whether individual members receive the journal or whether they need to be journal subscribers as well.* [W1B-028-137]

[9] I want to ask *what you think about the role of the father today* [S1A-072-29]

Indirect directives (orders, requests, and the like) may be reported by nominal finite clauses. The verb is then usually subjunctive (especially in American English) or it is used with a modal such as *should*:

[10] The project was first proposed four years ago and until recently the Quebec government had insisted *that the Canadian government help pay for the project.* [890911-0021-3]

[11] But they recommend *that any work by the water, electricity and gas authorities should be done before the scheme is started.* [W2C-017-82]

Suggest also allows an *-ing* participle clause as an indirect request:

[12] Mr. Bennett has suggested *sending drug dealers to military-style camps designed to build self-esteem.* [890906-0087-11]

Indirect directives are commonly infinitive clauses:

[13] The Louisiana attorney general and New Orleans district attorney have asked a federal district court *to allow them to revive laws making it a crime to perform abortions, punishable by as much as 10 years in prison.* [891012-0122-5]

[14] A marijuana smuggler is told *to work with AIDS patients.* [891012-0096-19]

[15] As a result, the FDA ordered importers *to detain most of China's canned-mushroom shipments for tests and began a nationwide recall of cans that had been linked to outbreaks.* [890927-0091-10]

Indirect exclamatives are reported by exclamative clauses introduced by *what* or *how*:

[16] My agent called me in this morning to tell me *how good he was.* [W1B-003-131]

Indirect speech is geared to the reporter's deixis: that is to say, it is geared to references to time, place, and participants from the point of view of the reporter and the person or persons being addressed by the reporter, and not to the original discourse that is being recorded. There are consequential referential shifts from the original discourse.

Personal pronouns, possessive pronouns, and reflexives are shifted to take account of the reporting situation. Hence, in **[17]** the original *I* and *my* of the speaker are shifted from first person to third person, and a possible original utterance might have had only either *my husband* or *Mark*:

> **[17]** Mrs Collier said *she*'d like to come down one day and uh get some knowledge of *her husband Mark* [S1A-028-236]

Similarly, in **[18]** the original *I* has been shifted to *you*, the addressee in the reporting situation:

> **[18]** And you said *you* were looking in the Guardian uhm on Monday obviously [S1A-034-205]

In **[19]** *I* replaces *she* or the name in the original discourse:

> **[19]** My mother said to my cousin apparently that *I* was getting fat [S1A-041-73]

And in **[20]** the instances of *I* and *my* replace *you* and *your* in the original discourse:

> **[20]** [. . .] the last doctor said that it was quite a lot to do with breathing through *my* nose because *I* couldn't breathe through *my* nose during the night when *I'm* sleeping [S1A-051-110]

Another type of shift from the original discourse to the reported or indirect speech is backshift: a shift from the original present tense to past tense. The original simple past or present perfect may also be shifted to past perfect. The relationship between the tenses in the reporting clause and the reported clause as a result of backshift is the sequence of tenses.

> **[21]** I felt a little consolation when a policewoman told me how lucky I *was* that the bullet fragments *were embedded* in my car door frame and dashboard rather than my head. [891011-0117-35]
>
> **[22]** And what he said was that alcohol *was* good for the memory [S2A-027-12]
>
> **[23]** Mr. Cohen, the new Drexel general counsel, says several attorneys have told him they *would* not *submit* detailed bills because of a concern the bills *would* later *be viewed* by the government. [891004-0013-48]
>
> **[24]** And he said that uh Mr Hook *had told* him that he *'d been* at a health farm for a fortnight worrying about what to do with his business and his uh private life [. . .] [S2A-070-57]
>
> **[25]** Andreotti said that 139 secret arms dumps *had been gathered* in over the last decade—but 12 *were* seriously *missing*. [W2C-010-35]

The past perfects in **[24]** and **[25]** could be replaced by simple pasts:

> **[24a]** He said that Mr Hook *told* him that he *was* at a health farm for a fortnight.
>
> **[25a]** Andreotti said that 139 secret arms dumps *were* gathered in over the last decade.

The original present may be retained if the content still applies at the time of the reporting situation:

[26] On Friday, Sen. Boren told a meeting of the Democratic committee members that he *intends* to offer an amendment to Sen. Bentsen's proposal that would reduce the capital gains rate. [891002-0002-20]

The report in the newspaper **[26]** evidently precedes the actual offer of an amendment. Similarly, in **[23]** the refusal to submit applies at the time of reporting, so that the pasts could be replaced by presents (*will not submit; will later be viewed*). In **[21]** the luck of the interviewee and the embedded fragments were still in evidence in the reporting situation, and so presents could have been used in that sentence too (*how lucky I am; the bullet fragments are embedded*). The same principle can be applied to **[22]**, where a generalization is stated (*alcohol is good for the memory*).

Further examples appear below of the retention of the original present tense forms:

[27] [. . .] The organisation ARK has said that sea-level *will rise* by one meter ⟨ , , ⟩ if present pollution levels and conditions *continue* [S1B-007-191]

[28] [. . .] Rabbi Sacks said at one point faith *is* not *measured* by acts of worship alone [S1B-028-79]

[29] Well you all know that Malthus said two hundred years ago ⟨ , ⟩ population when unchecked *increases* in a geometrical ratio [S2B-048-63]

[30] Zox said to me recently that he *doesn*'t *think* there *'s going to be* a rehearsal for the wedding. [W1B-015-39]

[31] Novell demonstrated NetWare and said that it *'s* a very fine network operating system. [W2B-036-105]

The simple present may be used—as an alternative to the simple past—in the reporting clause (cf. 5.22), as in:

[32] [. . .] but the referee *says* it wasn't straight [S2A-002-119]

Place and time references may also need to be adjusted to take account of their deixis in the reporting situation. For example, *there* in **[33]** may have been shifted from *here* in the original discourse:

[33] [. . .] like going in and being told one's never had an account *there* at all. [W2F-011-93]

6.19
Free direct speech and free indirect speech

The two minor modes of reporting are related to the two major modes.

Free direct speech is essentially direct speech without reporting clauses. It is employed in fiction for interior monologue, to represent a character's stream of thought. Present tense is used where appropriate, as in direct speech.

The thoughts of Cathy in **[1]** are in the present tense, and there is no backshift. But, as is typical in free indirect speech, the third person is used instead of the first person. The reporting of Cathy's thoughts constitutes a mixture of free direct speech (in tense) and free indirect speech (in person shift):

[1]   'Would you have liked something like that for your fiftieth?'
'Heavens, no! You know me. Not a man for surprises. I must be off. See you this evening.'
'See you this evening.'
Not a man for surprises. Cathy smiles to herself with the truth of that remark as she washes up the breakfast dishes. *So much is Will not a man for surprises that he is no more capable of giving them than of receiving. Her own fiftieth is not far away. It will not be long before he asks his regular question: 'What would you like for your birthday?' However outrageous or impossible the answer, he will get her what she wants. Only on one occasion, earlier in their marriage, when she asked for 'A surprise, please', has she seen him completely thrown, searching miserably for ideas. She must not put him through that agony again.*
But instead of considering possible suggestions, Cathy finds her thoughts still concerned with the surprise party. [W2F-019-94 ff.]

In general, free indirect speech has tense backshift verb forms as well as pronoun shift, but it retains some of the expressive features of direct discourse, such as vocatives, direct questions, and interjections. In **[2]**–**[4]** we see the free indirect speech merging with the narration:

[2]   Before leaving the house, he had gone down into the kitchen, and cut one thick slice of bread and butter, and he ate that, now, with one of the cheese triangles. As soon as he had finished, he wanted a drink. *He had been stupid not to find some sort of bottle. Well, there was no drink, it would be better to try and not think about it.* Instead he got up and crossed to the other side of the clearing. [*I'm the King of the Castle*, by Susan Hill (Harmondsworth: Penguin, 1974), p. 71]

[3]   My father refused to complete the financial aid papers; finally, in desperation, I stole the tax returns from the glove compartment of his Toyota and did them myself. More waiting. Then a note from the Dean of Admissions. *An interview was required, and when could I fly to Vermont?* I could not afford to fly to Vermont, and I wrote and told him so. Another wait, another letter. *The college would reimburse me for my travel expenses if their scholarship offer was accepted.* Meanwhile the financial aid packet had come in. [*The Secret History*, by Donna Tartt (Harmondsworth: Penguin, 1993), p. 11]

[4]   On the rare occasions he thought of Joyce, it was to reproach himself for stupidity. *There's no surer way to lose a good friend than to marry her. High-spirited, bouncy, generous Joyce had in middle age and close proximity become a bore; and as for sex, so good in experimental and lusty youth, that had switched to something akin to aerobics. But now, after the Bodmin Assizes, he had a free weekend. He would dawdle back to London, bird-watch on the way. Should he head for Slapton Ley and the Exe Estuary for migratory birds, or chance the cliffs of North Devon?* He drove as far as Launceston enjoying his indecision. [W2F-018-9 ff.]

Chapter 7
Text

Summary

Chapter 7 Summary

- Speech is the primary form of language, but in certain respects the written language is an autonomous system.

- The most common form of speech is casual conversation. Dialogues may be face-to-face (as is usual in normal conversations) or distanced (as in telephone conversations), they may be private or public. Monologues may be scripted or unscripted.

- The major distinction in writing is whether it is published—and therefore generally edited by others—or not published.

- Language use may be categorized according to register (the type of activity engaged in through language), level of formality, attitudes to the other participants or to the communication, relationships between participants, and the situational context.

- A text (a written text or spoken discourse) depends in part for its interpretation on intertextuality, the relationship of the text to other past or coexisting texts.

- The unity of a text is assured by its cohesion (lexical and grammatical devices for linking parts of a text) and its coherence (the continuity of meaning that enables one to make sense of a text).

- Situational deixis involves the use of expressions to refer directly to persons and objects in the situation and to temporal and locational features. Textual deixis involves the use of expressions to refer to other words in the text. Anaphoric references are to previous words, cataphoric references are to subsequent words.

- Reference, substitution, ellipsis, and logical connectives contribute to the cohesion of a text.

- Paragraphs present structural units of conceptually related sentences.

- Some texts have conventional textual patterns.

- Speech acts are often indirect, as in a question intended as a request.

- Interpretations of texts are dependent on understanding implications.

Speech and Writing

Language is communicated chiefly through speech, using the medium of sound, and writing, using the medium of vision. There are strong arguments for the claim that speech is the primary form of language:

1. Many languages—undoubtedly most in the history of human communication—have only been spoken. There are still many in present use that have never been written down.

2. The spoken language comes first in time. Many centuries may elapse before a language acquires a written form, if at all.

3. Where there is a written language, some speakers—in certain cultures the majority—are illiterate or only partially literate. In former times literacy was commonly confined to special groups, such as priests or clerks in legal and administrative positions. Even today, some societies have people who are paid to read and write letters. It is usual to employ experts for certain highly specialized kinds of writing, such as drafting statutes or drawing up legal documents.

4. We learn to speak before we learn to write. Children acquire speech by exposure to it; they generally have to be taught to read and write.

5. Speech is biologically based. The human vocal organs are specially adapted to speech. The adaptation has been at the expense of their other purposes, so that it is possible for an adult human (but not an animal) to choke to death on food.

6. Even highly literate individuals are likely to use speech more frequently than writing.

7. Writing systems are often intended to represent certain features of pronunciation: syllables in syllabic systems and individual sounds in alphabetic systems.

Reservations were raised in the past to the use of writing. It was said that reliance on written texts weakens memory and debilitates the mind. Written texts, it was claimed, acquired an undeserved authority, and those that were false or defective enjoyed a permanence that survived attempts at refutation; the only remedy for subversive writings was to burn them. Similar reservations were also voiced when printing was first invented, allowing the circulation of numerous copies of a written work. New technologies tend to be resisted: ballpoint pens were once forbidden in schools because of their alleged impairment of handwriting; we still hear objections to the use of calculators in schools as weakening the ability to do mental arithmetic; many older writers refuse to resort to computers for word processing.[1]

7.2
Writing as an autonomous system

In certain respects the written language is at least in part an autonomous system:

1. In present-day societies, the written language has social prestige and is highly valued. Notions of correctness in writing largely determine what is felt to be correct in speech. It is the standard language that is presented in the writing system; non-standard dialects are not used in official writing and they do not have an institutionalized orthography. The written language is studied in educational institutions, often to the complete or virtual neglect of the spoken language. Literacy is a requirement for skilled occupations.

2. The written symbols do not necessarily correspond fully to pronunciation. In English the lack of correspondence between spelling and pronunciation is often blatant (cf. 12.1–6), but there are also languages (such as Chinese) where no correspondence is to be found between written symbols and sounds.

3. Rapid reading is silent. Competent readers read much faster than they speak, since they recognize chunks of writing rather than individual words. Speed in reading is an important advantage of the written language.

4. Much of reading and writing in everyday life, outside education and work, has no analogue in speech. Consider such activities as writing cheques, compiling shopping lists, reading labels, checking invoices, filling out forms, leaving notes for family members, keeping personal records, reading instructions for installing and using household devices, finding a route on a map, consulting timetables. There are also graphic devices that are confined to writing: maps, diagrams, graphs, tables, complex formulae and equations.

5. It is possible to read and write a foreign language without being able to speak it. Similarly, those who endure from birth the handicap of being unable to speak or hear can nevertheless learn to read and write.

6. It is usual for older children and adults to learn new words and new grammatical constructions from the written language. We may be able to understand or use a word in writing without knowing how to pronounce it; for example, *inveigle* or *heinous*.

For certain functions the difference between speech and writing is likely to be eroded by two recent technologies: faxes ('facsimiles') and e-mail ('electronic mail'). When the speed of these two forms of communication is sufficiently enhanced, they will resemble telephone communication in the immediacy of interactions between participants. The widespread availability of telephones has already seriously reduced the use of personal letters.

7.3
Different kinds of speech

The most common form of speech is casual conversation in which two or more speakers interact face to face. Such dialogue is typically spontaneous, involving no preparation, and covering a range of topics (not necessarily connected) initiated by one or more speakers. Speakers often overlap, intricately when several participate. Some people may be present as acknowledged listeners without participating in the conversation, while others may simply be eavesdropping. Face-to-face conversation is generally supplemented by paralinguistic messages conveyed by body language, such as facial expressions and gestures, that indicate (for example) understanding or puzzlement, agreement or disagreement, or attitudes such as alarm, regret, impatience, and anger. Paralinguistic information on feelings and attitudes may also be conveyed by the tone of voice, the volume and speed of utterance. Accents communicate information on geographical origins and perhaps subsequent locations of speakers as well as on their social status.

In casual conversation the speakers are normally visible to each other. New technologies during this century have introduced various kinds of distanced communication, overcoming the previous limitation in the use of the spoken language. The most common kind involves two people using telephones. Telephone speakers often feel impelled to accompany their speech with appropriate facial expressions and gestures, as they are accustomed to doing in face-to-face conversation. The absence of visual contact prompts speakers to assure themselves that the other person is still on the line when it is their turn in the conversation. Similarly, it is usual for listeners to signal that they are attending to what is being said and can understand it by interjecting *yes*, *mm*, and the like. Longer silences are tolerated on television broadcasts than on radio broadcasts. The absence of the visual medium allows speakers to conceal their reactions to a greater extent, an advantage in certain situations.

More recent technologies have introduced telephone conference calls, where more than two speakers can participate, but this facility is not universally available. Drawing the conditions much closer to face-to-face conversation are videophones, an innovation that may well become the norm for telephones early in the next century.

Other forms of distanced two-way conversation are not as widespread as telephone conversations. Radio communication tends to be restricted to specialized situations and personnel, such as between airplane pilots and airport communication towers or between the police and their station bases. Wider use of radio occurs with the citizen bands available in some countries, where strangers communicate with each other (in the United States commonly among long-distance truck drivers, who may refer to each other by nicknames); some radio hams converse internationally. Both radio and television are generally one-way communications from their stations, but phone-in programmes approximate telephone conversations, though they differ in that participants are selected, topics are laid down by the presenters, a delaying device may introduce some censorship, and there are restrictions on time. Recent technological developments in cable television allow viewers in some countries to interact with others by television, enabling them (for example) to shop from home.

In previous centuries a major difference between speech and writing was that speech was fleeting whereas writing was permanent—or could be permanent if preserved. On the whole, this difference still holds true for most of the time that the spoken language is used. Conversations are not normally recorded and we usually have no need or wish to record them. However, the new technologies of audio and video recordings and recording equipment for playing them allow us to preserve speech permanently too, if we wish to do so. The present techniques for retrieving information from spoken material lag well behind those for retrieving information from written material whether in books—where we can skip, scan, or skim, re-read, and annotate—or in machine-readable form on computer screens. Recent progress in multimedia hardware and software and in hypertext programs suggests that in the not-too-distant future we will be able to retrieve information from sound and pictures as efficiently as from written material.

Conversations are typically private. Some kinds of dialogue are public, in that they are conducted before an audience. Examples of public dialogue range from broadcast discussion programmes and interviews that are heard at a distance by mass audiences, through debates in parliament and cross-examinations in law courts (though both of these may be broadcast in some countries) to committee meetings open to the public and college seminars that may be attended by casual visitors. Those who speak in public have generally prepared themselves for what they are going to say. Some may use notes or even read from scripts, perhaps thereby bringing features of the written language into their speech.

Monologues are typically public and prepared. They include lectures, speeches, talks, presentations by lawyers and summings-up by judges. Any of these may be unscripted or scripted, but broadcast news reports—another type of prepared public monologue—are generally scripted (though they may contain brief live reports by outside reporters, statements by public figures, or interviews). When monologues (for example, lectures or speeches) are published from scripts or recordings, they may be revised to bring the published version closer to printed English.

Midway between the spoken and written language are written representations of speech. These appear in plays, which are read privately or are spoken by actors, and in the dialogue to be found in novels and stories. The representations attempt to imitate, to a greater or lesser extent, characteristics of normal conversation.

7.4
Different kinds of writing

Written communication can be published writing or non-published writing. Non-published material is typically handwritten or typed. Published material is typically printed.

Non-published writing generally has a more restricted circulation than published writing. It may be addressed to just one person, as in social or business letters, though copies may be sent to other people. It may even be self-addressed as in diaries recording events, reflections, etc., or in self-reminder notes. Non-published writing therefore tends to be private. In the case of letters, it is generally interactional in the sense that letters elicit replies, but the interaction is not immediate, as in dialogue.

Non-published writing is generally unedited in that it is not usual for a professional editor to be engaged to correct the language. Consequently, non-published writing more reliably reflects the language of the writer. Of course the writers themselves have the opportunity to edit their own language or content, a task made easier in recent times by word processing. They may also seek advice from language reference works or from other people, to that extent departing from their private use of language.

Intermediate between published and non-published writing is the kind of material produced by institutions and commercial companies for distribution internally or to a targeted readership; for example: memoranda, reports, agendas. They are semi-private, since they are not available to the general public, and may even be marked 'confidential'.

Published material is in principle public, and it is generally sold. In practice, of course, its circulation varies immensely. It is edited, often by professional copy-editors, who may propose—or enforce—changes in the material according to the dictates of the house style of the publishing company and according to their own views of what is acceptable or desirable. The editing tends to induce conformity with the rules of standard written English.

Technological changes are producing innovations in publishing that cross the boundaries between speech and writing. Publishing companies are already engaged in developing multimedia electronic products that combine speech, writing, film, and graphics. Hypertext applications, sometimes accompanying multimedia and sometimes used by themselves, permit guided browsing through a text or through different texts, and are particularly valuable for reference works.

7.5
The dimensions of language use

Language may be categorized according to the type of activity engaged in through language (cf. 1.8). Registers (or genres) are defined in this way. In identifying registers, we may view them along a continuum from the very general to the very specific. For example, information writing covers academic writing, popular writing, and press news reports. Academic writing can be subdivided by general topic into humanities, social sciences, natural sciences, and technology. Humanities can be further subdivided into disciplines such as history and literary criticism—and so on. These subdivisions may correlate with differences in language.

Major register categories according to the purpose for which language is used include exposition, argumentation, narration, instruction, persuasion, regulation, entertainment. In practice, a particular spoken discourse or written text may be a mixture of these uses: a history text may include narration and exposition; a lecture exposition, argumentation, and entertainment. The major registers cut across speech and writing. So do some of the more specific registers, such as news reports, sports commentaries, editorials, which may occur in the press or on radio and television. Some registers are restricted to writing (dictionaries, statutes, contracts) and others to speech (science demonstrations, legal cross-examinations). Mixtures of registers are found: a broadcast news report may include interviews, a letter may combine business with social content. Spontaneous conversation is typically heterogeneous.

Distinctions are also found in the level of formality, ranging from the highly formal to the very casual. Attitudes to the other participants or to the communication may colour the language: politeness, hostility; seriousness, irony. So also may personal relationships such as that between spouses or between friends or the relationships of parent/child, teacher/student, doctor/patient, salesperson/customer. There are personality factors: people may be outgoing or shy. The situational context (or domain) may also influence the use of language: home, school, club, church.

7.6
Intertextuality

In this chapter, 'text' refers to both spoken and written language. A written text is a stretch of writing, while a spoken text—here called a discourse—is a stretch of speech.

A written text may be as long as a novel or a multi-volume encyclopedia; it may be as short as a one-word notice, such as *Exit*. A monologue discourse may be as long as an hour-long lecture or as short as the time announcement that can be elicited from answerphone, such as *Sunday three ten pm*. A dialogue discourse may be as long as a two-hour seminar or as short as the greeting *Good morning* exchanged by neighbours in passing.

To understand a text we need to know its context. The context of a written text includes the period and place in which it was composed, its author, and its intended audience—if this information is known. Fictional written texts may also have imaginary contexts: an assumed setting in time and place, a persona constructed as the author, and a fictional audience. The context of a discourse is the situation in which it occurs: its time and place, the presence of non-participants as well as those who speak, and any features in the situation that are referred to or are relevant in some other way to what is said. Imagine that a speaker points to a carton of milk and says either **[1]** or **[2]**:

> **[1]**   This is good for you.
>
> **[2]**   This is made from a tree.

For **[1]** the presence of milk is relevant, not the container or the material from which the container is made. For **[2]** it is the fact that the container is made from cardboard—not from glass or plastic—that is relevant.[2] The presence or absence of visual context is of course a crucial difference between radio and television. A sports commentator on the radio must describe the events and the surroundings and perhaps the reactions of the audience as well as commenting on what is happening. A television commentator knows what the viewers see on their screens and can therefore focus on commenting.

In the broadest sense, context involves intertextuality, which is more evident for written texts than for discourse. Intertextuality is the relationship between a text and other past or coexisting texts. The relationship is most clearly manifested in the conventions to which a written text is expected to conform. We recognize immediately a business letter from its layout, its headings, and its endings; confirmation follows from its style and its contents. We can usually distinguish at a glance an advertisement in a newspaper or magazine from a feature article or a news report; if there is a danger that we might fail to recognize that it is an advertisement, it is generally headed as such. The genres of poetry are signalled in various ways: layout, number of lines, rhyming schemes, style, and content; poets may exploit genre conventions in parody or in deviations that extend the conventions or create new genres. All writers bring to their writing their reading of other texts. They may acknowledge their debt by quotations or allusions or by references to books they have consulted or are recommending for further reading.

Discourses also display their dependence on intertextuality. What is appropriate for a sermon is not appropriate for an academic lecture; what passes as polite among strangers has a chilling effect on close friends. Whether published in newspapers or broadcast on radio or television, news reports allude to, or rely on, knowledge of news items that have been disseminated previously. Similarly, conversations between people that have met before presuppose knowledge of previous conversations and shared experiences.[3]

Connections across Sentences

7.7
Cohesion and coherence

The unity of a text is assured by its cohesion and its coherence.[4] Cohesion refers to lexical and grammatical devices for linking parts of a text. Coherence refers to the continuity of meaning that enables others to make sense of a text. Unless there is evidence to the contrary, listeners and readers assume that the texts they encounter are coherent and make the effort to interpret them as having unity.

A simple illustration of lexical cohesion appears in the first two sentences of a brief news item:

> **[1]** John Maynard Keynes, the century's most influential economist, once said that in his utopia members of his profession would be like dentists—useful but humble people. Utopia may be arriving with the administration of President-elect Bill Clinton. [*International Herald Tribune*, 21 December 1992, p. 7]

The sentences are cohesive solely through the repetition of the word *utopia*. For coherence, the implication in the second sentence is that under the new President's administration economists will be useful but not prominent. The implication derives from the implicit acceptance by the writer of the opinion expressed by Keynes (reported in the first sentence) on the place of economists in utopia. Readers infer that acceptance from the juxtaposition of the two sentences and interpret *utopia* as referring solely to this one feature of the future administration.

The first two sentences of another news item (on the same page of the *International Herald Tribune*) illustrate grammatical cohesion:

> **[2]** To stimulate or not to stimulate. That is the question vexing president-elect Bill Clinton, who says he will decide at the last possible moment, after he sees the latest statistics.

The two sentences are cohesive solely through the use of the pronoun *that*, the first word in the second sentence. The pronoun refers back to the whole of the first sentence. The beginning of this news item also exhibits a feature of intertextuality: a cliché allusion to Hamlet's soliloquy *to be or not to be.*

7.8
Lexical cohesion

The most striking uses of lexical cohesion are in parallel structures where combinations of words are repeated. Here is a simple instance, the headline of an advertisement for a brand of yoghurts:

[1]   No artificial colouring
No artificial flavouring
No artificial anything

Parallelism with identical or almost identical phraseology is a feature of sermons and political speeches. Here is John F. Kennedy in his inaugural address (20 January 1961):

[2]   And so, my fellow Americans: ask not what your country can do for you—ask what you can do for your country. My fellow citizens of the world: ask not what America will do for you, but what together we can do for the freedom of man.

Martin Luther King effectively introduced a series of visions of a changed American society with the repeated *I have a dream that one day* . . . (28 August 1963).

Parallelism may be found in dialogue, across speakers, as in this extract from a conversation:

[3]   A: Let's *have a sleepover* next week
B: Can we *have a sleepover*
A: Just *tee-shirts* and *teddies*
B: *Tee-shirts* for the guys and *teddies* for the girls
A: And *I'll bring the* cream *cheese*
B: *I'll bring the* whipped *cream* [ICE-USA-S1A-002]

There is strict parallelism only in the last pair of the three exchanges in **[3]**, but there is considerable lexical repetition in the other two exchanges as well; in the first with a change in grammatical structure, and in the second with expansion.

Most lexical cohesion is achieved in a more diffused way, without parallelism. In **[4]**, which is extracted from a legal cross-examination, the word *cigarette* is repeated exactly, but there is a slight variation in the other repetition—singular *hand* and plural *hands*:

[4]   A: But you only had one hand because you'd got a cigarette in the other
B: No I was holding on with both hands but the cigarette was in my two fingers [S1B-066-16]

A similar variation in inflection (*dub*/*dubbed*) appears in this extract from the opening sentences of a feature article:

[5]   To *dub* or not to *dub* has never been the question in Italy—or not until now. For decades every foreign film entering the country has been *dubbed* into Italian [. . .] [*International Herald Tribune*, 18 December 1992, p. 12]

You will notice another allusion to Hamlet's soliloquy.

The linked items may be synonymous, *slaughtering* and *killing* in **[6]**:

> **[6]** Europeans began *slaughtering* wolves from the moment they arrived in America. Indeed, the *killing* of wolves, like the *killing* of Indians, was perceived as a moral duty, a symbolic act in the subjugation of godless wilderness. ['The Return of the Wolf', by Richard Grant, *The Independent Magazine*, 19 December 1992, p. 27]

Antonyms provide the lexical link between the second and third sentences of **[7]** (here numbered for convenient reference), the contrast between *virtues* and *vices*:

> **[7]** (1) The popular family game of snakes and ladders originated as a system for the moral instruction of young people in India. (2) Virtues, in the shape of ladders, allowed players to reach their goal—heaven, or *nirvana*—quickly. (3) The vices, represented by snakes, forced players back down towards earth (or, in some versions, hell). [*The Times*, 26 December 1992, p. 3.11]

The contrast is highlighted in the headline to the feature item: *Vaunting virtue, slippery vice. Heaven* (2) and *hell* (3) are further examples of antonyms. The extract exhibits repetition across the three sentences: *ladders* in (1) and (2); *snakes* in (1) and (3); *players* in (2) and (3). Synonymy is expressed in the paraphrase of *in the shape of (ladders)* in (2) by *represented by (snakes)* in (3).

Other semantic relationships are also illustrated in this passage about the game of snakes and ladders. *Game* (1) is an activity in which *players* (2, 3) take part. *Virtues* (2) and *vices* (3) are subsumed under *moral* behaviour (1). This last relationship is clearly illustrated in **[8]**. *Fermentation* is a hyponym of the superordinate term *process* (cf. 8.13), a particular term being succeeded by a more general term.

> **[8]** Fermentation can then begin. A process taking six weeks at the least, and often a good deal longer [. . .] [advertisement, *The Independent Magazine*, 19 December 1992, p. 14]

Lexical cohesion may depend on general knowledge, as in these opening sentences of a feature article on space travel. Readers are expected to know that Albert Einstein was a genius and therefore to experience no difficulty in identifying *Albert Einstein* in (1) with *the gentle genius* in (3):

> **[9]** (1) Blame it on Albert Einstein. (2) In the very act of freeing us from the straitjacket of Newtonian physics, he slammed the door on our planetary prison. (3) It's a life sentence that the gentle genius imposed on us, with no parole. ['Space Hop? Dreams Are Good for You', by Hank Burchard, *International Herald Tribune*, 19–20 December 1992, p. 6]

The identification of *Albert Einstein* with *the gentle genius* is supported by grammatical devices. *It* in (1) refers forward to the whole of sentence (2), in which *he* refers back to *Albert Einstein*, and *us* in (3) refers back to *our* in (2). Metaphorical language clinches the identification. The prison metaphor that extends from (2) to (3) links the *he* who imprisoned us with *the gentle genius* who imposed a life sentence on us.

7.9
Situational and textual deixis

Deixis involves the use of expressions to refer directly to the situation within which an utterance is taking place, and their interpretation is therefore dependent on features of that situation. For example, the pronoun *I* is necessarily deictic, since it must refer to the speaker or writer: in a conversation, the reference of *I* shifts according to who is speaking. Deictic expressions typically refer to persons and objects in the situation and to temporal and locational features. When you say *Don't drop it*, you may be using the pronoun *it* to refer to something present in the situation that you have not previously named, and when you say *You can't sit here* the pronoun *you* refers to the person you are addressing and the adverb *here* may refer directly to a place visible to the person you are addressing, a place that you may not have mentioned before. The use of the imperative in *Don't drop it* introduces a reference to future time, a time later than that of the utterance.

The concept of deixis is sometimes extended from situational deixis (the use of expressions to point at some feature of the situation) to textual deixis (the use of expressions to point at other expressions in the text). Textual deixis contributes to cohesion because of its linkage to previous or subsequent words in the text. References to what comes earlier in the text are anaphoric, whereas references to what comes afterwards are cataphoric. In **[1]** *it* refers back to *the basket*, and is therefore anaphoric; whereas in **[2]** *here* refers forward to the whole of the following sentence, and is therefore cataphoric:

> **[1]** A: Would you like to put some of these things in *the basket*
> B: Okay I don't know how clean *it* is [ICE-USA-S1A-004]

> **[2]** *Here*'s a problem *Human language* ⟨ , , ⟩ *is it genetic* [S1B-003-6 f.]

Anaphoric and cataphoric reference can also apply within the same sentence, but in that case the reference does not contribute to cohesion across sentences:

> **[3]** And so Bob drafted *this questionnaire* and gave *it* to Dick [S1A-008-97]

> **[4]** I went to *Lindos* once and slept on a beach *there* [S1A-063-55]

Anaphoric and cataphoric expressions not only provide connections between sentences, they enable us to avoid repetition; *it*, for example, replaces the possible repetition of *the basket* in **[1]**. In many instances, avoiding repetition results in a substantial saving in words, so that they are also a means of abbreviation. For example, *it* in the second sentence of **[5]** refers back to all of the previous sentence from *that crucial aspects* onwards:

> **[5]** It is not often that crucial aspects of a nation's history remain almost totally hidden despite the efforts of generations of historians to bring to light what is important. But *it* can happen even in the case of something so fundamental as the Glorious Revolution of 1688–91, a turning-point not only in the history of England but also of Scotland, Ireland, the American colonies, the Dutch Republic and the European balance of power. ['History in the making', by Jonathan Israel, *The Independent*, 28 December 1992, p. 13]

By avoiding repeating what we have already said, we gain an additional bonus: we can focus the attention of listeners and readers on what is new.

Referring expressions are gainfully employed when the listener or reader is successful in making the intended connection. The following advertisement contains a grammatical pun, requiring the reader to identify different referents for *it* in the two sentences:

> **[6]** Rising damp
> we cure it
> we guarantee it

The reader will of course have no difficulty in interpreting the first sentence as 'we cure rising damp' and the second as 'we guarantee that we cure rising damp'. But referring expressions may be ambiguous—comically in **[7]**:

> **[7]** If the baby does not thrive on raw milk, boil *it*. [example by Otto
> Jespersen, cited in *The Complete Plain Words*, by Sir Ernest Gowers, 3rd
> edition revised by Sidney Greenbaum and Janet Whitcut (London: HMSO,
> 1986), p. 112]

7.10
Referring expressions

The most common referring expressions are drawn from pronouns (e.g. *she, it, this, that, these, those, some, none*), determiners (e.g. *the, this, that, these, those*), and adverbs (e.g. *here, there, then*).

The definite article *the* (cf. 4.33, 5.16) may be used anaphorically in sentence cohesion:

> **[1]** (1) A useful image of cell diversification is of an undulating landscape in
> which a ball rolls down pathways that branch [. ..] (2) At many branch
> points there may be just two new tracks, while at others there may be
> more. (3) *The* tracks can be thought of as patterns of gene activity and
> *the* ball as a developing cell. [*The Triumph of the Embryo*, by Lewis
> Wolpert (Oxford: Oxford University Press, 1991), p. 91]

In (3) *the* is attached to two nouns to identify them by anaphoric reference: *the ball* refers back to *a ball* in (1), and *the tracks* to *two new tracks* and *more* (*tracks*) in (2). In place of *the*, the demonstrative determiners might have been used: *these tracks* or *those tracks*, and *this ball* or *that ball*. *This* and *these* indicate closer proximity in physical distance or textual distance than *that* and *those*; since *ball* in (3) is further away from the previous mention of *ball* in (1), *this ball* is a less likely replacement of *the* than *that ball*.

In **[1]** the determiner is accompanied by repetition of the previously mentioned words *tracks* and *ball*. But there need not be any lexical repetition. In **[2]** *the* in *the negotiations* links the phrase to *These talks* in the previous sentence:

[2] These talks are the key to unlocking the outflow of money for investment from Japan. The failure of *the* negotiations has resulted in an appreciation of the yen. [*International Herald Tribune*, 29 August 1994, p. 1]

In both **[1]** and **[2]** the highlighted determiners are anaphoric. In **[3]**, *this* is cataphoric, pointing forward to the whole of the second sentence:

[3] Let me put it *this* way ⟨ , , ⟩ Initially observations on that vessel [. . .] were by police in South Wales ⟨ , , ⟩ Were the customs aware of these observations [S1B-063-226 ff.]

Pronouns are commonly used anaphorically to refer to a previous phrase, their antecedent:

[4] My cat, a ginger male, is lost. If you have seen *him*, please phone me. [notice attached to a tree in north-west London]

[5] When one feels an emotion, certain involuntary changes occur within us. *These* include changes in salivation, breathing, heart rate, perspiration and muscle tone. [W1A-017-14 f.]

[6] Steve checks over his uh shoulder to see if there are any dangers There are *none* whatsoever [S2A-006-87 f.]

The former and *the latter*, though not usually considered pronouns, have similar functions:

[7] There are two main components in coffee: soluble and insoluble substances. *The former* are the caffeine, sugar and proteins, *the latter* the oils and colloids. ['Italians know how to express it so well', by Chris Long, *The Independent*, 28 December 1992, p. 11]

The anaphoric reference may be to the whole of the previous sentence (cf. also **[5]** in 7.9):

[8] I had to find out where the controlled drugs were kept, and how they were ordered, delivered and paid for. *This* meant getting involved in administration [. . .] [W2F-004-38]

The relative pronoun *which* can begin a new sentence with the same anaphoric reference to a previous sentence as *that*:

[9] In a flat, faltering voice Louis XVI then read the formal declaration of war as though it were a death sentence upon himself. *Which* indeed it was. [*Citizens: A Chronicle of the French Revolution*, by Simon Schama (London: Penguin Books, 1989), p. 597]

The sentence introduced by *which* is a sentential relative clause (cf. 5.10). *Here* and *there* are also used for extended anaphoric reference:

[10] Christ brought us freedom from the curse of the law by becoming for our sake an accursed thing ⟨ , ⟩ for Scripture says the curse is on everyone who is hanged on the gibbet ⟨ , ⟩ The reference *here* is to the exhibition of the dead body not a lingering execution [S2B-028-32]

Personal pronouns may have cataphoric reference to a name in a subsequent sentence at the beginning of a narrative. This is a common device of suspension in fiction, but it is also found in newspaper and magazine features or news articles. Here is a striking example:

[11] *He*'s sitting on the sofa locked into a staring match with the television set as *he* digests *his* deli sandwich and daily dose of anti-inflammatories. There's a channel changer to fill the void in *his* racquet hand, and whenever *he* gets tired of watching golf, *he* can retire to the four-poster bed in a room *he* keeps as cold as Dracula's vault, the better to get *his* beauty sleep. Or, in *his* case, *his* power sleep.

"This is it, this is my life; it's like being a retired person," said Pete Sampras, the world's top-ranked tennis player and the defending champion of the U.S. Open [. . .] [*International Herald Tribune*, 29 August 1994, p. 17]

Pronouns and the adverbs *here* and *there* may have extended cataphoric reference:

[12] *It*'s a classic example of the right hand not knowing what its left is doing. A valuable nonproliferation initiative by the Clinton administration is being undermined by another of its pet projects. [*International Herald Tribune*, 29 August 1994, p. 8]

[13] *Here* are some of those thoughts. 6 November 1987: Today I went home, and [. . .] [W2B-001-117]

In certain stereotyped sentences, cataphoric *this* and *here* are interchangeable:

$$\left.\begin{array}{l} \textit{This} \text{ is} \\ \textit{Here} \text{ is} \end{array}\right\} \left\{\begin{array}{l} \text{the news.} \\ \text{what I mean.} \\ \text{how to do it.} \\ \text{how it goes.} \end{array}\right.$$

Similarly, *these* and *here* in these stereotyped sentences:

These/Here again are the main points of the news.
These/Here are the results.

More obviously cataphoric are *below*, *as follows*, and *the following*. Cataphoric *below* contrasts with its antonym, anaphoric *above*:

[14] Nerve injuries have been classified into various grades and these are discussed *below*. [W2A-026-63]

[15] You may find the *above* questions obvious, for which I apologise [. . .] [W1B-030-58]

7.11
Verb and predicate substitution

Do so, *do it*, *do the same*, and the like are often used as substitutes for a verb and (if present) any complements of the verb or adjuncts (adverbials that are not sentence adverbials, cf. 4.27). Since for their interpretation they depend on an antecedent, these substitutes contribute to cohesion.

[1] Perhaps she should stay away from Lesley today? But in her heart of hearts she knew that if she *did so* she would regret it later on. [W2F-003-38] ('stayed away from Lesley today')

[2] A: Don't you ever stick your finger in your ear ⟨ , , ⟩
 B: I don't think I *do it* in company but then I don't pick my nose in traffic jams either [S1A-080-86]

[3] [. . .] I didn't take any photographs ⟨ , , ⟩ I'm so bad at *doing that* [S1A-036-159]

[4] Turning to Miriam, she said, 'Begging your pardon, Miriam. I know Jane's your sister, but there's no denying she scandalised Henwood with her ways.'
 Trying to hide a smile, Miriam said, 'I seem to remember I *did the same* when I was Lottie's age.' [W2F-007-133]

So alone can be a substitute for a clause:

[5] A: Does insurance cover hotels
 B: I think *so* [S1A-021-18]

[6] A: Uhm ⟨ , ⟩ Matt's just left ⟨ , ⟩
 B: For Hertford
 A: Well I presume *so* [S1A-099-97]

[7] A: That's the effect isn't it
 B: I felt *so* [S1B-069-79]

[8] Was this prefix, Mocu-, an indication of status? It would seem *so* [. . .] [W1A-002-24]

[9] Anyhow are you coming to stay? If *so* when? [W1B-005-142]

The negative corresponding to pro-clause *so* is *not*:

[10] A: Is that a position that is likely to ensure ⟨ , ⟩ as I put it in my resignation letter ⟨ , ⟩ that we hold and retain a position of influence in this vital debate ⟨ , , ⟩
 B: I fear *not* [S2B-050-69 f.]

[11] A: I mistook you for a more intelligent kind of man
 B: I'm afraid *not* no [S1A-041-106]

[12] A: Uhm ⟨ , , ⟩ were your first ⟨ , ⟩ sexual relationships anything like you'd expected them to be ⟨ , , ⟩
 B: I guess *not* [S1A-072-167]

[13] A: Its a question of faith
 B: Maybe *not* [S1A-071-255]

7.12
Ellipsis

Ellipsis—the omission of material that can be recovered by the hearer or reader—plays a significant role in grammatical cohesion when the part to be recovered is indicated in the previous text. Sometimes, particularly in responses in conversation, most of the sentence is ellipted:

[1] A: What's that
 B: The jigsaw [S1A-057-11 f.]

[2] A: Who do you think this is really for ⟨ , , ⟩
 B: Well me [S1A-060-189 f.]

[3] A: Well I don't need a man at the moment ⟨ , ⟩
     B: Why [S1A-080-32 f.]

[4] A: Have you noticed they've been bleeding a lot recently
     B: Uhm Yeah they have [S1A-087-198 ff.]

Often all or most of the predicate is ellipted after an operator (cf. 5.18):

[5] A: So how come you've been treated differently
     B: Well I wasn't [S1A-060-8 f.]

[6] A: Didn't John used to deal with uhm ⟨ , , ⟩ divorce in his earlier days
     B: Did he [S1A-061-249 f.]

In this sports report, there is an accumulation of negative auxiliaries, each with a different ellipsis:

[7] A sobering thought for the festive season: if Mike Quinn were to maintain over a full campaign his Coventry scoring rate of 10 goals in six matches, he would finish with a total of 70. That would make him, in statistical terms, the greatest striker ever in the English game.
     He *can't, won't* and *isn't* . . . [*The Independent*, 28 December 1992, p. 19]

To supply the ellipsis, we have to re-read the two sentences of the preceding paragraph: 'He can't maintain over a full campaign his Coventry scoring rate of 10 goals in six matches, he won't finish with a total of 70, and he isn't the greatest striker ever in the English game.'

7.13
Place and time connectives

As might be expected, place and time connectives thread their way through descriptions and narratives. They indicate the locational and temporal relations between situations. First, examples of place connectives:

[1] Forty detectives and uniformed officers [. . .] had been given the task of blocking off each passage way. A firearms unit was also positioned *nearby* along with a dog handling unit. [W2C-011-55]

[2] In the 69th minute Wallace broke clear and raced towards the penalty area [. . .]. Burrows sprinted *across* from the left and brought him down about 25 yards from the goal. [W2C-004-37 f.]

[3] There are bound to be guards at the checkout, whether the alarm is out for us or not. We'll never get *past* looking how we do. [W2F-015-113]

Next, some examples of time connectives:

[4] The leak in the bathroom has been long-standing but earlier this year we accepted assurances that it had been cured. We even redecorated the bathroom. *Soon afterwards* we discovered that nothing in fact had been done to resolve the problem. [W1B-016-112 ff.]

[5] If you receive any interest on overdue tax demands, please forward them to me as I will then take up the matter with the Inspector. *Meanwhile*, I

hope to prepare the accounts and establish the exact liability for
1990/91 shortly. [W1B-023-92 f.]

[6] It was to no avail, but it helped Alice through the first aftermath of the
news. *Until then* Alice had felt paranoid and helpless, wounded by the
thought that someone in authority saw her as a threat. [W2F-009-40 f.]

The place adverbs *here* and *there* and the time adverb *then* often function
as pro-forms for place and time:

[7] In stage 4, the reef has grown most or all the way around the topographic
high to enclose a lagoon. Lime muds may accumulate *here* in this atoll-
like stage. [W2A-023-22]

[8] A: It's just beside the uhm Science Museum
B: You can buy geological maps from *there* [S1B-007-46]

[9] He could see gaps in the timbers that should have protected him and
through them the sea appeared like a monster's icy rolling eye. *Then* the
ship lurched up out of the trough and glistening bright light crashed in
upon him through the bars. [W2F-001-4 f.]

Relations in time are also shown by the maintenance or change in tense or
aspect (cf. 5.20). Here is an example:

[10] In the confident days when the Single European Act was approved, it *was*
possible to think in terms of structuring a European currency around the
Deutschmark. But today the Deutschmark *is* no longer looking such a
solid foundation. [W2E-008-74 f.]

The change from *was* to *is* accompanies the change from *in the confident days*
to *today*.

7.14
Co-ordinators

Sentences may begin with a co-ordinating conjunction that points back to a
previous sentence or set of sentences, as in **[1]** (where the sentences are
numbered for convenience of reference):

[1] (1) Then he could rein in the agencies that share responsibility to curb the
arms trade but do not share an unalloyed interest in doing so. (2) The
Commerce Department wants to expand trade, not regulate it. (3) The
Nuclear Regulatory Commission seeks to promote nuclear power, not just
prevent proliferation. (4) The Defense Department wants to keep arms
from falling into the wrong hands—but not at the expense of having
defense contractors go broke. (5) *And* the State Department's interest in
cultivating good relations with other countries can interfere with denying
them exports. [*International Herald Tribune*, 4 January 1993, p. 6]

And in (5) signals that its sentence is the final one in a set of four, each dealing
with a US government agency that shares responsibility for curbing the arms
trade but also has an interest in encouraging such trade. By setting out the four
points as separate orthographic sentences, the editorial gives greater
prominence to each agency's interest, stacking their individual vested interests

against their shared responsibility. The passage also illustrates the use of parallelism in cohesion: sentences (2)–(4) have similar syntactic structures and (2)–(5) are semantically parallel.

In **[2]** the reservation expressed in the final sentence of this feature article is reinforced by being stated in a separate paragraph. *But* highlights the writer's doubt:

> **[2]** If the Clinton-Gore team can effectively respond to the new global agenda—understanding, explaining and carrying out intelligent policies to meet new changes—it will have demonstrated true leadership.
>   *But* that is a big "if." ['The '90s Leaders Need Bigger Thinking', by Paul Kennedy, *International Herald Tribune*, 4 January 1993, p. 6]

While *but* in **[2]** relates just to a previous sentence (albeit in a previous paragraph), *but* in **[3]** relates to the set of three sentences that begin a book review. *But* marks a fact that is surprising in view of what has been said in the previous three sentences:

> **[3]** Trollope is our most popular and reprinted Victorian novelist. His new companions in the Abbey—Dickens, George Eliot and Hardy—may sell more copies of individual novels, but they cannot match the expansiveness of Trollope's appeal. Forty or more of his works are currently in print—some in as many as five different editions. *But* for a century, Trollopians have complained about the lack of a reliable life of their author. ['Trollopiad', by John Sutherland, *London Review of Books*, 9 January 1992, p. 12]

In **[4]** *or* introduces an alternative to the suggestion made in the previous sentence. The alternative is elaborated in the next sentence, so that *or* initiates a set of two sentences:

> **[4]** Personally, Marje, there is one more thing that bothers me. Since you had such a cracking story on your hands, why didn't you turn it into proper bodice-ripping fiction? *Or*, if that was not good enough, couldn't you have left our illusions intact and simply confessed to your diary? The passionate details could have been released in the future, if some nosy biographer turned up after your death. ['Marjorie Proops and the bodice-ripper scandal', by Margaret Maxwell, *The Independent*, 4 January 1993, p. 5]

7.15
Logical connectives

The co-ordinators in 7.14 point to certain types of connections between sentences or sets of sentences. Various expressions make explicit these and other types of connections, particularly in exposition and argumentation. Some examples of the types are listed below, together with illustrative sentences.

Listing

First(ly), second(ly), third(ly) . . .; first of all, in the second place, for one thing, equally, also, in addition, furthermore, what is more, moreover, above all, finally, lastly, to conclude, last but not least, in conclusion, to sum up

[1] While it sounds intriguing, I have to say no this time around for two reasons. *Firstly*, we simply have no promotional budget left [. . .] *Secondly*, personnel will also be a problem. [W1B-019-34 ff.]

Apposition (including exemplification)

that is to say, namely, for example, for instance

[2] On occasion Frankish rulers intervened directly in Britanny. *For example*, they issued diplomas for Breton monasteries, which conveyed to these Breton communities the same legal status and privileges that many Frankish churches enjoyed. [W1A-003-44 f.]

Result

consequently, so, therefore, as a result, in that case, then

[3] However no one has denied that conditioning has some role in learning. It is *therefore* highly worthy of close examination. [W1A-017-51 f.]

Reformulation

in other words, rather, put differently, alternatively

[4] The plant uses this nitrate to grow. *In other words*, the farmer has a source of 'free' nitrogen. [W2B-027-81 f.]

Contrast

on the contrary, on the other hand, instead

[5] Gowing made further enquiries to try to find out more, but he could not confirm the story. *Instead* he decided to write a novel based upon this incident and using his knowledge of political events in Poland to make his story authentic. [W2B-005-34 f.]

Concession

nevertheless, however, still, yet, in any case, all the same, at any rate, in spite of that

[6] At that time, my speech was good enough to pass muster in public so we had no worries on that score. *Nevertheless*, I had spent months wondering when, where, and how much to reveal to colleagues and the public. [W2B-001-38 f.]

A new topic can be introduced by explicit markers such as:

My next subject is . . .
What I'd like to talk about now is . . .
I'm going to deal first with . . .
I'd like to start by discussing . . .
Let us now turn to . . .
We must now move on to . . .
I've been meaning to tell you that . . .

We can put our main topic on hold while making a digression. Common markers of digression are *incidentally* and *by the way*.

> **[7]** 'We tried all kinds of crazy ideas for putting analogue and digital recordings on the same tape,' says Wirtz, 'but we found we can't do it—yet.' *Incidentally*, although the signal may sound the same after recording and playback, it certainly does not look the same when analysed electronically. [W2B-038-109 f.]

More explicit markers of digression are constructions such as *Before I answer, I'd like to say . . .*

We can return to the main topic by explicit markers such as *To get back to what I was saying . . .* or *As I was saying . . .*

Textual Patterns

7.16
Paragraphs

Let us now examine the conceptual relationships expressed by sentences or sets of sentences within a paragraph. (The sentences in the examples that follow are numbered for convenient reference.) Consider the pair of consecutive paragraphs in the following fictional description.

> **[1]** (1) Housekeeper, cleaner, butt, object of pity and scorn, Elisabet was somewhat younger than her master but even less prepossessing. (2) At least, Kobus hoped he was not deluding himself on that score. (3) She was skinny but big-bottomed; splay-legged; bent forward at the hips and bent upwards at the neck. (4) Denied a bridge to her nose, she had been endowed by way of compensation with exceptionally narrow, deep nostrils. (5) The upward twist of her neck made it all the easier for the onlooker to gaze into these; as well as to take note of the limited yet exaggerated range of expressions which crossed her little face.
>
> (6) There was a scowl of unavailing concentration; her puffed-cheek, closed-eye acknowledgement of pain; her rare grin of pleasure, when both her elongated yellow teeth were revealed; her generalised wrinkling up from chin to forehead, which showed that respect and wonder were going on within. (7) All these expressions were accompanied by more or less identical gasps. (8) She spoke little, and when she did it was difficult to follow her. (9) Her clothes were rags. (10) Her smell was not sweet. [*The God-Fearer*, by Dan Jacobson (London: Bloomsbury, 1992), pp. 7 f.]

The two paragraphs, which begin a new section early in the novel, are united by a shared topic. The topic is introduced in the first sentence—the topic sentence: it is the unattractiveness of Elisabet, who is said to be 'even less prepossessing' than her master Kobus. The second sentence implies that Kobus agrees with the narrator's evaluation. The subsequent sentences in the first paragraph and the whole of the second paragraph elaborate the topic. The writer presents in (3) a general impression of Elisabet, and then in (4)–(6) focuses on details; (5) refers to her 'limited yet exaggerated range of expressions', and these are particularized in (6). The remaining sentences move from a description of her body and facial expressions to the sounds she made (7) and (8); the condition of her clothes (9); and her smell (10). The pair of paragraphs start with a generalization in (1), which is then supported by particularization. On a smaller scale, the same relation of generalization and particularization exists between the second half of (5) and the whole of (6).

The topic sentence is commonly, though not invariably, the first sentence of a paragraph. It is so in **[1]** and again in **[2]**, which conveys a generalization (1) followed by an example in (2)–(4).

[2] (1) At times, those who govern also regard particular circumstances as too uncomfortable, too painful, for most people to be able to cope with rationally. (2) They may believe, for instance, that their country must prepare for long-term challenges of great importance, such as a war, an epidemic, or a belt-tightening in the face of future shortages. (3) Yet they may fear that citizens will be able to respond only to short-range dangers. (4) Deception at such times may seem to the government leaders as the only means of attaining the necessary results. [*Lying: Moral Choice in Public and Private Life*, by Sissela Bok (London: Quartet Books, 1980), p. 168]

In **[3]** it is the second sentence that is the topic sentence:

[3] (1) For the past ten years or so Derrida has been dividing his time between Paris and America, mainly through his visiting professorships at Yale and Johns Hopkins universities. (2) His following among American critics has grown apace, and it is now safe to say that he exerts a greater influence on them than any of his fellow French post-structuralists. (3) This is evident from the sheer volume of critical writing that nowadays bears the deconstructionist imprint, whether openly acknowledged or (more often) betrayed by certain characteristic turns of argument or phrase. (4) Derrida himself has entered with alacrity into the various discussions sparked off by his writing. (5) To disciples and opponents alike he has responded with a number of prolix and mind-wrenching texts designed for translation and wittily exploiting the inherent ambiguities of the medium. (6) In some of these essays the playful inclination—already well developed in his writing on Nietzsche—seems to outrun any content of serious argument. (7) But one needs to exercise a good deal of caution when applying such conventional measures of worth to texts that explicitly put them in question. (8) Perhaps the most radical effect of Derrida's writing has been to transform the very notion of what counts as 'serious' critical thought. [*Deconstruction: Theory and Practice*, by Christopher Norris (London: Methuen, 1982), p. 90]

The first sentence sets the situation in place and time. The topic sentence (2) conveys the extent of Derrida's influence on American critics, for which evidence is provided in (3). In (4)–(8) the writer describes and evaluates Derrida's reponses to the reactions of critics influenced by him.

In **[4]** the first two orthographic sentences might alternatively have been punctuated as one sentence with a colon between the two parts. As a pair they state the topic: the contrast between theorists and experimenters. The topic is restated more succinctly in (3), and then pairs of sentences elaborate the contrast by citing specific details illustrating the differing approaches of theorists and experimenters.

> **[4]** (1) Theorists conduct experiments with their brains. (2) Experimenters have to use their hands, too. (3) Theorists are thinkers, experimenters are craftsmen. (4) The theorist needs no accomplice. (5) The experimenter has to muster graduate students, cajole machinists, flatter lab assistants. (6) The theorist operates in a pristine place free of noise, of vibration, of dirt. (7) The experimenter develops an intimacy with matter as a sculptor does with clay, battling it, shaping it, and engaging it. (8) The theorist invents his companions, as a naïve Romeo imagined his ideal Juliet. (9) The experimenter's lovers sweat, complain, and fart. [*Chaos: Making a New Science*, by James Gleick (Harmondsworth: Penguin, 1988), p. 125]

The narrative paragraph in **[5]** has no topic sentence. The paragraph narrates a series of events in chronological order. Each event or set of events is followed by the contemporary mental reaction of the fictional child narrator—(2), (5), (8)–(9):

> **[5]** (1) We went first into my mother and father's bedroom; someone looked in a cupboard. (2) I thought—What are we searching for: something that has been lost in the uprising of the extremists? (3) My mother went to the end of the passage and knocked on the door of Helga and Magda's room; after a time Magda came out and stood with her back against the door; she put her arms out like a crucifix. (4) Rosa Luxemburg spoke to Magda in her soft purring voice and after a time Magda lowered her arms and put her head on Rosa Luxemburg's shoulder; she seemed to weep.
> (5) I thought—There are illustrations like this in stories about myths.
> (6) Someone opened the door into my bedroom; my mother seemed to protest; the door into my room was closed. (7) Then Rosa Luxemburg left Magda and held her arms out to me. (8) I thought—I am to become part of this odd story? (9) When I was in Rosa Luxemburg's arms she had a strange musty smell like something kept in a sack in an attic. [*Hopeful Monsters*, by Nicholas Mosley (London: Minerva, 1991), p. 9]

The paragraphs cited earlier in this section illustrate different conceptual relationships between sentences or sets of sentences. They are included in the following list of some major relationships.[5]

generalization	refutation
particularization	chronological narration
exemplification	description
supporting with factual evidence	definition
supporting with argumentation	offering solution
restatement	evaluation
elaboration	contrast
qualification	comparison
concession	summarization

Similar analyses apply to units within monologues.

7.17
Conventional textual patterns

Some types of written texts are patterned conventionally. Recipes are strikingly similar in the categories they contain, though the order of categories and the layout may vary in different publications:

container(s)
cooking time(s)
number of servings
ingredients with their measures
instructions, expressed in brief imperative sentences, that follow the sequence of actions

[1]   Corn Bread
MAKES 1 LOAF
[There follows a paragraph mentioning that there are different versions of corn bread, and that this is the author's version. Readers are told where cornmeal, one of the ingredients, is available.]
55g (2 oz) butter, melted
110g (4 oz) cornmeal
55g (2 oz) plain flour
30g (1 oz) caster sugar
1 tablespoon baking powder
A good pinch of bicarbonate of soda
225ml (8 oz) low-fat natural yoghurt
120ml (4 fl.oz) milk
2 eggs, beaten
  Grease a 1.5 litre (2½ pint) loaf tin with a little of the butter.
  Mix all the dry ingredients in one bowl and all the liquid ones in another.
  Quickly, and using as few strokes of a spoon as possible, fold the wet ingredients into the dry. Pour into the greased tin and bake in a preheated oven at 200 ºC/400 ºF, gas mark 6 for 35 minutes or until a skewer comes out dry when pushed into middle of the loaf.
  Allow to cool, then slice. ['The Cooking of America', by Richard Cawley, in *The Sunday Times Cook's Companion*, ed. Shona Crawford Poole and Richard Girling (London: Ebury Press, 1993), p. 173]

There are numerous written text types that are like recipes in having a highly conventionalized format. Among them are the main text of dictionaries and telephone directories; notices of births, engagements, marriages, and deaths; personal classified advertisements; listings for films, plays, and radio and television programmes; knitting instructions; descriptions of chess games; income tax forms.

Other conventional forms have somewhat looser structures. Articles in learned journals reporting experimental research have sections on hypotheses, methodology, description of experiment, discussion of results, conclusions, and they end with a list of references; the articles may be preceded by an abstract and include additional sections on previous work and suggestions for future research. Such journal articles are seen as subtypes conforming to a more general Problem–Solution pattern, which may also be extended to include the context in which the problem is situated and an evaluation of the solution.

News reports in newspapers have a conventional structure.[6] They begin with a headline or set of headlines printed in large bold type. The report proper begins with the lead, a sentence or paragraph introducing and summarizing the news. Other categories deal with the main event or events, the background of the events in the present situation and in past events, an evaluation of the events and an evaluation of the consequences; any of these categories may include attributions to sources and quotations from people on their reactions. Some categories are optional and are likely to be omitted in short news reports. The categories are partially illustrated in the following news report.

[2] Iraqi raid into Kuwait
     LONDON (Reuter)—Two hundred Iraqis crossed the Kuwaiti border in heavy transport vehicles early yesterday and seized armaments, including surface-to-surface missiles, from trenches before returning to Iraq, a local United Nations spokesman said.
       The raid came as Iraq prohibited an aircraft chartered by UN weapons inspectors from landing in Baghdad.
       The spokesman, Abdellatif Kabbaj, said the Iraqi raiders ignored protests by UN observers at the Umm Qasr border post, according to Kuna, the Kuwaiti news agency, monitored by the BBC. The trenches are guarded by the observers 24 hours a day in accordance with a UN Security Council resolution passed last November.
       "Kabbaj pointed out that the Iraqis had been able, in 90 minutes, to transport the contents of the [arms] depots to their vehicles and returned to Iraq," the agency said.
       The aim of the operation appeared to be the retrieval of Iraqi arms left behind after the Gulf war. An Iraqi vehicle crashed into a UN vehicle during the operation, but there were no casualties. [*The Independent*, 11 January 1993, p. 1]

The headline summarizes the report, which is further summarized—but in sentence form and at greater length—in the lead sentence. The lead conveys some of the kinds of information that are prescribed in journalism textbooks: who did it, what they did, where they did it, and when they did it.

The other news categories do not appear in sequential order. The second paragraph gives the current background to the main event: a simultaneous event in which Iraq also engaged in an act that contravened a decision of the UN. The third paragraph provides a detail on the main event (the Iraqis ignore protests by the UN observers) and then gives further background information, a reference to the current situation (the trenches are continuously guarded) intertwined with a reference to a past event (the Security Council resolution). In the next paragraph another detail is presented on the main event (the speed with which it happened), for which the news agency reporting it is quoted. The final paragraph comments on the event by suggesting a reason for the Iraqi action (the retrieval of Iraqi arms left behind after the Gulf War) and implies an evaluation of the only immediate consequences of the event (a car crash, but without casualties).

One notable feature of this news item is the care taken to attribute the information to various sources: the UN spokesman is quoted by the Kuwaiti news agency, which is monitored by the BBC. The item as a whole is based on a report from Reuter in London. The explanatory addition of *arms* to *depots* in the agency quotation is indicated as an editorial insertion by its enclosure in square brackets.

7.18
Speech acts

One way of looking at the uses of sentences and their interrelations is through speech act theory, which is most easily explained with illustrations from conversations (cf. 3.10).[7]

Here are examples of various speech acts performed by uttering declarative sentences:

[1] You should take an aspirin. (advice)

[2] I'm going to give you a bicycle for your birthday. (promise)

[3] It's going to rain. (prediction)

[4] You mustn't smoke in here. (prohibition)

[5] You may take another one. (permission)

The communicative force of the utterance depends on the particular context and the intention of the speaker. *Alice will be at my party* may be intended as a promise, an order for an immediate action, or general advice to be implemented whenever the situation arises. The hearer may of course misinterpret the intention of the speaker.

Finally, various functions may be realized by utterances that do not have the form of clauses (cf. 6.1). *No smoking* is a prohibition, *Hands up!* a command, *Taxi!* a request, *The Police!* a warning, *Hello* a greeting, *Out* may be a command or an umpire's declaration, *Congratulations* is itself a congratulation.

The performance of an utterance in a particular context with a particular intention is a speech act and the intention is its illocutionary force. Verbs—such as *apologize, warn,* and *advise*—explicitly denoting the illocutionary force are performative verbs. They normally convey the corresponding speech acts when they are used in the present tense in declarative sentences with *I* or *we* as subject of these verbs. The possible insertion of *hereby* is an indication that the utterance has the associated illocutionary force, though *hereby* is restricted to highly formal contexts. Thus, **[1]**–**[5]** might be prefaced by performative verbs:

[1a] I *advise* you to take an aspirin.

[2a] I *promise* you that I will give you a bicycle for your birthday.

[3a] I *predict* that it will rain.

[4a] I *forbid* you to smoke in here.

[5a] I *permit* you to take another one.

In saying **[2a]**, for example, I am making a promise and in saying **[3a]** I am making a prediction. The performative verbs may have the same illocutionary force when used in the passive:

[1b] You are *advised* to take an aspirin.

[4b] It is *forbidden* to smoke in here.

Past and perfect forms, however, are used in reports of the speech acts denoted by the performative verbs, so that as speech acts **[1c]** and **[4c]** have the status of reports:

[1c] I *advised* him to take an aspirin.

[4c] I *have forbidden* them to smoke in here.

Some performative verbs are conventionally used for the speech acts they denote:

[6] I hereby *adjourn* the meeting.

[7] I *name* this ship the Northern Star.

[8] I *bet* you ten dollars that I will get the job.

[9] I *declare* the winner to be Alison White.

In hedged performatives, uttering the sentence indirectly conveys the speech act denoted by the performative verb. For example, **[10]** refers to the obligation to congratulate, but the implication is that by uttering the sentence the speaker accepts the obligation to perform the speech act and the acceptance is the equivalent of performing it.

[10] I *must congratulate* you on passing the examination with honours.

Here are some further examples of hedged performatives:

[11] I *would like to apologize* for my lateness.

[12] *May I thank* you for your generous gift?

[13] I *have the honour of presenting* my niece.

[14] I *am happy to acknowledge* my debt to you for your constant advice.

[15] *It is a pleasure to welcome* you all to this historic meeting.

[16] I *regret to inform* you that you have been suspended from membership of the society.

[17] I *should like to tell* you all how grateful I am for being invited to participate in this inaugural meeting.

Except for the conventional uses exemplified in **[6]–[9]**, it is normal to perform speech acts (advise, warn, predict, etc.) without the use of performative verbs. Communicative functions are commonly conveyed indirectly. For example, the request to turn out the light might be made directly through the use of the imperative or the performative verb *request*:

[18] Turn out the light.

[19] I request you to turn out the light.

Utterance **[18]** is rather harsh for a request, though it could be softened by the addition of a tag question: *Turn out the light, will you?* or by the addition of *please*: *Turn out the light, please.* On the other hand, **[19]** is highly formal. However, there are numerous indirect ways of making the same request, for example:

[18a] Would you mind turning out the light?

[18b] Could you turn out the light?

[18c] should like you to turn out the light.

[18d] wonder whether you would be good enough to turn out the light.

[18e] Hadn't you better turn out the light?

[18f] How about turning out the light?

[18g] Have you forgotten to turn out the light?

[18h] What should you do when you leave the room?

Here are some further examples of possible indirect speech acts.

[20] Why don't you look at the brake lining? (advice)

[21] Do you have a match? (request for a match)

[22] It's getting cold in here. (request to close a window or to turn on a heater)

[23] There's a wild dog in the neighbourhood. (warning)

[24] It's stopped raining. (suggestion to go out)

Indirect speech acts tend to be more tactful ('saving face') or more polite than the corresponding direct speech acts. The question form of the request in **[21]** allows the hearer to reply *Yes* or *No*, as with questions that genuinely seek such responses. The hearer is asked whether he has a match, but the implication is that if he has one the speaker wants it. The indirect request is politer than a direct request since it gives the listener the opportunity of refusing indirectly by replying that he does not have a match (whether or not that is true). Politeness is similarly a motivation for the indirect formulation of the request in **[22]**, since it leaves it to the listener to infer the need to close a window or turn on a heater.

Here is a list of some common paired exchanges in conversation.[8]

greeting—greeting
farewell—farewell
request for *yes–no* information—*yes/no*
request for missing information—information supplied
request for action—accepted/rejected
request for permission—granted/refused
suggestion—accepted/rejected
offer/invitation—accepted/rejected
explanation—accepted/rejected
complaint—apology/excuse/rebuff
compliment—thanks
assertion—agreement/disagreement

In all instances there may be qualification in the response or amplification beyond what is required by the initial utterance. The second speaker may also evade responding directly.

Backchannels (or hearer signals) are common acknowledgements that the listener is following what is being said (cf. 6.1). They may also express agreement or diagreement. Here are some examples:

m, uhuh, yes, no, I see, right, OK, of course, exactly

The speaker may encourage the listener to continue listening by insertions such as *you see* and *you know*.

Some exchanges are fairly stereotyped: greetings, farewells, introductions, enquiries about health, openings of telephone conversations. There are also less restricted conventional formats in dialogue discourses as diverse as liturgies, legal cross-examinations, and panel games.

7.19
Implications

Implications are conventional in indirect speech acts (cf. 7.18). For example, the implication is that you are asking to be told the time when you ask someone *Can you tell me the time?*, and when you say *Do you know where the nearest post office is?* your expectation is that the hearer will understand that you want to know where it is. Literally, the questions are merely whether the hearer is able to tell the time and whether the hearer knows where the nearest post office is.

Agreement or disagreement is often implied. The suggestion in **[1]** may be followed by **[2]** or **[3]**:

[1]   Let's go to a movie.

[2]   Let me first phone my sister.

[3]   I'm afraid I have to hand in a paper tomorrow.

The implication in **[2]** is that the suggestion is accepted. ('OK, but I have something to do first'), whereas the implication in **[3]** is that it is rejected ('No, I don't have the time').

Here is a more complicated fictional example, set in South Africa (*A Sport of Nature*, by Nadine Gordimer, London: Jonathan Cape, 1987, p. 79). Olga and her husband Arthur are contemplating leaving the country. A guest from Italy ('the butterfly lady') recommends that they buy a place in Italy: 'a little pied-à-terre'. Olga replies:

[4]   The way things are going, it might have to be more than that!

The narrator comments:

[5]   Olga laughed when she said it, and the butterfly lady did not pause to take in the inference . . .

The inference that 'the butterfly lady' missed was that Olga and Arthur were contemplating moving their main residence abroad, so that they would need more than 'a little pied-à-terre'.

In **[6]** it is asserted in the first sentence that Brenda Clubine felt encouraged. The implication is that the subsequent sentences give the reason for her feeling encouraged.

> **[6]** When she arrived in California's prison for women in Frontera in 1983, convicted of killing her husband by hitting him with a bottle and stabbing him with a kitchen knife, Brenda Clubine felt encouraged. A surprising number of her fellow-prisoners had similar stories to tell. They had killed their husbands or lovers after enduring years of beatings, torment and humiliation. [. . .] Although the state had convicted most of them of first- or second-degree murder, they thought of themselves as victims. [*The Economist*, 16 January 1993, pp. 48 f.]

A listener may make the wrong inference, misinterpreting a previous speaker's implication, as in **[7]**:

> **[7]** 'And there's no door on the lavatory,' continued the good Earl. Silence. 'No door on the toilet?' gasped one of the models. 'Well, how do you get in then?' ['Nothing but the best', by Sue Arnold, *The Observer*, 27 December 1992, p. 12]

The first speaker intends his statement to be understood as reporting that the opening could not be closed off because a door was missing, perhaps originally there but subsequently removed. The model absurdly misunderstood him as reporting the absence of an opening.

Chapter 8
Words and their Meanings

Summary

Reference books on words (8.20)

Meaning (8.21)

Chapter 8 Summary

- Though the term *word* is an everyday word in English, there are problems in giving it a precise definition.

- More than half of the English words in common use today derive from the Old English period (450–1150). Other major sources of English vocabulary are words from Scandinavian, French, Latin, and Greek. Latin and Greek continue to provide elements from which new words are formed.

- Words acquire new meanings because of changes in society, the desire for euphemism, the need to express intensification, the abbreviation of a longer expression, and the adoption of specialized terms into the general language.

- Words shift in meaning when they become generalized or specialized, or acquire pejorative or ameliorative connotations, or are extended through metaphor or metonymy.

- Words may be semantically related as synonyms, which can be used interchangeably in at least some contexts; as antonyms, which may be contraries (allowing intermediate terms), contradictions (excluding intermediate terms), or converses (involving reciprocal relationships); through hyponymy, whereby a superordinate term covers its hyponyms (more specific terms); through a part–whole relationship, such as holds between *ceiling* or *floor* and *room*.

- Combinations may be free or idiomatic. Intermediate are collocations, words that tend to co-occur.

- Homonyms are distinct words that happen to have the same form. Homophones are homonyms that are pronounced the same but are spelled differently. Homographs are spelled the same but are pronounced differently. Homomorphs have the same form and are related in meaning but are different grammatically.

- Polysemes are words that differ in meaning but the meanings are felt to be related.

- The average number of words known by an educated adult has been estimated as at least 50,000 and perhaps as high as 250,000. Estimates depend on whether polysemes, grammatical forms of words, and compounds are counted separately.

- The vocabulary is said to consist of content words (comprising those in the open classes of nouns, full verbs, adjectives, and adverbs) and grammatical words (those in the closed classes).

- Dictionaries may be arranged alphabetically or semantically. General alphabetic dictionaries usually offer information on spelling, pronunciation, inflections, parts of speech, definitions, usage labels, and etymology. They are increasingly offering encyclopedic information.

■ The sense of a word is its cognitive meaning as determined by its place within the semantic system of the language. Its denotation is its relationship to entities, situations, and attributes that exist outside language. Its connotation is the emotive associations that it invokes. Reference is what a word—more commonly a phrase—refers to in a particular utterance.

Defining the Word

8.1
Words as units

Of all the linguistic terms in everyday English, *word* is one of the most frequently used.[1] We talk about the meaning of words, their spelling, their pronunciation; whether they are short or long, easy or difficult; what is the correct word or a better word for something. We may object to some words as dirty or offensive.

We have a perception of words as basic units of our language. Yet there are problems in giving a precise definition of the term *word*. In linguistic descriptions the morpheme is generally viewed as the basic unit for vocabulary and grammar rather than the word (cf. 9.36 f.).

In written English, words can be easily recognized. The orthographic word is isolated on either side by a space or a combination of a space and one or more punctuation marks. But, as we will soon see, there is some variability in writing and some arbitrary divisions into words. In the spoken language, words are not differentiated in the flow of speech sounds.

Several criteria have been proposed for identifying words:

1. In speech we can pause between words, perhaps inserting vocal pauses such as *uh*:

[1] Your—uh—dog—uh—is—uh—trampling—uh—on—uh—my—uh—flower-bed.

This is an exaggerated though possible instance of interruption by pauses. However, it would be odd to pause between parts of a word: between *trampl-* and *-ing* or between *flower-* and *-bed*. In **[2]**, extracted from a conversation, the verb *have* is isolated by pauses on either side:

[2] You uh ⟨ , , ⟩ have ⟨ , ⟩ ideas and it's not just for actual articles ⟨ , ⟩ uh ⟨ , ⟩ and you submit them to uh ⟨ , , ⟩ to magazines [S1A-066-171]

2. A word can occur in isolation as a response utterance:

[3] A: Who needs more of these
B: Potatoes [S1A-012-91 f.]

[4] A: Would she be free to do it today ⟨ , ⟩
B: No [S1A-017-41 f.]

[5] A: I just loved him dearly
B: Really [S1A-085-217 f.]

Not all words can function as utterances. Conspicuous exceptions are the articles *a* and *the*. They can serve as utterances in metalinguistic contexts only, when questions are being asked about the language:

[6] A: What is the definite article in English?
B: *The.*

3. A word has internal stability in that another word cannot be inserted within it. Occasionally, an expletive is exceptionally inserted within a polysyllabic word, for example, *bloody* in *abso-bloody-lutely*.

4. A word can be separated from words before and after it by being moved elsewhere in the sentence. *Find out* ('discover') is semantically a unit, but the two words are separable:

[7]   I just don't *find out* anything until it's happened or all signed and sealed
[S1A-082-17]

[7a]   I just don't *find* anything *out* until it's happened.

5. Inflections (cf. 9.35) are attached to the end of a word. In the expression *find out*, the inflections are attached to *find*: *finds*, *finding*. A few compound nouns, however, may take the plural inflection on the first segment, either only (*notaries public*) or as an alternative (*mothers-in-law/mother-in-laws*), cf. 4.7.

Certain problems remain. A compound is a word composed of other words, but there is not a sharp distinction between compounds and freely formed phrases (cf. 9.24). In writing, compounds may appear as two orthographic words (*hay fever*, *lager lout*) or vary in their orthography (*ice cream/ice-cream*, *for ever/forever*). We make useful distinctions between *all ready* and *already*, between *all ways* and *always*, and between *all together* and *altogether*; but *all right* has to serve also as a compound in formal writing, since the spelling *alright* ('ok') has not acquired full respectability: *Your answers were all right* is ambiguous between 'All your answers were correct' and 'Your answers were satisfactory'. Other arbitrary orthographic practices are highlighted in the pairs *no one/nobody*, *any time/sometime*, *in fact/indeed*. It is not surprising that some of these orthographically separate words are mistakenly run together, as are expressions such as *a lot* and *of course*.

There are also instances where two words are combined without forming a compound in the usual sense. The negative word *not* and a relatively small number of frequently occurring words (mostly verbs) can be contracted and attached to other words. Usually they are attached at the end as enclitics: *she's* (for *she is* or *she has*), *don't* (*do not*). Occasionally they are proclitics: *d'you* (*do you*), *'tis* (*it is*). The combination of both types of clitics appears in *'tisn't*. Although they are not isolated orthographically or in other respects, we can regard these clitics as reduced forms of words.

A different analytic problem arises with the group genitive (cf. 4.10):

the Queen of England's grandchildren
Tom and Paula's wedding

The genitive—represented by the apostrophe plus *s*—is attached to the last noun of the group, but it applies to the whole group: they are the grandchildren of the Queen of England, not England's grandchildren. Some grammarians have therefore argued that the group genitive is more like a word than an inflection.

What may be a word in one language may be an affix in another. There are languages (such as Hebrew) that have affixes corresponding to the English definite article *the* and certain conjunctions and prepositions.

Origins of Words

**8.2
Where English
words come
from**

In general, the relationship between words and their meanings is arbitrary and conventional. There is nothing in the sound of the English word *pig* to indicate the animal or in the sounds of *little* and *big* that would enable someone ignorant of English to assign the words to their correct meanings in English.[2]

It is normal for concepts to be expressed by different words in different languages. Where the same word or a very similar-sounding word appears in two languages, it is reasonable to assume one of three possibilities: (1) The word existed in the common language from which the two developed; English *father* and German *vater* descend from a common ancestor in Germanic; (2) One language borrowed the word from the other; *restaurant* is a loanword from French, borrowed in the nineteenth century; (3) The similarity is coincidental; there is no reason to relate *Britain* and *British* to the Hebrew word /brɪt/ ('covenant'), whereas *cider* and Hebrew /ʃexɑ:r/ ('strong drink') are ultimately related despite differences in sound, since *cider* is a Semitic word that entered English as a loanword from French after passing through Greek and Latin.

The contribution of onomatopoeia to the vocabulary of any language has been severely marginal. Onomatopoeia is a type of sound symbolism (or phonaesthesia, cf. 9.34) that associates the sound of a word with its meaning. We can recognize the imitation of sounds in words such as *boom, bubble, crack, ping-pong, pop, slap, tinkle.* The imitations in sounds are suggestive and not universal. Onomatopoeic words tend to be language-specific: cocks crow *cock-a-doodle-doo* in English, but *kikeriki* in German and /ɔ:ɔ:ɔ:/ in Chinese; a pistol goes *bang* in English but *v'lan* in French; the bell sounds *ding-dong* in English but *talan-talan* in Spanish. English people *giggle, titter,* or *chuckle,* whereas Japanese people *kusu-kusu.*

The original English word-stock comes from the Germanic language that the Anglo-Saxon invaders brought with them when they colonized Britain. It has been estimated that about 85 per cent of the words that are known to us from the Old English period have not been preserved in the English of today. These losses have been more than compensated for by the tens of thousands of loanwords adopted from other languages, in particular from French, Latin, and Greek.[3]

The most extensive way in which the English vocabulary has been augmented is through natural growth. New words have been created from old words by combining words or parts of words that are already in the language, including established loanwords. *Driveway* combines the words *drive* and *way*; *superstructure* the prefix *super-* with the word *structure*; *mortgagee* the suffix *-ee* with the word *mortgage*. Word-formation is the topic of Chapter 9.

Our vocabulary has also increased substantially through the addition of new meanings for old words and expressions. *Mouse* is used metaphorically for a computer device; *minder* has acquired a specialized sense for an adviser to politicians to protect them from making embarrassing mistakes. New meanings may also arise from translations of foreign expressions. A recent conspicuous example is *green*, 'concerned with the conservation of the environment', a translation from the German *grün*, which had acquired that ecological meaning in German. Recent loan translations into British English from French (as a result of legislation and regulations of the European Union) include *cohabitation*, 'sharing political power', and *subsidiarity*, 'allocation of powers to lower levels of government as far as possible'. Semantic change is treated later in this chapter.

8.3
Words from the Old English period

It has been estimated that more than half the words in common use today derive from the Old English period (450–1150). Among them are many that are classed as grammatical words (cf. 8.19): pronouns (e.g. *I, he, you*), conjunctions (*and, if, that*), auxiliary verbs (*can, may, will*), prepositions (*at, for, of, to*), and the negative word *not*. Below is a selection of other common words:

kinship nouns:	brother, child, daughter, father, mother, son, wife
other nouns:	book, day, food, house, light, man, meat, night, water, word, work
verbs:	be, drink, drive, eat, have, help, know, live, see, sit, sleep, stand, write
adjectives:	cool, full, good, long, old, slow, strong, young

The vocabulary that the Anglo-Saxon invaders brought with them was almost purely Germanic, but it contained at least fifty Latin loanwords found in other Germanic languages that were absorbed during the contacts between Germans and Romans before the invasion of Britain. Among those loanwords that have survived in present-day English are:

butter, cheese, dish, kitchen, mile, pound, street, wall, wine

Additional loanwords were adopted after the invasion, particularly after the introduction of Christianity into England at the end of the sixth century and its gradual spread throughout the country during the seventh century.

Many of the loanwords concerned the church and education. Among those that have survived are:

altar, candle, disciple, history, master, noon, paper, verse

Latin loanwords from other spheres include:

anchor, cap, cook, cucumber, fan, fever, fork, pear

It has been estimated that just over 500 Latin loanwords were present in Old English. Most have dropped out of the English vocabulary; others were lost and borrowed again at a later date, for example *sign*, reborrowed via French.

The conquered Celts left few traces on the English language apart from place-names or segments in place-names. Among the place-names derived from Celtic are *Cornwall, Devon, Dover, Kent, London, Thames, York.* Also from Celtic is the first segment in *Doncaster, Exeter, Gloucester, Lancaster, Winchester.* The second segment in these names comes from the Latin *castra* ('camp') and is likely to have been present in the Celtic names. Relatively few Celtic words were borrowed in later centuries. The most common are *clan, slogan,* and *whiskey* (or *whisky*) from Scotland; *galore, shamrock,* and *Tory* from Ireland; and *crag* from Wales.

The vocabulary of the Old English period that has survived contains many of the most frequently used words in present-day English. Frequency data can be obtained from three corpora (collections of language material), each containing one million words, that have been compiled in recent times: the Brown Corpus of written American English; the LOB (Lancaster-Oslo/Bergen) Corpus of written British English; and ICE-GB, the British corpus of the International Corpus of English. Table 8.3.1 sets out the frequency rankings of the fifty most frequent words in Brown, LOB, and ICE-GB.[4]

Only two of the words on the lists for Brown and LOB, the corpora of printed material, are not found in Old English texts: the Scandinavian loanwords *they* and *their*, which make their first appearance in texts in the early Middle English period. The ICE-GB list also contains two representations of sounds that occur very frequently in the spoken language: *uh* and *uhm* (sometimes transcribed *er* and *erm* in British English), which may fill a hesitation gap or be used as a backchannel (cf. 6.1). Almost all the items on the three lists are grammatical words (cf. 8.19). A few others—*uh, uhm,* and *well*—are used mainly as discourse signals for interaction with others or in the organization of speech. An apparent exception is *know*, but it owes its prominence in ICE-GB to its high frequency in the discourse signal *you know*, which occurs 1,318 times out of the total frequency of 2,796 for *know*. The twelfth on the list—*'s*—excludes the genitive; it comprises enclitics representing contractions of *is*, *has*, and *us* (in *let's*).

Table 8.3.1 Brown, LOB, and ICE-GB rankings of the fifty most frequent words in present-day English

Brown		LOB		ICE-GB	
1. the	26. from	1. the	26. have	1. the	26. uhm
2. of	27. or	2. of	27. are	2. of	27. at
3. and	28. have	3. and	28. which	3. and	28. we
4. to	29. an	4. to	29. her	4. to	29. not
5. a	30. they	5. a	30. she	5. a	30. there
6. in	31. which	6. in	31. or	6. in	31. so
7. that	32. one	7. that	32. you	7. I	32. or
8. is	33. you	8. is	33. they	8. that	33. by
9. was	34. were	9. was	34. an	9. it	34. which
10. he	35. her	10. it	35. were	10. you	35. from
11. for	36. all	11. for	36. there	11. is	36. what
12. it	37. she	12. he	37. been	12. 's	37. one
13. with	38. there	13. as	38. one	13. for	38. if
14. as	39. would	14. with	39. all	14. was	39 well
15. his	40. their	15. be	40. we	15. on	40. all
16. on	41. we	16. on	41. their	16. be	41. no
17. be	42. him	17. I	42. has	17. uh	42. an
18. at	43. been	18. his	43. would	18. as	43. do
19. by	44. has	19. at	44. when	19. this	44. had
20. I	45. when	20. by	45. if	20. but	45. has
21. this	46. who	21. had	46. so	21. have	46. can
22. had	47. will	22. this	47. no	22. with	47. about
23. not	48. more	23. not	48. will	23. he	48. would
24. are	49. no	24. but	49. him	24. are	49. been
25. but	50. if	25. from	50. who	25. they	50. know

8.4
Words from Scandinavian

Scandinavian settlement in England began in the middle of the ninth century, but was soon confined to the Danelaw, territory to the east of a line running from London to Chester. It is therefore in the north and east of the country that Scandinavian influence was greatest, and is still present in local dialects and place-names. Examples of dialect terms derived from Scandinavian that are absent from the standard language are:

bairn ('child')	lait ('look for')
ket ('rubbish')	lop ('flea')
kirk ('church')	lug ('ear')
kirn ('churn')	speel *or* spoal ('splinter')
laik *or* lake ('play')	stee ('ladder')

Common Scandinavian segments in English place-names are *thorp* ('settlement' or 'farm'), *by* ('village' or 'farm'), *thwaite* ('clearing'), and *toft* ('plot of ground'). Examples of names with these segments are:

Althorp, Bishopsthorpe, Northorpe, Thorpe
Derby, Grimsby, Ormesby, Rugby, Stokesby

Birthwaite, Easthwaite, Falthwaite, Thwaite
Bratoft, Eastoft, Lowestoft, Moortoft, Toft

The English and Scandinavian languages belong to the Germanic family. Many words that the Scandinavian settlers spoke were identical to, or closely resembled, their English cognates. Most of the Scandinavian loanwords make their first appearance in Middle English writings since virtually all extant writings from the earlier period emanate from outside the Danelaw, but they were probably in widespread use well before 1150.

For over two centuries many of the Scandinavian settlers were probably bilingual in Scandinavian and English. Their use of Scandinavian was reinforced by trade and further invasions by Scandinavian settlers. For a period of twenty-five years in the early eleventh century the whole of England was ruled by Danish kings. It is not surprising that some common words in English are the result of Scandinavian influence. Among them are the highly frequent words *law* and *wrong*, both of which make their first appearance in writings before the Norman Conquest.

Sometimes the Scandinavian form ousted an English cognate: *begin, egg, get, give, kettle, sister*. In other instances, semantic contamination occurred, so that an English word acquired the Scandinavian meaning: *bread* (Old English 'fragment'), *dream* (Old English 'joy'). Some Scandinavian words replaced unrelated English words: *anger, cut, knife, sky, take, window*. Still others coexist with their English counterparts, but usually differ in use: Scandinavian loanwords *dike, ill, scrub, skin, skirt* and English words *ditch, sick, shrub, hide, shirt*. The initial /sk/ in *scrub, skin, skirt, sky* is characteristic of words deriving from Scandinavian; among other loanwords with the same initial sounds are *scab, scant, scare, scorch, scowl, skill*.

The most important Scandinavian loanwords are the third person plural pronouns *they, them, their*; the plural Scandinavian *th-* forms were presumably felt to be more distinctive than the Old English *h-* forms, which might be confused with the singular pronouns in Old English; the Old English accusative forms, for example, were *hine* ('him'), *hīe* or *hēo* ('her'), *hit* ('it'), *hīe* or *hēo* ('them'). Other grammatical words adopted from Scandinavian include *both, same,* and *though*. Perhaps also indebted to Scandinavian influence was the spread of Northern *are*, replacing the plural *sindon* or *syndon* that was dominant in Old English writings.

Relatively few Scandinavian words have been adopted since the Middle English period. They include *fjord* (or *fiord*), *geyser, rug, saga, ski*. The most recent well-known importations are *smorgasbord* and *ombudsman*.

8.5
Words from French

Although a few French words were borrowed earlier, the vast majority of French loanwords entered English after the Norman Conquest of 1066. A new ruling class was then established whose native language was Norman French. French became a prestige language, used as an alternative to Latin in education, administration, and law. Until 1250 relatively few French words entered English; one estimate is merely 900 words. As the ruling class turned away from the sole use of French to become bilingual, they introduced into English a flood of French words. Over 10,000 French words were adopted during the Middle English period, most of them between 1250 and 1400, the period when French had to be learned rather than acquired as a native language. French loanwords came from two French dialects: Anglo-Norman (the dialect of Norman French that developed in England) and Central French (the French of Paris, which later became standard French). In some instances English has acquired doublets, one form from Anglo-Norman and the other from Central French. From Anglo-Norman are derived *cattle* and *warranty*, and from Central French the corresponding words *chattel* and *guarantee*.

The loanwords from French reflect the interests of the ruling class in administration, law, war, religion, fashion, food, trade, and cultural pursuits. Here are examples of loanwords in these spheres that have survived to the present day:

administration, allegiance, parliament, public, revenue, tax
acquit, court, crime, defendant, judge, jury, justice, pardon, sue, summon
army, enemy, guard, officer, peace, soldier, war
clergy, faith, prayer, religion, sermon, service
coat, costume, dress, fashion, frock, jewel, lace
boil, dinner, feast, fry, roast, supper, toast
bargain, butcher, customer, grocer, money, price, value
art, college, music, poet, prose, story, study

The names for some kinds of meat served at the table derive from French: *beef, bacon, mutton, pork, veal, venison*; the names of animals are retained from Old English: *bull, cow, deer, sheep, swine.*

Words have been borrowed from French since the Middle Ages but to a much lesser extent. Those adopted during the sixteenth century and the first half of the seventeenth century reflected the frequent travel in France by the wealthy and educated and their reading of French books: *bigot, detail, duel, essay, invite, invoice, prelude, ticket, vogue.* Later French loans tend to reveal their foreign origin in their spelling or pronunciation: *amateur, ballet, boulevard, bureau, café* or *cafe, cigarette, connoisseur, encore, entrepreneur, fiancé, massage, reservoir, restaurant, souvenir.* Recent borrowings include *aromatherapy* (though it could equally have been compounded from English words), *bustier* ('close-fitting bodice'), *fromage frais* ('low-fat dairy dessert').

8.6
Words from Latin and Greek

Some Latin loanwords were present in Old English (cf. 8.3). The influx of French during the Middle English period (cf. 8.5) introduced a multitude of words that ultimately derived from Latin. Hundreds of Latin words were also borrowed directly from Latin in the Middle English period, though it is often impossible to tell whether a particular Latin word (for example, *consist*, *explore*, *modest*) entered English directly or via French. The Latin borrowings were largely legal, religious, or scholarly terms. Among them are:

> admit, client, conviction, custody, discuss, equal, index, infinite, intellect, library, medicine, minor, opaque, prosecute, pulpit, scribe, scripture, simile, testimony

In the fifteenth century it became customary for writers—in particular poets—to introduce Latin loanwords as a decorative device. Some of these aureate terms have survived, such as *mediation* and *prolixity*.

The major introduction of words from Latin occurred during the Renaissance (1500–1650). Some 10,000 new loanwords entered English during that period, most of them directly from Latin. The Latin borrowings were intended to augment English vocabulary for scholarly discourse. Their absorption eased the transition from Latin to English for that purpose. Most of those that have survived are part of the general vocabulary. Among the numerous Latin loanwords are:

> adapt, appropriate, benefit, climax, compensate, confident, consult, digress, editor, exist, expectation, fact, fictitious, frequency, habitual, imitate, immature, instruct, investigate, invitation, offensive, quote, relapse, series, sporadic, susceptible, urge, vindicate

Most Greek words entered English via Latin or French:

> aristocracy, atmosphere, autograph, chaos, comedy, crisis, critic, dogma, drama, enthusiasm, harmony, machine, parenthesis, rhythm, system, theory

Some words came directly from Greek:

> acme, bathos, catastrophe, cosmos, criterion, idiosyncrasy, kudos, misanthrope, pathos, pylon, therm

The massive borrowing of words from foreign languages, particularly Latin, during the Renaissance provoked controversy. Some writers objected to the loanwords because of their obscurity. The inkhorn terms, as they were called, were ridiculed as pedantic. Instead of borrowing from other languages, purists advocated giving existing English words new meanings or forming new words from existing English words. Some also proposed reviving obsolete English words or drawing on words in regional dialects. In the course of time many of the ridiculed words have ceased to seem strange:

alien, concede, conscious, contaminate, defunct, idiom, ingenuity, integrated, negotiation, notoriety, segregated, strenuous, timid

Latin and Greek continue to be active in English in providing the segments from which new English words are formed, words that did not exist in the original languages:[5]

acupuncture, aerobics, agnostic, biorhythm, condominium, dinosaur, homophobia, macrobiotics, neurotic, retrovirus, telepathy

Classical elements have proved particularly valuable for forming innumerable scientific and medical terms. A number of classical prefixes and suffixes are commonly used in creating new words (cf. 9.6–22); for example:

anti-, de-, dis-, post-, pre-, pro-, re-
-al, -ant, -ial, -ic

Numerous Latin phrases are preserved in English, some of them particularly or exclusively in legal or medical usage.[6] In print it is usual to italicize most of the phrases, and in writing to underline them. Here is a selection of Latin phrases in common use among well-educated speakers of English:

ab initio	in memoriam	per se
ad hoc	in vitro	persona non grata
ad infinitum	ipso facto	post mortem
alma mater	magnum opus	prima facie
a priori	memento mori	pro forma
bona fide	modus operandi	pro rata
compos mentis	modus vivendi	quid pro quo
de facto	mutatis mutandis	sub judice
de jure	non sequitur	sui generis
ex officio	per annum	ultra vires
habeas corpus	per capita	vice versa
in camera	per cent (*or* percent)	
in loco parentis	per diem	

The three levels of distinctions in American university degrees are denoted by the Latin phrases *cum laude, magna cum laude, summa cum laude*. It is still customary for institutions to employ Latin for their mottoes.

Some abbreviations stand for Latin words or phrases; in most cases their full forms may be unknown to many users. Here are some common examples, most of them occurring only in written English:

AD	anno Domini
a.m.	ante meridiem
c. *or* ca.	circa
cf.	confer
e.g.	exempli gratia
et al.	et alii, et aliae, *or* et alia

etc.	et cetera
i.e.	id est
loc. cit.	loco citato
NB	nota bene
op. cit.	opere citato
p.m.	post meridiem
PS	post scriptum
QED	quod erat demonstrandum
q.v.	quod vide
s.v.	sub verbo
v. *or* vs.	versus

8.7
Synonyms from native, French, and Latin sources

The vocabulary of English has been enormously enriched by the absorption of words from French and Latin. In particular, English enjoys an abundance of synonyms or near-synonyms because of duplications from these two sources. We sometimes find triplets from native English/French/Latin sources:

tell/recount/relate
ask/question/interrogate
teach/train/instruct
fearful/cowardly/timid
friendly/amiable/amicable
kingly/royal/regal
shy/coy/diffident
freedom/liberty/latitude
liar/perjurer/fabricator
land/country/territory
tale/story/narrative

Each of the non-native sources may also offer synonyms. From French:

annul/cancel
reprimand/rebuke/reprove
hideous/horrible
humble/modest
anguish/distress/grief
joy/pleasure

From Latin:

concoct/fabricate
contradict/controvert
authentic/genuine

consequence/repercussion
acrimony/virulence/acerbity

Latin loanwords are generally more learned and formal, but stylistically there is often little to choose between native and French words. In some instances, the French or Latin loanword is stylistically neutral and more familiar than the native synonym. In the examples that follow, the first column gives a word that derives from Old English; the synonyms in the second column are from French, except for the Latin synonyms of *kin*:

mar	spoil
woe	trouble
bliss	joy
deem	judge, decide
kin	relative, family

Languages do not favour exact synonyms since it is uneconomical to have two words that do exactly the same work, so when stylistic differences are absent other differences emerge. It may be a matter of collocation, the company that a word habitually keeps (cf. 8.15): we talk about an oral contract rather than a spoken contract, friendly advice rather than amicable advice. Or there may be differences in meaning: where *carry* and *transport* overlap in situational use, *transport* is not appropriate when one speaks of carrying something over very short distances (for example, from one room in a building to another room) but is more appropriate than *carry* if a vehicle is used. Synonyms may also differ in their grammatical potential; you can teach, train, and instruct somebody, and you can teach somebody something, but you cannot train or instruct somebody something:

$$\text{She is} \begin{cases} \text{teaching us physics} \\ \text{teaching us to shoot} \\ \text{training us to shoot} \\ \text{instructing us in swimming} \end{cases}$$

At various periods hostility has been expressed to excessive importations from Latin or French. In the fifteenth century the aureate diction of some poets evoked a certain amount of disparaging comment, but the introduction of unfamiliar Latin words was a stylistic device that had little impact on the general vocabulary. During the Renaissance, purists condemned the inkhorn terms that were borrowed in huge numbers, mainly from Latin (cf. 8.6). In the eighteenth century there was opposition to accepting too many words from French, then the prestige language of Europe. Early in the nineteenth century, the Romantic movement's interest in the medieval period produced some attempts to replace French and Latin words by native formations; the purists succeeded only in adding a few words, notably *foreword* (as an alternative to *preface*) and *handbook* (a revival of an Old English word as an alternative to *manual*). It is not surprising that successes were few, since French and Latin words are deeply entrenched in the English vocabulary. The vast majority of

English speakers do not know whether a particular word derives from Old English, French, or Latin. Words from French such as *cancel*, *judge*, and *trouble* are fully naturalized, as are Latin words such as *contradict*, *discuss*, *family*.

8.8
Words from other languages

English has been hospitable to words from many other languages, though no languages have provided us with the huge numbers received from French and Latin. Within the confines of this book it is not possible to do more than touch on the most important of the languages that have contributed to the present English vocabulary.

In the sixteenth century and onwards, trade, exploration, colonization, and cultural contacts led to the borrowing of new words from a variety of languages. Major sources were the Romance languages of Spanish, Portuguese, and Italian. Since the Spanish and Portuguese were the European pioneers in exploration and colonization, many non-European words were transmitted into English through these two languages. Among the loanwords from Spanish and (to a lesser extent) Portuguese are:

> anchovy, armada, banana, barbecue, cafeteria, cannibal, canoe, canyon, cargo, cask, chilli (*or* chili), chocolate, cigar, cocaine, cockroach, cocoa, desperado, embargo, guitar, mosquito, negro, port (wine), potato, ranch, renegade, sherry, siesta, tango, tank, tobacco, tomato, vanilla

Many Spanish loanwords are found exclusively or predominantly in American English because of the proximity of Latin America, the absorption of Spanish-speaking areas during the period of expansion of the United States, and the more recent immigrations of millions of Spanish speakers from Mexico, Puerto Rico, and Cuba. Among these words are:

> chicano, frijoles, hacienda, patio, poncho, puebla, rodeo, tortilla

The numerous words from Italian include many musical terms as well as some names for foods. Here is a selection of Italian loanwords:

> aria, artichoke, bandit, broccoli, cameo, carnival, casino, concerto, duet, finale, ghetto, graffiti (*singular* graffito), incognito, inferno, influenza, larva, libretto, macaroni, maestro, mafia, malaria, paparazzi (*singular* paparazzo), piano, pizza, ravioli, regatta, replica, scampi, solo, soprano, spaghetti, studio, umbrella, vendetta, vermicelli, volcano

Trade relations and wars between England and the Low Countries, particularly in the sixteenth and seventeenth centuries, led to a number of loanwords from Dutch, Flemish, and Low German. Later loans came through contacts between the British and the South African Boers and between the

Americans and the early Dutch settlers in America. Among the loanwords from Dutch and kindred languages are:

apartheid, booze, boss, brandy, buoy, coleslaw, commando, cookie, cranberry, cruise, deck, decoy, dock, dollar, dope, easel, excise, freight, furlough, gin, kit, knapsack, landscape, luck, onslaught, pickle, reef, sketch, skipper, slim, smuggle, snap, snip, trek, waffle, wagon (*or, also in British English*, waggon), yacht

Some loanwords have come from High German, including a group of words for foods and drinks (most of them making their first appearance in American English through German-speaking immigrants):

delicatessen, ersatz, frankfurter, hamburger, hamster, lager, noodle, poodle, pretzel, pumpernickel, rucksack, sauerkraut, schnitzel, waltz, wiener

American English has coined a number of words with the German ending *-fest*: *bookfest, songfest, walkfest.*

The United States has had large numbers of Yiddish-speaking immigrants, who have introduced Yiddish words originating from German, Hebrew, and Slavic languages. Most of the words are confined to American English, but some have spread to other national varieties. Among the Yiddish loanwords are:

bagel, chutzpah (*or* hutzpah), gelt, goy, kibbitz, kvetch, maven (*or* mavin), megillah, nebbish, nosh, nudnik, schlep (*or* schlepp), schmo (*or* shmo), schmooze, schnozzle, shlock, shtick (*or* shtik), yenta

Until recent times, loanwords from Hebrew and Arabic have generally entered English through other languages. Most of the Hebrew words have religious significance:

amen, babel, cabbala (*or* cabala, kabbalah, kabala), camel, cherub, jubilee, manna, messiah, sabbath, satan, seraph, shibboleth

Many English first names are ultimately from Hebrew; for example: *Daniel, David, Elizabeth, John, Mary, Michael, Ruth, Susan.* The early translations of the Old Testament provided words such as *long-suffering, scapegoat,* and *stumbling-block.*

Words ultimately of Arabic origin include some that incorporate the Arabic definite article *al.* A number of the words are scientific or mathematical terms, an indication of the eminence of Arab scholarship in the Middle Ages:

admiral, albatross, alchemy, alcohol, alcove, algebra, alkali, almanac, amber, assassin, candy, cipher (*or* cypher), harem, hazard, lemon, magazine, nadir, safari, sherbet, sofa, syrup, zenith, zero

Conquest and trade by the British have brought words from oriental languages. India has been the largest contributor. Loanwords from the various Indian languages, some borrowed through other languages, include:

bungalow, cashmere, chutney, cot, curry, dinghy, ginger, guru, juggernaut, jungle, jute, loot, mango, pariah, polo, punch, pundit, pyjamas (*or* pajamas), shampoo, swastika, thug, toddy, veranda (*or* verandah), yoga

Loanwords from Persian have usually passed through other languages. They include:

arsenic, bazaar, caravan, chess, khaki, kiosk, magic, musk, paradise, rook, scarlet, shawl, spinach, tiger

From Chinese have come:

chop suey, chow, chow mein, ginseng, gung-ho, ketchup (*or* catchup *or* catsup), kung fu, tea, tofu (*via Japanese*), typhoon

From Japanese:

bonsai, geisha, hara-kiri (*or* hari-kiri), judo, haiku, ju-jitsu, kimono, sake, soy, soya, tofu, tycoon

Contacts between the European settlers and the native American Indians led to relatively few borrowings from Amerindian languages. Among them are:

chipmunk, hickory, moccasin, moose, pecan, racoon, skunk, squash, toboggan, totem

8.9
Recent loanwords

A collection of neologisms that entered English between 1941 and 1991 notes that most of its loanwords came from French, the main source of loans since the Norman Conquest. The author also points out that many words containing foreign elements are actually formed in English. An inspection of new words for the ten years 1981 to 1990 yielded only nine loanwords, three of them from French and the other six from six different languages.[7] The predominance of loanwords from French is confirmed in a dictionary of new words covering the decade ending 1991 that includes words that came into prominence during that period as well as words that were first recorded then. Of the thirty-nine loanwords, eight came from French. The nearest competitors were Spanish and Japanese, both with five. An examination of the dictionary highlights the paucity of foreign borrowings among the 750 entries.[8]

Changes in Meaning

8.10
New and old meanings

Words may acquire new meanings. Usually the new meanings coexist with the old. *Hand* is used for the end part of a human arm as well as for various derived meanings, such as for the hour or second pointers on a clock or watch and for a set of playing-cards dealt to a player. We did not lose the animal reference of *mouse* when we acquired its reference to a computer device. The verb *cram* could be used for forcing things into a receptacle long before it could be used for preparing for an examination by an intensive burst of study. The British informal drinking toast *cheers* is now also synonymous with *goodbye* and *thanks*. *Squid* is an American college slang synonym of *nerd* as well as denoting a sea creature.

Sometimes a new meaning eventually displaces an earlier meaning. Earlier meanings of *lewd*—such as 'untaught', 'foolish', 'ignorant', 'ill-mannered'—are obsolete. *Meat* no longer refers to food in general, except as an archaism in older translations of the Bible or in proverbs such as 'One man's meat is another man's poison'. Earlier uses of *silly*—'fortunate', 'happy', then 'blessed', 'holy', then 'pitiable'—are no longer available to us. The uses of *nice* in expressions such as *a nice distinction* and *a nice fit* are now likely to be misunderstood by most people. The homosexual meaning of *gay* has become predominant and is driving out earlier uses.

There are two main approaches to the study of semantic change in the vocabulary. We can examine the causes of change or the processes of change. We will look at each of these in turn.[9]

8.11
Causes of semantic change

A. External history

Words may acquire new meanings because of changes in society. In the feudal system a knight was a military servant of his lord; the feudal relationship no longer exists, but the word remains with a new significance: the title *knight* is conferred on a man by the British monarch in recognition of personal merit or services to the state. Although there is a continuity in the development of the institutions, terms such as *monarch*, *lord* ('peer of the realm'), and *Commons* have changed in their significance as the functions and powers of the institutions have changed. The anomalous use of the term *public school* in England for a certain type of private fee-paying school not under the control of the state or the local government can be explained by the changes in the management of these schools. When it was felt that *sex* over-emphasized the biological differences between males and females because the word was also used for 'sexual intercourse', the grammatical term *gender* acquired the additional role of signifying a more neutral division. *Class*, still used in general for any set or division, has been pressed into service for what is thought to be a major division in society. With changes in kinship relationships, *family* has acquired the more restricted sense of 'nuclear family' (as in 'working to support the family').

Technological changes may affect meanings. *Manuscript* may be used of texts written on the typewriter as well as by hand—in contrast to *print*—though *typescript* is also available if the distinction is needed. A more radical change affected the noun *manufacture*; the etymology (ultimately from Latin) specifies that the work was done by hand, and that was the first use of the word in English, but when it became usual for the production of goods and materials to be performed by machines, the common use of *manufacture* and *manufactured* excluded work by hand. *Car*, once used to denote a carriage, cart, or wagon, is used—particularly in British English—for a vehicle powered by an internal-combustion engine (also called *motor car* and particularly in American English *automobile*), when this type of vehicle became the usual means of private transport.

Scientific developments may affect meanings. *Atom* was once thought of as the ultimate indivisible particle of physical matter, but this conception changed when atoms were split. *Germ* was used vaguely for something that causes a disease; it now more specifically refers to a micro-organism. *Language*, at first restricted to human communication involving words and grammar, has also been applied to the communication systems of various other creatures (for example, dolphins and bees) as these have been shown to constitute complex systems.

B. Euphemism

The desire for euphemism motivates some acquisitions of new meanings. Euphemisms are a way of avoiding direct reference to subjects that are taboo or impolite or simply felt to be unpleasant in the community to which we belong, or they are a way of disguising activities and attitudes that others might consider offensive.[10]

Parts of the body and bodily processes attract euphemisms, drawing on existing words or expressions, some of them informal or slang. Here is a small selection from a vast repertoire:

> bottom, box, (family) jewels, knockers, tail
> sleep with, score, swing
> pass water, break wind, tinkle, the runs, be excused
> toilet, lavatory, bathroom (*American*), geography of the house (*British*)
> period, (be) expecting, (be in) labour

More delicate constitutions from an earlier period have left their mark in the euphemistic substitutions of *white* (meat) for the breast of a chicken and *dark* (meat) for the thigh.

Illness and death give rise to many euphemisms:

condition, social disease, stroke
(trouble with the) plumbing, waterworks, (give a) specimen
pass away, loss, the departed, casket (*American*), funeral director,
    memorial park (*American*)

People with a physical incapacity have been labelled with a series of euphemisms, including *handicapped* and *disabled*. Current notable euphemisms are *differently abled* in Britain and *physically challenged* in the USA.

War has brought a plethora of euphemisms, many of them to avoid referring directly to killing. Here are just a few examples:

armed reconnaissance	friendly fire
carpet bombing	neutralize
collateral damage	pacify
degradation	police action
cleanse	surgical strike

Similarly, *redeploy*, *retire*, and *withdraw* conceal the ignominy of retreat. (*Secret*) *agent* and *operative* are dignified terms for spies. The fighting in Yugoslavia that began in the early 1990s has given rise to the euphemistic expression *ethnic cleansing*.

Taboos on certain swear words have resulted in phonetic disguises;[11] for example:

shoot, shucks	(shit)
darn	(damn)
golly, gosh	(God)
gee, jeez	(Jesus)
crikey	(Christ)
heck	(hell)

Rhyming slang is another disguising device, the disguise being particularly effective if the rhyming word is left out, as in these examples:

berk (Berkeley *or* Berkshire hunt)	(cunt)
cobblers (awls)	(balls)
hit (and miss)	(piss)
raspberry (tart)	(fart)
Tom (tit)	(shit)

C. Intensification

From time to time we feel the need to express our approval or disapproval in strong terms. Words have been pressed into this service that depart from their earlier meanings, sometimes—as in the case of *awful*—ousting previous uses. Below are some instances of approving and disapproving adjectives accompanied by illustrative nouns. They are used mainly in speech.

fabulous speech	awful meal
fantastic dress	dreadful teacher
gorgeous day	horrible weather
marvellous play	revolting book
phenomenal success	rotten party
smashing story	
terrific show	
wonderful lesson	

Successive generations seek out new terms. Among recent expressions of approval are *awesome*, *bad*, *brilliant* (also *brill*), *cool*, *radical* (also *rad*), *wicked*.

Adverbs may also have acquired new meanings in becoming intensifiers:

awfully good	highly intelligent
badly needed	terribly nice
deeply worried	terrifically patient

Whereas the adjective *awful* retains its disapproving meaning—as in *awful meal*—the adverb *awfully* has flattened into a general intensifier synonymous with *extremely* or perhaps merely *very*.

D. Collocation

The tendency for words to collocate—co-occur frequently with other words (cf. 8.15)—can result in a particular word being used alone with the meaning of the pair of words. *Private* derives from the collocation *private soldier*, *wellington* from the collocation *wellington boot*. In appropriate contexts, *the pill* will be understood as referring to the contraceptive pill. To propose to somebody is to propose marriage to that person. A woman who is expecting is expecting a baby. *Intercourse* is generally understood to refer to sexual intercourse, a point missed by the foreign student who wrote that he enjoyed coming to a summer school in London because it gave him the opportunity to have intercourse with people from many countries.

Below are some examples of recent words used with the meaning of the collocation. The omitted words of the full forms are given in parentheses:

cable (television)	(shopping) mall
(wheel) clamp	Patriot (missile)
jet(-propelled aircraft)	soap (opera)
landfill (site)	(space) shuttle
laptop (computer)	

E. Technical and general use

The nineteenth and twentieth centuries have witnessed an explosion of technical terms, due to the enormous expansion in scientific and technological studies and in their practical applications. Technical terms are expressions in use within a specialized field of knowledge or activity. There is no clear dividing line between technical terms and terms in general use, since technical terms may pass into the general vocabulary, and general words and expressions may in addition acquire a technical meaning.

Some technical terms are restricted to usage within their field. We are not likely to encounter in non-specialized contexts plant terms such as *embryophyta* and *phaeophyta*, chemical terms such as *titration* and *basicity*, or linguistic terms such as *hyponym* and *denominal*. Of course, many technical terms are in general educated use with roughly the same meaning: *deciduous, fungus, gene, neologism, prehensile, ruminant, tort*. However, when some technical terms have come into more general use they have acquired a different meaning among non-specialists. For example, in general use the psychological term *complex* denotes an obsession, while *inferiority complex* refers simply to a sense of inferiority; the legal term *alibi* has been extended to mean an excuse of any kind; the mathematical term *parameter* is commonly used for a measurable or quantifiable feature; *spectrum*, a term in physics and optics, is in general use to mean a wide range.

When everyday expressions are adopted as technical terms, they are defined precisely and may then become distinct from their more general use. Examples are *mass* (physics), *salt* (chemistry), *complement* (grammar), *dedicated* (computers), *benign* (medicine), *frame* (film).

8.12 Processes

A. Generalization and specialization

Generalization involves a shift in the meaning of a word that makes it more inclusive. The legal term *alibi* has extended its use to any kind of excuse, *pilot* is now used primarily for the person who operates an aircraft in addition to its use for the person who takes charge of a ship entering a harbour, and *marathon* refers to any activity involving difficulty and long duration.

Specialization results in a restriction of meaning. *Starve* used to refer to dying by any means, *science* to all kinds of knowledge, *cattle* to all livestock. *Mutton* has precluded the use of *sheep* to refer to the animal as food. In American and Australian English *corn* is typically restricted to maize.

B. Pejoration and amelioration

These two processes involve an evaluative shift, pejoration moving to a less favourable connotation and amelioration to a more favourable connotation.

Silly is an early instance of pejoration. In Old English *sǽlig* meant 'happy', 'blessed'; by the Early Modern period it had deteriorated evaluatively to mean 'deserving of pity', 'helpless'; 'weak', 'insignificant'; 'unlearned', 'ignorant'. *Cræftig* had the favourable senses 'skilful', 'ingenious' in Old English, not the later pejorative connotation of *crafty*. Similarly, *cunning* meant 'learned', 'clever' in Middle English. *Officious* started off with the meanings 'eager to please' and 'dutiful', true to its Latin etymology, but soon acquired the modern pejorative meaning. More recent times have seen the acquisition by *propaganda* and then *appeasement* of pejorative connotations.

Shrewd provides a contrast to *crafty* and *cunning*: it began pejoratively in Middle English in the meaning 'wicked', 'vicious', then shifted to 'cunning' before acquiring its present favourable connotation; *shrew* and *shrewish* remain pejorative. Other examples of amelioration are *fond*, which once meant 'foolish', and more recently *aggressive*. The current slang terms *bad* and *wicked* are striking instances of amelioration.

C. Metaphoric extension

The metaphoric extension of a word is probably the most common process by which a word acquires an additional meaning. When the new meaning has become established its metaphorical relationship may no longer be noticed: the metaphor is a dead metaphor. The similarity that gives rise to the new meaning is generally one of form or function.

The formal similarity may be in shape:

bulb (of electric lamp)	hand (of clock)
cake (of soap)	leg (of table)
eye (of needle)	mouse (for computer)
fork (of road)	mouth (of river)

It may be in spatial relationship:

bottom (of road)	face (of building)
brow (of hill)	foot (of bed)
coat (of paint)	head (of table)

Or the metaphor may combine shape and spatial relationship:

arm (of chair)	leg (of table)
cap (of bottle)	vein (in marble)

A remoter spatial relationship is conveyed by *rainbow* ('an arch of contiguous colours') in *rainbow coalition*, and by *shoot* ('discharge something') in *shoot oneself with a drug*, or *shoot a question at somebody*.

The similarity may be functional:

bump (from job)	menu (on computer screen—also similar in
cannibalize (a vehicle)	layout)
ceiling (for prices)	mule (drugs courier)
(ethnic) cleansing	(computer) program
demolish (an argument)	root (of problem)
(brain) drain	sow (dissent)
(acids) eat	spoonfeed (students)
(DNA) fingerprint	(be in) suspense
grasp (an idea)	toy (boy)
gulf (between factions)	(computer) virus

The similarity may be evaluative, as in these expressions when they are applied to people:

angel	honey
arse-hole	mouse
baby	pig
bitch	prick
cat	swine
cow	witch
heel	

Or there may be a combination of evaluation with some physical similarity, as in *couch potato* and *infect* (with ideas).

D. **Metonymic extension**

Another common process is metonymy. A word acquires a new meaning as an entity or attribute that is substituted for something with which it is associated. Here are common kinds of metonymic relationships that have resulted in new meanings.

part for whole:
  (new) blood ('people'), (new) face ('person'), (another) hand ('person')
concrete for abstract:
  bench ('judiciary'), brain ('intellect'), crown ('monarchy'), seat ('membership'), turf ('horse-racing')
abstract for concrete:
  falsehood ('lie'), performance ('event'), terror (referring to a person), trust ('organization')
eponym (named after a person or place):
  bikini, boycott, dunce, lynch, pasteurize, platonic, sadist, sandwich, sherry, valentine
place for institution:
  Downing Street ('the British Prime Minister'), the City ('British financial institutions'), Paris ('the French Government'), Washington ('the American administration')
transferred epithet (transferred from a person):
  curious (response), happy (occasion), hopeful (turn of events), miserable (weather), red-eye (flight), sad (result), sick (building syndrome)

Another kind of metonymy appears in *white-collar crimes*, i.e. crimes by white-collar workers.

The various kinds of conversion (cf. 9.29) involve some changes of meaning that are metonymic. For example, *to orphan* means 'to make somebody into an orphan', *a bore* is 'somebody or something that bores'. However, the change of proper noun to common noun sometimes implies a comparison and is then metaphoric:

He is a veritable *Hitler*.

She is the *Einstein* of our time.

When shall we build *Jerusalem* in England's green and pleasant land?

Semantic Relationships between Words

8.13
Semantic relationships

A. Synonymy

Words can be grouped into sets that share some relationship of meaning. The thesaurus is a reference book that arranges the vocabulary into conceptual categories that display words and phrases that are associated in meaning, though the term has also been used of alphabetical dictionaries of synonyms. The relationships that are most widely recognized are synonymy and antonymy.[12]

Synonyms are expressions that are identical or similar in meaning and that can be used interchangeably in at least some contexts (cf. 8.7). The verbs *buy* and *purchase* are synonyms:

They $\left\{ \begin{array}{l} \text{bought} \\ \text{purchased} \end{array} \right\}$ an expensive house.

They differ stylistically in that *purchase* is formal. They also differ grammatically in that only with *buy* can we insert an indirect object:

She bought *me* a birthday present.

The nouns *order* and the more formal *command* are synonymous in the sense of directive, but *order* is more inclusive. Only *order(s)* can be used in these contexts:

I will not take orders from anybody.

My orders ['orders given to me'] are to requisition this building.

Commandment is restricted to a divine command. *Now* can only be replaced by *nowadays* when it means 'in these times':

I can't tell you now.

What will happen now?

They now knew that he was guilty.

B. Antonymy

Antonyms share a negative relationship within the same field of meaning. *Cold* and *hot* are antonyms in the semantic field of temperature: if something is cold, it is not hot; if it is hot, it is not cold. The two terms are gradable on the temperature scale: my food can be very cold or it can be cooler than yours. There are also other gradable terms on the scale between *cold* and *hot*, so that if something is not cold it is not necessarily hot, and if it is not hot it is not necessarily cold:

hot—warm—lukewarm—cool—cold

Where intermediate terms are possible, as with *cold* and *hot*, the antonyms are contraries. Here are some other examples of contraries:

huge—large—medium-sized—small—tiny
wet—moist—dry
probable—possible—unlikely
hate—dislike—like—love

Sometimes the set of antonyms may contain some words that are not gradable; for example, the extremes in this set:

always—frequently—occasionally—rarely—never

Contradictories (also called complementaries) are binary antonyms. Examples are:

male—female
dead—alive
animate—inanimate
married—unmarried
stay—leave
inside—outside

These normally exclude intervening terms: one is either male or female, dead or alive. Nevertheless, it is sometimes possible to squeeze in middle terms in exceptional circumstances or with certain connotations:

male—hermaphrodite—female
dead—more dead than alive—half-dead—very much alive—alive
outside—half-in—inside

Antonymous pairs that are morphologically related in that one term has a negative prefix (cf. 9.9) may be either contradictories or contraries. Examples of contradictories:

continue   discontinue
curable   incurable
legal   illegal
ripe   unripe
punctual   unpunctual

Examples of contraries:

approve	disapprove
friendly	unfriendly
happy	unhappy
intelligent	unintelligent
wise	unwise

Converses are opposites where there are reciprocal relationships. A typical example is the pair *buy* and *sell*:

Tom bought the car from Norma.
Norma sold the car to Tom.

Other examples of pairs of verbs that are converses:

give   receive
lend   borrow

The same verb may be used for both directions of the action:

Sylvia rented the apartment to Diane.
Diane rented the apartment from Sylvia.

I loaned the stereo to Robert.
Robert loaned the stereo from me.

Certain pairs of terms for kinship and social relationships may also constitute converses:

wife	husband
parent	child
grandparent	grandchild
doctor	patient
teacher	student
lawyer	client

If Sandra is Paul's wife, then Paul is Sandra's husband. Similarly, if Ronald is Elizabeth's teacher, then Elizabeth is Ronald's student. The same term is sometimes available for both directions. If Kelvin and Sheila are colleagues, then Kelvin is Sheila's colleague and Sheila is Kelvin's colleague. Other converses that are identical are *friend, partner, associate, room-mate, cousin, sibling*. So also for verbs and combinations with verbs: *marry, be related to, be associated with*. Adjectives and verbs denoting similarity or difference may be identical converses: *resemble, differ, equal; similar to, identical with, different from, equal to*. Some terms for spatial and temporal relations are also converses:

in front of   behind   before   after
above   below

If I am in front of the screen, then the screen is behind me. If Milton lived after Shakespeare, then Shakespeare lived before Milton. Terms that may be identical converses for spatial relations include *near, next to, opposite*.[13]

Some sets of terms within the same semantic field are not considered as antonyms, though they are incompatibles. They are incompatibles because the use of one term excludes the other. If a dress is green it cannot be blue, though a dress can be partly green and partly blue. Whereas *black* and *white* are considered antonyms, *green* and *blue* are not. Other examples of incompatibles are the terms for days of the week, military ranks, numbers, rooms in a house (*bedroom, kitchen, bathroom*, etc.), departments in a university or college (*History, Mathematics, Physics*, etc.).

C. **Hyponymy**

Hyponymy is a relationship of inclusion: a general term (a superordinate or hypernym) covers terms that are more specific (its hyponyms). The word *meat* refers to a type of food: the superordinate term is *food*, and *meat* is its hyponym. There is of course more than one type of food: *meat, fish, fowl, fruit, vegetables* are co-hyponyms of *food*. Since each of these in turn have hyponyms, we have a hierarchy of hyponymy for *food*. *Fruit*, for example, includes the co-hyponyms *berry* and *citrus fruit*; among the co-hyponyms of *berry* are *strawberry, gooseberry, blackberry, raspberry*, and among the co-hyponyms of *citrus fruit* are *orange, grapefruit, tangerine*. 'I bought some oranges' entails 'I bought some citrus fruit', which in turn entails 'I bought some fruit', and that entails 'I bought some food' and ultimately 'I bought something'. The hyponymy hierarchy allows us to be as specific or as general as we wish.

Here are some other examples of superordinates followed by some of their co-hyponyms:

go:	walk, run, ride, drive, fly
walk:	stroll, saunter, amble, march
get:	buy, borrow, steal
cook:	bake, boil, fry, grill, poach, roast
religion:	Christianity, Islam, Judaism, Hinduism, Buddhism
fuel:	oil, gas, electricity, coal, wood

Not all words have superordinates. For example, there is no term to cover the adjectives *happy* and *sad*, though the nouns *emotion* or *feeling* might be considered quasi-superordinates for these and other adjectives in the same semantic field. Similarly, there are no superordinates for *teacher/student, old/young, live/die*. In kinship terms we lack a superordinate in ordinary use for *brother* and *sister*, though the technical term *sibling* is sometimes pressed into service for this purpose. Consequently, we normally have to ask 'Have you any brothers or sisters?', whereas we can ask 'Have you any children?' without specifying whether they are sons or daughters. There may also be some variation in the use of superordinates. *Vegetable* is ordinarily felt to be a superordinate of *potato* and *tomato*. However, a restaurant menu may specify *vegetables* and *potatoes* as separate sets of items. *Tomato* is technically a fruit, but we treat it as a vegetable. Similarly, nuts are technically fruit, but in ordinary use we do not consider them as such.

In certain instances involving sexual distinctions, a term may be a superordinate and a hyponym of itself. *Dog*, for example, may be used for both sexes of the animal ('I have recently bought a dog') or just for the male dog ('Is it a dog or a bitch?'). Similarly, *man* is sometimes used—but less so than in the past, to avoid accusations of sexism—as a synonym for the noun *human*: 'man's inhumanity to man'; 'All men are born equal'.

D. Part–whole relationships

The distinction between hyponymy and part–whole relationships is sometimes blurred, but some clear examples can be given. The parts of the body include the arms, legs, and the head; the head includes the face; the face includes the eyes, nose, and mouth. In the hyponymous relationship of *food* and *fruit*, we can say 'A fruit is a kind of food'; but we cannot say 'A head is a kind of body', or 'A face is a kind of head', or 'A mouth is a kind of face'. Here are some other examples of the part–whole relationship:

aircraft: fuselage, engine, rudder, wing, wheel
shoe: heel, sole, instep, lining, tongue
revolver: barrel, bore, cylinder, trigger, butt, hammer
room: door, window, ceiling, floor

Combinations of Words

8.14 Free combinations and idioms

The semantic relationships illustrated in 8.13 appear in sets of words from which a choice has to be made by the speaker or writer. Depending on our intended meaning and other factors (such as style), we choose whether to say *buy* or *purchase*, *like* or *dislike*, *stroll* or *amble*, *heel* or *sole*. The choices constitute the paradigmatic dimensions of the vocabulary: sets (or paradigms) of options available to the user. In contrast, the syntagmatic dimension presents the possible or obligatory sequences of words as they appear in speech or writing.

Most combinations of words are free, though there may be grammatical constraints. The noun *day* can go with a large range of adjectives: *fine* ('It was a fine day'), *sunny*, *wet*, *long*, *sad*, *boring*—to take just a few examples. The verb *write* can be used with nouns such as *letter*, *essay*, *paper*, *article*, *report*, *card*, *memo*, *reply*, *protest*, *objection*, *defence*, *attack*, *apology*; *letter*, in turn, can combine with many other verbs such as *read*, *study*, *see*, *remember*, *forget*, *post*, *mail*, *file*, *discard*, *tear*, *fold*, *begin*, *end*.

Some combinations are idiomatic in that the meaning of the whole cannot be deduced from the meanings of the parts:[14]

a red herring	kick the bucket
out of the blue	hit the roof
a piece of cake	up the spout
a rough diamond	cut dead
a flash in the pan	run of the mill
a lame duck	on the wagon

Idioms need not be entirely frozen. There may be some lexical variability:

hit the roof *or* hit the ceiling
out of the blue *or* out of a clear blue sky
kick one's heels *or* cool one's heels
hit a nerve *or* touch a nerve
keep your shirt on *or* keep your hair on

Or there may be grammatical variability:

a rough diamond *or* rough diamonds
kick, kicks, kicked, *or* kicking one's heels
take somebody to the cleaners *or* somebody was taken to the cleaners

Proverbs and sayings tend to be frozen:

A stitch in time saves nine
Out of sight, out of mind
Forewarned is forearmed
Every dog has its day
Don't count your chickens before they're hatched

There are numerous standard similes, though these may allow some variation:

as busy as a bee	as sick as a dog
as clear as crystal *or* as clear as daylight	as strong as a horse *or* as strong
as cool as a cucumber	as an ox
as hot as hell	as ugly as sin
as keen as mustard	

There are also numerous relatively fixed expressions (catch phrases and the like), some of which can be interpreted literally:

a whole new ball game	Read my lips
gloom and doom	Tell it like it is
slow but sure	Don't make me laugh
Did the earth move for you?	Keep your shirt on
Go on, make my day	and a good thing too

Fro is preserved only in the phrase *to and fro*, and similarly *kith* only in *kith and kin*.

Many phrasal verbs, prepositional verbs, and phrasal-prepositional verbs (cf. 5.34–7) are idiomatic to varying degrees. Here are just a few examples:

bring up ('rear')	make out ('understand')
catch on ('understand')	make up ('end quarrel')
come by ('acquire')	put up with ('tolerate')
fall out ('quarrel')	take out on ('vent anger on')
go into ('investigate')	

8.15
Collocations

Between free combinations and idioms are loose combinations of words, where the meanings of the whole can generally be predicted from the parts. These collocations—words that frequently co-occur—vary in the extent to which they do co-occur. The standard seasonal greetings are *Merry Christmas* and *Happy New Year*, although *Happy Christmas* seems possible, *Merry New Year* or indeed *Merry Birthday* are odd. We can ask for *black coffee* (not *brown coffee*) and *white wine* (not *yellow wine*); the words need not be juxtaposed: 'Would you prefer your coffee to be black?' The choices are lexical choices, to do with words and not meaning. There is nothing in the meanings of *merry* and *happy* that make the collocations in the greetings predictable, and similarly there is nothing in the meaning of *black* that makes it more suitable than *brown* to collocate with *coffee* or in the meaning of *white* that makes it more suitable than *yellow* to collocate with *wine*.

The phrasal verb *turn on* collocates with (among other items) *light, gas, radio*, and *television*. That is to say, if we hear or read *turn on*, among the items we might expect nearby are those nouns. These items constitute, in part, the collocational range of *turn on*. In this instance, there is some mutual expectancy: the presence of *television* predicts the presence of *turn on*, though probably less strongly than the reverse; other items that collocate with *television* include *turn off, switch on, switch off, watch*. The expectancy may be very much stronger in one direction. In the list below, the adjective predicts the noun far more than the reverse:

rancid butter	gammy leg
stale bread	addled brains
callow youth	pungent smell

On the other hand, the noun is more predictive in the collocation *dumb blonde*.

A particular type of collocation is found in binomials, the co-ordination of expressions in a relatively fixed order. Here are some examples:

black and white	law and order
cup and saucer	men and women
free and easy	odds and ends
ladies and gentlemen	pots and pans

Synonyms may have different collocations. *Schoolchildren* are *truant* (or *play truant*) from *school*, and there may be complaints about their *truancy*; *workers* are *absent* from *work*, and there may be complaints about *absenteeism*. Of course it is also possible to say that *workers* are *truant*, but that is a less frequent collocation, whereas *schoolchildren* perhaps collocates with *absent* as frequently as with *truant*. *Students* are *expelled* (in some British universities they are *rusticated* or *sent down*), *workers* are *fired* or *sacked*, and *soldiers* are *dismissed* from the army. A *banker* has *customers*, but a *lawyer* has *clients*. Intensifying adverbs have their favourite verbs: *badly* collocates with *need* and *want*, *entirely* with *agree*, *completely* with *forget*, and *greatly* with *admire*.

The examples of co-occurring words in this section and in the previous section suggest that in much of our everyday use of the language we draw on prefabricated units rather than selecting words individually. Just as we may allude to a literary source by saying 'August is the cruellest month', so we may allude to an established collocation; for example, *virtuous circle* in the following citation:

> It seems to be easier to stabilise inflation at low levels, partly, perhaps, because this creates a virtuous circle of low inflationary expectations.
> [*The Economist*, 7 November 1992, p. 21]

Other examples of allusions to collocations are these headlines in one issue of *The Economist* (17 October 1992):

> Will more be merrier?
>
> Gin and tunics
>
> Shrinking pains

In the widest sense, collocation covers frequent co-occurrence of words at any distance from each other in the same spoken discourse or the same written text, or perhaps in some part of a discourse or text. If we encounter the word *dinner* in a conversation, among the words that we might expect to hear in its vicinity are *time, ready, table, serve, prepare, cook, dish*. If we encounter the word *dinosaur* in a book, we might expect to find in its vicinity *museum, fossil, skeleton, extinct*. *Cancer* collocates with *smoking, malignant, chemotherapy, tumour, cell*. In one meaning *star* collocates with *Hollywood* and *film*, in another meaning with *astronomy, space, telescope, visible, planet*. The company that a word keeps contributes to its interpretation.

Homonymy and Polysemy

8.16
Homonymy

Homonyms are distinct words that happen to have the same form. For example, the noun *bank* represents two words: *bank* where money is deposited (derived from French *banque*) and *bank* of a river (probably derived from Old Norse *banke*). In this instance the two words are pronounced the same, spelled the same, and belong to the same word class. Other examples of homonyms are *duck* (a swimming-bird) and *duck* ('bend quickly'), *ear* (of a face) and *ear* (of a cereal), *peep* ('make a feeble shrill sound') and *peep* ('look cautiously'), *bear* (a large mammal) and *bear* ('carry'). The homonyms of both *duck* and *bear* belong to different word classes, noun and verb.

When two lexical items are pronounced the same but are spelled differently, they are called homophones. Here are just a few examples:

altar, alter	one, won
brake, break	peace, piece
cell, sell	right, write
die, dye	sail, sale
hair, hare	sight, site
knew, new	threw, through
meat, meet	weak, week

Since pronunciations vary, what may be a homophone for one speaker may not be for another. Those who use a rhotic accent (retaining /r/ before a consonant or in final position) will pronounce *father* and *farther* differently, whereas for speakers with a non-rhotic accent the two words are homophonous. In some dialects *ate* and *eight* are homophones; in other dialects the vowels of the two words are distinguished as /ɛ/ and /eɪ/ respectively. Stylistic differences may also affect pronunciation: *than* and *then* may be pronounced identically in casual speech, a possible cause for the misspelling of *than* as *then*.

Homographs are spelled the same but pronounced differently.[15] *Lead* represents two nouns: the *lead* /liːd/ attached to a dog and the metal *lead* /lɛd/; the same written form is also used as a verb: to *lead* /liːd/ the patrol. As a verb, *row* can mean 'propel (a boat) with oars' /rəʊ/ or 'quarrel' /raʊ/. The spelling system makes more distinctions than the sound system, so there are fewer homographs than homonyms. Here are some further examples of homographs:

does:	present singular of *do* /dʌz/, plural of *doe* /dəʊz/
read:	present tense /riːd/, past tense /rɛd/
sewer:	'conduit' /suːə(r)/, 'one who sews' /səʊə(r)/
sow:	'scatter seed' /səʊ/, 'female adult pig' /saʊ/
tear:	'pull apart' /tɛː(r)/, 'drop from eye' /tɪə(r)/

Homomorphs are words with the same form that are related in meaning but are distinct grammatically. Most frequently the pairs of words are related by means of conversion (cf. 9.29); for example: the verb *laugh* and the noun *laugh*, the adjective *calm* and the verb *calm*. Other examples of homomorphs are the adjective *fast* ('a *fast* car') and the adverb *fast* ('They drove *fast*'); the adverb *past* ('They went *past*') and the preposition *past* ('They went *past* our house'); the adverb *since* ('I haven't seen them *since*'), the preposition *since* ('I haven't seen them *since* last April'), and the conjunction *since* ('I haven't seen them *since* I was a child'). Homomorphs may be different grammatical forms of the same word: *put* as present tense and past tense. In some instances the relationship in meaning is unclear, although there is an etymological connection, and therefore their status as homomorphs is in doubt; for example, *but* as conjunction ('They do nothing *but* complain'), preposition ('We've had nothing *but* trouble from them'), and adverb ('She is *but* a child'), where the meaning relationship of the adverb to the other two is obscure.

8.17
Polysemy

The two meanings of *bank* relate quite obviously to two distinct words, which are therefore undoubtedly homonyms. We expect the homonyms to be given separate entries in dictionaries. But it is not always clear whether two words are distinct: some people, for example, might see a relationship between the homonyms of *ear* ('The ear of corn looks like the ear of an animal') and the homonyms of *duck* ('The verb refers to an action that ducks habitually perform').

In many instances the semantic relationship is clear. *Hand* (of a human) and *hand* (of a clock) are polysemes rather than homonyms, and so are *grasp* (a stick) and *grasp* (an idea). These two meanings of *hand*, as well as many others, appear under one entry in dictionaries. Polysemy refers to multiple meanings of a word. We think of one meaning as literal or basic and the others as extended meanings that are derived from the first. As a brief inspection of a dictionary shows, words generally have more than one meaning and some have very many meanings. The most frequent words tend to be the most polysemous. Consider just a few of the meanings that can be distinguished for the verb *have*:

be in possession of:	have a car
be in a relationship to:	have a daughter
experience:	have a headache
cause:	have the television repaired
hold:	have a party
give birth to:	have a baby

Homonyms are coincidental in language, and might be considered a defect; they may introduce ambiguity without any compensating advantage. Polysemes are essential in language; they immensely reduce the number of words we need to learn and store in our memory.

Homonymy and polysemy are common intentional components of ambiguity in literature and, more generally, of wordplay in language.[16]

Numbers of Words

8.18
The size of the vocabulary

The average number of words known by an educated adult has been estimated as at least 50,000 and perhaps as high as 250,000.[17] Webster's *Third New International Dictionary* (published 1961) claims to have over 450,000 words.

Both these sets of figures raise questions on matters that have been considered earlier in this chapter. What counts as a word? Do we take polysemous words to be one word or do we take each polyseme as a separate word? If we count polysemes, how many should we assign to words such as *have* and *give*? The bigger the dictionary, the more definitions will be provided for such words.

Do we count the grammatical forms of a word as separate words? Is it sufficient for this purpose to list the verb *dance*, or should we regard *dance, dances, danced, dancing* as separate words? The same point applies to nouns (*woman, women, woman's, women's*), adjectives (*tall, taller, tallest*), and pronouns (*they, them, their*).

Problems also arise in what to include as a compound (cf. 9.24). Are we to count *hot dog* as a word as well as *hot* and *dog*? And are idiomatic phrasal verbs such as *make up* ('invent') to be listed separately?

The high estimates for words known by educated adults refer to passive knowledge of vocabulary: words that are recognized or whose meaning is inferred from the word's components. The number of words that any individual actually uses will be much smaller.

Dictionaries do not include all the words that educated adults know. In the past, taboo words were generally excluded, and even now many slang and dialect words may not be admitted. For instance, the 1991 edition of *Collins English Dictionary* (nearly 1,800 pages) has an entry for *rental* but not in the British teenage slang sense 'parental'; it does not note *bizzies* ('police'), used by young Geordies, or the British market-trader's *bunce* ('profit'). Merriam Webster's *Collegiate Dictionary* (the tenth edition, published in 1993) does not include such examples of American college slang as *squid* (though it has its synonyms *dork* and *nerd*) and *grinder* ('difficult course').

General dictionaries do not include all scientific and technical words, which are best catered for in specialized dictionaries. In chemistry alone, it has been estimated that there are over six million named compounds, and more are continually being added. Even for the general vocabulary, since it takes some time before new words are noted and researched, dictionaries are always somewhat out of date.

The same points have to be taken into consideration if we attempt to estimate the number of words in the English language. We also have to consider whether we are dealing with just one national variety or whether we include words in all national varieties, even when the words do not have currency outside one country.

Some of these considerations apply equally when we look at the vocabulary of a particular speech or piece of writing or the collected works of one author. If a student's paper is limited to 1,000 words or a novel is cut down to 50,000 words, the reference is to the number of running words in the text: each occurrence of a word is counted separately. On the other hand, if Shakespeare's vocabulary in his works is estimated at between 15,000 and 24,000 words whereas Milton's vocabulary is said to be between 7,000 and 8,000 words, the reference is to distinct words.[18] The distinct words are types and the instances of the types are tokens: for example, there may be 85 tokens of the type *you* in a text. The higher the ratio of types to tokens, the richer the vocabulary. The relative frequency is expressed in the type : token ratio. In counting types and tokens, decisions have to be taken about polysemy and grammatical variants.

Two Major Types of Words

8.19
Content words and grammatical words

The vocabulary is often categorized as consisting of content words and grammatical words. Content (or full or lexical) words—most of the words in the language—are said to carry in the main the semantic content of the vocabulary, whereas the grammatical (or function or form) words chiefly carry the grammatical relationships. Though linguists may vary over details, the content words are usually said to comprise words belonging to the major word classes: nouns, main verbs, adjectives, and adverbs. The grammatical words belong to the minor word classes: pronouns, determiners, auxiliary verbs, prepositions, and conjunctions.

This distinction correlates with the distinction between open classes and closed classes. The major word classes are readily open to new words. The minor classes, however, do not easily admit new members. Witness the difficulty of finding a neutral personal pronoun to replace *he* and *she*. However, a few new members have been recently added to closed classes, for example *plus* as a conjunction.

The grammatical words have important grammatical functions in relation to content words or units containing content words (for example, *a* and *the* introduce noun phrases, and *and* links phrases and clauses), but they generally also have semantic content. We are aware of the semantic contrasts between the pronouns *he* and *she*, the prepositions *up* and *down*, and the auxiliaries *may* and *must*. Perhaps the clearest example of a purely grammatical word is the infinitival *to*, as in *to pay*.

Reference Books on Words

8.20
The contents of dictionaries

Dictionaries are reference books on the vocabulary. They range in size from the scholarly 20-volume *Oxford English Dictionary* (second edition 1989) to pocket dictionaries. Some, including the *Oxford English Dictionary*, are available as software for use on personal computers.

Dictionaries may be arranged alphabetically (from word to meaning) or semantically (from meaning to word). Semantically arranged dictionaries—such as the various books called *Roget's Thesaurus*—also require an alphabetical index. One type of thematic dictionary is a pictorial dictionary, which is generally limited to nouns and noun phrases.

Dictionaries may be monolingual (limited to the vocabulary of one language), or bilingual (offering definitions or synonyms in the other language), or even multilingual. Some monolingual English dictionaries are intended for the foreign learner.

The typical dictionary is alphabetically arranged and covers the general vocabulary but may include some specialized terms and also some words from slang or non-standard dialects. Specialist dictionaries deal with a particular aspect of the vocabulary. They include dictionaries of pronunciation, words that may be confused, new words, difficult words, abbreviations, idioms, slang, taboo words, words from non-standard dialects, or from disciplines such as law or linguistics.

The general dictionary usually offers the following information:

1. Spelling, including any variants, e.g. *yoghurt, yogurt*. The variation may be in capitalization, e.g. *Aids, AIDS*. Hyphens are indicated, e.g. *air bag, air-bed*. Some dictionaries also indicate where end-of-line hyphens may be used.

2. Pronunciation, using some kind of phonetic transcription. Variants may be indicated, e.g. /ˈvɪtəmɪn/, /ˈvʌɪtəmɪn/. It is usual to supply stress marks for polysyllabic words.

3. Inflections, such as the plural of irregular nouns and the past and the *-ed* participle of irregular verbs. Where the inflections conform to regular rules, they are usually not given. However, inflected forms are included if the consonant is doubled when the inflection is added; e.g. *big—bigger—biggest*; *permit—permitted—permitting*.

4. Parts of speech, such as noun and verb. Except in dictionaries for foreign learners, grammatical information is minimal.

5. Definitions for each of the senses that are distinguished. Multi-word expressions are also listed and defined under the entry for the dominant word in the expression; e.g. *cod-liver oil* under *cod*; *dirty dog* under *dog*; *order about* under *order*; *go on record* under *record*.

6. Usage labels, indicating restrictions of time (archaic, obsolete), place (British, Australian), register (medical, historical, literary), style (informal, slang, taboo). There may also be usage notes to explain points of usage, such as when to use *who* or *whom* and the difference between *imply* and *infer*.

7. Etymology, indicating the history of words, referring to earlier periods of English and to languages from which they were borrowed.

General dictionaries are increasingly including encyclopedic information, such as information on names of people and places. Among the encyclopedic entries on just one page of *Collins English Dictionary* (3rd edition, 1991) are *Gance* (French film director), *Gand* (French name for Ghent), *Gandhi*, *Ganges*, *Gang of Four*, *Gangtok* (city in NE India).

Meaning

8.21
Sense, denotation, reference

Meaning and *sense* have been used interchangeably in this chapter in ways that are usual in everyday language. In linguistics and philosophy these and related words may be used variously as technical terms. Within the scope of this chapter it is not appropriate to enter into a discussion of the use of such terms, but it may be helpful to refer to a few concepts about meaning.

The sense of a word is its cognitive meaning as determined by its place within the semantic system of the language. The word *mother* has the sense 'parent and female', in contrast to *father* 'parent and male', both of the words contrasting with *child*, *son*, and *daughter* in a set of related kinship terms. *Football* is definable as a ball game with certain characteristics, in contrast with other words for ball games, such as *basketball* and *netball*. *Come* is a verb of movement in contrast with *go*; *sad* is an adjective of emotion, a synonym of *unhappy* and an antonym of *happy*; *down* and *up* are contrasting pairs of prepositions of direction; *and* and *or* are contrasting co-ordinating conjunctions, the first indicating merely a link between two items and the second a disjunction. Words may have more than one sense. In one sense, *brother* is a kinship term, in another it is a religious term.

The denotation of a word is the relationship between the word and the set of entities, situations, and attributes that exist outside the language. In its most common use the word *cat* denotes (or refers to) a class of small four-legged domesticated animals; the adjective *round* denotes a particular shape; *talk* denotes a type of activity. The word *unicorn* denotes a mythical animal, a being in an imaginary world. Even if we do not believe in fairies or demons, the words *fairy* or *demon* have denotations for us. Words are often fuzzy at the edges in their denotation. The set denoted by a word may have very typical members but there may also be items about which people are in doubt whether they belong to the set. The word *bird* obviously denotes robins, pigeons, and sparrows, but is a bat a bird? Trousers and skirts are prototypical for *clothes*, but shoes and gloves seem peripheral to the set. When is it appropriate to refer to a person as being *old*? Can we agree on which countries to call *democracies*? Where on a leg does a *foot* begin? Can we distinguish precisely between *run* and *jog*?

Whereas every word has one or more senses, not every word has a denotation. For example the articles *a* and *the* and the conjunctions *and* and *because* have senses that can be defined for their use in the language, but they do not denote anything outside the language.

The connotation of a word is the emotive associations that a word evokes. Contrast the typical connotations of *mother*, *stepmother*, and *mother-in-law*. There may, however, be individual connotations, based on experience, that contradict the stereotypical connotations.

Reference is what a word—more commonly a phrase—refers to in a particular utterance. Somebody may call out:

> Your dog is jumping on me. Get the beast off me.

The phrase *your dog* refers to a particular dog in the situation. If the sentences were said in a different situation, *your dog* might refer to a different dog. We infer that *the beast* in the second sentence refers to the same dog as *your dog* does. The reference of the two phrases is the same (they are co-referential) in the particular context, but the senses of the two phrases are different. The person might have used a pronoun (*it*, *him*, *her*) instead of *the beast*, which would also be co-referential with *your dog*. We can interpret the sense of each word or phrase out of context and may also be able to infer which are co-referential without knowing what they refer to.

Chapter 9
The Formation of Words

Summary

Other types of word-formation (9.29–34)

Morphology (9.35–9)

Chapter 9 Summary

- Words may be simple or composite. Composite words are composed of smaller units.

- Affixes—prefixes and suffixes—are attached to the base of a word. The root is what remains when all affixes are removed. Some words are compounds, consisting of more than one base.

- New words may be borrowed from other languages or from other national varieties of the language, or they may result from the addition of new meanings to existing words. New words are also created from existing words by various processes of word-formation.

- The four main processes of word-formation are prefixation, suffixation, compounding, and conversion.

- Combining forms, such as *astro-* and *-logy*, resemble both affixes and bases.

- Prefixes are grouped semantically: supportive and opposing, reversative and deprivative, negative, pejorative, place, size, time, status, number. There are also class-changing prefixes.

- Suffixes tend to be class-changing. They are grouped according to the resulting word class: verbs, adjectives, concrete nouns, abstract nouns, adverbs.

- Compounds are distinguished from phrases conceptually, by being written solid or hyphenated, or by their stress pattern. It is best to take account of all three criteria. Compounds are found in all word classes, but particularly in nouns and adjectives.

- Conversion is the process of shifting a word to a different word class without adding an affix. The major types of shifting are nouns from verbs, verbs from nouns, and verbs from adjectives.

- Minor processes of word-formation are back-formation (dropping what is thought to be a suffix), clipping (omission of one or more syllables), creation of acronyms (words derived from initial letters of parts of a word or phrase), blends (compounds formed from parts of words), onomatopoeia, and conversion of proper names.

- Morphology is the study of the internal structure of words. Its two major branches are word-formation and inflection.

- Morphemes are abstract units in the structure of words. They are represented by morphs, actual forms of a word or a part of a word. Variant members of a set of morphs (e.g. *in-* of *incompetence* and *il-* of *illegal*) are allomorphs of the same morpheme.

- The choice of allomorphs depends on three types of conditioning: phonetic (determined by the following or preceding sound), lexical (dependent on the particular word), and grammatical (dependent on the word class). Some allomorphic variation may be ascribed to stylistic conditioning, and some to free variation.

- A portmanteau morph represents more than one morpheme but cannot be divided into morphs. An empty morph (e.g. *to* in *to say*) has no meaning. A suppletive morph is a form from a different root used in the paradigm of a particular word (e.g. *go, went*). A zero morph signifies the absence of a morph to represent a morpheme expected in the grammatical system.

- A free morph can occur by itself as a word. A bound morph is always combined with another morph.

- A paradigm is a set of grammatically related forms of verbs. Paradigms for verbs are conjugations, and those for nouns are declensions.

The Structure of Words

9.1
Simple words and composite words

Some of the most frequent words in our language are simple: they cannot be divided into smaller meaningful segments: *and, the, if, on.* Most words, however, are composite in that they have a recognizable internal structure.[1] We know that the adjective *unhappy* consists of *un-* plus *happy* because *happy* occurs as a word by itself and *un-* is found with the same negative meaning in other words (*untidy, unwell, unkind*). A different *un-*, reversative in meaning, appears in the verbs *uncover, undress, unlock, untie.*

9.2
Affix, prefix, suffix, base, root

Unhappy consists of the word *happy* to which the affix *un-* has been attached. If the affix comes at the beginning (like *un-* in *unhappy*) it is a prefix, if it comes at the end (like *-ly* in *happily*) it is a suffix. *Unhappily* therefore has both a prefix and a suffix.

The segment to which an affix is attached need not occur as a word itself:

capture = capt + ure

We find *capt* in other words—*captive, captor, captivate, recapture*—each of them with affixes that appear elsewhere. *Capt* is the root of these words, but unlike *happy* it does not exist as a word. The root is what remains when we strip all the affixes from a word.

More precisely, we attach affixes to the base of a word, which is not necessarily identical with its root. The word *recapture* has the structure *re-* plus *capture*; the prefix *re-* is attached not to the root *capt* but to the base *capture*. The structure of a complex word that has a base distinct from its root is illustrated by the diagram **(Fig. 9.2.1)** for *undoubtedly*. The diagram shows that the root *doubt* is the base for *doubted*, that *doubted* is the base for *undoubted*, so *undoubted* (and not the obsolete word *doubtedly*) is the base for *undoubtedly*

In a further complication, some words are compounds, consisting of more than one base: *backache, dry-clean, mother-in-law.* The bases of compounds may have their own affixes: *printmaker, non-profit-making.* In some instances, the affix applies to the compound as a whole rather than to one of the bases: *kindhearted, matter-of-factly*; we know *-ed* is attached to *kindheart-* and *-ly* to *matter-of-fact-* because we do not have *hearted* and *factly.*

It is often unclear what the root of a word is, particularly for many borrowings from Greek and Latin, since their etymology is not known to most speakers of the language, or for words that in the course of centuries have

Fig. 9.2.1 Structure of a complex word

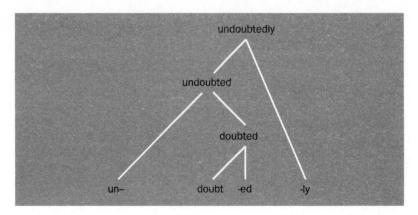

changed their form or meaning. Does *handsome* consist of the root *hand* (perhaps related to the word *hand*) and the suffix *-some* (which is a suffix in *toothsome, awesome, troublesome*) or should we rather say that it is an unanalysable whole for present-day speakers? Is there a shared root in *exceed, proceed, succeed* or in *accept, except, precept*? Answers will depend on how much weight is given to etymology and how much to the contemporary meanings.

For this chapter, such questions can be left aside, since we are mainly concerned with how new words are formed in our own period. In 9.35–9 you will find a broader conspectus on the study of word-structure.

Sources of New Words and Meanings

9.3
Borrowings and existing resources

A major source for new words in our language, especially in earlier periods, is the acceptance of words from other languages (cf. 8.2–9). Among loanwords that have been acquired or have achieved prominence during the last decade are *perestroika* and *glasnost* from Russian, *bimbo* and *galleria* from Italian, *intifada* and *fatwa* from Arabic, *karaoke* and *futon* from Japanese, *fromage frais* from French. Words or expressions may also come from another national variety of English. American English, in particular, is a rich source of words and expressions for other varieties of English. They are spread through the mass media and may be rapidly assimilated without people being aware of their origin. *Yuppie, fax, headhunt,* and *safe sex* are several of the numerous successful entrants in recent times from the United States. Other national varieties have contributed too: British English has benefited from the useful Australian expressions *go walkabout* and *wheelie-bin*.

Our vocabulary stock also increases substantially through the addition of new meanings to existing words or expressions, such as the metaphorical extensions of *menu* for a set of options in a computer program and of *paste* for a computer process of transferring text (cf. 8.10–12).

Finally, new words and expressions are created from the resources of the language itself. They are formed from existing words in a variety of ways. Word-formation is the topic of this chapter and will be treated in detail in subsequent sections.

Main Types of Word-Formation

9.4
Prefixation, suffixation, compounding, conversion

Present-day English has four main processes that result in the formation of new words:

1. prefixation: the addition of a prefix in front of a base; for example: *pro-life, recycle, deselect*
2. suffixation: the addition of a suffix at the end of a base; for example: *ageism, marginalize, additive*
3. Compounding (or composition): the combination of two or more bases; for example: *hands-on* (as in *hands-on experience*), *helpline, spin doctor*
4. conversion: the change of a base from one word class to another without any change in form; for example: the verbs *email, fax,* and *microwave* derive from the nouns of the same form.

Minor types of word-formation are discussed in 9.30–4.

Prefixation and suffixation are types of affixation (or derivation) that differ most obviously in positioning but also in another important respect.[2] Typically, prefixation is class-maintaining in that it retains the word class of the base. Retention when a prefix is added is illustrated by the noun pair *choice/pro-choice*, the adjective pair *green/ungreen*, and the verb pair *select/deselect*. Suffixation tends to be class-changing. Change when a suffix is added is illustrated by the shift from the adjective *fat* to the noun *fattism*, the verb *lug* to the adjective *luggable*, and the verb *highlight* to the noun *highlighter.* There are exceptions in both directions. Prefixation brings about a shift from the adjective *sure* to the verb *ensure*, from the noun *mask* to the verb *unmask*, and from the noun *friend* to the verb *befriend*. Suffixation has no effect on the word class of the noun pairs *martyr/martyrdom*, *author/authorships*, and *host/hostess*, or the adjective pairs *kind/kindly* and *economic/economical*, though there is a shift in subclass from concrete noun to abstract noun in the first two noun pairs.

Affixation, compounding, and conversion may co-occur. The adjective *red-handed* ('They were caught red-handed') is composed of the phrase *red hand* to which the suffix *-ed* has been added to form a compound; the adjective compound *user-friendly*, composed of two words with their own suffixes (*-er* and *-ly*), is the base for the noun compound *user-friendliness*, while the compounds *user-unfriendly* and *user-unfriendliness* have a prefix in their second segment as well; from the noun compound *necklace* in its metaphorical use (in the context 'killing by burning a tyre around the victim's neck') has been formed the verb compound *necklace* by conversion, and the verb in turn has become the base for the compound noun *necklacing* by suffixation.

Inflections—those suffixes that change the grammatical forms of words (cf. 9.35)—generally come at the very end of a compound or suffixed word:[3]

> reader-friendly/reader-friendlier/reader-friendliest
> headhunt/headhunts/headhunted/headhunting
> marginalize/marginalizes/marginalized/marginalizing

Affixes and processes of word-formation are productive when they are commonly used to form new words: we might think of the suffix *-ness* for making new nouns or the negative prefixes *un-* and *non-*. On the other hand, we rarely find new nouns formed with the suffix *-hood* or new adjectives with the suffix *-ly*, so these two have severely limited productivity.

This chapter deals with word-formation in ordinary language and therefore excludes, for example, affixes that are used only in scientific and technical vocabulary.

9.5
Combining form

Straddling affixation and compounding are processes involving combining forms. Combining forms are segments that do not occur as separate words in the language (cf. 9.39, bound morphs) and like affixes they are attached before or after another segment to constitute a word. They are usually neo-classical; that is to say, they are mostly segments originating from Latin and Greek that are used to form words in English. Examples of initial combining forms are *Anglo-, astro-, bio-, electro-, Euro-, psycho-, tele-*; examples of final combining forms are *-cide, -cracy, -gram, -graph, -logy, -phile, -phobe*. These may be combined with established English words: *biochemistry, electromagnetism, psychotherapy, Eurosceptic, teleconference, meritocracy, futurology, escapologist*. In this way, elements from the classical languages enjoy a new life in English, forming words that did not exist in the original languages. Apart from their use in non-specialized language, combining forms are a common feature of scientific terminology, particularly in chemistry and pharmacology.

Initial combining forms generally end in a vowel, mostly *o*, though other vowels are also found, e.g. *agriculture, docudrama*. When a new initial combining form is created, it tends to end in *o*. It may be shortened for that purpose from a longer word: *eco-*, from *ecology* and *ecological*, provides the first segment of *ecosystem* and *ecocentric; Euro-*, from *Europe* and *European*, yields *Eurocrat* and *Eurospeak*. If that possibility is not available, the combining vowel *o* is added to convert the first segment into a combining form, as in *speedometer, futurology, meritocracy, Francophone*.

Combining forms resemble affixes in being initial or final segments of words. However, two combining forms can be joined to form a word (*psychology, homophobe, Eurocrat, astronaut*), just as two bases can be conjoined in a compound word, whereas it is not possible to have a word consisting of just a prefix and a suffix. Indeed, final combining forms regularly combine only with initial combining forms: *-logy*, for example, requires an initial combining form such as *psycho-, socio-, anthropo-, futuro-, escapo-*. Hence, *pigeoncide* (attested in a news item in the British daily *The Independent*, 2 January 1991, p. 1) is irregular, though intelligible, as would be *spacenaut* in place of *astronaut*.

Prefixes

9.6
Recent coinages

It is convenient to treat initial combining forms that occur frequently together with prefixes. Many of these initial segments are commonly used nowadays to form new words. The alphabetical list below presents recent coinages for a number of prefixes and initial combining forms.

anti-choice	hypertext	pan-African
bicultural	interface	paramedic
co-presenter	intra-uterine	postmodernism
counter-culture	macrobiotic	preschooler
deselect	maxiseries	proactive
difunctional	megastar	reflag
disinvest	microsurgery	retrofire
eco-tourism	minibreak	supergun
Eurosceptic	multimedia	ungreen
ex-directory	neo-colonialism	unisex
gigabyte	non-proliferation	up-market

Prefixes presumed no longer productive, except possibly as deliberate archaisms, can sometimes be resurrected. Witness the recent use of *a-* in the adjective *adither*:

> The Labour Party, however, is already adither over the desirability of complying as fully as Mr King suggests with Resolution 678. [W2E-001-18]

Co-ordination of prefixes is possible with a few related prefixes:

> pro- and anti-war   pre- and post-1945   micro- and midi-computers

The sections that follow contain semantic groupings of prefixes, including some initial combining forms and initial segments that appropriately belong with them even if by some criteria they are more properly analysed as initial bases in compounds.

9.7
Supportive and opposing

pro-	('on the side of'):	pro-choice, pro-life, pro-market
anti-	('against', 'counteracting'):	antibody, anti-abortion, anticoagulant
	('spurious'):	anti-hero, antichrist
contra-	('against'):	contraception, contraindicate
	('contrasting'):	contraflow, contradistinction

counter-	('in opposition to'):	counteract, counter-example, counter-espionage

Pro- and *anti-*, the most common prefixes in this set, are antonyms. They can be freely used with nouns and adjectives to express support or opposition.

9.8
Reversative and deprivative

de-	('reverse of something'):	decriminalize, deselect, decontaminate
	('remove something'):	debug, defrost, delouse
	('depart from' or 'cause to depart from'):	deplane, detrain, decamp
dis-	('reverse of something'):	disqualify, disinvite, disenfranchise
	('remove something'):	disarm, disillusion, disambiguate
un-	('reverse of something'):	unscramble, untie, unlock
	('remove something'):	unleaded, unmask, unhouse

The reversative sense may be illustrated by *decriminalize*, which denotes the act of undoing the previous act of making something criminal. To *debug* has a deprivative sense: it means to remove bugs (literally, insects, and metaphorically, either hidden microphones or defects in a system). The departure sense of the prefix *de-* is rarely used to form new words. A creative use of reversative *un-* appeared in the headlines *Vietnam unblackballed* (*The Economist*, 25 July 1992, p. 59).

When they exist, the antonyms of these prefixed words are mostly the corresponding unprefixed words: *disarm/arm*, *unleaded/leaded*. In the departure sense, the corresponding antonyms (where they exist) have the prefix *en-* or (before bases beginning with *b* or *p*) *em-*: *decamp/encamp*, *deplane/emplane*.

9.9
Negative

a-	('not'):	atheist, asymmetric
	('not affected by'):	amoral, apolitical, asexual
dis-	('not'):	disloyal, distrust, disagree

in-	('not'):	illegal, incapable,
il- (before *l*)		imperfect, irregular
im- (before *b*, *m*, or *p*)	('absence of'):	intolerance, impatience,
ir- (before *r*)		injustice
non-	('not'):	non-aggression, non-interference, non-stop
	('not regarded as'):	non-person, non-event
un-	('not'):	unfair, unproductive

The antonyms are the corresponding unprefixed words. There are some interesting sets of related words that illustrate differences between these negative prefixes. Both *amoral* and *immoral* are antonyms of *moral*, but in careful usage *amoral* refers to behaviour to which standards of morality cannot be applied (for example, the behaviour of animals, which are assumed not to have a moral code). *Non-American* is a neutral descriptive term, whereas *un-American* denotes behaviour that is judged not to conform to assumed American norms; *non-scientific* is neutral ('not connected with science') and *unscientific* is evaluative ('not conforming to scientific standards of investigation'). *In-* and *dis-* are generally found in words of Latin or French origin. *Un-* and *non-* are the two regular negative prefixes for new words.[4]

Inflammable is derived from *inflame*, where *in-* is a causative prefix, and means 'capable of being set on fire'. Because confusion with the negative prefix could be dangerous, it has usually been replaced on substances and manufactured objects by *flammable*, the negative ('not capable of being set on fire') being *non-flammable* or *non-inflammable*.

Irregardless has two negative affixes, the prefix *ir-* and the suffix *-less*. Since *regardless* is well-established in the language, objections have been voiced against *irregardless*, which is intended to have the same meaning but has the redundant prefix.

The prefix *non-* comes from Latin via French, as do the words *negative* and *null*. A large number of words make use of the Old English words *nā* ('not', 'not at all') and *ne* ('not' or 'nor'):

no	neither	nobody	naught (*or* nought)
nor	never	nothing	naughty
not	none	nowhere	

In Old English a number of verbs had negative forms, produced by prefixing *n-* (contracted from *ne*) to the normal form and displacing the initial *w* if present. Thus, *ne* + *is* became *nis*, *ne* + *wǣs* became *nǣs*, and *ne* + *wolde* became *nolde*. The corresponding negative forms in Modern English have *n't* (contracted from *not*) attached at the end, with other changes in some instances: *isn't*, *wasn't*, *wouldn't*, *can't*, *won't*. The older negative form is preserved in *willy-nilly* ('whether one likes it or not'), literally 'I am willing, I am unwilling'.

9.10
Pejorative

crypto-	('concealed'):	crypto-fascist, crypto-Catholic, cryptography
mal-	('improper'):	malpractice, malformation, malnutrition
	('badly'):	maltreat, malfunction, maladjusted
mis-	('wrong'):	mismanagement, misinformation, mismarriage
	('wrongly'):	miscalculate, misgovern, mishandle
pseudo-	('false'):	pseudo-education, pseudo-intellectual, pseudo-science
	('imitation'):	pseudo-Elizabethan, pseudo-Gothic

Words formed with the prefixes *crypto-* and *pseudo-* can contrast neatly. A crypto-Catholic is a Catholic who conceals his religious affiliation; a pseudo-Catholic is a non-Catholic who pretends to be a Catholic.

Unlike *mal-* (which originated as a prefix in borrowings from French), *mis-* is a frequent prefix. *Disinformation* has a more restricted meaning than *misinformation*; it refers to the intentional spreading of false or distorted information, usually by governmental agencies and particularly by intelligence agencies.

9.11
Place

ante-	('before'):	antechamber, ante-room
circum-	('around'):	circumnavigate, circumlocution, circumcision
extra-	('outside', 'beyond'):	extramarital, extracurricular, extrasensory
fore-	('in front'):	forefinger, forecourt, foreskin
	('front part of'):	forehead, forefront, foreground
in-, il-, im-, ir-	('in'):	ingathering, indoors, in-patient
	('into'):	immigrate, ingrown, import
inter-	('between'):	interracial, international, interdisciplinary
intra-	('inside'):	intramural, intra-uterine, intravenous
mid-	('middle'):	midfield, mid-point, midway
out-	('out of', 'outside'):	outdoor, out-patient, outlook
	('surpass'):	outdistance, outbid, outnumber

over-	('from above', 'outer'):	overthrow, overshadow, overcoat
	('excessive')	overemphasis, overenthusiasm
	('excessively')	over-anxious, overcharge, overfish
retro-	('backwards'):	retroflex, retrorocket, retroject
sub-	('below'):	subway, subsoil, subconscious
	('secondary'):	sub-editor, subdean
	('below the norm'):	subhuman, substandard, subzero
	('subordinate part (of)'):	subcommittee, sub-plot, sublet, subtitle
super-	('above'):	superstructure, superimpose, superterrestrial
	('beyond the norm'):	superhuman, supergun, superstar
	('excessive'):	superconformity, superconfidence
	('excessively'):	supersensitive, superabundant, supercritical
supra-	('above'):	supranational, supramundane
sur-	('above'):	surtax, surcharge, surtitle
tele-	('at a distance'):	telecommunication, telephoto, television
trans-	('across'):	transatlantic, transnational, transsexual
ultra-	('beyond'):	ultraviolet, ultrasonic
	('excessively', 'extremely'):	ultra-modest, ultra-thin, ultra-modern
under-	('below'):	underground, undercarriage, underclothes
	('too little'):	undercharge, underpay, undercook
	('subordinate'):	under-secretary, underclass

Some of these prefixes have metaphorical extensions of their literal meanings of relative place, indicating relative status or relative intensification. Others indicate time as well as place (cf. 9.13).

Not surprisingly, some of these prefixes form contrasting pairs of words: *extramural/intramural, international/intranational, indoors/outdoors, overeat/undereat, substructure/superstructure.*

In some of the new words with *tele-*, the prefix is an abbreviation of various words: *telemarketing* ('marketing by telephone'), *teleprompter* ('prompter next to a television camera'), *teleconference* ('conference where participants are linked by telecommunication devices'), *teleprinter* ('printer for telegraph messages').

The adverb *overly* is an alternative to the prefix *over-* in its 'excessively' sense, particularly in American and Scottish usage. It premodifies adjectives: *overly eager, overly scrupulous.*

9.12 Size

macro-	('large'):	macrocosm, macro-organism, macro-economics
mega-	('very large'):	megastar, megastore
micro-	('small'):	micro-computer, microsurgery, microtransmitter
	('minute'):	micro-organism, microgram, microscope
midi-	('medium'):	midibus, midi-computer
mini-	('small'):	miniseries, minibreak, minicab

Hyper- ('huge and complex') should be added to these for its use in a set of words for stores ranging in size: *mini-market, supermarket, megastore, hypermarket. Maxi-* (shortened from *maximum*) indicates the longest in a set of words for lengths of skirts or coats: *miniskirt, midiskirt, maxiskirt*; these have been shortened to the words *mini, midi, maxi. Micro-* and *macro-* form pairs of antonyms: *microcosm/macrocosm, macroeconomics/microeconomics, microscopic/macroscopic*; *micro* and *macro* are themselves used as words in computer language. *Mega* is written as a separate word in phrases such as *mega bore*, and colloquially quite independently in the sense 'very good' ('She was mega').

9.13 Time

ante-	('before'):	antenatal, antedate
ex-	('former'):	ex-wife, ex-president, ex-colony
fore-	('before'):	foresee, foretell, foreplay
mid-	('middle'):	mid-afternoon, midwinter, midnight
neo-	('new', 'recent form of'):	neo-colonialism, neo-conservative, neo-impressionist
post-	('after'):	post-war, post-modernism, post-structuralist
pre-	('before'):	prepay, pre-existing, predate, preview, preschool
re-	('again'):	reprint, reapply, replay, renew,

We find contrasting pairs of words with *pre-* and *post-*: *pre-war/post-war*, *pre-tax/post-tax*, *predate/post-date*. Of the three prefixes meaning 'before', *pre-* is the one most used to form new words. It also competes with the others in a few words: the words in the pairs *antenatal/prenatal*, *forejudge/prejudge*, *foreordain/pre-ordain* are synonyms.

Re- appears as an English prefix in words that contrast with borrowings from French or Latin. In such contrast, the English prefix *re-* is pronounced /riː/ whereas the initial syllable of the loanwords may begin /rɪ/ or /rɛ/ or /rə/, and the English prefix is differentiated by being spelled with a hyphen: *re-cover* ('provide with a new cover')/*recover*, *re-form/reform*, *re-creation/recreation*, *re-fuse/refuse*, *re-lay/relay*, *re-mark/remark*, *re-present/represent*, *re-serve/reserve*, *re-sign/resign*.

Two prefixes that are less common (in non-scientific language) are *proto-* ('first', 'original'), as in *prototype*, and *retro-* ('back in time'), as in *retroactive*. *Retro-* has had some recent popularity in the sense 'fondness for past style or fashion', both as a word on its own, and (with the same sense) as a prefix in words such as *retro-culture* and *retro-rock*.

9.14 Status

arch-	('chief'):	archbishop, archangel, arch-rival
co-	('joint'):	co-author, co-founder, co-presenter
pro-	('deputy'):	proconsul, pro-vice-chancellor
vice-	('deputy'):	vice-president, vice admiral, vice-chancellor

To these may be added the metaphorical application of some place prefixes: *overseer*, *subdean*, *under-secretary*.

In formations from the sixteenth century, *arch-* is generally pejorative, as in *arch-hypocrite*. *Pro-* meaning 'substitute for' appears in the non-personal noun *pronoun*.

9.15 Number

mono-	('single', 'one'):	monotheism, monorail, monoplane
uni-	('one'):	unidirectional, unidimensional, unilateral
poly-	('many'):	polysyllabic, polytheism, polygraph
multi-	('many'):	multi-faith, multinational, multimillionaire
semi-	('half'):	semicircle
	('partly'):	semi-automatic, semi-conscious, semi-official

demi-	('half'):	demisemiquaver
	('partly'):	demigod
hemi-	('half'):	hemisphere, hemistich
bi-	('two'):	bifocal, bilingual, bilateral
di-	('two'):	dioxide
duo-, *du-*	('two'):	duologue, duplex
tri-	('three'):	tripartite, triangle, triennial

Mono-, *poly-*, *hemi-*, and *di-* are generally confined nowadays to forming new words in scientific discourse. Exceptions are *monophonic* in contrast with *stereophonic*, usually abbreviated to *mono* and *stereo*, and *polytechnic*, which in reference to a type of British college was abbreviated to *poly* (but since 1992 these have assumed the title of *university*). Neither *demi-* nor *duo-* are productive prefixes. For non-scientific language, the productive prefixes in this list are *uni-*, *multi-*, and *semi-*. Curiously, *unisex* does not refer to one sex but to either sex.

We find contrasting pairs in *monogamy/polygamy*, *monotheism/polytheism*, *monosyllabic/polysyllabic*, *monolingual/bilingual*. Number prefixes form many sets: *duple/triple/multiple*; *monologue/duologue* ('precisely two'), *dialogue* ('two or more'); *unicycle/bicycle/tricycle*; *unilateral/bilateral/trilateral/quadrilateral*; *triplets/quadruplets* (also shortened to *quads*), *quintuplets* (also *quins*), *sextuplets*, *septuplets*; *duet/trio/quartet/quintet* etc.; *sexagenarian/septuagenarian/octogenarian/nonagenarian*. The last months of our present calendar indicate their origin in the Roman calendar, where the year began in March and the months were once the seventh to tenth months: *September, October, November, December*. Etymologically related to *December* is *decimate* ('kill one in ten of', originally referring to the punishment for mutiny in the Roman army); it has developed the extended sense 'kill a large proportion of', which is often rejected as incorrect.

Words prefixed by *bi-* that refer to time frequency may be ambiguous; for example, *biweekly* or *bimonthly* may be taken to mean 'every two' or 'twice in one'. It is safer to use a paraphrase: 'every two weeks' or 'twice a week', etc. *Bicentenary* and *bicentennial* are unambiguously 'two hundredth'.

9.16
Class-changing

Two prefixes have as their primary effect the change of the word class. They are rarely used nowadays to form new words.

| *be-* | (for transitive verbs from nouns): | besiege, beguile, bewitch |
| | (intensifying the force of verbs): | besmear, bewail, bespatter |

	(for transitive verbs from adjectives):	belittle, becalm, befoul
	(for participle adjectives from nouns):	bespectacled, beribboned
en-, em-	(for transitive verbs from nouns, 'put in'):	encode, endanger, ensnare
	(for intransitive verbs from nouns, 'put oneself onto or into'):	enlist, embark, enrol
	(for transitive verbs from nouns, 'make into'):	enslave, ennoble
	(for transitive verbs from adjectives, 'make'):	enlarge, embitter, enrich, ensure

9.17
Miscellaneous

Here are some common productive prefixes that do not fit into previous sections.

auto-	('self'):	autograph, autopilot, auto-suggestion
bio-	(abbreviation of *biology* and *biological*):	biodegradable, biofeedback, biodiversity
eco-	(abbreviation of *ecology* and *ecological*):	ecosystem, eco-tourism
Euro- ⎫ *euro-* ⎭	(abbreviation of *Europe* and *European*):	Eurocurrencies, Eurosceptic, Europhile
para-	('ancillary'):	paramilitary, paramedic, paralegal
	('beyond the scope of'):	paranormal, parapsychology
self-		self-motivating, self-denial, self-satisfaction

Most of these are also written as separate words. The nouns *auto* and *para* have specialized meanings: *auto* as an abbreviation of *automobile*, and *para* as an abbreviation of *paratrooper* or *paragraph*.

Suffixes

9.18
Recent coinages

By analogy with prefixes (cf. 9.6), we may include with suffixes also final combining forms (cf. 9.5) and some recurring final segments that might be regarded as parts of compounds.

One of the major functions of most suffixes is to signal word class: a word ending in *-ism* is a noun, one ending in *-ize* is a verb. Suffixes commonly bring about a shift in class. *Informant* is a deverbal noun (a noun derived from the verb *inform*), whereas *freedom* is a de-adjectival noun. *Logical* is a denominal adjective (derived from the noun *logic*), *choosy* a deverbal adjective. *Modernize* is a de-adjectival verb, *hospitalize* a denominal verb. Both *snob* and *snobbery* are nouns, but *snob* is a concrete personal noun, *snobbery* an abstract noun. *Host* and *hostess* are nouns distinguished by gender.

An interesting method of creating new suffixes has become quite common in recent times. The end of a specific word is sliced off as a suffix carrying with it a major component of the meaning of the parent word and generating sets of words. Watergate was identified with a major political scandal in the USA in the early 1970s, and the word *Watergate* referred to that scandal. The word came to be used for other (mainly political) scandals, and subsequently *-gate* has spawned many other (usually ephemeral) words for scandals: *Koreagate, Westlandgate, Irangate, Iraqgate*. *Alcoholic* has given rise to terms for other types of addiction: *workaholic, shopaholic, chocoholic*. On the basis of *marathon* many new words have been formed for activities involving endurance, generally to raise funds for charities: *telethon, walkathon, readathon, sellathon*. Perhaps because of a misanalysis of *hamburger* (a derivative from the name of the city *Hamburg*) as composed of *ham + burger*, the suffix *-burger* has been applied to a certain kind of fast food: *beefburger, cheeseburger, fishburger, nutburger, tunaburger*. The computer term *hardware* has generated (among other words) *software, shareware, freeware, wetware, liveware*.

Below is a list of recent words formed by suffixation. The words are listed in the alphabetic order of the suffixes.

microwave*able*	wrinkl*ie*	retur*nik*
faction*al*	gentr*ify*	retro*philia*
gentrific*ation*	network*ing*	homo*phobe*
yuppie*dom*	wimp*ish*	homo*phobia*
finger-dri*ed*	able*ism*	homo*phobic*
fax*ee*	surviva*list*	franco*phone*
leader*ene*	recyclabil*ity*	child*proof*
bagg*er*	confront*ive*	share*ware*
bimb*ette*	privat*ize*	street*wise*
additive-*free*	eco*mania*	glitch*y*
kisso*gram*	user-friendli*ness*	

The sections that follow are arranged by word class, within which semantic groups are distinguished. The largest number of suffixes are noun suffixes. There are only a few verb or adverb suffixes.

Suffixes are more numerous than prefixes. Within the scope of this chapter the focus is on just those suffixes that continue to be productive in the general language.

9.19
Verb suffixes

-ify	beautify, purify, classify, personify
-ize, -ise	capitalize, modernize, popularize, terrorize

Only *-ize*/*-ise* is a very productive suffix. Both it and *-ify* are added to either adjective or noun bases. Other verb suffixes include the denominal *-ate*, still productive for creating scientific words (*chlorinate*), and the chiefly de-adjectival *-en* (*quieten*), which is no longer productive.

Some writers on style criticize the excessive use of words ending in *-ize* or the corresponding noun suffix *-ization*. New words formed with these suffixes are sometimes ridiculed, usually because they are associated with bureaucratic writing; *finalize*, *hospitalize*, and *prioritize* are among those that have evoked complaints in recent times, while others (for example, *privatize* and *privatization*) have apparently entered the language without opposition. As with all coinages, if they allow us to express a concept more economically they will be accepted.

For most verbs, *-ize* is the only American spelling. The predominant British spelling is still *-ise*, but *-ize* has become the house style for some British publishers, including Oxford University Press.

9.20
Adjective suffixes

-able	readable, profitable, reliable
-al, -ial	accidental, managerial, musical
-ed	cultured, heavy-handed, eagle-eyed
-ful	powerful, careful, resentful
-ic	Arabic, aristocratic, dramatic
-ish	Swedish, feverish, youngish, moreish (*or* morish)
-less	careless, harmless, restless
-like	childlike, statesmanlike, godlike
-y	funny, sleepy, choosy

Among the adjective suffixes that are no longer productive or only mildly productive are *-ary* (*inflationary*), *-ate* (*affectionate*), *-en* (*golden*), *-ive* (*attractive*), *-ly* (*friendly*), *-ory* (*inflammatory*), and *-ous* (*monotonous*).

The *-ed* suffix is distinct from the *-ed* inflection for the past and participle of verbs. It is attached to nouns or noun phrases to form adjectives: from the noun *gable* we derive the adjective *gabled* as in 'gabled house', from the noun phrase *short sight* the adjective *short-sighted*. *Wet-handed* in the example below alludes to the established word *red-handed*:

> Caught wet-handed, a Cape Coral resident argued against a ticket for watering her lawn.

The suffix *-able* is always attached to native English words. The much rarer suffix *-ible* (pronounced identically) appears primarily in words borrowed from French which end in *-ible* and in words borrowed from Latin which end in *-ibilis*. If in doubt as to whether to use *-able* or *-ible*, consult a dictionary. Dictionaries may give alternative spellings for a few of the words.

Many words ending in *-ish* that convey the meaning 'having the characteristics of' are pejorative (*fiendish, brutish, prudish*). Compare also *childish* with the neutral *childlike*. The pejorative meaning is not inherent in ethnic adjectives (*British, Jewish, Polish*) and is also absent in adjectives when the suffix conveys an approximative meaning (*youngish, smallish, reddish, sixtyish*).

Some words ending in *-ic* contrast with words having the same base but the suffix *-ical*:

economic:	economic situation, economic rent, economic theory
economical:	economical life-style, economical in buying goods, economical car
historic:	historic events, historic building
historical:	historical novel, historical approach, historical research

Other contrasts include *classic/classical, comic/comical, electric/electrical, politic/political, psychic/psychical*.

Some additional suffixes are used in forming small sets of words. They include *-free* (*gluten-free*), *-friendly* (*ozone-friendly*), *-genic* (*telegenic*), *-holic* (*chocoholic*), *-proof* (*baby-proof*).

9.21
Suffixes of concrete nouns

-ant, -ent	informant, claimant, solvent
-ee	trainee, mortgagee, absentee
-er	teacher, carer, toaster
-ery, -ry	brewery, machinery, weaponry

| *-ing* | clothing, flooring, drawing |
| *-ist* | socialist, novelist, sexist |

These suffixes chiefly form personal nouns. Other suffixes that are at best only mildly productive are *-an/-ian* (*African, Australian*), *-crat* (*Eurocrat*), *-eer* (*racketeer*), *-ess* (*hostess*), *-ette* (*kitchenette*), *-ie/-y* (*toughie, softy*), *-ite* (*suburbanite*), *-let* (*playlet*), *-ling* (*weakling*), *-ster* (*gangster*), *-ware* (*shareware*).

In certain words the suffix is spelled *-or* or *-ar* rather than *-er*. For some words there are variant spellings in *-er* and *-or* (perhaps linked to different senses of the word): *adapter/adaptor, conjurer/conjuror, converter/convertor, mortgager/mortgagor*. Some words in *-or* or *-ar* were borrowed from French or Latin without there being an English verb base: *doctor, emperor, tailor, bursar, scholar*. In other instances, verbs have been created by back-formation (cf. 9.30): *burglar/burgle, editor/edit, hawker/hawk, pedlar/peddle* (also *peddler* in American English), *scavenger/scavenge*. But there are nouns in *-or* and *-ar* that are derived from an English verb base: *conqueror, educator, exhibitor, liar, operator, visitor*.

Nouns in *-ant* and *-er/-or/-ar* generally denote a personal agent—the person who performs the action denoted by the verb base: *claimant* ('person who claims'), *contestant, baker, waiter*. Some denote impersonal agents or instruments: *disinfectant, pollutant, strainer, typewriter*. Corresponding to the active suffix *-er/-or* in some words is the passive suffix *-ee*: *examiner/examinee, franchiser* (also *franchisor*)*/franchisee, mortgager/mortgagee, nominator/nominee, payer/payee, trainer/trainee, tutor/tutee*. However, some established nouns in *-ee* have an active meaning: *absentee, escapee, refugee*; *retiree* may be interpreted as either active ('one who has retired') or passive ('one who has been retired'). Less well-established nouns with the active meaning arouse objections from some: *returnee, standee*. *Amputee* has been objected to because it is the limb that has been amputated and not the person, but it has survived objections. The opposing meanings of the *-ee* suffix can lead to confusion. A book reviewer in *The Sunday Times* was obviously confused, misusing *nominee* as active:

> He was elected to the austere American Academy and Institute of Arts and Letters in spite of having Allen Ginsberg as his nominee. (Ginsberg, we are told, also nominated his boyfriend [. . .]). [*The Sunday Times*, 10 March 1991, p. 6.3]

The suffix *-ist* forms nouns for a person connected with a particular occupation or activity (*cartoonist, cyclist, hygienist, psychiatrist, violinist*) or for an adherent of a particular ideology or attitude (*capitalist, leftist, materialist, nationalist, racist*). In the occupational or behavioural sense the corresponding abstract nouns end in *-y* (*archaeology, bigamy, botany, dentistry, psychiatry*) or *-ics* (*economics, physics*); in the ideological sense they end in *-ism* (*communism*, cf. 9.22).

The suffixes *-ery/-ry* form collective nouns for objects (*confectionery, cutlery*) or place nouns (*brewery, nursery*); *grocery* can refer to either a food that you buy) or a place (where you shop). The suffix *-ing* forms nouns for objects (*bedding, building*). Both *-ery/-ry* and *-ing* are also used to form abstract nouns, cf. 9.22.

9.22
Suffixes of abstract nouns

-age	postage, spillage, drainage
-al	betrayal, dismissal, deferral
-ation, -ion	collaboration, authorization, objection
-dom	freedom, martyrdom, officialdom
-ery, -ry	snobbery, chemistry, summitry
-ing	cleaning, gardening, manufacturing
-ism	idealism, favouritism, ageism
-ity	responsibility, technicality, publicity
-ment	arrangement, embarrassment, bewilderment
-ness	usefulness, carelessness, willingness
-ship	dictatorship, editorship, scholarship

Among the suffixes for abstract nouns that are at best only mildly productive are *-acy* (*intimacy*), *-ance/-ence* (*utterance, existence*), *-ancy/-ency* (*truancy, decency*), *-babble* (*psychobabble*), *-ful* (*mouthful*), *-hood* (*statehood*), *-line* (*chatline*), *-speak* (*Eurospeak*), *-thon* (*talkathon*).

Abstract nouns in *-ity* derive from adjectives ending in *-al/-ial, -able/-ible*, and *-ar*: *brutality, technicality, superficiality; profitability, responsibility; regularity, peculiarity*. Abstract nouns in *-acy, -ancy*, and *-ency* derive respectively from adjectives in *-ate, -ant*, and *-ent*: *accuracy, intimacy; relevancy, vacancy; agency, decency*.

The most productive abstract noun suffixes are *-ing* and *-ness*. From virtually any activity verb may be derived an *-ing* noun referring to the activity of the verb or to the occasion when the activity occurred:

> I enjoyed the *playing*.
> We attended the last *hearing*.
> Were you at their *wedding*?
> Nobody heard her *warnings*.

Abstract nouns in *-ness* can be freely formed from adjectives, but *-ness* competes with nouns in *-ity, -cy*, or *-tion*. Where an abstract noun already exists with these suffixes (such as *brutality* and *decency*), it is felt clumsy to form a noun in *-ness* (*brutalness, decentness*). However, sometimes a pair of such nouns has developed different meanings, so that both may be needed: *casualness/casualty, correctness/correction*.

9.23
Adverb suffixes

-ly   amiably, candidly, surprisingly

The *-ly* suffix can be freely added to adjective bases to form adverbs, though it is not added to adjectives ending in *-ly*, such as *friendly*. It is occasionally used with phrases, the most common example being *matter-of-factly*. Below is a conspicuous example of an adverb neologism, *transbroomstickally* (from *The Times*, 6 June 1992):

> [I]t comes as no real surprise to discover that partners who live together *transbroomstickally* before getting married are more likely to finish up in the divorce court.

The only other adverb suffix that deserves a mention is *-wise*:

> Anybody got any problems *notewise* on that [S1A-026-223] ('from the point of view of the musical notes')

Compounds

9.24
Compounds and phrases

A compound is a word consisting of two or more bases (cf. 9.2): *postcard*, *picture postcard*. Compounds contrast with phrases, which consist of two or more words that are grammatically related: *a large card*, *beautiful pictures*.

The distinction between *postcard* and *large card* can be viewed conceptually. *Postcard* is a word that we expect to find in a dictionary because it is the name of an object; *large* and *card* refer to separate concepts and would not appear as one entry in a dictionary, since *large* independently ascribes a descriptive feature to innumerable objects. Similarly, the compounds *blackbird* and *blackboard* are names of objects, neither of which are necessarily black in colour; they differ from the combinations of adjective *black* plus noun (written as separate words) in *black bird* and *black board*. *Cooking apples* ('apples for cooking') and *eating apples* ('apples for eating') are compounds naming major classes of apples by a feature of those classes that is important for human beings. The phrase *rotting apples* ('apples that are rotting'), on the other hand, does not present a characteristic feature of a class of apples, but a descriptive feature that can apply to any apples and to innumerable other things; analogous phrases are *running water, crying baby, sinking ship, sleeping patients*. *Sleeping partner* is ambiguous between phrase ('partner who is sleeping') and compound ('partner who does not take an active role'), whereas *sleeping pill* (also written *sleeping-pill*) is unambiguously a compound.

The conceptual criterion is not entirely satisfactory, since it is subjective and therefore open to disagreement in specific instances. On conceptual grounds we might be unsure whether to count as compounds such expressions as *black pepper, white people, summer school, winter vacation*. We cannot rely on dictionaries to tell us. They vary considerably in what multi-word expressions they include and they do not indicate which they regard as compounds.

Orthographic practice has been urged as evidence that an expression is perceived as a compound. It is true that expressions that are written solid (*postcard*) or hyphenated (*bird-watching*) can reliably be considered compounds. But the vagaries of orthographic practice in this respect are notorious. To take just one example, three spellings for this compound appear in dictionaries:

open:	*paper knife*
hyphenated:	*paper-knife*
solid:	*paperknife*

Other instances of pairs that are commonly found with either open or hyphenated spellings are *cease fire/cease-fire, ice cream/ice-cream, paper clip/paper-clip, sleeping bag/sleeping-bag, water ski/water-ski*. Secondly, many words that are not written solid or hyphenated should properly be counted as compounds on conceptual grounds. Apart from those mentioned earlier, these include *fancy dress, hay fever, hot dog, house arrest, space flight, travel guide*.

Another criterion is word stress. Generally, words have one main stress. Compounds tend to have their main stress on the first base (if there are only two bases), here indicated by the superscript vertical line: ˈ*blackbird,* ˈ*databank*. The same tendency applies if the compound is written as two words: ˈ*news conference,* ˈ*travel agent*. In contrast, two-word phrases tend to have the main stress on the second word: *good* ˈ*conference, personal* ˈ*agent*. But stress patterns are also not wholly reliable. First, there is considerable individual variation in the positioning of stresses. Secondly, there is variation across national varieties. For example, British English tends to have *hot* ˈ*dog* and *class-*ˈ*conscious*, while American English tends to have ˈ*hot dog* and ˈ*class-conscious*. Also, compounds consisting of an adjective or adverb as the first base and a participle as the second base normally have the main stress on the second base: *flat-*ˈ*footed, well-*ˈ*meaning*.

There are numerous exceptions to the typical stress pattern of compounds for which no generalizations or explanations can be offered. For example, names of streets have the main stress on the second word, except for names with the word *street* itself:

Edgware ˈRoad
Highfield ˈAvenue
Park ˈLane
Manor ˈDrive
ˈChurch Street

It seems odd to regard only those names with *street* as compounds.

Here are a few individual contrasts:

'black spot	black 'market
'Christmas card	Christmas 'Day
'power base	power 'steering
'rock salmon	lemon 'sole
'white people	white 'lie

Since no one criterion alone is adequate, it is best to take account of all three criteria in deciding what to regard as compounds.

9.25
Recent coinages

Below are some examples of compounds that have been coined in recent times:

alpha test	ozone hole	sound bite
brat pack	passive smoking	spin doctor
compassion fatigue	phonecard	thirtysomethings
cook-chill	photo opportunity	toyboy
junk food	safe sex	venture capitalism
lager lout	shell suit	zero option
magnet school	smart card	
neighbourhood watch	snail mail	

Nonce coinages are frequent. Outside their context, they may be opaque. It would be impossible to find an interpretation for *boiled-frog approach* in isolation, but its meaning is clear in the context of a quotation by an American management psychologist:

[1] "Some [companies] take the 'boiled-frog approach,' " in which managers turn up the productivity heat. "People get used to hotter and hotter water." [*International Herald Tribune*, 25–6 June 1992, p. 1]

Here are two more nonce coinages:

[2] I am of Scots-English ancestry, a breed as common as sparrows, but in America a man can always better himself through marriage and so, a few years ago I married a Dane. I learned to speak Danish just well enough to get into trouble and I visit the *motherland-in law* whenever possible and try to improve myself. ['They Eat and Talk Together (How Odd!) but Think Apart', by Garrison Keillor, *International Herald Tribune*, 7 September 1993, p. 7]

[3] In Washington, President Bill Clinton strongly endorsed Mr. Yeltsin's handling of the standoff.
   "I think so far they've done quite well," Mr. Clinton said. "I don't think that any of us should be here basically *armchair quarterbacking* the unfolding events." [*International Herald Tribune*, 30 September 1993, p. 1]

The opaqueness applies equally to many—if not most—established compounds. We have to learn what they mean, though their components may provide a clue or a reminder. We could not, for example, interpret *smart card* or *magnet school* simply by knowing their components. Humourists have played on false interpretations: *turncoat* ('a reversible jacket'), *blunderbuss* ('an awkwardly placed kiss'); so also for affixed words: *liability* ('the ability to lie').[5]

9.26
Compounds in word classes

Compounds are found in all word classes:

nouns:	pop group, whistle-blower, date-rape
adjectives:	class-ridden, heart-breaking, homesick
verbs:	babysit, dry-clean, cold-shoulder
adverbs:	good-naturedly, however, nowadays
pronouns:	anyone, everything, nobody
numerals:	sixty-three, nine-tenths
prepositions:	as for, because of, next to
semi-auxiliaries:	be going to, had better, have got to
conjunctions:	except that, rather than, whenever

New coinages are mainly nouns and adjectives.

Historically, compound verbs are derived chiefly from nouns. They may be derived by conversion (cf. 9.29), simply a shift in word class from a noun compound without any other change: *blackmail, cold-shoulder, daydream*. Or they may be derived by back-formation (cf. 9.30), the removal of a suffix: *babysit* (from *babysitting* or *babysitter*), *double-park* (from *double parking*), *shoplift* (from *shoplifting*).

Some of the prepositions, semi-auxiliaries, and conjunctions are not strictly compounds because the segments can be separated by the insertion of other words: *because (however) of; was (perhaps) going to; except (I think) that.*

As with prefixes (cf. 9.6), some initial segments of compounds can be co-ordinated:

English- and French-speaking
mothers- and fathers-in-laws
eating or cooking apples

Some compounds, chiefly nouns and adjectives, are reduplicatives: the segments are identical (*clever-clever*) or near-identical. If near-identical, they differ in the initial consonant (*teeny-weeny*) or more commonly in the medial vowel (*tick-tock*). They tend to be very informal and some are restricted to nursery language (*chuff-chuff, din-din*) or pseudo-baby talk intended affectionately (*mumsie-wumsie*). They may (1) imitate sounds (*quack-quack, bow-wow*), (2) suggest movements up and down or back and forth, perhaps also imitating sounds (*flip-flop*, *ping-pong*), and from that literal use metaphorical instability (*hocus-pocus*, *mishmash*), and (3) intensify (*goody-goody*, *hush-hush*). American English has borrowed from Yiddish the reduplicative device in which *schm-* appears at the beginning of the second word to deride the use of the first word: *chairman-schmairman*, *architects-schmarchitects*.

9.27
Compound nouns

In the most common type of compound noun the final segment denotes the general class of entities to which the compound belongs: *travel guide* is a kind of guide, *pop group* a kind of group, *Dover sole* a kind of sole, *blackbird* a kind of bird. This relationship is absent from—or at least not transparent in—many compounds: *whistle-blower* is someone who blows the whistle metaphorically, *summer house* denotes a building but not a house, *hotdog* certainly does not refer to a dog in the usual sense, and *washer-dryer* refers to an object that combines equally the functions of a washer and a dryer.

The relationships between the segments of compound nouns can often be explained in grammatical terms. A segment may be a noun, a verb or a word derived from a verb, or an adjective. The relationship, for example, may be that of subject + verb, verb + object, or subject + predicative. Examples appear below.

subject + verb:	bee sting ('bee stings'), headache, snowfall
verb + subject:	answerphone ('phone answers'), playboy, washing machine
verb + object:	chewing gum ('chews gum'), cooking apple, know-all
object + verb:	air-conditioner ('conditions air'), sightseeing, travel guide

Note the contrast between *call-girl* ('calls girl') and *call-boy* ('boy calls').

subject + object:	cable car ('the cable operates the car'), compassion fatigue ('(excessive) compassion causes fatigue'), hay fever ('hay causes fever')
object + subject:	honey-bee ('bee produces honey'), news agency ('agency distributes news'), pop group ('group plays pop')
verb + instrument:	hearing aid ('hears with an aid'), plaything, washcloth
instrument + verb:	gunfight ('fights with a gun'), fly-fishing, word play
verb + place:	dance hall ('dances in a hall'), driveway, swimming pool

place + verb:	boat ride ('rides on a boat'), factory worker, home help
verb + time:	closing time ('closes at that time'), payday ('pays on that day'), rush hour
time + verb:	daydreaming ('dreams during day'), night worker, spring-cleaning

Many compounds are composed of two nouns or an adjective plus a noun, where the verb *be* can link the two segments in a subject + predicative relation.

adjective + noun:	passive smoking ('the smoking is passive'), smart card, white lie
noun + noun:	
'B is A'	booster shot ('the shot is a booster'), junk food, willow tree
'B is like A'	magnet school ('the school is like a magnet'), shell suit, toyboy
'B is for A'	ashtray ('the tray is for ash'), raincoat, safety belt
'B is part of A'	door handle ('the handle of a door'), fingertip, table leg

One type of compound noun, whose first segment may be a noun or an adjective, refers to an entity indirectly by a characteristic:

loudmouth:	('person who has a loud mouth')
hunchback:	('person who has a hunched back')
paperback:	('book that has a paper cover')

9.28 Compound adjectives

Most compound adjectives end in an adjective (*sea-sick*), an *-ing* participle (*soul-destroying*), or an *-ed* participle (*well-dressed*). One common type is formed by adding the *-ed* suffix to a compound noun (*short-sighted*, cf. 9.20).

The grammatical relationships between the segments of compound adjectives can be explained in the same way as for compound nouns (cf. 9.27).

object + verb:	English-speaking ('speaks English'), germ-resistant, soul-destroying
place/time/cause + verb:	far-reaching ('reaches far'), home-made ('made at home'), frost-bitten ('bitten by frost')
noun + adjective:	
'A is B'	footsore ('the foot is sore'), heart-sick, top-heavy
'as B as A'	dirt-cheap ('as cheap as dirt'), jet black, paper-thin

The first segment in this relationship has an intensifying force ('extremely cheap').

> *'B in respect of A'*   camera-shy ('shy in respect of cameras'), colour-blind, power-mad

Some compounds imply a co-ordination relationship:

> *'A and B'*   aural-oral, bitter-sweet, deaf-mute

These may be associated with words containing initial combining forms: *Anglo-Irish, psycho-linguistic, socio-economic.*

Here are some examples of compounds formed by adding an *-ed* suffix to a compound noun: *foul-mouthed, right-angled, single-minded.*

Other Types of Word-Formation

9.29
Conversion

Conversion is the process of shifting a word to a different word class without adding an affix. It resembles suffixation, which usually has the same effect. For example, from the adjective *humid* is derived the verb *humidify* ('make humid') by suffixation. Analogously, from the adjective *wet* is derived the verb *wet* ('make wet') by conversion. Conversion similarly produces from the concrete noun *water* the verb *water* ('provide with water'), and from the verb *swim* the abstract noun *swim* (as in 'I'm going for a swim'). Most instances involve the conversion of nouns to verbs or of verbs to nouns.

With suffixation it is easy to see which word came first; it is obviously the word to which the suffix was added (but cf. back-formation, 9.30). Historical research on the direction of conversion can sometimes find evidence for which word entered the language first. For example, we know that the verb *talk* appeared about three centuries before the noun *talk*. Even without the historical evidence, we are likely to feel that the verb is the base, perhaps because the noun fits into a set of abstract nouns that refer to an event or activity denoted by verbs: *have a chat/drink/fight/look/quarrel/sleep/swim/walk/wash.* It would be difficult to define some of these nouns—for example, *smoke* in *have a smoke*—without referring to the verb. We might explain the noun *bore* as denoting someone who habitually bores others; we would hardly explain the verb *bore* as referring to what a bore does. On the other hand, the verb *carpet* in the sense 'provide with a carpet' clearly derives from the noun.

Relative frequency may also support our intuition. We are aware that the noun *party* is much more frequent than the verb *party*, which suggests that the verb was converted from the noun. Three recent instances of conversion of nouns to verbs are *fax*, *parent*, and *video*.

The major types of conversion are listed below.

1. Nouns from verbs

state:	dislike, doubt, know (as in *in the know*)
action:	laugh, offer, walk
agent:	bore ('person or thing that bores'), rebel, sneak
affected:	drink ('what someone drinks'), find, reject
instrument:	cure ('something one uses to cure'), polish, wrap
place:	dump ('where something is dumped'), haunt, stop (as in *bus stop*)

2. Verbs from nouns

to produce:	echo, knot, tunnel
to make into:	cash, clone, orphan
to put into/on:	box, garage, shelve
to provide with:	butter, finance, label
to remove:	peel ('to remove the peel'), skin, weed
to do something with:	bomb, comb, hammer
to transport by:	cart, ship, wire
to go by:	bicycle, motor, ski
to act as:	bully, mother, tutor

3. Verbs from adjectives

to become:	faint, idle, slim
to make:	calm, clean, smooth

There are occasional uses of conversion involving other word classes and involving constructions:

> They tried to *out* him. (adverb to verb)
> That course is a *must* for someone like you. (auxiliary to noun)
> Don't give me any *ifs* or *buts*. (conjunctions to nouns)
> I haven't yet learned the *ins* and *outs* of the business.
>   (adverbs/prepositions to nouns)
> I don't have the *know-how*. (verb plus adverb to noun)

Here are some recent examples:

> The theory is that humans, who are after all only *jumped-up* animals, emit a chemical *come-hither* from their sweat glands when they are in the mood for mating. [*The Observer Life*, 17 October 1993, p. 4] (verb + adverb to adjective and to noun)

> "Yes, this may be a *de facto* presidency," someone said. "But Al Gore will have to accept he is not one of the *co-es*." [*The Independent*, 22 January 1993, p. 11] (prefix to noun)

> A constant refrain from *has-been* and *never-were* journalists is that investigative journalism is dead. [*The Sunday Times*, 24 January 1993, p. 3] (auxiliary + verb and adverb + verb to adjectives)

> But I do get chemically depressed and during this separation I got depressed. *I-lost-20lb-in-three-weeks* depressed. It was bad. [*The Times, Life magazine*, 1 May 1994, p. 8, quoting Hollywood agent] (sentence to intensifier)
>
> Gunnell prefers the serious *taking-care-of-business* approach, but she is increasingly out of fashion. [*The Times*, 7 August 1992, p. 14] (participle clause to adjective)
>
> The dowdy and apologetic *I'm-a-servant-of-the-proletariat* look has gone for good. [*The Times*, 7 August 1992, p. 14] (sentence to adjective)

One change of subclass is worth mentioning, that of proper noun to common noun:

> She's going to buy a *Rover*.
> They're auctioning a couple of *Picassos*.
> Pass me your *Shakespeare*.

These common nouns refer to instances of products bearing the name. But some names of products have been generalized to refer to other products having the same function; for example, *hoover* and *xerox*, used both as nouns and (by conversion) as verbs.

9.30
Back-formation

Back-formation is the process of deriving words by dropping what is thought to be a suffix or (occasionally) a prefix. It applies chiefly to the coining of verbs from nouns. Recent back-formations include the adjective *abled* from *disabled* and the verb *explete* from *expletive*.

Some people find new back-formations ugly and have objected to them for that reason. Most derivations by back-formation are well-established, and their origin by that process is recognized only by those who have studied the history of the language. Only a very few common back-formations are still felt to be such by at least some people—chiefly perhaps *emote* (from *emotion*), *enthuse* (*enthusiasm*), *liaise* (*liaison*). Although *editor* appeared before *edit*, in a description of current English it is appropriate to analyse *editor* as derived from *edit* by the addition of the suffix *-or*.

The two major sources of back-formation are (1) nouns (including compound nouns) ending in *-er/-or/-ar* or *-ing*, and (2) nouns ending in *-tion* or *-ion*. It is not always possible to determine for the first group whether the source is the agent suffix or the *-ing* suffix. Examples of these two groups are given below, followed by a miscellaneous group (3).

(1a)   burgle, commentate, edit, peddle, scavenge, sculpt, swindle
(1b)   air-condition, babysit, brainstorm, brainwash, browbeat, dry-clean, house-hunt, housekeep, sightsee, tape-record

(2)   articulate, assassinate, coeducate, demarcate, emote, intuit, legislate, marinate, orate, vaccinate, valuate

(3)   diagnose (from *diagnosis*), enthuse (*enthusiasm*), laze (*lazy*), liaise (*liaison*), reminisce (*reminiscence*), statistic (*statistics*), televise (*television*)

Back-formation of verbs from compounds is particularly common.

9.31 Clipping

Clipping is a shortening of a word by the omission of one or more syllables. What is left may be the beginning of a word (*exam* from *examination*), less frequently the end (*phone* from *telephone*), and infrequently the middle (*flu* from *influenza*). They are usually informal, though they may lose their informality when they usurp the place of the full form: *bus* (from *omnibus*), *mob* (from *mobile*, shortened from the Latin *mobile vulgus*), *pants* (from *pantaloons*). Even when the full form is still current, the clipping may predominate and may be felt to be neutral in style, so that the full form is stylistically marked as formal: *lunch* (*luncheon*), *plane* (*airplane/aeroplane*), *pram* (*perambulator*), *stereo* (*stereophonic*), *taxi* (*taxicab*, from *taximeter cab*).

Here are some further examples of clippings:

bike (bicycle)
decaf (decaffeinated coffee)
fan (fanatic)
fax (facsimile)
fridge (refrigerator)
hyper (hyperactive)
intercom (intercommunication system)
lab (laboratory)
medic (medical student/doctor)
memo (memorandum)
mike (microphone)
movie (moving picture)
photo (photograph)
pub (public house)
zoo (zoological gardens)

The American clipping of *mathematics* is *math* while the British clipping is *maths*.

Names may also be clipped: *Liz/Beth/Betsy* (*Elizabeth*), *Fred* (*Frederick*), *Tom* (*Thomas*), *Frisco* (*San Francisco*).

Generally, clippings originate in some group where the abbreviation is easily understood. They may remain confined to the group or percolate into the general language.

9.32
Acronyms

Acronyms are another abbreviatory device. They are words—generally nouns—formed from the initial letters of parts of a word or phrase. The letters may be pronounced as words (*AIDS*, also *Aids*, from *Acquired Immune Deficiency Syndrome*) or they may be pronounced as a series of letters (*UN*), in which case they are sometimes distinguished from acronyms by being called initialisms or alphabetisms.

Acronyms have been a very productive method of creating new words in the last few decades. They are commonly used for names of organizations, and often the name has been chosen because it lends itself to an appropriate acronym: *ASH* (*Action on Smoking and Health*). Sometimes people know what the acronym refers to without knowing what the initials stand for: *radar* (*radio detection and ranging*). One of the dangers of acronyms for communication is that people may not understand them, since the initials give no clue to the composition of the words. If there is any doubt on this score, it is best when writing to add the full form or a paraphrase in parentheses.

Here are some further examples of acronyms:

AI	artificial intelligence
a.s.a.p.	as soon as possible
CD-ROM	compact disk, read-only memory
ECU	European Currency Unit
EEG	electroencephalogram
e.g.	*exempli gratia* ('for example' in Latin)
HIV	human immunodeficiency virus
NIMBY, nimby	not in my backyard
PC	personal computer
PS	postscript
RSVP	*répondez s'il vous plaît* ('please answer' in French)
scuba	self-contained underwater breathing apparatus

There may also be combinations of acronyms with words: *email* (*electronic mail*).

9.33
Blends

Blends are yet another abbreviatory device, which has also been productive in the last few decades. They are compounds formed from bits of two words: *brunch* from the combination of *breakfast* and *lunch*.

Here are some further examples:

bit	binary + digit
camcorder	camera + recorder
contraception	contra + conception

geep	goat + sheep
glitterati	glitter + literati
modem	modular + demodulator
motel	motor + hotel
smog	smoke + fog
transistor	transfer + resistor

Two medieval blends are *don* (*do* + *on*) and *doff* (*do* + *off*).

9.34
Miscellaneous

Two other ways in which words are formed are briefly mentioned:

1. onomatopoeia—words felt to be suggestive of the sounds they refer to (cf. 9.26 for reduplicatives): bubble, burp, clatter, hiss, mutter, splash;
2. words from proper names: bowdlerize, boycott, braille, caesarean, lynch, pasteurize, platonic, sadist, sandwich.

It is very rare for new words to be created without being composed of existing words or parts of words. Two examples are *gas* and *googol* (10^{100}), though *gas* is said to be modelled on *chaos*.

Phonaesthemes are combinations of sounds found in sets of words with some vague associations in meaning, often through onomatopoeia. Many words in -*ump* suggest heaviness and hardness in an object or a sound: *hump, lump, rump, bump, dump, stump, thump*. In contrast, words in -*ip* suggest a light, sharp movement or sound: *clip, nip, dip, flip, tip, drip, snip, zip*. Notice also the -*i*-/-*o*- contrasts in *clip-clop, flip-flop, tip-top* that we also find in *tick-tock* and *ping-pong*. Some words in *sle-* or *sli-* have in common a suggestion of trim and thin: *slim, slender, slick, slit, sliver*. Some in *sk-* or *sc-* suggest a frisky movement: *skip, skim, scurry, scuttle, scour, scamper, scoot, skedaddle*. Phonaesthemes have played a part in the creation of new words; for example, it has been suggested that *hassle* was formed in imitation of the set *bustle, hustle, rustle; tumble* may have given rise to *stumble* and *fumble*, and *fiddle* to *twiddle* and *diddle*. See also n. 4 for prefixoids.

Morphology

9.35
Word-formation and inflection

Morphology is the study of the internal structure of words. The two major branches of morphology are word-formation (or lexical morphology) and inflection (or inflectional morphology). Word-formation deals with the creation of new words, whereas inflection deals with the grammatical forms of the same word. *Pluggable* is derived by the addition of the suffix *-able* to the root *plug*, *unplug* adds the prefix *un-* to the same root, and *sparking-plug* combines the two words *sparking* and *plug*. On the other hand, the suffix *-s* in the noun *plugs* is an inflection; *plug* is the singular form of the noun and *plugs* is the plural form.

In one obvious sense, *plug* and *plugs* are different words: they are pronounced and spelled differently. We can say that *plug* and *plugs* are different grammatical words belonging to the same lexical word. In a dictionary (or lexicon), *plug* and *plugs* will share an entry; since the plural is formed by a regular inflectional rule, only the very largest of dictionaries will refer to the plural inflection. By contrast, we would expect the lexical words *plug*, *unplug*, *pluggable*, and *sparking-plug* to appear in different places in the dictionary.[6]

9.36
Morpheme, morph, allomorph

The basic unit for morphological (or morphemic) description is the morpheme, the smallest unit required for grammatical and lexical analysis.

Morphemes are abstract units, established for the analysis of word structure. When a word segment represents one morpheme in sound or writing, the segment is a morph. *Infamous*, for example, consists of three morphs *in-*, *fam(e)*, *-ous*, each representing one morpheme; *harmful* contains two morphs; and *house* just one.

A morpheme may be represented by more than one morph: the morpheme realized by the prefix *in-* of *incompetent* is also found in *il-* of *illegal*, *im-* of *impatient*, and *ir-* of *irregular*. Similarly, there are different morphs for the root morphemes in the pairs *peace/pacifist*, *long/length*, *omit/omission*, *appear/apparent*.

Variant members of a set of morphs are allomorphs of the same morpheme: *in-*, *im-*, and *ir-* are allomorphs of a particular prefix morpheme. The negative prefix morpheme of *infamous* differs from the directional prefix morpheme of *indoors* and *income*, but it also has allomorphs in *il-* (*illuminate*), *im-* (*immigrant*), and *ir-* (*irrupt*, cf. *interrupt*). Dictionaries usually give the two prefixes as separate entries, perhaps adding different number superscripts or subscripts. In linguistic descriptions morphemes are distinguished where necessary by being placed in braces: {and}, {fame}, {in₁}. No significance is attached to which allomorph is used to display the morpheme.

An inflectional morpheme corresponds to a grammatical category: the inflectional suffix in *students* represents the plural morpheme, also found with different allomorphs in *churches* and *oxen*.

9.37
Conditioning of allomorphs: phonetic, lexical, grammatical

The choice of allomorphs depends on three types of conditioning: phonetic (or phonological), lexical (or morphological), and grammatical.

Phonetic conditioning may involve either progressive assimilation (determined by the following sound) or regressive assimilation (determined by the preceding sound). The allomorphs of the negative prefix *in-* are conditioned by the sound that follows the prefix: *il-* before /l/, *im-* before /m/ or /p/, *ir-* before /r/, and *in-* before any other sound:

il-	*im-*	*ir-*	*in-*
illegal	immature	irrational	inadequate
illegibly	immorality	irregularity	independence
illiteracy	impolitely	irresistible	informally
illogical	impossible	irresponsible	invalid

As noted in the previous section, the same conditioning applies to allomorphs of another prefix morpheme with directional, intensive, or causative meanings: *il-* (*illuminate, illustrate*), *im-* (*immigrate, imprison*), *ir-* (*irrigate, irritate*), *in-* (*inflame, invade*). We can also hear the effect of a following /p/ on the pronunciation of *ten* in *tenpence* and *Saint* in *Saint Paul*: /tem/ and /sm/ respectively.

The allomorphs of the regular plurals of nouns are conditioned by the sound that precedes the plural inflection (cf. 4.6): /ɪz/ after a sibilant (*kisses*); /z/ after voiced sounds (cf. 10.3) other than sibilants (*dogs*); and /s/ after voiceless sounds other than sibilants (*cats*). The same conditioning applies to the allomorphs of the third person singular present of verbs (*teaches, knows, writes*), the allomorphs of genitives of nouns where an *s* has been added (*church's, women's, priest's*), and the allomorphs of the contracted forms of *is* and *has* (*Joyce's taken it; she's leaving; The ticket's too expensive*).

Lexical conditioning applies when the choice of allomorph depends on the particular word. The plural allomorph *-en* of *oxen* is unique to that word, since it is a fossil from an earlier period of the language, like (for example) *men* and *teeth*. Similarly, plural allomorphs of other irregular nouns, some of them borrowed from foreign languages, cannot be predicted by rules but refer to the particular word; for example: *larva/larvae, curriculum/curricula, thesis/theses, kibbutz/kibbutzim.*

Allomorphs of irregular forms of verbs may also be lexically conditioned. Irregular verbs have allomorphs of the past tense or of the *-ed* participle or both:

	regular	irregular			
	walk	see	take	put	sing
past	walked	saw	took	put	sang
participle	walked	seen	taken	put	sung

The contexts for the past and participle are shown below:

Norman walked/saw his dog.

Norman has walked/seen his dog.

In the two sentences, *walked* conforms to a regular rule for inflecting past and participle forms, whereas *saw* and *seen* are unpredictable forms from the verb *see*.

Lexical conditioning applies to words and roots as well as affixes. The indefinite article has allomorphs that vary according to whether a vowel or consonant follows (*a garden, an orchard*) and according to whether the word is unstressed or (less usually) stressed: /ə/, /ən/, /eɪ/, /an/. Compare the allomorphs of the base in *fraction, fracture*, and *fragile, fragment*, or in the base *please, displease*, and *pleasant, pleasure.*

Grammatical conditioning is recognizable in the shift of stress in some verbs of two syllables that are converted into nouns (cf. 10.11). The stress shifts to the first syllable of the noun. Whereas the unstressed first syllable of the verb generally has the reduced vowel /ə/, the stressed first syllable of the noun has a full vowel. The noun–verb pairs include *convert, convict, escort, extract, permit, present, rebel, record, reject, suspect.* There is some variation in the stress patterns across and within national varieties of English.

Another example is the change from the final voiceless consonants /s/, /f/, /θ/ to the voiced /z/, /v/, /ð/ when some nouns are converted into verbs:

their use /s/ → they use /z/
our belief /f/ → we believe /v/
my mouth /θ/ → we mouth /ð/

Some allomorphic variation may be ascribed to stylistic conditioning, perhaps often in combination with phonetic conditioning. Contractions are characteristic of informal speech and some are conventionally represented in writing:

she is → she's   they will → they'll
do not → don't   do you → d'you

Most of the variants in grammatical words, however, are not usually represented in writing, for example /kən/ for *can* and /əv/ or /ə/ for *of*.

Finally, there may be free variation in the alternation of some morphs. The past and -ed participles of *bet* and *dream* may be irregular or regular: *bet* or *betted, dreamt* or *dreamed*. Some nouns have regular as well as irregular plural inflections:

cacti/cactuses   formulae/formulas
curricula/curriculums   appendices/appendixes

9.38
Portmanteau morph, empty morph, suppletive morph

A portmanteau morph corresponds to a bundle of morphemes. The word *am* is a portmanteau morph: it contains the morphemes {*be*}, {present}, {1st person}, and {singular}, but it cannot be segmented into morphs. Similarly, *men* consists of the morphemes {*man*} and {plural}, and *took* of the morphemes {*take*} and {past}.

In contrast, some morphs have been said to have no meaning. The *to* used to introduce infinitives is an empty morph. It is generally obligatory in certain types of infinitival constructions; for example: *I want to be your friend*; *We asked her to represent us*; *To open the door, insert your identification card*. Where in a relatively few cases *to* is optional, it seems to make no difference to meaning whether or not it is present: *I helped him (to) fill in the form*. Another empty morph is the -o- found in combining forms: *Anglo-French, psychology, pseudo-Elizabethan*.

It has been claimed that *it* in cleft sentences (*It was on Monday that I last saw her*, cf. 4.38) and *there* in existential sentences (*There is somebody asking for your signature*, cf. 4.39) are empty morphs, since *it* and *there* are introduced in constructions that rearrange basic structures (*I last saw her on Monday*; *Somebody is asking for your signature*). The *it* that is used as subject in sentences denoting time, weather, and distance has been called 'prop *it*', 'empty *it*', and 'expletive *it*', all indications that it has been analysed as serving simply to fill the obligatory function of subject in an independent clause when there is no other candidate for that function.

A suppletive (or suppletive morph) is a form from a different root that is used in a paradigm, a grammatically related set of forms. Suppletion is postulated for only a few morphemes in English, but they occur in highly frequent words. The verb *be* is composed of words that come from three distinct roots, all of them present in Old English: *be, been, being; is, am, are; was, were. Go* has a suppletive past tense form *went*, which joined the paradigm from the verb *wend* during the Middle English period. The comparatives and superlatives of four highly frequent adjectives are suppletives in Modern English as they were in Old English:

good   better, best
bad   worse, worst

much	more, most
little	less, least

The same suppletives are used for the adverbs *well, badly, much, little*.

Some linguists recognize a zero morph where a morpheme is expected in the grammatical system but no morph is there. The absence of a relative pronoun in *a letter I wrote* (compare *a letter that I wrote*) is noted by postulating a zero relative pronoun. The plural of *sheep* is identical with the singular *sheep*, though (say) the plural of *cow* is *cows*; the plural noun *sheep* has been said to have a zero morph. More controversially, a zero article has been postulated for plural nouns and for non-count nouns (e.g. *sugar*) to fill the paradigm of indefinite and definite articles:

a garden	gardens	sugar
the garden	the gardens	the sugar

9.39
Free morph, bound morph

A free morph can occur by itself as a word, whereas a bound morph is always combined with another morph. Affixes are always attached to a base and are therefore bound morphs: the prefix *en-* in *enjoy*, the suffix *-ity* in *activity*, and the inflectional suffix *-s* in *tasks*. Roots may be free morphs: *tidy* in *untidy*, *move* in *movement*, *own* in *owner*. However, roots are often bound morphs. The classic example of a bound root morph is *cran-* in *cranberry*, a unique morph found nowhere else in the language. Other examples are *twi-* (*twilight*) and *leng-* (an allomorph of *long* in *length*, *lengthen*, *lengthy*).

Bound root morphs typically appear in words borrowed directly or ultimately from Latin and Greek. It is easy to recognize the bound root morph *-mit-* in *admit, commit, omit, permit, submit, transmit*, and the allomorphic variant in the corresponding suffixed words *admission, commission, omission, permission, submission, transmission*. Another example is *-pel-* in *compel, dispel, expel, impel, repel*, and the allomorphic variant in *compulsory, expulsion, impulse, repulse*. We can acknowledge that pairs of words such as *admit/admission* share the same root morpheme even if we do not know what meaning to assign to the morpheme without looking up the etymology of the words. In any event, meanings may have changed for some or all the words from their meanings in the source languages: *edify* and *edification* have an etymology in common with *edifice* but the words have diverged considerably in meaning.

Some affixes were originally free root morphs. In Old English these are words as well as suffixes: *dōm, hād, lic*. From them derive the present-day suffixes in *freedom, kingdom; childhood, falsehood; friendly, heavenly*.

The reverse may also happen. Some affixes have also become words: *ex* (former spouse or lover), *isms, ologies, pseud(s), minis, macros, micros*. The nonce-word *wasm* was created by analogy with the word *ism* in the following newspaper headline, producing a punning that gives new meaning to *ism*:

> State socialism: an 'ism' that became a 'wasm'.

9.40
Paradigm, conjugation, declension

A paradigm is a set of grammatically related forms of a word. Paradigms can be established in English for verbs, nouns, adjectives, and (to a limited extent) adverbs.

Paradigms for verbs are conjugations. We conjugate a verb when we give its variant forms. For example, the conjugation of regular verbs may be exemplified by the verb *play*:

> play
> plays
> playing
> played

To each of these forms we may ascribe its grammatical functions (cf. 4.14). The irregular verb *drive* has five forms in its conjugation:

> drive
> drives
> driving
> drove
> driven

The functions of *played* are distributed between *drove* (simple past) and *driven* (*-ed* participle). In *play* the forms are differentiated solely by inflections. In *drive*, there is a change of vowel in *drove* and a combination of vowel change and inflection in *driven*. In the verb *go* the paradigm drawns on suppletion (a form from a different root) for the simple past *went* (cf. 9.38).

Paradigms for nouns are declensions. For regular nouns there is little variation in declension. We can decline *girl* in the written language with four forms (*girl, girl's, girls, girls'*), but in the spoken language there are only two forms, since the genitive singular *girl's* and the two plurals are pronounced the same. Irregular nouns may display all four forms in speech as well as in writing (*man, man's, men, men's*).

The terms *conjugations* and *declensions* are useful in highly inflected languages, where there may be several well-defined conjugations of verbs and declensions of nouns and adjectives. The terms are not usually applied to present-day English grammar because there are few inflections in these word classes.

There is a paradigm for adjectives that are inflected for comparison: *old*, *older, oldest.* There are also some adjectives that are irregularly inflected; for example: *good, better, best.* A relatively few adverbs are also inflected for comparison: (*work*) *hard, harder, hardest; badly, worse, worst.*

Finally, there are paradigms of pronouns, particularly personal pronouns; for example: *I, me, my.*

Chapter 10
Sounds and Tunes

Summary

Phonetics (10.1–2)

Consonants (10.3–5)

Vowels (10.6–8)

Phonemes (10.9)

Word stress (10.10–14)

Intonation (10.15–16)

Sounds and tunes in verse (10.17–18)

Chapter 10 Summary

- Phonetics is the study of sounds used in the communication of human languages. Its three branches are articulatory phonetics (dealing with the production of sounds), acoustic phonetics (dealing with the transmission of sound waves), and auditory phonetics (dealing with the perception of sounds).

- In the production of sounds, air ascends from the lungs through the windpipe and vocal cords. Also involved are the organs of speech within the mouth: the soft palate, the hard palate, the alveolar ridge, the tongue, the lips, and the top front teeth.

- Consonants typically obstruct the flow of air. To describe them we take account of the articulator (usually the tongue or lips), the place of articulation, the manner of articulation, and whether they are voiced or voiceless.

- In accordance with their manner of articulation, consonants may be stops, fricatives, affricates, nasals, or approximants.

- There are some differences between English accents in the use of consonants or in their pronunciation. The major distinction is between rhotic and non-rhotic accents. Non-rhotic accents drop the /r/ when it is followed by a consonant or a pause.

- Vowels are described according to the positions of the tongue inside the mouth as they are being articulated and by the shape of the lips. Vowels may be short or long; single vowels, diphthongs, or triphthongs.

- Two sets of vowels are described: Received Pronunciation and General American. Some reference is made to other sets.

- Phonemes are abstract sound units. Variant pronunciations that represent the same phoneme are its allophones.

- If a word is polysyllabic, one of its syllables carries the primary or only stress and another syllable may have secondary stress. The stress pattern may be affected by the grammatical class of the word. In many instances it is possible to predict the stress pattern of a word.

- Many grammatical words occur in two forms: a stressed form and an unstressed form.

- English is said to be a stress-timed language, where stress occurs (or is perceived to occur) at roughly equal intervals.

- A tone unit is a segment of speech that contains a nuclear tone, a distinctive movement of pitch. Tone units tend to correspond to units of grammar and units of information. The most important part of the information is indicated by the location of the nuclear tone.

- The most frequent nuclear tones are falling and rising tones. The tones may signal grammatical distinctions and attitudes.

- Repetition of identical or near-identical sounds is characteristic of verse, and may be conventional and systematic. The most common conventional devices are rhyme and alliteration. Others are assonance, consonance, reverse rhyme, and pararhyme. Sound patterning is also employed in (for example) headlines, proverbs, and advertisements.

- Rhythm is the patterning of stressed and unstressed syllables that occurs in connected speech. Metre, a formal convention of much of English verse, is a regular patterning that ignores the variability usual in speech.

Phonetics

10.1
The branches of phonetics

Phonetics is the study of the sounds used in the communication of human languages.[1] Phoneticians distinguish three branches of their discipline:

1. articulatory phonetics, which deals with the production of sounds
2. acoustic phonetics, which deals with the movement of air caused by the transmission of sounds from the speaker's mouth to the listener's ear
3. auditory phonetics, which deals with the perception of sounds by the brain after they have been received by the ear.

Articulatory phonetics is based on anatomy and physiology and uses their methodologies. Acoustic phonetics borders on physics. Auditory phonetics may be viewed also as a subdiscipline of psychology. All three branches of phonetics use laboratories and experimental techniques.

Phonetics is applied in foreign language teaching, speech therapy (for the deaf, stroke patients, and others with speech defects), and in automatic speech recognition and synthesis. This last application includes devices for converting written material into speech and speech into written form, and for verifying the identity of speakers through their voiceprints. Most work in these areas has been done on English.

10.2
The organs of speech

We produce speech by interfering with the movement of air, originating from the lungs, that we breathe out through the nose or mouth. Air ascends from the lungs through the windpipe (or trachea), at the top of which stands the larynx.

The larynx is a cartilaginous and muscular box containing the vocal cords (or vocal folds or vocal lips). These are two bands of elastic tissue lying opposite each other across the windpipe. They are attached to the front wall of the larynx (which protrudes, particularly in men, as the Adam's apple) but are movable at the back. They can be moved towards each other to cover the top of the windpipe completely, thereby blocking the passage of air; or they can be drawn apart so that there is a gap (glottis) between them and they therefore do not interfere with the movement of air; or they can be closed partially, causing friction. The glottal stop is the sound in the middle of *water* (indicated by the spelling *wa'er*) in accents such as Cockney; it is produced when the closed cords are suddenly opened to release air. The vocal cords are drawn apart for sounds such as [p] and are half-open for [h]. They can also be made to vibrate (opening and closing rapidly) while held loosely together. The effect of the continuous vibration is to produce voiced sounds. The English sounds [z] as in *zip* and [s] as in *sip* are pronounced identically except that [z] is voiced, produced while the vocal cords are vibrating. We can feel the vibration by putting our fingers on the sides of the larynx or by putting our hands over our ears as we produce a buzzing sound with [z].

The other main organs of speech are inside the mouth:

1. The soft palate (or velum) is at the back of the top of the mouth. During normal breathing the soft palate is lowered, allowing air to pass through the nose. It is also lowered during the production of the nasal consonants [m], [n], and [ŋ]. It is raised during the production of oral sounds, preventing air from passing into the nose.

2. The hard palate is the hard roof of the mouth in front of the soft palate.

3. The alveolar ridge is at the very front of the palate. It is the rough ridge immediately behind the top front teeth.

4. The tongue is particularly important as an articulator because of its extreme mobility and its use in the production of most sounds. It is roughly divided into three parts, indicating its position at rest relative to the three parts of the palate: the blade is below the alveolar ridge, the front below the hard palate, and the back below the soft palate. The tip of the tongue sometimes has a function in articulation.

5. The lips are also highly mobile. They come together in [p], touch the teeth in [f], are rounded in [u:] as in *two*, are spread in [i:] as in *see*, or are simply apart as in the pronunciation of *ah*.

6. The top front teeth are touched by the tongue in producing the English dental sounds.

Consonants

10.3
English
consonants

In general, the difference between consonants and vowels is that consonants are sounds made by obstructing the flow of air whereas vowels are sounds made without obstruction. A second difference is that vowels generally constitute the nucleus of syllables whereas consonants are generally at the peripheries of syllables. We have syllables consisting simply of the vowel nucleus, as in the monosyllabic words represented by the spellings *I, a, oh, ah*. We have syllables with one or more consonants before the vowel (*be, tree*), one or more after the vowel (*it, old*), and one or more on either side (*brink, streets*). However, in some pronunciations there are syllabic consonants (consonants that can constitute a syllable by themselves; for example: [l̩] in metal [mɛtl̩], [ŋ] in kitten [kɪtn̩]). A third conspicuous difference is the effect on the form of the preceding indefinite article: *a* before words with initial consonant sounds, as in *play* and *weather*, *an* before words with initial vowel sounds, as in *uncle* and *hour*.

To describe English consonants we have to take account of the active articulator, the organ that moves in the production of the sound (usually the tongue or lips); the place of articulation, i.e. the location of the passive or fixed articulator with which the active articulator comes into contact (as when the tip of the tongue touches the upper front teeth); the manner of articulation, i.e. the type and extent of obstruction in the flow of air; and the distinction between voiced and voiceless consonants, the voiced consonants requiring vibration of the vocal cords. The distinction in voice is particularly important, since it differentiates consonants in several pairs.

Table 10.3.1 displays the phonetic set for a sample of English consonants. The column headings indicate the main articulators apart from the tongue, and the horizontal terms indicate the manner of articulation and the presence or absence of voicing.

Table 10.3.1 English consonants

		bilabial	labiodental	dental	alveolar	palato-alveolar or post-alveolar	palatal	velar	glottal
stop	voiceless	p			t			k	
	voiced	b			d			g	
fricative	voiceless		f	θ	s	ʃ			h
	voiced		v	ð	z	ʒ			
affricate	voiceless					tʃ			
	voiced					dʒ			
nasal	voiced	m			n			ŋ	
liquid	voiced				l	r			
semi-vowel	voiced	w					j		

The sounds of the consonants are exemplified below:

Stops

p *p*an   t *t*ill   k *k*ilt
b *b*an   d *d*ill   g *g*ilt

The glottal stop [ʔ] is most easily recognized in the pronunciation of *water* and *daughter* in certain accents, sometimes represented by the spellings *wa'er* and *daugh'er*.

Fricatives

f *f*at   θ *th*in   s *s*eal   ʃ fa*sh*ion   h *h*at
v *v*at   ð *th*is   z *z*eal   ʒ revi*s*ion

Our spelling system does not differentiate between voiceless [θ] (as in *thin*, *thirty*, *thistle*) and voiced [ð] (as in *this*, *the*, *then*).

Affricates

tʃ *ch*in
dʒ *g*in

Nasals

m *m*ail   n *n*ail   ŋ si*ng*

In some accents, the *ng* of *sing* is pronounced [ŋ], contrasting with the final consonant [n] of *sin*. [ŋ] occurs only at the end of a syllable.

Liquids

l *l*ap   r *r*ap

Semi-vowels

w *w*et   j *y*et

Liquids and semi-vowels are approximants. The liquid [l] is often called a lateral approximant or simply a lateral. The semi-vowels are pronounced like vowels but function like consonants. They occur only in front of a vowel; for example, [w] in *water* and *twinkle*, and [j] in *yes* and *cure*. They behave like consonants in requiring the form *a* of the indefinite article (*a well, a yawn*), and they do not function as the nucleus of a syllable.

10.4
The articulation of consonants

The place of articulation indicated by the column headings in Table 10.3.1 may be summarized in this way:

1. bilabials: the lips come together
2. labiodentals: the lower lip touches the upper front teeth
3. dentals: the tip of the tongue touches the upper front teeth
4. alveolars and palato-alveolars: the tip or blade of the tongue touches the alveolar ridge
5. palatals: the front of the tongue approaches or touches the hard palate
6. velars: the back of the tongue touches the soft palate (or velum)
7. glottals: the vocal cords come together either completely as for [ʔ] or partially as for [h].

The types of manner of articulation indicated by the horizonal terms may be summarized in this way:

1. stops (or plosives): total closure, during which air pressure builds up behind the closure, followed by a sudden release (or plosion)
2. fricatives: partial closure, forcing the air to escape through a narrow passage and thereby producing a turbulent (or friction) sound

3. affricates: as indicated by the phonetic symbols, combinations of stops and fricatives—total closure followed immediately by a slow release that produces a friction sound

4. nasals: lowering of soft palate and total closure within the mouth, forcing the air to pass through the nose only

5. approximants: the articulators come close but no audible friction is produced. In the production of lateral [l], air is allowed to escape around the sides of the tongue.

The names of the consonants refer to the place of articulation, and—where the distinction is relevant—to whether the consonants are voiced or voiceless. For example, [p] and [b] are bilabials, [p] and [t] are stops, [p] and [f] are voiceless. More fully, [p] is a voiceless bilabial stop, [z] is a voiced alveolar fricative, [tʃ] is a voiceless palato-alveolar affricate.

10.5
Accent differences in consonants

Below are specified some important instances of regional or social variation that apply to English consonants. There are fewer differences for consonants than for vowels.

1. There is a major distinction between rhotic and non-rhotic accents. Non-rhotic accents drop the /r/ when it is followed by a consonant, as in *part*, or by a pause, as in 'They haven't gone *far*'. The /r/ is retained when followed by a vowel (as in *peril*), even if the vowel is in the next word, as in 'They are *far* away by now'. Rhoticity is dominant among accents. Non-rhoticity is typical of most of England and Wales, Australia, South Africa, New Zealand, and some parts in the east and south of the United States. There are several types of pronunciations of /r/, often within the same accent.

2. In Indian English the alveolar stops [t] and [d] are retroflex, pronounced with the tip of the tongue curled back and raised upward. Indian English also has dental stops,[t̪] and [d̪], which are used in place of [θ] and [ð].

3. In the English of Scotland, Ireland, Wales, and South Africa, there is an additional consonant, the voiceless velar fricative [x] in words such as *loch*. It is also found in some pronunciations of Yiddishisms adopted into American English, such as *chutzpah*.

4. In American English, in words spelled with a medial -t- or -tt-, such as *butter* and *metal*, the medial sound is typically pronounced in the same way (or almost the same way) as [d], so that *metal* sounds like *medal*, and *latter* like *ladder*. Also, [t] is often dropped from medial [nt] in words such as *winter*, so that *winter* sounds the same as *winner*.

5. Words ending in -*ing*, such as *making*, may end with [n] or [ŋ]. In general, the pronunciation with [n]—widely referred to as 'dropping the *g*'—correlates with a lower level of socio-economic class and a lower level of

formality. The lower prestige form is sometimes indicated in spelling by an apostrophe in place of the final *g*, as in *makin'*.

6. In some regional accents in Australia, England, Wales, and the West Indies, [h] is dropped at the beginning of a word or syllable, as in *happy* or *behind*.

7. The Cockney accent replaces [θ] by [f], as in *think* (homonymous with *fink*), *Arthur, both*. It replaces [ð] by [v], but usually only when it is medial or final, as in *rather, mother, smooth*; initial [ð], as in *this*, is commonly replaced by [d]. The same replacements are found in some accents in the south of the United States and in Black English. These pronunciations are indicated in the non-standard spellings *muvver* and *dis*. The two consonants are variously pronounced in the different regional varieties of African English; [θ] as [t] (*tree* and *three* then being homophones) or as [s], and [ð] in *they* as [d] or as [z].

Vowels

10.6
The set of Received Pronunciation vowels

Traditionally, the vowels are described according to the positions of the tongue inside the mouth as the vowels are being articulated, but in practice the distinctions between vowels are based on how they sound and the relative positions of the tongue that we infer from what we hear. We also take account of the shape of the lips, whether they are rounded (as in *ooh*); spread (as in *ease*), or neutral (as in *ah*); whether the vowel is short, like [ɪ] in *pit*, or long, like [i:] in *peat*; and whether it is a pure or single vowel (or monophthong) such as [ɪ] in *it*, or a diphthong (involving a glide from one vowel to another), such as [ʌɪ] in *ice*.

Fig. 10.6.1 is a vowel chart, which is used to indicate the position of the tongue in producing vowel sounds. The chart is an abstraction from possible positions of the tongue. The location of the vowels correlates roughly with the highest part of the tongue (front, centre, or back) when the sound is made and its position in the mouth: high (close to the palate), mid, or low (far from the palate). The vowel symbols in the chart are those used in the *New Shorter Oxford English Dictionary* (Oxford: Clarendon Press).

RP (Received Pronunciation, i.e. generally accepted pronunciation) is an accent that is typical of educated speakers of British English, though by no means all educated speakers use it. It is not associated with any particular region of the country, but it is associated with speakers from the upper and upper-middle social classes. It is used by a small minority of British speakers, estimates varying from 3 to 10 per cent according to how broadly it is defined.

RP is the accent that is commonly taught to foreign learners of English and is usual for news broadcasters on the BBC. As with other accents, there is a great deal of variability among RP speakers, so the chart should be considered a generalization.[2] The exemplification of vowels that follows applies to typical RP pronunciations.

Fig. 10.6.1 Vowel chart

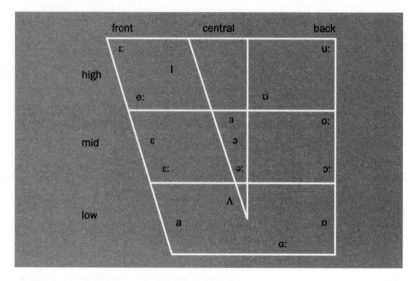

The pure vowel sounds are:

Front vowels

high	i:	b*eat*	ɪ	b*it*
mid	ɛ	b*et*	ɛ:	h*air*
low	a	b*at*		

Central vowels

ə: h*er*   ə *ago*   ʌ r*u*n

Back vowels

high	u:	*too*	ʊ	p*u*t
mid	ɔ:	s*aw*		
low	ɑ:	*arm*	ɒ	d*o*t

Some of the pure vowel sounds correspond to two or three letters in the spellings of the particular words exemplifying them. RP is a non-rhotic accent, so that the *r* that ends a word in *her* or precedes a consonant in *arm* is not given its consonantal value.

The short vowels are:

ɪ b*it*   ɛ b*et*   a b*at*   ə *ago*   ʊ p*u*t   ʌ r*u*n   ɒ d*o*t

The long vowels are:

i: b*eat*   ə: h*er*   ɛ: h*air*   u: *too*   ɔ: s*aw*   ɑ: *arm*

The colons indicate that these are long vowels. Short vowels and long vowels differ in relative length: the difference is manifested when they occur in the same context, preceded or followed by the same sounds. For example, the vowel in *bead* is longer than that in *bid*, and similarly the vowel in *beat* is longer than that in *bit*. But because vowels are generally longer before a voiced sound, such as [d], than before a voiceless sound, such as [t], the vowel in *bid* is longer than the one in *bit*, and similarly the vowel in *bead* is longer than that in *beat*. As a result, the lengthened short vowel in *bid* may well be longer than the shortened long vowel in *beat*. Another difference between short and long vowels relates to constraints on a short vowel in a stressed monosyllabic word. If a short vowel appears in a stressed monosyllable, it must be followed by a consonant; for example, [ɪ] in *bit*. A long vowel may occur in a stressed monosyllable, so we can have [i:] in *bee* as well as in *beat*.

The lips are slightly spread for these vowels:

    ɪ b*it*   ɛ b*et*   ɛ: h*air*   a b*at*   i: b*eat*

They are rounded for these vowels, strongly for [u:]:

    ɒ d*ot*   ʊ p*ut*   ɔ: s*aw*   u: t*oo*

They are neutral for these vowels:

    ə *ago*   ʌ r*un*   ə: h*er*   ɑ: *arm*

The diphthongs are sounds that glide from one vowel to another. The second vowel, shorter in duration, is [ə], [ɪ], or [ʊ]:

    ɪə f*ear*   ʊə p*oor*
    eɪ b*ait*   ʌɪ t*ie*   ɔɪ t*oy*
    əʊ sn*ow*   aʊ c*ow*

The diphthongs and triphthongs are long vowels. Mention might be made here of two triphthongs, where the glide continues to a third vowel:

    ʌɪə t*ire*   aʊə s*our*

10.7 The set of General American vowels

GA (General American) is not a regional or class accent, but an abstraction from what is typical of English pronunciation in the United States in contrast to British RP.[3]

The pure vowel sounds are:

Front vowels

    high   i: b*eat*   ɪ b*it*

mid   e: b*ait*
        ɛ   bet
low   a   b*at*

Central vowels

        ɜ   h*er*
        ə   *ago*
        ʌ   r*u*n

Back vowels

high   u: *too*   ʊ   p*u*t
mid   o: b*oat*   ɔ: b*ough*t
low   ɑ: p*o*t

The lips are spread for:

i: b*eat*   ɪ bit   ɛ bet   a b*at*

They are rounded for:

ʊ p*u*t   ɔ: s*aw*   o: b*oat*   u: *too*

They are neutral for:

ɜ h*er*   ə *ago*   ʌ r*u*n   ɑ: p*o*t

The short vowels are:

ɪ b*i*t   ɛ bet   a b*at*   ɜ her   ə *ago*   ʌ r*u*n

The diphthongs, which are long vowels, are:

aʊ *cow*   ʌɪ t*ie*   ɔɪ t*oy*

The long vowels are:

i: b*eat*   e: b*ait*   u: *too*   ɔ: s*aw*   ɑ: p*o*t   o: b*oat*

In many sets of words roughly the same vowel is used in both GA and RP, but in other sets the two accents differ. *Path, dance, can't,* and numerous other words are pronounced with the vowel [a] in GA and [ɑ:] in RP, so that GA does not distinguish *can't* from *cant.* Most American speakers distinguish between the [ɑ:] of words like *cot* and the [ɔ:] of words like *caught,* though some have an intermediate vowel that serves for both sets of words. The RP distinction in [ɒ] and [ɑ:] between the vowel sounds in *hot* and *heart* and between *cot* and *cart* is generally not made in GA. Many American speakers do not distinguish between the short vowels in *ago* and *run.*

The GA pure long vowel [o:] corresponds to the RP diphthong [əʊ], as in *boat, home, no.* Similarly, the GA pure long vowel [e:] corresponds to the RP diphthong [eɪ], as in *bait, shave.*

In a number of words GA has [u:] where RP has the combination [ju:]; for example, *duke, new, tune.* In a few words, such as *clerk* and *Berkeley,* GA [ɜr] corresponds to RP [ɑ:]. There are also several idiosyncratic differences, such as the pronunciation of the medial vowel of *tomato*: [eɪ] in GA, [ɑ:] in RP; *ate* in RP is usually [ɛt], in GA [eɪt]; *vase* has the vowel [ɑ:] in RP, and usually [e:] in GA.

RP is a non-rhotic accent, whereas GA is rhotic. As a result, some RP diphthongs correspond to sequences of a pure vowel plus [r] in GA: *fear* has [ɪə] in RP and [ɪr] in GA; *poor*, [ʊə] in RP and [ʊr] in GA.

10.8
Accent differences in vowels

Within the scope of this chapter, it is possible to refer to only a few of the numerous differences in vowels in various regional accents.

1. Scottish English is highly distinctive. While vowels may vary in length according to context, the contrasts between short and long vowels, as found elsewhere, are absent. The same vowel [u] is used for both *full* and *fool*; [ɔ] for *cot* and *caught*; [a] for *can* and *calm*.

2. Regional accents in Australia, England (in the Midlands and South East, including Cockney) have diphthongs that differ from those of RP and GA: [ʌɪ] for the vowel in *paper*, which is homophonous with *piper*; [ɔɪ] for the vowel in *child* and *buy*, the latter homophonous with *boy* (a merger also found in some regional Irish accents); [aʊ] for the vowel in *no*, which is homophonous with *now*.

3. Caribbean English does not distinguish between *beer* and *bare*, the vowel being [e:] or [ie] according to the region. There is a tendency to use unreduced non-central vowels where other accents use reduced central vowels, such as [ə]; for example, [a] in the second syllable of *woman*.

4. African varieties of English do not have a contrast between [ɪ] and [i:], giving rise to numerous pairs of homophones, such as *ship/sheep*, *sin/seen*, *bit/beat*, *live/leave*.

Phonemes

10.9
Phonemes and their allophones

Despite the variations, we can recognize a limited set of sound units that are distinctive. These sound units are the phonemes of the accent of the language.

The phonemes are distinctive in that if we substitute one phoneme for another we can produce a different word. For example, the word *ban* consists of a sequence of three phonemes; /b, a, n/. If we replace the initial consonant /b/ by /p/ we get the different word *pan*; if we replace the vowel /a/ by /ɪ/ we get *bin*; and if we replace the final consonant /n/ by /t/ we get *bat*. In this way we can show that /b, p/, /a, ɪ/, and /n, t/ are contrastive in English, and are therefore phonemes.

Phonemes are abstract sound units. A phoneme is manifested by a number of phones (or sounds), and variants of a particular phoneme are allophones of that phoneme. Phonemes are conventionally placed between virgules (slanting lines), whereas phones and allophones are enclosed within square brackets. In previous sections of this chapter, the phonetic transcription has been broad, a transcription restricted to a simple set of symbols that are used for the representation of phonemes. A narrow transcription uses more specific symbols or adds superscripts and subscripts. For example, the three main allophones of /l/ are shown in a narrow transcription as [l], [l̥], and [ɫ].

The concepts of phoneme and allophone become clearer by analogy with the letters of the alphabet. We recognize that a symbol is *a* despite considerable variations in size, colour, and (to a certain extent) shape. The representation of the letter *a* is affected in handwriting by the preceding or following letters to which it is joined. Writers may form the letter idiosyncratically and may vary their writing according to whether they are tired or in a hurry or nervous. The variants in the visual representations are analogous to the allophones of a phoneme, and what is distinctive in contrast to other alphabetic letters is analogous to the phoneme.

Allophonic variation may depend on the phonetic environment, the sounds preceding or following an allophone. If two allophones never occur in the same phonetic environment, they are in complementary distribution. For example, the phoneme /k/ is pronounced differently in *key* and *coo*, influenced by the vowel that follows it. It is easy to feel the difference in the position of the tongue when we say [k] as if we are going to say *key* and when we say [k] as if we are going to say *cow*. For *key* the tongue is forward into the hard palate in anticipation of the following high front vowel; for *cow* the tongue is retracted low down on the soft palate in anticipation of the following mid back vowel. In many accents, including RP and GA, there are distinct allophones of /l/. Clear [l], which is close in sound to a front vowel, is an allophone of /l/ that occurs before vowels, as in *leap* and *look*; dark [ɫ], which is close in sound to a back vowel, occurs after vowels, as in *peal* and *milk*; voiceless [l̥] follows /p/ or /k/ in a stressed syllable, as in *play* and *sprinkler*. As final examples, /n/ is realized by the dental allophone [n̪] when followed by the dental fricatives /θ, ð/, as in *tenth*; similarly /t/ and /d/ are realized by the dental allophones [t̪, d̪] when followed by /θ, ð/, as in *eighth*.

Allophonic variation may arise from individual differences in pronunciation of the same word that do not affect the meaning, in which case the allophones are in free variation. For example, the final consonant of the stop /t/ in *Take it!* may be followed by a sudden release (or plosion) or it may be unreleased; the unexploded allophone is symbolized by the addition of a small circle as a superscript: [t°]. Free variants are allophones that occur in the same phonetic environment. They may be produced by the same person on different occasions.

Other factors may affect the production of sounds. There are anatomical differences in the shape and size of vocal organs, individual differences as well as general differences in sex and age. The realization of phonemes may also be affected by the tempo and volume of utterances or by emphasis.

Word Stress

10.10
Stressed syllables

Syllables may be stressed or unstressed. In a monosyllabic word, there can be only one stressed syllable. Polysyllabic words vary in which of their syllables are stressed. We stress the first syllable of *capitalize, generally, microbe, supermarket*; the—or a—middle syllable of *dictatorial, glaucoma, politician, potato*; the final syllable of *below, contain, engineer, unforeseen*. If a word has two or more syllables, it may have a secondary stress. The primary (or only) stress is indicated by ' before the syllable, and the secondary stress by , before the syllable. The stress patterns of the words mentioned above are shown here:

'capita,lize	,dicta'torial,	be'low
'generally	,glau'coma	con'tain
'mic,robe	,poli'tician	,engi'neer
'super,market	po'tato	,unfore'seen

Stress is produced by an increase in muscle energy during articulation. The stressed syllable is perceived as more prominent than unstressed syllables in the word. Several factors may enter into the perception of prominence. They include pitch movement on the syllable; the type of vowel (for example [ə] does not normally occur in stressed syllables, and [ɪ] and [ʊ] rarely occur in stressed syllables of polysyllabic words); the length of the vowel (longer vowels are more prominent).

10.11
Stress patterns and word class

Stress is relevant to grammar as well as phonetics, since the stress patterns in some words may be affected by their grammatical word class. Some disyllabic verbs are distinguished from corresponding nouns or adjectives in that the verbs take the primary stress on the second syllable whereas the nouns and adjectives take it on the first syllable. There is often also some accompanying change in a vowel. Here are some examples, all of them words of classical origin (cf. 10.12):

noun/adjective	verb
'ac‚cent	‚ac'cent
'com‚bine	com'bine
'con‚duct	con'duct
'convict	con'vict
'frequent	fre'quent
'object	ob'ject
'perfect	per'fect
'pro‚duce	pro'duce
'pro‚ject	pro'ject
'rebel	re'bel
're‚cord	re'cord
'subject	sub'ject
'trans‚port	‚trans'port

Several disyllables have the same stress pattern for both noun and verb or have a varying pattern; for example *contact, contrast, comment*. The present tendency seems to be to move the stress in disyllabic verbs of Latin origin to the first syllable. That tendency, which is also found in words of more than two syllables, whether they are verbs or nouns, is exemplified in the disputed pronunciations of *contribute, controversy, dispute, distribute, research*.

Words of more than two syllables also display different stress patterns according to their word class. Some examples follow.

noun/adjective	verb
'attri‚bute	at'tri‚bute
'estimate	'esti‚mate
'moderate	'mode‚rate
'prophecy	'prophe‚sy
'repri‚mand	‚repri'mand
'separate	'sepa‚rate

10.12
Predicting word stress

Attempts have been made to establish the rules for determining where to place the primary stress and (if relevant) the secondary stress. The rules are extremely complex and admit numerous exceptions. It is beyond the scope of this chapter to deal with this topic in any detail, but a few general remarks are in order.

The English vocabulary consists primarily of native words of Germanic origin to which have been added an enormous number of loanwords originating directly or indirectly from Latin or Greek. Different stress rules apply to Germanic and classical words. Germanic words typically take primary stress on the first syllable of their root, and that stress position is usually retained when prefixes and suffixes are added:

'holy	'live	'sweet	'heaven
'holiness	'living	'sweeter	'heavenly
un'holy		'sweetest	

Classical words also generally retain the stress on the same syllable (not necessarily the first) when Germanic suffixes are added, if the words have just a primary stress:

'generous	'organize	'editor
'generously	'organizer	'editorship
but ˌgene'rosity	*but* ˌorgani'zation	*but* ˌedi'torial

Nouns or adjectives of classical origin that have two or more syllables generally have the primary stress on the penultimate syllable (one from the end) or the antepenultimate syllable (two from the end) when a suffix is added. The position of the stress depends on the affix:

	antepenultimate	*penultimate*
'photograph	pho'tography	ˌphoto'graphic
	pho'tographer	
'nation	ˌnatio'nality	ˌnationa'listic
'national		
'logic	ˌlogi'cality	lo'gician
'logical		
'origin	o'riginal	oˌrigi'nation
	oˌrigi'nality	

There are considerable variations in word stress between and within national varieties. For example, American English stresses the first syllable of *laboratory* and *inquiry*, whereas British English stresses the second syllable.

10.13
Strong and weak forms

Whereas all content words carry a primary stress on one syllable, many grammatical words (cf. 8.19)—such as most of the pronouns and auxiliary verbs—occur in two forms: a strong or stressed form and a weak or unstressed form. For example, the strong form of the indefinite article *a* is [eɪ], whereas the weak form is [ə]. The weak forms are the ones normally used.

The strong forms are used in these circumstances:

1. When the words are cited:

   How many instances of the word *a* [eɪ] can you find in this paragraph?

2. When the words are in contrast:

   He is not a [eɪ] suspect, he is the [ðiː] suspect.

3. When the words are emphasized:

   You must [mʌst] tell me.

4. When the units to which the words are related are fronted or omitted:

   Who were you speaking to [tuː, tʊ]?
   ('You were speaking to X')

   They were taken advantage of [ɒv].
   ('X took advantage of them')

   If you won't do it, I will [wɪl]
   ('If you won't do it, I will do it')

Here are some common weak forms:

a	[ə]	*have*	[həv, əv, v, ə]
am	[m, əm]	*must*	[məst]
an	[n̩, ən]	*not*	[n̩t, n̩]
and	[ənd, ən, n̩]	*of*	[əv, ə]
as	[əz]	*some*	[səm]
at	[ət]	*to*	[tə] + consonant
but	[bət]		[tʊ] + vowel
can	[kən]	*was*	[wəz]
could	[kəd]	*will*	[l]
from	[frəm]		

Below are examples of weak forms in connected speech:

I*'m* [m] ready, *but* [bət] I*'d* [d] prefer *to* [tə] get *some* [səm] food first, or *at* [ət] least *a* [ə] cup *of* [ə] coffee.

It*'s* [s] best *to* [tə] tell *him* [ɪm] before *the* [ðə] meeting.

Bob *and* [n̩] Henry *must* [məst] know where *he's* [ɪz] staying.

I couldn*'t* [n̩] say which *of* [ə] them*'s* [ðəmz] *from* [frəm] Manchester.

Words that are distinct from each other in their strong forms may become homophones in their weak forms. The example sentences above show that [n̩] can represent *and* and *not*, and that [ə] can represent *a* and *of*. Both *of* and *have* have the weak forms [ə] and [əv], a convergence that can cause the misspelling of *have* as *of* in combinations such as *I could have told you that. What's she like?* is ambiguous, depending on what strong form corresponds to the [s] of *What's*: *What is she like?* or *What does she like?* Similarly, *He's paid today* corresponds to either *He is paid today* or *He has paid today*.

The weak forms exhibit various kinds of reductions from the strong forms; omission of vowels and consonants, shortening of the lengths of sounds, and replacement of vowels by [ə].

Some weak forms are represented by standard contracted spellings in writing; for example: *'m, 've, 'll, n't, 's*. There are also non-standard spellings of weak forms; for example: *a* for *of* in *cuppa coffee*; *n* for *and* in *fish'n'chips*; *'em* (derived from older *hem*, rather than *them*) in *Get 'em*.

10.14
Rhythm

In connected speech, the alternation of stressed and unstressed syllables often conveys a rhythm, with stressed syllables providing the beat:

> El'even 'hundred 'people in 'fifty con'stituencies were 'asked 'how they'd 'vote.

In this example, there is virtually a regular pattern of unstressed syllables followed by stressed syllables. The major exception is the set of four unstressed syllables consisting of the three syllables of *constituencies* that follow the first syllable of that word and the unstressed *were*.

It has been suggested that speakers of English tend to keep (or are perceived to keep) a similar amount of time between stressed syllables, so that the time taken by two or more unstressed syllables is (or is perceived to be) roughly equivalent to that taken by one stressed syllable. English is therefore said to be a stress-timed language, in contrast to languages such as French that are syllable-timed, since they give approximately the same time to each syllable. However, varieties of African and Indian English are generally syllable-timed.

The time equivalence between stressed syllables is very approximate indeed. It is also affected by hesitations, rapid changes of tempo, and emphasis. The equivalence is most apparent in some rhetorical styles of public speaking.

Intonation

Intonation involves patterns of pitch prominence in connected speech. The most important prominence is generally conveyed by a tone (a distinctive movement of pitch) that starts on a stressed syllable—the nuclear syllable or nucleus—and may continue over several syllables. A tone unit is a segment of speech that contains a nuclear tone. In what follows the nuclear syllable is in capitals.

Tone units generally correspond to grammatical units: phrases, clauses, or short sentences. Plausible ends of the tone units below are marked by vertical lines.

Phrases

> He is putting some distance between HIS ideas| and those of his COLleagues|

Clauses

> As soon as I got out of the WAter| I began to SHIver|

Sentences

> I DON'T have an insurance policy| I've NEver had one|

In these examples, there are separate tone units for the phrase beginning with *and*, for the initial subordinate *as*-clause, and for the two parallel sentences beginning with *I*. A tone unit may consist of just one word; for example: *Yes* or *No* as responses, or *unfortunately* in:

> UnFORtunately| I've caught a COLD|

Tone units function as units of information that are offered by the speaker to the listener. The most important part of the information is indicated by the location of the nuclear tone. Take the question:

> Where are you this week?

A possible reply would be:

> I'm in COLchester this week.

The information required by the question is conveyed by *Colchester*, and the tone begins on the nuclear syllable *COL*, which is the stressed syllable of the word. We can see that *Colchester* is the most important information, since an appropriate reply could have been limited to that name. Similarly, the question:

> What are you reading?

might elicit the reply:

> I'm NOT reading.

NOT conveys the most important information, a denial of the implication of the question.

The most important information in a tone unit tends to be information that has not been mentioned or implied before or that the listener could not know from the situation or from general knowledge.

There is a tendency to put the most important information at the end of a tone unit, its climax. Hence, the tone will tend to occur on the last stressed syllable of the unit.

> What are you doing NOW?
>
> I'm just cleaning my TEETH.
>
> The play was pretty DREAry.
>
> My last examination was on THURSday.

The tone is generally on the stressed syllable of just one word, but the focus of information—the part that the listener's attention is directed to—may extend over more than one word. For example, a question–answer exchange might be:

> What are you DOing?
> I'm just cleaning my TEETH.

Here *I'm* is implied in the question, and the focus is *just cleaning my teeth*.

When the tone is not on the last stressed unit, it has special function, such as marking emphasis, as in an earlier example in this section:

> I DON'T have an insurance policy| I've NEver had one|

Or for contrast, as in another earlier example:

> He is putting some distance between HIS ideas| and those of his COLleagues|

His is being contrasted with *of his colleagues.*

10.16
Direction of tone

The most common tone by far is the falling tone, where the pitch movement is downward. It is therefore considered the neutral tone. It conveys the impression of completeness. On the other hand, the rising tone (the second most frequent tone) conveys the impression of incompleteness. In what follows, the direction of the tone is indicated by an arrow immediately before the word carrying the tone.

The contrast between the two impressions given by falls and rises is most clearly seen in lists. All the items in a list except the last have rises, indicating that more items are coming, whereas the last item has a fall, indicating that the list is now complete:

↗ SALmon| ↗TROUT| ↗TURbot| ↗HALibut| ↗HERring|

↗ TEN| ↗TWENty| ↗THIRty| ↗FORty| ↗FIFty| ↗SIXty| ↘SEventy|

Similarly, in alternative questions, where the listener is presented with alternatives to choose from in the reply, the first alternative has a rise and the second a fall.

Did you have ↗MUMPS| or ↘MEAsles?|

A rise is also common, though not invariable, in *yes–no* questions:

Have you had ↗MUMPS?

Initial clauses tend to have a rise, to show that more is to come:

When I started my ↗caREER| there was ↘NO unemployment|

You ↗TRAIN the troops for six months| you send them ↗aBROAD for six months| and then you bring them ↘BACK again|

A rise may allow for a more polite request or invitation, since it conveys a lack of finality:

↗TELL us

Come around ↗toNIGHT

The other tones, which are far less frequent, are mostly combinations of fall and rise. The fall-rise often conveys doubt or encouragement:

We could have gone straight to the ∨↗poLICE

I ∨↗MIGHT

They are very ∨↗exPENsive| for what you ↘GET out of them|

∨↗CAREful

It is often used for an initial short adverbial:

∨↗SurPRIsingly| no one was ↘THERE|

∨↗FRANKly| I was ↘BORED|

In all ∨↗probaBIlity| you are too ↘LATE|

Even ∨↗SO| there's a lot to be done ↘inTERnally|

The level tone, which is a variant of the rise, tends to convey lack of interest:

It's ‾OKAY

It might be used with *yes* and *no* in responses to a series of routine questions at an interview.

The rise-fall, which is a variant of the fall, may communicate various strong feelings, such as enthusiasm, indignation, and sarcasm:

You were simply ∧↘WONderful

What ∧↘aGAIN

That's ∧↘NICE

There is also a combination of fall-plus-rise where the tones are carried by two nuclear syllables, indicating two places of information prominence in the one tone unit:

↘YOU ↗SHOULD

The ↘SIMplest way to ↗DO it| is to use your ↘HANDS|

From the discussion of the tones in this section, it is clear that the directions of tones play some part in signalling both grammatical and attitudinal distinctions. They serve in large measure to reinforce what is conveyed by the grammar. Questions expecting the answer *yes* or *no* (*Are you ready?*) tend to end in a rise, whereas *wh*-questions expecting to extract information from the listener (*What's your name?*) tend to end in a fall. But these tendencies may be countered by the speaker's wish to convey certain attitudes. There may be other factors that are yet to be discovered.

Sounds and Tunes in Verse

10.17
Sound patterns in verse

Repetition of identical or near-identical sounds is characteristic of poetic language and of verse in general.[4] The repetition may be conventional and systematic, as in rhymed or alliterative verse. Rhyme, alliteration, and other conventional devices take account of syllable structure.

The English syllable consists of a vowel (V), which may be preceded by one or more consonants and may be followed by one or more consonants. A simplified notation gives the formula (C)V(C), where C stands for an optional consonant cluster. The conventional devices for sound repetition in English verse require that one or two parts of the CVC structure vary in the stressed syllable that carries the sound patterning. For example, rhyme requires that only the vowel and the final consonant cluster be identical: *ran/man*, *swung/flung*. The rhyme pattern can therefore be represented as C**VC**, where the bold **VC** represents the identity of sounds. It is the sounds that are identical, not the spellings: *pane* and *rain* rhyme. The absence of a consonant cluster in the rhyming pair is regarded as an equivalence: *lie* and *try* rhyme, since the final consonant cluster is absent in both words. As in the other conventional devices for the repetition of sounds, the rhyme generally starts from the stressed syllable: *re'main* rhymes with *Spain*.

Using the CVC formula, we obtain the sound patterns listed below.

C**VC** rhyme

    r**age**/p**age**   destr**oy**/j**oy**   s**eemed**/scr**eamed**   f**all**/**all**   **I**/l**ie**

CVC alliteration

    take/**t**ea   **l**iving/**l**ighting   **st**umble/**st**agger   a**d**azzle/**d**im

CVC assonance

bait/main   growl/mount   sea/beneath

CVC consonance (or half-rhyme)

ran/sun   sent/can't   clasped/lisped

CVC reverse rhyme

soft/song   strange/straight   free/freeze

CVC pararhyme (or slant rhyme)

hall/hell   laughed/left   grained/ground   toil/all

Alliteration was a common linking convention between half-lines in Old English verse and it was conventional in the alliterative verse in parts of England during the fourteenth century. Since the Old English period, rhyme has been the dominant verse convention for systematic sound patterning, marking words at the ends of lines.

In alliterative verse, the absence of an initial consonant cluster is alliterative. *Abraham* and *ombihtum* alliterate in this line from an Old English poem paraphrasing the first half of Genesis, although they begin with different vowels:

> Ðā Abraham spræc   tō his ombihtum
> (Then Abraham spoke to his servants)

There may be partial alliteration in that the consonantal cluster is not fully identical in the words:

> . . . and **b**end
> Your force to **b**reak, **b**low, **b**urn, and make new.
> [John Donne, 'Batter my heart', 3 f.]

> The **f**air breeze blew, the white **f**oam **f**lew,
> The **f**urrow **f**ollowed **f**ree;
> [Samuel Taylor Coleridge, 'The Rime of the Ancient Mariner', 104 f.]

Rhymes begin on the stressed syllables of the paired words, and include any unstressed syllables that follow the stressed syllables. If there are no unstressed syllables, the rhymes are monosyllabic or masculine:

st**alk**/w**alk**   car**essed**/br**east**   broc**ade**/displ**ayed**

If one unstressed syllable follows, the rhymes are disyllabic or feminine:

fl**ower**/p**ower**   h**oary**/gl**ory**   int**entions**/inv**entions**

Polysyllabic rhymes, with more than two unstressed syllables, are most likely to occur in light or satirical verse:

met**iculous**/rid**iculous**   b**illion**/s**illion**

Rhymes may extend over more than one word:

> She snatch'd it, and refused another m**orsel**,
> Saying, he had gorged enough to make a h**orse ill**.
> [Lord Byron, 'Don Juan', Canto II, 7 f.]

When the rhyming pair are sharply different in their grammatical forms the effect is humorous, as in the Byron example or in the rhyming couplet that concludes Canto III of Alexander Pope's 'The Rape of the Lock':

> The meeting points the sacred hair diss**ever**
> From the fair head, for ever, and for **ever**!

In this concluding sombre couplet from a Hopkins poem, the rhyming pair are more nearly matched grammatically:

> It is the blight man was b**orn for**,
> It is Margaret you m**ourn for**.
> [Gerard Manley Hopkins, 'Spring and Fall: To a Young Child', 14 f.]

In his 'Essay on Criticism', Part II (lines 365–73, here renumbered 1–9), Alexander Pope illustrates the use of sound patterning in verse to reinforce meaning:

> 1. The sound must seem an Echo to the sense:
> 2. Soft is the strain when Zephyr gently blows,
> 3. And the smooth stream in smoother numbers flows;
> 4. But when loud surges lash the sounding shore,
> 5. The hoarse, rough verse should like the torrent roar:
> 6. When Ajax strives some rock's vast weight to throw,
> 7. The line too labours, and the words move slow;
> 8. Not so, when swift Camilla scours the plain,
> 9. Flies o'er th' unbending corn, and skims along the main.

Here the patterning is localized rather than being a conventional form for the verse. The repeated fricatives in line 2 are suggestive of the gentle turbulence of the wind; the combination of sibilants with nasals in line 3 suggests greater smoothness. In contrast, the meaning of line 4 is supported by the diphthongs in the stressed words *loud* and *sounding* and by the voiced consonants in the stressed words *loud*, *surges*, and *sounding*. In line 6 the image of Ajax's striving is reinforced by both the stress pattern and the syntactic order. Five successive stressed monosyllables ('strives some rock's vast weight') slow down the line, which is also slowed by the abnormal positioning of the direct object 'some rock's vast weight' before its verb 'throw'. Line 9 contrasts with line 6: although it is an alexandrine (with twelve syllables), it has fewer stresses and it displays normal word order.

Sound patterning is employed in uses of language other than verse. Here are some instances of alliteration drawn from headlines in *The Independent* for just one issue (10 December 1992):

> Ill met by moonlight in Mogadishu
> Digging dirt can land you in doo-doo
> Rights for the wrong reasons
> Beastly tidings for Buxton
> Kop confused by King Kenny's return

Sound patterns also occur in such diverse uses of language as proverbs ('Time and tide wait for no man', 'Birds of a feather flock together'), and advertisements: 'Guinness is good for you'; 'SHE is a woman and a lover, SHE is a worker and a mother' (advertisement for the magazine *SHE*); 'In Touch with Tomorrow—Toshiba'. Rhyming slang alludes to an intended word through a phrase that rhymes with it: *cut and carried* for 'married', *Mona Lisa* for 'freezer', *stand at ease* for 'cheese'.

10.18 Rhythm and metre

Rhythm represents the patterning of stressed and unstressed syllables that normally occurs in connected speech. It also involves pitch changes, including those associated with nuclear tones in tone units (cf. 10.15 f.). In ordinary speech there are various degrees of stress, varying jumps or drops in pitch, and varying durations of pitch movements in the tones. Rhythm takes account of syntactic units.

Metre is a regular patterning of alternations of stressed and unstressed syllables that ignores the variability usual in speech. It is a formal convention of much of English verse. In Old English alliterative verse the number of unstressed syllables associated with a stressed syllable is not constrained.

The traditional approach to metre uses terminology borrowed from the analysis of quantitative metres (based on the length of syllables) in Greek and Latin poetry. The units within a line are feet. Feet consisting of two syllables are duple, those consisting of three syllables are triple. In the list of main types of foot given below, an unstressed syllable is symbolized by 'x' and a stressed syllable by '/'.

x / iamb   x x / anapaest
/x trochee   / x x dactyl
/ / spondee

Lines are characterized by the number of feet in them. The lines most frequently used are:

3 feet trimeter
4 feet tetrameter
5 feet pentameter
6 feet hexameter or alexandrine

The most common metrical form in English poetry is iambic pentameter. It is exemplified in the first line of Thomas Gray's 'Elergy Written in a Country Churchyard':

> The curfew tolls the knell of parting day
> x   / l x / l   x   / l x / l x   / l

The traditional foot-scansion has been criticized because the foot is not a perceptual unit and because rhythmic effects transcend the boundaries of feet. However, no alternative metrical scansion has yet gained general acceptance.[5]

Chapter 11
Punctuation

Summary

Punctuation and the spoken language (11.1–3)

Punctuation for separating and for enclosing (11.4–8)

Periods (11.9–11)

Question marks (11.12)

Exclamation marks (11.13)

Colons (11.14–16)

Semicolons (11.17)

Chapter 11 Summary

■ There are numerous graphic displays that are unique to human communication. The conventions of punctuation reflect only crudely—if at all—the pauses and intonational patterns that occur in speech.

■ The present punctuation system for English was essentially in place during the second half of the seventeenth century. It is linked more to grammatical structure than to the rhythms of speech.

■ Punctuation marks do not necessarily coincide with pauses in speech. They occasionally indicate intonational features.

■ The two major functions of punctuation marks are to separate and to enclose. There is a hierarchy of separation marks and a hierarchy of enclosing marks. The most frequently used marks are the comma and the period.

■ The separation marks are periods, question marks, exclamation marks, colons, semicolons, commas, and dashes.

■ The enclosing marks come in pairs, though one of the pair may be absorbed by a more major mark. The enclosing marks are parentheses, dashes, commas, and quotation marks.

■ Two punctuation marks apply to words. They are apostrophes and hyphens.

Punctuation and the Spoken Language

11.1
Written communication

There are numerous graphic displays that are unique to written communication: footnotes and indexes; tables, diagrams, maps, and graphs; photographs and cartoons; formulae and equations. Some variations in printed texts may have communicative—and not merely aesthetic—significance: print size, spacing between letters, roman versus italic, normal versus bold.

One set of writing systems in English bears some relationship to systems in the spoken language: the conventions for spelling, which are discussed in Chapter 12, correspond in some measure to the sounds used in speech. On the other hand, the conventions for punctuation, the topic of this chaper, reflect only crudely—if at all—the pauses and intonational patterns that occur in speech (cf. 11.3).

11.2
The development of English punctuation

The beginnings of the punctuation systems used now in Europe can be traced back to punctuation practices in classical Greece and Rome, which influenced the punctuation used by medieval European scribes. However, there was a great deal of variability and inconsistency in both classical and medieval periods: variability and inconsistency in the number and form of punctuation signs and in their use even within the same work.

The unsystematic punctuation that was common in medieval manuscripts continued into the early period of printing. In some instances, more than one compositor was employed to set a work and the compositors might vary in the punctuation that they added to what they found in the manuscripts of authors. It has been claimed, for example, that several compositors worked on Shakespeare's First Folio, the different hands manifesting themselves in the variable punctuation of parts of the printed text. Indeed, it is likely that Shakespeare's punctuation was augmented by others before the manuscripts reached the compositors: perhaps by the prompter, to guide the actors in their rendering of the lines; and by the professional scribes, who produced a fair copy of the text for the acting company.

The present punctuation system for English was essentially in place during the second half of the seventeenth century. It owes its standardization in the first place to the work of printers and subsequently to the guidelines set by publishing companies. Some variation continues to the present day. Relatively minor differences, though conspicuous, distinguish American and British punctuation, the two systems that influence punctuation practices elsewhere in the English-speaking world. In addition, some publishers maintain house styles, and copy-editors often impose on the manuscripts of authors their own prescriptions.

The earliest punctuation systems tended to reflect a division into sense units that were expected to correlate at their boundaries with pauses in speech. They provided an aid to reading aloud and for some religious texts a guide to chanting. With the increased publication of printed books, the punctuation system was adapted for silent reading and was linked more to grammatical structure than to the rhythms of speech.

11.3
Punctuation, pauses, and intonation

There is a widespread belief that the comma is equivalent to a pause in speech and even that the semicolon, colon, and period (or full stop) represent progressively longer pauses than the comma. It is true that a reader is often likely to pause after such punctuation marks when reading aloud from a script, though there is no strict hierarchy in length of pause. However, in unscripted monologue (even when the speaker is prepared or knows the topic well) and certainly in casual conversation we may expect to find numerous pauses where punctuation marks would not occur: these may reflect the speaker's hesitations, which are common even among practised speakers. Such pauses and also intonation breaks (which mark the ends of intonation units but may sound like pauses to the untrained ear) vary considerably in their placement, depending on factors apart from familiarity with the topic, such as the personality of the speaker, the speaker's mood, the tempo of the speech, and the relationship between participants in the discourse.

There are, however, circumstances apart from hesitations where pauses or intonation breaks occur in speech but punctuation marks are not allowed in writing. One example is the position immediately after a long subject. In **[1]** a pause (or some other kind of break) is expected in speech between *discussed* (the end of the subject of the sentence) and the verb *concerns*, but punctuation rules forbid the separation of the subject from the rest of the sentence by a single punctuation mark:

> **[1]** The question that does remain to be discussed concerns notions of political responsibility and ethics. [W2A-017-6]

Similarly, it would not be surprising to find a pause in speech between *was* and *that* in **[2]**, but punctuation rules forbid the insertion of a single comma between the verb *be* and the subject predicative (cf. 3.18):

> **[2]**   The prediction was that broking firms would expand their operations and that very many new companies would be created. [W2A-005-56]

In the next example, a pause or intonation break would be normal in speech between *also* and *that*, but rules intervene, preventing us from inserting a single comma before a *that*-clause functioning as an extraposed subject (cf. 4.38):

> **[3]**   It should be noted also that the rate of protein turnover is influenced by the activity of the thyroid gland. [W2A-024-28]

On the other hand, punctuation marks may be found where pauses would normally not occur. In **[4]** a pause is unlikely between *that* and *after* (though likely between *time* and *that*, where a comma is disallowed):

> **[4]**   Sears predicted at the time that, after an initial surge triggered by an advertising blitz, sales would not be affected at all. [891005-0012-13]

Similarly, a pause is unlikely before *in fact* in **[5]**, even though a pair of commas encloses the expression:

> **[5]**   Many analysts, in fact, said they thought IBM did not go far enough in lowering expectations. [890928-0146-3]

Nevertheless, there are occasions when punctuation marks indicate intonational features that are not otherwise conveyed in the text. For example, question marks signal the presence of a question and therefore the intonation appropriate to a question. If the grammatical form shows that the sentence is a question, the question mark is redundant, as in **[6]**:

> **[6]**   Is this an indication that the social structure within the church mirrored that in secular society? [W1A-002-25]

But a question mark is required otherwise, as in **[7]**:

> **[7]**   Well I did it—I asked for a hard piece and she said "A really hard one?" [W1B-010-55]
>
> **[8]**   Perhaps she should stay away from Lesley today? [W2F-003-37]

Similarly, an exclamation mark is redundant when the sentence is exclamative in form:

> **[9]**   How lovely to be writing to you again! [W1B-003-106]

But the punctuation signals the appropriate intonations in **[10]**–**[13]**, without of course detailing what they could be:

> **[10]**   I miss you! [W1B-001-35]
>
> **[11]**   I've not had a permanent job for almost two years now! [W1B-001-164]
>
> **[12]**   Muchas gracias for your letter which came this morning. It was nice to hear from you—when I finally got it open! [W1B-004-64]
>
> **[13]**   'Come in, come in. Tom, look who's here . . . Aunty Emma!' [W2F-003-48 f.]

If the presence of the punctuation marks is optional, they may suggest some intonation pattern in a spoken version, though not necessarily a particular pattern. Consider the use of the optional dash in **[14]** to express a dramatic pause before a self-correction:

> **[14]** The night of the accident she'd been upset, distracted—no, upset: after dinner, she hadn't been able to settle to anything. [W2F-016-86]

In the following examples, notice the effect of the suspension periods in **[15]**, and the parentheses in **[16]**, and the pairs of commas in **[17]**:

> **[15]** I was passing, and . . . I'm sorry, I shouldn't be here. [W2F-009-88]

> **[16]** I've come to Haight Street (home of the hippies I told you about) to get a haircut. [W1B-011-71]

> **[17]** She asked if she might see a hand-mirror, please, and when it was placed in her hand she started fussing, quite urgently, with her hair. [W2F-010-66]

Punctuation for Separating and for Enclosing

11.4
The functions of punctuation

We can distinguish two major functions for punctuation marks: either they separate or they enclose.[1]

Marks that separate occur singly and set apart juxtaposed units. In **[1]** the period signals the end of the first sentence and therefore separates the two sentences, in **[2]** the semicolon separates the two main clauses that have been juxtaposed in one orthographic sentence, and in **[3]** the commas separate the three adjectives:

> **[1]** Until now we have been a rural planet in which most of mankind has lived close to the land and to nature. By the end of the century we will be transformed into an urban planet which will be mainly man-made and include 3 thousand million people competing for limited space in its towns and cities. [W2B-018-7 f.]

> **[2]** I was sorry to hear about your traumatic experience; it must have been very harrowing. [W1B-011-5]

> **[3]** She had always disliked this building. To her it was cold, unsanctified, sinister. [W2F-005-85 f.]

There are several enclosing marks that set apart a unit that is included in a larger unit. In **[4]** there are two appositives, the first enclosed by a pair of dashes and the second by a pair of commas, while in **[5]** the appositive is enclosed by parentheses.

[4] You can try an experiment on reaction by sitting in a chair with castors—an office chair or a wheelchair—and throwing a heavy object, such as a brick or a book, away from you. [W2B-035-19]

[5] It was based on the fact that a colour picture contains both luminance (light or brightness) and the colour. [W2B-034-108]

Theoretically, enclosing marks always occur in pairs, but a comma or dash is omitted at the beginning of a sentence, as in **[6]**, and is absorbed by a more major punctuation mark when it occurs at the end, as in **[7]**:

[6] Frankly, those reasons are not good enough. [W2B-013-54]

[7] He did notice the flowers, apparently. [W2F-019-67]

Contrast these two examples of enclosed adverbs with **[8]**, where both commas are present:

[8] Then, unhappily, my thoughts are unoriginal. [W2F-018-93]

Parentheses, on the other hand, may enclose one or more sentences—one sentence in **[9]** and two in **[10]**—or occur at the end of the sentence before the period, as in **[11]**:

[9] The operatives identified pro-choice Democrats and emphasized the abortion issue among them. (Special-election procedures allow cross-party voting.) In a district where 33% of the voters are registered Democrats, the only Democratic candidate on the ballot received 6.6%; the remainder voted for Ms. Hunter. [891013-0006-28]

[10] The novels in particular intrigued Alice, because she sensed that to read some of them might afford insights, but Eleanor so consistently downplayed them that she soon stopped asking about them. (A search through library catalogues—with an unmistakably furtive feeling—revealed nothing. None of the titles was even listed, and the only authors with the name Hamilton were other people.) [W2F-009-47 ff.]

[11] Much of Mr. Lane's film takes a highly romanticized view of life on the streets (though probably no more romanticized than Mr. Chaplin's notion of the Tramp as the good-hearted free spirit). [891102-0153-10]

Periods marking the ends of enclosed sentences come within the parentheses, as in **[9]** and **[10]**. The period follows the closing parenthesis if the enclosed unit functions as part of the sentence, as does the *though*-clause in **[11]**.

Several marks have a specifying function, sometimes in addition to other functions. For example, the question mark not only separates between sentences (like the period) but also specifies that its sentence is a question. Pairs of quotation marks not only enclose but also specify that the enclosed content is direct speech. The apostrophe in *neighbours'* specifies that the word is in the genitive plural in contrast to the genitive singular *neighbour's* and the non-genitive plural *neighbours*.

11.5
The written text

A text is a self-contained communicative unit. Written texts range in size from a multi-volume encyclopedia to a road sign consisting of one word such as 'STOP'. Large texts are visually divided into smaller units. Books, for example, are divided into chapters for the main body of the text, though there is also obligatory front matter and there may be optional back matter. Chapters may in turn be divided into sections, as in this book, and perhaps into subsections or a hierarchy of subsections.

The visually distinct units that are common to the majority of varieties of written texts are the paragraph, the sentence, and the word. Since the word and the sentence in orthography (the writing system) are not always equivalent to the word and the sentence in grammar, it is sometimes necessary to refer to them as the orthographic word and the orthographic sentence. The paragraph, on the other hand, is a conceptual entity that is not defined in grammar, so that there is no such unit as a grammatical paragraph.

Punctuation also separates or encloses units other than the paragraph, sentence, and word; but the others are not as visually distinct or as well-established.

A word is separated from words before and after it by a space or by a combination of a space with one or more punctuation marks preceding or following the space:

> I'm *surprised* how   a '*routine*' that I
> We can, *however*, say   '*Good*'. And should I

Punctuation marks—apostrophes, hyphens, capitals, and abbreviation periods—may also perform functions for words, internally or at the peripheries:

> they *can't*   my *T-shirt*
> '*twas* too early   *custom-built* furniture
> the *minister's* brief   *F*— off!
> our *sons'* birthdays   You *c—t*!
> her *ex-husband*   *Prof.* Carter

A sentence begins with a capital and usually ends with a period; less usually it ends with a question mark or exclamation mark or some indication of interruption or suspension such as a dash or ellipsis dots. The sentence—or a set of sentences—may also be enclosed by opening and closing quotation marks or by opening and closing parentheses. Between two sentences there may be a longer space than is normal between two words.

The beginning of a new paragraph is signalled by indentation (also called indention) or by a larger space after the previous paragraph than is normal between lines or by a combination of indentation and spacing. In print (and sometimes in typescript) the first paragraph of a chapter or section normally begins without indentation, since indentation is unnecessary to signal the beginning of such a paragraph. The end of a paragraph is signalled by leaving blank the space remaining after the last sentence. If the end of the paragraph coincides with the end of the line, the signal for the end of the paragraph in block style is extra spacing before the next paragraph; this signal is obscured when the end of the line also coincides with the end of the page.

11.6
The separating punctuation hierarchy

Sentences, clauses, and phrases constitute a grammatical hierarchy in that a sentence consists of one or more clauses and a clause of one or more phrases. However, for punctuation we have to distinguish the orthographic sentence from the grammatical sentence. For example in both **[1]** and **[2]** we have two orthographic sentences separated by periods, but only in **[1]** do we have also two grammatical sentences:

[1]   Things never work out the way we would like them to. Like fallen leaves that the wind sweeps to and fro, we are indiscriminately swayed by our unsubstantial and frivolous emotions. [W1B-001-37 f.]

[2]   You're no doubt working extremely hard. At avoiding the things you dislike and doing the things you do best. [W1B-001-4 f.]

The second orthographic sentence in **[2]** is a grammatical phrase, not a grammatical sentence (cf. 11.9).

The norm in punctuation is for the orthographic sentence to be also a grammatical sentence. But the writer can often exercise the option of combining two sentences into one, for example by replacing the period in **[1]** by a semicolon. The effect would be to signal to the reader that the two units were more closely connected than the sentences on either side of them. In **[3]** we have two independent clauses separated by a semicolon:

[3]   The paint was peeling everywhere; it would be a surprise if it wasn't. [W2F-006-34]

The two clauses in **[3]** could equally have been made into two orthographic sentences separated by a period.

Commas are often used to separate co-ordinated units (but cf. 11.18–21). The co-ordination may be syndetic (with a co-ordinator) **[4]** or asyndetic (without a co-ordinator) **[5]**:

[4]   These images come mainly from poems, novels, articles, cartoons, postcards, and posters [. . .] [W2A-009-21]

[5]   Brett looked down at the stiff cold collar, inspected the fittings. [W2F-001-78]

The hierarchy of separation marks is shown below together with the units that they normally separate:

mark   *unit*
1. period, question mark, exclamation mark   sentence

2. colon	sentence(s), independent clause, phrase
3. semicolon	independent clause
4. dash	independent clause, phrase
5. comma	subordinate clause, phrase

Marks are sometimes used to separate units other than those specified, either for special purposes or for stylistic effects. For example semicolons are used in [6] and [7] to separate phrases when internal commas obscure the major units:

[6]   Airlines that could be affected include Continental Airlines, a unit of Texas Air Corp., Houston; Pan American World Airways, a unit of Pan Am Corp., New York; and Trans World Airlines, New York. [891005-0119-30]

[7]   More police, more jails, more-stringent penalties, increased efforts at interception, increased publicity about the evils of drugs—all this has been accompanied by more, not fewer, drug addicts; more, not fewer, crimes and murders; more, not less, corruption; more, not fewer, innocent victims. [890929-0138-4]

Independent clauses that are asyndetically co-ordinated (i.e. without a co-ordinator) are normally not separated by commas, but commas may be used to reinforce parallel structures, as in [8]:

[8]   He loved his mother, he feared his father.

The separation punctuation hierarchy is useful in distinguishing superordinate from subordinate units. In [9], for example, the colon is the superordinate mark, which introduces a list of units separated by semicolons:

[9]   They never expressly forswore reunification but never stood up for it either, hiding behind alibis: Reunification is, at best, a long way off; it can be achieved only with the support of "our neighbors,"; it is possible only within "a European solution." [890918-0062-19]

Semicolons and separating commas readily occur in a series of more than two units. Unlike the other separating marks, the colon can introduce a unit consisting of more than one sentence (cf. 11.15).

11.7
The enclosing punctuation hierarchy

In parallel with the hierarchy for separation marks, we can establish a hierarchy for enclosing marks:

mark	*unit*
parentheses	sentence(s), clause, phrase
dashes	sentence, clause, phrase
commas	subordinate clause, phrase

The most frequent kind of parentheses is ( ), usually called brackets in British English. For other kinds of parentheses, see 11.26.

The enclosing marks are correlative. Parentheses (and other types of bracketing) come in pairs, the closing mark being different in shape from the opening mark. Theoretically, the dashes and commas are in pairs, but one or other of the pair may be absorbed by a more major punctuation mark or omitted at the beginning of a sentence.

Parentheses are placed above dashes in the hierarchy because they can enclose two or more sentences. And while the units enclosed by all three correlative pairs can be omitted without affecting the acceptability and meaning of the remainder, those enclosed by parentheses are most easily dispensed with.

One enclosed unit can be embedded within another. As examples **[1]**–**[4]** demonstrate, there is no hierarchy dictating which marks should enclose the superordinate and subordinate units.

> **[1]** One of the fastest growing segments of the wine market is the category of superpremiums—wines limited in production, of exceptional quality (or so perceived, at any rate), and with exceedingly high prices. [891102-0121-8]

> **[2]** Copying media coverage of the Olympics, this film dogs the steps of Aleksei Sultanov, the young Soviet athlete—oops, musician—who won last spring's tournament—oops, piano competition. [891012-0165-21]

> **[3]** When inserted again this year, the provision was not even challenged on the Senate floor, as conservatives relied—mistakenly—on the House ultimately stripping out the language. [891012-0054-38]

> **[4]** Mum's coming up for a few days and then Daddy's joining us on the bank holiday weekend (back to the camp bed for me—we've only one bed!). [W1B-004-34]

Quotation marks are also correlative, and like parentheses the opening and closing marks are always present. Quotation marks fall into a different category from the three sets of marks in the enclosing hierarchy, since their primary function is not enclosure but specification: they specify that the enclosed content is direct speech or a quotation (cf. 11.30).

11.8
Frequencies of punctuation marks

Of the separating and enclosing punctuation marks, the most frequently used are the comma and the period. One study of American punctuation[2] cites frequency counts based on samples totalling about 72,000 words that were drawn in equal proportions from three styles of writing in print: journalism, learned writing, and fiction. The figures for the punctuation marks are:

commas	4,054 (46.8%)
periods	3,897 (45%)

dashes	189 (2.2%)
pairs of parentheses	165 (1.9%)
semicolons	167 (1.9%)
question marks	84 (1%)
colons	78 (0.9%)
exclamation marks	25 (0.3%)

Together, the comma and the period accounted for over 90% of the marks. None of the other marks came anywhere near their frequency.

Comparable figures are given below for percentages in a British set of texts—the written component of ICE-GB, which consists of 200 texts totalling approximately 400,000 words (see Ch. 8, n. 4):

commas	19,485 (41.9%)
periods	18,632 (40.1%)
dashes	1,347 (2.9%)
opening parentheses	2,090 (4.5%)
closing parentheses	2,118 (4.6%)
semicolons	743 (1.6%)
question marks	810 (1.7%)
colons	806 (1.7%)
exclamation marks	444 (1%)

Again, the most frequent punctuation marks by far are the commas and periods. There are higher percentages for parentheses in particular in ICE-GB than in the American samples, but that may be due to differences in the types of texts: the texts in ICE-GB were drawn from a wider selection of text categories. In the American texts the parentheses always came in pairs, but in the British texts the closing parentheses sometimes came singly, after a section or list number or letter.

The sections that follow examine in turn the individual separating and enclosing marks and then consider the factors that influence choices where they are available.

Periods

11.9
Periods at the ends of sentences

The period (commonly called full stop in British English) is the most usual punctuation mark for the end of an orthographic sentence. The relatively infrequent alternatives are the question mark and the exclamation mark. Since these two marks replace the sentence period they are generally not followed by a period even when quotation marks intervene:

[1]   He looked slowly round at the crew and said, 'Anyone know if it's raining in Rio?' [W2B-004-108]

It is acceptable and quite usual—particularly in official and business letters—to put a period at the end of a request that is politely framed as-a question:

[2]   Would you kindly telephone the above number to make an appointment. [W1B-017-65]

[3]   In the meanwhile, may I just confirm a few administrative details. [W1B-030-85]

Question marks are possible in **[2]** and **[3]**, but they suggest genuine queries.

It is sound practice to resort to exclamation marks sparingly and to prefer a period unless the sentence is intended to be read as undoubtedly exclamatory in tone. Imperative sentences normally end in a period:

[4]   'Bring him out here,' instructed Miss Pickerstaff. [W2F-012-87]

A period may end an orthographic sentence that is not a grammatically independent sentence. Here is a series of fragments in the form of noun phrases, each in an orthographic sentence for separate emphasis:

[5]   But there is also punishment and self-imposed pain here—guilt, perhaps, at taking the role of breadwinner away from the father. *Anxiety. Solitude. Defilement. Despair. Blacking.* All these things come together, and we are left with the image of the young boy writhing in agony on the rat-infested floor. [W2B-006-8 ff.]

This type of fragment is often found in advertisements:

[6]   Thai now flies smooth as silk to Istanbul. *Twice a week.* [*International Herald Tribune*, 23 September 1994, p. 18]

Elliptical sentences and non-sentences (cf. 6.1) are particularly common in dialogue:

[7]   'Actually I was thinking of having a rest afterwards,' I said.
         '*A rest?*' she said incredulously. '*On the first day of our holiday?*' [W2F-013-28 ff.]

[8]   'What you mean? What can they do to me? I mean really.'
         '*Really deport you.*'
         '*How?*'
         '*Extradition.*' [*Adolf's Revenge*, by Lynne Alexander (London: Abacus, 1994), p. 82]

Periods are customarily omitted after addresses and dates that head letters and after addresses on envelopes. They are always omitted after the name that ends a letter.

It is usual not to have a period in titles of books and other works and in newspaper headings or subheadings, even if these take the form of sentences that would elsewhere end in a period:

[9]   Fossils Provide Closest Clue to Missing Link [*International Herald Tribune*, 23 September 1994, p. 1]

More conspicuously, the heading in **[10]** consisting of two sentences has the period at the end of only the first sentence:

[10] Researchers have been bewitched by the elegance of nucleic acids and proteins. Now they are opening their eyes to the subtleties of sugar [*The Economist*, 24 September 1994, p. 119]

It is sometimes claimed that there is a rule against starting a sentence with *and* or *but*, but they are frequently used by experienced writers. Though inexperienced writers may overuse *and* and *but* at the beginnings of sentences and their usage may be unjustified, skilled writers can use these conjunctions with confidence to smooth the flow of the discourse.

11.10
Abbreviation periods

A period may be placed after initial letters or after a shortened form of a word to indicate an abbreviation:

B.A.	Mon.
U.K.	Dec.
C.O.D.	Fig.
a.m.	Prof.
A.D.	Gen. (General *or* Genesis)
	Hon. Sec.

The period is not used for acronyms where the initials are pronounced as a word and the word has established currency:

AIDS (Acquired Immune Deficiency Syndrome; also writtens as *Aids*)
WASP (White Anglo-Saxon Protestant)
NOW (National Organization for Women)
UNESCO (United Nations Educational, Scientific, and Cultural Organization)
VAT (Value-added Tax)

Increasingly, the abbreviation period is omitted—particularly in British English—even when the acronym is pronounced as a sequence of letters (sometimes called an alphabetism or an initialism):

AC/DC (Alternating Current/Direct Current)
NHS (National Health Service)
IRA (Irish Republican Army)
FDA (Food and Drug Administration)
NEA (National Endowment for the Arts)
BBC (British Broadcasting Corporation)
GMT (Greenwich Mean Time)

OUP (Oxford University Press)
DNA (deoxyribonucleic acid)

Similarly, periods are often omitted in British English in alphabetisms such as *BA, UK, PhD, am, PC* (Police Constable), *QC* (Queen's Counsel), *MP* (Member of Parliament).

In British usage there has long been a tendency to omit the period when the final letter is present as well as the first letter, in which case the shortening is regarded as an orthographic contraction:

Mr   Mrs   Dr   Rd   St (Street *or* Saint)   Ltd

The tendency is being extended in some British printed matter (particularly newspapers) to other forms of shortening, though it is more usual to provide periods:

Lt.Col.   Capt.   Co.   sq.ft.   Inc.   Rev.

Initials for personal names normally take periods: J. R. Pearson. The periods are omitted after the initials in some typing and printing styles.

In British usage, the day of the month may be written as an ordinal numeral (*1st May, 8th June*) as well as a cardinal numeral (*1 May* or *May 1*). A period is usually not inserted after the abbreviated ordinal.

Numerals for abbreviated dates may be separated by periods, but virgules (slanting lines or solidi) and dashes (en-dashes in print) are common alternatives:

8.3.95   8/3/95   8–3–95

The dates here represent August 3, 1995 in American English and 8 March 1995 in British English, since the references to day and month are differently ordered in the two varieties. Periods are generally used in British English for time abbreviations as well, where American English uses colons:

9.30   9:30

They are also used before decimals (and are then called decimal points) and between units of money:

15.30 per cent   £18.50 $27.99

Scientific and technological works generally follow an international system of abbreviations for measures, chemical elements, and the like. No periods are used for the abbreviations:

kg (kilogram)   s (second)   sq (square)
Hz (hertz)   m (minute)   O (oxygen)

If an abbreviation period coincides with a sentence period, only one period is used:

If the 20-point limit is triggered after 1:30 p.m. Chicago time, it would remain in effect until the normal close of trading at 3:15 p.m. [891102-0104-6]

11.11
Ellipsis and suspension periods

A sequence of (normally) three periods is used for omissions in quotations and for hesitation or suspense. They are termed ellipsis dots, ellipsis points, or ellipsis periods; the terms suspension dots or suspension periods are sometimes reserved for hesitations and suspense.

Ellipsis periods indicate that the writer has omitted something from a quotation. It may be at the beginning of the quotation [1], in the middle [2], or at the end [3]:

[1] Another alteration is: '. . . weep, and you sleep alone'. [W2B-010-44]

[2] One dictionary defines dowager as 'a wealthy or dignified elderly woman . . . a widow possessing property or a title obtained from her husband'. [W2B-022-13]

[3] In section 40 it states "After the formation of the filament and during its formation, arsenic [. . .] will flow from the electrodes and heavily dope the filament . . ." [W2A-034-54]

If the omission comes at the end of a sentence, a fourth period is commonly added (particularly in American English and for scholarly writing in British English) for the usual sentence period.

Suspension periods indicate hesitations and pauses of various kinds and breaks in sentence structure that may be followed by a new start:

[4] Bereavement is so . . . yes it does feel like fear. [W1B-010-25]

[5] The accident, caused by human error and negligence, is on record as "the world's worst nuclear accident" . . . yet. [W2A-030-6]

[6] 'Now if only Peter could give me a child like that I'd get pregnant tomorrow. The only trouble is . . .' her look now enveloped Peter as well, 'his children have turned out so badly.' [W2B-004-44 f.]

[7] 'He vanished,' Anne said, 'Just like Tommy did. He said he was going to look for him, so I suppose he's over here somewhere, unless . . .' Sally shook her head. [W2F-002-40]

[8] But drinking coffee and reading in an undusted room, children and mother still in their night-clothes, the breakfast dishes undoubtedly unwashed in the sink if not still on the table—it was . . . Emma sought for a civilized word . . . sloppy. [W2F-003-62]

A dash can similarly indicate a break in structure, but it suggests a sharper break than do suspension periods (cf. 11.23).

Question Marks

11.12
The functions of question marks

A question mark is placed at the end of a sentence to signal that the sentence is a question. It therefore has a dual purpose: it marks the end of a sentence (thereby replacing the sentence period and indeed including the period in its appearance) and it specifies that the sentence is a question:

[1] Is this an indication that the social structure within the church mirrored that in secular society? [W1A-002-25]

[2] What have you two been up to? [W1B-002-78]

[3] Is Joe still annoying everyone or has she learned to keep her big mouth shut? [W1B-002-28]

Sentences **[1]**–**[3]** have the structures of various types of questions (cf. 3.5): a *yes–no* question **[1]**, expecting the answer *yes* or *no*; a *wh*-question **[2]**, requesting the supply of missing information; an alternative question **[3]**, asking for a choice.

The questions may be elliptical:

[4] Seen anyone else I know? [W1B-002-36]

[5] You spendthrift! Anyhow why not? [W1B-004-81]

[6] Any ideas? [W1B-007-50]

[7] Looking forward to your move to Cambridge? [W1B-013-93]

[8] More coffee? [W2F-019-87]

A tag question (cf. 3.6), which requires a question mark, is attached at the end of a sentence that is not a question:

[9] It won't be too long before you come over, will it? [W1B-008-137]

[10] 'You don't mind, do you?' [W2F-003-81]

[11] They haven't come back, either, have they? [W2F-006-132]

[12] You love me, don't you? [W2F-016-97]

A declarative question (cf. 3.10), which has the function of a question though not the form, also ends in a question mark:

[13] Perhaps this represents cash advanced? [W1B-020-18]

[14] You must be glad to have Keith back? [W2F-003-112]

[15] I said quickly, 'You believe in using drugs to suppress all pain?' [W2F-004-92]

[16] Jaycee was a male? [W2F-006-178]

[17] I thought you telephoned ahead? [W2F-012-26]

[18] 'You did pick your passport off the floor?' [W2F-015-104]

A tag question may sometimes not have question form:

[19] 'What have you been up to with this then, eh?' [W2F-001-65]

Punctuation conventions require that a question mark not be used for indirect questions:

[20] I don't know whether you've had any work lately.

[21] They told him what the topic should be.

See also 11.13 for exclamatory questions.

A question mark in parentheses is occasionally used to express doubt about a part of the sentence that comes immediately before it:

[22] The concern with 'authenticity' and 'integrity' expresses itself in, for example, gridded metal-framed canopies in the arcades, supported by steel (?) rods emerging out of free-standing stone pillars [. . .] [W2A-005-108]

Exclamation Marks

11.13
The functions of exclamation marks

The exclamation mark is placed at the end of a sentence to signal that the sentence is a forceful utterance. Like the question mark (cf. 11.12), it has a dual purpose, since it also marks the end of a sentence. It is used for certain kinds of utterances, typically in personal letters between intimates, informal notices, and representations of dialogues:

1. **Exclamatory sentences introduced by *how* or *what***

   [1] What an appropriate introduction to San Francisco! [W1B-012-15]

   [2] How lovely to be writing to you again! [W1B-003-106]

   [3] How boring! [W1B-004-103]

2. **Exclamatory questions**

   [4] Aren't things different now! [W2B-022-7]

3. **Expressions of surprise or shock**

   [5] You can only have showers on week-days after supper, and you have to pay 5 Francs each time—I couldn't believe it! [W1B-002-126]

   [6] The architecture here is dramatically different from that in Manhattan. You can see the sky! [W1B-012-26 f.]

4. **Conventional form of wishes and curses**

   [7] Good luck to Simon for his exams! [W1B-004-99]

   [8] Happy Birthday! [W1B-006-98]

   [9] Congratulations! [W1B-014-69]

[10] If only it would! [W2F-003-44]

[11] Damn the Belgian refugees! [W2F-005-33]

5. Urgent warnings or alarms

[12] Look, Benjamin! [W2F-012-93]

[13] 'Shoot him! Shoot him!' [W2F-012-130]

[14] The wheelchair woman cried, 'Not like that!' [W2F-018-88]

6. Vocatives (cf. 5.15) when used alone

[15] 'The neighbours will hear you. Or do you want people to know how you behave towards me?'
    'Susan!' [W2F-008-145]

7. Interjections (cf. 4.47)

[16] Oh dear! [W1B-005-124]

[17] Hi again! [W1B-009-29]

[18] "Humph!" she said to herself. [W2F-005-101]

[19] Well, well! [W2F-005-123]

[20] 'Oh no!' [W2F-006-153]

Here are some other examples:

[21] I miss you! [W1B-001-35]

[22] I've not had a permanent job for almost two years now! [W1B-001-164]

[23] You spendthrift! [W1B-004-80]

[24] The rent costs next to nothing and the area is superb—about time too! [W1B-008-136]

[25] I'm here at last! [W1B-013-44]

[26] I shall regret this for the rest of my life! [W1B-015-24]

[27] 'She wouldn't do that!' [W2F-006-155]

Exclamation marks are occasionally used within sentences:

[28] However, usually (and ideally!) the industrial contract is of a thoroughly standard kind. [W1B-029-30]

They are also occasionally used in parentheses in informal writing to indicate that what appears in an immediately preceding part of the sentence is surprising.

[29] There are about 50 other girls, most appear to be younger than me (!) and are very unfriendly. [W1B-002-120]

In informal writing we occasionally find combinations of two or more exclamation marks **[30]** or combinations of question marks with exclamation marks **[31]**:

[30] (Gosh, the things which satisfy us, as we get older . . . !!) [W1B-001-160]

[31] Has he mended the door yet?! [W1B-002-45]

Colons

11.14
The major functions of colons

The colon has three major functions:

1. to introduce identifications
2. to introduce examples
3. to introduce, especially in formal style, quotations or direct speech.

The colon separates two units: it is attached to the end of one unit and introduces the unit that follows, which may consist of several parts. Within the second unit, the identifications, examples, and quotations are separated by semicolons or commas. (But see 11.15 for the punctuation in itemized lists set out in columns.)

In **[1]** the colon introduces a list of items that identify the three spectral bands:

[1] This arrangement allows measurements to be made in three spectral bands: solar, near infrared and (by subtraction) visible. [W2A-029-47]

[2] Today they face a further threat to their survival: starvation. [W2C-002-40]

The colon introduces an identification (one item rather than a list) in **[2]** and an example in **[3]**:

[3] There are numerous variables that can contribute towards an increasing totalitarianism within a new religious movement: one fairly obvious one is physical isolation. [W2A-012-55]

A period or a semicolon is more usual than a colon when an explicit expression is present, such as *for example* in **[4]**, though the period would ordinarily be used only when the expression is followed by a sentence:

[4] Some we won: for example, a standardized mineral-carrying rail wagon was agreed on. [W2B-016-87]

The colon is followed by a quotation in **[5]** and by direct speech in **[6]** and **[7]**:

[5] It is disappointing, therefore, that the submitted design should fall far short of its clearly stated goal: 'to discover an architectural form that can accommodate all these functions, activities and contexts at once'. [W2A-005-73]

[6] Atkinson said yesterday: "I'm happy here." [W2C-004-105]

[7] One dealer said: "Even as late as yesterday I suppose the market had a 90% belief in war. That 10% of optimism has now been stamped out." [W2C-013-13]

A comma would be more usual than a colon in **[6]**, where the direct speech consists of just one short sentence and the style is not formal.

A colon appears in **[8]**–**[10]**, but a period or semicolon would be common alternatives when what follows the colon could be an independent sentence.

In **[8]** the second unit (which follows the colon) is a conclusion; in **[9]** an elaboration; in **[10]** an explanation or reason:

> **[8]** Similarly, the behavioural model does not support the illness or sick concept either, but assumes that a person's observable actions determine whether he/she is normal or abnormal: one is abnormal if one acts abnormally. [W1A-007-34]

> **[9]** The raid turns into a fiasco: Butch shoots the other two gang members because they are running off with the loot, and is then wounded himself. [W2B-009-122]

> **[10]** One of the members of our local diving club once surfaced in an oil slick and said that he really felt for the birds: the stuff matted his hair, filled his ears and tasted foul. [W2B-029-20]

The colon may be superordinate to the semicolon in the hierarchy of separation punctuation (cf. 11.6); the point is illustrated in **[11]** below. Equally, the semicolon may be superordinate to the colon **[12]**.

> **[11]** The production of seeds by a plant is dependent on three processes: first, pollination; then, fertilisation of the ovule (embryo sac) by fusion of the female gamete (egg cell) with a male gamete from a pollen grain to produce an embryo; and finally, development and maturation of seed. [W2B-030-55]

> **[12]** The book is a series of letters purportedly written but not sent by a modern Arthurian officer; the last letter is melodramatically incomplete: the enemy are rapidly encroaching. [W2A-009-50]

11.15
Punctuation accompanying colons

An itemized list following a colon is commonly set out in a column or with separate indentations for each item:

> **[1]** To install the application:
> 1. Put the *OED2* compact disc in the CD drive.
> 2. Run Windows.
> 3. Put the floppy disk distributed with the package in your floppy-disk drive.
> 4. Run File Manager and double click on the drive icon for your floppy-disk drive.
> 5. Double click on the program file SETUP.EXE.
> 6. Follow the instructions on the screen. [*The Oxford English Dictionary Second Edition on Compact Disc* (Oxford: Oxford University Press, 1994), p. 3]

A dash is sometimes superfluously combined with a colon that introduces a list (:—).

Listed items may be enumerated by numbers (roman—upper or lower case—or arabic) or by letters (upper or lower case). The numbers or letters may be followed by a period (as in the above example), or be enclosed in a pair of parentheses, or be set off by just the closing parenthesis. In printed documents and forms and in advertising, other signals may be used for marking each item in the list, such as a bullet •.

The unit before the colon may signal explicitly that a list is to follow by referring to the presence of listing or by using the expressions *as follows* or *the following*.

When the units before the colon can be an independent sentence, the colon replaces a possible sentence period:

[2]   Of all scenes that evoke rural England, this is one of the loveliest: An ancient stone church stands amid the fields, the sound of bells cascading from its tower, calling the faithful to evensong. [891102-0103-3]

[3]   But yesterday's factory orders report had good news on that front: it said factory inventories fell 0.1% in September, the first decline since February 1987. [891102-0157-26]

In American usage it is usual for the sentence after the colon to begin with a capital [2], though occasionally it begins with a lower case letter [3]. British usage prefers lower case:

[4]   Extremes meet: unity disperses into multiplicity. [W2A-004-79]

[5]   This is a rather long book: some of the characters are weak, and the dialogue is heavy at times. [W2B-005-35]

If there are two or more sentences after the colon, as in [13] below, it is usual to begin with a capital. Note also the punctuation of [1] above.

In both American [6]–[7] and British usage [8]–[9], however, direct speech and quotations that follow a colon begin with a capital:

[6]   The mathematics section of the widely used California Achievement Test asks fifth graders: "What is another name for the Roman numeral IX?" [891102-0147-3]

[7]   The judge declined to discuss his salary in detail, but said: "I am going to be a high-priced lawyer." [891102-0143-47]

[8]   Or, as a member of the US Supreme Court is reported to have said about pornography: 'I can't define it, but I know it when I see it.' [W2A-035-75]

[9]   The witness replied, "Not altogether." [W2C-019-56]

American guides to usage advise against inserting a colon or any other punctuation if the first unit is not a complete sentence. However, the colon is common in such contexts in British punctuation, as in [10]–[11]:

[10] To track environmental change the gene pool must be able to: a) maintain and continuously update an adequate reserve of variants [. . .] [W1A-009-32]

[11] What is the structure and composition of the link, is it: single crystal, part poly and part single crystal or a mixture of microcrystallites and dielectric? [W2A-034-36]

The colon is unnecessary and intrusive in [11], where the listed items are not numbered. It would not be a mistake to omit the colon in these contexts in British English even when the list is displayed, as in [12]:

[12] The *OED2* application comes with a full installation program which
- creates a directory on your hard disk
- copies all the required files into that directory
- installs the *OED2* fonts in Windows
- creates an *OED2* program group and item in Windows. [*The Oxford English Dictionary Second Edition on Compact Disc* (Oxford: Oxford University Press, 1994), p. 2]

Punctuation usage varies for ends of items set out as a list. Questions must be given question marks, as in **[13]**:

[13] So in carrying out your survey, try to find the answers to the following questions:
What kind of heating is installed?
Does it operate efficiently and keep the house warm in winter?
How old is it and what condition is it in?
Is it safe? [. . .] [W2D-012-49 ff.]

Otherwise the choices are periods **[1]**, no punctuation except for a period at the end **[12]**, or no punctuation at all **[14]**:

[14] You can choose to pay:
—the whole amount on 3rd May
—two instalments on 3rd May and 3rd November
—eight monthly instalments from 3rd May to 3rd December [invoice from Thames Water Utilities 1994]

Another less common option is to use semicolons except for a period after the last item.

11.16
The minor functions of colons

Here are some conventional uses of the colon:

1. In times, to separate hours from minutes, especially in American usage:

9:30   14:15

Periods are more usual in British usage, but colons are always used for the 24-hour clock.

2. In titles, to separate subtitle from title:

Teaching Grammar: A Guide to the National Curriculum
Bully for Brontosaurus: Reflections in Natural History

A common alternative is a period. On the book cover and title page the difference between title and subtitle may be expressed by a difference in fount or type size.

3. In biblical references, to separate chapter from verse:

Genesis 11: 1–9   2 Kings 10: 12–25

4. In the salutation for letters, especially in American usage (where British usage generally has a comma):

Sir: Dear Mr Taylor:

American English uses a comma too for informal personal letters.

5. In bibliographies, between place of publication and publisher's name:

Oxford: Oxford University Press
Amsterdam: Rodopi

6. In ratios, between the proportions:

. . . the three substances in the proportions of 3 : 2 : 1.5 parts by weight respectively

7. In various abbreviated forms, to separate a heading from accompanying information:

PS: I forgot to say that . . .
NOTE: You will find . . .
Tel: . . .   Fax: . . .   Telex: . . .
Present: . . .   Our Ref: . . .
Admission: Members £5, Guests £7.50
X-ray of chest: no abnormality found
1st prize: . . .

Semicolons

11.17
The functions of semicolons

The main function of the semicolon is to separate two or more independent clauses that are placed next to each other within a sentence:

[1] The government counts money as it is spent; Dodge counts contracts when they are awarded. [891102-0157-49]

[2] Arbitrage does not cause volatility; it responds to it. [891102-0073-22]

[3] She was the widow of a curate from the south of France; with her daughter she kept a small day school and had a few paying guests. [W2B-002-14]

[4] On the one hand, it would be a relief to have it off my chest; on the other, I felt that I would be committing professional hara kiri on air. [W2B-001-41]

[5] Like Sir Winston, Randolph was a prodigious drinker and smoker; unlike him, he was also impulsive, quick-tempered and grandly irresponsible. [891004-0157-18]

A sentence period can always be used in place of a semicolon that separates independent clauses, but a semicolon is preferable if the two or more units are felt to be closer to each other than to sentences on either side of them. For the option of using commas between parallel independent main clauses, see 11.18, 11.20; a colon is a less likely alternative and is restricted to separating not more than two clauses.

The clauses separated by semicolons are often co-ordinated; asyndetically (without a co-ordinator) **[1]**–**[5]** or syndetically (with a co-ordinator) **[6]**–**[7]**:

> **[6]** It is, he says, just a hunch; *but* as we have seen, Broecker's hunches have an uncanny knack of coming true. [W2B-025-41]

> **[7]** It is hardly probable that anything can be proved; it is even possible that there is nothing to prove; *and* unwarranted investigation might cause undeserved stress. [W2F-011-2]

When there is a sequence of three or more units, some writers use a comma instead of a final semicolon before the co-ordinator:

> **[8]** John Garrison sang solidly and affectingly as Edmund; Gloria Parker, as Dahlia, was the other cast standout; Marla Berg, as Eleanor, was an adept actress if a somewhat thin and colorless soprano, *and* Imre Pallo conducted the rough-and-ready-sounding Ohio Chamber Orchestra. [891012-0062-46]

When co-ordinators are present, commas can be used instead of semicolons, but semicolons are required to mark the units if the clauses have internal commas that might obscure the structure of the sentence, as in **[8]**. Commas are considered incorrect—and are particularly stigmatized in American English—if a linking expression other than a co-ordinator or semi-co-ordinator (cf. 11.18) is used. In **[9]** the semicolon is required because the linker is *instead*:

> **[9]** In Australia itself, airline pilots said they were withdrawing a 30% pay-hike demand that is at the heart of a dispute disrupting Australia's domestic air services; *instead*, the pilots are seeking an unspecified increase based on a 25% increase in productivity. [891005-0100-20]

When three or more clauses are separated by semicolons, the clauses are likely to constitute a list:

> **[10]** The wooden watchtowers are crumbling; the entire area is overgrown with weeds; the remains of the crematoriums are barely marked and cannot be approached because of surrounding debris. [891011-0167-54]

> **[11]** We sit in the car instead of walking; we use the lift instead of the stairs; we spend the evening sitting in front of the television. [W2B-022-9]

> **[12]** All this explains why early satellite launch vehicles were used for only one mission; why they consisted of multiple stages; and why they could carry only a very small payload. [W2B-035-59]

When the semicolon separates independent main clauses, which is its major function, it competes chiefly with the period. When the semicolon separates other units, they come in sets of three or more and the chief competitor is the comma. (See also 11.14 for the colon.) Semicolons are preferred over the more usual comma when the units have internal commas, since the semicolons mark the superordinate units more clearly. In **[13]** the units are subordinate *that*-clauses; in **[14]** they are noun phrases:

> **[13]** Italians have also learned that General Giovanni De Lorenzo, as secret service chief, compiled secret dossiers, including tapes and photographs, on some 150,000 people; that his successor, General Vito Miceli, received an $800,000 handout from the Americans, that Miceli was linked to an abortive coup in 1970 led by Prince Valerio Borghese, a war-time mini-sub commander. [W2C-010-66]

> **[14]** And executives at stations in such major markets as Washington; Providence, R.I.; Cleveland; Raleigh, N.C.; Minneapolis, and Louisville, Ky., say they may very well not renew "Cosby." [891102-0132-16]

In **[15]** the semicolon separates two sets of noun phrases, each set with internal commas:

> **[15]** They had been replaced by a range of lesser varieties laid out over scraps of plastic on the ground: Russian chocolates, curling irons, cutlery, shower nozzles, juice extractors; plus East German fishing rods, a Czechoslovak carpet, a Turkish fire extinguisher. [890928-0009-77]

Semicolons may separate units other than independent clauses even if there are no internal commas. They are used in place of commas to emphasize distinct points in a series:

> **[16]** If the Japanese companies are seriously considering their survival, they could do at least three things to improve the situation: raise salaries higher than those of financial institutions; improve working conditions (better offices and more vacations, for example); accept and hire more labor from outside Japan. [891102-0098-14]

> **[17]** She is a home-maker; a wonderful mother; a marvellous cook. [W2F-019-39]

Commas for Separating

11.18
Commas for separating two independent clauses

Commas are by far the most frequently occurring punctuation marks within sentences. They are the lightest of the marks and the most versatile, used to separate units and in a variety of contexts to isolate units. They are also the most flexible of marks, since writers often have the choice whether or not to insert them. Commas offer scope for assisting readers to understand the text. Writers show their skill in punctuation by their judicious use of commas: too many commas slow down reading and can obstruct comprehension; too few can promote ambiguity.

If two main clauses are linked by a co-ordinating conjunction, a separating comma is generally used before the conjunction:

[1] It is recognised that natural selection acts on phenotypes and not on genotypes, *and* it is acknowledged that behaviour constitutes a significant part of phenotype expression. [W1A-009-3]

[2] It sounds an excellent idea to take a boat over to Dusseldorf, *and* I do hope that the boat owners will be able to undertake this project. [W1B-019-100]

[3] But nobody knows who he is, *or* if they do they are keeping it to themselves. [W2B-005-109]

[4] Is this something recent, *or* have you felt this way for a while? [W2F-004-74]

[5] She might not know the cause, *but* she could weigh up the symptoms and what she found when she examined me. [W2B-001-76]

[6] The diet may be deficient in calcium, but their bodies will compensate by absorbing more and excreting less. [W2B-022-1]

The linkers *so, yet,* and *nor* may also be preceded by a comma, though it is quite usual for them to follow a more major mark when the clauses are lengthy:

[7] We are happy to give a randomly selected jury power over the life or death of individuals, *so* why not give a similarly randomly selected panel power over the nation? [W2B-014-71]

[8] The governor could not make it, *so* the lieutenant governor welcomed the special guests. [891102-0184-12]

[9] Transfer payments are already unwieldy for budget management, *yet* such new burdens as child care are in the works. [891012-0107-30]

[10] That would indicate that IBM expects to make up ground in the fourth quarter, *yet* analysts do not believe the problems will go away that fast. [890928-0146-15]

[11] No one knows exactly how many new religions there are, *nor* does anyone know how many members are in each movement. [W2A-012-1]

[12] We do not know the advantages or handicaps of having a high or low rate of whole body protein turnover, *nor* do we know the effects on it of a habitually low energy intake. [W2A-024-24]

A comma may sometimes be absent, particularly if the co-ordinator is *and* and the clauses are short:

[13] Poorly-sorted coarse sands occur around the patch reefs *and* muddy fine sands cover the lagoon floor. [W2A-023-13]

[14] She asked Eddie if he wanted a cup of tea *but* he said no. [*Cowboys and Indians*, by Joseph O'Connor (London: Sinclair-Stevenson, 1991), p. 178]

Two independent clauses are occasionally juxtaposed, separated by a comma without a co-ordinator, particularly if they are short and parallel:

[15] Justine occasionally received a flowered, coyly folded letter from one of her fading Action friends, tattooed with slogans like "Hippies are cool, greasers are fools." [*Two Girls, Fat and Thin*, by Mary Gaitskill (London: Chatto & Windus, 1991), p. 137]

[16] It was nobody's fault, that was the thing to remember. [*Cowboys and Indians*, by Joseph O'Connor (London: Sinclair-Stevenson, 1991), p. 207]

11.19
Commas for separating two units other than independent clauses

If two units other than independent clauses are linked by co-ordinators, there is usually no punctuation between the units:

[1] The inadequacies of our own relationship of father *and* son, the real *but* stifled affection, the things we never said to each other, the gestures felt *but* unmade, were no doubt responsible for my desire to find out what I flinched from. [W2F-014-15]

[2] Instead it has been decided to try to improve conditions and regimes for prisoners by building new jails *and* by management reorganisation. [W2C-001-80]

[3] Cut the meat into even-sized cubes, leaving on any fat *but* removing all gristle. [W2D-020-25]

[4] What are you doing for the summer, staying in Paris *or* going home? [W1B-001-109]

[5] I described how I first noticed the symptoms *and* how I first heard from the doctor that it was no ordinary problem. [W2B-001-53]

[6] The CIA's job is to find out what led the agent there *and* who killed him. [W2B-005-59]

Commas are occasionally found, particularly with *but* and *or*, perhaps to emphasize contrast or alternatives:

[7] When my plate was clean I asked her if she would mind telling him when she got the chance that I couldn't stand snails or garlic, *but* that this was no reflection on his excellent cooking. [W2F-013-90]

[8] It lasted on the whole for 250 years: nothing like it had been known before, *or* has been repeated since. [W2A-001-49]

[9] Bands which contain either no sound at all, *or* sound which is masked, need less coding. [W2B-038-33]

Commas—or a more major punctuation mark—are always used in asyndetic co-ordination (without a co-ordinator):

[10] When she was able *to move, to shake herself free again*, she stumbled downstairs. [W2F-020-70]

[11] He looked down into the white-tiled portal where the ticket inspector yawned, *scratching his head, briefly returning Michael's glare from his booth*. [W2F-008-87]

11.20
Commas for separating three or more units

A series of three or more units can be co-ordinated by *and* or *or*:

[1]   Statistical data can be portrayed in many ways—as just lists of figures, *or* diagrams *or* if a spatial element is involved as a map. [W1A-006-39]

[2]   Emperor tamarins are about the same size as the other species, which is to say about the size of a good handful, *and* are clothed in black and reddish brown, *and* sport a long flowing moustache of white. [W2B-021-37]

The co-ordination exemplified in **[1]** and **[2]** is polysyndetic co-ordination, where the co-ordinator is repeated between the units.

More usually the co-ordination is syndetic (with a co-ordinator) or asyndetic (without a co-ordinator). Here are examples of asyndetic co-ordination:

[3]   The audience roared in approval, the children cheered and shook their fists in the air, their mothers protectively stroked their brows. [*Two Girls, Fat and Thin*, by Mary Gaitskill (London: Chatto & Windus, 1991), p. 236]

[4]   I hope I can perform again *somewhere, sometime, somehow* . . . [W1B-008-31]

[5]   Flipping through this book, one discovers that almost every ailment— *rheumatism, cataracts, eczema, convulsions, sciatica*—responds to sustained doses of laxatives. [*International Herald Tribune*, 28 September 1994, p. 5]

[6]   Meanwhile, *sitting in the sky boxes, running the concessions, selling hot dogs to the crowd*, are the *lawyers, politicians, race-mongers white and black, opportunists of every variety*. The rest of us watch while the wrestlers sweat and thunder. We watch thanks to the biggest cashier-in of all, the *huge, dish-linked, lap-topped, ad-powered, fame-fueled, deadline-tooled* media luring us so far into *the myths, the dream, the beastliness, the spectacle,* that we hardly notice the fact that we've become the spectacle ourselves. [*International Herald Tribune*, 27 September 1994, p. 3]

There are two punctuation styles for syndetic co-ordination. The A, B and C style (which omits the comma between the last two units) is the general British convention. The A, B, and C style (which inserts the final comma) is the general American convention, except that the A, B and C style is usual in American journalism. The insertion of the final comma is increasing in British practice. The general American A, B, and C style is shown in **[7]**–**[8]** and the journalistic American A, B and C style is shown in **[9]**–**[10]**:

[7]   The new geometry mirrors a universe that is rough, not rounded, scabrous, not smooth. It is geometry of the pitted, pocked, *and* broken up, the twisted, tangled, *and* intertwined. [*Chaos: Making a New Science*, by James Gleick (New York: Viking Penguin, 1987), p. 94]

[8]   Although the work in this tradition started in philosophy, it soon spread to linguistics, psychology, *and* artificial intelligence. [*Arenas of Language Use*, by Herbert H. Clark (Chicago: University of Chicago Press, 1992), p. xii]

[9] Under the stars and moons of the renovated Indiana Roof ballroom, nine of the hottest chefs in town fed them Indiana duckling mousschino, lobster consommé, veal mignon *and* chocolate terrine with a raspberry sauce. [891102-0184-19]

[10] The U.S., claiming some success in its trade diplomacy, removed South Korea, Taiwan *and* Saudi Arabia from a list of countries it is closely watching for allegedly failing to honor U.S. patents, copyrights *and* other intellectual-property rights. [891102-0173-1]

The omission of the final comma is sometimes justified on the grounds that it is redundant in the presence of a co-ordinator. However, the comma is occasionally needed to indicate the correct grouping. Here are examples from American journalism, where the A, B, and C style has been selected instead of the usual A, B and C style:

[11] One of his favorite groups of shorts is the "junk-yard play," involving buyers of junk bonds, bank lenders to junk-bond issuers, *and* others. [891012-0014-43]

[12] One of his central, and more familiar, tenets is that children, despite their terrible hygiene and inability to spell, are somehow superior in wisdom and spirituality to those of us who can drive, open bank accounts, *and* procreate. [891011-0146-46]

In [11] the presence of the comma prevents the misreading 'bank lenders to others'. In [12] the comma emphasizes the three separate privileges of adults.

11.21
Commas for separating adjectives

Special consideration needs to be given to a series of adjectives that premodify nouns. If the adjectives are linked by a co-ordinator, their punctuation follows the conventions outlined in 11.19 and 11.20. The absence of a co-ordinator may be interpreted as asyndetic co-ordination or there may be a hierarchy of modification in which one adjective modifies another adjective or the rest of the noun phrase (cf. 5.2).

Some usage guides require commas when the adjectives are asyndetically co-ordinated, as shown by the possibility of inserting co-ordinators between them and reversing the order of the adjectives. The punctuation then follows the general rule for asyndetic co-ordination. Here are some examples of asyndetically co-ordinated adjectives (or adjective phrases) that premodify nouns:

[1] But conventional as Ms. Anderson has become, she can still make the *inspired, ironic, off-beat* observation now and then, as when she offers her off-center interpretation of the Star-Spangled Banner. [891011-0138-29]

[2] Although Congress could ultimately fall back on a *much cheaper, stripped-down* set of benefits, it is not likely to tackle *high-cost, broad-based* medical issues anytime soon. [891004-0119-3]

[3] So he designed a *computerized, digital* wristwatch that tells how high the tide is now and how high it is going to be at any date and time during the coming year. [890928-0098-29]

[4] It seems strange that there is an ice-rink in the middle of such a *hot, dusty* city. [W1B-009-39]

If the adjectives are not asyndetically co-ordinated, commas are not required:

[5] Peasant farmers are being pushed onto increasingly marginal land as a direct result of the failure to carry out *effective agrarian* reform. [W1A-013-57] ('agrarian reform that is effective')

[6] It's great to hear about Michael—love puts a *whole new* complexion on things, doesn't it? [W1B-013-66]

[7] They tended to consist of that minority of the 'middling sorts' of society who had lost faith in the *old religious* ways and were seriously worried about their personal salvation. [W2A-006-92]

In the phrase *high-cost, broad-based medical issues* in **[2]**, the adjectives *high-cost* and *broad-based* are asyndetically co-ordinated, but not *medical*: the two adjectives modify *medical issues* as a unit. A similar example is **[8]** where the sets of adjectives modify *younger man* and *older guy* as units:

[8] "Hardball" is a buddy show about undercover cops that teams a *cocky, longhaired younger* man with a *bull-headed, paunchy older* guy. [890918-0036-39]

In **[9]** *bright* modifies *yellow*:

[9] He turned suddenly and ran, to reappear a moment later with a *bright yellow* racing car. [W2F-003-54]

The insertion of a comma between the two adjectives would indicate the interpretation 'a racing car that was bright and yellow'.

In practice, even edited printed writing does not always follow the distinctions. In **[10]** the adjectives *multi-national* and *trans-frontier* are presumably intended to be asyndetically co-ordinated, but there is no comma between them. The same applies to the three adjectives in **[11]**.

[10] One of the most widespread *multi-national trans-frontier* pollution problems over the last decade has been acid rain. [W2A-030-47]

[11] Don Boswell at the Record has an opening for a *bright vital young* reporter [. . .] [W2F-014-73]

On the other hand, the comma between *early* and *major* in **[12]** seems odd, since presumably the intended interpretation is 'the early works among the major works':

[12] All Freud's *early, major* works on normal psychology reveal that the dynamics of the mind rely on unconscious forces rather than intelligence [. . .] [W2A-002-14]

Similarly, there is hierarchical modification rather than asyndetic co-ordination in **[13]**.

[13] Lord Denning has clothed his opposition to the application of the legal rule in a *vivid, narrative* presentation of the facts. [W2A-007-68]

Dashes for Separating

11.22
The major functions of dashes

Like the colon, the dash separates two units only, but it signals a sharper break between the units and it is also used in contexts where a comma is equally appropriate.

One such context is when the second unit is linked to the first by a co-ordinator (*and*, *or*, or *but*):

[1] In Scandinavia, after centuries of conflict, Swedish and Norwegian leaders deliberately chose to seek a path of friendship and cooperation—and disciplined their communications consistently. [W2A-017-72]

[2] A loss made all the greater, from his own account, by the spectacle of seeing his older sister win a prize—or, rather, two prizes. [W2B-006-53]

[3] Police said the jogger could be just a friend—or the killer himself. [W2C-020-83]

[4] Perhaps in the industrial and political climate of the day it wasn't possible—but I doubt whether it was even recognized at the time as being something important to strive for. [W2B-016-60]

[5] We've got to come back and finish the job—and I think we can do it. [W2C-014-18]

The co-ordinated units in **[4]** and **[5]** are main clauses.

An independent clause can follow a dash without a co-ordinator:

[6] He wouldn't thank me for continuing to be with him for these reasons—it's so dishonest. [W1B-015-96]

[7] Several of the tasks that brains can perform well have strong commercial potential—for example, automatic speech recognition and synthesis are already used in many applications. [W2A-032-33]

[8] Remember this—official figures show that two million houses in England alone are inadequately heated. [W2D-012-48]

[9] There wasn't anything glamorous or sophisticated about her—she was just a typist in Barnsley's office. [W2F-011-75]

[10] Americans today spend $15,000 like pocket change—they do not think much about it. [891102-0105-12]

A colon would be a more formal alternative to the dash; an initial capital is not an option after the dash, though a capital is possible for independent clauses after colons in British English and usual after colons in American English.

Semicolons are another more formal alternative, particularly for **[7]**, but not for **[8]** since *this* points forward to the second unit.

In casual writing, for example in personal letters between family members or close friends, we sometimes find elliptical sentences or fragments separated by a dash:

> **[11]** Saw you glance at the camera tonight—didn't notice it first time through.
> [W1B-008-14]

> **[12]** A rather different evening on Wednesday—dinner champagne (a good imitation of it, anyway!) and excellent jazz at Kimball's. [W1B-011-54]

11.23
The minor functions of dashes

Apart from the separating function (cf. 11.22) and the enclosing function (cf. 11.27), the dash has a number of minor conventional uses:

1. To combine with a colon that introduces a list (:—)

This combination does not occur frequently now.

2. In representation of dialogue, to represent a pause

> **[1]** 'We—' he indicated Peter and himself—'will be in Hong Kong.' [W2B-004-74]

> **[2]** 'Did—' Dee groped for their names—'did Jaycee and Maggie go to classes today?' [W2F-006-116]

> **[3]** 'Let's just say—' she paused, sighed winsomely, looking aged. 'Let's just say they're from someone who cares' [W2F-008-6]

3. In representation of dialogue, to indicate that a person is interrupted or does not finish the sentence

> **[4]** 'I wonder if a computer could handle—'
> 'I think you'll find the administrator more than happy to talk to you about his work,' he said. [W2F-004-125]

4. In representation of dialogue, to indicate a break in the sentence structure followed by a new start in the structure

> **[5]** I don't know what's happened to—I mean, I don't know where she is or why she isn't back. [W2F-006-142]

5. In representation of dialogue, to indicate hesitation, stammering or stuttering

> **[6]** 'I—I'm not sure.' [W2F-006-119]

> **[7]** 'We're going to do all right, Co—Cora,' she murmured to herself. [W2F-006-249]

6. To indicate a missing letter or letters or a word that has been suppressed

> f—ing   Mr B— T—   Senator —

7. To indicate various uses of inclusive numbers and the like (the shorter en-dash)

1995–99	March–June 1990
1–5 p.m.	20 November–1 December
verses 10–15	Genesis 1: 10–2: 5
pages 95–102	28–15 victory

When the concluding date is in the unpredictable future, nothing follows the dash:

Professor of English (1994–)

Parentheses

11.24
Parentheses for enclosing

Parentheses (more commonly called brackets—sometimes round brackets—in British English) are used to enclose content that the writer sets out apart so that it does not interrupt the flow of the sentence. In the examples given below, the enclosed content constitutes an explanation or a rephrasing in less technical language **[1]**–**[4]**, an exemplification **[5]**–**[6]**, an identification or specification **[7]**, an elaboration **[8]**–**[9]**, a concession **[10]**–**[11]**, a comment **[12]**, a justification **[13]**–**[14]**:

[1] Qualifying earnings may also be credited (treated as paid)—for example, on account of sickness or unemployment—but only to the level needed to make the year a qualifying one. [W2D-004-17]

[2] We can send two representatives and additional observers (who can participate but not vote). [W1B-024-60]

[3] Release studies are conveniently performed in vitro using either small slices of brain, or synaptosomal preparations (pinched-off nerve endings). [W2A-027-3]

[4] Totally absorbed, the ringers stare straight ahead, using peripheral vision (they call it "rope sight") to watch the other ropes and thus time their pulls. [891102-0103-30]

[5] [. . .] and the 1970 Chronically Sick and Disabled Persons Act placed a further set of obligations on local authorities, with regard to community care provision (for example, assessment for a telephone). [W2A-013-52]

[6] I think it is disgraceful, for example, that Mrs T is given so little credit for stamping out the disgusting—not to say dangerous—practice of eating partially cooked or even sometimes raw eggs (as in foreign confections such as omelettes and mayonnaise). [W2B-014-3]

[7] The American transnational corporations (Ford, General Motors and Chrysler), the Japanese giants (Nissan, Toyota and Honda specifically), and the European "National champions" including VW, Rover, Fiat and Renault are fighting for dominance or survival. [W2A-015-26]

[8] Sprinkle the cornflour over the meat and add the garlic (cut in half), soy sauce and rosemary. [W2D-020-56]

[9] We took a shuttle bus from the airport (door-to-door service) driven by a rather creepy guy. [W1B-012-7]

[10] Either that or my (admittedly simplistic) approach is faulty. [W1B-020-9]

[11] She always fell in with any plan for excursions or picnics (although she was always expected to pack up the picnic basket). [W2F-017-11]

[12] Undeterred, Microsoft continued refining Windows, and in November 1987 (I guess Microsoft likes November launches!) Windows 2.0 was released. [W2B-036-12]

[13] The commonest causes of death are heart disease (31.9 per cent) and malignant cancers (17.6 per cent). [W2A-019-62]

[14] We (I assume you are in this with me at this point) need to get three words—"for examination only"—eliminated from the law. [891102-0084-59]

Parentheses and dashes signal a sharper break in the continuity of a sentence than do commas. The combination of these pairs of marks allows for one enclosed unit to be embedded within another, as in **[5]** (where the parentheses unit is embedded in a commas unit). Parentheses and dashes, unlike pairs of commas, can enclose a sentence, as in **[4]**. Notice that the embedded sentence in **[4]** does not have an initial capital.

Unlike dashes, parentheses can enclose a sentence that is not embedded in another sentence and therefore has its own period within the enclosing parenthesis, as in **[15]**:

[15] The Artist hangs out in Greenwich Village, on a strip of Sixth Avenue populated by jugglers, magicians and other good-natured hustlers. (This clearly is not real life: no crack dealers, no dead-eyed men selling four-year-old copies of Cosmopolitan, no one curled up in a cardboard box.) [891102-0153-13]

Furthermore, more than one sentence can be enclosed within one set of parentheses, each ending in its own period, question mark, or exclamation mark.

11.25
The minor functions of parentheses

Parentheses have a range of minor uses, some of which are related to the major functions described in 11.24. They enclose:

1. **An abbreviation that will subsequently be used in the text**

   [1] The break in the redox potential profile, known as the redox potential discontinuity (RPD) occurred at shallower depths in finer sediments. [W2A-022-49]

2. **A translation or equivalence of an expression**

   [2] It is an allied strength that he takes so flexible yet responsible a view of what should be understood by that innocent word *sense* ('to aid the sense') [...] ['High Punctuation', by Christopher Ricks, *London Review of Books*, 14 May 1992, p. 9—italics in original]

   [3] The city had expected to pay about 11 million yen ($77,000), but Fujitsu essentially offered to do it for free. [891102-0141-26]

   [4] A typical Eldorado weighed about 4600 lb (2086 kg). [W2B-037-67]

See also related examples in 11.24.

3. **References to other places in a text**

   [5] On 11 and 12 September 1985 the centre of an anticyclone was situated over Denmark and produced clear skies over the North Sea (Fig.1). [W2A-029-31]

Similarly:

(p.125)   (opposite)   (above left)   (below)
(Table 15)   (on next page)   (Chapter 3)   (cf. page 15)

4. **Bibliographical references to other texts or bibliographical details about other texts**

   [6] Judging from the Americana in Haruki Murakami's "A Wild Sheep Chase" (Kodansha, 320 pages, $18.95), baby boomers on both sides of the Pacific have a lot in common. [891102-0156-1]

   [7] These trends are of major concern to a government with a strong policy objective to control public expenditure on all its social programmes (Thain and Wright, 1990) and to reduce the level of direct state involvement in service provision (Flynn, 1989). [W2A-013-10]

Styles of bibliographical references are usually determined by the publishers of books and journals. In some styles, brackets [ ] are used instead of parentheses.

5. **Various identificatory or locatory references**

   [8] Sen. John Danforth (R., Mo.) praised the department's actions, noting that rollover crashes account for almost half of all light-truck deaths. [891102-0128-13]

   [9] I enclose an official union order form (# U2081) for the work. [W1B-028-57]

   [10] These are located in reception (our street entrance) and the cashier's office (4th floor). [W1B-028-104]

> **[11]** Do please contact either Julie Green (X 3136) or myself (X 3228) if you have any queries. [W1B-019-124]

6. Numerals or letters that enumerate sections of a text or items on a list

Brackets (cf. 11.26) are an alternative in this use. In a list, the opening parenthesis or bracket may be omitted.

7. In formulas, to show which items belong together

$$(a+b)^2 \quad (a+b+c)\,(x+y)$$

When enclosed items are embedded within other enclosed items, the different extents of enclosure may be indicated with the use of other types of bracketing, such as [ ] and braces { }.

11.26
Other types of bracketing

Brackets [ ] (commonly called square brackets in British English) are the most frequent type of bracketing apart from parentheses. Their distinctive (though not necessarily most frequent) use is to indicate an editorial insertion in a quotation:

> **[1]** Gervase continues: 'The two [chapels] of St Anselm and St Andrew, formerly placed in a circle on each side of the church, prevented the breadth of the choir from proceeding in a straight line [. . .]' [W2B-003-84]

In this first of several sentences quoted from Gervase, the author has inserted '[chapels]'—either missing in the original or replacing a less familiar expression—as a help to the reader, but has indicated that the insertion is an editorial interpolation by enclosing it in brackets. In **[2]** the author feels constrained to point out that the italics are added:

> **[2]** Strictly speaking, it should be: '*lay on*, Macduff; / And damn'd be he that first cries, "Hold enough!" ' [my italic] (Shakespeare, Macbeth, V.iii.33). [W2B-010-114]

As often in this volume, omission of a part of a quotation is indicated by three ellipsis periods within brackets.

In **[3]** the conventional '[sic]' ('thus' in Latin) draws attention to something surprising in a sentence taken from a quoted text.

> **[3]** Vincent felt great sympathy for the mother, fell in love with the daughter Ursula [sic], and spent a happy time with them, as the cheerful tone of his letters clearly shows. [W2B-002-15]

Two common uses of brackets are as alternatives to parentheses in bibliographical references and in the enumeration of sections of a text or items on a list; in the enumeration use, the opening bracket may be omitted. One technical use of brackets (which can be found in Ch. 10) is to enclose transcriptions of sounds in a language.

Apart from parentheses and brackets there are a number of other types of bracketing for enclosing content, but these have technical uses in particular subject areas. As with parentheses and brackets, they occur in pairs and typically the opening and closing marks have a different shape. Here are a few examples:

{ } braces
⟨ ⟩ angle (or diamond) brackets
/ / oblique brackets or slants

Dashes for Enclosing

11.27
Enclosing dashes

Dashes are enclosing marks as well as separating marks (cf. 11.22). In their enclosing function they resemble parentheses (cf. 11.24), signalling a sharper break from the rest of the sentence than do commas:

[1] I'm studying Computer Operating Systems at the moment—MS DOS & UNIX for example—as well as two modules in Communication Studies. [W1B-001-97]

[2] It's really embarrassing at the moment because everyone in the street—and I mean everyone—has cut their lawn. [W1B-004-28]

[3] When the war did break out, such images were not so much forgotten—it was soon termed the Great War—as distorted by propagandist caricature. [W2A-009-17]

[4] The average daily calorie intake is only 1901—a figure which is dangerously near the minimum necessary to sustain life—and 90 per cent of the population is undernourished. [W2A-019-64]

[5] Was it because she knew—or suspected—more than she was admitting? [W2F-006-103]

In **[1]**–**[5]**, the pairs of dashes could be replaced by pairs of parentheses. Pairs of commas are also possible replacements except in **[3]**, because the enclosed unit is an independent sentence. In **[6]** the internal commas rule out replacement by a pair of commas since they would obscure the structure of the sentence:

[6] It is unrealistic to expect human nature to change, to expect humanity—overnight, over millennia, ever—to mature and transcend what appears to be one of our most basic bio-sociological drives. [W2A-017-17]

If the second of the enclosing dashes comes at the end of a sentence, it is absorbed by the period or its equivalent:

> **[7]** The term 'acid rain' is a short-hand version of acid deposition—the fallout of acidic material from the atmosphere. [W2A-030-60]
>
> **[8]** When did you last hear from her—any of you? [W2F-006-96]
>
> **[9]** It was nice to hear from you—when I finally got it open! [W1B-004-64]

The second dash is also absorbed by a semicolon, as in **[10]**, and by a colon, as in **[11]**:

> **[10]** Timber is a crop that grows and dies—often in a lifetime; it is meant to be used for the benefit of man—it is "renewable forever." [891005-0112-18]
>
> **[11]** "If you continue to do this, the investor becomes frightened—any investor: the odd lotter, mutual funds and pension funds," says Larry Zicklin, managing partner at Neuberger & Berman. [891102-0074-60]

Commas for Enclosing

11.28
Enclosing commas

Commas are used to enclose as well as to separate (cf. 11.18–21). They signal a less sharp break from the rest of the sentence than do parentheses (cf. 11.24) or dashes (cf. 11.27), and the writer can often choose between the three types of enclosing marks. Unlike parentheses and dashes, commas cannot enclose a sentence; on the other hand, they are regularly used to enclose an initial element in a sentence.

Enclosing commas come in pairs, as in **[1]**:

> **[1]** Nothing, so far as she could see, had been disturbed. [W2F-020-24]

However, if the enclosed unit comes at the beginning of the sentence, the first comma is omitted:

> **[2]** Among 33 men who worked closely with the substance, 28 have died—more than three times the expected number. [891102-0191-13]

And if it comes at the end, the second comma is absorbed by the period:

> **[3]** I long for your skin on mine, your face touching mine. [W1B-007-116]

The omission illustrated in **[2]** occurs also when the initial comma is preceded by other major marks of punctuation, such as a colon, semicolon, or dash. Similarly, the absorption of the second comma is applied when other major marks of punctuation follow it. However, the second comma is retained in the presence of a closing parenthesis:

> **[4]** If you were primarily here to receive full-time education (and would normally be elsewhere), you will not be regarded as having been ordinarily resident here. [W2D-003-44]

Punctuation conventions disallow the presence of a comma immediately before an opening parenthesis, since a unit enclosed by parentheses cannot be embedded initially within another unit. For the punctuation of commas in relation to quotation marks, see 11.30.

Enclosing commas (or more major enclosing marks) are conventionally used for:

1. **Vocatives**

   [5] 'You'll bend over that table, lad,' he said. [W2F-001-95]

   [6] 'Tiger, wait!' Anne shouted, but the boy didn't stop. [W2F-002-161]

2. **Tag questions** (cf. 3.6)

   [7] 'Morphine's a controlled drug, isn't it?' [W2F-004-99]

   [8] 'You don't mind, do you?' [W2F-003-81]

3. **Adverbial clauses that are verbless or have a participle as their verb** (cf. 6.13)

   [9] And Chile, while retaining a rather large primary sector, has an extraordinarily large proportion of its population employed in the tertiary services sector. [W2A-019-25]

   [10] As already mentioned, land redistribution schemes are very unpopular with landowners. [W1A-013-64]

   [11] [. . .] the upper classes were privileged, enjoying a sort of benefit of clergy. [W2A-001-80]

   [12] There were no truths, however revered, that Coleridge allowed to lie bed-ridden in the dormitory of his soul. [W2A-003-15]

   [13] Surviving evidence suggests a preference for capitals, whether square or rustic, for non-Christian texts [. . .] [W2A-008-31]

4. **Adverbial finite clauses** (cf. 6.13) **when they are in medial position within their host clause**

   [14] Why, if Edward I consistently sought peace, did Anglo-French relations degenerate from relative harmony into outright hostility in 1294? [W2A-010-68]

5. **Appositives** (cf. 5.11)

   [15] 'Oh, I should think so,' said one of them, a jolly, red-faced girl. [W2F-004-172]

   [16] A son, Alistair, was born in 1900. [W2F-017-50]

   [17] Similar situations apply in India, a country in the World Bank's lower middle-income group of 35–40 countries. [W1A-014-21]

   [18] Dugongs, or sea cows, are declining in numbers throughout their fairly wide geographical range. [W2B-029-52]

Enclosing commas are commonly used for:

6. **Expressions that comment on the sentence or link it to other sentences** (cf. 4.27)

   [19] Nevertheless, civilian society was largely fed on a diet of heroic stories and atrocity tales. [W2A-009-28]

[20] Curiously, the birth certificate showed that the baby was born at 87 Hackford Road, while the father was resident at number 17 in the same street. [W2B-002-39]

[21] Tragically, Haiti suffers uniquely from the terrible scourge of AIDS [. . .] [W2A-019-71]

[22] If Romanesque cathedrals were dark, this was not a deliberate search for sacred gloom; on the contrary, their designers lit them as well as they could. [W2B-003-19]

[23] In any case, these are my initial thoughts. [W1B-018-116]

[24] Conversely, if one seeks peaceful coexistence, the prescription is blatantly obvious [. . .] [W2A-017-33]

7. **Initial adverbial finite clauses** (cf. 6.13)

[25] When I look around at my friends, virtually all of them seem to have got careers. [W1B-001-167]

[26] If I were you, I'd apply for the York position just for the experience. [W1B-014-43]

8. **Other initial adverbials if they are long**

[27] As a first-aid measure for a patient in petit mal status, a paper bag placed over the mouth and nose may be helpful. [W2B-023-155]

9. **Adverbial finite clauses introduced by causal *since*, contrastive *while*, *whereas*, *although*, *though*, and purpose *so that* even when they are in final position**

[28] The sandflats are regarded as the province of marine biologists, while the dunes are investigated by terrestrial biologists. [W2A-022-9]

[29] At present, there is no universally accepted surgical nomenclature for the various constituents of a peripheral nerve, although a long-accepted anatomical terminology has been based on microscopic findings. [W2A-026-32]

For commas with non-restrictive relative and appositive clauses, see 5.8–11.

11.29
Commas for avoiding misinterpretation

Commas are sometimes needed to prevent misinterpretation, even if the meaning may become evident in the context:

[1] As scientific involvement increases, knowledge increases and advancements are likely. [W1A-007-76]

The absence of the comma from **[1]** might lead to the initial reading for the first part of the sentence: 'As scientific involvement increases knowledge'. Similarly in **[2]**, the absence of the final comma before *and* would suggest a co-ordination of the final unit with *lack of oxygen* instead of with the series that begins with *certain eye injuries*:

[2]   These include certain eye injuries, electrical injuries requiring medical attention, loss of consciousness due to lack of oxygen, and any injury resulting in twenty-four hours in hospital [. . .] [W2A-018-5]

Below are some invented examples that show how the presence of a comma can forestall a misinterpretation:

[3]   The Romans had slaves, like other ancient peoples.

[4]   The minimum salary has been fixed for the grade above, that of principal.

[5]   However, much as he wanted the job, he was unwilling to move to another city.

[6]   When the demands are high, prices will rise.

[7]   After this has been done, clearly the next task should be to consider upon what evidence such conclusions must rest.

[8]   She slipped her shoes on quickly, deciding to open the door herself.

The headline in [9] is a play on the difference made by the presence or absence of a comma:

[9]   No, Canada
Or no Canada? [*The Economist*, 17–23 October 1992, p. 20]

Quotation Marks

11.30
Quotation marks for quotations

Quotation marks (also called inverted commas and sometimes quote marks) are primarily used to indicate the exact words of a speaker or writer in quotations, including direct speech (cf. 6.17 f.). Quotation marks come in pairs. In handwriting and in perhaps most printed material the opening mark and the closing mark are usually differentiated in shape, but some typewriters and computer keyboards provide the same shape for both marks. In British English there is an increasing tendency to employ single marks as the norm and double marks for quotations within quotations. In American English, in contrast, double marks are the norm and single marks are used for quotations within quotations.

Here is an example of the two types of quotation marks in British English [1] and American English [2]:

[1]   'You said, "not certain"?' [W2F-010-49]

> **[2]** Says Mr. Novack in Allentown: "When you go into a store and buy bananas that say, 'No cholesterol,' you know there is a concern out there." [891012-0100-50]

If a sentence (or more than one sentence) consists entirely of direct speech except perhaps for a reporting clause, the closing quotation mark comes after a period, question mark, or exclamation mark that belongs to the direct speech:

> **[3]** The policeman said, 'I'd like your full name and address, please.' [W2F-009-97]

> **[4]** Mr Bennett raises the question, "Do you think it was a mistake to repeal Prohibition?" [890929-0138-64]

> **[5]** 'You're lying, Edward, aren't you? You're not going to let me see him!' [W2F-012-40 f.]

If the reporting clause is at the end of the sentence, the period that would have ended the direct speech is replaced by a comma:

> **[6]** "A couple of my law clerks were going to pass me in three or four years, and I was afraid I was going to have to ask them for a loan," the judge quipped in an interview. [891102-0143-38]

However, a question mark or exclamation mark remains before the reporting clause:

> **[7]** "What sector is stepping forward to pick up the slack?" he asked. [891102-0157-15]

> **[8]** 'Tiger, wait!' Anne shouted, but the boy didn't stop. [W2F-002-161]

If a sentence of direct speech is interrupted by a reporting clause, a comma ends the first part and is followed by a closing quotation mark:

> **[9]** "People are going over to cable anyway," he says, "so why not see our product there as well?" [890928-0074-12]

The comma ends the first part even if the sentence of direct speech would not have any punctuation there:

> **[10]** "How long," he recalls asking himself, "could it take to finish one drink?" [891004-0157-22]

The punctuation that follows the medial reporting clause depends on what would be the punctuation of the sentence or sentences in direct speech. In **[11]** the part following the reporting clause is intended as a new sentence and therefore the medial reporting clause is followed by a period:

> **[11]** 'It can't be far away,' said Mary Jane, swivelling her head. 'Isn't that a castle on top of the cliff?' [W2F-013-12 f.]

A semicolon may also follow the reporting clause.

If a sentence containing direct speech or any other type of quoted material within quotation marks contains more than a reporting clause, British and American English differ in their punctuation conventions. In British English, the closing punctuation mark belongs to the sentence as a whole and is put outside the quotation marks:

> **[12]** The motto of the market is 'Let the buyer beware'. [W2A-019-70]

There may therefore be a punctuation mark before the closing quotation mark and another after it:

> **[13]** One often raised question about OS/2 is 'Why does it require so much money?'. [W2B-036-78]

However, the final punctuation is often omitted in such combinations. See **[1]** above. In **[14]** the period is outside the closing quotation mark because the sentence of direct speech is not given in full within quotation marks:

> **[14]** Their victory, he said, 'will mean the police were guilty of perjury, that they were guilty of violence and threats, that the confessions were erroneous'. [W2E-007-89]

The same convention applies to the comma after quoted expressions:

> **[15]** In his brief address inside the church, the curate spoke of her being 'with the hosts of angels'; after her recent 'troubles', she was now 'crowned with glory'. [W2F-010-69]

In American English, the final quotation marks always follow a period or a comma:

> **[16]** One writer, signing his letter as "Red-blooded, balanced male," remarked on the "frequency of women fainting in peals," and suggested that they "settle back in their traditional role of making tea at meetings." [891102-0103-65]

> **[17]** Last December, he made his Metropolitan Opera debut leading "The Tales of Hoffman"; he returns this winter to do "Samson and Delilah" and "Faust." [890815-0053-54]

If direct speech extends over more than one paragraph, the convention is to place opening quotation marks at the beginning of each paragraph and closing quotations marks only at the end of the final paragraph.

A long quotation may be set out from the rest of the text as a block quotation or extract. It is then usual to omit quotation marks. In handwritten or typed material, the block quotation is usually distinguished by having all the lines identically indented from the left (unless there is further indentation for the beginnings of paragraphs); the typist may also leave less space between the lines than in the text. Printers may further indicate the block quotation by using a smaller type.

11.31
The minor functions of quotation marks

Quotation marks also enclose:

1. Cited words or expressions

[1] What is the difference between an 'award' and a 'grant'? [W2D-003-8]

[2] 'What do you mean by "lately"?' Dee pounced on the word. [W2F-006-127 f.]

[3] The phrase 'to sock it to someone' originally meant 'to put something bluntly' (and was used as such by Mark Twain). [W2B-010-56]

For the citation of single words, italics are often used in print, normally represented by underlining in handwriting or typing.

2. Paraphrases and translations

An example of a paraphrase enclosed in quotation marks appears in **[3]**. Here is an example of a translation:

[4] Literally 'water of life', *aqua vitae*, originally an alchemist's term, appears to be the most amusing euphemism ever invented for hard liquor. [*Nil Desperandum: A Dictionary of Latin Tags and Useful Phrases*, by Eugene Ehrlich (London: Guild Publishing, 1986), p. 4]

3. 'So-called' expressions

Expressions are sometimes highlighted by being enclosed in quotation marks to indicate that the author does not accept responsibility for the wording. It is often possible to preface them with *so-called*. The expressions may represent someone else's view, may be intended ironically, or may be a neologism or slang. Here are some examples:

[5] By adopting this slogan, which originated in the 'permissive' 1960s, women have turned their own interest in the personal to their advantage. [W2B-009-4]

[6] In the 'good old days' our great-great-grandmothers walked several miles to the village [. . .] [W2B-022-4]

[7] It also seems allowable to beg if you are a 'deserving person'. [W1A-002-56]

[8] What is chilled is the speech of anyone whose views might "offend" the "victims" of those look-alike, think-alike white males. [891012-0112-23]

[9] As the parents of deaf children have to be, in a sense, "super-parents," so deaf children themselves have to be even more obviously, "super-children." [*Seeing Voices*, by Oliver Sacks (London: Picador, 1990), p. 18]

In printed material, titles of works are italicized if they are separate publications—for example, books, long poems, newspapers, operas, plays, films, musical compositions; titles of works that are parts of longer works are in roman type and are enclosed in quotation marks—for example, chapters, articles, short stories, short poems, songs, radio or television programmes. The distinction is not always kept in handwritten material, where quotation marks are often used for all such titles. However, it is clearer to employ underlining (the manuscript equivalent of italics) in place of quotation marks in sentences where apostrophes or other quotation marks are required.

Punctuation of Words

11.32
Apostrophes

The main use of the apostrophe is to signal the genitive (or possessive) case of nouns (cf. 4.10–12). The general rule is that to form the genitive singular we add an apostrophe and an *s*, to form the genitive plural we add an apostrophe only (unless the plural does not end in *s*, as is the case for a few irregular nouns). The genitive relation can usually be paraphrased with *of* ('the *boy's* mother'—'the mother of the boy'), but like the relation expressed with *of* it encompasses a range of meanings.

Here are examples of the genitive singular, with possible paraphrases in parentheses:

Jill's house (the house owned by Jill *or* lived in by Jill)
Freud's theories (the theories espoused by Freud)
Einstein's contributions to science (the contributions to science made by Einstein)
her daughter's career (the career followed by her daughter)
the author's later novels (the later novels written by the author)
the university's future (the future envisaged for the university)
the chairman's secretary (the secretary working for the chairman)
the baby's bib (the bib worn by the baby)
the judge's sentence (the sentence passed by the judge)
the prisoner's sentence (the sentence received by the prisoner)
in an hour's time (in a time lasting an hour)
the judge's interrupting the witness (the interrupting of the witness by the judge)

Here are examples of the genitive plural:

my parents' car (the car owned *or* hired by my parents)
the voters' decision (the decision taken by the voters)
the bankers' huge loss (the huge loss suffered by the bankers)
the developing countries' objections (the objections voiced by the developing countries)
a two hours' flight (a flight lasting two hours)
the officers' acquittal (the acquittal given to the officers)

If the plural does not end in an *s*, we form the genitive plural by adding an apostrophe and an *s*:

the children's school fees (the school fees required for the children)
women's rights (rights claimed for women)
the people's opinions (the opinions held by the people)
the police's reactions (the reactions exhibited by the police)

Like the genitives of singular nouns, the genitives of indefinite pronouns ending in *-body* or *-one* (such as *somebody, anyone*, cf. 4.44) are formed by the addition of an apostrophe and an *s*: *somebody's fault* (the fault ascribable to somebody). But the possessive pronouns (cf. 4.34 f.) form their genitives sometimes without an *s*, e.g. *my, mine, her, our*, and always without an apostrophe, i.e. *hers, ours, yours, its*. The spelling *it's* is not the genitive of *it*, but a contraction of *it is* ('It's late') or *it has* ('It's eaten my fish').

There are a few exceptions to the general rules:

1. Traditionally, singular common nouns ending in an 's' sound that combine with *sake* take the apostrophe alone

for goodness' (appearance', conscience') sake

Alternatively, particularly in British English, the apostrophe may be omitted.

2. There is divided usage over singular proper names ending in *-s*

Some follow the general rule for the singular:

Dickens's novels   Jones's children

but make an exception for *Moses* and *Jesus*, because the two words already have two *s* letters:

Moses' rebuke   Jesus' teachings

and traditionally also for Greek names of more than one syllable that end in *-s*:

Aristophanes' characters   Socrates' death

Others use only an apostrophe in all cases, therefore allowing:

Dickens' novels   Jones' children

Plural proper names follow the general rule for plurals ending in *-s* by taking only the apostrophe:

the Thompsons' new house   the Joneses' children

3. Plurals of letters are usually formed by adding apostrophe and *s* if doing so avoids confusion

A's and *B*'s   *i*'s and *y*'s

The apostrophe is sometimes added when there is no confusion, but this practice is considered unnecessary. Hence, it is better to add simply *s* in instances such as the following:

in the 1980s   the three Rs   But me no *but*s

The group genitive (cf. 4.10) is attached at the end of a modifying *of*-phrase:

the head of the police's absence (cf. the head's absence)

the Queen of England's wealth
the Tower of London's opening hours

This end-attachment similarly occurs in informal style after other modifiers:

the woman in the corner's dress
the man on their left's face

The genitive is also attached at the end of co-ordinated nouns that constitute a unit:

Norman and Alice's wedding
my son and daughter-in-law's trip to Australia

The genitive noun may be used without a following related noun:

That is my son's car. → That car is my son's.

It is so used to refer to a place:

Where is St. Paul's?
I'm going to the dentist's.
We'll see you at Gerry's tonight.

From this use have developed plural forms for large companies—without the apostrophe:

They're shopping at Harrods.

The apostrophe is also used to indicate a contraction. The apostrophe marks the place where one or more letters have beeen omitted:

she'll	couldn't	o'clock
we've	isn't	d'you
he's	won't	'fraid not
they'd	aren't	'cause ('because')

11.33
Hyphens in compounds

The main function of the hyphen is to link words that form a compound word. Compounds may be 'open', written as separate words (e.g. *washing machine*), 'hyphenated', linked by a hyphen (e.g. *tax-free*), or 'solid', written as one word (e.g. *handkerchief*). Also to be considered are hyphens that attach some prefixes to an existing word to form a new word (e.g. *ex-husband*). American English tends to use fewer hyphens than British English, but British practice is increasingly following American practice in this respect.

Practice varies considerably on the use of hyphens. Some general guidance follows, but for particular combinations you should consult a large dictionary.

1. **In compounds used attributively (i.e. to modify a following noun), a hyphen is inserted if it is needed to clarify which words belong together** [3]

> a long-dead pet
> a first-class performance
> a well-known artist
> twentieth-century novels
> a small-scale production.

The hyphen is not needed if the two words do not come before the noun:

> The pet is long dead.
> Your performance was first class.
> She was well known.
> The novels were written in the twentieth century.
> The production was on a small scale.

It is also not needed if the first word is an adverb ending in *-ly* and can therefore be recognized as modifying the second word: *a tastefully furnished room* (contrast *a well-furnished room*).

An adverb or adjective preceding an attributive compound is not hyphenated:

> a very well-known artist
> an early twentieth-century novel

2. **Adjective compounds on the pattern 'adjective or noun + noun + -ed suffix' are generally hyphenated even if they come after a noun, but they are also sometimes written solid**

> They were middle-aged.
> The children were long-haired.
> He is simple-minded.
> The packet was king-sized.

Compounds such as *middle-aged* are not written solid, to avoid juxtaposing the vowels.

3. **Most adjective compounds whose second word is an *-ing* or *-ed* participle are either hyphenated or more usually (especially in American English) written solid even when they come after a noun**

> easy-going/easygoing   far-fetched/farfetched
> good-looking/goodlooking fresh-baked/freshbaked
> life-saving/lifesaving   home-grown/homegrown

Some tend to be hyphenated in both British and American English, for example *fact-finding, custom-built.*

4. **Noun compounds on the pattern 'verb with an *-er* or *-ing* suffix + adverb' are hyphenated**

passer-by   summing-up

Where the first word is without these suffixes, the compounds may be hyphenated: *break-in, follow-up, follow-through, stand-in;* but many such compounds are usually solid: *breakdown, breakthrough, breakup.*

5. Compounds expressing an 'and' relation are hyphenated

    bitter-sweet   Anglo-Irish   deaf-mute
    tragic-comic   socio-economic   secretary-treasurer

6. Number compounds are hyphenated

    fifty-three   three-eighths

but

    two hundred   five thousand

Note the use of the hyphens in:

    four twenty-fifths   thirty-three fiftieths

and for attributive use in:

    a one-day-old baby
    thirty-odd students
    a 70-mile-an-hour speed limit

7. Compounds in which the first element is a single capital are hyphenated

    T-shirt   F-word
    U-turn   X-rated
    X-ray (*or* x-ray)

8. A hyphen is usual after a few prefixes

    ex-wife   ex-partner   ex-girlfriend
    half-breed   half-life   half-truth
    quasi-judicial   quasi-mystical   quasi-public
    self-appointed self-perpetuating self-restraint

However, *selfsame* is written solid and there are exceptions and variants for *half* (e.g. *halfback*).

    A hyphen is usual if the prefix precedes a capital or a digit:

    pre-1960s   anti-English   un-American

It is required to distinguish different words (cf. 9.13):

    re-form ('form again')   reform ('improve')

In British English it is sometimes used to prevent mispronunciation, e.g. *co-operation, pre-eminent,* but there is an increasing tendency to follow the American practice of writing such words solid.

9. Two or more hyphenated forms may be linked

    pro- and anti-Vietnam demonstrations

> middle- or old-aged patients
> mothers- and fathers-in-law

11.34
Hyphens in word divisions

In handwritten material it should not be necessary to divide words at ends of lines. When lines are justified in print or typing, word divisions are sometimes required. British English divides words according to etymology where the etymology is clear, and otherwise according to pronunciation; American English gives priority to pronunciation, the division into syllables. The contrast appears in the divisions for words such as *psychologist* and *knowledge*: British *psycho-logist* and *know-ledge*, American *psychol-ogist*, *knowl-edge*. However, British practice may be moving towards American practice and for most words the application of the different principles yields the same results. Some dictionaries indicate word divisions for entries of more than one syllable.

Here are some general recommendations:

1. **Divide hyphenated compounds at the hyphen**

   self-perpetuating (*not* self-perpet-uating)

   Divide solid compounds at the join between the parts:

   micro-analysis (not microan-alysis)

2. **Prefer a division after a prefix**

   over-simplify (*not* oversim-plify)
   dis-interested (*not* disin-terested)

3. **Avoid divisions that might confuse the reader by suggesting a different word or a different pronunciation**

   manu-script (*not* man-uscript)

   Leave undivided the words that might otherwise cause problems to the reader:

   flower   women   offer

4. **In general, divide between two or more consonants**

   regret-ting   elec-tron
   profes-sor   terres-trial
   mas-sacre   pros-perity

   But do not divide between two consonants that form one sound. The correct division is shown here:

wea-ther   ranch-ers   sul-phur
crack-ers research-able   rough-est

5. Divide before the ending -*ing*

writ-ing   offer-ing   cross-ing
show-ing   rock-ing   fish-ing

But when the final consonant is doubled before -*ing*, divide between the two consonants:

permit-ting   plan-ning   put-ting
plug-ging   slip-ping   recur-ring

If the word ends in an -*le* syllable before the -*ing* suffix is added, divide before *l* or another consonant plus *l*:

wrig-gling   puz-zling   chuck-ling
ram-bling   fon-dling   trick-ling

6. Do not divide these endings when they constitute one syllable

-ceous   -cious   -sion
-cial   -geous   -tial
-cion   -gion   -tion
-cian   -gious   -tious

Chapter 12
Spelling

Summary

Chapter 12 Summary

- Correct spelling is viewed nowadays as an indicator of a good education. It has not always been assumed that each word has—or should have—a unique spelling. There is some variation in spelling even today.

- English spelling is a mixture of systems: principally an original system going back to Old English, new conventions introduced by French scribes after the Norman Conquest, and spellings derived from Greek and Latin during the Renaissance period.

- The connection between spelling and pronunciation has been weakened because changes in pronunciation since the seventeenth century have generally not been reflected in changes in spelling.

- Some words have been respelled to accord with their Latin etymologies and contain letters that were never pronounced. On the other hand, some spellings have influenced pronunciation.

- The spelling system often gives precedence to spelling–meaning relationships over spelling–sound correspondences.

- English spelling has been credited with reducing the amount of homonymy, thereby easing comprehension and reducing the chances of ambiguity.

- Attempts to reform English spelling have not met with success.

- Different types of cues are required by readers and spellers.

- Spelling equivalents are given for each phoneme: consonants, short vowels, long vowels, and diphthongs.

- Some general spelling rules are stated.

A Historical Introduction

12.1
Standard spelling

Spelling is commonly considered a reliable indicator of a writer's education. It is assumed that somebody who is good at spelling will tend to be good at using the language in general. Not surprisingly, to spell accurately—particularly unusual words—we need to read widely and perhaps also to engage in varied kinds of writing. However, a weak speller is not necessarily illiterate in other respects. Occasional errors in spelling are common among even the highly educated, and good writers may be poor spellers. Some people at the top of their profession rely on their secretaries to ensure that their spelling—perhaps also their punctuation—is correct, though their writing may otherwise be efficient.

Correct spelling is highly valued in our society. Poor spelling may arouse ridicule and reduce the chances of obtaining employment and promotion, at least in jobs that require some writing. When parents and employers criticize the standards of English in school-leavers, spelling mistakes tend to head the list of faults.

It has not always been assumed that each word has—or should have—a unique spelling. To take a celebrated example, Shakespeare is often cited for spelling his own name in various ways. Our present spelling conventions reach back, in the main, to the work of printers. By about 1650 some printers had their own house styles for spellings, and by 1700 a stable spelling system existed for print, though handwriting continued to exhibit variant spellings. Spelling books and dictionaries promoted the notion of correct spellings in personal use. Samuel Johnson's dictionary of 1755, which followed the norms of the printers, was accepted as the authority for private use in Britain by the end of the eighteenth century. In the USA, Noah Webster's spelling book of 1783 and his dictionary of 1828 influenced the development of distinctive American spellings.

Nowadays we expect greater uniformity in spelling than in any other aspect of the English language. Yet the spelling of standard English is by no means invariant even today. Open a large contemporary dictionary at random and you are likely to find in the spread of two pages one or more sets of variant spellings. There are of course the well-known differences between British and American English, but both national varieties recognize doublets such as *adviser/advisor*, *judgment/judgement*, *discussable/discussible*, *encylopedia/encyclopaedia*, *yoghurt/yogurt*. British dictionaries cite variants for British English such as *realise/realize*, *aether/ether*, *jail/gaol*, *fetus/foetus*. American dictionaries cite variants for American English such as *ameba/amoeba*, *ax/axe*, *distill/distil*, *OK/okay*. Other national varieties (principally Canadian, Australian, and New Zealand English) have adopted spelling variants from the two major standards of English.[1]

12.2
The sources of spelling conventions

The Germanic tribes that colonized Britain from the middle of the fifth century brought with them a set of angular letters called runes; these were mainly inscribed on wood, stone, or metal for magical purposes. The Roman alphabet found in Anglo-Saxon manuscripts was introduced by Christian missionaries from Ireland; it was augmented by several characters that catered for sounds peculiar to Old English.[2] But the unique equivalences of sounds and letters were disrupted as additional sound–spelling correspondences were superimposed on the original spelling system and as the pronunciation of English sounds changed.

After the Norman Conquest, new spelling conventions were introduced by the French scribes from the Continental tradition, usually first in words borrowed from French and then spreading (not always consistently) to native words. These include *qu* in *queen* for earlier *cw*, *wh* for earlier *hw*, as in present day *what*; *v* for the sound in present day *live*, previously spelled *f*, which served (as it does nowadays) for the /v/ in *of* as well as the /f/ in *life*; *ch* for the sound in *child*, usually spelled by Anglo-Saxon scribes as *c*; *z* for the initial sound in the name of the letter, a sound that previously was generally represented by *s*, which is still the common spelling today, as in *dogs* /z/; *sh* for the initial sound in *ship*, for earlier *sc*; *c* for the initial /s/ in *city* in addition to the continuing use of *s* for the same sound, giving us today *mice* alongside of *mouse*; *gh* to spell a velar or palatal fricative, sounds like the final consonant of Scots *loch*, but the spelling is retained in words where the sound was changed or lost, for example *laugh* and *though*; *gu* for the combination of sounds /gw/ in *sanguine*; *ou* for the sound /u:/ that was used earlier in *house*.

During the Renaissance period (1500–1650 approximately) numerous words were borrowed from other languages, particularly from Greek (which was then an essential component of the scholarly curriculum), Latin, and French. The influx of loanwords increased the use of non-native spellings, some of which had existed in English in earlier periods. Certain spelling conventions entered the English writing system from Greek via Latin transliterations of Greek letters. The initial *ch* in *Christ* and *chaos* is the Latin rendering of the Greek letter χ (*chi*); the Greek letter resembled English *X* and appears in the abbreviation *Xmas* for *Christmas*. The Latin use of *ph* for the Greek letter ϕ (*phi*) is found in words deriving from Greek such as *philosophy* and *phenomenon*. *Ps* is the Latin spelling of the Greek letter ψ (*psi*) and appears in words of ultimately Greek origin such as *psalm* and *psychology*. Other English spellings that betray the Greek origin of the words include *pn* in *pneumonia*, *mn* in *mnemonic*, *pt* in *pterodactyl*, *rh* in *rhetoric*, *rrh* in *catarrh*, *ae* in *aegis*, and *oe* in *phoenix*.

Greek and Latin elements continue to be used to form English words, heightening the prominence of alternative spelling conventions. Most of the later formations are restricted to technical vocabularies, but many are used in ordinary language; for example: *chemotherapy*, *phase out*, *psychiatrist*. A feature article on the centenary of the British Pteriodological Society, devoted to the collection and study of ferns, playfully alludes to the classical spelling in its heading 'Pterrible names, fiendishly complicated sexual lives' and in the comment 'Pteriodological is a pterrible mouthful' (*The Independent*, 3 August 1991, p. 39). A 1990 volume of words and meanings that have recently entered the language in non-technical contexts lists a number of words containing elements with the *ph* spelling that are already used in the language; they include *glasphalt, hydrophonic, photo-ageing, radiophobia, workaphile*. In this way the dead classical languages live on in English and in many other languages.

Loanwords from languages other than French, Greek, and Latin have contributed a few spelling conventions to English. For example, the initial *sch*, instead of the usual *sh*, is found in borrowings from German and Yiddish, as in *schnitzel* and *schlock*. From Italian come the use of *c* in *cello* and *concerto* and of *ae* in *maestro*; from Spanish, the initial *ll* in *llama* and *llano*; from Persian, the initial *kh* in *khaki*.

12.3 Changes in pronunciation

It took over two centuries (roughly 1450–1700) for English to acquire a stable spelling system. During that period, and subsequently, major changes occurred in the pronunciation of English that disturbed the links between the conventional spellings and the sounds they were intended to represent. Starting in the fifteenth century and ending about 1600, a series of changes—traditionally known as the Great Vowel Shift—affected the long vowels. In Middle English the vowel sounds had Continental values, and the same letter was used to represent a short vowel and its corresponding long vowel; for example, the letter *i* was used for both the short vowel sound /ɪ/ in present-day *bit* and the long vowel sound /iː/ in *beet*. After the Great Vowel Shift the phonetic connection was disrupted: the *i* in *bite* is a diphthong /ʌɪ/, not related in a straightforward way to the *i* in *bit*. Similarly, the same letters are used without a simple short/long phonetic relationship in *mat/mate, met/mete, not/note*, though we have retained the final -*e* that marked the previous vowel as a long vowel.

One type of change that occurred during the seventeenth and eighteenth centuries was the loss of a sound in a cluster, resulting in a 'silent' letter in the spelling. The initial sounds in /kn/ and /gn/ were lost, so that *k* and *g* are not pronounced in words such as *knee, kneel, knife, knight, knit, knob, knock, know*; *gnat, gnaw, gnome*. Similarly, the *w* in *wr* is no longer pronounced in words such as *wrap, wrestle, wrist, write, wrong*. The second sounds in the clusters /mb/ and /mn/ were lost in words such as *bomb, climb, comb, dumb, tomb, womb*; *autumn, column, condemn, hymn, solemn*. By analogy, the combination *mb* was confusedly used in place of simple *b* where there was no etymological justification; e.g. *crumb, limb, numb, thumb*. The sound of /l/ was lost in the modals *should* and *would*; the spelling was introduced in late Middle English for the modal *could* (from *coude*) by analogy with the two modals and without etymological justification, as we can see by comparing these three past tense forms with their present tense forms: *can/could, shall/should, will/would.*

One significant change that affected some areas of the English-speaking world in the eighteenth century was the loss of the sound /r/ before a consonant or in final position, as in *beard* and *beer.* The loss or retention of /r/ in these environments is a major difference between regional varieties of the language, and within a regional variety both possibilities may be in use, one being considered superior. Accents that drop /r/ are called non-rhotic; those that retain /r/ are rhotic. Broadly speaking, non-rhotic accents are common in England and Wales and in most of the Commonwealth countries where English is the native language, whereas rhotic accents are common in the United States, Scotland, and Ireland.

The lost /r/ in non-rhotic accents reappears in certain environments when it is followed by a word beginning with a vowel, as in *far away, for us, car engine.* It also reappears within related words where *r* is followed by a vowel, a useful spelling reminder to those with non-rhotic accents: *water, watering; refer, reference; vigour, vigorous; peculiar, peculiarity.* By analogy, an 'intrusive /r/' appears in non-rhotic accents in the same environments even though it is not etymologically justified; for example, in *law/r/ and order, America/r/ and Europe.*

Another significant loss—the vowel in the regular verb inflection *-ed*— began to occur in late Middle English, but is not reflected in present-day spelling. The syllable /ɪd/ is pronounced when the inflection follows /d/ or /t/ as in *padded* and *trotted,* but otherwise the vowel is dropped. The inflection is pronounced /d/ after voiced sounds other than /d/, e.g. *condemned* and *stayed,* and /t/ after voiceless sounds other than /t/, e.g. *passed* and *hoped.* We therefore have three pronunciations for the *-ed* spelling: /ɪd/, /d/ and /t/. Although the *-es* spelling for noun and verb inflections generally corresponds to the syllabic pronunciation /ɪz/, as in *changes* (except where the *-e-* results from a change of *-y* to *-ie-* as in *cries*), the *-s* spelling varies between /z/ after voiced sounds (e.g. *dogs, lies*), and /s/ after voiceless sounds (e.g. *cats, puffs*).

Some sound changes resulted in the merging of two previously different sounds. The different spellings reflect their history before the merger, giving us modern homophones such as *meet/meat, see/sea.* Similar mergers are reflected in the two sets of homophones *pane/pain, wave/waive* and *toe/tow, sole/soul.* Some words did not participate in the general mergers: the spelling *ea* is used for the merged sound /iː/ in *meat, please, tea, teach,* but the merger did not affect other words with the *ea* spelling: those pronounced /eɪ/, such as *break, great, steak,* now homophones of *brake, grate, stake,* or those pronounced /ɛ/, such as *bread, dead, head, sweat,* resulting in the homophones *bread/bred.* The sound changes spread gradually to individual words, and some regional accents or social variants within regions preserve older pronunciations. Alexander Pope rhymed *tea* with *obey* in this couplet from *The Rape of the Lock,* written in the early eighteenth century:

> Here thou, great Anna! whom three realms obey,
> Dost sometimes counsel take—and sometimes tea.

The pronunciation of *tea* /eɪ/ exhibited here is still used by some speakers in Ireland and England.

12.4
Analogical spellings and spelling pronunciations

In the Renaissance period, certain words were respelled to accord with their Latin etymologies: *b* was introduced in *debt, doubt, redoubt, subtle; c* in *indict; p* in *receipt*. These inserted letters have never been represented in pronunciations of those words.

On the other hand, some added letters led eventually to spelling pronunciations of the words, pronunciations based on analogies with regular spelling–pronunciation correspondences. In the same period, *h* was added after *t* in a number of nouns, and the new spelling has resulted in a change of sound; for example: *apothecary, authentic, author, catholic, theatre* (spelled *theater* in American English), *throne*. A similar spelling change for *Thames* and *Thomas* (compare *Tom*) has not affected the initial sound /t/, but the *th* in *Anthony*, pronounced /t/ in British English (compare *Tony*), is pronounced /θ/ in American English, as in other proper nouns, for example *Dorothy*.

Many spelling pronunciations coexist today with more traditional pronunciations: *arctic* with the first *c* pronounced as /k/, traditionally not pronounced; *often* with /t/, traditionally without; *Sunday* and other words ending in *-day* with the final vowel pronounced as in the word *day*, traditionally as in *sandy*. Spelling pronunciations bring the sounds of words closer to their spellings. They balance the opposite tendency, where sound changes distance sounds of words from their spellings.

Spelling and Pronunciation Today

12.5
Spelling for meaning

In 12.2 and 12.3 two major reasons have been given why our spellings of words do not have a consistent one-to-one correspondence with the sounds we make in pronouncing the words: (1) our spellings reflect a mixture of spelling conventions, so that the same sound may be represented by various alphabetic letters or combinations of letters, and conversely a particular letter or combination of letters may reflect more than one pronunciation; (2) for the most part, our spellings do not take account of the changes in pronunciation that have affected English since the fifteenth century.

In this section we will examine another major reason for the lack of spelling–sound correspondences: our spelling system often gives precedence to spelling–meaning relationships over spelling–sound correspondences.

In general, the spelling preserves the stability of the word even though in everyday speech the word may be pronounced in more than one way by the same speaker in different contexts. For example, some function words (words that play an important function in the grammar) are regularly pronounced differently when unstressed (the usual pronunciation) than when stressed. We use the stressed form when we cite the word in isolation or for emphasis or contrast. Here are several examples of stressed forms with one or more unstressed variants (or weak forms):

	stressed	*unstressed*
a	/eɪ/	/ə/
and	/and/	/ənd/, /ən/
can	/kan/	/kən/
of	/ɒv/	/əv/, /ə/
the	/ði:/	/ðə/
you	/ju:/	/jʊ/, /jə/

Only in some instances are spelling contractions available in the writing system to represent, in whole or part, the reductions in pronunciation, as in *n't* (*not*) or *'s* (*is* or *has*).

In addition, in the flow of everyday speech, variants often occur with other types of words, depending on the speed and informality of the speech. As a consequence individual sounds or syllables may be omitted; for example, the final consonant in the first word of *good morning* and *left school*, a vowel in the middle of *dangerous* and *medicine*, and the middle syllable of *library* and *average*. In some instances, assimilation may take place; for example, from alveolar to bilabial in *Saint* /sm/ *Paul* (where the final cluster /nt/ is otherwise often reduced to /n/ in casual speech) and from alveolar to palato-alveolar in *his* /hɪʒ/ *shop*. (See 10.3 for nasal and voiced consonants.)

The spelling of words often signals that they are related in meaning even when their pronunciation obscures the relationship. The spellings of the -*ed* and -*s* inflections for regular verbs and the -*s* inflection for regular nouns are constant despite the differences in pronunciation, which are induced by preceding sounds (cf.12.3). Other examples appear in related sets of words such as:

medicine, medicinal; medic, medical, medicate, medication
sign, signer; signal, signatory, signature
nation; national, nationality, nationalize
photograph, photographic; photographer, photography

Finally, the same spelling may represent different pronunciations across the English-speaking world. One major difference is that between rhotic and non-rhotic accents (cf. 12.3). Another example is the different pronunciations in Britain and the United States of the words represented by *laboratory*: the British stress on the second syllable contrasts with the American stress on the first syllable, the distinction in stress resulting in different pronunciations of the vowels. Even within the same country there are regional and social dialects. So we find the vowel in *book* as /ʊ/ or /uː/ and in *bath* as /ɑː/ or /a/, the second syllable of *bullet* as /ɪt/ or /ət/, and retention or dropping of the initial consonant in *happy*, as well as rhotic and non-rhotic accents.

On the whole, national differences in spelling are minor and do not affect mutual intelligibility. Non-standard dialects do not have institutionalized spellings, though there have been attempts in dialect poetry and in fictional dramatic dialogue to indicate non-standard pronunciations; for example: the dropping of *h* (*'e*), the pronunciation /n/ for the final consonant in the ending *-ing* (*goin'*), the substitution of /f/ for /θ/ (*fink*). The common spelling system has the undoubted advantage of conveying meaning directly, ignoring the manifold variability in pronunciation.

12.6
Homonyms, homophones, homographs

English spelling has been credited with reducing the amount of homonymy that occurs in speech, thereby easing comprehension in the written language and reducing the chances of ambiguity.

Homonyms are sets of two or more words that are pronounced or spelled identically but have different meanings (cf. 8.16). For example, *seal* may refer to a type of animal or to a device for closing something tightly; *fair* may refer to a place of entertainment or to displaying the quality of impartiality or to being light in colour. In these two instances there is identity in both pronunciation and spelling.

Very often, however, the spellings show the differences even though the pronunciations are the same. Here are a few examples of such homophones: *aid/aide, berry/bury, buy/by, cereal/serial, chews/choose, frees/freeze/frieze, hear/here, know/no, meat/meet, write/right/rite/wright, scent/sent/cent, son/sun*. Spellings may also differentiate homophonous word combinations, such as *their* from *they're* or *syntax* from the compound *sin tax*. Homophones are not necessarily constant across all English accents: words that sound the same in one regional or social accent may sound different in others. Some speakers of English, for example, pronounce these words identically while others do not: *orphan/often, where/wear, father/farther, ate/eight, ladder/latter, marry/merry/ Mary, hostel/hostile*. Even for the same speaker, pairs that are homophones in normal speech may be distinguished quite easily when it is necessary to do so to avoid ambiguity; for example, *affect/effect, accept/except*.

English also has homographs (also called heteronyms), words pronounced differently but spelled the same; for example: *does* /dʌz/, the -*s* form of the verb *do*, or /dəʊz/, the plural of the noun *doe*; *lead* /liːd/, the verb meaning 'guide', or /lɛd/, the name of a metal. Among the homographs are a number of words where the stress varies in speech according to whether the word is functioning either as a verb or as a noun or adjective (cf. 10.11); for example: *conduct, convict, permit, rebel, absent, frequent, perfect*. Similarly, some words related in meaning are spelled identically even though they differ in the pronunciation of a vowel (the verb *live* and the adjective *live* as in *live wire*) or a consonant (the verb *use* and the noun *use*). For this type of homograph, the identical spelling preserves the meaning relationship between the two words while the pronunciations signal their syntactic difference.

On the whole, English has more homonyms in speech than in writing. Admittedly, homonyms are usually distinguished in context and are therefore not a major obstacle for communication, but the spelling distinctions may be helpful for the reader. They are another way in which spellings take into account meanings rather than just sounds.

12.7
Spelling reform

Calls for changes in English spelling first appeared in the middle of the sixteenth century. Some of the proposals of the early reformers have left permanent effects on English spelling. Spelling reform movements continue to advocate new spelling systems: radical reforms require the replacement of the present alphabet by a new set of symbols that have a regular one-to-one correspondence with sounds; a more moderate approach supplements the existing alphabet with new symbols; the most realistic goal is to retain the present alphabet but use the letters more regularly.

The majority of English words conform to regular rules of sound–spelling correspondences, but there are enough exceptions to create the impression that English spelling is chaotic. Irregularities affect many of the words that are most frequently used: consider the unpredictability of the spellings of *are, one, two, have, were, some, come, says, does* (from the verb *do*). Spelling reform would save a great deal of the time that children now spend in learning to read and to spell and reduce the emotional strain that many of them endure, and it would similarly help adult illiterates in the English-speaking world. A more regular spelling system would also remove a formidable obstacle to the learning of English by foreigners.

Movements for the reform of English spelling currently exist in the USA and Britain but they have failed to attract sufficient political support. Opposition to reform comes from those who are unwilling to learn a new spelling system and also from those who see no pressing need for the change. It has also been argued that the change would inhibit access to printed sources in the old spelling. But for many who are proficient in the present spelling system it is simply that unfamiliar spellings look wrong. If a reformed system were introduced, there would undoubtedly be an awkward and costly transitional period when old and new spelling systems existed side by side. A major problem for language reform in general is that English-speaking countries do not have language academies or other authoritative language regulatory agencies; such bodies would be needed to decide among competing reformed spelling systems. It is essential that major English-speaking countries agree on reforms; otherwise, they would no longer have a common spelling system (albeit with minor variations). It is difficult to imagine the procedures that could be instituted for bringing about a consensus on spelling reforms.

The essential linguistic problem involved in reaching a consensus is the need to account for variation in sound systems across and within countries. Contrasts in pronunciation within one system may not exist in another. For example, rhotic accents distinguish *sauce* and *source*, but in non-rhotic accents the two words may sound the same (cf. 12.11); similarly, most American speakers pronounce *palm* and *pot* with the same vowel, but most British speakers pronounce the two words with different vowels.

Some simplifications of British spellings have occurred in recent times under the influence of American spellings. The ligatures *æ* and *œ* have disappeared; so, for example, *encyclopædia* has given way to *encyclopaedia*, which is now giving way to *encyclopedia* (without the *ae* digraph), and *-ize*, *-ization* is frequently replacing the traditional British *-ise*, *-isation*. Eventually regularized spellings of brand names, advertising copy, and shop notices may accustom people to non-standard variations. On the other hand, the widespread use of spelling checkers in computer software may inhibit spelling variants and may be felt to reduce the need for spelling reform. It may eventually lead to a more unified international spelling of English through American influence, since most spelling checkers are American.

There is much to be said for a return to the earlier tolerance of spelling variation in non-printed writing, but this requires a change in public attitudes to spelling that would be difficult to achieve. More attainable would be the gradual regularization of anomalous spellings. The notorious *ough* cluster could be respelled according to its pronunciation; perhaps *tho* (*although*), *thru* or *thrue* (*through*), *enuf* (*enough*), *cof* (*cough*), *drowt* (*drought*), *bawt* (*bought*). Simpler and more regular variants, where they exist in English-speaking countries, could be encouraged: *plow* (*plough*), *analog* (*analogue*), *jail* (*gaol*), *traveled* (*travelled*), *draft* (*draught*), *omelet* (*omelette*). In the absence of authoritative agencies that could command respect throughout the English-speaking world, spelling reform will be successful only through a long and gradual process initiated by publishers.

12.8 Reading and spelling

The proficient reader draws on cues from the general subject matter and the immediate context as well as visual recollections of whole words. Such a reader does not need to decode the parts of each word into their sound equivalents, and except for unfamiliar words absorbs the written text in chunks of perhaps a half-line or more. The good reader derives meaning directly from the text, bypassing the conversion of the written forms into sound. That is what we mean by silent reading.

Good spellers, on the other hand, need to know the regular equivalents in writing for each sound or combinations of sounds and to remember the many exceptions. There are often a number of possible letters or combinations of letters for a particular sound; the good speller must remember exactly the choice required for a particular word. For example, the vowel sound of *shoe* could potentially be rendered by such spellings as *shew* (cf. *shrew*), *shue* (cf. *blue*), *shoo* (cf. *zoo*), and *shu* (cf. *flu*). The last three spellings, however, could have only the one sound correspondence found in *shoe*, so that a competent reader would be able to read the word correctly in those three spellings.

In what follows, we will be looking at spelling from the point of the writer; that is to say, we will start from the sounds and find the major equivalencies in spelling.[3]

Sound–Spelling Correspondences

12.9 Consonants

The description in this section and 12.10 f. follows the convention that phonemes (cf. 10.9) are enclosed in slashes and letters in diamond brackets. In some instances the spelling equivalent consists of more than one letter, usually a digraph such as *sh* or *th*.

1. /p/ is normally spelled ⟨p⟩ and to a lesser extent ⟨pp⟩: *pip, appeal.* An exceptional spelling is *hiccough*, more usually spelled regularly *hiccup*. In addition ⟨ph⟩ is often pronounced /p/ before ⟨th⟩ in a few words, e.g. *diphtheria, diphthong.*

2. /b/ is normally spelled ⟨b⟩ and to a lesser extent ⟨bb⟩: *book, ribbon.*

3. /t/ is normally spelled ⟨t⟩ and to a lesser extent ⟨tt⟩: *pet, written.* The past and participle inflection ⟨ed⟩ is pronounced /t/ when the preceding phoneme is voiceless if it is not /t/, e.g. *hoped, popped.* Examples of unusual spellings: *two, receipt, debt, doubt, indict, pterodactyl, yacht.* There is also the exceptional ⟨th⟩ in *posthumous* and *thyme* and in certain names, e.g. *Thames, Thomas, Anthony.*

4. /d/ is normally spelled ⟨d⟩ and to a lesser extent ⟨dd⟩. The past and participle inflection ⟨ed⟩ is pronounced /d/ when the preceding phoneme is voiced if it is not /d/, e.g. *sowed*, and /ɪd/ when the preceding phoneme is /d/ or /t/, e.g. *flooded, potted*.

5. /k/ is most frequently spelled ⟨k⟩ before front vowels (cf. 10.6) and ⟨c⟩ otherwise: *king, keep, call, cute*. Before the letters ⟨i⟩ and ⟨e⟩, the spelling ⟨k⟩ occurs, but not ⟨c⟩. Less frequent spellings:

⟨ck⟩	pick
⟨qu⟩ /kw/	quiet
⟨qu⟩	conquer
⟨que⟩	cheque
⟨ch⟩	chaos
⟨x⟩ /ks/	six
⟨cc⟩	account

6. /g/ is normally spelled ⟨g⟩ or ⟨gg⟩: *go, rigged*. Less frequent spellings:

⟨gu⟩	guest
⟨gh⟩	ghost
⟨x⟩ /gz/	examine

7. /tʃ/ is normally spelled ⟨ch⟩, e.g. *church*, and to a lesser extent ⟨tch⟩, e.g. *batch*. Another common spelling is ⟨t⟩ before *i* or *u*, e.g.: *question, statue, furniture, ritual, century*. There is also the exceptional ⟨c⟩ in the Italian loanwords *cello* and *concerto*.

8. /dʒ/ is most frequently spelled ⟨j⟩, ⟨g⟩, or ⟨ge⟩: *job, gin, rage, garage*. Less frequent equivalents are ⟨dge⟩, ⟨dg⟩ or ⟨dj⟩: *judge, dodgy, adjust*. Exceptional spellings: ⟨di⟩ and ⟨gg⟩ in *soldier, suggest, exaggerate*.

9. /f/ is normally spelled ⟨f⟩ and to a lesser extent ⟨ff⟩: *fit, stiff*. In words with elements of Greek origin, the usual spelling is the digraph ⟨ph⟩: *philosophy, telegraph*. The exceptional ⟨gh⟩ spelling appears in a few very common words, e.g. *tough, laugh*.

10. /v/ is normally spelled ⟨v⟩: *vain*. The ⟨ve⟩ spelling appears in a few very common words: *active, have, live* (verb), *give; love, dove, glove, shove*. Exceptional is the ⟨f⟩ spelling in *of*.

11. /θ/ (voiceless) and /ð/ (voiced) are both spelled ⟨th⟩: *think, that*.

12. /s/ is most frequently spelled ⟨s⟩ and ⟨ss⟩, and to a lesser extent ⟨c⟩: *rats, pass, city*. ⟨c⟩ and the minority spelling ⟨sc⟩ in this correspondence occur virtually only before the vowel letters ⟨i⟩, ⟨y⟩, and ⟨e⟩: *cite, cycle, cent; science, scythe, obscene*. ⟨x⟩ may represent the cluster /ks/, as in *box*.

13. /z/ is most frequently spelled ⟨s⟩ and to a lesser extent ⟨z⟩, ⟨zz⟩, and ⟨ss⟩: *has, zoo, buzz, possess*. In this use, initial ⟨s⟩ does not occur. On the other hand, final ⟨s⟩ is common in noun and verb inflections after voiced phonemes: *dogs, prays, discusses*. Initial ⟨x⟩ may be pronounced /z/, as in *xenophobia, xerox, xylophone*. In the initial combination ⟨ex⟩, ⟨x⟩ may represent the cluster /gz/, as in *exist*.

14. /ʃ/ is most frequently spelled by ⟨t⟩, ⟨s⟩, ⟨ss⟩, or ⟨c⟩ when these are

followed by ⟨i⟩ at the juncture of a suffix from Latin: *attention, expulsion, discussion, officious*. Another common spelling is the digraph ⟨sh⟩, which is generally associated with this phoneme: *shape*. ⟨ch⟩ is a minority spelling, found in words of French origin: *chef*.

15. /ʒ/ is most frequently spelled ⟨s⟩ and to a lesser extent (and usually before ⟨e⟩) ⟨g⟩: *usual, massage*.

16. /h/ is normally spelled ⟨h⟩. A minority spelling ⟨wh⟩ is found in a few words, several of them occurring very frequently, e.g. *who, whose, whole*.

17. /m/ is normally spelled ⟨m⟩ or ⟨mm⟩: *mirror, commit*. Exceptional spellings: ⟨mb⟩, ⟨mn⟩, and ⟨gm⟩: *dumb, condemn*, and *phlegm*. When a suffix is added, the ⟨n⟩ in ⟨mn⟩ and the ⟨g⟩ in ⟨gm⟩ are no longer silent: *condemnation, phlegmatic*.

18. /n/ is normally spelled ⟨n⟩ or ⟨nn⟩: *note, runner*. Exceptional spellings: ⟨kn⟩, ⟨gn⟩, and ⟨pn⟩: *knife, sign, pneumatic*. There is also the odd spelling ⟨mn⟩ in *mnemonic* and words derived from it. When a suffix is added, the ⟨g⟩ in ⟨gn⟩ is no longer silent: *resignation*.

19. /ŋ/ is spelled ⟨n⟩ if the sounds /k/ or /g/ follow. Otherwise, it is spelled ⟨ng⟩, the usual spelling: *sing. drink, single* (though these may also be pronounced with /n/ instead of /ŋ/.

20. /l/ is normally spelled ⟨l⟩ or ⟨ll⟩: *list, called*.

21. /r/ is normally spelled ⟨r⟩ or ⟨rr⟩: *real, carry*. Exceptional spellings: ⟨wr⟩ and ⟨rh⟩ in *write, rheumatism*.

22. /w/ is normally spelled ⟨w⟩: *water*. Less frequent spellings are ⟨u⟩, particularly in the combinations ⟨qu⟩ and ⟨gu⟩, and ⟨wh⟩: *quite, language, suite, wheel*. The ⟨wh⟩ occurs initially in a number of highly frequent words; for example: *what, when, whether, which, why*. Some people, however, pronounce these words with initial /hw/. The sound /w/ occurs in some words spelled with ⟨oi⟩ that have been borrowed in recent times from French: *bourgeois, repertoire*. There is also the exceptional spelling *one*.

23. /j/ is spelled ⟨y⟩: *year, yes, yet*.

12.10
Short vowels

Correspondences between vowels and letters are complicated by regional, social, and idiosyncratic variation.

It is traditional to distinguish between short vowels (such as /a/ in *rat*) and long vowels (such as /eɪ/ in *rate*). The correspondence in spelling may be discontinuous; for example, in *rate* ⟨a...e⟩ the ⟨e⟩ comes at the end of the syllable and marks the ⟨a⟩ as representing a long vowel.

1. /ɪ/ is most frequently spelled ⟨i⟩: *pit*. Other frequent spellings are ⟨y⟩ and ⟨e⟩: *city, blanket*. But for many speakers, the final vowel in words such as *city* may be /iː/. Less frequent spellings include:

⟨a⟩   spinach
⟨a...e⟩   manage
⟨ey⟩   alley
⟨ie⟩   calorie

Unusual spellings include:

⟨o⟩   women
⟨u⟩   busy
⟨ui⟩   biscuit
⟨ee⟩   been (a possible pronunciation when unstressed)

2. /ε/ is normally spelled ⟨e⟩: *pet*. Another frequent spelling is ⟨ea⟩: *deaf*. Less frequent are ⟨ai⟩, ⟨a⟩, and ⟨eo⟩: *said, any, leopard*. Unusual spellings include *friend, bury,* and (one British pronunciation) *ate*.

3. /a/ is virtually always spelled ⟨a⟩: *pat*. Exceptional spellings include:

⟨i⟩   meringue
⟨ai⟩   plaid
⟨au⟩   laugh (American English)

4. /ʊ/ is most frequently spelled ⟨u⟩ or ⟨oo⟩: *put, good*. The exceptional spelling ⟨ou⟩ occurs in the three modal auxiliaries *could, should, would*. Some words have the variant pronunciation /uː/, e.g. *book*, and in some accents the phoneme /ʊ/ has merged with /uː/.

5. /ʌ/ is most frequently spelled ⟨u⟩: *cut*. Less frequent are ⟨o⟩ and ⟨ou⟩: *brother, trouble*.

6. British /ɒ/ is normally spelled ⟨o⟩: *top*. The American pronunciation is usually /ɑː/. A less frequent spelling is ⟨a⟩: *want*. Unusual spellings include ⟨au⟩, ⟨ou⟩, and ⟨ow⟩: *sausage, cough, knowledge*.

7. /ə/, called schwa, is the reduced vowel commonly used in unstressed syllables. It is spelled by various vowel letters or combinations of letters. Some examples are listed below, where the relevant letters are italicized. In non-rhotic accents, a following ⟨r⟩ in the same syllable is to be included in the representation of schwa.

c*o*ver   *a*broad
f*o*rget   tod*a*y
li*a*r   fam*ou*s
s*u*rprise   elem*e*nt
col*ou*r   posit*io*n
fut*ure*   deliri*u*m
ac*re*   defic*i*t

12.11
Long vowels and diphthongs

In non-rhotic accents, an /r/ that at one time was pronounced after a vowel has been lost before a consonant or in final position, whereas in rhotic accents the original /r/ has been retained (cf. 10.5). The spelling with ⟨r⟩ complicates the task of speakers of non-rhotic accents, who may pronounce *roar* and *raw* identically, although the /r/ reappears in *roaring* where it is no longer in final position. In (9)–(14) below, the phonemes are combined with /r/ for rhotic accents.

1. /ʌɪ/ is most frequently spelled ⟨i...e⟩, ⟨y⟩, or ⟨y...e⟩: *bite, fly, type.* Generally ⟨i⟩ occurs initially or medially, whereas ⟨y⟩ occurs finally. A less frequent spelling is ⟨igh⟩: *high, fight.*

2. /i:/ has several frequent spellings:

⟨e⟩	legal
⟨e...e⟩	gene
⟨ee⟩	beef
⟨ea⟩	teach

Less frequent spellings include:

⟨ae⟩	aegis
⟨i⟩	visa
⟨i...e⟩	magazine
⟨ie⟩	field
⟨oe⟩	foetus

The digraph spellings ⟨ae⟩ and ⟨oe⟩ for /i:/ are often replaced by ⟨e⟩, especially in American English. For many speakers the final ⟨y⟩ in words such as *city* and *cosy* is pronounced /i:/.

3. /eɪ/ is most frequently spelled ⟨a...e⟩ or ⟨a⟩: *case, danger.* Other frequent spellings are ⟨ay⟩ and ⟨ai⟩: *may, plain.* Less frequent spellings include several for late French loanwords:

⟨é⟩	café
⟨e...e⟩	suede
⟨er⟩	foyer
⟨et⟩	beret
⟨ée⟩	matinée

Other infrequent spellings include:

⟨ea⟩	great
⟨ei⟩	reign
⟨ey⟩	obey
⟨eigh⟩	eight

4. /aʊ/ is normally spelled ⟨ou⟩ or ⟨ow⟩: *loud, crowd.* Infrequent spellings are:

⟨ou...e⟩   house
⟨ough⟩   drought

5. British /əʊ/ and American /oː/ are normally spelled ⟨o⟩, ⟨o...e⟩, or ⟨oe⟩: *radio, note, toe*. Less frequent spellings are ⟨ow⟩ and ⟨oa⟩: *follow, coat*. Infrequent spellings include some late French loanwords:

⟨ot⟩   depot
⟨eau⟩   bureau
⟨au⟩   chauffeur

6. /uː/ is most frequently spelled:

⟨u⟩, ⟨u...e⟩, or ⟨ue⟩   lucid, rude, clue
⟨oo⟩, ⟨oo...e⟩   food, choose
⟨o⟩, ⟨o...e⟩   do, prove

Less frequent spellings are:

⟨ew⟩   crew
⟨ou⟩   youth
⟨ui⟩   fruit
⟨eu⟩   rheumatic

See also /juː/ below.

7. /ɔɪ/ is spelled either ⟨oi⟩ or ⟨oy⟩: *poison, employ*.

8. The combination /juː/ is most frequently spelled ⟨u⟩, ⟨u...e⟩, ⟨ue⟩, or ⟨ew⟩: *music, cube, due, hew*. The /j/ is dropped, especially in American English, in many words with the combination /juː/, resulting in the pronunciation /nuː/ for *new* rather than /njuː/.

9. /ɑː/ in non-rhotic accents, such as RP (Received Pronunciation in British English, cf. 10.6), is most frequently spelled ⟨a⟩ or ⟨ar⟩: *class, car*. However, the vowel in words such as *class* is generally /a/ in American English (like the vowel in *cat*). In rhotic accents, such as generally American English, ⟨ar⟩ in *car* is pronounced /ɑːr/. In American English /ɑː/ is also spelled ⟨o⟩ or ⟨a⟩: *doll, watch*. Less frequent spellings include ⟨ear⟩ in non-rhotic accents and ⟨ea⟩ in rhotic accents, e.g. *heart*; and ⟨al⟩, e.g. *half*, though in American English generally pronounced with the vowel /a/.

10. /ɔː/ in non-rhotic accents is most frequently spelled ⟨or⟩, ⟨ore⟩, ⟨ar⟩, ⟨our⟩, or ⟨a⟩: *for, core, war, four, salt*. In rhotic accents, the spellings of /ɔː/ exclude ⟨r⟩ since the ⟨r⟩ corresponds to the actual pronunciation of /r/. Less frequent spellings are ⟨au⟩ and ⟨aw⟩: *author, saw*. Infrequent spellings include:

⟨augh⟩   caught
⟨ough⟩   fought

11. non-rhotic /ɜː/ and rhotic /ɜːr/ are most frequently spelled ⟨er⟩: *revert*. Less frequent spellings are:

⟨ur⟩   nurse
⟨ir⟩   bird

⟨or⟩ work
⟨ear⟩ earth

Infrequent spellings include:

⟨our⟩ journey
⟨eur⟩ entrepreneur
⟨yr⟩ myrtle

12. non-rhotic /ɪə/ and rhotic /ɪr/ or /ɪə/ are most frequently spelled:

⟨ea(r)⟩ idea, fear
⟨er⟩ period
⟨ere⟩ here
⟨ia(r)⟩ media, peculiar
⟨ee⟩ beer

13. non-rhotic /ɛ:/ and rhotic /ɛ:r/ are most frequently spelled:

⟨ar⟩ rarity
⟨are⟩ care
⟨air⟩ hair

A less frequent spelling is ⟨ear⟩: *pear, wear.* Two very common words have idiosyncratic spellings: *there, where.*

14. non-rhotic /ʊə/ and rhotic /ʊr/ are frequently spelled ⟨oor⟩, ⟨ure⟩, or ⟨ur⟩: *poor, sure, security.* However, many RP speakers pronounce words such as *poor* and *sure* with the vowel /ɔ:/. The phoneme /j/ sometimes precedes the sequence /ʊə/, as in the words *cure, curious, endure, furious.*

12.12
Some spelling rules

Spelling rules tend to be complex with many subrules and exceptions. Nevertheless, it may be helpful to attempt some generalizations.

A. Doubling of consonant letter before suffix

If you add a suffix to a word, double the final consonant letter before the suffix under these conditions:

1. the suffix starts with a vowel letter:
   forget/forgetting, *cf.* forgetful
2. the word ends in a single consonant letter that represents a single sound:
   red/redder, *cf.* old/older, box/boxer
3. a single vowel letter comes before the final consonant letter:
   stop/stopped, *cf.* stoop/stooped
4. the stress is on the final syllable both before and after the suffix is added:
   refer/referred, *cf.* refer/reference, rapid/rapidity

There are variant spellings for many words ending in an unstressed syllable to which *-ed* or *-ing* is added. Most of the words end in *l*, such as *travel, label*. British English requires doubling (*travelled, labelling*), whereas American English follows the regular rule by preferring a single consonant (*traveled, labeled*). Other examples with similar variation: *marvelous/marvellous, traveler/traveller, worshiper/worshipper, diagramed/diagrammed, programer/programmer*. The spelling of words derived from *gas* is inconsistent: *gaseous* and *gasify* (both infringing the doubling rule) contrast with *gasser* and *gassy*. There is variation between *-s-* and *-ss-* in inflected forms of *bias, bus, focus*, and *gas*, except that *gas* has the variants *gases/gasses* but only the one form for *gassed* and *gassing*. There are variants of the inflected forms of *benefit* (*benefited/benefitted*), though doubling appears to be more usual in American English.

To preserve the /k/ sound, final ⟨c⟩ is usually spelled ⟨ck⟩ when a suffix is added: *panic/panicky, mimic/mimicked*.

B. Dropping of silent final *-e*

Drop the silent ⟨e⟩ at the end of words if you add a suffix beginning with a vowel letter:

have/having	deplore/deplorable
fame/famous	mediate/mediation
fertile/fertility	medicine/medicinal

Keep the ⟨e⟩ when the suffix begins with a consonant letter:

hope/hopeful	false/falsehood
base/basement	lecture/lectureship
care/careless	scarce/scarcely

If the word ends in ⟨ie⟩ and the suffix begins with ⟨i⟩, drop the ⟨e⟩ but also change the ⟨i⟩ to ⟨y⟩ to avoid ⟨ii⟩:

die/dying	tie/tying
lie/lying	vie/vying

Exceptions where you keep ⟨e⟩:

1. The letters ⟨c⟩ and ⟨g⟩ are generally pronounced /s/ and /dʒ/ respectively when they are followed by one of the vowel letters ⟨e⟩, ⟨i⟩, or ⟨y⟩: *cell, city, cycle; gem, gin, gymnasium*. To signal these pronunciations, ⟨e⟩ is generally kept when a suffix is added beginning with another vowel letter, notably ⟨a⟩ or ⟨o⟩:

noticeable	courageous
peaceable	knowledgeable

If the suffix begins with ⟨e⟩, ⟨i⟩, or ⟨y⟩, the ⟨e⟩ is dropped in accordance with the regular rule:

notice/noticed/noticing   rage/raging

2. Keep the ⟨e⟩ in *singeing* (from *singe*) and *swingeing* (from *swinge*) to distinguish them from *singing* (from *sing*) and *swinging* (from *swing*). Similarly, keep the ⟨e⟩ in *dyeing* to distinguish it from *dying* (from *die*).

3. In a number of words, there are irregular variants where ⟨e⟩ is kept. They include the set of words to which the suffix ⟨able⟩ has been added:

likable/likeable	movable/moveable
livable/liveable	ratable/rateable

The irregular retention of ⟨e⟩ may be due to the association of the suffix with the word *able* and hence the feeling that these words are compounds. The rule for dropping ⟨e⟩ before a vowel letter applies only when a suffix is added and not when two words are joined to form a compound such as *whereas*.

In a few words, the irregular variant is preferred. The most common instances are *ageing*, *matey*, and *mileage*. The word *acreage* has only this spelling with ⟨e⟩.

Exceptions where you drop ⟨e⟩ before a consonant letter:

1. Six words irregularly drop ⟨e⟩:

argue/argument	nine/ninth
awe/awful	true/truly
due/duly	whole/wholly

2. In some words ending in ⟨ge⟩, there are variants without ⟨e⟩, particularly in American English, when the suffix begins with a consonant letter:

abridgement/abridgment
acknowledgement/acknowledgment
judgement/judgment

C. Changing of final ⟨y⟩ to ⟨i⟩ before suffix

The general rule is that when a word ends in a consonant letter plus ⟨y⟩, change the ⟨y⟩ to ⟨i⟩ before adding a suffix:

happy/happiness	cry/cried
industry/industrious	story/stories
fifty/fiftieth	beauty/beautiful

Keep the ⟨y⟩ when the word ends in a vowel letter plus ⟨y⟩:

enjoy/enjoyment	play/played
annoy/annoyance	spray/sprays

Exceptions when you keep the ⟨y⟩:

1. before the suffix ⟨ing⟩:

cry/crying   apply/applying

2. before the genitive '*s*:

the story's end   the industry's complaint

3. when the suffix -*ness* is added to a few words of one syllable:

dryness   shyness   slyness

4. in *busyness* ('state of being busy') to distinguish it from *business* ('industrial or commercial operation', etc.).
Exceptions when you change ⟨y⟩ to ⟨i⟩:

daily   paid   slain
laid   said

The change from *say* to *said* also involves a vowel change: /eɪ/ to /ɛ/.

D. ⟨i⟩ before ⟨e⟩ except after ⟨c⟩

This is the spelling rule that most people remember from their schooldays. The rule in full is: When the vowel sound is /iː/, represent the sound by spelling ⟨ie⟩, but after ⟨c⟩ spell it ⟨ei⟩.

⟨ie⟩	⟨ei⟩ after ⟨c⟩
achieve	ceiling
believe	conceit
brief	deceit
diesel	deceive
field	perceive
niece	receipt
priest	receive
siege	
thief	

Exceptions with ⟨ei⟩ as the spelling of /iː/ when it does not come after ⟨c⟩: *caffeine, codeine, counterfeit, protein, seize.*
In several words with ⟨ei⟩ there are variant pronunciations, one of which is /iː/:

either   neither   inveigle

Weird, whose vowel is the diphthong /ɪə/, is another exception.
Exceptions with ⟨ie⟩ after ⟨c⟩:

1. Words in which ⟨y⟩ has changed to ⟨i⟩ keep ⟨ie⟩ even after ⟨c⟩:

agency/agencies   policy/policies   fancy/fancied

2. The word *species* is an exception. Note the spelling ⟨ie⟩ in words representing a diphthong or a sound other than /iː/:

financier   science   sufficient   conscience   efficiency

For most words that do not have the pronunciation /iː/ and where ⟨c⟩ does not precede, the usual order is ⟨ei⟩:

neighbour   reign   weigh

The most common exception is *friend*.

Notes
Chapter 1

1. There are now a sizeable number of books dealing with English throughout the world. A useful reference work is *The Oxford Companion to the English Language*, edited by Tom McArthur (Oxford: Oxford University Press, 1992). A range of statistics on the uses of English appears in *English: A World Commodity*, by Brian McCallen (London: The Economist Intelligence Unit, 1989). A summary account of differences between national standard varieties of English can be found in *International English: A Guide to Varieties of Standard English*, by Peter Trudgill and Jean Hanna (London: Edward Arnold, 2nd edn., 1985). Among other general works on English internationally are *The Story of English*, by Robert McCrum, William Cran, and Robert MacNeil (London: Faber & Faber, 2nd edn., 1992), *The Other Tongue: English Across Cultures*, edited by Braj B. Kachru (Urbana: University of Illinois Press, 2nd edn., 1992), *The New Englishes*, by John Platt, Heidi Weber, and Ho Mian Liam (London: Routledge & Kegan Paul, 1984), *English as a World Language*, edited by Richard W. Bailey and Manfred Görlach (Ann Arbor: University of Michigan Press, 1982), *The English Language Today*, edited by Sidney Greenbaum (Oxford: Pergamon, 1985). Devoted to English internationally are the quarterly magazine *English Today* (Cambridge University Press) and the scholarly journals *World Englishes* and *English World-Wide*.

2. On the history of English and other languages in the British Isles and their present status and uses, see *Language in the British Isles*, edited by Peter Trudgill (Cambridge: Cambridge University Press, 1984).

3. See *Language in the British Isles*, ch. 25, for details on the newer minority languages.

4. See *Language in the British Isles*, ch. 14.

5. On the English language in the countries mentioned in 1.3 and 1.4, see the books listed in n. 1 of this chapter. For the United States in particular, see *Language in the USA*, edited by Charles A. Ferguson and Shirley Brice Heath (Cambridge: Cambridge University Press, 1981).

6. *Pidgins and Creoles*, by Loreto Todd (London: Routledge, 2nd edn., 1992) is a succinct account that focuses on English-based pidgins and creoles.

7. Current views favour regarding Black English as a development of a creole English that was indebted in its origins to West African languages. See the discussion in *Pidgins and Creoles*, by Loreto Todd, pp. 61–5.

8. The statistics are taken from *The Economist Pocket World in Figures* (London: Hamish Hamilton, 4th (1995) edn., 1994), p. 22.

9. The international presence of English has not been welcomed everywhere. In some countries English has been viewed as having a malign influence on local languages, contaminating their purity by infiltrating large numbers of foreign words. Official resistance to English loanwords is fiercest in France, where there have been moves by the government to bar their use in the media, advertising, and official documents. Most media reaction in France has declared the restrictions unenforceable. More generally, French officialdom has been concerned with the preservation of French as an international language and the threats from English and other languages to the retention of French by the francophone countries in Africa and the Americas.

10. The International Corpus of English is a research project into standard varieties in about twenty countries, most of which have English as a second language. It is co-ordinated by Sidney Greenbaum and his colleagues at the Survey of English Usage, University College London.

11. *Webster's Dictionary of English Usage* (Springfield, Mass.: Merriam-Webster, 1989) is recommended for those who wish to know the historical background to usage controversies, the views of writers who have commented on disputed usages, and the evidence for present-day usage. A recent practical usage guide for quick reference is the *Longman Guide to English Usage*, by Sidney Greenbaum and Janet Whitcut (London: Penguin, 1996). The best of the newspaper commentators on language is William Safire, who writes a weekly column in *The New York Times*, which is reprinted in *The International Herald Tribune*. He has published several books based on his column and has included in his books the letters generated by his observations.

12. On issues concerned with the standard language, see *Authority in Language*, by James Milroy and Lesley Milroy (London: Routledge, 2nd edn., 1991). On grammars in relation to the standard language, see 'A Grammarian's Responsibility', in *Good English and the Grammarian*, by Sidney Greenbaum (London: Longman, 1988), ch. 3.

13. On variation according to use, see *Investigating English Style*, by David Crystal and Derek Davy (London: Longman, 1969).

14. A lively and enlightening discussion of jargons appears in *Jargon: Its Uses and Abuses*, by Walter Nash (Oxford: Blackwell, 1993).

15. On correct English and good English, see *Bad Language*, by Lars Andersson and Peter Trudgill (Oxford: Blackwell, 1990) and 'Good English', in *Good English and the Grammarian*, by Sidney Greenbaum (London: Longman, 1988), ch. 1. Excellent analyses of abuses of language appear in *Language—The*

Loaded Weapon, by Dwight Bolinger (London: Longman, 1980). On swearing, see *Swearing: A Social History of Foul Language, Oaths and Profanity in English*, by Geoffrey Hughes (Oxford: Blackwell, 1991). On political correctness, see *The Official Politically Correct Dictionary and Handbook*, by Henry Beard and Christopher Cerf (London: Grafton, 1992) and *The Politically Correct Phrasebook*, by Nigel Rees (London: Bloomsbury, 1993). A history of sexist bias in English and attempts to counter it appears in *Grammar and Gender*, by Dennis Baron (New Haven: Yale University Press, 1986).

Chapter 2

1. The earlier work is by the eminent Danish linguist Otto Jespersen (Copenhagen: Munksgaard, 1909–49). The more recent work is by Randolph Quirk, Sidney Greenbaum, Geoffrey Leech, and Jan Svartvik (London: Longman, 1985).

2. The grammars of non-standard varieties have not been researched to anywhere near the extent that standard varieties have been. Summary accounts of the grammars of British non-standard varieties can be found in *English Accents and Dialects*, by Arthur Hughes and Peter Trudgill (London: Edward Arnold, 1989), *The Dialects of England*, by Peter Trudgill (Oxford: Basil Blackwell, 1990), and *Real English: The Grammar of English Dialects in the British Isles*, edited by James Milroy and Lesley Milroy (London: Longman, 1993). Selective information on the grammars of American non-standard varieties appears in *Dialects and American English*, by Walt Wolfram (Englewood Cliffs, NJ: Prentice Hall, 1991). Essays on aspects of non-standard dialects in the USA, Canada, Australia, and the British Isles appear, with summary introductions, in *Dialects of English: Studies in Grammatical Variation*, edited by Peter Trudgill and J. K. Chambers (London: Longman, 1991). Works that deal with these grammars focus on certain features that display differences from standard varieties. It is assumed that most of the grammar will be identical for all varieties.

3. Among the numerous introductions to linguistics, mention may be made of *Language and Linguistics: An Introduction*, by John Lyons (Cambridge: Cambridge University Press, 1981) and *General Linguistics: An Introductory Survey*, by R. H. Robins (London: Longman, 4th edn., 1989). *Teach Yourself Linguistics*, by Jean Aitchison (London: Hodder & Stoughton, 4th edn., 1992), is a highly readable, wide-ranging, elementary introductory text. On language universals, see *Language Universals and Linguistic Typology*, by Bernard Comrie (Oxford: Basil Blackwell, 2nd edn., 1989).

4. Chomsky's Government and Binding Theory retains two syntactic levels, but these are termed D-structure (formerly deep structure) and S-structure (formerly surface structure), which are related by movement transformations. Surface structures (in the new sense) result from the application of rules that determine the phonetic form of the S-structures. In his more recent Minimalist framework, Chomsky dispenses with the distinction between D-structure and S-structure and no longer uses these two terms.

   The Language Instinct: The New Science of Language and Mind, by Steven Pinker (London: Allen Lane, 1994) presents an excellent, wide-ranging account of language that is heavily influenced by Chomsky's approaches to language.

5. The sentence is uttered by Butt the Hoopoe in *Haroun and the Sea of Stories*, by Salman Rushdie (London: Granta Books, 1991), p. 71.

6. Accounts of English traditional grammars appear in *The English Reference Grammar: Language and Linguistics, Writers and Readers*, edited by Gerhard Leitner (Tübingen: Max Niemeyer, 1986); *Grammatical Theory in Western Europe 1500–1700: Trends in Vernacular Grammar*, by G. A. Padley (Cambridge: Cambridge University Press, 1985); *English Grammatical Categories and the Tradition to 1800*, by Ian Michael (Cambridge: Cambridge University Press, 1970). A comprehensive study of English teaching in earlier periods, including the teaching of English language, is to be found in *The Teaching of English: From the Sixteenth Century to 1870*, by Ian Michael (Cambridge: Cambridge University Press, 1987).

Chapter 3

1. The major reference grammar of present-day English is *A Comprehensive Grammar of the English Language*, by Randolph Quirk, Sidney Greenbaum, Geoffrey Leech, and Jan Svartvik (London: Longman, 1985). An abridgement of that work, with some revisions, is *A Student's Grammar of the English Language*, by Sidney Greenbaum and Randolph Quirk (London: Longman, 1990). Other recent general grammars that are worth consulting are *A New Approach to English Grammar, on Semantic Principles*, by R. M. W. Dixon (Oxford: Clarendon Press, 1991) and the 2-volume *English Grammar: A Function-Based Introduction*, by T. Givón (Amsterdam: John Benjamins, 1993).

2. Caution is necessary in the use of the term *verb*. In traditional practice, it is applied in two ways: (1) for a part of speech (*contains* is a verb in the verb

phrase *contains* and *given* in the verb phrase *has been given*) and (2) for a major constituent in a sentence or clause (*contains* in **[1]**; *'ve been given, have,* and *may be reduced* in **[4]**). See also n. 9.

3. *Yes–no* questions have also been called polarity questions, polarity being the system of positive/negative contrast. *Wh*-questions have also been called information questions.

4. In early periods of English, questions such as **[8a]** would have been formed by subject–verb inversion, without the support of the auxiliary *do*, and this was still possible in Elizabethan times. Thus, Shakespeare's Hamlet asks:

Stay'd it long?

The present-day equivalent is:

Did it stay long?

The use of *do* as a dummy auxiliary began in the fourteenth century as an option instead of the fronting of the main verb, it became the preferred option by the middle of the sixteenth century, and it finally became obligatory by the early eighteenth century. The increased use of *do* reflected the increased rigidity of word order in English. The insertion of the dummy auxiliary allowed both the verb–subject order that signalled *yes–no* questions (*did it . . .*) and the subject–(main) verb order (*. . . it stay*). It also paralleled the pattern found with auxiliaries in questions (*It should stay, Should it stay?*). However, the main verb *be* has continued to follow the earlier pattern of subject–verb inversion without *do*-support, if no auxiliary is present:

Are they naughty?

But if an auxiliary accompanies *be*, there is subject–operator inversion:

Have they been naughty?

British English allows both options for the main verb *have*, but American English generally follows the regular pattern with *do*-support:

Have you enough to eat?

Do you have enough to eat?

In informal style *have . . . got* is more common in British English:

Have you got enough to eat?

Analogous uses of *do*-support apply elsewhere when present-day English requires an auxiliary, as in verb negation (cf. 3.11).

The older forms of questions and verb negation without *do*-support are occasionally found in present-day English either in solemn oration, in an imitation of the style of the King James Bible and the Common Prayer Book, or in jocular style. The oratorical use is exemplified in John Kennedy's often-quoted words from his 1961 inaugural address:

> And so, my fellow Americans *ask not* what your country can do for you;
> ask what you can do for your country.

The jocular use is exemplified in this brief news item about new lavatories in Northumbria:

> The view from the washbasins, the company's recreation manager, Chris
> Spray (*we kid you not*), enthuses, is 'spectacular'. [*The Independent*,
> 25 August 1992, p. 17]

5. Not all prepositions can be fronted in *wh*-questions. For example, the prepositions that follow the verb *be* are retained in final position:

> *What* was the food *like*?

So also:

> *What* did you say that *for*? ('Why did you say that?')

6. The imperative auxiliary *let's* and the main verb *let* co-occur in this example:

> '*Let's let* the Khmer Rouge become outlaws or rebels,' Mr. Jennar said,
> and enforce the building 'of democracy and the building of rehabilitation of
> the country.' [*International Herald Tribune*, 6–7 February 1993, p. 5]

7. The classic works on speech act theory are by philosophers: *How To Do Things With Words*, by J. L. Austin (Oxford: Oxford University Press, 1962), *Speech Acts*, by John R. Searle (Cambridge: Cambridge University Press, 1969), *Expression and Meaning: Studies in the Theory of Speech Acts*, by John R. Searle, chs. 1 and 2 (Cambridge: Cambridge University Press, 1979). For a concise account by a linguist of various theories dealing with speech acts and a critique of them, see *Pragmatics*, by Stephen C. Levinson (Cambridge: Cambridge University Press, 1983), ch. 5.

8. This is an example of a hedged performative, where a modal auxiliary is used to express (for example) the obligation, ability, or willingness to perform the speech act designated by the performative verb, but at the same time the speaker intends what he says to constitute the performance of that speech act.

9. The term *verb phrase* is also used for the verb plus its complements (if any). *Predicate* may be similarly used, but may also be extended to include adverbials that are closely attached to the sentence. The verb of the sentence is sometimes called the predicator.

10. British English also allows the direct object to come first if both objects are pronouns. The normal order—indirect object followed by direct object—occurs in this example:

> Well if you give *me* (O) *it* (O) tomorrow I might be able to do some
> tomorrow morning [. . .] [S1A-038-155]

The exceptional order—direct object followed by indirect object—is shown below:

> Give *it* (O) *me* (O) tomorrow.

11. Subject predicative has also been called subject complement and object predicative has also been called object complement. *Complement* has been replaced by *predicative* to avoid confusion, because *complement* has a more generalized sense. *Predicative* has been traditionally used for predicative adjectives and predicative nouns (or nominals) when these are functioning to complement a copular verb.

12. It has been argued that gender as a grammatical category does not exist in English, since the only candidates for gender distinctions are a few pronouns, and their choice is overwhelmingly determined by sex reference, whereas choices in grammatical gender are determined by agreement with words according to their subclass (e.g. the noun agreeing with an adjective or verb). The choice of reflexive pronoun in the following two sentences depends on extralinguistic information, not on agreement with the noun *friend*:

> Your friend is washing herself.
> Your friend is washing himself.

Chapter 4

1. The exception is the main verb *beware*, which is not inflected. Among auxiliaries and semi-auxiliaries, there are no inflections for *must, ought to, had better* (or *better*), *had best* (or *best*). The uninflected *got to* (*gotta* in non-standard spelling) is an informal variant of *'s got to, 've got to, 'd got to*.

2. In this sense the verb is a constituent of a sentence or clause just as are the subject and direct object. See Ch. 3, nn. 2 and 9.

3. Infinitival *to* is a separate word, and therefore adverbials (especially single adverbs) sometimes intervene between it and the infinitive. The interruption results in what is traditionally known as the split infinitive.

   [1] But it's the sense of freedom of being able *to* just *lie* down if you want to roll over [S1A-003-88]

   [2] How could people be so insensitive as *to* not *know* they've got wax in their ears [S1A-080-77]

[3] But you'd need to think carefully about the number of support people required *to* actually *administer* ⟨ , ⟩ a process like this [S1B-020-195]

[4] Certainly all the members of the panel here tonight are too young *to* really *remember* the Second World War [. . .] [S1B-035-31]

[5] Boeing Co. said that it is discussing plans with three of its regular Japanese suppliers *to* possibly *help* build a larger version of its popular 767 twin-jet. [891102-0152-1]

[6] Some associates suspect that the 40-year old Mr Trumka would like *to* someday *head* the nation's largest labor group. [891005-0019-14]

[7] When must states make retroactive refunds of collected taxes that are later found *to* unconstitutionally *interfere* with interstate commerce? [891002-0001-26]

[8] They want to plug into the EC power grid, get a piece of Europe's Eureka high-tech research program and set up as an export platform for South Korea *to* conveniently *manufacture* and ship its wares into the EC. [890928-0009-124]

The split infinitive has been objected to because infinitival *to* has been perceived as part of the infinitive. This perception was at one time influenced by a knowledge of Latin grammar, which does not have an infinitival *to*. In some contexts splitting the infinitive avoids ambiguity. For example, if in a written form of **[4]**, *really* was placed before *to* it could be misunderstood as focusing on *too young*, though in speech the intended focus could be conveyed intonationally. In other contexts, the infinitive must be split, unless the sentence is rephrased. This applies to **[5]** and **[8]** and to the longer interruption in **[9]** below:

[9] Who would cherish them as friends, when we have new, clean, up-to-date people *to*, if you like, *look* up to—people such as Richard Branson, Gary Lineker, Paul McCartney? [*The Sunday Times*, 14 February 1994, p. 5.1]

Chapter 5

1. Genitive noun phrases generally have a determiner function: *the girls' parents* parallels *their parents*. They can also be premodifiers, as in *a girl's school* (cf. 4.12).

2. The intensifiers *so*, *that*, and *too* followed by an adjective can come at the beginning of a noun phrase:

[1] Certainly it was *so prominent a* punctuation in the landscape that one was positively drawn towards it. [W2F-005-74]

[2] I'd had a ⟨ , , ⟩ reasonable lunch but not *that good a* lunch [S2A-044-22]

[3]   I think you're putting that in *too simplistic a* form [S1B-031-93]

So may correlate with a *that*-clause after the head noun, as in **[1]**, or with a *to*-infinitive clause introduced by the subordinator *as*. *Too* may correlate with a *to*-infinitive clause.

3.   The adverb *else* is only a postmodifier. It follows indefinite pronouns and adverbs compounded with *some*, *any*, or *no*, interrogative pronouns (cf. 4.43), and interrogative adverbs (cf. 4.26):

> **[1]**   I don't know what *else* I'll go to though [S1A-005-68]
>
> **[2]**   Well do it somewhere *else* [S1A-010-145]
>
> **[3]**   I don't know anyone *else* who could do it [S1A-021-11]
>
> **[4]**   Where *else* do you look John [S1A-034-207]

The genitive inflection is on *else* rather than on the pronoun:

> **[5]**   Is it part of your responsibility or someone *else's* responsibility to check whether the people who're running the hotel appear on the face of it to be competent and up to the job [S1B-067-30]

4.   Extraposition of the postmodifying *of*-phrase would have forestalled the embarrassing suggestion reported without comment in this news item:

> A press release informs us that he hopes to raise the issue of "street children and those sold into sex slavery *with Foreign Office ministers*". [*The Independent*, 19 June 1992, p. 19]

Whereas the *of*-phrase is a postmodifier of the head noun *issue*, the *with*-phrase is an adverbial of the infinitive clause. It would be better still to place the *with*-phrase after *to raise*.

5.   The quasi-independent status of the sentential relative clause is indicated by its ability to be punctuated as an independent sentence in writing **[1]** and even to head a new paragraph **[2]**:

> **[1]**   You'll get a letter from me tomorrow and no doubt be embarassed [*sic*] when the lady gives it to you. *Which* reminds me, do you want me to post your toothbrushes? [W1B-006-82 f.]
>
> **[2]**   The news is not all bad. The Bank judges that six countries got the macroeconomic fundamentals right: . . .
> *All of which* is quite some achievement. (*The Economist*, 5 March 1994, p. 22]

6.   Exceptional titles that follow names include the (chiefly) American designations *Senior* (*Sr.*) and *Junior* (*Jr.*) to distinguish between fathers and sons with the same first names, as in *Martin Luther King, Jr.*; subsequent generations are given Roman numerals, as in *Sen. John D. Rockfeller IV* (read as 'the fourth'). *Major* and *minor* are sometimes used in British schools after family names of brothers in the same school (e.g. *Smith minor*). The courtesy title *Esq.* (abbreviation of *Esquire*) is occasionally used in addresses on letters

with the full name when no other title is used with the name (e.g. *John Black, Esq.*).

7. Descriptive phrases consisting of the definite article *the* and an adjective or numeral may follow the names of monarchs; *Elizabeth I* ('the first'), *William the Conqueror*. Those of the type *Ivan the Terrible* and *Elizabeth I* are postmodifiers (compare: *the terrible Ivan, the first Elizabeth*), whereas in *William the Conqueror, the Conqueror* is an appositive (compare *the poet Longfellow*).

8. Appositive clauses are to be distinguished from relative clauses (cf. 5.9). Appositive clauses are self-contained, whereas in relative clauses the relative item functions within the clause. For example in the appositive clause **[1]** *that* is a subordinator and does not function (say as subject or direct object) in the clause:

> **[1]**   Police say they can't confirm a TV report *that the building had been hit by automatic fire* [S2B-016-95]

We can extract the appositive clause without its subordinator and make it an independent sentence:

> **[1a]**   The building had been hit by automatic fire.

We can show that it is an appositive by demonstrating its copular link with the preceding noun phrase:

> **[1b]**   The TV report is *that the building had been hit by automatic fire.*

We can insert an appropriate apposition marker, in this case *namely*. On the other hand, the *that*-clause in **[1c]** is a relative clause:

> **[1c]**   Police say that they can't confirm a TV report *that we all saw last night.*

Here *that* is a relative pronoun functioning as direct object in the relative clause. We can replace it by the relative pronoun *which*, which refers back to the antecedent *a TV report* ('We all saw the TV report last night').

9. Certain types of clauses that have a non-finite verb phrase as their verb can serve as independent complete utterances. They mainly occur in informal conversation. Here are some examples of questions whose verb is non-finite, an *-ing* participle **[1]**–**[2]** and an infinitive **[3]**:

> **[1]**   *How about pouring* a pint of oil over their heads or something [S1B-079-290]
>
> **[2]**   *What about putting* legs on it and making it into an enclosed table type of arrangement [S1B-073-238]
>
> **[3]**   *Why change* things [S1A-017-2]

10. Some grammarians have argued that the perfect is a tense rather than an aspect, since it refers to a period or point in time: the past of the speaker/writer or a preceding past time. Others have considered it an aspect because it is retrospective in at least some of its uses.

11. The absence of an operator for negation shows that the verb is subjunctive even though it has the same form as the indicative:

> And every last one of the six who had children said he would prefer they *not smoke*. [*International Herald Tribune*, 19 April 1994, p. 6]

The indicative requires the dummy operator *do*: 'they *do not smoke*' or 'they *did not smoke*'.

12. For a readable and enlightening study of multi-word verbs, see *The Phrasal Verb in English*, by Dwight Bolinger (Cambridge, Mass.: Harvard University Press, 1971).

13. Prepositional objects are sometimes termed oblique objects. In some analyses, prepositional objects that correspond to indirect objects are also termed indirect objects: 'I gave a book *to her*' (cf. 'I gave *her* a book').

14. The difference between the adjective and the adverb as premodifiers is starkly posed in a report of a printing mistake:

> Foul-up corner, part two. From this week's *Fashion Weekly*, on an earlier article about the Hackett chain: "In paragraph eight we referred to the company as 'a *terrible* British company', this should of course have read 'a *terribly* British company . . .' " [*The Independent*, 13 November 1992, p. 27] (italics in original)

The adverb *terribly* has become an intensifier, having lost its pejorative connotation. The adjective modifies the unit *British company* ('a British company that is terrible'), whereas the adverb modifies only the adjective *British* ('a company that is terribly British').

15. Adjectives functioning as complements of prepositions are virtually confined to fixed expressions. They should all perhaps be regarded as nominal adjectives (cf. 4.23). Here is a list of such expressions, arranged according to the preposition:

at best	in brief
at large	in common
at worst	in full
	in general
for better or worse	in particular
for certain	in private
for free	in public
for good	in secret
for real	in short
for sure	
	of old
from bad to worse	on high

There are also a few expressions with determiners, e.g. *all of a sudden, in the extreme, to the full.*

16. The preposition *but* ('except') is occasionally found with ellipsis of its complement, the ellipsis being recoverable from the preceding context:

> The campaign for the European election on Sunday was easy to ignore, but the new European Parliament will be anything *but*. [*International Herald Tribune*, 13 June 1994, p. 4] ('anything *but* easy to ignore')

Chapter 6

1. The concept of a sentence is discussed in *Syntax*, by P. H. Matthews (Cambridge: Cambridge University Press, 1981), ch. 2.

2. For co-ordination and subordination, see *A Comprehensive Grammar of the English Language*, by Randolph Quirk, Sidney Greenbaum, Geoffrey Leech, and Jan Svartvik (London: Longman, 1985), chs. 13–15.

3. If verb phrases include complements of the verbs, as in some analyses, then the subordinate clauses in **[2]–[5]** would also be constituents of phrases.

4. A subordinate clause may be embedded in a phrase (cf. 6.3). In one approach, the sentence is simple if the only subordinate clauses occurring in the sentence are in phrases. If complements of verbs are taken as constituents of phrases, this approach would extend the notion of simple sentence considerably.

5. An adverbial that is not a clause may also extend its scope to more than one main clause. Below, three co-ordinated main clauses are within the scope of the initial adverbial:

> *Here in wonderful London*, the sun shines, the birds sing *and* the streets are still paved with gold. [W1B-001-20]

6. On clause complexes, see *An Introduction to Functional Grammar*, 2nd edition, by M. A. K. Halliday (London: Edward Arnold, 1994), ch. 7. We could define a clause cluster as a set of clauses related by parataxis or hypotaxis, as Halliday does for clause complex. Certainly we would want to include within a clause cluster most of the paratactically related clauses listed in 6.5. There is, however, a problem with juxtaposed clauses. For example, should all the juxtaposed clauses in citation **[1]** in 6.5 be considered as belonging to one cluster, or just the two linked by *For example*? In the written language we might follow the clues provided by punctuation, so that citations **[2]** and **[3]** in 6.5 are regarded as having one cluster each because the clauses are linked by punctuation that is internal to an orthographic sentence. In the spoken language we may need

to take account of intonation linkage that suggests that the cluster has not been completed. If we attempt to establish logical connections as the basis of a clause cluster, we may find ourselves designating a complete written text or speech as a cluster.

7. Many Americans cannot use *nor* with a co-ordinator. For them, *nor* itself is a co-ordinator. However, it differs from the other co-ordinators in that, like *neither*, it causes subject–operator inversion, as in **[7]** in 6.8.

8. *So* is frequently used as a pro-clause for a *that*-clause functioning as direct object, and similarly *not* as a negative pro-clause (cf. 7.11). The *that*-clause is generally a complement of a verb of saying, cognition, or perception:

> **[1]** He was happy to return to Manfield Terrace and to Norma, and often said *so*. [W2F-014-37] ('and often said *that he was happy to return to Manfield Terrace and to Norma*')

> **[2]** A: Oh I would imagine she would have left by now if she said twenty minutes
>   B: You would have thought *so* [S1A-039-157]

> **[3]** A: Uhm ⟨ , , ⟩ were your first ⟨ , ⟩ sexual relationships anything like you'd expected them to be ⟨ , ⟩
>   B: I guess *not* [S1A-072-167]

A similar range of verbs of cognition and perception (but not verbs of saying) are involved in transferred negation, the transfer of negation from the subordinate clause to the host clause. The negative in *I don't think they know you* can negate the host clause ('I'm not of that opinion')—and it clearly does so if *think* is stressed—or it can negate by transferred negation the subordinate clause ('I think they don't know you'), though the negative force is weaker in transferred negation than when the subordinate clause is directly negated. Compare also the direct negation in *They don't know you, I think.* Here are some examples of transferred negation:

> **[4]** I *don't suppose* anyone can guess what this is [S2A-051-90] ('I suppose no one can guess what this is')

> **[5]** I *don't believe* that's correct [S1B-069-60]

> **[6]** The vet *didn't think* she would live but she's nearly 7 months old now. [W1B-014-93]

Transferred negation applies also with complements that are *to*-infinitive clauses and finite clauses or *-ing* participle clauses introduced by *as if, as though,* or *like*:

> **[7]** [. . .] I *don't expect to* make a profit [. . .] [S1B-078-60] ('I expect not to make a profit')

> **[8]** Anne *didn't seem to* be listening. [W2F-002-18]

> **[9]** You *don't look as if* you need it [S1A-075-13]

> **[10]** [. . .] they all of them *didn't feel like* doing their exams because he died like the night before a lot of uh the exams [S1A-093-180]

Can't seem to and *couldn't seem to* transfer also the meaning of the modal:

> **[11]** [. . .] I honestly feel great now, although my stomach *can't seem to* handle anything stronger than fruit at the moment! [W1B-005-50] ('my stomach seems not to be able to handle')

The pro-clause *so* is commonly used in transferred negation:

> **[12]** A: Are you going grey
> B: I don't think *so* [S1A-068-104]

It is less formal than direct negation with *not*:

> **[12a]** I think *not*.

9. Some grammarians have considered the nominal relative clause to be a noun phrase rather than a clause. They analyse the nominal relative item as consisting of a pronoun or general noun phrase that is fused with a relative item as in these examples drawn from citations in 6.12: '*the things that* the market wants to see' **[34]**, 'things that looked like 20 different types of fish' **[35]**, 'any person who needs to be bribed to get on that plane' **[36]**. In this alternative analysis, the nominal relative clause is regarded as a noun phrase whose head (*what* in **[34]**–**[35]** and *whoever* in **[36]**) is a fused relative with a built-in antecedent, and the head is followed by the rest of a postmodifying relative clause.

10. Some participles—*assuming, judging, considering, supposing*—are commonly used in adverbial clauses with an understood generic subject:

> As usual, the second half is expected to be better, *assuming that the recession is shallow* [. . .] [W2C-005-82]

> [. . .] *judging by the experimental evidence*, any reduction of lean body mass is likely to be mainly at the expense of slowly metabolizing tissues, particularly muscle. [W2A-024-14]

> The baby tortoise, so tiny when Pete christened him on the docks at Southampton, was now the size of a large soup plate which, *considering how many of our plants he'd devoured over the years,* was hardly surprising. [W2B-004-38]

> *Supposing we want to create a large commercial monopoly for some reason* we'll come back to why in a few moments how would we do it [S1B-005-89]

11. Complements of verbs may have the same form as adverbial clauses and express the same kinds of meanings as they do. For example:

> There was even animated, dewy-eyed talk of a hurried return to the First Division and startling mention of the "rich rewards of Europe", with the footballing folk of Newcastle urged to put their money *where their mouths are* [. . .] [W2C-004-69]

See the subsection on manner clauses in 6.14.

12. Conditional clauses exhibit a number of parallels with subordinate interrogative clauses (cf. 6.12):

    1. Both indicate that information is missing. For conditional clauses, the missing information is about the fulfilment of the condition. In fact, we can often rephrase a conditional construction as a question with its response:

    > You're going to have huge trouble if you've infected me.

    > Have you infected me? If so, you're going to have huge trouble.

    2. The semantic and formal distinctions between the three types of interrogative clauses (*yes–no*, alternative, *wh-*) are analogous to those between the three types of conditional clauses (direct, alternative, *wh-*).

    3. *If* and *whether* are used as subordinators in both interrogative and conditional clauses.

    4. Rhetorical questions (cf. 3.5) are paralleled by rhetorical conditions:

    > Is there anybody stronger than me?

    > If anybody is stronger than me, I'll eat my hat.

13. *If* can be a subordinator in an abbreviated conditional clause with the pro-clause *so* or *not* (cf. n. 8 to this chapter):

    > Should you buy a separate transport unit and, *if so*, which one? [W2B-040-3]

    > Seen anyone else I know? *If not*, then what the hell have you been doing?!! [W1B-002-37]

14. *If* may be used concessively (usually in abbreviated clauses) as well as conditionally. It may be synonymous either with *even if* [1] or with *even though* [2]:

    [1] Unfortunately there remain some strong *if not stronger* arguments in favour of the opposite view: that an excessive show of force inevitably leads to war. [W2C-003-86] ('even if they are not stronger')

    [2] But can't that fantastic technical ingenuity [. . .] at last be applied to civilian production turning *if not swords into ploughshares* F Fifteens into kidney machines [S2B-034-77] ('even though not turning swords into ploughshares')

15. *The* in proportion clauses is not the definite article. It derives from the use in Old English of the instrumental case *þȳ* of the demonstrative pronoun in expressions of comparison ('*by that* the faster, *by that* the better').

16. The concept of complementation has been extended to adjectives and nouns by analogy with its use with verbs. As with verbs, complements of adjectives and nouns need not be obligatory. Indeed, very few adjectives (e.g. *fond of*) or nouns (e.g. *lack of*) require a complement. But just as the same verb (e.g. *eat*) may be used as either intransitive (without any complement) or transitive (with a direct object as complement), so specific adjectives or nouns may occur with or without a complement.

With respect to complement clauses, clauses are considered to be complements if their form is determined by the subclass of adjective or noun; for example, whether the complement is finite, what subordinator is used, what forms of verbs are possible. Thus, the adjectives *aware* and *sure* are followed by *that*-clauses, though if the host clause is negative *sure* can also take interrogative clauses. Similarly, nouns such as *impression* belong to a subclass that can take appositive clauses. Another criterion for complementation is that when the complements are omitted the sentence, though grammatical, is felt to be semantically incomplete, as in *Are you sure?* Further evidence is provided by resemblances, in meaning and perhaps also in form, to verbs with the same complements. So, *you are aware that she is abroad* parallels *You know that she is abroad*, and *their decision to leave early* parallels *they decided to leave early*.

17. On reported speech, with particular reference to indirect and free indirect speech, see *The Fictions of Language and the Languages of Fiction*, by Monika Fludernik (London: Routledge, 1993).

Chapter 7

1. On the move from speech to written technologies, see *Orality and Literacy*, by W. J. Ong (London: Methuen, 1982), and *Worlds of Reference*, by Tom McArthur (Cambridge: Cambridge University Press, 1986).

2. This example appears in *Understanding Utterances*, by Diane Blakemore (Oxford: Blackwell, 1992), pp. 42 f.

3. Pragmatics is the study of the principles governing language use in context. For a general introduction, see *Pragmatics*, by Stephen C. Levinson (Cambridge: Cambridge University Press, 1983). For a brief but comprehensive study of texts in communication, see *Introduction to Text Linguistics*, by Robert de Beaugrande and Wolfgang Dressler (London: Longman, 1981). While asserting the importance of other aspects of intertextuality, some present-day literary critics deny the relevance of information about the author and the period of composition for the interpretation of literary texts, but this is an approach that is unlikely to endure.

4. Coherence and cohesion are discussed in *Introduction to Text Linguistics*, referred to in n. 3. For a detailed study of cohesion, see *Cohesion in English*, by M. A. K. Halliday and Ruqaiya Hasan (London: Longman, 1976); more succinct accounts appear in *A Comprehensive Grammar of the English*

Language, by Randolph Quirk, Sidney Greenbaum, Geoffrey Leech, and Jan Svartvik (London: Longman, 1985), ch. 19, and in *An Introduction to Functional Grammar*, by M. A. K. Halliday, 2nd edition (London: Edward Arnold, 1994), ch. 9.

5. Among the numerous books on rhetoric and composition, mention might be made of three: *Classical Rhetoric for the Modern Student*, by Edward J. Corbett, 2nd edition (New York: Oxford University Press, 1971); *Rhetoric: The Wit of Persuasion*, by Walter Nash (Oxford: Blackwell, 1989); *Designs in Prose: A Study of Compositional Problems and Methods*, by Walter Nash (London: Longman, 1980).

6. This description of the structure of news reports draws on 'News Schemata', by Teun A. van Dijk, in *Studying Writing: Linguistic Approaches*, ed. Charles R. Cooper and Sidney Greenbaum (Beverly Hills, Calif.: Sage, 1986), pp. 155–85.

7. For references to books on speech acts, see Ch. 3, n. 7.

8. For a thorough and systematic introduction to conversational interactions, see *An Introduction to Spoken Interaction*, by Anna-Brita Stenström (London: Longman, 1994).

Chapter 8

1. Two general books on English vocabulary are recommended. *Words in the Mind: An Introduction to the Mental Lexicon*, by Jean Aitchison (Oxford: Basil Blackwell, 1987), is written from a psycholinguistic perspective. *Vocabulary: Applied Linguistic Perspectives*, by Ronald Carter (London: Allen & Unwin, 1987) is of particular value for the teaching of modern English vocabulary.

2. Words based on existing words (e.g. *piglet*, *pigwash*) are not arbitrary, though the meanings of the derived words may not always be transparent.

3. The most important reference source for the history of English words is the massive *Oxford English Dictionary* (*OED*), published by Oxford University Press. It is now available in a second edition that incorporates the four supplementary volumes that were published in the period 1972–86 and also some new material. The second edition has been published in book form and on CD-ROM. Though dated, *A History of Foreign Words in English*, by Mary S. Serjeantson (London: Routledge & Kegan Paul, 1935) remains useful, and it was consulted for this chapter. Among other works consulted are two general

histories of English: *A History of the English Language,* by Albert C. Baugh and Thomas Cable, 4th edition (Englewood Cliffs, NJ: Prentice-Hall, 1993) and *The Origins and Development of the English language,* by Thomas Pyles and John Algeo, 4th edition (San Diego: Harcourt Brace Jovanovich, 1993). Recommended on changes of meaning in English words is *Words in Time: A Social History of the English Vocabulary,* by Geoffrey Hughes (Oxford: Basil Blackwell, 1988).

4. Each of the three corpora contains 500 texts (samples of language that have actually been used), and each text contains about 2,000 running words. The Brown and LOB corpora, which are roughly parallel in their composition, consist of printed material published in 1961. ICE-GB consists of language produced during the four years 1990–3: 300 texts (600,000 words) of spoken material and 200 texts (400,000 words) of written material. The spoken categories include conversations, public dialogues (such as legal cross-examinations and parliamentary debates), unscripted monologues (such as lectures and legal summings-up), and scripted monologues (such as lectures and broadcast news). The written categories include manuscript as well as printed material. The sources for the 500 texts in ICE-GB are listed at the end of this book.

5. At one time there were objections against formations that combined segments originating from different languages; for example, words that combined Latin with Greek elements or classical elements with native elements. Among the combinations that Fowler condemned as hybrids in his usage guide were the following words, which few people would see as problematic:

> amoral, bureaucracy, climatic, coastal, floatation [*sic*], gullible, pacifist, speedometer, tidal

(See the entry 'hybrid derivatives' in *A Dictionary of Modern English Usage,* by H. W. Fowler (Oxford: Clarendon Press, 1926).) In his revised version published in 1965, Sir Ernest Gowers retains these words under the entry 'hybrids and malformations', except for the spelling emendation *flotation,* and adds a word of his own—*automation.*

6. For an explanation of Latin tags, phrases, maxims, and proverbs, see *A Dictionary of Latin Tags and Phrases,* by Eugene Ehrlich (London: Guild Publishing, 1985).

7. The book in question is *Fifty Years Among the New Words: A Dictionary of Neologisms, 1941–1991,* ed. John Algeo (Cambridge: Cambridge University Press, 1991). Excluded were words formed from segments already existing in English, such as *Legionellosis.* The three French loans were *magicienne, messagerie,* and *minited.* The other loans were *bhangra* (Hindi), *intifada/intifadah* (Arabic), *lambada* (Portuguese), *perestroika* (Russian), *primo* (Spanish), and *rumtaske* (Norwegian). As with all neologisms, only time will tell which—if any—of these will become permanent in English.

8. The work consulted is *The Oxford Dictionary of New Words: A Popular Guide to Words in the News*, by S. Tulloch (Oxford: Oxford University Press, 1991).

9. The processes of change can also be viewed as indications of the effects of change: the extension ('process') of a meaning results in its extension ('effect'). On the use of metaphor and metonymy in everyday language, see *Metaphors We Live By*, by George Lakoff and Mark Johnson (Chicago: University of Chicago Press, 1980).

10. On euphemisms, see *Euphemism and Dysphemism: Language Used as Shield and Weapon*, by Keith Allan and Kate Burridge (Oxford: Oxford University Press, 1991); *The Faber Dictionary of Euphemisms*, by R. W. Holder, 2nd edition (London: Faber & Faber, 1989); *In Other Words: A Thesaurus of Euphemisms*, by Judith Neaman and Carole Silver, 2nd edition (London: Angus & Robertson, 1990); *A Dictionary of Euphemisms and Other Doubletalk*, by Hugh Rawson (New York: Crown Publishers, 1981).

11. For a recent account of the history of swearing in English, see *Swearing: A Social History of Foul Language, Oaths and Profanity in English*, by Geoffrey Hughes (Oxford: Blackwell, 1991).

12. On semantic relationships, see *Semantics*, by John Lyons (Cambridge: Cambridge University Press, 1977), vol. i, ch. 8, on which I have drawn for some examples.

13. Pairs of adjectives and adverbs that are contraries can serve as converses in comparative constructions:

> Ron is older than Susan.
> Susan is younger than Ron.
>
> Kenneth plays better than Norman.
> Norman plays worse than Kenneth.

14. There are numerous dictionaries of idioms. Among recent ones are *Oxford Dictionary of Current Idiomatic English*, i. *Verbs with Prepositions and Particles* (1975), by A. P. Cowie and R. Mackin (published in 1993 under the title *Oxford Dictionary of English Idioms*); ii. *Phrase, Clause and Sentence Idioms*, by A. P. Cowie, R. Mackin, and I. R. McCaig (Oxford: Oxford University Press, 1983); *Longman Dictionary of English Idioms*, by Thomas Hill Long (London: Longman, 1979); *A Dictionary of Contemporary Idioms*, by Martin H. Manser (London: Macmillan, 1983); *NTC's American Idioms Dictionary*, by Richard A. Spears (Lincolnwood, Ill.: National Textbook Company, 1987).

15. In some descriptions *homophone* and *homograph* are defined differently. If two items are pronounced the same, they are considered homophones regardless of their spellings; if they are spelled the same, they are considered homographs regardless of their pronunciation. Hence, according to this treatment the

homonyms of *bank* are also both homophones and homographs, depending on whether one is discussing the sound system or the writing system.

16. The classic work on ambiguity in English literature, and in particular in English poetry, is *Seven Types of Ambiguity: A Study of its Effects in English Verse*, by William Empson (London: Chatto & Windus, 1953). On wordplay in general, see *The Language of Humour: Style and Technique in Comic Discourse*, by Walter Nash (London: Longman, 1985) and *Puns*, by Walter Redfern (Oxford: Basil Blackwell, 1984).

17. The estimates are derived from researches reported in *Words in the Mind: An Introduction to the Mental Lexicon*, by Jean Aitchison (Oxford: Basil Blackwell, 1987), pp. 6–7. Aitchison (personal communication) cites results of a project on children's vocabulary in which she was involved to show that the average 11-year-old knows at least 10,000 words and the average 14-year-old knows at least 20,000 words.

18. The estimates are cited in *Growth and Structure of the English Language*, by Otto Jespersen, 8th edition (Oxford: Basil Blackwell, 1935), pp. 194–5.

Chapter 9

1. A recent general work on the structure of words is *English Word-Formation*, by Laurie Bauer (Cambridge: Cambridge University Press, 1983). An older account can be found in *An Introduction to Modern English Word-Formation*, by Valerie Adams (London: Longman, 1973). The classic work is *The Categories and Types of Present-Day English Word-Formation: A Synchronic–Diachronic Approach*, by Hans Marchand (Munich: Oscar Beck, 1969).

2. English rarely makes use of infixes (insertions within words), for example *abso-bloody-lutely, im-fucking-possible, un-fucking-believable*.

3. A few noun compounds make their plural in the first segment (e.g. *mother-in-law*), but the regular plural may also be used in some of these compounds, particularly in informal style (cf. 4.7).

4. To these negative prefixes may be added prefixoids that have a negative feeling about them. Prefixoids are sound sequences that resemble genuine prefixes without qualifying for the status of prefix, since their etymology is not known to the vast majority of speakers. Examples of sets of negative prefixoids are *deny, despair, despise, detest, disdain, disgust, distress, object, obliterate, obnoxious, obstruct, obtrude*.

5. The examples are taken from *Word Warps: A Glossary of Unfamiliar Terms*, by David Diefendorf (London: Muller, Blond & White, 1986).

6. If the senses of words derived by suffixation can be predicted with confidence, many dictionaries will save space by putting the words under the entry for their base, perhaps without further definition (*portability* and *portably* under *portable*). Words derived by prefixation (*unclear* from *clear*) will be given in their alphabetical positions. Compounds may be cited separately or under the entry for their head segment: *sparking-plug* under *plug*, since a sparking-plug is a type of plug, not a type of sparking.

The noun *plug* and the verb *plug* are also different lexical words, each with its own set of inflections: the noun *plug/plugs* and the verb *plug/plugs/plugged/plugging*; but for economy they may appear under the same entry. Larger dictionaries assign distinct senses of an item or different etymologies to separate entries (for example, the noun *plug* and the verb *plug* in their several senses).

Chapter 10

1. Three introductory textbooks on phonetics are recommended: *A Course in Phonetics*, by Peter Ladefoged, 3rd edition, international edition (Fort Worth: Harcourt Brace, 1993), which takes account of British and American English and their regional variants and also refers to other languages, is linguistically orientated but wide-ranging; *The Speech Chain: The Physics and Biology of Spoken Language*, by Peter B. Denes and Elliot N. Pinson, 2nd edition (New York: W. H. Freeman, 1993) draws on various disciplines to explain what happens in spoken communication; *Patterns of Spoken English: An Introduction to English Phonetics*, by Gerald Knowles (London: Longman, 1987) focuses on English, drawing on various national varieties, and deals amply with connected speech. Differences between British and American pronunciation are recorded in the *Longman Pronunciation Dictionary*, by J. C. Wells (London: Longman, 1990). For British pronunciation, see *An Introduction to the Pronunciation of English*, by A. C. Gimson, 4th edition, revised by Susan Ramsaran (London: Edward Arnold, 1980). For American pronunciation, see *The Pronunciation of American English*, by Arthur J. Bronstein (New York: Appleton-Century-Crofts, 1960). The standard work on the pronunciation of English world-wide is the three-volume *Accents of English*, by J. C. Wells (Cambridge: Cambridge University Press, 1982).

2. Public attention has recently been focused on the spread among the younger generation of the middle and upper social classes in South East England of an accent that is intermediate between RP and Cockney, the traditional accent of

working-class Londoners. This accent has been called Estuary English, to indicate its main location in the basin of the River Thames. Two features are particularly associated with Estuary English. One is the vocalization of /l/ when it does not precede a vowel, as in *little* [lɪʊ], *belt* [bɛʊt]. Sometimes, instead [ə] is inserted, as in *oil* [ɔɪəl], *feel* [fiːəl]. The other feature is the frequent use of the glottal stop as an allophone of /t/ at the end of a word: *cut it out* [kʌʔ ɪʔ aʊʔ].

3. Though for convenience of comparison, the same distinction in length is made here for GA as for RP, vowel length is less important in GA and the length colons are usually omitted in transcriptions of American vowels. More usually in American classification, the short vowels are said to be lax while the long vowels and the diphthongs are said to be tense. The terms refer to the relative degree of tension in the tongue and other muscles during the articulation of the vowels. In general, American tense vowels are shorter in duration than the corresponding RP long vowels.

4. On sound patterns in verse, see *A Linguistic Guide to English Poetry*, by Geoffrey N. Leech (London: Longman, 1969), ch. 6, which has been consulted for this section.

5. *Rhythmic Phrasing in English Verse*, by Richard D. Cureton (London: Longman, 1992) contains critiques of current theories and traditional views of verse rhythm and presents a new comprehensive theory.

Chapter 11

1. A scholarly account of major aspects of American punctuation based on a computer corpus of printed texts appears in *A Linguistic Study of American Punctuation*, by Charles F. Meyer (New York: Peter Lang, 1987). A theoretical treatment of American punctuation can be found in *The Linguistics of Punctuation*, by Geoffrey Nunberg (Stanford University, Calif.: Center for the Study of Language and Information, 1990). *You have a Point There*, by Eric Partridge (London: Routledge, 1953) is a comprehensive guide to British punctuation with a chapter on differences in American punctuation by John W. Clark, but it is somewhat dated. Usage guides tend to include advice on punctuation, but a comprehensive investigation into British practice is long overdue.

A scholarly history of punctuation in Western Europe appears in *Pauses and Effect: An Introduction to the History of Punctuation in the West*, by M. B. Parkes (Aldershot, Hants: Scholar Press). *But I Digress: The Exploitation of*

Parentheses in English Printed Verse, by John Lennard (Oxford: Clarendon Press, 1991) discusses the functions of just one punctuation mark in English poetry, with detailed critical analyses of the works of Marvell, Coleridge, and Eliot.

2. The frequencies are taken from the book by Meyer (p. 7) referred to in n. 1.

3. If the hyphen is used to link an open compound with an affix or another word, the result can be odd. It may wrongly suggest that only one part of the compound is linked:

> the next *New York-Los Angeles* flight
>
> the *post-Cold War* world
>
> *A White House-Size Logistical Drama* [*International Herald Tribune*, 13 September 1993, p. 6—headline]

Chapter 12

1. Two major scholarly works on English spelling have appeared recently: *American English Spelling: An Informal Description*, by D. W. Cummings (Baltimore: Johns Hopkins University Press, 1988) and *English Spelling—A Survey*, by E. Carney (London: Routledge, 1994), which is based on British spelling and pronunciation, but takes account of differences in American English. For the historical background, see *A History of English Spelling*, by D. G. Scragg (Manchester: Manchester University Press, 1974).

2. One of the early additions has survived into present-day English as a curious vestige of the runic þ (called 'thorn') in the archaic pretensions of shop names such as *Ye Olde Tea Shoppe*. The thorn spelled both the sounds represented by modern *th* in *this* and *thin*, but it was eventually replaced by *th* because it could easily be confused with *y* in manuscripts. The *Y* of *Ye* in *Ye Olde Tea Shoppe* reflects the earlier spelling, when the word was intended to be pronounced as *the*. On the whole, the Old English alphabet successfully represented the sound system in the language when it was first used.

3. For sound–spelling correspondences I have drawn on the information in the book by Carney referred to in n. 1.

Appendix: Sources of Citations in ICE-GB

The identity number for each text appears in the left-hand column. If there are subtexts, their numbers appear in the second column. If the second column displays a range of numbers, e.g. 1–5, this indicates that each subtext in the range is derived from the same source.

The identification of participants as extra-corpus indicates that they are excluded from the corpus proper (perhaps because they are not British) but are retained for their contribution to the context. The number of participants and their sex—m(ale) or f(emale)— are noted for conversations.

The descriptions contain some abbreviations. Those that are not universally known and seem to be relevant to an appreciation of the type of text are listed below with their full forms.

AUT	Association of University Teachers
BMA	British Medical Association
CUP	Cambridge University Press
GLR	Greater London Radio
HMSO	Her Majesty's Stationery Office
ITV	Independent Television
LAGB	Linguistic Association of Great Britain
RADA	Royal Academy of Dramatic Art
RSA	Royal Society of Arts
SEU	Survey of English Usage
UCL	University College London
UCLU	University College London Union

S1A-001 to S1A-090: Direct Conversations

S1A-001		Instructor and dance student, Middlesex Polytechnic, Apr. 1991 [m, f]
S1A-002	1	Instructor and dance students, Middlesex Polytechnic, Apr. 1991 [m, 2f]
S1A-002	2	Instructor and dance student, Middlesex Polytechnic, Apr. 1991 [m, f]
S1A-003		Instructor and dance student, Middlesex Polytechnic, Apr. 1991 [m, f]
S1A-004		Instructors at Middlesex Polytechnic, Apr. 1991 [2m]
S1A-005		Student friends, 12 Mar. 1991 [2f]
S1A-006		Workmates, 20 Mar. 1991 [m, f]
S1A-007		Family conversation, 8 June 1991 [3m, 2f]
S1A-008		Friends, 7 June 1991 [m, f]
S1A-009		Mother and son, 2 July 1991 [m, f]
S1A-010		Mother and daughter 5 July 1991 [2f]
S1A-011	1	Friends, 9 June 1991 [m, 2f]
S1A-011	2	Colleagues' conversation, 3 Dec. 1991 [2f]
S1A-012		Conversation among members of a barbershop quartet, 9 June 1991 [4m]
S1A-013		Marketing discussion, Apr. 1991 [2f, 3m]
S1A-014		Friends, July 1991 [m, 2f]
S1A-015		Friends, recorded in a pub, 12 June 1991 [m, f]
S1A-016		Marketing discussion, Apr. 91 [2f, 3m]
S1A-017		Friends, July 1991 [m, 2f]
S1A-018		Friends, 12 Apr. 1991 [m, 2f]
S1A-019		College friends, 2 June 1991 [2m, 4f]
S1A-020		Friends, Aug. 1991 [4m]
S1A-021	1–2	Friends, 3 July 1991 [2m, 2f + 3 extra-corpus]
S1A-022		Family conversation, 10 June 1991 [m, 3f]
S1A-023		Family conversation, 8 Oct. 1991 [m, f]
S1A-024		University professor and PhD student, 7 Nov. 1991 [2m]
S1A-025		Brother and sister, Mar. 1991 [m, f]
S1A-026		Conversation during singing practice, 9 June 1991 [4m]
S1A-027		Friends, 10 Nov. 1991 [2m, 2f]
S1A-028		Birthday party conversation, July 1991 [2m, 3f]
S1A-029		Programmers' conversation at SEU, 15 Nov. 1991 [5m + 1 extra-corpus]
S1A-030		Flatmates' conversation, 21 Nov. 1991 [4m]
S1A-031		Friends, 27 Nov. 1991 [2f]
S1A-032	1–2	Family conversation, 12 Oct. 1991 [2m, 2f]
S1A-033		Careers interview, 4 Mar. 1992 [2m]
S1A-034		Careers interview, 5 Mar. 1992 [m, f]
S1A-035		Careers interview, 5 Mar. 1992 [m, f]
S1A-036		Colleagues, February 1991 [2f]
S1A-037		Student friends, May 1991 [2f]
S1A-038		Flatmates, October 1991 [m, f]
S1A-039		Flatmates, October 1991 [2f]
S1A-040		Flatmates, 7 Dec. 1991 [m, 4f]
S1A-041		Flatmates, 7 Dec. 1991 [2m]
S1A-042		Flatmates, 4 Dec. 1991 [3f]
S1A-043		Friends, 21 Oct. 1990 [2m]
S1A-044		Friends, 21 Oct. 1990 [2m]
S1A-045	1–3	Friends, 23 Apr. 1991 [2m]
S1A-046		Family conversation, Nov. 1991 [2m, 2f]
S1A-047		Christmas dinner family conversation, 25 Dec. 1991 [m, 2f]
S1A-048		Friends, 5 Jan. 1992 [3f]
S1A-049		Friends, 12 June 1991 [3f]

S1A-050		Counselling interview, 26 Feb. 1991 [m, f]
S1A-051	1	Doctor and patient, 12 Nov. 1991 [m, f]
S1A-051	2	Doctor and patient, 12 Nov. 1991 [2m]
S1A-051	3	Doctor and patient, 12 Nov. 1991 [m, f]
S1A-051	4	Doctor and patient, 12 Nov. 1991 [2m]
S1A-052	1–2	Researchers and photographer, June 1991 [3m]
S1A-053		Friends, 6 Jan. 1992 [2m, f]
S1A-054		Friends, 27 Nov. 1991 [2f]
S1A-055		Conversation in canteen, 20 Jan. 1992 [2m, 3f]
S1A-056	1–4	Mealtime conversation, 7 Feb. 1992 [2m, f + 1 extra-corpus]
S1A-057		Birthday party (family), 8 Feb. 1992 [2m, f]
S1A-058	1–2	Family conversation, Jan. 1992 [2m, f, + 1 extra-corpus]
S1A-058	3	Dinner party conversation, Feb. 1992 [m, f]
S1A-059		Counselling interview, Feb. 1991 [2m]
S1A-060		Counselling interview, 10 Oct. 1990 [m, f]
S1A-061		Colleagues' lunchtime conversation, Feb. 1992 [2m]
S1A-062		Counselling interview [m, f]
S1A-063		Colleagues' conversation [2m, 2f]
S1A-064		Conversation among students of speech and drama, Nov. 1991 [3f]
S1A-065		Friends, 18 Nov. 1991 [2f]
S1A-066		Careers interview, 29 Jan. 1992 [m, f]
S1A-067		Friends, 8 Nov. 1991 [2f]
S1A-068		Students' Union Office conversation, 6 Mar. 1992 [2m, f]
S1A-069	1–2	Students' Union Office conversation, 6 Mar. 1992 [m, f]
S1A-070		Students' Union Office conversation, 6 Mar. 1992 [2m]
S1A-071		Conversation in a restaurant, Mar. 1992 [2m, 2f]
S1A-072		Psychology research interview, Apr. 1991 [m, f]
S1A-073		Lunchtime conversation, 10 Nov. 1991 [2m, 2f]
S1A-074	1	Conversation in a travel agent's office, 10 Dec. 1991 [2m, f]
S1A-074	2	Conversation in a travel agent's office, 10 Dec. 1991 [2m]
S1A-074	3	Conversation in a travel agent's office, 10 Dec. 1991 [m, 2f]
S1A-074	4	Conversation in a travel agent's office, 10 Dec. 1991 [2m, f]
S1A-074	5	Office conversation, 10 Feb. 1992 [m, 2f]
S1A-074	6	Office conversation, 10 Feb. 1992 [m, f]
S1A-074	7	Office conversation, 10 Feb. 1992 [2m, f]
S1A-075		Psychology research interview, Apr. 1991 [m, f]
S1A-076		Psychology research interview, Apr. 1991 [m, f]
S1A-077		Office conversation, 24 Mar. 1992 [2m, 2f]
S1A-078	1	UCLU Rights and Advice Office, 6 Mar. 1992 [m, f]
S1A-078	2	UCLU Rights and Advice Office, 6 Mar. 1992 [m, 2f]
S1A-078	3	UCLU Rights and Advice Office, 6 Mar. 1992 [m, f]
S1A-078	4	UCLU Rights and Advice Office, 6 Mar. 1992 [m, 2f]
S1A-079		UCLU Rights and Advice Office, 5 Mar. 1992 [m, 2f]
S1A-080		Friends, May 1992 [2f]

S1A-081		Family conversation, Apr. 1992 [m, f + 1 extra-corpus]
S1A-082		Students of speech and drama, Mar. 1992 [m, 2f]
S1A-083		Tennis coaches, Apr. 1992 [2f]
S1A-084		Students, Mar. 1992 [m, 2f]
S1A-085		Friends, Mar. 1992 [m, f]
S1A-086		Friends, Apr. 1992 [3f]
S1A-087	1–2	Dentist and patient, Mar. 1992 [2m]
S1A-088		Dentist and patient, Mar. 1992 [2m]
S1A-089	1	Dentist and patient, Mar. 1992 [2m]
S1A-089	2–4	Doctor and patient, 12 Nov. 1991 [m, f]
S1A-090	1	Students' conversation, Mar. 1992 [m, 3f]
S1A-090	2	Students' conversation, Mar. 1992 [3f]

S1A-091 to S1A-100: Distanced Conservations

S1A-091		Friends, Aug. 1991 [2f]
S1A-092		Friends, Aug. 1991 [m, f]
S1A-093		Sisters, 26 June 1991 [2f]
S1A-094		Niece and aunt, 28 July 1991 [2f]
S1A-095	1	Brothers, 8 Aug. 1991 [2m]
S1A-095	2	Mother and son, 8 Aug. 1991 [m, f]
S1A-095	3	Brothers, 8 Aug. 1991 [2m]
S1A-095	4	Mother and son, 8 Aug. 1991 [m, f]
S1A-096		Friends, Feb. 1992 [m, f]
S1A-097		Friends, Oct. 1991 [2m]
S1A-098	1	Friends, 4 Dec. 1991 [2f]
S1A-098	2	Friends, 4 Dec. 1991 [m, f]
S1A-098	3	Friends, 4 Dec. 1991 [2f]
S1A-099	1–2	Friends, 20 Jan. 1992 [m, f]
S1A-100	1	Secretary and lawyer, Oct. 1991 [m, f]
S1A-100	2	Secretaries, Oct. 1991 [2f]
S1A-100	3	Friends, 20 Jan. 1992 [2m]

S1B-001 to S1B-020: Classroom Lessons

S1B-001		Jewish and Hebrew Studies, 3rd year, UCL, 16 May 1991
S1B-002		Linguistics, 1st year, UCL, 24 Oct. 1991
S1B-003		Psychology, 1st year, UCL, 22 Oct. 1991
S1B-004		Community Medicine, 2nd year, UCL, 12 Mar. 1991
S1B-005		History, 3rd year, UCL, 18 Nov. 1991
S1B-006		Geology, 1st year, UCL, 28 Oct. 1991
S1B-007		Geography, 2nd year, UCL, 18 Nov. 1991
S1B-008	1–3	Slade School Workshop, 2nd year, UCL, 29 Nov. 1991
S1B-009		Anatomy, 2nd year, UCL, 22 Nov. 1991
S1B-010		Surgery, 4th year, UCL, 19 May 1992
S1B-011		Public Law, 1st year, UCL, 14 Oct. 1991
S1B-012		Linguistics supervision with Ph.D student, Cambridge University, 6 Dec. 1992
S1B-013		Mathematics, 2nd year, UCL, 10 Feb. 1992
S1B-014		History of Art, 1st year, UCL, 16 Oct. 1991
S1B-015		Anatomy, 2nd year, UCL, 29 Nov. 1991
S1B-016		Psychology, 1st year, UCL, 24 Oct. 1991
S1B-017		Archaeology, 3rd year, UCL, 20 Mar. 1992
S1B-018		Slade School Workshop, 2nd year, UCL, 29 Oct. 1991
S1B-019		Greek and Latin, 1st year, UCL, 4 May 1992
S1B-020		Biochemistry, 3rd year, UCL, 11 May 1992

S1B-021 to S1B-040: Broadcast Discussions

S1B-021	1	*Sport on Four*, BBC Radio 4, 27 Apr. 1991
S1B-021	2	*Andrew Neil on Sunday*, LBC Radio, 21 July 1991
S1B-022		*Thames Special: A Question for London*, ITV, 17 June 1991
S1B-023		*Richard Baker Compares Notes*, BBC Radio 4, 27 Apr. 1991
S1B-024		*Start the Week*, BBC Radio 4, 12 Nov. 1990
S1B-025		*Gardeners' Question Time*, BBC Radio 4, 24 Feb. 1991
S1B-026		*Midweek with Libby Purves*, BBC Radio 4, 15 May 1991
S1B-027		*Question Time*, BBC 1 TV, 17 Jan. 1991
S1B-028		*The Persistence of Faith*, BBC Radio 4, 27 Jan. 1991
S1B-029		*Tea Junction*, BBC Radio 4, 5 Apr. 1991
S1B-030		*The Moral Maze*, BBC Radio 4, 27 Apr. 1991
S1B-031		*The Moral Maze*, BBC Radio 4, 2 Apr. 1991
S1B-032		*Richard Baker Compares Notes*, BBC Radio 4, 9 Feb. 1991
S1B-033		*The Scarman Report*, BBC Radio 4, 16 June 1991
S1B-034		*Panorama*, BBC 1 TV, 29 Apr. 1991
S1B-035		*Any Questions?*, BBC Radio 4, 9 Nov. 1990
S1B-036		*Any Questions?*, BBC Radio 4, 2 Feb. 1991
S1B-037		*Issues*, BBC Radio 3, 10 Nov. 1990
S1B-038		*BBC Radio 4 News* (extended Gulf War edition), 30 Jan. 1991
S1B-039		*Andrew Neil on Sunday*, LBC Radio, 13 Oct. 1991
S1B-040		*The Wilson Years*, BBC Radio 4, 31 Oct. 1990

S1B-041 to S1B-050: Broadcast Interviews

S1B-041		*Mavis Catches up with . . . Robert Runcie*, ITV, 13 June 1991
S1B-042	1	*Aspel & Co.*, ITV, 16 Mar. 1991
S1B-042	2	*The Radio 2 Arts Programme*, BBC Radio 2, 9 Feb. 1991
S1B-043		*On the Record*, BBC 1 TV, 25 Nov. 1990
S1B-044	1–2	*Kaleidoscope*, BBC Radio 4, 21 Feb. 1991
S1B-044	3	*Kaleidoscope*, BBC Radio 4, 14 Feb. 1991
S1B-045		*Third Ear*, BBC Radio 4, 7 Jan. 1991
S1B-046		*Desert Island Discs*, BBC Radio 4, 16 June 1991
S1B-047		*The Reith Lecture*, BBC Radio 4, 7 Nov. 1990
S1B-048		*Bookshelf*, BBC Radio 4, 6 Jan. 1991
S1B-049		*Tough Cookies*, BBC Radio 4, 1 Nov. 1990
S1B-050		*Third Ear*, BBC Radio 4, 11 Feb. 1991

S1B-051 to S1B-060: Parliamentary Debates

S1B-051		Hugo Summerson *et al.*, 2 Mar. 1990
S1B-052		Public Expenditure Debate, 8 Nov. 1990
S1B-053		Margaret Thatcher *et al.*, 30 Oct. 1990
S1B-054		Overseas Debate, 25 July 1990
S1B-055		Employment Debate, 26 June 1990
S1B-056		Welsh Debate, 29 Oct. 1990
S1B-057		Employment Debate, 11 Dec. 1990
S1B-058		Tony Newton *et al.*, 26 Nov. 1990
S1B-059		Education/Employment Debate, 24 July 1990
S1B-060	1	Abortion Debate, 2 Apr. 1990
S1B-060	2	Foreign Policy Debate, 16 Jan. 1991

S1B-061 to S1B-070: Legal Cross-Examinations

S1B-061	Court of Chancery, Hansen Engines *v.* Sainsbury, 17 July 1990, cross-examination of plaintiff by defence counsel
S1B-062	Queen's Bench, Hawkes *v.* Arend, 19 Nov. 1990, cross-examination of prosecution witness by plaintiff's counsel and judge
S1B-063	Queen's Bench, Wallings *v.* Customs & Excise, 4 Oct. 1990, cross-examination of defence witness by plaintiff's counsel and judge
S1B-064	Queen's Bench, Lehrer *v.* Lampitt, 5 July 1990, cross-examination of prosecution witness by defence counsel and judge
S1B-065	Queen's Bench, Lehrer *v.* Lampitt, 5 July 1990, cross-examination of defence witness by plaintiff's counsel and judge
S1B-066 1	Queen's Bench, Heidi Hoffmann *v.* Intasun Holidays, 25 Oct. 1990, cross-examination of plaintiff by defence counsel
S1B-066 2	Queen's Bench, Heidi Hoffmann *v.* Intasun Holidays, 25 Oct. 1990, cross-examination of plaintiff's witness by plaintiff's counsel
S1B-067	Queen's Bench, Heidi Hoffmann *v.* Intasun Holidays, 25 Oct. 1990, cross-examination of defence witness by plaintiff's counsel and judge
S1B-068 1	Queen's Bench, Tull *v.* Olanipekun and other, 25 Mar. 1991, cross-examination of police officer by defence counsel and judge
S1B-068 2	Queen's Bench, Tull *v.* Olanipekun and other, 25 Mar. 1991, cross-examination of expert witness by two defence counsels and judge
S1B-069	County Court, Scott Cooper *v.* Manulite, 23 July 1990, cross-examination of defence witness by plaintiff's counsel
S1B-070	Queen's Bench, Hawkes *v.* Arend, 19 Nov. 1990, cross-examination of expert witness by barrister and judge

S1B-071 to S1B-080: Business Transactions

S1B-071		Architect and 2 clients, 4 June 1991
S1B-072		Solicitor and client, 6 June 1991
S1B-073		Builder and 2 clients, 24 June 1991
S1B-074	1–3	Insurance company and client, 25 Mar. 1992
S1B-075		UCL Arts Faculty Meeting, 5 Feb. 1991
S1B-076		Business discussion between SEU and CUP, Jan. 1991
S1B-077		AUT Meeting, UCL, 16 Oct. 1991
S1B-078		UCL Mature Students' Society AGM, 20 Feb. 1992
S1B-079		UCLU Social Committee meeting, 6 Mar. 1992
S1B-080	1–2	Insurance company and clients, 25 Mar. 1992

S2A-001 to S2A-020: Spontaneous Commentaries

S2A-001		*Soccer*, BBC Radio 5, 21 May 1991
S2A-002		*Sport on Five*, BBC Radio 5, 2 Feb. 1991
S2A-003		*Football Extra*, BBC Radio 5, 7 Jan. 1991
S2A-004		*Rugby League*, BBC 1 TV, 10 Nov. 1990
S2A-005	1–5	*The Grand National*, BBC Radio 5, 6 Apr. 1991
S2A-006	1	*The Epsom Derby*, BBC Radio 5, 5 June 1991

S2A-006 2–5   *Racing from Newmarket*, Channel 4, 20 June 1991
S2A-007 1–13 *Athletics*, ITV, 26 July 1991
S2A-008 1   *Snooker*, BBC 1 TV, 11 Feb. 1991
S2A-008 2–6   Meeting of John McCarthy with Perez De Cuellar, LBC Radio, 11 Aug. 1990
S2A-008 7   *Athletics*, ITV, 26 July 1991
S2A-009   *Champion Sport*, BBC Radio 5, 6 Mar. 1991 (boxing)
S2A-010   *International Soccer Extra*, BBC Radio 5, 23 May 1991
S2A-011   *Trooping the Colour*, BBC Radio 4, 15 June 1991
S2A-012 1–7   *Sunday Sport*, BBC Radio 5, 19 May 1991 (motor racing)
S2A-013 1–4   *Sunday Sport*, BBC Radio 5, 19 May 1991 (cricket)
S2A-013 5   *Sunday Sport*, BBC Radio 5, 19 May 1991 (motor racing)
S2A-014   *International Soccer Extra*, BBC Radio 5, 23 May 1991
S2A-015   *LBC Sport*, LBC Radio, 10 Aug. 1991 (soccer)
S2A-016 1–5   *Tour de France*, Channel 4, 20 June 1991
S2A-017   *Capital FM Soccer*, 30 Oct. 1991
S2A-018   *LBC Sport*, LBC Radio, 3 Aug. 1991 (soccer)
S2A-019   *The Gulf Ceremony*, BBC Radio 4, 21 June 1991
S2A-020 1   *The Maundy Thursday Service at Westminster Abbey*, BBC Radio 4, 28 Mar. 1991
S2A-020 2   *National Service of Remembrance and Thanksgiving*, Glasgow Cathedral, BBC Radio 4, 4 May 1991

S2A-021 to S2A-050: Unscripted Speeches

S2A-021   Sir Peter Newsam, 'Teaching the Teachers', Frederick Constable Memorial Lecture, RSA, 22 May 1991
S2A-022   Simon James, 'The Ancient Celts Through Caesar's Eyes', British Museum Lecture, 22 Dec. 1990
S2A-023   John Banham, 'Getting Britain Moving', RSA Lecture, 29 Apr. 1991
S2A-024   Patsy Vanags, 'Greek Temples', British Museum Lecture, 1 May 1991
S2A-025   Dr A. Chandler, 'Earthquakes and Buildings: Shaken and Stirred', UCL Lunchtime Lecture, 14 Mar. 1991
S2A-026   David Jeffries, 'Joseph Hekekyan', UCL Lunchtime Lecture, 7 Feb. 1991
S2A-027   Prof. Hannah Steinberg, 'An Academic's Path through the Media', UCL Lunchtime Lecture, 5 Mar. 1991
S2A-028 1   Wyndham Johnstone, UCL staff training presentation, 10 June 1991
S2A-028 2   Mark David Abbott, UCL staff training presentation, 10 June 1991
S2A-028 3   Dr D. M. Roberts, Introduction to Prof. Peter Cook's Inaugural Lecture, UCL, 1 May 1991
S2A-029 1   Nicole Gower, UCL staff training presentation, 17 June 1991
S2A-029 2   Andy Betts, UCL staff training presentation, 17 June 1991

S2A-029 3   Andrew Newton, UCL staff training presentation, 20 June 1991
S2A-030   John Local, 'Prosodic Phonology' (lecture), 21 June 1991
S2A-031 1   Hilary Steedman, 'Towards a Quality Workforce', RSA Lecture, 23 Jan. 1991
S2A-031 2   Sir John Cassells, 'Towards a Quality Workforce', RSA Lecture, 23 Jan. 1991
S2A-032   John Hutchins, 'Eurotra and Some Other Machine Translation Research Systems', King's College London, 25 Apr. 1991
S2A-033 1   Katy Ash, UCL staff training presentation, 20 June 1991
S2A-033 2   D. R. L. Edwards, UCL staff training presentation, 20 June 1991
S2A-033 3   A. N. Lansbury, UCL staff training presentation, 14 June 1991
S2A-034 1   Andrew Wood, UCL staff training presentation, 17 June 1991
S2A-034 2   Mark Morrissey, UCL staff training presentation, 11 June 1991
S2A-034 3   R. Ramsay, UCL staff training presentation, 11 June 1991
S2A-034 4   Dr Jane Stutchfield, UCL staff training presentation, 20 Dec. 1991
S2A-035 1   Sharon Spencer, UCL staff training presentation, 12 June 1991
S2A-035 2   Lindsay James, UCL staff training presentation, 12 June 1991
S2A-035 3   Harriet Lang, UCL staff training presentation, 4 Dec. 1991
S2A-036   Dr M. Weitzmann, Hebrew and Jewish Studies seminar, UCL, 16 May 1991
S2A-037   Dr D. M. Roberts, 'The Relationship between Industrial Innovation and Academic Research', UCL Lunchtime Lecture, 15 Oct. 1991
S2A-038   Sir Peter Laslett, 'The Third Age', RSA Lecture, 6 Feb. 1991
S2A-039   Andrew Phillips, 'Citizen Who, Citizen How?', RSA Lecture, 27 Mar. 1991
S2A-040   Prof. Peter Cook, 'The Ark', Inaugural Lecture, School of Architecture, UCL, 1 May 1991
S2A-041   Prof. A. L. Cullen, Barlow Memorial Lecture, UCL, 23 Oct. 1991
S2A-042   Prof. Elkins, 'The Immunological Compact Disc', UCL Lunchtime Lecture, 22 Oct. 1991
S2A-043   Prof. Rapley, 'Studying Climate Change from Outer Space', UCL Lunchtime Lecture, 12 Nov. 1991
S2A-044   Prof. Twining, 'Lawyers' Stories', UCL Lunchtime Lecture, 28 Jan. 1991
S2A-045   Gerald Grosvenor, Duke of Westminster, 'Managing a Great Estate', RSA Lecture, 27 Nov. 1991
S2A-046 1   Graham Rose, UCL staff training presentation, 12 Dec. 1991
S2A-046 2   Andrew Shaw, UCL staff training presentation, 19 Dec. 1991
S2A-046 3   Dr Mark Cope, UCL staff training presentation, 20 Dec. 1991

S2A-047		C. Macaskill, UCL staff training presentation, 17 Dec. 1991
S2A-048		Dr Tait, 'Write with Your Hand, Read with Your Mouth: Scribes and Literacy in Ancient Egypt', UCL Lunchtime Lecture, 24 Oct. 1991
S2A-049		Prof. John Burgoyne, 'Creating a Learning Organisation', RSA Lecture, 8 Jan. 1992
S2A-050	1–2	Photojournalist's reminiscences, Apr. 1991

S2A-051 to S2A-060: Demonstrations

S2A-051		Dr C. A. King, 'Movement in the Microscopical World', UCL Lunchtime Lecture, 28 Feb. 1991
S2A-052		George Hart, 'New Kingdom Paintings and Reliefs', British Museum Lecture, 23 Apr. 1991
S2A-053		David Delpy, 'Looking into the Brain with Light', UCL Lunchtime Lecture, 21 Nov. 1991
S2A-054	1–2	'Pass your Motorbike Test' (commercial video, Duke Video Ltd.), 1990
S2A-055	1–3	*Top Gear*, BBC 2 TV, 7 Mar. 1991
S2A-056	1–2	Virginia Ball, demonstration of laryngograph, UCL staff training presentation, 17 Dec. 1991
S2A-057	1–2	Prof. Bindman, demonstration of eighteenth-century caricatures, History of Art Dept., UCL, 16 Oct. 1991
S2A-058	1	Dr Clive Agnew, demonstration of WordPerfect, Dept. of Geography, UCL, 18 Nov. 1991
S2A-058	2	Dr Nick Walton, demonstration of planetary nebulae, UCL staff training presentation, 16 Jan. 1992
S2A-058	3	Avril Burt, demonstration of a wound model, UCL staff training presentation, 16 Jan. 1992
S2A-059		Barbara Brend, 'Persian Manuscripts', British Library Gallery talk, 23 Nov. 1990
S2A-060		Rowena Loverance, 'The Mosaics of Torcello', British Museum talk, 15 Dec. 1990

S2A-061 to S2A-070: Legal Presentations

S2A-061		Queen's Bench, Keays v. Express Newspapers, 11 July 1990, judge's summation
S2A-062		Queen's Bench, Ford v. Kent County Council, 29 June 1990, judge's summation
S2A-063		Queen's Bench, Proetta v. Times Newspapers, 22 June 1990, judge's ruling
S2A-064	1	Slipper v. BBC, Queen's Bench, 26 June 1990, judge's address to prosecution lawyer
S2A-064	2	Slipper v. BBC, Queen's Bench, 26 June 1990, submission by plaintiff's counsel
S2A-065		Queen's Bench, CL Line Inc v. JMS Overseas (St Vincent) Ltd., 20 Mar. 1991, judge's summation
S2A-066	1	Queen's Bench, Astor Chemicals v. GEC Technology, 27 Mar. 1991, judgment
S2A-066	2	Queen's Bench, VHO v. Coral Sea Enterprises, 21 Mar. 1991, judgment
S2A-067		Queen's Bench, Cooke v. Bournecrete, 21 Feb. 1991, judgment
S2A-068	1–2	Queen's Bench, Walling v. Customs & Excise, 4 Oct. 1990, submission by plaintiff's counsel
S2A-069		County Court, Bankruptcy Order, 25 July 1990, judgment
S2A-070		Queen's Bench, 24 Oct. 1990, judgment

S2B-001 to S2B-020: News Broadcasts

S2B-001		*Channel 4 News*, 4 Feb. 1991
S2B-002		*Channel 4 News*, 11 Feb. 1991
S2B-003		*News at Ten*, ITV, 23 Nov. 1990
S2B-004		*The Six O'Clock News*, BBC Radio 4, 2 Feb. 1991
S2B-005		*The Six O'Clock News*, BBC Radio 4, 9 Feb. 1991
S2B-006		*Today*, BBC Radio 4, 7 Nov. 1990
S2B-007		*The World at One*, BBC Radio 4, 5 Nov. 1990
S2B-008		*BBC Radio 4 News*, 17 Jan. 1991
S2B-009		*The World this Weekend*, BBC Radio 4, 25 Nov. 1990
S2B-010		*Newsnight*, BBC 2 TV, 15 Jan. 1991
S2B-011		*News at Ten*, ITV, 23 Nov. 1990
S2B-012		*The PM Programme*, BBC Radio 4, 2 Jan. 1991
S2B-013		*Channel 4 News*, 4 Feb. 1991
S2B-014		*The World this Weekend*, BBC Radio 4, 24 Feb. 1991
S2B-015	1	*Radio Bedfordshire News*, 19 Jan. 1991
S2B-015	2	*Radio Oxford News*, 19 Jan. 1991
S2B-016	1	*LBC Radio News*, 4 Aug. 1991
S2B-016	2	*Capital Radio News*, 25 Feb. 1991
S2B-016	3	*Chiltern Radio News*, 13 Feb. 1991
S2B-016	4	*GLR Newshour*, 7 Nov. 1990
S2B-017		*The World Tonight*, BBC Radio 4, 5 Nov. 1990
S2B-018	1	*The Nine O'Clock News*, BBC 1 TV, 28 Jan. 1991
S2B-018	2	*The World this Weekend*, BBC Radio 4, 24 Nov. 1990
S2B-019		*The World at One*, BBC Radio 4, 1 Nov. 1990
S2B-020	1	*News at One*, BBC 1 TV, 22 Nov. 1990
S2B-020	2	*Newsview*, BBC 2 TV, 24 Nov. 1990

S2B-021 to S2B-040: Broadcast Talks

S2B-021	1–4	LBC Radio, journalists' monologues on presidential wealth, 7 July 1991
S2B-022	1	*The River Thames*, ITV, 21 June 1991
S2B-022	2	*Nature*, BBC 2 TV, 5 Mar. 1991
S2B-023	1	*Can You Steal It?*, BBC Radio 1, 2 Mar. 1991
S2B-023	2	*Spirit Level*, Radio Oxford, 20 Jan. 1991
S2B-023	3	*From Our Own Correspondent*, BBC Radio 4, 27 Apr. 1991
S2B-024	1	*Viewpoint '91: Poles Apart*, ITV, 30 Apr. 1991
S2B-024	2	*40 Minutes*, BBC 2 TV, 8 Nov. 1990
S2B-025		*For he is an Englishman*, BBC Radio 4, 5 Feb. 1991
S2B-026		*The World of William*, BBC Radio 4, 5 Nov. 1990
S2B-027		*Castles Abroad*, ITV, 21 June 1991
S2B-028	1	*Lent Observed*, BBC Radio 4, 19 Mar. 1991
S2B-028	2	*Lent Observed*, BBC Radio 4, 26 Feb. 1991
S2B-029		*The Reith Lecture, No. 2*, BBC Radio 4, 21 Nov. 1990
S2B-030	1	*Address to the Nation*, BBC Radio 4, 17 Jan. 1991
S2B-030	2	*Address to the Nation*, BBC Radio 4, 18 Jan. 1991
S2B-030	3	*Labour Party Political Broadcast*, BBC 1 TV, 13 Mar. 1991
S2B-030	4	*Social Democratic Party Political Broadcast*, Channel 4, 13 Mar. 1991
S2B-031	1–2	*The BBC Radio 4 Debate: The Police Debate*, 10 Feb. 1991

S2B-031	3	*The Week's Good Cause*, BBC Radio 4, 30 Mar. 1991
S2B-032	1	*Opinion: King or Country*, BBC Radio 4, 7 Nov. 1990
S2B-032	2	*The BBC Radio 4 Debate: The Police Debate*, 10 Feb. 1991
S2B-033		*Barry Norman's Film '91*, BBC 1 TV, 12 Mar. 1991
S2B-034		*Analysis*, BBC Radio 4, 16 May 1991
S2B-035	1–2	*The BBC Radio 4 Debate: The Class Debate*, 24 Feb. 1991
S2B-036	1–2	*The BBC Radio 4 Debate: The Class Debate*, 24 Feb. 1991
S2B-037		*The Scarman Report*, BBC Radio 4, 16 June 1991
S2B-038	1	*Medicine Now*, BBC Radio 4, 12 Mar. 1991
S2B-038	2	*Medicine Now*, BBC Radio 4, 19 Mar. 1991
S2B-038	3	*The Week's Good Cause*, BBC Radio 4, 17 Mar. 1991
S2B-039	1–3	*From Our Own Correspondent*, BBC Radio 4, 2 Apr. 1991
S2B-040	1–3	*From Our Own Correspondent*, BBC Radio 4, 27 Apr. 1991

S2B-041 to S2B-050: Scripted Speeches

S2B-041	1	The Queen's Speech at the Opening of Parliament, 31 Oct. 1991
S2B-041	2	Budget Speech, House of Commons, 19 Mar. 1991
S2B-042		Hugh Denman, 'Is Yiddish a Real Language?', UCL Lunchtime Lecture, 12 Mar. 1991
S2B-043		Dr Wendy Charles, 'Anglo-Portuguese Trade in the Fifteenth Century', Royal Historical Society Lecture, UCL, 11 Oct. 1991
S2B-044	1	Census Office, 'The Census: It Counts Because You Count' (Public information video)
S2B-044	2	Camden Adult Education Authority, Audio Prospectus, 1990–1
S2B-045		Peter McMaster, 'The Ordnance Survey: 200 Years of Mapping and On', RSA Lecture, 10 Apr. 1991
S2B-046		Prof. Freeman, 'Who Owns my Cells?', UCL Lunchtime Lecture, 17 Oct. 1991
S2B-047		Shirley Williams, RSA Lecture, 28 Mar. 1992
S2B-048		Sir Peter Baldwin, 'Transoceanic Commerce', The Thomas Gray Memorial Lecture, RSA, 20 May 1991
S2B-049		Prof. Palmer, 'Firthian Prosodic Phonology', LAGB Lecture, 22 June 1991
S2B-050		Sir Geoffrey Howe, Resignation Speech, House of Commons, 13 Nov. 1990

W1A-001 to W1A-010: Non-Printed: Student Essays

W1A-001	Rodwell, Tom, 'What happened to the British in the 5th and 6th centuries?', 1st year, Dept. of History, UCL, 1991
W1A-002	Monks, T. J., 'Discuss the value of Adamnan's Life of Columba for evidence of the structure of society and the nature of politics in seventh-century Ireland and Scotland', 1st year, Dept. of History, UCL, 1991
W1A-003	Cunnington, Tara, 'To what extent if any did the Franks "rule" Brittany in the early Middle Ages?', 1st year, Dept. of History, UCL, 1991
W1A-004	Lawrence, Anthony, 'Amnesia: Theory and Research', 3rd year, Dept. of Psychology, UCL, 1991
W1A-005	Elkan, David, 'Programs for the Survey of English Usage', BA dissertation, Dept. of Computer Science, UCL, 1990
W1A-006	1	Reed, Jacqueline, 'Why is the Milankovitch theory currently favoured as an explanation of glacial/interglacial cycles?', 2nd year, Dept. of Geography, UCL, 1991
W1A-006	2	Tribe, S., 'Outline the principal problems of presentation and interpretation associated with the depiction of statistical data in the form of choropeth maps', 2nd year, Dept. of Geography, UCL, 1991
W1A-007		Beech, Sandra, 'The medical model is alive and well despite numerous criticisms. Discuss', 1st year, Dept. of Psychology, UCL, 1991.
W1A-008		' "Perfect" Man, "New" Woman and Sacred Art', MA dissertation, Dept. of the History of Art, UCL, 1991
W1A-009	1	Vale, Barbara, 'Why has intelligence evolved?', 1st year, Dept. of Psychology, UCL, 1991
W1A-009	2	Plewes, Anthony, 'To what extent, if at all, can a Pictish identity be established?', 1st year, Dept. of History, UCL, 1991
W1A-010		Warner, A., 'Narrative Texts and Intellectual and Cultural Sources', 1st year, Dept. of English, UCL, 1991.

W1A-011 to W1A-020: Non-Printed: Examination Scripts

W1A-011	1–3	2nd year Anthropology, 25 May 1990
W1A-012	1–3	2nd year Anthropology, 25 May 1990
W1A-013	1–3	2nd year Geography of Development and Poverty, 1990
W1A-014	1–2	2nd year Geography of Development and Poverty, 1990
W1A-015	1–4	2nd year Geography of Development and Poverty, 1990
W1A-016	1–3	3rd year Psychology, 23 Apr. 1990
W1A-017	1–3	3rd year Psychology, 1990
W1A-018	1–3	1st year English Literature, May 1991
W1A-019	1–4	3rd year Post-1945 American and European Art, 19 June 1990
W1A-020	1–5	1st year Structural Geology, 1990.

W1B-001 to W1B-015: Non-Printed: Social Letters

W1B-001	1	Sean to Matthew, 1990
W1B-001	2	Sean to Anne-flo, 1990
W1B-001	3	Sean to Darren, 1990
W1B-001	4	Sean to Nordine, 1990
W1B-001	5	Ruthie to Laura, 26 June 1991
W1B-002	1	Jane to Emma, Apr. 1991
W1B-002	2	Bryan to Emma and Ginny, 1991
W1B-002	3	Anne Marie to Emma, 1991
W1B-002	4	Nigel to Emma, 1990

W1B-003	1	Isabelle to 'Thing', 1991
W1B-003	2	Isabelle to D.B. 1991
W1B-004	1	Ruthie to Laura, 18 Apr. 1991
W1B-004	2	Swoo to Laura, 7 July 1991
W1B-004	3	Swoo to Laura, 25 July 1991
W1B-004	4	Ian to Laura, 26 May 1991
W1B-004	5	Ian to Laura, 15 May 1991
W1B-005	1	Mary to Laura, 7 May 1991
W1B-005	2	Isabelle to David, 5 June 1991
W1B-005	3	Joey to Laura, 1991
W1B-005	4	Swoo to Laura, 30 June 1991
W1B-005	5	Swoo to Laura, 27 Sept. 1991
W1B-006	1	Isabelle to Laura, 14 July 1991
W1B-006	2	Isabelle to Laura, 1991
W1B-006	3	Dee to Laura, 1991
W1B-006	4	Ian to Laura, 26 July 1991
W1B-006	5	Andy to friend, 1991
W1B-006	6	Ellie to Laura, 21 June 1991
W1B-007	1–4	Isabelle to Laura, 1991
W1B-008	1–2	Isabelle to Laura, 1991
W1B-008	3	Sean to Françoise, 1990
W1B-008	4	Sean to Anne Marie, 1990
W1B-008	5	Sean to Lydia and Valeria, 1990
W1B-008	6	Sean to Anne-flo, 1990
W1B-008	7	Peter to Simon, 5 Nov. 1990
W1B-009	1	Swoo to Laura, 21 July 1991
W1B-009	2	Swoo to Laura, 14 July 1991
W1B-009	3	Ruthie to Simon, 2 Aug. 1991
W1B-009	4	Jane to Laura, 5 Aug. 1991
W1B-009	5	Ellie to Laura, 24 July 1991
W1B-010	1	Isabelle to D.B., 20 June 1991
W1B-010	2	Jane to F.F., 23 July 1991
W1B-010	3	Gill to Laura, 11 Aug. 1991
W1B-010	4	Dee to Laura, 5 Aug. 1991
W1B-011	1	B.C. to Bea and Dera, 13 July 1991
W1B-011	2	B.C. to Mike, 24 Aug. 1991
W1B-011	3	Ellie to Laura, 1991
W1B-012	1	B.C. to Mike, 18 Aug. 1991
W1B-012	2	B.C. to Mike, 12 Aug. 1991
W1B-013	1	B.C. to Mike, 22 Aug. 1991
W1B-013	2	B.C. to Rachel, 19 June 1991
W1B-013	3	Helen to Laura, 20 Aug. 1991
W1B-014	1	June to Yibin, 23 Aug. 1991
W1B-014	2	June to Yibin, 12 Aug. 1991
W1B-014	3	Alan to Yibin, 25 Aug. 1991
W1B-014	4	Tony to Yibin, 28 Aug. 1991
W1B-014	5	Nichola to Laura, 7 Sept. 1991
W1B-014	6	Karen to Laura, 1991
W1B-014	7	A. A. Leigh to Tony and Joan, 7 Dec. 1990
W1B-014	8	A. A. Leigh to Gordon, 14 Apr. 1991
W1B-015	1–3	Andy to friend, 1991
W1B-015	4	Andy to cousin, 1991
W1B-015	5	B.C. to boyfriend, 1991

W1B-016 to W1B-030: Non-Printed: Business Letters

W1B-016	1	RNLI to Emma Whitby-Smith, 19 Mar. 1991
W1B-016	2	Bank to client, 19 Feb. 1991
W1B-016	3	Financial advisers to client, 29 Apr. 1991
W1B-016	4	Job applicant to interview board, 31 Jan. 1991
W1B-016	5	Linguistics Society to member, 20 June 1991
W1B-016	6	Museum to job applicant, 3 July 1991

W1B-016	7	BBC to SEU, 3 July 1991
W1B-016	8	Client to building contractor, 4 July 1991
W1B-016	9	Client to solicitor, 5 Nov. 1990
W1B-016	10	Letter from Army Squadron, 10 Aug. 1991
W1B-017	1	Doctor to company, 2 Jan. 1991
W1B-017	2	Doctor to colleague, 8 Jan. 1991
W1B-017	3	Doctor to colleague, 11 Jan. 1991
W1B-017	4	Doctor to architect, 18 Jan. 1991
W1B-017	5	Doctor to colleague, 21 Jan. 1991
W1B-017	6	Doctor to student, 21 Jan. 1991
W1B-017	7	Doctor to colleague, 30 Jan. 1991
W1B-017	8	Doctor to patient, 1 Feb. 1991
W1B-017	9	Doctor to company, 5 Feb. 1991
W1B-017	10	Doctor to student, 20 Feb. 1991
W1B-017	11	Doctor to student, 20 Feb. 1991
W1B-017	12	Doctor to architect, 7 Mar. 1991
W1B-017	13	Doctor to colleague, 14 Mar. 1991
W1B-017	14	Doctor to company, 18 Mar. 1991
W1B-017	15	Doctor to colleague, 20 Mar. 1991
W1B-017	16	Doctor to patient, 5 Apr. 1991
W1B-017	17	Doctor to patient, 5 Apr. 1991
W1B-017	18	Doctor to colleague, 18 Apr. 1991
W1B-017	19	Doctor to colleague, 29 Mar. 1991
W1B-017	20	Doctor to company, 7 May 1991
W1B-017	21	Doctor to colleague, 8 May 1991
W1B-018	1	Doctor to colleague, 15 May 1991
W1B-018	2	Doctor to patient, 15 May 1991
W1B-018	3	Doctor to colleague, 16 May 1991
W1B-018	4	Doctor to colleague, 16 May 1991
W1B-018	5	Doctor to colleague, 29 May 1991
W1B-018	6	Doctor to colleague, 30 May 1991
W1B-018	7	Doctor to student, 4 June 1991
W1B-018	8	Doctor to colleague, 7 June 1991
W1B-018	9	Doctor to colleagues (circular), 18 July 1991
W1B-018	10	Doctor to student, 25 July 1991
W1B-018	11	Doctor to student, 26 July 1991
W1B-018	12	Doctor to colleague, 26 July 1991
W1B-018	13	Doctor to colleague, 26 July 1991
W1B-018	14	Doctor to colleague, 26 July 1991
W1B-018	15	Doctor to student, 26 July 1991
W1B-018	16	Theatre manager to theatre company, 12 Apr. 1991
W1B-018	17	Theatre manager to company, 11 Apr. 1991
W1B-018	18	Theatre manager to personnel office, UCL, 5 Apr. 1991
W1B-018	19	Theatre deputy manager to job applicant, 8 Mar. 1991
W1B-018	20	Theatre deputy manager to company, 8 Mar. 1991
W1B-018	21	Theatre accountant to bank, 4 Mar. 1991
W1B-019	1	Bookshop manager to customer, 19 Apr. 1991
W1B-019	2	Bookshop operations director to customer, 22 Apr. 1991
W1B-019	3	Bookshop sales manager to company, 9 Aug. 1990
W1B-019	4	Bookshop personnel officer to job applicant, 25 June 1991
W1B-019	5	Bookshop personnel officer to job applicant, 31 July 1991
W1B-019	6	Bookshop personnel officer to job applicant, 12 Aug. 1991

W1B-019	7	Bookshop personnel officer to job applicant, 12 Aug. 1991
W1B-019	8	Tourist Authority to client, 12 Apr. 1991
W1B-019	9	Tourist Authority to client, 8 Feb. 1990
W1B-019	10	Tourist Authority to client, 2 Aug. 1991
W1B-019	11	Tourist Authority to client, 30 July 1991
W1B-020	1	Client to accountant, 10 July 1991
W1B-020	2	Client to security company, 1 Feb. 1990
W1B-020	3	Client to insurance company, 28 Jan. 1991
W1B-020	4	Client to Electricity Board, 23 Jan. 1990
W1B-020	5	Client to solicitor, 25 Apr. 1990
W1B-020	6	Letter to planning officer, 4 Feb. 1990
W1B-020	7	Letter to colleague, 1 May 1990
W1B-020	8	Client to solicitor, 3 July 1990
W1B-020	9	Letter to neighbour, 3 July 1990
W1B-021	1	Theatre manager to insurance company, 14 Feb. 1991
W1B-021	2	Theatre manager to theatre group, 31 May 1991
W1B-021	3	Theatre administrator to accountant, 30 May 1991
W1B-021	4	Theatre manager to electrical engineer, 31 May 1991
W1B-021	5	Theatre front-of-house manager to company, 29 May 1991
W1B-021	6	Theatre manager to job applicant, 15 Apr. 1991
W1B-021	7	Theatre manager to Finance Manager, 14 May 1991
W1B-021	8	Theatre manager to Film Institute, 14 May 1991
W1B-021	9	Theatre manager to colleague, 2 May 1991
W1B-021	10	Theatre deputy manager to whom it may concern, 17 Apr. 1991
W1B-021	11	Theatre technician to RADA, 12 Apr. 1991
W1B-022	1	Librarian to publisher, 5 Nov. 1990
W1B-022	2	Librarian to publisher, 20 Dec. 1990
W1B-022	3	Client to accountant, 12 Feb. 1991
W1B-022	4	Client to accountant, 20 June 1991
W1B-022	5	Client to accountant, 2 July 1991
W1B-022	6	Accountant to client, 15 Feb. 1991
W1B-022	7	Accountant to client, 8 Mar. 1991
W1B-022	8	Accountant to client, 26 Apr. 1991
W1B-022	9	Accountant to client, 8 May 1991
W1B-022	10	Accountant to client, 18 June 1991
W1B-022	11	Accountant to client, 28 June 1991
W1B-022	12	Client to estate agent, 13 Mar. 1990
W1B-022	13	Lecturer to college administrator, 1991
W1B-022	14	Lecturer to college administrator, 1991
W1B-023	1	Accountant to Inspector of Taxes, 20 June 1990
W1B-023	2	Accountant to client, 14 Dec. 1990
W1B-023	3	Accountant to Inspector of Taxes, 6 Feb. 1991
W1B-023	4	Accountant to Inspector of Taxes, 18 Mar. 1991
W1B-023	5	Accountant to client, 20 Mar. 1991
W1B-023	6	Accountant to Inspector of Taxes, 21 Mar. 1991
W1B-023	7	Accountant to client, 4 Apr. 1991
W1B-023	8	Accountant to client, 7 May 1991
W1B-023	9	Accountant to Inspector of Taxes, 17 June 1991
W1B-023	10	Accountant to client, 17 June 1991
W1B-023	11	Accountant to client, 17 June 1991
W1B-023	12	Accountant to client, 17 June 1991
W1B-023	13	Accountant to Inspector of Taxes, 25 June 1991
W1B-023	14	Accountant to client, 27 June 1991
W1B-023	15	Union president to union member, 19 Apr. 1991
W1B-024	1	Union president to union members (circular), 26 Jan. 1990
W1B-024	2	Union president to Research Council, 3 Feb. 1990
W1B-024	3	Union president to College Finance Office, 19 Mar. 1990
W1B-024	4	Union president to College management, 26 Mar. 1990
W1B-024	5	Union president to union members (circular), 21 Feb. 1991
W1B-024	6	Union president to Council member, 8 Mar. 1991
W1B-024	7	Union president to union member, 13 Mar. 1991
W1B-024	8	Union president to union member, 19 Apr. 1991
W1B-024	9	Union president to union member, 19 Apr. 1991
W1B-025	1	Research director to colleague, 1991
W1B-025	2	Research director to colleague, 1991
W1B-025	3	Research director to publisher, 1991
W1B-025	4	Research director to publisher, 1991
W1B-025	5	Research director to publisher, 1991
W1B-025	6	Union president to union members (circular), 29 May 1991
W1B-025	7	Union president to union members, 10 June 1991
W1B-025	8	Union president to BMA, 24 June 1991
W1B-025	9	Letter to planning officer, 26 June 1991
W1B-026	1	Careers adviser to company, 24 Apr. 1990
W1B-026	2	Careers adviser to company, 19 June 1990
W1B-026	3	Careers adviser to company, 23 Aug. 1990
W1B-026	4	Careers adviser to company, 13 Sept. 1990
W1B-026	5	Careers adviser to company, 21 Sept. 1990
W1B-026	6	Careers adviser to company, 30 Nov. 1990
W1B-026	7	Careers adviser to company, 12 Dec. 1990
W1B-026	8	Careers adviser to company, 12 Dec. 1990
W1B-026	9	Careers adviser to company, 7 May 1991
W1B-026	10	Letter to local authority, 15 May 1991
W1B-026	11	Client to company, 14 Dec. 1990
W1B-026	12	Client to insurance company, 26 Aug. 1990
W1B-026	13	Letter to bowling club, 18 Apr. 1991
W1B-026	14	Letter to bowling club, 1 May 1991
W1B-026	15	Client to travel agent, 28 Jan. 1991
W1B-026	16	Client to bank, 15 Apr. 1991
W1B-026	17	Letter to academic society, 14 Dec. 1990
W1B-026	18	Client to insurance company, 16 Feb. 1991
W1B-026	19	Letter to bowling club, 25 Apr. 1991
W1B-026	20	Letter to bowling club, 7 Feb. 1990
W1B-027	1	Letter to colleague, 22 May 1990
W1B-027	2	Letter to Criminology Society, 19 Jan. 1990
W1B-027	3	Letter to local authority, 26 Feb. 1990
W1B-027	4	Letter to chief planner, 6 July 1991
W1B-027	5	Letter to editor, RIPA Report, 5 Oct. 1990
W1B-027	6	Client to insurance company, 6 Aug. 1990
W1B-027	7	Client to construction company, 25 Aug. 1990
W1B-027	8	Client to construction company, 14 Feb. 1990
W1B-027	9	Client to decorators, 8 Apr. 1991
W1B-027	10	Client to suppliers, 8 Jan. 1990
W1B-027	11	Client to hotel, 3 Mar. 1991
W1B-027	12	Client to clothing company, 10 Feb. 1990
W1B-028	1	Union officer to UCL Security, 15 July 1991
W1B-028	2	Union officer to UCL Safety Office, 9 May 1991

W1B-028	3	Union officer to cleaning company, 28 May 1991
W1B-028	4	Union officer to cleaning company, 21 June 1991
W1B-028	5	Union officer to flooring company, 6 June 1991
W1B-028	6	Union officer to committee, 26 June 1991
W1B-028	7	Union officer to UCL Security, 27 Mar. 1991
W1B-028	8	Union officer to UCLU Film Society, 15 July 1991
W1B-028	9	Union officer to police, 26 June 1991
W1B-028	10	Letter to district council, 1991
W1B-028	11	Client to bank, 1991
W1B-028	12	Client to insurance company, 1991
W1B-028	13	Letter to Economics Association, 1991
W1B-029	1	Acting managing director to Finance Division, 28 June 1991
W1B-029	2	Managing director to academic, 22 May 1991
W1B-029	3	Acting managing director to colleague, 1 Feb. 1991
W1B-029	4	Acting managing director to academic, 25 Jan. 1991
W1B-029	5	Businessman to patent agent, 18 Jan. 1991
W1B-029	6	Theatre deputy manager to security officer, 2 Apr. 1991
W1B-030	1	Businessman to client, 21 Sept. 1990
W1B-030	2	Businessman to client, 11 Sept. 1990
W1B-030	3	Businessman to academic, 7 Jan. 1991
W1B-030	4	Education administrator to conference delegate, 21 June 1991
W1B-030	5	Conference co-ordinator to delegate, 15 May 1991
W1B-030	6	Conference co-ordinator to delegate, 11 May 1991
W1B-030	7	Continuing Education co-ordinator to academic, 31 July 1991

W2A-001 to W2A-010: Printed: Learned: Humanities

W2A-001	Brunt, P. A., *Roman Imperial Themes*, Clarendon Press (1990), 110–17
W2A-002	Collier, Peter, 'The Unconscious Image', in Peter Collier and Judith Davies (eds.), *Modernism and the European Unconscious*, Polity Press (1990), 20–7
W2A-003	Davidson, Graham, *Coleridge's Career*, Macmillan (1990), 1–6
W2A-004	Hill, Leslie, *Beckett's Fiction: In Different Words*, Cambridge University Press (1990), 1–8
W2A-005	Haldane, John, 'Architecture, Philosophy and the Public World', *The British Journal of Aesthetics*, 30/3 (July 1990), 4–10
W2A-006	Hutton, Ronald, *The British Republic, 1649–1660*, Macmillan (1990), 25–31
W2A-007	Jackson, Bernard S., 'Narrative Theories and Legal Discourse', in Christopher Nash (ed.), *Narrative in Culture: The Uses of Storytelling in the Sciences, Philosophy, and Literature*, Routledge (1990), 23–31
W2A-008	McKitterick, Rosamond, 'Carolingian Uncial: A Context for the Lothar Psalter', *The British Library Journal*, 16/1 (Spring 1990), 1–9
W2A-009	Onions, John, *English Fiction and Drama of the Great War, 1918–1939*, Macmillan (1990), 30–7

W2A-010	Vale, Malcolm, *The Angevin Legacy and the Hundred Years War 1250–1340*, Blackwell (1990), 175–82

W2A-011 to W2A-020: Printed: Learned: Social Sciences

W2A-011	Campbell, Adrian, and Warner, Malcolm, 'Management Roles and Skills for New Technology', in Ray Wild (ed.), *Technology and Management*, Cassell (1990), 111–17
W2A-012	Barker, Eileen, 'New Lines in the Supra-Market: How Much Can we Buy', in Ian Hamnett (ed.), *Religious Pluralism and Unbelief: Studies Critical and Comparative*, Routledge (1990), 31–7
W2A-013	Mackintosh, Sheila, Means, Robin, and Leather, Philip, *Housing in Later Life: The Housing Finance Implications of an Ageing Society*, SAUS (1990), 109–15
W2A-014	Ferlie, Ewan, and Pettigrew, Andrew, 'Coping with Change in the NHS: A Frontline District's Response to AIDS', *Journal of Social Policy*, 19/2 (Apr. 1990), 191–8
W2A-015	Davenport, Eileen, Benington, John, and Geddes, Mike, 'The Future of European Motor Industry Regions: New Local Authority Responses to Industrial Restructuring', *Local Economy*, 5/2 (Aug. 1990), 129–37
W2A-016	Shannon, John, and Howe, Chris, 'Controlling a Growing Firm', *International Journal of Project Management*, 8/3 (Aug. 1990), 163–6
W2A-017	Bloom, William, *Personal Identity, National Identity and International Relations*, Cambridge University Press (1990), 128–36
W2A-018	Hutter, Bridget M., and Lloyd-Bostock, Sally, ' The Power of Accidents: The Social and Psychological Impact of Accidents and the Enforcement of Safety Regulations', *British Journal of Criminology*, 30/4 (Autumn 1990), 409–17
W2A-019	Calvert, Peter, and Calvert, Susan, *Latin America in the Twentieth Century*, Macmillan (1990), 186–200
W2A-020	King, Anthony D., *Global Cities: Post-Imperialism and the Internationalization of London*, Routledge (1990), 53–9

W2A-021 to W2A-030: Printed: Learned: Natural Sciences

W2A-021	Horan, N. J., *Biological Wastewater Treatment Systems: Theory andOperation*, Wiley (1990), 107–21
W2A-022	Little, Colin, *The Terrestrial Invasion: An Ecophysiological Approach to the Origins of Land Animals*, Cambridge University Press (1990), 86–95
W2A-023	Tucker, Maurice E., and Wright, V. Paul, *Carbonate Sedimentology*, Blackwell (1990), 28–34
W2A-024	Waterlow, J. C., 'Mechanisms of Adaptation to Low Energy Intakes' in G. A. Harrison and J. C.

Waterlow (eds.), *Diet and Disease in Traditional and Developing Societies*, Cambridge University Press (1990), 5–14

W2A-025 Hart, J.W., *Plant Tropisms and other Growth Movements*, Unwin Hyman (1990), 23–32

W2A-026 Smith, P. J., 'Nerve Injury and Repair' in F. D. Burke, D. A. McGrouther, and P. J. Smith, *Principles of Hand Surgery*, Longman (1990), 143–53

W2A-027 Dockray, G. J., 'Peptide Neurotransmitters', in W. Winlow (ed.), *Neuronal Communications*, Manchester University Press (1990), 108–16

W2A-028 Jennings, D. M., Ford-Lloyd, B. V., and Butler, G. M., 'Morphological Analysis of Spores from Different *Allium* Rust Populations', *Mycological Research*, 94/1 (Jan. 1990), 83–8

W2A-029 Kilsby, C. G., 'A Study of Aerosol Properties and Solar Radiation during a Straw-Burning Episode using Aircraft and Satellite Measurements', *Quarterly Journal of the Royal Meteorological Society*, 116/495 (July 1990), pt. B, 1173–85

W2A-030 Park, Chris, 'Trans-Frontier Pollution: Some Geographical Issues', *Geography*, 76/330 (Jan. 1991), 26–32

W2A-031 to W2A-040: Printed: Learned: Technology

W2A-031 Roberts, D., and Roberts, A. M., 'Blind Shaft Drilling at Betws Colliery', *The Mining Engineer*, 149/345 (June 1990), 463–6

W2A-032 Nightingale, C., and Hutchinson, R. A., 'Artificial Neural Nets and their Application to Image Processing', *British Telecom Journal*, 8/3 (July 1990), 81–5

W2A-033 Frost, A. R, 'Robotic Milking: A Review', *Robotica*, 8 (1990), 311–14

W2A-034 Neale, Ron, 'Technology Focus: A Reflow Model for the Anti-Fuse', *Electronic Engineering*, 63/772 (Apr. 1991), 31–40

W2A-035 Campbell, J. A., 'Three Novelties of AI: Theories, Programs and Rational Reconstructions', in Derek Partridge and Yorick Wilks (eds.), *The Foundations of Artificial Intelligence: A Sourcebook*, Cambridge University Press (1990), 237–43

W2A-036 McNab, A., and Dunlop, Iain, 'AI Techniques Applied to the Classification of Welding Defects from Automated NDT Data', *British Journal of Non-Destructive Testing*, 33/1 (Jan. 1991), 11–16

W2A-037 Drury, S. A., *A Guide to Remote Sensing: Interpreting Images of the Earth*, Oxford University Press (1990), 22–43

W2A-038 Knowles, Dick, 'Mapping a Mascot 3 Design into Occam', *Software Engineering Journal*, 5/4 (July 1990), 207–13

W2A-039 Burcher, R. K., 'The Prediction of the Manœuvring Characteristics of Vessels', *Philosophical Transactions of the Royal Society*, 334/1634 (13 Feb. 1991), 79–88.

W2A-040 Lord, C. J. R., 'Brayebrook Observatory, Part 1', *Journal of the British Astronomical Association*, 101/1 (Feb. 1991), 42–5

W2B-001 to W2B-010: Printed: Popular: Humanities

W2B-001 Worsnip, Glyn, *Up the Down Escalator*, Michael Joseph (1990), 127–35

W2B-002 1 Bailey, Martin, *Young Vincent: The Story of Van Gogh's Years in England*, W. H. Allen (1990), 26–32

W2B-002 2 Thomson, Richard, *Camille Pissarro: Impressionism, Landscape and Rural Labour*, The Herbert Press (1990), 19–24

W2B-003 Johnson, Paul, *Cathedrals of England, Scotland and Wales*, Weidenfeld & Nicolson (1990), 48–52

W2B-004 Stark, Graham, *Remembering Peter Sellars*, Robson Books (1990), 183–93

W2B-005 McCormick, Donald, and Fletcher, Katy, *Spy Fiction: A Connoisseur's Guide*, Facts on File (1990), 111–17

W2B-006 Ackroyd, Peter, *Dickens*, Sinclair-Stevenson (1990), 83–8

W2B-007 Sword, Keith, *The Times Guide to Eastern Europe: The Changing Face of the Warsaw Pact*, Times Books (1990), 144–50

W2B-008 Greenfield, Edward, Layton, Robert, and March, Ivan, *The Penguin Guide to Compact Discs*, Penguin (1990), 412–17

W2B-009 Breen, Jennifer, *In Her Own Write: Twentieth-Century Women's Fiction*, Macmillan (1990), 88–103

W2B-010 Rees, Nigel, *Dictionary of Popular Phrases*, Bloomsbury (1990), 142–54

W2B-011 to W2B-020: Printed: Popular: Social Sciences

W2B-011 Nugent, Nicholas, *Rajiv Gandhi: Son of a Dynasty*, BBC Books (1990), 54–60

W2B-012 Lord Young, *The Enterprise Years: A Businessman in the Cabinet*, Headline (1990), 49–55

W2B-013 Icke, David, *It Doesn't Have To Be Like This: Green Politics Explained*, Merlin Press (1990), 46–54

W2B-014 Jones, Terry, 'Credit for Mrs Thatcher', in Ben Pimlott, Anthony Wright, and Tony Flower, *The Alternative: Politics for a Change*, W. H. Allen (1990), 189–93

W2B-015 Watkins, Alan, *A Slight Case of Libel: Meacher v Trelford and Others*, Duckworth (1990), 15–23

W2B-016 Thompson, Peter, *Sharing the Success: The Story of NFC*, Collins (1990), 37–45

W2B-017 Johnson, Paul, *Child Abuse: Understanding the Problem*, Crowood Press (1990), 11–19

W2B-018 McGraw, Eric, *Population: The Human Race*, Bishopsgate Press (1990), 12–26

W2B-019 Holman, Bob, *Good Old George: The Life of George Lansbury*, Lion Publishing (1990), 100–7

W2B-020 Poulter, Sebastian, *Asian Traditions and English Law: A Handbook*, Trentham Books (1990), 129–35

W2B-021 to W2B-030: Printed: Popular: Natural Sciences

W2B-021 Nichols, John, *The Mighty Rainforest*, David & Charles (1990), 56–65

W2B-022 Nicol, Rosemary, *Everything You Need To Know About Osteoporosis*, Sheldon Press (1990), 68–75

W2B-023 Lever, Ruth, *A Guide to Common Illnesses*, Penguin Books (1990), 167–76

W2B-024 Haines, Andrew, 'The Implications for Health', in Jeremy Leggett (ed.), *Global Warming: The Greenpeace Report*, Oxford University Press (1990), 149–57

W2B-025 Gribbin, John, *Hothouse Earth: The Greenhouse Effect and Gaia*, Bantam Press (1990), 154–64

W2B-026 Giles, Bill, *The Story of Weather*, HMSO (1990), 30–42

W2B-027 Mabey, David, Gear, Alan, and Gear, Jackie, *Thorson's Organic Consumer Guide: Food You Can Trust*, Thorsons Publishing Group (1990), 29–35

W2B-028 Sparks, John, *Parrots: A Natural History*, David & Charles (1990), 157–68

W2B-029 Dipper, Francis, 'Earth, Air, Fire, Water, Oil and War', *BBC Wildlife*, 9/3 (Mar. 1991), 191–3

W2B-030 Griggs, Pat, *Views of Kew*, Royal Botanic Gardens, Kew and Channel Four Television (1990), 14–21

W2B-031 to W2B-040: Printed: Popular: Technology

W2B-031 1 Trask, Simon, 'JD800', *Music Technology* (June 1991), 26–32

W2B-031 2 Goodyer, Tom, 'Spirit Studio', *Music Technology* (June 1991), 50–4

W2B-032 Denison, A. C., 'Is Anybody There?', *Practical Electronics* (June 1991), 16–20

W2B-033 Royall, David, and Hughes, Mike, *Computerisation in Business*, Pitman Publishing (1990), 95–102

W2B-034 Poole, Ian, 'The History of Television', *Practical Electronics* (June 1991), 21–4

W2B-035 Ashford, David, and Collins, Patrick, *Your Spaceflight Manual: How You Could be a Tourist in Space within Twenty Years*, Headline Publishing (1990), 33–44

W2B-036 1 Morse, Ken, 'From Little Acorns . . .', *Personal Computer World* (Feb. 1991), 237–8

W2B-036 2 Bancroft, Ralph, 'One of the Crowd', *Personal Computer World* (Feb. 1991), 249–50

W2B-037 Robson, Paul, *The World's Most Powerful Cars*, Apple Press (1990), 1–3

W2B-038 Fox, Barry, 'Digital Compact Cassette: The Whole Story', *Hi-Fi News & Record Review* (Mar. 1991), 41–7

W2B-039 Southgate, T. N., *Communication: Equipment for Disabled People*, Oxfordshire Health Authority (1990), 27–37

W2B-040 Colloms, Martin, 'Transports: The Best on Test', *Hi-Fi News & Record Review* (Mar. 1991), 69–71

W2C-001 to W2C-020 : Press News Reports

W2C-001 1 Brown, Colin, and Jones, Judy, 'Ministers knew of MoD intervention in Wallace affair', *The Independent*, 1 Nov. 1990, p. 2

W2C-001 2 Cusick, James, 'Lockerbie lawyers say timing of TV report "suspicious" ', *The Independent*, 1 Nov. 1990, p. 3

W2C-001 3 Mills, Heather, 'Home Office ready to consider code on rights of prisoners', *The Independent*, 1 Nov. 1990, p. 8

W2C-001 4 Hughes, Colin, 'Pay-offs for dockworkers "400% above original cost" ', *The Independent*, 1 Nov. 1990, p. 5

W2C-001 5 Anon, 'Detective "set up man accused of blackmail" ', *The Independent*, 1 Nov. 1990, p. 5

W2C-002 1 Hogg, Andrew, 'The children who know only war and starvation', *Sunday Times*, 28 Oct. 1990, p. 21

W2C-002 2 Lees, Caroline, 'Heads challenge McGregor on curriculum', *Sunday Times*, 28 Oct. 1990, p. 3

W2C-003 1 Young, Hugo, 'When Tory jaw-jaw turns to war-war', *The Guardian*, 6 Nov. 1990, p. 20

W2C-003 2 Dixon, Norman F., 'Will the trigger pull the finger in the Gulf?', *The Guardian*, 6 Nov. 1990, p. 21

W2C-004 1 Barden, Leonard, 'Karpov slips up', *The Guardian*, 1 Nov. 1990, p. 16

W2C-004 2 Lacey, David, 'United expose Liverpool rearguard', *The Guardian*, 1 Nov. 1990, p. 16

W2C-004 3 Bierley, Stephen, 'Magpies make a big issue of 18m', *The Guardian*, 1 Nov. 1990, p. 16

W2C-004 4 Bateman, Cynthia, 'Soccer', *The Guardian*, 1 Nov. 1990, p. 16

W2C-005 1 Cowe, Roger, 'Yorkshire banks on homely service as it treks south', *The Guardian*, 6 Nov. 1990, p. 14

W2C-005 2 Stoddart, Robin, 'Interest rate hopes lift the market', *The Guardian*, 6 Nov. 1990, p. 14

W2C-005 3 Milner, Mark, 'Bank governor puts regulation at forefront of debate', *The Guardian*, 6 Nov. 1990, p. 14

W2C-006 1 Wintour, Patrick, 'Brittan offers new European option', *The Guardian*, 5 Nov. 1990, p. 1

W2C-006 2 Dyer, Clare, 'Empty chairs prevent replay of Bar victories', *The Guardian*, 5 Nov. 1990, p. 2

W2C-006 3 White, Michael, 'PM plans counter-attack in Queen's Speech debate', *The Guardian*, 5 Nov. 1990, p. 1

W2C-006 4 Brindle, David, 'Boost for hospital building fund', *The Guardian*, 5 Nov. 1990, p. 1

W2C-007 1 'Steel: the cold economic truth', *The Times*, 11 Nov. 1990

W2C-007 2 'Justice for criminals', *The Times*, 10 Nov. 1990

W2C-007 3 'Blood in the oil', *The Times*, 13 Nov. 1990

W2C-008 1 'Well met in Moscow', *The Times*, 12 Nov. 1990

W2C-008 2 'The son rises', *The Times*, 12 Nov. 1990

W2C-008 3 'Chancellor buys votes', *The Times*, 9 Nov. 1990

W2C-008 4 'Testing the UN', *The Times*, 9 Nov. 1990

W2C-009 1 Morris, Nigel, 'Subsidy cut spells woe', *Wembley Observer*, 27 Dec. 1990, p. 1

W2C-009 2 Morris, Nigel, 'Centre gets a last chance', *Wembley Observer*, 27 Dec. 1990, p. 2

W2C-009 3 Morris, Nigel, 'Taxpayers' card "bribe"', *Wembley Observer*, 27 Dec. 1990, p. 3

W2C-009 4 Anon, 'Weather aborts poll tax march', *Wembley Observer*, 27 Dec. 1990, p. 3

W2C-009 5 Anon, 'Still barred from committee service', *Wembley Observer*, 27 Nov. 1990, p. 3

W2C-009 6 Porter, Toby, 'Ambulance service in crisis: claim', *Wembley Observer*, 27 Nov. 1990, p. 5

W2C-009 7 White, Marcia, 'Streets sweep nets 68 truants', *Wembley Observer*, 27 Nov. 1990, p. 7.

W2C-010 1 Scobie, William, 'Secret army's war on the Left', *The Observer*, 18 Nov. 1990, p. 11

W2C-010 2 Flint, Julie, 'Lebanon sets its hopes on the Second Republic', *The Observer*, 18 Nov. 1990, p. 16

W2C-011 1 Court reporter, 'Killer used knife like a bayonet, court told', *Willesden and Brent Chronicle*, 8 Nov. 1990, p. 1

W2C-011 2 Conroy, Will, 'Police smash drugs ring', *Willesden and Brent Chronicle*, 8 Nov. 1990, p. 5.

W2C-011 3 Walsh, Jennie, 'Residents win first stage of battle to halt development', *Willesden and Brent Chronicle*, 8 Nov. 1990, p. 10

W2C-011 4 Court reporter, 'Judge sends armed robber to secure special hospital', *Willesden and Brent Chronicle*, 8 Nov. 1990, p. 13

W2C-012 1 Beugge, Charlotte, 'Home thoughts on insurance for going abroad', *Daily Telegraph*, 19 Jan. 1991, p. 19

W2C-012 2 Hughes, Duncan, 'Wartime Investments', *Daily Telegraph*, 19 Jan. 1991, p. 19

W2C-012 3 Whetnall, Norman, 'Shares end in state of uneasy calm', *Daily Telegraph*, 19 Jan. 1991, p. 21

W2C-012 4 Cowie, Ian, 'Reality as euphoria starts to evaporate', *Daily Telegraph*, 19 Jan. 1991, p. 23

W2C-012 5 Rankine, Kate, 'Tace chief agrees to quit in March', *Daily Telegraph*, 19 Jan. 1991, p. 23

W2C-013 1 Osborne, Peter, 'Dealers batten down the hatches', *Evening Standard*, 16 Jan. 1991, p. 23

W2C-013 2 Smith, Paul, 'Dealing slump puts jobs in firing line', *Evening Standard*, 16 Jan. 1991, p. 25

W2C-013 3 McCrystal, Amanda, 'Europe dodges the credit rating knife', *Evening Standard*, 16 Jan. 1991, p. 25

W2C-013 4 Hamilton, Kirstie, 'Murdoch faces new debt crisis', *Evening Standard*, 16 Jan. 1991, p. 26

W2C-013 5 Blackstone, Tim, 'First Leisure in the money', *Evening Standard*, 16 Jan. 1991, pp. 26–7

W2C-014 1 Hart, Michael, 'Salako expects to finish the job', *Evening Standard*, 22 Jan. 1991, p. 50

W2C-014 2 Stammers, Steve, 'Clark finds small consolation', *Evening Standard*, 22 Jan. 1991, p. 50

W2C-014 3 Thicknesse, John, 'Gooch's timely win', *Evening Standard*, 22 Jan. 1991, p. 51

W2C-014 4 Blackman, Peter, 'Graf meets her match', *Evening Standard*, 22 Jan. 1991, p. 51

W2C-014 5 Jones, Chris, 'Ryan in the clear over Buckton injury', *Evening Standard*, 22 Jan. 1991, p. 51

W2C-014 6 Allen, Neil, ' "Famous Five" go off to form their own club', *Evening Standard*, 22 Jan. 1991, p. 51

W2C-015 1 McKenzie, Eric, 'Steel plant union leader vows to fight on', *The Scotsman*, 25 Feb. 1991, p. 6

W2C-015 2 Scott, David, 'Council house mortgage plan seen as threat to rural areas', *The Scotsman*, 25 Feb. 1991, p. 6

W2C-015 3 Wilson, Sarah, 'Region acts over racial fostering problem', *The Scotsman*, 25 Feb. 1991, p. 7

W2C-015 4 Kennedy, Linda, 'Rat clearance plan to lure puffins back to island', *The Scotsman*, 25 Feb. 1991, p. 7

W2C-015 5 Chisholm, William, 'Tenants launch campaign to block homes sell-off', *The Scotsman*, 25 Feb. 1991, p. 7

W2C-016 1 Houlder, Vanessa, 'L&M turns 134m of debt into equity', *Financial Times*, 25 Feb. 1991, p. 19

W2C-016 2 Lascelles, David, 'Banks hope to net a saving', *Financial Times*, 25 Feb. 1991, p. 19

W2C-016 3 Rawstorne, Philip, 'Reduced importance of the brewer's pub tie', *Financial Times*, 25 Feb. 1991, p. 20

W2C-017 1 Payton, Richard, 'Youngsters find it tough to buy home', *Western Mail*, 2 Mar. 1991, p. 4

W2C-017 2 Anon, 'Car hit couple on country road', *Western Mail*, 2 Mar. 1991, p. 4

W2C-017 3 Betts, Clive, 'Joint bid may force out HTV', *Western Mail*, 2 Mar. 1991, p. 5

W2C-017 4 Anon, 'Traffic plan for town opposed', *Western Mail*, 2 Mar. 1991, p. 7

W2C-017 5 'Top scientist will launch county's space age project', *Western Mail*, 2 Mar. 1991, p. 7

W2C-018 1 McGregor, Stephen, 'Decisions, decisions: Major faced with double dilemma after poll disaster', *Glasgow Herald*, 9 Mar. 1991, p. 1

W2C-018 2 Clark, William, MacDonald, George, 'No Tory seat is safe, says Hattersley', *Glasgow Herald*, 9 Mar. 1991, p. 7

W2C-018 3 Horsburgh, Frances, 'More interest kindled in plan to assist tenants buying home', *Glasgow Herald*, 9 Mar. 1991, p. 3

W2C-019 1 Anon, 'Street fights injure eight in Belgrade', *Yorkshire Post*, 12 Mar. 1991, p. 5

W2C-019 2 Anon, 'Yeltsin under fresh attack by hardliners', *Yorkshire Post*, 12 Mar. 1991, p. 5

W2C-019 3 'Crackdown in troubled townships', *Yorkshire Post*, 12 Mar. 1991, p. 5

W2C-019 4 'Mandela witness "in dream world"', *Yorkshire Post*, 12 Mar. 1991, p. 5

W2C-019 5 Braude, Jonathan, 'Boatpeople talks planned', *Yorkshire Post*, 12 Mar. 1991, p. 5

W2C-019 6 'Wife's nose for trouble', *Yorkshire Post*, 12 Mar. 1991, p. 5

W2C-019 7 'Flat deaths tragedy', *Yorkshire Post*, 12 Mar. 1991, p. 5

W2C-020 1 Deans, John, 'Council tax will still punish the big spenders', *Daily Mail*, 22 Apr. 1991, pp. 1–2

W2C-020 2 Harris, Paul, 'Charles looks to happy days at Happylands', *Daily Mail*, 22 Apr. 1991, p. 3

W2C-020 3 ' "Graffiti art" student joined gang of spray can raiders', *Daily Mail*, 22 Apr. 1991, p. 5

W2C-020 4 Rose, Peter, 'Jogger mystery after "perfect son" murder', *Daily Mail*, 22 Apr. 1991, p. 5

W2C-020 5 'Laureate too ill for royal poem', *Daily Mail*, 22 Apr. 1991, p. 2

W2C-020 6 'Major belt for Owen', *Daily Mail*, 22 Apr. 1991, p. 2

W2C-020 7 'Travel in London dearest in Europe', *Daily Mail*, 22 Apr. 1991, p. 2

W2D-001 to W2D-010: Printed:

Administrative/Regulatory

W2D-001 Department of Social Security, 'NHS Sight Tests and Vouchers for Glasses', HMSO (Apr. 1990), 4–11

W2D-002 Department of Social Security, 'Unemployment Benefit', HMSO (Apr. 1990), 11–16

W2D-003 Department of Education and Science and The Welsh Office, 'Grants to Students: A Brief Guide 1990–1', HMSO (Aug. 1990), 2–11

W2D-004 Department of Social Security, 'National Insurance for Employees', HMSO (Apr. 1990), 2–7

W2D-005 Department of Social Security, 'A Guide to Family Credit', HMSO (Apr. 1990), 4–19

W2D-006 1 British Library Board, 'Regulations for the Use of the Reading Rooms' (July 1990)

W2D-006 2 UCL Library, 'Access and Borrowing Rights for Members of UCL within other Libraries of the University of London' (1990)

W2D-007 London School of Economics and Political Science, 'Calendar 1990–1' (1990), 184–99

W2D-008 University of London, 'Regulations on University Titles', *University of London Calendar 1990–1* (1990), 331–41

W2D-009 Department of Transport, 'Travel Safely by Public Transport', HMSO (Apr. 1991), 2–11

W2D-010 Driver and Vehicle Licensing Agency, 'Registering and Licensing your Motor Vehicle', HMSO (Jan. 1990)

W2D-011 to W2D-020: Printed: Skills/Hobbies

W2D-011 Branwell, Nick, *How Does Your Garden Grow?: A Guide to Choosing Environmentally Safe Products*, Thorsons Publishing Group (1990), 59–63

W2D-012 Collard, George, *Do-it-Yourself Home Surveying: A Practical Guide to House Inspection and the Detection of Defects*, David and Charles (1990), 104–17

W2D-013 Rich, Sue, *Know about Tennis*, AA Publishing (1990), 26–42

W2D-014 Cheshire, David, *The Complete Book of Video*, Dorling Kindersley (1990), 22–7

W2D-015 Hughes, Charles, *The Winning Formula*, The Football Association and Collins Publishing (1990), 108–12

W2D-016 Pipes, Alan, *Drawing for 3-Dimensional Design: Concepts, Illustration, Presentation*, Thames & Hudson (1990), 28–36

W2D-017 Batten, David, *An Introduction to River Fishing*, Crowood Press (1990), 37–42

W2D-018 Carroll, Ivor, *Autodata Car Manual: Peugeot 309 1986–90*, Autodata Ltd. (1990), 29–42

W2D-019 Jackson, Paul, *Classic Origami*, Apple Press (1990), 31–63

W2D-020 Barry, Michael, *The Crafty Food Processor Cook Book*, Jarrold Publishing (1990), 72–86

W2E-001 to W2E-010: Press Editorials

W2E-001 1 'The purpose of the war', *Evening Standard*, 28 Jan. 1991, p. 7

W2E-001 2 'Belittling Europe', *Evening Standard*, 31 Oct. 1990, p. 7

W2E-001 3 'Challenge to tyranny', *Evening Standard*, 16 Jan. 1991, p. 7

W2E-001 4 'A doomed dictator', *Evening Standard*, 22 Jan. 1991, p. 7

W2E-002 1 'Britain at war', *Sunday Times*, 28 Oct. 1990, p. 5

W2E-002 2 'The duty of the banks', *Sunday Times*, 28 Oct. 1990, p. 5

W2E-003 1 'Unity: who can provide it?', *The Guardian*, 5 Nov. 1990, p. 22

W2E-003 2 'The best big bang', *The Guardian*, 5 Nov. 1990, p. 22

W2E-003 3 'More to share than the burden', *The Guardian*, 29 Jan. 1991, p. 18

W2E-004 1 'Heseltine's misguided detractors', *The Independent*, 15 Nov. 1990, p. 26

W2E-004 2 'Bush needs public support', *The Independent*, 15 Nov. 1990, p. 26

W2E-004 3 'A certain election loser', *The Independent*, 1 Nov. 1990, p. 26

W2E-004 4 'Dishonesty at the top', *The Independent*, 1 Nov. 1990, p. 26

W2E-005 1 'The voice of authority', *Daily Telegraph*, 17 Jan. 1991, p. 16

W2E-005 2 'Socialist folly', *Daily Telegraph*, 17 Jan. 1991, p. 16

W2E-005 3 'The epitaph of Sir Geoffrey Howe', *Daily Telegraph*, 14 Nov. 1990, p. 20

W2E-005 4 'Allied advantage', *Daily Telegraph*, 19 Jan. 1991, p. 12

W2E-006 1 'Voters make all kinds of marks', *The Scotsman*, 9 Mar. 1991, p. 10

W2E-006 2 'Galleries in the dark', *The Scotsman*, 9 Mar. 1991, p. 10

W2E-006 3 'Paper warriors', *The Scotsman*, 9 Mar. 1991, p. 10

W2E-006 4 'The final test of Allied aims', *The Scotsman*, 25 Feb. 1991, p. 8

W2E-006 5 'Fighting recession', *The Scotsman*, 25 Feb. 1991, p. 8

W2E-007 1 'Keeping cool while the war hots up', *The Observer*, 27 Jan. 1991, p. 20

W2E-007 2 'A stark choice that can't be avoided', *The Observer*, 13 Jan. 1991, p. 14

W2E-007	3	'Putting justice to rights', *The Observer*, 17 Mar. 1991, p. 20
W2E-008	1	'United in disarray', *Yorkshire Post*, 12 Mar. 1991, p. 10
W2E-008	2	'Unhappy landings', *Yorkshire Post*, 12 Mar. 1991, p. 10
W2E-008	3	'No concessions', *Yorkshire Post*, 9 Apr. 1991, p. 10
W2E-008	4	'While Europe waits', *Yorkshire Post*, 9 Apr. 1991, p. 10
W2E-009	1	'Now let Irish government act', *Daily Mail*, 26 Oct. 1990, p. 8
W2E-009	2	'Exporters love EC', *Daily Mail*, 26 Oct. 1990, p. 8
W2E-009	3	'Embarrassing', *Daily Mail*, 26 Oct. 1990, p. 8
W2E-009	4	'Those who don't ask don't get', *Daily Mail*, 30 Jan. 1991, p. 6
W2E-009	5	'A better way of taxing', *Daily Mail*, 22 Apr. 1991, p. 6
W2E-009	6	'Storming home', *Daily Mail*, 22 Apr. 1991, p. 6
W2E-009	7	'Simple truth', *Daily Mail*, 22 Apr. 1991, p. 6
W2E-009	8	'Mr Heseltine spells it out', *Daily Mail*, 24 Apr. 1991, p. 6
W2E-009	9	'Sanctions must go', *Daily Mail*, 24 Apr. 1991, p. 6
W2E-010	1	'A President adrift', *Sunday Times*, 21 Oct. 1990, p. 7
W2E-010	2	'Over to Major', *Sunday Times*, 19 May 1991, p. 5

W2F-001 to W2F-020: Printed: Creative

W2F-001	Enters, Ian, *Up to Scratch*, Weidenfeld & Nicolson (1990), 80–6
W2F-002	Harris, Steve, *Adventureland*, Headline Publishing (1990), 308–16
W2F-003	Robertson, Denise, *Remember the Moment*, Constable (1990), 182–94
W2F-004	Puckett, Andrew, *Terminus*, Collins (1990), 34–41
W2F-005	Lees-Milne, James, *The Fool of Love*, Robinson Publishing (1990), 86–93
W2F-006	Babson, Marian, *Past Regret*, Collins (1990), 40–6
W2F-007	Thompson, E. V., *Lottie Trago*, Macmillan (1990), 12–19
W2F-008	Sayer, Paul, *Howling at the Moon*, Constable (1990), 142–9
W2F-009	Priest, Christopher, *The Quiet Woman*, Bloomsbury (1990), 8–13
W2F-010	Frame, Ronald, *Bluette*, Hodder and Stoughton (1990), 244–51
W2F-011	Caudwell, Sarah, 'An Acquaintance with Mr Collins', in *A Suit of Diamonds*, Collins (1990), 47–60
W2F-012	Dobbs, Michael, *Wall Games*, Collins (1990), 258–65
W2F-013	Owens, Agnes, 'Patience', in Alison Fell (ed.), *The Seven Cardinal Virtues*, Serpent's Tail (1990), 135–42
W2F-014	Symons, Julian, *Death's Darkest Face*, Macmillan (1990), 199–209
W2F-015	Napier, Mary, *Powers of Darkness*, Bodley Head (1990), 215–28
W2F-016	Clay, Rosamund, *Only Angels Forget*, Virago Press (1990), 98–106
W2F-017	Lambton, Anthony, 'Pig', in *Pig and Other Stories*, Constable (1990), 127–40
W2F-018	Wesley, Mary, *A Sensible Life*, Bantam Press (1990), 355–64
W2F-019	Melville, Anne, 'Portrait of a Woman', in *Snapshots*, Severn House (1990), 1–10
W2F-020	Kershaw, Valerie, *Rockabye*, Bantam Press (1990), 154–61

Glossary

accent   An accent is the set of features of pronunciation that is used by a speaker of the language. A regional accent is an accent that is characteristic of a particular location (e.g. country, city, rural area). A social accent is an accent that is characteristic of a particular social group, which may be defined by educational level or social class. There are also ethnic accents, which are associated with ethnic groups.

accusative case   See **case**.

acronym   An acronym is a word formed from the initial letters of parts of a word or phrase. It may be pronounced as a word (*AIDS*, from *Acquired Immune Deficiency Syndrome*). If it is pronounced as separate letters (*PC*, from *personal computer*), it is sometimes called an initialism or an alphabetism.

active   See **passive**.

adjective   An adjective is a word such as *wise* that typically can premodify a noun such as *decision* (*a wise decision*) and function as **subject predicative** after a **copular verb** such as *be* or *seem* (*The decision is/seems wise*). When used as the premodifier of a noun, the adjective is attributive; when used as subject predicative, it is predicative. Adjectives that can be used both attributively and predicatively are central adjectives. Most adjectives can be intensified by adverbs such as *very* (*very wise/informative*) and permit **comparison** either inflectionally (*wiser, wisest*) or periphrastically (*more informative, most informative*). The inflectional forms are comparative (*wiser*) or superlative (*wisest*). Adjectives that accept intensification and comparison are gradable adjectives. See also **gradability, nominal adjective**.

adjective phrase   An adjective phrase has an adjective such as *heavy* or *informative* as its head. Within the adjective phrase the adjective may be premodified (*too heavy*) or postmodified (*afraid of spiders*) or both premodified and postmodified (*too heavy to carry, extremely afraid of spiders*).

adjunct   An adjunct is an **adverbial** (an optional element) that is integrated to some extent in sentence or clause structure. The major semantic subclasses of adjuncts are space, mainly referring to location (*in* my city) or direction (*to New York*); time, mainly referring to time location (*on Monday*), duration (*permanently*), or frequency (*every week*); process, mainly conveying the manner in which the action denoted by the verb is performed (*smoothly*); focus, adverbials that focus on a particular unit (*only, mainly, utterly*). Adverbials that are not adjuncts are sentence adverbials, either **conjuncts** or **disjuncts**.

adverb   An adverb is a word that typically functions as a premodifier of an adjective or another adverb or as an **adverbial**. *Very* is an adverb that can be a premodifier of an adjective (*very sharp*) or another adverb (*very carelessly*). *Often* is an adverb that functions as an adverbial (*They often complained about the noise*). Many adverbs can be either premodifiers (*too loud, too loudly*) or adverbials (*I too have complained*), though not necessarily with the same meaning. Adverbs that have the same form as adjectives can take **comparison** inflections: comparative ('work *harder*'), superlative ('work *hardest*').

adverbial   An adverbial is an optional element in sentence or clause structure. There may be more than one adverbial in a sentence or clause. Adverbials are either sentence adverbials or **adjuncts**. Sentence adverbials are loosely attached to the sentence or clause. They are either **conjuncts** or **disjuncts**.

adverbial clause   An adverbial clause is a clause that functions as an **adverbial** in sentence or clause structure.

adverb phrase   An adverb phrase has an adverb such as *badly* or *luckily* as its head. The adverb may be premodified (*so quickly, very luckily*), or postmodified (*quickly enough, luckily for me*), or both premodified and postmodified (*very luckily for me*).

affix   An affix is a segment that is not itself a word but is attached to a word. If it is attached to the beginning of a word it is a prefix (*un-* in *undecided*), and if it is attached to the end of a word it is a suffix (*-ize* in *polarize*). Suffixes that represent grammatical categories, such as plural for nouns and past for verbs, are inflections (*-s* in *computers* and *-ed* in *revealed*). The process of adding affixes to form new words is affixation or derivation.

allomorph   An allomorph is a variant form of the same **morpheme**. For example, there is a negative prefix whose usual allomorph is *in-* (*incompetent*), but it also has allomorphs in *il-* (*illegal*), *im-* (*impatient*), and *ir-* (*irregular*). In phonetic conditioning, the choice of allomorph is determined by a neighbouring sound (as in the allomorphs of the negative prefix *in-*). In lexical conditioning, the choice depends on the particular word (the *-en* inflection in *taken*). In grammatical conditioning, the variation depends on the grammatical class of the word (the different stress pattern—and consequent pronunciation differences—of the verb *rebel* and the noun *rebel*). In stylistic conditioning, the choice of allomorph depends on the style (the informal contraction *n't* in *isn't*).

allophone   An allophone is a pronunciation variant of the same **phoneme** (abstract sound unit). Allophonic variation may depend on the sound that precedes or follows an allophone (the different way that /l/ is usually pronounced in *lick* and *milk*). Very often allophones are in free variation, varying with the same speaker on different occasions. Differences in pronunciation are also affected by physical differences between speakers as well as by general differences in sex and age.

alphabetism   See **acronym**.

alternative condition   An alternative condition presents two or more conditions ('*Whether you buy the house or rent it*, you'll find the monthly payments too expensive').

alternative question   An alternative question offers two or more choices for the response (*Do you want to stay a little longer or go home straightaway? Which would you prefer, coffee or tea?*).

anaphoric   Anaphoric reference is a reference to a preceding expression (*it* referring to *a draft* in *I'll write a draft and show it to you for your comments*). Cataphoric reference is a reference to a following expression (*she* referring to *the doctor* in *As soon as she had finished questioning the patient, the doctor phoned for an ambulance*). See also **deixis**, **ellipsis**.

antecedent   The antecedent of an expression is the expression that it refers to. The antecedent of *who* in *the official who spoke to us so rudely* is *the official*, and the antecedent of *she* is *the doctor* in *The doctor will see you as soon as she is ready*.

anticipatory *it*   Anticipatory *it* takes the position (usually a subject) that might have been occupied by a clause. Instead of the clausal subject in *That they refused to sign our petition is surprising*, anticipatory *it* is introduced as subject and the clause is extraposed (postponed to the end) in *It is surprising that they refused to sign our petition*.

apposition   Apposition is a relationship between two units that refer to the same entity or overlap in their reference. Typically the units are noun phrases and are juxtaposed (*George Washington, the first president of the United States*). Sometimes an apposition marker introduces the second unit (*namely, that is to say, for example*). In co-ordinative apposition the two units are linked by *or* or (less usually) *and* (*eeg, or brain wave trace*).

aspect Aspect is a grammatical category referring primarily to the way that the time denoted by the verb is regarded. English has two aspects: the perfect aspect and the progressive (or continuous) aspect. The perfect aspect is expressed by a combination of the auxiliary *have* and the *-ed* participle (*has mentioned, have called, had seen*); it is used to locate the time of a situation as preceding that of another situation (*She has mentioned it several times since she arrived*). The progressive aspect is expressed by a combination of the auxiliary *be* and the *-ing* participle (*is mentioning, was calling, were seeing*); it is chiefly used to focus on the duration of a situation (*He was calling for help*). The two aspects may be combined, the perfect followed by the progressive (*He had been calling for help*). See also **participle**.

asyndetic co-ordination See **co-ordination**.

auxiliary An auxiliary (or auxiliary verb or helping verb) is one of a small set of verbs that combine with a **main verb** to form the perfect or progressive **aspect** or the **passive**, or to convey distinctions of modality (such as possibility and permission), and to function as **operator** for forming negative sentences and questions. The three primary auxiliaries are *be, have,* and *do. Be* is used to form the progressive (*was making*) and the passive (*was made*), and *have* to form the perfect (*has made*). *Do* is used to perform the functions of an operator when no auxiliary is otherwise present (*Did they make it?, They didn't make it*). The modals (or modal auxiliaries) are *can, could, may, might, shall, should, will, would, must*. In addition, there are a number of marginal auxiliaries (*dare, need, ought to, used to*) that share some of the characteristics of the auxiliaries and a larger group of semi-auxiliaries (auxiliary-like verbs) that convey similar notions of time, aspect, and modality (e.g.: *be going to, have to, had better*).

back-formation Back-formation is the process (or the result of the process) of deriving new words from existing words by dropping what is thought to be a suffix. Thus, *edit* is a back-formation from *editor* and *diagnose* is a back-formation from *diagnosis*. Most back-formations are verbs coined from nouns.

backshifting Backshifting is a shifting in the tense of the verb of a reported clause in indirect speech. *She said Pam was looking well* reports an utterance such as *Pam is looking well*, where the verb (*is*) is in the present tense. Similarly, the simple past and the present perfect may be backshifted to the past perfect: *Pam played well* and *Pam has played well* may both be reported as *She said Pam had played well*. The present tense may be retained if the situation (including an expressed opinion) holds at the time of reporting: *She said Pam writes well*. Backshifting also takes place in **conditional clauses**.

base The base of a word is the segment to which a prefix or suffix is attached: the suffix *-able* is attached to the base *enjoy*, and the prefix *un-* is attached to the base *enjoyable*. Compounds have more than one base: *dry-clean*. The root of a word is what remains when all affixes are stripped from a word. Thus, *agree* is the root of both *agrees* and *disagreeable*.

base form The base form of the verb is the uninflected form (*remain, take, write*), the form to which inflections are added (*remained, takes, writing*), except that for the highly irregular verb *be* the base form is *be*. The base form is used for: (1) the present tense except for the third person singular (*They remain in good spirits*), but *be* has the equivalents *am* and *are*; (2) the imperative (*Remain here*); (3) present subjunctive (*I recommended that he remain here*); (4) infinitive, which may be the bare infinitive (*You must remain here*) or the *to*-infinitive (*I want you to remain here*).

blend A blend is a word formed from segments of two or more words that have been fused: *brunch* from *breakfast* and *lunch, smog* from *smoke* and *fog*.

bound morph See **morpheme**.

case Case is a grammatical category in which distinctions in the forms of words indicate grammatical relationships between words. In present-day English, case distinctions apply only to nouns and certain pronouns. For nouns, the only case form is the genitive (or possessive) case (as in *man's* and *men's*), all other forms having no inflection (common case). Certain pronouns, chiefly personal pronouns, distinguish between subjective case (*I*, *we*), objective case (*me*, *us*), and genitive case (*my*, *our*), though the genitives of personal pronouns are often separately designated as possessive pronouns. Old English had additional cases and they extended to adjectives and determiners. The cases in Old English (with their characteristic uses) were nominative (for the subject of a sentence or clause), accusative (for the direct object), the genitive, the dative (for the indirect object), and the instrumental (usually not distinct from the dative, to express the means employed in an action or the manner of the action).

cataphoric   See **anaphoric**.

clause   A clause is a construction that typically consists minimally of a subject and a verb (*I laughed*), though in an imperative clause the subject is generally absent but implied, so that minimally only the verb needs to be present (*Sit*). A clause may be within a larger construction: co-ordinated with another clause (the two clauses co-ordinated by *and* in *I paid this time and you can pay next time*), or subordinated within another clause (the subordinate *whether*-clause in *They asked whether I would pay*), or within a phrase (the *that*-clause in the noun phrase *the company that employed me*). In all the examples given so far, the clauses are **finite** in that their verb phrase is finite. But clauses may be non-finite (the infinitive clause in *I wanted to pay*, the *-ing* participle clause in *I enjoy paying*, and the *-ed* participle clause in *They wanted the house sold before the end of the year*) or verbless (the *when*-clause in *When in Rome, do as the Romans do*). A set of clauses interrelated by co-ordination or subordination (or minimally one clause that is independent of any such links) constitutes a sentence (or—a less misleading term for the spoken language—a clause cluster).

clause cluster   See **clause**.

cleft sentence   A cleft sentence is a sentence that is cleft (split) so as to put the focus on one part of it. The cleft sentence is introduced by *it*, which is followed by a verb phrase whose main verb is generally *be*. The focused part comes next, and then the rest of the sentence is introduced by a **relative pronoun**, **relative determiner**, or **relative adverb**. If we take the sentence *Tom felt a sharp pain after lunch*, two possible cleft sentences formed from it are *It was Tom who felt a sharp pain after lunch* and *It was after lunch that Tom felt a sharp pain*.

clipping   Clipping is a shortening of a word by the omission of one or more syllables. What is left may be the beginning of the word (*lab* from *laboratory*), less frequently the end (*bus* from *omnibus*), and rarely the middle (*flu* from *influenza*).

clitic   A clitic is a word that cannot occur independently but must be attached to another word. Clitics in English are contracted forms of words (*n't* for *not*, *'ll* for *will*). Generally they are attached at the end as enclitics (*wasn't*, *we're*), but they may also be attached at the beginning as proclitics (*d'you*, *'tis*). A combination of proclitic and enclitic appears in *'tisn't*.

closed class   Closed classes are in contrast with open classes, and both denote classes of words (or parts of speech) that are required for grammatical description. A closed class is a set of words that is small enough to be listed fully and that does not readily admit new members. The closed classes that are generally recognized for English include **auxiliaries**, **conjunctions**, **prepositions**, **determiners**, and **pronouns**. The four open classes, which readily admit new members, are nouns, adjectives, verbs, and adverbs. Closed-class words are termed grammatical words or function words because of their importance in grammatical relations, whereas open-class words have been called lexical or content words.

coherence   Coherence refers to the continuity of meaning that enables others to make sense of a written text or of a stretch of speech.

cohesion   Cohesion refers to lexical and grammatical devices for linking parts of a written text or spoken discourse. Lexical devices include repetition of words or substitution of synonymous expressions. Grammatical devices include use of pronouns and ellipsis.

co-hyponym   See **hyponymy**.

collective noun   A collective noun denotes a group of people, animals, or institutions. A singular collective noun may be treated as plural (more commonly in British English than in American English) and therefore take a plural verb and (particularly) plural pronouns when the focus is on the group as individuals: *The enemy have brought in more of their paratroops.*

collocation   Collocation refers to the tendency for certain words to co-occur : *wine* with *white, red, dry,* and *sweet*; *agree* with *entirely*; *vicious* with *attack* and *circle.*

combinatory co-ordination   See **co-ordination**.

combining form   A combining form is a segment that does not occur as a separate word but is attached before or after another word or segment to form a new word. Combining forms generally originate from Latin or Greek. Initial combining forms mostly end in -*o* (*psycho-* in *psychopath, socio-* in *sociology, bio-* in *biochemistry*) but other vowels are also found (*tele-* in *television, agri-* in *agriculture*).

common noun   See **proper noun**.

comparative   See **adjective, adverb**.

comparative clause   Comparative clauses are introduced by the subordinators *as* or *than*. They correlate with a preceding comparative element: *more* or the -*er* comparative inflection, *less*, or *as* (*more tolerant than I thought*; *cleverer than his brothers are*; *less important than the other items on the agenda were*; *as tall as she is*).

comparison   Comparison applies to adjectives or adverbs that are gradable. There are three directions of comparison: higher (*taller than Sue*), same (*as tall as Sue*), lower (*less tall than Sue*). There are three degrees of comparison: absolute (*tall*), comparative (*taller*), superlative (*tallest*). The superlative *least* is used to express the lowest direction, *least tall* contrasting with *tallest*.

complement   A complement is a phrase or clause whose form is determined by the word it complements. For example, the verb *asked* in *She asked me three questions* admits two complements: *me* (**indirect object**) and *three questions* (**direct object**), whereas the verb *answered* in *I answered her questions* admits just one complement: *her questions* (direct object).   Apart from direct and indirect objects, complements of verbs may be **subject predicative** (*responsible* in *Jeremy is responsible*) or object predicative (*responsible* in *I consider Jeremy responsible*). Prepositions generally require complements (*my parents* in *from my parents*). Complements also occur with adjectives (*of tomato juice* in *fond of tomato juice*) and nouns (*whether it is hers* in *the question whether it is hers*). See also **preposition**.

complex sentence   A complex sentence consists of a **main clause** that has one or more subordinate clauses. The *that*-clause is a subordinate clause in the complex sentence 'Everybody thought *that he had won*'.

complex-transitive verb   A complex-transitive verb has two complements: a **direct object** and an object predicative: *They named us* (direct object) *the winners* (object predicative). See also **subject predicative**.

compound   A compound is a word formed from a combination of two or more words (strictly speaking, two or more **bases**). Compounds may be written solid (*turncoat, mouthpiece*), hyphenated (*mother-in-law, cook-chill*), or as separate orthographic words (*smart card, junk food*). Noun compounds generally have their main stress on the first word.

compound sentence   A compound sentence is a sentence that consists of two or more **main clauses** (each of which could be an independent sentence) that are linked by co-ordination, the co-ordinator generally being *and, but,* or *or* ('It has only been a week *and* I feel lonesome without you').

conditional clause   Most conditional clauses are introduced by the subordinator *if.* Conditions may be open (or real), leaving completely open whether the condition will be fulfilled (*You're going to be in trouble if you've infected me*). Or they may be hypothetical (or unreal or closed), expressing that the condition has not been fulfilled (for past conditions), is not fulfilled, or will not be fulfilled. Hypothetical conditions take backshifted tenses: for present and future conditions, the past is used in the conditional clause and a past modal (generally *would*) in the host clause ('If I *had* my dictionary, I *would look* up the word'); for past conditions, the **past perfect** is used in the conditional clause and a past perfect modal (generally *would have*) in the host clause ('If I *had seen* them, I *would have invited* them to eat with us'). Subjunctive *were* is sometimes used instead of indicative *was* in the conditional clause, particularly in formal style ('If she *were* here, you would not need me'). Conditional clauses may also have **subject–operator inversion** without a subordinator, generally when the operator is *had, were,* or *should* ('*Had* I known, I would have told you'). See also **backshifting**, **alternative condition**, ***wh*-conditional clause**.

conjunct   Conjuncts are sentence **adverbials** that indicate logical relationships between sentences or between clauses. They are mainly adverbs (e.g. *therefore, however, nevertheless*) or prepositional phrases (e.g. *on the other hand, in consequence, in conclusion*). See also **disjunct**.

conjunction   Conjunctions are either co-ordinators (or co-ordinating conjunctions) or subordinators (or subordinating conjunctions). The central co-ordinators are *and, or,* and *but.* Co-ordinators link units of equal status, which may be clauses or phrases (including single words): *I recognized them, but they didn't remember me; out of work and in trouble; soft or hard.* Often considered as marginal co-ordinators are *nor* and *for.* The co-ordination may be emphasized by a correlative expression: *both . . . and; either . . . or; not (only) . . . but (also); neither . . . nor.* Subordinators link subordinate clauses to their host clauses. Among the many subordinators are *if, since, because, although*: *I can lend you some money if you have none on you.* Subordinators are sometimes emphasized by a correlative expression in the following clause: *if . . . then; because . . . therefore; although . . . nevertheless; whether . . . or; as . . . so.*

connotation   The connotation of a word is the emotive associations that a word evokes, as opposed to its denotation (the meaning relationship that a word has in its reference to entities outside language).

content word   See **closed class**.

continuous   See **aspect**.

converse   The converse of a term is its opposite in a reciprocal relationship: *buy/sell, husband/wife, above/below.*

conversion   Conversion is the term in word-formation for creating a new word by shifting an existing word to a different word class without adding a prefix: the noun *drink* from the verb *drink,* the verb *butter* from the noun *butter,* the verb *clean* from the adjective *clean.*

co-ordination   Co-ordination is the linking of two or more units that would have the same function if they were not linked. When co-ordinators such as *and* are present, the co-ordination is syndetic: *I enjoy classical music, jazz, and pop music.* When co-ordinators are not present but are implied, the co-ordination is asyndetic:

'*Distinguished guests, colleagues, friends,* I welcome you all.' If three or more units are co-ordinated and the co-ordinator is repeated between each unit, the co-ordination is polysyndetic: 'The cake contains *eggs and flour and cheese and honey and spices.*' Co-ordination of noun phrases may be segregatory or combinatory. In segregatory co-ordination each noun phrase could function separately in a paraphrase involving the co-ordination of the clauses: '*Bomb warnings and drugs courier baggage* were mentioned' → '*Bomb warnings* were mentioned and *drugs courier baggage* was mentioned.' This is not possible in combinatory co-ordination: '*Peter and Laura* first met at a dance'. Combinatory co-ordination is also found with adjectives: 'a *red, white, and blue* flag.'   See also **conjunction**.

co-ordinative apposition   In co-ordinative apposition the two noun phrases that are in apposition are linked by the co-ordinator *and* or *or*: *eeg or electroencephalogram*; *She is the book's author and Mr. Deng's youngest daughter.*

co-ordinator   See **conjunction**.

copular verb   A copular (or linking) verb is complemented by a **subject predicative** in sentence or clause structure. The most common copular verb is *be*; others include *become* (*my friend*), *feel* (*tired*), *get* (*ready*), *seem* (*happy*). A copular prepositional verb is a prepositional verb (combination of verb plus preposition) that is complemented by a subject predicative: *sound like* (*you*), *turn into* (*a monster*), *serve as* (*mitigating circumstances*).

correlative   See **conjunction**.

count noun   A count (or countable) noun is a noun that has both singular and plural forms (*book/books*) and can take determiners (as appropriate) that accompany distinctions in number (*a /this book, many /these books*).

creole   A creole develops from a pidgin when the pidgin becomes the mother tongue or a first language of the community. A pidgin is a link language between speakers of mutually unintelligible languages that is formed from a mixture of languages and it has a limited vocabulary and a simplified grammar. When a pidgin is creolized, the vocabulary is expanded and the grammar is elaborated.

dative case   See **case**.

declarative   A declarative (or declarative sentence) is the most common type of sentence type, typically used in the expression of statements and generally requiring subject–verb order: *It was raining last night*; *Nobody saw us*; *Cindy is the best candidate.* The other sentence types, with which it is contrasted, are interrogative, imperative, and exclamative. A declarative question is a declarative that has the force of a question. In speech it ends with rising intonation, and in writing it ends with a question mark: *You accept their word?*

definite   A definite noun phrase conveys the assumption that the hearer or reader can identify what it refers to. Identification may be assumed when (for example) the phrase refers to something previously mentioned or uniquely identifiable from general knowledge or from the particular context. Definite reference is associated with the use of the definite article *the*, the personal pronouns, the demonstratives, and proper names. Definite reference contrasts with indefinite reference, commonly signalled by the indefinite article *a /an* ('I bought *a* used car last week for the family, but *the* car (or *it*) is giving me a lot of trouble').

definite article   The definite article is *the*. With singular noun phrases it contrasts with the indefinite article *a /an* (*a house, the house*). With plural noun phrases it contrasts with the zero article, i.e. the absence of an article or other determiner (*the houses, houses*), or with the indefinite determiner *some* (*the houses, some houses*).

deixis   Deixis may be situational or textual. Situational deixis denotes the use of expressions to point to some feature of the situation, typically persons or objects in the situation and temporal or locational features. For example, the pronoun *I* is necessarily deictic, referring to the speaker and writer and shifting its reference according to who is speaking or writing. Similarly, *here* and *now* may be situationally bound as is the use of tenses that take as their point of reference the time of speaking or writing. Textual deixis denotes the use of expressions to point to other expressions in the linguistic context. References to what comes earlier are anaphoric, whereas references to what comes later are cataphoric. See also **anaphoric**.

demonstrative   The demonstrative pronouns and determiners are singular *this* and *that* and their respective plurals *these* and *those*.

denotation   See **connotation**.

deontic   Deontic (or root or intrinsic) meanings of the modals refer to some kind of human control over the situation, such as permission or obligation (*may* in *You may sit down now* or *must* in *I must tell you about it*). Deontic meanings contrast with epistemic meanings, which refer to some kind of evaluation of the truth-value of the proposition such as possibility or necessity (*may* in *It may rain later* or *must* in *That must be your sister*). Each of the modals has both kinds of meaning. See also **auxiliary**.

dependent genitive   See **genitive**.

derivation   See **affix**.

determiner   Determiners introduce noun phrases. They convey various pragmatic and semantic contrasts relating to the type of reference of the noun phrase and to notions such as number and quantity. In their positional potentialities they fall into three sets: predeterminers (e.g. *all, both*), central determiners (e.g. *a/an, the, my, this*), and postdeterminers (e.g. *two, many, several*). Most of the words that function as determiners also function as pronouns (e.g. *this, some, all*).

direct object   A direct object is a **complement** of a transitive verb. It generally follows the verb in a declarative sentence (*my car* in *Norman has borrowed my car*). It can be made the subject of a corresponding passive sentence (*My car has been borrowed by Norman*) and can be elicited by a question with *who(m)* or *what* in company with the subject and verb (*What did Norman borrow? My car*). The direct object is typically the entity affected by the action.

direct speech   Direct speech quotes the actual words used by somebody, and in writing it is enclosed in quotation marks: (*Charles asked me*,) '*What shall I do next?*'. Indirect speech reports the substance of what was said or written: (*Charles asked me*) *what he should do next*.

disjunct   Disjuncts are sentence adverbials, either style disjuncts or content disjuncts. Style disjuncts comment on the act of speaking or writing, and may be adverbs (*bluntly, honestly, personally*), prepositional phrases (*in all fairness, in short, between you and me*), non-finite clauses (*frankly speaking, putting it bluntly, to be truthful*), and finite clauses (*if I may say so, since you ask me*): '*Honestly*, I didn't do it'; '*Since you ask me*, I wouldn't mind a drink'. Content disjuncts comment on the truth-value of what is said (*possibly, undoubtedly, in all probability*) or evaluate it (*unfortunately, to my delight, what is more disappointing*): 'Our side will *undoubtedly* win'; '*Unfortunately*, the deadline has passed'.

ditransitive   See **transitive verb**.

double genitive   See **genitive**.

doubly transitive phrasal-prepositional verb   See **phrasal-prepositional verb**.

doubly transitive prepositional verb   See **prepositional verb**.

dummy operator   Auxiliary *do* is a dummy operator, since it functions as an operator in the absence of any other auxiliary when an operator is required to form questions (*My sister likes them → Does my sister like them?*), to make the sentence negative (*My* *sister doesn't like them*), or to form an abbreviated clause (*My sister likes them, and I do too*).

ellipsis   Ellipsis is the omission of a part of a normal structure. The ellipted part can be understood from the situational context (ellipsis of *have you* in *Got any suggestions?*) or the textual context, where it may be anaphoric (dependent on what precedes: *May I drive? Yes, you may*) or cataphoric (dependent on what follows: *If you don't want to, I'll drive*). See also **anaphoric**.

emphatic reflexive   See **reflexive pronoun**.

empty morph   See **morpheme**.

enclitic   See **clitic**.

end focus   The principle of end focus requires that the most important information comes at the end of the sentence or clause.

end weight   The principle of end weight requires that a longer unit follow a shorter unit if the choice is available. See also **extraposed postmodifier**.

epistemic   See **deontic**.

exclamative   An exclamative (or exclamative sentence) is a sentence type in which the exclamative element is fronted, introduced by *what* (followed by the rest of the noun phrase) or by *how* (otherwise): *What a good time we had; How kind you are*.

existential *there*   Existential *there* is used in a rearrangement of the sentence in which the subject is postponed, the effect being to present the postponed (notional) subject as new information: *Too many cars are ahead of us* → *There are too many cars ahead of us*. If the sentence consists only of the subject and the verb *be*, then only the existential sentence is normally possible: *There's still time*.

extraposed postmodifier   An extraposed postmodifier is a postmodifier in a noun phrase (generally a noun phrase functioning as subject) that is postponed to a later position in the sentence, in accordance with the principle of **end weight**: *A tape recording in which a huge ransom was demanded was received* → *A tape recording was received in which a huge ransom was demanded*.

extrinsic   See **deontic**.

finite   A verb is finite if it displays tense, the distinction between present and past tense: *cares/cared, take/took*. A verb phrase is finite if the first (or only) verb in the phrase is finite, all other verbs being non-finite: *is caring/was caring, has taken/had taken*. A clause is finite if its verb is finite: *I cared about what they thought of me; I generally take a nap after lunch*. The non-finite verb forms are the infinitive, the *-ing* participle, and the *-ed* participle.   See also **aspect, clause, infinitive, participle**.

free morph   See **morpheme**.

function word   See **word class**.

GA   GA (General American) is an abstraction from what is typical of the pronunciation of English in America.

gender   Gender is a grammatical category in which contrasts are made within a word class (in present-day English restricted to certain pronouns and determiners) such as personal/non-personal, masculine/feminine/neuter. The most conspicuous gender contrasts in present-day English are found in the third person singular personal pronouns *he/she/it*.

General American   See **GA**.

generic   In generic reference, noun phrases are used in generalizations to refer to all members of the class denoted by the phrases that are relevant in the context: '*Coffee* contains *caffeine*'; '*The poor* are always with us'; '*Apples* are good for you'; '*An apple* a day keeps *the doctor* away'.

genitive   The genitive (or possessive) case applies to nouns and some pronouns. The genitives for *child* are singular *child's* and plural *children's*, and for *girl* they are singular *girl's* and plural *girls'*. Genitives may be dependent or independent. A phrase with a dependent genitive is dependent on a following noun phrase: 'the child's parents', parallel with 'her parents'. The independent genitive is not dependent in this way, though a following noun may be implied: 'I'm going to my cousin's.' The double genitive is a combination of a genitive and an *of*-phrase: 'that article of Estelle's.' The group genitive applies not just to the noun to which it is attached: 'an hour and a half's sleep'; 'the president of the company's resignation'. See also **case**.

gerund   The gerund is an *-ing* participle that shares characteristics of a noun and a verb. *Finding* is a gerund in 'It depends on Algeria's *finding* more efficient ways to run its factories'. Like a noun it is preceded by a genitive (*Algeria's*) that is dependent on it, but like a verb it takes a direct object (*finding more efficient ways to run its factories*). The genitive is often replaced by a noun in the common case (*Algeria*). In the same context, possessive pronouns (*their* in *their finding*) are often replaced by pronouns in the objective case (*them finding*).

gradability   Gradable words allow intensification and comparison. *Clever* is gradable because we can intensify it up or down on a scale of cleverness (*very clever, quite clever, somewhat clever*) and it can be compared (*cleverer, cleverest, as clever, more clever*). On the other hand, *animate* is not gradable.

group genitive   See **genitive**.

homograph   Homographs are two (or more) distinct words that happen to be spelled the same. *Tear* represents two words that are pronounced differently, one being a noun ('drop from the eye') and the other a verb ('pull apart') or a noun derived from a verb.

homomorph   Homomorphs are words that are related in meaning and are pronounced and spelled the same but are distinct grammatically. For example, the verb *laugh* and the noun *laugh* are homomorphs.

homonym   Homonyms are distinct words that have the same form. *Bank* (where money is deposited) and *bank* (of a river) are homonyms. In this instance, they are spelled and pronounced the same and belong to the same word class (nouns). See also **homograph**, **homomorph**, **homophone**.

homophone   Homophones are distinct words that are spelled differently but happen to be pronounced the same. *One* and *won* are homophones.

host clause   See **subordinate clause**.

host phrase   See **subordinate clause**.

hypernym   See **hyponymy**.

hyponymy   Hyponymy is a relationship of inclusion in the hierarchy of a set of words. A general term (a superordinate or hypernym) includes within its reference terms that are more specific (hyponyms). *Food* is a superordinate of *fruit*, and *fruit* in turn is a hyponym of *food*. There are other hyponyms of *food*, and these (e.g. *vegetable, fish, meat*) constitute a set of co-hyponyms of *food*.

hypotaxis   Hypotaxis is in contrast with parataxis. Parataxis is a relationship between two or more units that are of equal grammatical status, as in co-ordination (*books and magazines*), whereas hypotaxis is a relationship between two units, one of which is dependent on the other, as in modification (the relationship between the relative *that*-clause and its noun head *books* in *books that I have read*).

hypothetical condition   See **conditional clause**.

hypothetical subjunctive   See **subjunctive**.

illocutionary force See **speech act**.

imperative An imperative is a sentence (or clause) type. The verb is in the **base form**, and typically the subject is absent, though *you* is implied as subject: *Look over there.* The term 'imperative' is also used for the verb functioning in the imperative sentence (*look* in *Look over there*, *be* in *Be quiet*).

indefinite article The indefinite article is *a* before consonant sounds (*a house*) and *an* before vowel sounds (*an hour*). See also **definite article**.

indefinite determiner/pronoun Indefinite determiners and indefinite pronouns have indefinite reference. Some indefinite determiners and pronouns have the same form (*some, any, either, neither, all, both*), but *no* is only a determiner and others (e.g. *none, someone*) are only pronouns. See also **definite**.

indefinite reference See **definite**.

independent genitive See **genitive**.

indicative See **mood**.

indirect object An indirect object is a **complement** of a transitive verb. It normally comes between the verb and the **direct object** (*Jean* in *I gave Jean the old computer*). It can be elicited by a question introduced by *who(m)* (*Who do you give the old computer (to)? — Jean*), and can be made subject of a corresponding passive sentence (*Jean was given the old computer*). The indirect object typically has the role of recipient or beneficiary of the action.

indirect speech See **direct speech**.

indirect speech act See **speech act**.

infinitive The infinitive has the **base form** of the verb. It may be preceded by infinitival *to* (*to be, to say*), but the bare infinitive (without *to*) is used after modals (*can say*), the **dummy operator** *do* (*did say, doesn't know*), and the imperative auxiliary *do* (*Do tell us*).

infinitive clause An infinitive clause is a clause whose verb is an **infinitive** ('I want *to learn Chinese*').

inflection An inflection is an **affix** that expresses a grammatical relationship, such as the plural *-s* in *candidates* and the *-ed* ending in *wanted*. In English, inflections are always suffixes.

initialism See **acronym**.

instrumental case See **case**.

interjection An interjection is an exclamatory emotive word that is loosely attached to the sentence or used as an utterance by itself, such as *oh* and *boo*.

interrogative An interrogative (or interrogative sentence) is a sentence type in which there is **subject–operator inversion** (the operator coming before the subject), as in *Do you know them?* (in contrast to the **declarative** word order in *You know them*). The exception is if the subject is a *wh*-item in *wh*-questions, in which case the subject retains its position, as in *Who knows them?* (in contrast to *Who do they know?*). Interrogatives are typically used to ask questions.

interrogative adverb The interrogative adverbs are *how, when, where,* and *why*. They are used to form *wh*-questions: *How did you find it? When did you last see her?*

interrogative determiner/pronoun The interrogative pronouns are *who, whom, whose, which,* and *what*. The interrogative determiners are *which, what,* and *whose*. Like the interrogative adverbs, they are used to form *wh*-questions: *Who wants to play? Whose desk is this?*

intertextuality Intertextuality is the relationship between a text and other past or coexisting texts. That relationship accounts for the conventions of genres and intentional deviations from conventions and for allusions.

intransitive phrasal verb	See **phrasal verb**.

intransitive verb	An intransitive verb is a verb that does not have a **complement**.

intrinsic	See **deontic**.

left dislocation	In left dislocation, an anticipatory noun phrase ('a phrase dislocated to the left') is followed by a pronoun that occupies the normal position for the phrase: '*Your mother, she* was just misunderstood'. In right dislocation, an anticipatory pronoun is in the normal position and an explanatory phrase appears later: '*They*'re not great social animals, *computer scientists.*'

lexical cohesion	See **cohesion**.

lexical word	See **closed class**.

main clause	A main clause is a clause that is not subordinate to another clause. It may be coextensive with the sentence or it may be co-ordinated with one or more other main clauses.

main verb	The main (or lexical) verb is the head of the verb phrase (*smoking* in *may have been smoking*) and is sometimes preceded by one or more auxiliaries (*may have been* in *may have been smoking*).

mandative subjunctive	See **subjunctive**.

marginal auxiliary	See **auxiliary**.

marker of apposition	See **apposition**.

mass noun	See **count noun**.

modal auxiliary	See **auxiliary**.

monotransitive	See **transitive**.

monotransitive phrasal-prepositional verb	See **phrasal-prepositional verb**.

monotransitive prepositional verb	See **prepositional verb**.

mood	Engish has three moods of verbs: indicative, **imperative**, and **subjunctive**. The indicative applies to most verbs in **declarative** sentences and to verbs in **interrogatives** and **exclamatives**. The imperative and the present subjunctive have the base form of the verb, and the past subjunctive is confined to *were*. See also **subjunctive**.

morph	See **morpheme**.

morpheme	A morpheme is an abstract unit established for the analysis of word structure. It is a basic unit in the vocabulary. A word can be analysed as consisting of one morpheme (*sad*) or two or more morphemes (*unluckily*; compare *luck, lucky, unlucky*), each morpheme usually expressing a distinct meaning. When a morpheme is represented by a segment, that segment is a morph. If a morpheme can be represented by more than one morph, the morphs are **allomorphs** of the same morpheme: the prefixes *in-* (*insane*), *il-* (*illegible*), *im-* (*impossible*), *ir-* (*irregular*) are allomorphs of the same negative morpheme. A portmanteau morph represents more than one morph: *men* is a combination of the morpheme for *man* plus the plural morpheme. An empty morph is a morph that lacks meaning; for example, the *-o-* in combining forms such as *psychology*. A suppletive morph is a morph from a different root that is used in a grammatical set; for example, *went* is the suppletive past of the verb *go*. A zero morph is postulated where a morpheme is expected in the grammatical system but is not represented; for example, the zero relative pronoun in *a letter I wrote* (compare *a letter that I wrote*). A free morph is one that occurs independently as a word, whereas a bound morph is always combined with one or more other morphs to form a word: inflections such as the plural *-s* are bound morphs, as are the suffix *-ness* in *goodness* and the bound root morph *cran-* in *cranberry*.

morphology	Morphology is the study of the structure of words.

multi-word verb A multi-word verb is a combination of a verb with one or more other words to form an idiomatic unit. The most common multi-word verbs are **phrasal verbs** (e.g. *give in*) and **prepositional verbs** (e.g. *rely on*).

nominal adjective A nominal adjective is an adjective that functions as the head of a noun phrase. Like adjectives in general, nominal adjectives may be modified by an adverb (*very sick* in *They looked after the very sick*) and take comparative and superlative forms (*poorer* in *She employed the poorer among them*, *best* in *The best is yet to come*).

nominal clause Nominal clauses have a range of functions similar to those of noun phrases. For example, they can be the subject of a sentence: the *that*-clause in *That they believe him is doubtful*, and the *whether*-clause in *Whether or not I am invited is irrelevant*.

nominal relative clause A nominal relative clause (or independent relative clause or free relative clause) is a clause whose introductory *wh*-word is a fusion of a **relative pronoun** or **relative determiner** with an implied **antecedent**: *Whoever said that* ('Any person who . . .') *needs his head examining*; *What you want* ('The thing that you want') *is too expensive*; *They don't know how to behave* ('the way that they should behave'). See also **relative clause**.

nominal relative determiner/pronoun Nominal relative pronouns and determiners introduce **nominal relative clauses**. There are twelve nominal relative pronouns: *who, whom, whoever, whomever, whosoever, whomsoever, which, whichever, whichsoever, what, whatever, whatsoever*. *Which* and *what* and their compounds can also be determiners.

nominative case See **case**.

non-count noun A non-count (or uncountable or mass) noun does not have a plural form; for example: *furniture, happiness, information*. Many nouns that are generally non-count can be treated as count when they are used to refer to different kinds (*French wines*) or to quantities (*two coffees*, 'two cups of coffee'). See also **count noun**.

non-finite See **finite**.

non-generic See **generic**.

non-restrictive See **restrictive**.

non-rhotic accent See **rhotic accent**.

non-specific See **specific**.

non-standard See **standard English**.

noun A noun is a word that (alone or with modifiers) is capable of functioning as subject (*rice* in 'Rice is grown in this country'), or direct object ('I like *rice*'), or complement of a preposition ('This is made from *rice*').

noun phrase A noun phrase is a phrase whose head (possibly its only word) is a noun (*coffee* in 'I prefer *black coffee*'), a pronoun (*that* in 'I prefer *that*'), or a nominal adjective (*elderly* in 'I prefer catering for *the elderly*'). See also **nominal adjective**.

nuclear tone A nuclear tone is the most prominent movement of pitch within a tone unit, a segment in an utterance that contains a distinct sequence of tones. The most common nuclear tones are falls (or falling tones) and rises (or rising tones).

object See **direct object, indirect object**.

objective case See **case**.

object predicative See **subject predicative**.

operator The operator is a verb that is being used for negation, interrogation, emphasis, and abbreviation. When the **main verb** *be* is the only verb in the verb phrase, it can function as operator (*is* in *He isn't in* and *Is he in?*). In British English in particular, the main verb *have* can similarly function as operator (*has* in *Has he any children?*). Otherwise, the operator is the first (or only) auxiliary in the verb phrase (*may* in *May I come in?* and *is* in *Is it raining?*). In the absence of another potential operator, the **dummy operator** *do* is introduced (*did* in *Did you see them?*).

optative subjunctive   See **subjunctive**.

orthographic   An orthographic word is the written form of a word as conventionally spelled and separated from other words. An orthographic sentence is a sentence in writing, usually signalled by an initial capital letter and a final stop (period, question mark, or exclamation mark).

paradigm   A paradigm is a set of grammatically related forms, such as the five forms of the irregular verb *drive*: *drive, drives, driving, drove, driven*.

parataxis   See **hypotaxis**.

part of speech   See **word class**.

participle   There are two participles: the *-ing* participle (or present participle) and the *-ed* participle (or past participle). Both are non-finite forms of verbs. The *-ing* participle always ends in *-ing* (*shouting, singing, writing*). The *-ed* participle ends in *-ed* in regular verbs (*shouted*), where it is identical with the simple past (*They shouted at him, He was shouted at*), but it need not have an *-ed* ending in irregular verbs (*sung, written*). The *-ing* participle is used to form the progressive aspect (*He was shouting*), and the *-ed* participle is used to form the perfect aspect (*She has written*) and the passive (*It was sung beautifully*). Both participles function as the verb in non-finite clauses: *-ing* participle clauses ('*Writing letters* is a chore') and *-ed* participle clauses ('*Written in an unknown script*, the inscription posed a challenge to scholars'). See also **aspect, passive**.

particle   A particle is a word that does not take inflections and does not fit into the traditional word classes; for example, the negative particle *not* and infinitival *to*. Particles also include the words that are used to form **multi-word verbs** (*in* in *give in, at* in *look at, up* and *with* in *put up with*), though further analysis may differentiate them as adverbs and prepositions.

passive   Passive voice is contrasted with active voice. Voice applies only to transitive verbs (those taking an object). The active is the norm. An active sentence will generally take the order subject-verb-object (or possibly two objects, the indirect followed by the direct): *Most students take the examination; Sandra took all the money*. The corresponding passive sentence will have the active object (*the examination; all the money*) as subject, the active subject (*Most students; Sandra*) will optionally appear after the verb in a *by*-phrase, and the active verb phrase will be turned into a passive phrase by the introduction of the auxiliary *be* followed by the *-ed* participle of the main verb: *The examination is taken* (*by most students*); *All the money was taken* (*by Sandra*). For all regular verbs and for many irregular verbs the *-ed* participle is identical with the simple past: *Paul invited all the teachers* → *All the teachers were invited* (*by Paul*). See also **direct object, indirect object**.

past   See **tense**.

past perfect   The past perfect is a combination of the past of the perfect auxiliary *have* followed by the *-ed* participle: *had revealed, had made, had seen, had been* (*crying*). See also **aspect**.

past progressive   The past progressive is a combination of the past of the progressive auxiliary *be* with the *-ing* participle of the following verb: *was phoning, were having, were being examined*. See also **aspect**.

past subjunctive   See **subjunctive**.

perfect   See **aspect**.

performative verb   A performative verb is a verb used to perform the **speech act** it denotes. For example: *I apologize* constitutes an apology.

person Three persons are distinguished. The first person indicates the speaker(s) or writer(s); the second person indicates the hearer(s) or reader(s); the third person indicates any others. The distinctions apply to noun phrases and verbs. For example: *I* is the first person singular of the personal pronoun, and *am* is the corresponding first person singular of the present tense of *be*. In the plural, the first person *we* may be inclusive (including hearer(s)/reader(s)) or exclusive (including others). Similarly, the second person *you* may include others, though not speakers or writers.

personal pronoun The personal pronouns are *I/me, you, he/him, she/her, it, we/us, they/them*.

phoneme The English phonemes are the abstract contrastive sound units that are postulated for a description of the sound system of English.

phonetics English phonetics is the study of the sounds used for communications in English.

phonology English phonology is the study of the English sound system.

phrasal-prepositional verb A phrasal-prepositional verb is a **multi-word verb** in which a verb combines with an adverb and a preposition to form an idiomatic unit. Monotransitive phrasal-prepositional verbs have just one object, a prepositional object (*'look down on* somebody', meaning 'despise'). Doubly transitive phrasal-prepositional verbs take two objects (*'let* somebody *in on* something').

phrasal verb A phrasal verb is a **multi-word verb** in which a verb is combined with an adverb to form an idiomatic unit. The phrasal verb may be intransitive, without an object (*shut up* 'keep quiet', *give in* 'surrender'), or transitive (*'point out* something', *'make up* something'). With transitive phrasal verbs the adverb may precede or follow the object ('find *out* the truth', 'find the truth *out*'), though if the object is a pronoun the adverb generally follows the object ('find it *out*').

phrase The phrase comes between the word and the clause in the hierarchy of grammatical units. Five phrase types are distinguished: **noun phrase, verb phrase, adjective phrase, adverb phrase, prepositional phrase.**

pidgin See **creole.**

polysemy Polysemy refers to the range of meanings denoted by a word. *Hand* is polysemous, denoting (for example) the hand of a human being and the hand of a watch, meanings that are perceived as related. Polysemy contrasts with homonymy, where words having the same form are perceived as distinct and unrelated in meaning. See also **homonym.**

polysyndetic See **co-ordination.**

portmanteau morph See **morpheme.**

possessive pronoun The possessive pronouns are the possessives of the **personal pronouns.** They may be dependent (*my, your, his, her, its, our, their*) or independent (*mine, yours, his, hers, its, ours, theirs*).

postdeterminer See **determiner.**

pragmatics Pragmatics is the study of the use of the language and its interpretation in situational contexts.

predeterminer See **determiner.**

predicate Sentences and clauses are often divided into the subject and the predicate. The predicate consists of the verb and its **complements** and **adverbials** that are functioning as **adjuncts**. In the sentence *I met a girl on the train today*, *I* is the subject and the rest of the sentence is the predicate. Excluded from the predicate are sentence adverbials: **conjuncts** such as *therefore* and *however*, and **disjuncts** such as *perhaps* and *on the other hand*.

prefix   See **affix**.

preposition   A preposition is a word that introduces a prepositional phrase, which consists of a preposition and the prepositional complement. In *for your sake, for* is a preposition and the noun phrase *your sake* is its complement. Prepositional complements may also be *-ing* participle clauses (*trying harder* in *by trying harder*) and *wh*-clauses (*whether I will be available* in *about whether I will be available*).

prepositional complement   See **preposition**.

prepositional object   A prepositional object is the object of a **prepositional verb** (*the painting* in *I looked closely at the painting*) or the object of a **phrasal-prepositional verb** (*your insults* in *I've put up with your insults for too long*). In both instances, the object is introduced by a preposition.

prepositional phrase   See **preposition**.

prepositional verb   A prepositional verb is a **multi-word verb** in which a verb combines with a **preposition** to form an idiomatic unit. Monotransitive prepositional verbs take one object, a **prepositional object** (*a grant* in *I applied for a grant*). Doubly transitive verbs take two objects: a **direct object** and a **prepositional object**. In *Nobody will blame you for the mistake, you* is the direct object and *the mistake* is the prepositional object (introduced by the preposition *for*). A copular prepositional verb takes a **subject predicative** as its complement, a *waste of time* in *It looks like a waste of time* (compare *It looks wasteful*, where *looks* is a **copular verb**).

present   See **tense**.

present perfect   The present perfect is a combination of the present tense of the perfect auxiliary *have* with the *-ed* participle of the following verb: *has seen, have owned*. See also **aspect**.

present progressive   The present progressive is a combination of the progressive auxiliary *be* with the *-ing* participle of the following verb: *am saying, is taking, are eating*. See also **aspect**.

present subjunctive   See **subjunctive**.

principal parts of verbs   The principal parts of a main verb are the three forms of verbs that are sufficient for deriving a list of all forms of the verb. The principal parts are the **base form** (*sail, see, drink, put*), the past (*sailed, saw, drank, put*), and the *-ed* participle (*sailed, seen, drunk, put*). From the base form we can derive the *-s* form (*sails, sees, drinks, puts*) and the *-ing* participle (*sailing, seeing, drinking, putting*).

proclitic   See **clitic**.

progressive   See **aspect**.

pronoun   Pronouns are a closed class of words that have a range of functions similar to those of nouns; for example they can serve as subject (*I* in *I know Paula*) or direct object (*me* in *Paula knows me*). Typically they point to entities in the situation or to linguistic units in the previous or following context. Many pronouns have the same form as corresponding determiners: *some* is a pronoun in *I have some with me*, whereas it is a **determiner** in *I have some money with me*. See also **demonstrative, indefinite determiner/pronoun, interrogative determiner/pronoun, nominal relative determiner/pronoun, personal pronoun, possessive pronoun, quantifier, reciprocal pronoun, reflexive pronoun, relative pronoun, *wh*-pronoun**.

proper noun   Proper nouns contrast with common nouns. Proper nouns have unique reference. They name specific people, places, etc. (*Esther, New York*).

quantifier   The primary quantifiers can function either as **pronouns** or as **determiners**: *many, more, most, a few, fewer, fewest, several, enough, much, more, most, a little, less, least, enough, few, little*. There are also compound quantifiers that function only as pronouns; for example: *a bit, a lot, a couple*.

Received Pronunciation   See **RP**.

reciprocal pronoun   The reciprocal pronouns are *each other* and *one another*.

reduced relative clause   See **relative clause**.

reduplicative   Reduplicatives are compounds formed by the combination of identical words (*hush-hush*) or near-identical words (*flip-flop*). The second segment is sometimes not an existing word but one invented for the purpose (*chairman-schmairman*).

reflexive pronoun   In standard English the reflexive pronouns are *myself, ourselves, yourself, yourselves, himself, herself, itself, themselves*. Singular *ourself* and *themself* are also used sometimes.

register   A register is a variety of the language that relates to the type of activity for which the language is used. Major registers at the highest level of abstraction include exposition, narration, instruction, argumentation. More specific registers include news reports, personal letters, legal language, advertising.

relative adverb   Relative adverbs are used to introduce **relative clauses**. The relative adverbs are *when, where*, and *why*: 'the hotel *where* I stayed', 'the occasion *when* we first met', 'the reason *why* he did it'.

relative clause   Relative clauses postmodify nouns ('the house *that I own*'), pronouns ('those *who trust me*'), and nominal adjectives ('the elderly *who are sick*'). Sentential relative clauses relate not to any of those items but to a sentence, a clause, or a part of a clause: 'I missed them, *which is a pity*.' Relative clauses may be **restrictive** or non-restrictive, but sentential relative clauses are only non-restrictive. Relative clauses are introduced by a relative item—a **relative adverb**, a **relative determiner**, or a **relative pronoun**. Reduced relative clauses are non-finite clauses that correspond to the full (finite) relative clauses: 'the person *to see*' ('the person *that you should see*'), 'the patient *waiting in the next room*', 'the work *set for tomorrow*'.

relative determiner   Relative determiners are used to introduce **relative clauses**. The relative determiners are *whose* and *which*: 'the patient *whose* records were misplaced', 'The complaint has been formally lodged, in *which* case I'd like a copy'.

relative pronoun   Relative pronouns are used to introduce relative clauses. The relative pronouns are *who, whom, which, that*, and zero: 'the candidate *who* was rejected', 'the meal *which* I prepared', 'a book *that* I've just read'. When *that* is omitted, the relative is the zero relative: 'a book I've just read'.

restrictive   Modification may be either restrictive or non-restrictive. Modification is restrictive when the modifier is intended to restrict the reference of the noun phrase. In *hair that grows slowly*, the postmodifying relative clause *that grows slowly* distinguishes that type of hair from other types. In 'This is Peter West, *who edits a men's magazine*', the relative clause *who edits a men's magazine* is non-restrictive, since it does not restrict the reference of *Peter West* but instead contributes information about Peter West.

rhotic accent   Non-rhotic accents drop the /r/ when it is followed by a consonant sound, as in *part*. They also drop the /r/ at the end of a word when it comes before a pause. Rhotic accents retain the /r/.

right dislocation   See **left dislocation**.

root   See **base**.

RP   RP (an abbreviation for Received Pronunciation) is an **accent** that is typical of educated speakers of British English, though by no means all educated speakers use it. It is not associated with any particular region of the country, but it is associated with speakers from upper and upper-middle social classes.

segregatory co-ordination   See **co-ordination**.

semi-auxiliary   See **auxiliary**.

sentence   See **clause, orthographic**.

sentential relative clause   See **relative clause**.

sequence of tenses   Sequence of tenses applies to indirect speech. It is the relationship between the tenses of the verbs in the reporting clause and the reported clause as a result of backshift of the verb in the reported clause. See **direct speech**, **backshifting**, **tense**.

simple past   See **tense**.

simple present   See **tense**.

simple sentence   A simple sentence consists of one **main clause**, without any subordinate clauses: *No fingerprints were found anywhere in the house.*

situational deixis   See **deixis**.

situational ellipsis   See **ellipsis**.

specific   A noun phrase has specific reference when it refers to a specific person, thing, place, etc. The reference in *a novel* is non-specific in 'I have always wanted to write *a novel*', since it does not refer to a particular novel.

speech act   The performance of an utterance (spoken or written) in a particular context with a particular intention is a speech act. The intention is the illocutionary force of the speech act. The illocutionary force of *You may smoke in here* is (for one plausible interpretation) permission and for *You mustn't smoke in here* it is prohibition. See **performative verb**.

spelling pronunciation   A spelling pronunciation is a pronunciation that is influenced by the spelling; for example, the pronunciation of the second syllable of *Sunday* as in *day* rather than as in the second syllable of *ready*.

split infinitive   A split infinitive is the separation between infinitival *to* and the infinitive verb by the insertion of one or more words. For example, *really* splits the infinitive in 'to *really* understand'. See **infinitive**.

standard English   Standard English is the national variety of English in countries such as the United States and England and is not restricted to any region within the country. It is to be distinguished from **accents** with which it may be pronounced. Standard English is pre-eminently the language of printed matter, and is the dialect of English that is taught in the education system. Other dialects of English used in the country are non-standard.

stranded preposition   A preposition is stranded when it is left by itself, without a following prepositional complement. *With* is a stranded preposition in 'It will be dealt *with* at once'. It is followed by the prepositional complement *it* in 'I will deal *with it* at once'. See **preposition**.

subject   The subject of a sentence (or clause) is the constituent that normally comes before the verb in a **declarative** sentence (*They* in 'They have told you about it') and changes positions with the operator (**subject–operator inversion**) in an *interrogative* sentence ('*Have they* told you about it?). Where applicable, the verb agrees in number and person with the subject: '*I am* ready' (the subject *I* is first person singular and so is *am*), '*He cares* about you' (the subject *he* is third person singular and so is *cares*).

subjective case   See **case**.

subject–operator inversion   In subject–operator inversion, the subject and the **operator** change places. For example, the declarative sentence '*You have* spent all of it' has the normal word order, whereas the corresponding interrogative sentence '*Have you* spent all of it?' exhibits subject–operator inversion: the operator *have* comes before the subject *you*.

subject predicative   A subject predicative is the **complement** of a **copular verb** such as *be* or *seem*. It may be an adjective phrase, an adverb phrase, or a prepositional phrase as well as a noun phrase or a **nominal clause**: 'Paula feels *very self-conscious*' (adjective phrase), 'Norman is *outside*' (adverb), '*I am out of breath*' (prepositional phrase), 'Amanda is *my best friend*' (noun phrase), 'My advice is *to say nothing*' (nominal clause). A complex-transitive verb has two complements: a direct object and an object predicative. In 'I made *my position clear*', *my position* is the direct object and *clear* is the object complement. The predicative relationship between the object and its complement is analogous to that between the subject and the subject predicative in '*My position* is *clear*'.

subject–verb agreement   See **subject**.

subjunctive   There are two subjunctives: the present subjunctive and the past subjunctive. The present subjunctive has the **base form** of the verb, and the past subjunctive is restricted to *were*. The present subjunctive has three uses. The optative subjunctive expresses a wish: 'God *help* the Republic'; contrast the indicative *helps* in 'God *helps* the Republic'. The suppositional subjunctive expresses a supposition, and is used chiefly with conditional and concessive clauses: 'I can teach him, even though it *be* inconvenient for me.' The mandative subjunctive is used in *that*-clauses that convey an order, request, or intention: 'They demanded that he *appear* before them for interrogation.' The past subjunctive *were* is the hypothetical subjunctive, used in hypothetical **conditional clauses** and some other hypothetical constructions: If I *were* you, I wouldn't go.'

subordinate clause   Subordinate clauses are grammatically dependent on a host (or superordinate) clause or host phrase and generally function as a constituent of their host. In the sentence (coterminous with a **main clause**) 'I wonder *whether they are at home*', the *whether*-clause is a subordinate clause. In the noun phrase 'the lunch *that I've just finished*', the relative clause *that I've just finished* is a subordinate clause.

subordinator   See **conjunction**.

suffix   See **affix**.

superlative   See **comparison**.

suppletion   Suppletion is the use of a word from a different root to complete a **paradigm**, a grammatically related set of forms. Suppletive *went* (from the verb *wend*) is the past of the verb *go*. See also **morpheme**.

syndetic co-ordination   See **co-ordination**.

tag question   Tag questions are attached to sentences that are not **interrogatives**. Typically, they are abbreviated *yes–no* questions: 'You can do it, *can't you?*', 'It hasn't reached you yet, *has it?*'

tense   Tense is a grammatical category referring to the time of a situation. English has two tenses that are signalled by the form of the verb: present and past. The tense distinction is made on the first or only verb in the verb phrase: *sings/sang, is/was crying, has/had made*. The simple present is the present tense when there is only one verb (the **main verb**): *sings, shows, writes, catches*. Analogously, the simple past is the past tense when there is only one verb: *sang, showed, wrote, caught*.

textual deixis   See **deixis**.

textual ellipsis   See **ellipsis**.

***to*-infinitive**   See **infinitive**.

***to*-infinitive clause**   See **infinitive**.

tone unit   A tone unit is a segment of speech that contains a **nuclear tone**.

transitive phrasal verb   See **phrasal verb**.

transitive verb   A transitive verb is a verb that has a **direct object** or an **indirect object** or both as its complement(s). *Heard* is a transitive verb in 'I've heard the news', since *heard* is followed by the direct object *the news*. *Lend* is a transitive verb in 'Lend me your pen', since it is followed by the indirect object *me* and the direct object *your pen*.

A monotransitive verb has just one object. A ditransitive verb has two objects: an indirect object and a direct object. A **complex-transitive verb** has a direct object and an object predicative. See also **subject predicative**.

verb   The term is used in two ways: (1) A verb is a word that displays contrasts such as **tense, aspect, mood, voice**, number (singular/plural), and **person**. It is generally inflected to offer non-finite forms: **infinitive** (write), -*ing* participle (writing), -*ed* participle (written). A non-finite **main verb** (or lexical verb) may combine with one or more **auxiliaries** (or auxiliary verbs) in a verb phrase: *may write, has been writing, could have written, was being written*. (2) A verb (consisting of a verb phrase) combines with the subject of the sentence to constitute a minimum sentence: *I* (subject) *won* (verb); *Dinner* (subject) *is served* (verb); *No complaints* (subject) *have been received* (verb); *All the guests* (subject) *have been complaining* (verb). If a sentence contains more than one clause, it is usual for each clause to have its own verb: 'The sun *is shining*, but I *predict* that it *will rain* before we *leave*.' See also **participle, verbless clause**.

verbless clause   A verbless clause is a clause-like structure except that it does not have a verb: 'Let me have your comments today, *if possible*'; '*When in doubt*, ask me'. See also **clause**.

verb phrase   A verb phrase is a phrase whose head is a **main verb** (or lexical verb). The main verb may be preceded within the verb phrase by one or more **auxiliaries** or **semi-auxiliaries**: *speaks, is speaking, is going to speak*.

vocative   A vocative is an optional addition to the basic sentence (or clause) structure, and is used to address directly the person or persons spoken to: 'You have a smudge on your nose, *Robin*.'

voice   Voice is a grammatical category which distinguishes between active and passive. The distinction applies to both clauses and verb phrases. See **passive**.

***wh*-adverb**   The *wh*-adverbs are used (1) for questions and interrogative clauses: *how, when, where, why*; (2) for exclamative sentences and clauses: *how*; (3) for **relative clauses**: *when, where, why, whereby, whereupon*, and the two archaic adverbs *whence, wherein*; (4) for **nominal relative clauses**: *how, when, why, where*; (5) for ***wh*-conditional clauses**: *however, whenever, wherever*.

***wh*-conditional clause**   A *wh*-conditional clause leaves open the number of possible conditions: '*Whatever you've been doing*, you've been doing the right thing' ('if you've been doing X, if you've been doing Y, . . .').

***wh*-determiner**   The *wh*-determiners are (1) for questions and interrogative clauses: *which, what, whose*; (2) for **exclamative** sentences and clauses: *what*; (3) for **relative clauses**: *whose, which*; (4) for **nominal relative clauses**: *which, what*; (5) for ***wh*-conditional clauses**: *whatever, whichever*. See **determiner**.

***wh*-pronoun**   The *wh*-pronouns are used (1) for questions and interrogative clauses: *who, whom, whose, which, what*. (2) for **relative clauses**: *who, whom, which*; (3) for **nominal relative clauses**: *who, whom, whoever, whomever, whosoever, whomsoever, which, whichever, whichsoever, what, whatever, whatsoever*; for ***wh*-conditional** clauses: *whoever, whomever, whosoever, whomsoever, whatever, whichever*.

***wh*-question**   *Wh*-questions and *wh*-interrogative clauses are introduced by a *wh*-word, which may be alone or within a phrase: '*Who* is next?'; '*To what* do I owe this visit?'; 'They asked me *which way* they should go'.

***wh*-word**   *Wh*-words are words beginning with *wh*-, but they also include *how* and its compounds (such as *however*).

word class   A word class (or part of speech) is a class of words, such as noun and verb, that share characteristics. Word classes may be open classes (open to new words) or **closed classes** (which generally do not admit new words). Classes may be divided into subclasses; for example, within nouns the distinction between common nouns and proper nouns.

word-formation   Word-formation refers to the processes of forming new words from existing words or segments of words.

word order   Word order is the order of constituents within a phrase, clause, or sentence. For example, in a **declarative sentence** the normal word order is subject, verb, direct object: *All the workers* (subject) *have signed* (verb) *the petition* (direct object).

***yes–no* question**   A *yes–no* question is a question that typically may be appropriately answered by *yes* or *no*. *Yes–no* questions have **subject–operator inversion**, in which the **operator** comes before the subject: '*Are* (operator) *you* (subject) ready?'; '*Have* (operator) *they* (subject) finished their breakfast?'; '*Do* (operator) *we* (subject) pay for ourselves?'

zero article   A zero article (or zero determiner) is postulated for noun phrases where no article (or other determiner) is present. It is a device for simplifying the grammar by assuming a contrast that is elsewhere present in the singular: the contrast between the definite article *the* and the indefinite article *a/an* is extended to the plural, as in *a student*, *the student*, (zero article) *students*, *the students*. See also **definite article**, **morpheme**.

zero relative   The zero relative (or zero relative pronoun) is postulated at the beginning of a relative clause when no **relative pronoun** is overtly present. For example, the relative pronouns *which* and *that* introduce the relative clauses in 'computer games *which* I enjoy'; 'the car *that* they have just bought'. The same clauses are said to be introduced by a zero relative when these pronouns are omitted.: 'computer games I enjoy'; 'the car they have just bought'. See also **morpheme**.

Index

All references are to chapters, sections within chapters, or notes associated with chapters. A reference to a chapter number is followed by *passim*, indicating that the topic is dealt with throughout the chapter. A reference to a note is presented as a chapter number followed by the note number for that chapter. Notes for all the chapters appear in chapter order at the end of the book.

References for a chapter, including notes, are separated by commas. Sets of references for different chapters are separated by semicolons. Major references are given in **bold**.